JONES & BARTLETT LEARNING
CDX Automotive

LIGHT VEHICLE

Tasksheet Manual for NATEF Proficiency

2013 NATEF Edition

Kirk T. VanGelder

ASE Certified Master Automotive Technician & LI
NATEF Evaluation Team Leader
Certified Automotive Service Instructor
Vancouver, Washington

JONES & BARTLETT
LEARNING

World Headquarters
Jones & Bartlett Learning
5 Wall Street
Burlington, MA 01803
978-443-5000
info@jblearning.com
www.jblearning.com

Jones & Bartlett Learning books and products are available through most bookstores and online booksellers. To contact Jones & Bartlett Learning directly, call 800-832-0034, fax 978-443-8000, or visit our website, www.jblearning.com.

Substantial discounts on bulk quantities of Jones & Bartlett Learning publications are available to corporations, professional associations, and other qualified organizations. For details and specific discount information, contact the special sales department at Jones & Bartlett Learning via the above contact information or send an email to specialsales@jblearning.com.

Production Credits

Chief Executive Officer: Ty Field
President: James Homer
Chief Product Officer: Eduardo Moura
Executive Publisher: Kimberly Brophy
Acquisitions Editor–CDX Automotive: Ian Andrew
Managing Editor–CDX Automotive: Amanda J. Mitchell
Associate Editor: Olivia MacDonald
Production Editor: Jessica deMartin
Senior Marketing Manager: Brian Rooney
VP, Manufacturing and Inventory Control: Therese Connell
Composition: Laserwords Private Limited, Chennai, India
Cover Design: Kristin E. Parker
Cover Image: © William Attard McCart/YAY Micro/age fotostock
Printing and Binding: Edwards Brothers Malloy
Cover Printing: Edwards Brothers Malloy

ISBN: 978-1-284-02679-5

6048

Printed in the United States of America
17   10 9 8 7 6

Contents

Section AO:
General Safety

CONTENTS

General Safety

© 2015 Jones & Bartlett Learning, LLC, an Ascend Learning Company

Student/intern information:

Name _____ Date _____ Class _____

Learning Objective/Task	CDX Tasksheet Number	2013 MLR NATEF Reference Number; Priority Level	2013 AST NATEF Reference Number; Priority Level	2013 MAST NATEF Reference Number; Priority Level
• Identify general shop rules and procedures.	C451	OA1; P-1	OA1; P-1	OA1; P-1
• Identify marked safety areas.	C456	OA6; P-1	OA6; P-1	OA6; P-1
• Identify the location and the types of fire extinguishers and other fire safety equipment; demonstrate knowledge of the procedures for using fire extinguishers and other fire safety equipment.	C458	OA7; P-1	OA7; P-1	OA7; P-1
• Identify the location and use of eye wash stations.	C459	OA8; P-1	OA8; P-1	OA8; P-1
• Identify the location of posted evacuation routes.	C460	OA9; P-1	OA9; P-1	OA9; P-1
• Locate and demonstrate knowledge of material safety data sheets (MSDS).	C465	OA15; P-1	OA15; P-1	OA15; P-1
• Draw a diagram of the shop and label all parts.	NN00	N/A	N/A	N/A

Time off_____

Time on_____

Total time_____

Materials Required

- Program's shop policy and other safety information
- MSDS book
- Fire extinguisher(s) from the shop
- Material Safety Data Sheets for the products listed

Some Safety Issues to Consider

- Comply with personal and environmental safety practices associated with clothing; eye protection; hand tools; power equipment; proper ventilation; and the handling, storage, and disposal of chemicals/materials in accordance with local, state, and federal safety and environmental regulations.
- Shop rules and procedures are critical to your safety. Please give these your utmost attention.
- Marked safety areas play an important role in maintaining a safe work environment. Always understand and heed marked safety areas.
- Fire blankets are an important component of fire safety in the shop. Always know their location, purpose, and use.
- Fire extinguishers come in a variety of types and sizes. It pays to understand the differences before they are needed.

- Eye wash stations are an important component of shop safety. Always know their location, purpose, and use.
- Pre-planned evacuation routes are an important component of shop safety. Always know the location of all evacuation routes for your shop.
- Being able to locate information in an MSDS is critical to your safety and health. Make sure you are familiar with their location and use.

Performance Standard

0—No exposure: No information or practice provided during the program; complete training required

1—Exposure only: General information provided with no practice time; close supervision needed; additional training required

2—Limited practice: Has practiced job during training program; additional training required to develop skill

3—Moderately skilled: Has performed job independently during training program; limited additional training may be required

4—Skilled: Can perform job independently with no additional training

MLR OA1   **AST** OA1   **MAST** OA1

Time off_____

Time on_____

Total time_____

CDX Tasksheet Number: C451

1. **List the location(s) of the following items.**

    a. **Program's general shop rules and policies:**

    b. **Material Data Safety Sheets (MSDS) book:**

    c. **Procedure for operation of a fire extinguisher:**

    d. **Procedure for operation of a vehicle hoist:**

2. **List the shop's policy for the wearing of safety glasses while in the shop:**

3. **List the shop's policy for driving vehicles:**

4. List the shop's policy for clothing in the shop:

5. List the shop's policy for jewelry in the shop:

6. **Pass the shop's safety test and record your score here:** _____

7. Have your supervisor/instructor verify satisfactory completion of this procedure, any observations found, and any necessary action(s) recommended.

Performance Rating

CDX Tasksheet Number: C451

0	1	2	3	4
□	□	□	□	□

Supervisor/instructor signature _____ Date _____

MLR 0A6   **AST** 0A6   **MAST** 0A6

Time off_____

Time on_____

CDX Tasksheet Number: C456

Total time_____

1. **Research the uniform color code system used to designate safety areas in a shop. List each color and its designation:**

    a. **Color:** _____ **designates:** _____

    b. **Color:** _____ **designates:** _____

    c. **Color:** _____ **designates:** _____

    d. **Color:** _____ **designates:** _____

2. **Label all of the marked safety areas on the diagram of the shop at the end of this section.**

3. Have your supervisor/instructor verify satisfactory completion of this procedure, any observations found, and any necessary action(s) recommended.

Performance Rating

CDX Tasksheet Number: C456

☐	☐	☐	☐	☐
0	1	2	3	4

Supervisor/instructor signature _____ Date _____

Identify the location and the types of fire extinguishers and other fire safety equipment; demonstrate knowledge of the procedures for using fire extinguishers and other fire safety equipment.

MLR	AST	MAST
OA7	OA7	OA7

Time off_____

Time on_____

Total time_____

CDX Tasksheet Number: C458

1. Research the types, location, and use of fire extinguishers.
   a. **List the different types of fire extinguishers (dry chemical, CO_2, etc.) available:**
      i. **Type:** _____ **; for use on what class of fire:** _____
      ii. **Type:** _____ **; for use on what class of fire:** _____
      iii. **Type:** _____ **; for use on what class of fire:** _____
      iv. **Type:** _____ **; for use on what class of fire:** _____

   In the above list, put a star next to the type(s) of fire extinguishers in this shop.

2. **List the steps for proper use of a fire extinguisher:**

3. Research the location, purpose, and use of fire blankets in your shop.
   a. **Describe the purpose of a fire blanket (under what circumstances should a fire blanket be used?):**

   b. **Describe how a fire blanket puts out a fire:**

4. **Label the location of all fire extinguishers on the diagram of the shop at the end of this section.**

5. **Label the location of the fire blanket(s) on the diagram of the shop at the end of this section.**

6. Have your supervisor/instructor verify satisfactory completion of this procedure, any observations found, and any necessary action(s) recommended.

Performance Rating

CDX Tasksheet Number: C458

0	1	2	3	4

Supervisor/instructor signature _____ Date _____

MLR
OA8

AST
OA8

MAST
OA8

Time off_____

Time on_____

Total time_____

CDX Tasksheet Number: C459

1. Research the location, purpose, and use of eye wash stations in your shop.

   a. **Describe the purpose of an eye wash station:**

   b. **Describe the proper use of an eye wash station (including time):**

   c. **What type of eye injury would use of an eye wash station NOT be appropriate for?**

2. **Label the location of the eye wash station(s) on the diagram of the shop at the end of this section.**

3. Have your supervisor/instructor verify satisfactory completion of this procedure, any observations found, and any necessary action(s) recommended.

Performance Rating

CDX Tasksheet Number: C459

0	1	2	3	4

Supervisor/instructor signature _____ Date _____

© 2015 Jones & Bartlett Learning, LLC, an Ascend Learning Company

MLR OA9   **AST** OA9   **MAST** OA9

Time off_____

Time on_____

Total time_____

CDX Tasksheet Number: C460

1. Research the location and purpose of evacuation routes.

   a. **Describe the purpose of evacuation routes:**

2. **Label the evacuation route(s) on the diagram of the shop at the end of this section. Also label the location of the posted evacuation route diagram(s).**

3. Have your supervisor/instructor verify satisfactory completion of this procedure, any observations found, and any necessary action(s) recommended.

Performance Rating

CDX Tasksheet Number: C460

| 0 | 1 | 2 | 3 | 4 |

Supervisor/instructor signature _____ Date _____

Locate and demonstrate knowledge of material safety data sheets (MSDS).

MLR	AST	MAST
OA15	OA15	OA15

Time off_____

Time on_____

Total time_____

CDX Tasksheet Number: C465

1. **List the safety precautions when handling motor oil:**

2. **List the flash point of gasoline/petroleum:** _____ °F/°C

3. **List the firefighting equipment needed to put out a gasoline/petroleum fire:**

4. **List the first aid treatment for battery acid in the eyes:**

5. **List the first aid treatment for ingestion of anti-freeze (ethylene glycol):**

6. **Label the location of the MSDS books on the diagram of the shop at the end of this section.**

7. Have your supervisor/instructor verify satisfactory completion of this procedure, any observations found, and any necessary action(s) recommended.

Performance Rating

CDX Tasksheet Number: C465

0	1	2	3	4

Supervisor/instructor signature _____ Date _____

Time off_____

Time on_____

Total time_____

CDX Tasksheet Number: NN0O

1. **On a full-sized piece of paper, draw a diagram of the shop and label each of the following:**

   a. **Marked safety areas (floor lines, etc.)** _____ **(X when finished)**
   b. **Location of the fire blanket(s)** _____ **(X when finished)**
   c. **Location of all fire extinguishers** _____ **(X when finished)**
   d. **Location of the exhaust fan switch(es)** _____ **(X when finished)**
   e. **Location of the electrical disconnect switch(es)** _____ **(X when finished)**
   f. **Location of the eye wash station(s)** _____ **(X when finished)**
   g. **Location of the MSDS books** _____ **(X when finished)**
   h. **Evacuation route(s)** _____ **(X when finished)**
   i. **Location of the master air shut-off valve** _____ **(X when finished)**
   j. **Location of the over-head door switch(es)** _____ **(X when finished)**

2. Have your supervisor/instructor verify satisfactory completion of this task.

Performance Rating

CDX Tasksheet Number: NN0O

0	1	2	3	4

Supervisor/instructor signature _____ Date _____

General Safety: Personal Safety

Student/intern information:

Name _____ Date _____ Class _____

Learning Objective/Task	CDX Tasksheet Number	2013 MLR NATEF Reference Number; Priority Level	2013 AST NATEF Reference Number; Priority Level	2013 MAST NATEF Reference Number; Priority Level
• Comply with the required use of safety glasses, ear protection, gloves, and shoes during lab/shop activities.	C461	OA10; P-1	OA10; P-1	OA10; P-1
• Identify and wear appropriate clothing for lab/shop activities.	C462	OA11; P-1	OA11; P-1	OA11; P-1
• Secure hair and jewelry for lab/shop activities.	C463	OA12; P-1	OA12; P-1	OA12; P-1

Time off_____

Time on_____

Total time_____

Materials Required
- Regular safety glasses
- Gloves
- Shoes

Some Safety Issues to Consider
- Comply with personal and environmental safety practices associated with clothing; eye protection; hand tools; power equipment; proper ventilation; and the handling, storage, and disposal of chemicals/materials in accordance with local, state, and federal safety and environmental regulations.
- Shop rules and procedures are critical to your safety. Please give these your utmost attention.

Performance Standard
0—No exposure: No information or practice provided during the program; complete training required

1—Exposure only: General information provided with no practice time; close supervision needed; additional training required

2—Limited practice: Has practiced job during training program; additional training required to develop skill

3—Moderately skilled: Has performed job independently during training program; limited additional training may be required

4—Skilled: Can perform job independently with no additional training

▶ TASK Comply with the required use of safety glasses, ear protection, gloves, and shoes during lab/shop activities.

MLR OA10 **AST** OA10 **MAST** OA10

Time off_____

Time on_____

Total time_____

CDX Tasksheet Number: C461

1. Describe the safety glasses policy for your shop (be specific):

2. Describe the policy related to ear protection in the shop (be specific):

3. Describe the policy related to gloves for your shop (be specific):

4. Describe the policy related to work shoes for your shop (be specific):

5. These tasks require observation of the student over a prolonged period. Ask your instructor to give you a date for your evaluation.

    a. Write that date here: _____

6. Continue with your projects, complying with the safe use of safety glasses, gloves, shoes, clothing, and hair containment during all lab/shop activities.

7. On or after that date, have your instructor verify satisfactory completion of these tasks.

Performance Rating

CDX Tasksheet Number: C461

☐	☐	☐	☐	☐
0	1	2	3	4

Supervisor/instructor signature _____ Date _____

▶ TASK Identify and wear appropriate clothing for lab/shop activities.

MLR OA11 | AST OA11 | MAST OA11

Time off_____

Time on_____

Total time_____

CDX Tasksheet Number: C462

1. Describe the clothing requirements for your shop (be specific):

2. **These tasks require observation of the student over a prolonged period. Ask your instructor to give you a date for your evaluation.**

   a. **Write that date here:** _____

3. Continue with your projects, complying with the safe use of safety glasses, gloves, shoes, clothing, and hair containment during all lab/shop activities.

4. On or after that date, have your instructor verify satisfactory completion of these tasks.

Performance Rating

CDX Tasksheet Number: C462

☐	☐	☐	☐	☐
0	1	2	3	4

Supervisor/instructor signature _____ Date _____

▶ **TASK** Secure hair and jewelry for lab/shop activities.

MLR OA12 **AST** OA12 **MAST** OA12

Time off_____

Time on_____

Total time_____

CDX Tasksheet Number: C463

1. List your shop's policy concerning securing hair in the shop (be specific):

2. List your shop's policy concerning jewelry in the shop (be specific):

3. **These tasks require observation of the student over a prolonged period. Ask your instructor to give you a date for your evaluation.**

    a. **Write that date here:** _____

4. Continue with your projects, complying with the safe use of safety glasses, gloves, shoes, clothing, and hair containment during all lab/shop activities.

5. On or after that date, have your instructor verify satisfactory completion of these tasks.

Performance Rating

CDX Tasksheet Number: C463

0	1	2	3	4

Supervisor/instructor signature _____ Date _____

General Safety: Tool Safety

Student/intern information:

Name _____ Date _____ Class _____

Learning Objective/Task	CDX Tasksheet Number	2013 MLR NATEF Reference Number; Priority Level	2013 AST NATEF Reference Number; Priority Level	2013 MAST NATEF Reference Number; Priority Level
• Identify tools and their usage in automotive applications.	C466	OB1; P-1	OB1; P-1	OB1; P-1
• Identify standard and metric designation.	C467	OB2; P-1	OB2; P-1	OB2; P-1
• Utilize safe procedures for handling of tools and equipment.	C452	OA2; P-1	OA2; P-1	OA2; P-1
• Demonstrate safe handling and use of appropriate tools.	C468	OB3; P-1	OB3; P-1	OB3; P-1
• Demonstrate proper cleaning, storage, and maintenance of tools and equipment.	C469	OB4; P-1	OB4; P-1	OB4; P-1
• Demonstrate proper use of precision measuring tools (e.g., micrometer, dial-indicator, dial-caliper).	C896	OB5; P-1	OB5; P-1	OB5; P-1

Time off_____

Time on_____

Total time_____

Materials Required

- Standard toolkit and other tools as required
- Precision measuring tools: micrometer, dial-indicator, dial-caliper, etc.

Some Safety Issues to Consider

- Comply with personal and environmental safety practices associated with clothing; eye protection; hand tools; power equipment; proper ventilation; and the handling, storage, and disposal of chemicals/materials in accordance with local, state, and federal safety and environmental regulations.
- Tools allow us to increase our productivity and effectiveness. However, they must be used according to the manufacturer's procedures. Failure to follow those procedures can result in serious injury or death.

Performance Standard

0—No exposure: No information or practice provided during the program; complete training required

1—Exposure only: General information provided with no practice time; close supervision needed; additional training required

2—Limited practice: Has practiced job during training program; additional training required to develop skill

3—Moderately skilled: Has performed job independently during training program; limited additional training may be required

4—Skilled: Can perform job independently with no additional training

Time off_____

Time on_____

Total time_____

CDX Tasksheet Number: C466

1. **Using the following list, describe the specific function/purpose of each of the following tools and any disadvantages/problems with using the tool, if any:**

    a. **Open-end wrench:**

    b. **Box-end wrench:**

    c. **Socket:**

    d. **Ratchet:**

    e. **Torque wrench:**

    f. **Slotted screwdriver:**

    g. **Phillips screwdriver:**

h. Tap:

i. Die:

j. Feeler blade:

k. Line wrench/flare-nut wrench:

l. Allen wrench:

m. Torx screwdriver or socket:

n. Hacksaw:

o. Oil filter wrench:

p. Compression gauge:

q. DVOM/DMM:

r. Test light:

s. Diagonal side cutters:

t. Locking pliers:

u. Needle-nose pliers:

v. Brake spoon:

w. Micrometer:

x. **Dial indicator:**

y. **Anti-freeze hydrometer:**

z. **Snap-ring pliers:**

3. Have your supervisor/instructor verify satisfactory completion of this procedure, any observations found, and any necessary action(s) recommended.

Performance Rating

CDX Tasksheet Number: C466

0	1	2	3	4
☐	☐	☐	☐	☐

Supervisor/instructor signature _____ Date _____

Time off_____

Time on_____

Total time_____

CDX Tasksheet Number: C467

1. Complete the following conversions from metric to standard and vice versa using the conversion charts below.

Volume

Volume is the amount of space occupied by a three-dimensional object. The metric system uses liters (l) or cubic centimeters (cc or cm³). The Imperial system uses gallons (gal) and quarts (qt) for "wet" volume and cubic feet (ft³) for "dry" volume. You'll need to determine volume any time you fill a vehicle's reservoir with liquid. This includes petrol/gasoline, coolant, oil, transmission fluid, or lubricant.

Volume Conversions	
Imperial-Imperial	4 US qt = 1 US gal 1 ft³ = 7.48 US gal 1 ft³ = 6.22 UK gal
Metric-Metric	1 L = 1000 cc 1 cc = 0.001 L
Imperial-Metric	1 in.³ = 16.387 cc 1 US gal = 3.78 L 1 UK gal = 4.54 L 1 US qt = 0.95 L
Metric-Imperial	1 L = 61.0237 in.³ 1 L = 0.035 ft³ 1 L = 0.26 US gal 1 L = 0.21 UK gal 1 L = 1.05 qt

2. **Knowledge Check: Convert the following:**
   a. **3.0 L = _____ in.³**
   b. **350 in.³ = _____ L**
   c. **3.0 gal = _____ L**
   d. **9 L = _____ gal**

Mass

Mass is a unit or system of units by which a degree of heaviness is measured. The metric system uses grams (g), kilograms (kg), and tonnes (t). The Imperial system uses ounces (oz), pounds (lb), and tons (T). In the workshop, you will use these measurements to determine the lifting capacity of equipment like hydraulic and engine hoists and floor jacks.

Mass Conversions	
Imperial-Imperial	16 oz = 1 lb 2000 lb = 1 T
Metric-Metric	1000 g = 1 kg 1000 kg = 1 t
Imperial-Metric	1 oz = 28.3 g 1 lb = 453 g 2.2 lb = 1 kg 1 T = 0.907 t
Metric-Imperial	1 t = 1.10 T

3. **Knowledge Check: Convert the following:**
   a. 8 oz = _____ g
   b. 475 g = _____ oz
   c. 6.6 lb = _____ kg
   d. 4500 kg = _____ lb

Torque

Torque is the twisting force applied to a shaft. The metric system uses the Newton meter (Nm). The Imperial system uses the inch-pound (in-lb) and the foot-pound (ft-lb). Vehicle manufacturers specify torque settings for key fasteners on the engine and wheels. You will need to follow the specifications or you could strip threads or break bolts. Torque is also an important concept when discussing engine performance. A foot-pound (ft-lb) is the twisting force applied to a shaft by a lever 1 foot long with a 1-pound mass on the end. A Newton meter (Nm) is the twisting force applied to a shaft by a level 1 meter long with a force of 1 Newton applied to the end of the lever. (1N is equivalent to the force applied by a mass of 100.)

Torque Conversions	
Imperial–Imperial	12 in-lb = 1 ft-lb 1 in-lb = 0.08 ft-lb
Imperial–Metric	1 ft-lb = 1.34 Nm
Metric–Imperial	1 Nm = 0.74 ft-lb 1 Nm = 8.8 in-lb

4. **Knowledge Check: Convert the following:**
   a. 48 in-lb = _____ ft-lb
   b. 15 ft-lb = _____ in-lb
   c. 65 ft-lb = _____ Nm
   d. 142 Nm = _____ ft-lb

Pressure

Pressure is a measurement of force per unit area. The metric system uses kilopascals (kPa) and bar. The Imperial system uses pounds per square inch (psi) and atmospheres. *Vacuum* is a term given to a pressure that is less than atmospheric pressure. The Imperial system measures vacuum in inches of mercury (" Hg) or inches of water. The metric system measures vacuum in millimeters of mercury (mm Hg). You'll need to understand pressure conversions when filling tires and replacing air-conditioning refrigerants or using a vacuum gauge.

Pressure Conversions	
Imperial–Imperial	14.7 psi = 1 atmosphere 1" Hg = 14" H_2O 0" Hg = 1 atmosphere
Metric–Metric	100 kPa = 1 bar
Imperial–Metric	1 psi = 6.89 kPa 1 atmosphere = 101.3 kPa 1" Hg = 25.4 mm Hg 1 atmosphere = 1.013 bar

5. **Knowledge Check: Convert the following:**
   a. 14.7 psi = _____ kPa
   b. 650 kPa = _____ psi
   c. 22 psi = _____ bar
   d. 5.5 bar = _____ psi

6. Have your supervisor/instructor verify satisfactory completion of this procedure, any observations found, and any necessary action(s) recommended.

Performance Rating

CDX Tasksheet Number: C467

0	1	2	3	4

Supervisor/instructor signature _____ Date _____

▶ **TASK** Utilize safe procedures for handling of tools and equipment.

MLR OA2 | AST OA2 | MAST OA2

Time off_____

Time on_____

Total time_____

CDX Tasksheet Number: C452

1. **These tasks will require observation of the student over a prolonged period after the initial check. Ask your instructor to give you a date for your evaluation.**

   a. **Write that date here:** _____

2. Continue with your other projects, utilizing safe handling of tools and equipment including proper cleaning, maintenance, and storage of the tools and equipment until the date of your evaluation.

3. On or after that date, have your instructor verify satisfactory completion of each task.

Performance Rating

CDX Tasksheet Number: C452

0	1	2	3	4

Supervisor/instructor signature _____ Date _____

▶ TASK Demonstrate safe handling and use of appropriate tools.

MLR OB3   AST OB3   MAST OB3

Time off _____

Time on _____

Total time _____

CDX Tasksheet Number: C468

1. **These tasks will require observation of the student over a prolonged period after the initial check. Ask your instructor to give you a date for your evaluation.**

    a. **Write that date here:** _____

2. Continue with your other projects, demonstrating safe handling, proper cleaning, maintenance, and storage of the tools until the date of your evaluation.

3. On or after that date, have your instructor verify satisfactory completion of each task.

Performance Rating

CDX Tasksheet Number: C468

0	1	2	3	4

Supervisor/instructor signature _____ Date _____

▶ TASK Demonstrate proper cleaning, storage, and maintenance of tools and equipment.

MLR OB4   **AST** OB4   **MAST** OB4

Time off_____

Time on_____

Total time_____

CDX Tasksheet Number: C469

1. **These tasks will require observation of the student over a prolonged period after the initial check. Ask your instructor to give you a date for your evaluation.**

    a. **Write that date here:** _____

2. Continue with your other projects, demonstrating safe handling, proper cleaning, maintenance, and storage of the tools until the date of your evaluation.

3. On or after that date, have your instructor verify satisfactory completion of each task.

Performance Rating

CDX Tasksheet Number: C469

☐	☐	☐	☐	☐
0	1	2	3	4

Supervisor/instructor signature _____ Date _____

► **TASK** Demonstrate proper use of precision measuring tools
(e.g., micrometer, dial-indicator, dial-caliper).

MLR OB5　**AST** OB5　**MAST** OB5

Time off_____

Time on_____

Total time_____

CDX Tasksheet Number: C896

1. **These tasks will require observation of the student over a prolonged period after the initial check. Ask your instructor to give you a date for your evaluation.**

   a. **Write that date here:** _____

2. Continue with your other projects, demonstrating safe handling, proper cleaning, maintenance, and storage of the tools until the date of your evaluation.

3. On or after that date, have your instructor verify satisfactory completion of each task.

Performance Rating

CDX Tasksheet Number: C896

0	1	2	3	4

Supervisor/instructor signature _____ Date _____

General Safety:
Vehicle Protection and Jack and Lift Safety

Student/intern information:

Name _____ Date _____ Class _____

Vehicle used for this activity:

Year _____ Make _____ Model _____

Odometer _____ VIN _____

Learning Objective/Task	CDX Tasksheet Number	2013 MLR NATEF Reference Number; Priority Level	2013 AST NATEF Reference Number; Priority Level	2013 MAST NATEF Reference Number; Priority Level
• Identify purpose and demonstrate proper use of fender covers and mats.	C473	OC2; P-1	OC2; P-1	OC2; P-1
• Utilize proper ventilation procedures for working within the lab/shop area.	C455	OA5; P-1	OA5; P-1	OA5; P-1
• Identify and use proper placement of floor jacks and jack stands.	C453	OA3; P-1	OA3; P-1	OA3; P-1
• Identify and use proper procedures for safe lift operation.	C454	OA4; P-1	OA4; P-1	OA4; P-1
• Ensure vehicle is prepared to return to customer per school/company policy (floor mats, steering wheel cover, etc.).	C476	OD1; P-1	OD1; P-1	OD1; P-1

Time off_____

Time on_____

Total time_____

Materials Required
- Vehicle
- Fender, seat, steering wheel, and carpet covers
- Floor jack
- Jack stand(s)
- Wheel chocks
- Vehicle hoist
- Shop rag
- Possible cleaning supplies

Some Safety Issues to Consider
- Comply with personal and environmental safety practices associated with clothing; eye protection; hand tools; power equipment; proper ventilation; and the handling, storage, and disposal of chemicals/materials in accordance with local, state, and federal safety and environmental regulations.
- Floor jacks and jack stands must have a capacity rating higher than the load lifted.
- Floor jacks and jack stands must be used on a hard, level surface. Do not attempt to lift or support a vehicle under any other conditions.

- Jacks are designed to lift a vehicle, not to support it. Always use jack stands once the vehicle has been lifted.
- Have the jack stands ready, and at hand, prior to lifting the vehicle.
- Vehicle hoists are important tools that increase productivity and make the job easier. But they also can cause severe injury or death if used improperly. Make sure you follow the hoist's and vehicle manufacturers' operation procedures. Also, make sure you have your supervisor's/instructor's permission to use a vehicle hoist.
- It is critical that the vehicle be returned to the customer in proper working order. Double-check your work before releasing the vehicle to the customer.

Performance Standard

0–No exposure: No information or practice provided during the program; complete training required

1–Exposure only: General information provided with no practice time; close supervision needed; additional training required

2–Limited practice: Has practiced job during training program; additional training required to develop skill

3–Moderately skilled: Has performed job independently during training program; limited additional training may be required

4–Skilled: Can perform job independently with no additional training

Identify purpose and demonstrate proper use of fender covers and mats.

MLR OC2 | **AST** OC2 | **MAST** OC2

Time off_____

Time on_____

Total time_____

CDX Tasksheet Number: C473

1. **Identify the purpose of the following items:**

    a. Fender cover:

    b. Seat cover:

    c. Steering wheel cover:

    d. Carpet cover/floor mat:

2. Properly prepare a vehicle for service or repair, using the above covers.

3. Have your supervisor/instructor verify satisfactory completion of this procedure, any observations found, and any necessary action(s) recommended.

Performance Rating

CDX Tasksheet Number: C473

0	1	2	3	4

Supervisor/instructor signature _____ Date _____

▶ **TASK** Utilize proper ventilation procedures for working within the lab/shop area.

Time off_____

Time on_____

Total time_____

CDX Tasksheet Number: C455

1. **List the OSHA personal exposure limit for carbon monoxide over an 8-hour work period:** _____ **ppm**

2. Properly position a vehicle in a work stall.

3. Properly connect the exhaust extraction system to the vehicle exhaust.

4. Turn on, or verify that the extraction system is on.

5. With your instructor's permission, start the vehicle and verify the extraction equipment is secure and operating properly.

6. Have your instructor verify your previously given answer, and proper exhaust extraction usage. **Supervisor/instructor's initials:** _____

7. Turn off the vehicle, return the exhaust hoses to their proper storage places, and shut off the extraction system if it isn't being used anymore.

8. Have your supervisor/instructor verify satisfactory completion of this procedure, any observations found, and any necessary action(s) recommended.

Performance Rating

CDX Tasksheet Number: C455

0	1	2	3	4

Supervisor/instructor signature _____ Date _____

▶ TASK Identify and use proper placement of floor jacks and jack stands.

Time off_____

Time on_____

Total time_____

CDX Tasksheet Number: C453

1. Research the jacking and lifting procedures for this vehicle in the appropriate service manual.

   a. Draw a diagram of the vehicle's lift points:

2. Check to make sure the vehicle is on a hard, level surface. If not, move it to a safe location.

3. Install wheel chocks. Prepare the floor jack and stands for use.

4. Lift and support one end of the vehicle on jack stands according to the manufacturer's procedure.

   a. Have your instructor initial to verify proper jack stand placement:

   _____

5. Lift the vehicle and remove the jack stands. Return the jack and stands to their proper storage places.

6. Return the vehicle to its beginning condition and return any tools you used to their proper locations.

7. Have your supervisor/instructor verify satisfactory completion of this procedure, any observations found, and any necessary action(s) recommended.

Performance Rating

CDX Tasksheet Number: C453

0	1	2	3	4

Supervisor/instructor signature _____ Date _____

MLR	AST	MAST
0A4	0A4	0A4

Time off_____

Time on_____

Total time_____

CDX Tasksheet Number: C454

Vehicle, if different than above:

Year _____ Make _____ Model_____

Odometer_____ VIN_____

1. Position the vehicle in proper relation to the lift, taking into consideration the center of gravity of the vehicle.

> **NOTE** Check the vehicle for unusual loading, such as heavy loads in the trunk or truck bed. If you find this situation, notify your instructor immediately.

2. Position the lift arms in the proper location as specified by the manufacturer.

3. Raise the lift until one of the arms lightly contacts the lift point. Check the position of the lift arms to make sure they are in contact with (or just about to contact) the proper points.

> **NOTE** Make sure the lift arms are not touching or pinching anything they shouldn't be in contact with, including the rocker panel, running boards, and fuel or brake lines, etc.

4. If the arms are in the proper position, raise the vehicle a few inches off the ground. Using a strong part of the vehicle, moderately shake the vehicle to make sure it is stable.

> **NOTE** If the vehicle shifts position at all or is out of balance, lower the vehicle and reset the lift arms or reposition the vehicle.

5. If the vehicle is stable, lift the vehicle to the height indicated by your instructor and engage the locks or lower the lift onto the locks. **Instructor/Supervisor Initial _____**

6. Verify that there are no obstacles under the vehicle, and that all doors are closed. Lower the vehicle and move the lift arms out of the way of the vehicle.

7. Return the vehicle to its beginning condition and return any tools you used to their proper locations.

8. Have your supervisor/instructor verify satisfactory completion of this procedure, any observations found, and any necessary action(s) recommended.

Performance Rating

CDX Tasksheet Number: C454

| 0 | 1 | 2 | 3 | 4 |

Supervisor/instructor signature _____ Date _____

► TASK Ensure vehicle is prepared to return to customer per school/company policy (floor mats, steering wheel cover, etc.).

MLR OD1   AST OD1   MAST OD1

CDX Tasksheet Number: C476

> **NOTE** A properly protected vehicle and good work habits will make this task much easier.

1. Double check that all work has been completed. Nothing can be missing, loose, or leaking.

   a. Student initial when completed: _____

2. If your instructor deems it necessary, test-drive the vehicle to be sure of proper repair and operation of the vehicle.

   a. Have your instructor initial here: _____

3. Double check that all tools are put away and stored properly.

   a. Student initial when completed: _____

4. Remove all fender covers, seat covers, floor covers, and steering wheel covers. Return them to their storage place or dispose of them properly, depending on the type of cover.

   a. Student initial when completed: _____

5. Check the exterior of the vehicle for greasy fingerprints or grime. Clean with an appropriate cleaner. Follow your shop's policies on this procedure.

   a. Student initial when completed: _____

6. Check the following interior locations for dirt or greasy spots. Clean with an appropriate cleaner. Follow your shop's policies on this procedure:

   a. Carpet and floor mats. Student initial when completed: _____
   b. Seats. Student initial when completed: _____
   c. Steering wheel and parking brake handle. Student initial when completed: _____
   d. Door panel and handles. Student initial when completed: _____

7. If the vehicle is ready to return to the customer, the vehicle may need to be moved out of the shop. Get your instructor's permission to move the vehicle to the customer pick-up area.

   a. Have your instructor initial here: _____

8. Return to your work stall and clean up the floor, benches, and related area.

   a. Student initial when completed: _____

9. Have your supervisor/instructor verify satisfactory completion of this procedure, any observations found, and any necessary action(s) recommended.

Performance Rating

0	1	2	3	4

Supervisor/instructor signature _____ Date _____

General Safety: Vehicle, Customer, and Service Information

Student/intern information:

Name _____ Date _____ Class _____

Vehicle used for this activity:

Year _____ Make _____ Model _____

Odometer _____ VIN _____

Learning Objective/Task	CDX Tasksheet Number	2013 MLR NATEF Reference Number; Priority Level	2013 AST NATEF Reference Number; Priority Level	2013 MAST NATEF Reference Number; Priority Level	Time off _____
• Proper vehicle identification information: Define the use and purpose of the VIN, engine numbers, and data code; locate the VIN, and apply knowledge of VIN information.	471	N/A	N/A	N/A	Time on _____
• Identify information needed and the service requested on a repair order.	C472	OC1; P-1	OC1; P-1	OC1; P-1	
• Demonstrate use of 3 Cs (concern, cause, and correction).	C474	OC3; P-1	OC3; P-1	OC3; P-1	Total time _____
• Review vehicle service history.	C475	OC4; P-1	OC4; P-1	OC4; P-1	

Materials Required

- Vehicle
- Service information
- Completed repair order assigned by your instructor
- Several repair orders for the same vehicle from repairs/services performed over an extended period of time
- Scheduled maintenance chart for this vehicle
- Blank repair order

Some Safety Issues to Consider

- Comply with personal and environmental safety practices associated with clothing; eye protection; hand tools; power equipment; proper ventilation; and the handling, storage, and disposal of chemicals/materials in accordance with local, state, and federal safety and environmental regulations.

Performance Standard

0–No exposure: No information or practice provided during the program; complete training required

1–Exposure only: General information provided with no practice time; close supervision needed; additional training required

2–Limited practice: Has practiced job during training program; additional training required to develop skill

3–Moderately skilled: Has performed job independently during training program; limited additional training may be required

4–Skilled: Can perform job independently with no additional training

▶ TASK Proper vehicle identification information: Define the use and purpose of the VIN, engine numbers, and data code; locate the VIN, and apply knowledge of VIN information.

Additional Task

Time off_____

Time on_____

Total time_____

CDX Tasksheet Number: 471

1. **Research the location and description of the VIN in an appropriate service manual.**

    a. **Location of VIN:** _____

    b. **VIN:** _____

2. **Using the VIN on the vehicle assigned to you, identify the following information. (Write both corresponding VIN code designation and what it represents.)**

    a. **Country of origin:** _____

    b. **Location of manufacturing plant:** _____

    c. **Passenger restraint system:** _____

    d. **Engine designation:** _____

    e. **Model year:** _____

3. **Which position in the VIN is the model year?** _____

4. **Which position in the VIN is the engine designation?** _____

5. Have your supervisor/instructor verify satisfactory completion of this procedure, any observations found, and any necessary action(s) recommended.

Performance Rating

CDX Tasksheet Number: 471

☐	☐	☐	☐	☐
0	1	2	3	4

Supervisor/instructor signature _____ Date _____

▶ **TASK** Identify information needed and the service requested on a repair order.

MLR OC1 | **AST** OC1 | **MAST** OC1

Time off_____

Time on_____

Total time_____

CDX Tasksheet Number: C472

1. **Familiarize yourself with the assigned repair order. Locate and list the following information below.**

   a. **Date:** _____

   b. **Customer:** _____

   c. **Address:** _____

   d. **Daytime phone number:** _____

   e. **Year:** _____

   f. **Make:** _____

   g. **Model:** _____

   h. **Color:** _____

   i. **License and state:** _____

   j. **Odometer reading:** _____

   k. **VIN:** _____

   l. **Customer concern(s)/service requested:**

2. **Did the customer sign the repair order authorizing the repairs?**
   Yes: _____ **No:** _____

3. Return the sample repair order to its proper storage place.

4. Have your supervisor/instructor verify satisfactory completion of this procedure, any observations found, and any necessary action(s) recommended.

Performance Rating

CDX Tasksheet Number: C472

0	1	2	3	4

Supervisor/instructor signature _____ Date _____

Demonstrate use of 3 Cs (concern, cause, and correction).

MLR OC3   **AST** OC3   **MAST** OC3

Time off _____

Time on _____

Total time _____

CDX Tasksheet Number: C474

1. **Using the following scenario, write up the 3 Cs as listed on most repair orders. Assume that the customer authorized the recommended repairs.**

   A customer complains that his vehicle is leaving what looks like oil spots on the landlord's driveway after he ran over something in the road a few days ago. You check the engine oil find that it is about 1/2 a quart low, but looks pretty clean, like it was changed recently. The engine oil life monitor indicates 92% oil life remaining. You safely raise and secure the vehicle on the hoist. While visually inspecting the underside of the vehicle, you notice oil dripping off of the engine oil drain plug. Checking the torque of the drain plug shows that the drain plug isn't loose. Closer inspection reveals a shiny spot on the aluminum oil pan near the drain plug. There is a small crack in the oil pan that is seeping oil and dripping slowly off of the drain plug.

2. **Concern/complaint:**

3. **Cause:**

4. **Correction:**

5. Have your supervisor/instructor verify satisfactory completion of the previous answers, and any necessary action(s) recommended.

Performance Rating

CDX Tasksheet Number: C474

0	1	2	3	4

Supervisor/instructor signature _____ Date _____

MLR OC4   **AST** OC4   **MAST** OC4

Time off_____

Time on_____

CDX Tasksheet Number: C475

Total time_____

1. **Familiarize yourself with the repair history as listed on the repair orders and answer the following questions.**

    a. **What was the first date this vehicle was serviced?** _____

    b. **What was the last date this vehicle was serviced?** _____

    c. **What was the most major repair performed?**

    d. **Was this vehicle ever returned for the same problem more than once? Yes:** _____ **No:** _____

        i. **If so, for what and how many times?** _____

    e. **Compare this list to the scheduled maintenance chart and list any missed maintenance tasks between the first service and the last service:**

2. Have your supervisor/instructor verify satisfactory completion of this procedure, any observations found, and any necessary action(s) recommended.

Performance Rating

CDX Tasksheet Number: C475

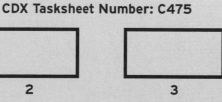 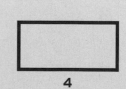

| 0 | 1 | 2 | 3 | 4 |

Supervisor/instructor signature _____ Date _____

General Safety: SRS and ABS Safety

Student/intern information:

Name _____ Date _____ Class _____

Vehicle used for this activity:

Year _____ Make _____ Model_____

Odometer_____VIN_____

Learning Objective/Task	CDX Tasksheet Number	2013 MLR NATEF Reference Number; Priority Level	2013 AST NATEF Reference Number; Priority Level	2013 MAST NATEF Reference Number; Priority Level
• Demonstrate awareness of the safety aspects of supplemental restraint systems' (SRS) electronic brake control systems, and hybrid vehicle high-voltage circuits.	C464	OA13; P-1	OA13; P-1	OA13; P-1
• Demonstrate awareness of the safety aspects of high-voltage circuits (such as high-intensity discharge [HID] lamps, ignition systems, injection systems, etc.).	C895	OA14; P-1	OA14; P-1	OA14; P-1

Time off_____

Time on_____

Total time_____

Materials Required

• Vehicle with SRS and anti-lock brake system (ABS)
• Special tools or equipment, if specified

Some Safety Issues to Consider

• Comply with personal and environmental safety practices associated with clothing; eye protection; hand tools; power equipment; proper ventilation; and the handling, storage, and disposal of chemicals/materials in accordance with local, state, and federal safety and environmental regulations.
• Deployment of the SRS system could cause serious injury or death. Follow all of the manufacturer's procedures before working on this system.
• The ABS system may hold brake fluid under extremely high pressure. Follow the manufacturer's procedures to relieve this pressure before working on this system.
• Hybrid and electric vehicles have batteries with VERY high voltage, which can kill you if handled improperly. Always get permission from your supervisor/instructor before working on, or near, the system. Also, ALWAYS follow the manufacturer's procedure when servicing a hybrid or electric vehicle.

Performance Standard

0–No exposure: No information or practice provided during the program; complete training required

1–Exposure only: General information provided with no practice time; close supervision needed; additional training required

2–Limited practice: Has practiced job during training program; additional training required to develop skill

3–Moderately skilled: Has performed job independently during training program; limited additional training may be required

4–Skilled: Can perform job independently with no additional training

MLR	AST	MAST
OA13	OA13	OA13

Time off_____

Time on_____

Total time_____

CDX Tasksheet Number: C464

1. **Research the following procedures for a hybrid vehicle in the appropriate service information.**

   a. List the precautions when working around or on the SRS system on this vehicle:

   b. List the steps to disable the SRS system on this vehicle:

   c. List the steps to enable the SRS system on this vehicle:

   d. List the precautions when working on or around the electronic brake control system on this vehicle:

e. **Identify the high-voltage circuit wiring on this vehicle. What color is the wire conduit?**

f. **List or print out the high-voltage disable procedure for this vehicle.**

2. Have your supervisor/instructor verify satisfactory completion of this task.

Performance Rating

CDX Tasksheet Number: C464

0	1	2	3	4

Supervisor/instructor signature _____ Date _____

▶ **TASK** Demonstrate awareness of the safety aspects of high-voltage circuits (such as high-intensity discharge [HID] lamps, ignition systems, injection systems, etc.)

MLR OA14   **AST** OA14   **MAST** OA14

Time off_____

Time on_____

Total time

CDX Tasksheet Number: C895

Vehicle used for this activity:

Year _____ Make _____ Model_____

Odometer_____ VIN_____

1. **Using appropriate service information, identify system voltage and safety precautions associated with high-intensity discharge headlights, ignition systems, and injection systems.**

   a. **HID lamp voltage:** _____ **volts**

   b. **List the safety precautions required when working on HID system:**

   c. **Maximum secondary ignition system voltage:** _____ **volts**

   d. **List the safety precautions required when working around ignition systems:**

   e. **Injection system voltage (on a vehicle with a high-voltage injection system):** _____ **volts**

   f. **List the safety precautions required when working around high-voltage injection systems:**

2. Have your supervisor/instructor verify satisfactory completion of this task.

Performance Rating

CDX Tasksheet Number: C895

0	1	2	3	4

Supervisor/instructor signature _____ Date _____

General Safety: Associated Studies

Student/intern information:

Name _____ Date _____ Class _____

Learning Objective/Task	CDX Tasksheet Number	2013 MLR NATEF Reference Number; Priority Level	2013 AST NATEF Reference Number; Priority Level	2013 MAST NATEF Reference Number; Priority Level
• Recognize different vehicle types and body components.	N/A	N/A	N/A	N/A
• Complete an accident report	N/A	N/A	N/A	N/A
• Identify vehicle needs and obtain customer agreement	N/A	N/A	N/A	N/A
• Conduct research to find specific information related to the automobile industry	N/A	N/A	N/A	N/A
• Complete work order to include customer information, vehicle identifying information customer concern related service history, cause, and correction	C590	OC5; P-1	OC5; P-1	OC5; P-1

Time off_____

Time on_____

Total time_____

Materials Required

- A range of vehicles of the designated types, which are fitted with different configurations
- Customer (may be role player in simulated environment)
- Vehicle for inspection
- Vehicle labor guide and service information data
- Blank repair order
- Service information

Some Safety Issues to Consider

- Comply with personal and environmental safety practices associated with clothing; eye protection; hand tools; power equipment; proper ventilation; and the handling, storage, and disposal of chemicals/materials in accordance with local, state, and federal safety and environmental regulations.

Performance Standard

0—No exposure: No information or practice provided during the program; complete training required

1—Exposure only: General information provided with no practice time; close supervision needed; additional training required

2—Limited practice: Has practiced job during training program; additional training required to develop skill

3—Moderately skilled: Has performed job independently during training program; limited additional training may be required

4—Skilled: Can perform job independently with no additional training

Time off_____

Time on_____

Total time_____

CDX Tasksheet Number: N/A

1. **Inspect a range of vehicles or illustrations (including computer-based), identify the following types of vehicles, and complete the table below.**

Vehicle Type	Year	Make	Model
Convertible			
Four-wheel drive			
Cube van			
Minivan			
Front-engine RWD			
Mid-engine RWD			
Rear-engine RWD			
Front-engine FWD			

2. **Now inspect a range of vehicles or illustrations (including computer-based), identify the following vehicle body parts, and complete the table below.**

Component	Year	Make	Model
Sun roof			
Tailgate			
Rear spoiler			
Hinged doors			
Sliding doors			
Satellite navigation			
Aerodynamic headlights			

3. Have your supervisor/instructor verify satisfactory completion of this procedure, any observations found, and any necessary action(s) recommended.

Performance Rating

CDX Tasksheet Number: N/A

0	1	2	3	4

Supervisor/instructor signature _____ Date _____

Time off_____

Time on_____

Total time_____

CDX Tasksheet Number: N/A

1. Use your school's accident report form to complete this task.

   a. Sam, another student, cut himself while helping you service a customer's car. Can you help Sam with the paperwork? (Use the following information to fill out the school's accident report. Add pertinent details as required on the form.)

Date	Today
Time	4:45 PM
Name	Sam Smith
Location	Work Bay 1B
Description	A cut on the left thumb
Treatment	Applied first aid, cleaned the wound and used a Band-Aid to cover the wound, no stitches were required
Insurance Claim	No

2. Have your supervisor/instructor verify satisfactory completion of this procedure, any observations found, and any necessary action(s) recommended.

Performance Rating

CDX Tasksheet Number: N/A

0	1	2	3	4

Supervisor/instructor signature _____ Date _____

Time off_____

Time on_____

Total time_____

CDX Tasksheet Number: N/A

Vehicle used for this activity:

Year _____ Make _____ Model _____

Odometer _____ VIN _____

1. Carry out the following tasks involving personal interaction with a customer while being observed by your supervisor/instructor.

    a. Making appropriate notes, obtain enough relevant information from the customer to enable you to understand the customer's perception of his or her vehicle's condition (customer concern/complaint). Note your findings here:

    b. Provide the customer with advice and information in relation to the following and summarize each point:

    i. The potential courses of action to rectify any issues:

    ii. The implications of any course of action (positive or negative):

    iii. The most appropriate vehicle repair and/or service procedures for his or her vehicle:

    iv. The estimated cost of the service or repair:

c. Prior to accepting the vehicle for the repair, obtain and record the customer's agreement to the following on the repair order:

   i. A description of the work to be undertaken

   ii. The company's terms and conditions of acceptance, if any

   iii. The estimated cost

   iv. The estimated time of completion, or contact with the customer for an update

d. Confirm your customer's understanding of the scope of work to be performed.

e. Have the customer sign the repair order.

f. Where additional work on the vehicle is required, make contact with the customer and obtain his or her approval prior to undertaking the additional work. Document the agreed course of action on the repair order.

2. Ask your supervisor/instructor to provide feedback and indicate satisfaction with your performance.

   a. Was the advice and information accurate, current, and relevant? Was it presented clearly in a form and manner that the customer would understand? Yes: _____ No: _____

     i. Observations:

   b. Did the student demonstrate positive communication skills and actively encourage the customer to ask questions and seek clarification during the conversations? Yes: _____ No: _____

     i. Observations:

3. Have your supervisor/instructor verify satisfactory completion of this procedure, any observations found, and any necessary action(s) recommended.

Performance Rating

CDX Tasksheet Number: N/A

0	1	2	3	4

Supervisor/instructor signature _____ Date _____

© 2015 Jones & Bartlett Learning, LLC, an Ascend Learning Company

▶ TASK Conduct research to find specific information related to the automotive industry.

Additional Task

Time off_____

Time on_____

Total time_____

CDX Tasksheet Number: N/A

1. While servicing a customer's car, your supervisor/instructor notices that the front tires are wearing out and will need to be replaced soon. Your supervisor/instructor asks Sam, another technician, to take note of the tire specifications so he can get information to inform your customer about the cost and availability. Here is a series of numbers and letters displayed on the side of the tires. Can you help Sam interpret these codes?

P   205   /   65   R   15   89   H

Tire Code	Explanation
P	
205	
65	
R	
15	
89	
H	

2. Have your supervisor/instructor verify satisfactory completion of this procedure, any observations found, and any necessary action(s) recommended.

Performance Rating

CDX Tasksheet Number: N/A

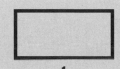 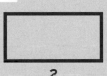 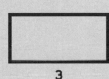 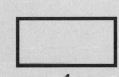

| 0 | 1 | 2 | 3 | 4 |

Supervisor/instructor signature _____ Date _____

© 2015 Jones & Bartlett Learning, LLC, an Ascend Learning Company

Complete work order to include customer information, vehicle identifying information, customer concern, related service history, cause, and correction.

MLR	AST	MAST
OC5	OC5	OC5

Time off_____

Time on_____

Total time_____

CDX Tasksheet Number: C590

Vehicle used for this activity:

Year _____ Make _____ Model _____

Odometer _____ VIN _____

1. Use your company's repair order to complete this task.

   Fred Smith brings in a 2008 Hyundai Santa Fe AWD, with a 3.3 L engine, automatic transmission, 72,426 miles on the odometer, silver paint, VIN 5NMSH73E28H192794. It needs some work before going on a 3000-mile trip. He would like an estimate of repairs needed and has agreed to let your technician inspect the vehicle while you write up the repair order. He gives you the following information:

   a. Home address: 1234 NE Main Street, Anytown, CA 13579
   b. Cell phone: (111) 222-1234
   c. Work phone: (111) 333-4567
   d. Vehicle license number: CDX – 111

2. The customer listed the following concern/complaints:

   a. Small oil leak from under the engine
   b. Small coolant leak from under the engine
   c. Squealing noise coming from the front brakes

3. The technician found the following conditions:

   a. Both valve covers have leaking gaskets.
   b. The water pump is leaking from the shaft and the bearing is worn.
   c. The front brake pads are worn down to the wear indicators, the rotors are a bit under specifications, and the calipers are starting to seep brake fluid past the caliper piston seal and need to be replaced.

4. **Complete the repair order as if all tasks were completed including parts, their cost, and labor.**

5. Have your supervisor/instructor verify satisfactory completion of this procedure, any observations found, and any necessary action(s) recommended.

Performance Rating

CDX Tasksheet Number: C590

0	1	2	3	4
□	□	□	□	□

Supervisor/instructor signature _____ Date _____

Section A1:
Engine Repair

CONTENTS

Engine Repair: Vehicle, Customer, and Service Information

Student/intern information:

Name_____ Date_____ Class_____

Vehicle used for this activity:

Year _____ Make _____ Model_____

Odometer_____VIN_____

Learning Objective/Task	CDX Tasksheet Number	2013 MLR NATEF Reference Number; Priority Level	2013 AST NATEF Reference Number; Priority Level	2013 MAST NATEF Reference Number; Priority Level
• Complete work order to include customer information, vehicle identifying information, customer concern, related service history, cause, and correction.	C885		1A1; P-1	1A1; P-1
• Research applicable vehicle and service information, such as internal engine operation, vehicle service history, service precautions, and technical service bulletins.	C002	1A1; P-1	1A2; P-1	1A2; P-1
• Identify hybrid vehicle internal combustion engine service precautions.	C900	1A7; P-3	1A9; P-3	1A9; P-3
• Demonstrate the use of the 3 Cs (concern, cause, and correction).	NN01	N/A	N/A	N/A

Time off_____

Time on_____

Total time_____

Materials Required

- Blank work order
- Vehicle with available service history records
- Depending on the type of concern, special diagnostic tools may be required. See your supervisor/instructor for instructions to identify what tools may be required.

Some Safety Issues to Consider

- Diagnosis of this fault may require test-driving the vehicle on the school grounds. Attempt this task only with full permission from your instructor and follow all the guidelines exactly.
- When running any vehicles in the shop, make sure you use the shop's exhaust ventilation system to discharge all exhaust gas safely outside.
- Lifting equipment such as vehicle jacks and stands, vehicle hoists, and engine hoists are important tools that increase productivity and make the job easier. However, they can also cause severe injury or death if used improperly. Make sure you follow the manufacturer's operation procedures. Also, make sure you have your supervisor's/instructor's permission to use any particular type of lifting equipment.

- Comply with personal and environmental safety practices associated with clothing; eye protection; hand tools; power equipment; proper ventilation; and the handling, storage, and disposal of chemicals/materials in accordance with local, state, and federal safety and environmental regulations.

Performance Standard

0—No exposure: No information or practice provided during the program; complete training required

1—Exposure only: General information provided with no practice time; close supervision needed; additional training required

2—Limited practice: Has practiced job during training program; additional training required to develop skill

3—Moderately skilled: Has performed job independently during training program; limited additional training may be required

4—Skilled: Can perform job independently with no additional training

▶ **TASK** Complete work order to include customer information, vehicle identifying information, customer concern, related service history, cause, and correction.

AST
1A1

MAST
1A1

Time off_____

Time on_____

Total time_____

CDX Tasksheet Number: C885

1. Using a vehicle with an engine-related customer concern, complete the work order, specifying the following:

   a. Customer information:

   b. Customer concern:

   c. Vehicle identifying information:

   d. Any related service history, etc.:

2. Determine the cause of the concern and list it on the work order.

3. List the action(s) needed to correct the concern, on the work order.

4. Have your supervisor/instructor verify satisfactory completion of the work order, any observations found, and any necessary action(s) recommended.

Performance Rating

CDX Tasksheet Number: C885

0	1	2	3	4

Supervisor/instructor signature _____ Date _____

▶ TASK Research applicable vehicle and service information, such as internal engine operation, vehicle service history, service precautions, and technical service bulletins.

MLR 1A1 | AST 1A2 | MAST 1A2

Time off_____

Time on_____

Total time_____

CDX Tasksheet Number: C002

1. Using the VIN for identification, use the appropriate source to access the vehicle's service history in relation to prior related internal engine work or customer concerns.

   a. List any related repairs/concerns, and their dates:

2. **Using the VIN for identification, access any relevant technical service bulletins for the particular vehicle you are working on in relation to any internal engine updates, precautions, or other service issues. List any related service bulletins and their titles:**

3. Have your supervisor/instructor verify satisfactory completion of this procedure, any observations found, and any necessary action(s) recommended.

> **NOTE** The following sign-off goes along with the first task on this tasksheet and can also be signed off once all of the other tasks in this tasksheet are completed.

Performance Rating

CDX Tasksheet Number: C002

0	1	2	3	4

Supervisor/instructor signature _____ Date _____

Identify hybrid vehicle internal combustion engine service precautions.

MLR
1A7   **AST**
1A9   **MAST**
1A9

Time off_____

Time on_____

CDX Tasksheet Number: C900

Vehicle used for this activity:

Year _____ Make _____ Model_____

Odometer_____ VIN_____

Total time_____

1. **Research the precautions when servicing an internal combustion engine on a hybrid vehicle in the appropriate service information. List all precautions:**

2. Have your supervisor/instructor verify satisfactory completion of the procedure, any observations found, and any necessary action(s) recommended.

Performance Rating

CDX Tasksheet Number: C900

0	1	2	3	4

Supervisor/instructor signature _____ Date _____

Demonstrate the use of the 3 Cs (concern, cause, and correction).

Time off_____

Time on_____

Total time_____

CDX Tasksheet Number: NN01

1. Using the following scenario, write up the 3 Cs as listed on most repair orders. Assume that the customer authorized the recommended repairs.

   An 8-year-old vehicle has been brought to your shop with an engine repair concern. The customer tells you that the vehicle runs rough at all speeds and conditions, and has gotten worse over the past couple of weeks. The malfunction indicator lamp (MIL) is blinking when the engine is running. The customer thought the malfunction was due to bad gas; he ran the tank out and refilled it with good gas from a very reputable station, but the car still runs rough after using half of a tank. The customer authorizes your shop to perform a diagnosis and you find the following:

   a. The vehicle is about 8 years old and has nearly 165,000 miles on it, but is in good overall condition.
   b. There is a diagnostic trouble code P0303, which indicates an engine misfire on cylinder #3.
   c. All of the spark plugs are moderately worn and show signs of moderate oil fouling, and the spark plug wires are original.
   d. Cylinder compression is about 25 psi on cylinder #3. The other cylinders are within specifications, but on the low side.
   e. A cylinder leakage test shows 85% leakage on cylinder #3 past the exhaust valve. The other cylinders show about 25% leakage past the piston rings.
   f. The engine mounts are oil-soaked due to a leaking valve cover and oil pan gaskets.
   g. The rear main seal shows signs of significant leakage.
   h. The oil light sometimes flickers when the engine is fully warmed up and idling, even though the oil is near the full mark.
   i. The radiator has a small coolant leak in the core.

   > **NOTE** Ask your instructor whether you should use a copy of the shop repair order or the 3 Cs in this manual to record this information.

2. **Concern:**

3. **Cause:**

4. Correction:

5. Other recommended service:

6. Have your supervisor/instructor verify satisfactory completion of this procedure, any observations found, and any necessary action(s) recommended.

Performance Rating

CDX Tasksheet Number: NN01

☐	☐	☐	☐	☐
0	1	2	3	4

Supervisor/instructor signature _____ Date _____

Engine Repair: Fastener Repair

Student/intern information:

Name_____ Date_____ Class_____

Vehicle used for this activity:

Year _____ Make _____ Model_____

Odometer_____VIN_____

Learning Objective/Task	CDX Tasksheet Number	2013 MLR NATEF Reference Number; Priority Level	2013 AST NATEF Reference Number; Priority Level	2013 MAST NATEF Reference Number; Priority Level
• Perform common fastener and thread repair, to include: remove broken bolt, restore internal and external threads, and repair internal threads with thread insert.	C886	1A6; P-1	1A7; P-1	1A7; P-1

Time off_____

Time on_____

Total time_____

Materials Required

- Vehicle or simulator with a damaged fastener/thread
- Fastener repair tools specific to the job

Some Safety Issues to Consider

- Power drills are powerful, and the drill bit can grab, especially when enlarging an existing hole. Always follow all safety precautions when drilling.
- Use the proper lubricant when drilling and tapping.
- Comply with personal and environmental safety practices associated with clothing; eye protection; hand tools; power equipment; proper ventilation; and the handling, storage, and disposal of chemicals/materials in accordance with local, state, and federal safety and environmental regulations.

Performance Standard

0—No exposure: No information or practice provided during the program; complete training required

1—Exposure only: General information provided with no practice time; close supervision needed; additional training required

2—Limited practice: Has practiced job during training program; additional training required to develop skill

3—Moderately skilled: Has performed job independently during training program; limited additional training may be required

4—Skilled: Can perform job independently with no additional training

© 2015 Jones & Bartlett Learning, LLC, an Ascend Learning Company

Perform common fastener and thread repair, to include: remove broken bolt, restore internal and external threads, and repair internal threads with thread insert.

MLR	AST	MAST
1A6	1A7	1A7

Time off_____

Time on_____

Total time_____

CDX Tasksheet Number: C886

> **NOTE** Your instructor may prefer that you perform this task on a mock-up or piece of scrap metal. Ask your instructor how he or she would like you to proceed.

1. **Identify the damaged fastener and its location, and list the information here:**

2. **Research the appropriate method of extracting the broken fastener, and list it here:**

3. **Using the appropriate method, remove the broken bolt from its location. List your observation(s):**

4. **Restore internal and external threads as required, and list your results:**

5. Have your supervisor/instructor check your work. **Supervisor's/instructor's initials:** _____

6. **Repair internal threads with a thread insert using the recommended method. List the steps below:**

7. Have your supervisor/instructor verify satisfactory completion of this procedure, any observations found, and any necessary action(s) recommended.

Performance Rating

0	1	2	3	4

Supervisor/instructor signature _____ Date _____

Engine Repair: Engine Mechanical Testing

Student/intern information:

Name_____ Date_____ Class_____

Vehicle used for this activity:

Year _____ Make _____ Model_____

Odometer_____VIN_____

Learning Objective/Task	CDX Tasksheet Number	2013 MLR NATEF Reference Number; Priority Level	2013 AST NATEF Reference Number; Priority Level	2013 MAST NATEF Reference Number; Priority Level
• Inspect engine assembly for fuel, oil, coolant, and other leaks; determine necessary action.	C004	1A3; P-1	1A4; P-1	1A4; P-1
• Verify operation of the instrument panel engine-warning indicators.	C898	1A2: P-1	1A3; P-1	1A3; P-1
• Perform cranking sound diagnosis.	NN09	N/A	N/A	N/A
• Perform engine vacuum tests; determine necessary action.	C392	8A2; P-1	8A5; P-1	8A5; P-1
• Perform cylinder power balance tests; determine necessary action.	C393	8A3; P-2	8A6; P-2	8A6; P-2
• Perform cylinder cranking and running compression tests; determine necessary action.	C709	8A4; P-1	8A7; P-1	8A7; P-1
• Perform cylinder leakage tests; determine necessary action.	C395	8A5; P-1	8A8; P-1	8A8; P-1

Time off_____

Time on_____

Total time_____

Materials Required

- Vehicle or simulator
- Vacuum gauge
- Tachometer (hand-held if the vehicle is not equipped with an in-dash tachometer)
- Insulated spark plug wire pliers (if using this method to disable the cylinders)
- Scan tool (if using this method to disable the cylinders)
- Compression tester
- Cylinder leakage tester
- Stethoscope
- Flashlight

Some Safety Issues to Consider

- You will be working under the hood of a running vehicle. Keep your hands and fingers away from moving belts, fans, and other parts.
- Be sure to only disconnect the proper vacuum hose. Many other hoses look alike but could carry gasoline or hot coolant under high pressure.

- During this test, you may be disabling the ignition or fuel systems. Be sure you only do so for the minimum amount of time to get your readings. Operating the engine with cylinders disabled may lead to damage of the catalytic converter or other parts. If in doubt, ask your supervisor/instructor.
- If you disable the cylinders by disconnecting the spark plug wires, you may expose yourself to extremely high voltage (up to 100,000 volts). Reduce the possibility of electrical shock by using appropriate insulated spark plug wire pliers.
- When running any vehicles in the shop, make sure you use the shop's exhaust ventilation system to discharge all exhaust gas safely outside.
- Always follow your supervisor's/instructor's directions on how to get the piston to top dead center. Failure to do so could cause injury or damage to the vehicle.
- Use caution when turning the engine to top dead center. If you do this by hand, be sure your fingers, hands, etc. stay clear of belts and pulleys that could cause severe pinching.
- Make sure the ignition switch is in the "off" position and the key is removed from the ignition switch during this job to prevent someone from inadvertently cranking the engine over while you are working on it.
- Comply with personal and environmental safety practices associated with clothing; eye protection; hand tools; power equipment; proper ventilation; and the handling, storage, and disposal of chemicals/materials in accordance with local, state, and federal safety and environmental regulations.

Performance Standard

0–No exposure: No information or practice provided during the program; complete training required

1–Exposure only: General information provided with no practice time; close supervision needed; additional training required

2–Limited practice: Has practiced job during training program; additional training required to develop skill

3–Moderately skilled: Has performed job independently during training program; limited additional training may be required

4–Skilled: Can perform job independently with no additional training

MLR 1A3   **AST** 1A4   **MAST** 1A4

Time off_____

Time on_____

Total time_____

CDX Tasksheet Number: C004

> **NOTE** If the vehicle's engine assembly is coated with leaking fluids and road dirt, you may need to pressure wash the engine before inspecting it for leaks. Some very small leaks, or leaks on engines that have a lot of accumulated residue, may be diagnosed with the use of a fluorescent dye and ultraviolet light. Check with your supervisor/instructor about which procedure to perform. Follow the dye check equipment manufacturer's instructions if you are performing this test.

> **NOTE** Fluid leaks can be hard to locate. Remember that gravity tends to pull any leaking fluid down. You will need to identify the highest point of the leak to locate its source. Fluids can also be flung from rotating parts, sprayed under pressure from pinhole leaks, or blown by airflow far from the source. Investigate carefully.

1. **Check for fluid leaks under the hood. List any leaks (component leaking and type of fluid):**

2. Safely raise and secure the vehicle on a hoist.

3. **Inspect the engine, cooling system, fuel system, transmission/transaxle, and any differentials for leaks. Identify the type of fluid leaking and the source of the leak for the following items:**

   a. **Engine:**

   b. **Fuel system:**

   c. **Cooling system:**

d. Transmission/transaxle:

e. Steering system:

f. Differentials:

4. Determine any necessary action(s):

5. Have your supervisor/instructor verify satisfactory completion of this procedure, any observations found, and any necessary action(s) recommended.

Performance Rating

CDX Tasksheet Number: C004

0	1	2	3	4
☐	☐	☐	☐	☐

Supervisor/instructor signature _____ Date _____

Verify operation of the instrument panel
engine-warning indicators.

Time off_____

Time on_____

Total time_____

CDX Tasksheet Number: C898

1. **Research the operation of instrument panel gauges/indicator lights in the appropriate service information. List each of the warning indicators:**

2. **Turn the ignition to the "run" position (engine not running). List the status of each gauge/indicator:**

3. **Start the engine and allow it to run for a few minutes. List the status of each gauge/indicator:**

4. **List any gauges/indicators that are showing a fault and the fault indicated:**

5. Have your supervisor/instructor verify satisfactory completion of this procedure, any observations found, and any necessary action(s) recommended.

Performance Rating

CDX Tasksheet Number: C898

0	1	2	3	4

Supervisor/instructor signature _____ Date _____

Time off_____

Time on_____

Total time_____

CDX Tasksheet Number: NN09

1. Disable the ignition or fuel system so that the engine will crank, but not start.

> **NOTE** Some vehicles can be put into "clear flood" mode by depressing the throttle to the floor before turning the ignition key to the "run" position. This prevents the fuel injectors from being activated. If your vehicle is equipped with this mode, hold the throttle down to the floor and try cranking the engine over (make sure you are prepared to turn off the ignition switch if the engine starts). You can also disable the engine by disconnecting the fuel injectors or ignition coils.

2. Crank the engine over for approximately 5 seconds and listen to the cranking sound.

> **NOTE** The engine should crank over at a normal speed. Too fast could mean low compression caused by bent valves or a slipped timing belt or chain. Too slow could mean a seized piston or bearing, or a faulty starting system. An uneven cranking sound may indicate grossly uneven compression pressures in the cylinders.

3. **List your observation(s):**

4. **Determine any necessary action(s):**

5. Have your supervisor/instructor verify satisfactory completion of this procedure, any observations found, and any necessary action(s) recommended.

Performance Rating

CDX Tasksheet Number: NN09

0	1	2	3	4

Supervisor/instructor signature _____ Date _____

▶ **TASK** Perform engine absolute (vacuum/boost) manifold pressure tests; determine necessary action.

MLR 8A2 **AST 8A5** **MAST 8A5**

Time off_____

Time on_____

Total time_____

CDX Tasksheet Number: C392

1. Find an appropriate vacuum hose to connect into.

> **NOTE** Make sure the vacuum hose is connected to the intake manifold vacuum and you are not disconnecting anything that will affect the operation of the engine. If possible, the use of a vacuum tee will allow you to take the reading while allowing the vacuum to get to its intended device.

2. Running Vacuum Test

    a. Describe the purpose of this test, the components or functions the test checks, and what the results might indicate:

    b. Start the engine, allow it to idle, and note the vacuum reading:
    _____

      i. Is the vacuum gauge needle relatively steady? Yes: _____ **No:** _____

    c. Carefully raise the engine RPM to 2000 RPM and note the vacuum reading: _____

      i. Is the vacuum gauge needle relatively steady? Yes: _____ **No:** _____

      ii. The vacuum reading should be higher at 2000 RPM than at idle. Is it? Yes: _____ **No:** _____

    d. Determine any necessary action(s):

3. Have your supervisor/instructor verify satisfactory completion of this procedure, any observations found, and any necessary action(s) recommended.

Performance Rating

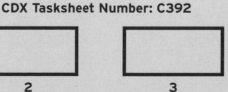

CDX Tasksheet Number: C392

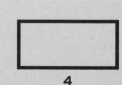

| 0 | 1 | 2 | 3 | 4 |

Supervisor/instructor signature _____ Date _____

MLR 8A3 | **AST** 8A6 | **MAST** 8A6

CDX Tasksheet Number: C393

1. Research the best option for disabling the cylinders on this vehicle in the appropriate service Information. The list that follows contains the most common methods. Choose the one that you plan on using.

    a. **Disconnect individual spark plug wires or ignition coils.** _____

    b. **Disconnect individual fuel injectors (multi-port fuel injection only).** _____

    c. **Use a diagnostic scope to disable cylinders through the ignition primary circuit.** _____

    d. **Use a scan tool on vehicles with power balance capabilities.** _____

    e. **Use short sections of vacuum hose and a test light (option for waste spark ignition systems).** _____

2. **Determine from the service information if this vehicle has an idle control system. If it does, list how to best disable the system during this test:**

3. Have your supervisor/instructor check the above answers. **Supervisor's/instructor's initials:** _____

4. **If this vehicle is equipped with an idle control system, disable it and set the idle speed to an appropriate RPM.**

    a. **List the RPM here:** _____

5. **Disable the cylinders one at a time and record the RPM drop (not the RPM) of each cylinder.**

    a. **RPM drop:** ---_____ ---_____ ---_____ ---_____ --- _____ ---_____ ---_____ ---_____

6. **Determine any necessary action(s):**

7. Have your supervisor/instructor verify satisfactory completion of this procedure, any observations found, and any necessary action(s) recommended.

Performance Rating

CDX Tasksheet Number: C393

0	1	2	3	4

Supervisor/instructor signature _____ Date _____

Perform cylinder cranking and running compression tests; determine necessary action.

Time off_____

Time on_____

Total time_____

CDX Tasksheet Number: C709

1. Research the procedure and specifications for performing both a cranking compression test and a running compression test on this vehicle in the appropriate service information.

2. **List the conditions that must be met for the cranking compression test to be accurate (you may paraphrase):**

3. Specifications

   a. **Minimum compression pressure:** _____ **psi/kPa or %**
   b. **Maximum variation:** _____ **%**

4. **Cranking Compression Test: Perform the cranking compression test following the specified procedure. The top row in the table below is a standard test and the bottom row is a wet test using a small amount of clean engine oil. The wet test would normally be performed on engines that fail the standard test. List the readings obtained for each cylinder in the table.**

Cylinder	#1	#2	#3	#4	#5	#6	#7	#8
Standard test (psi/kPa)								
Wet test(psi/kPa)								

   a. **Calculate the difference between the highest and lowest cylinders (dry test):** _____ **%**

5. **Running Compression Test: Perform the running compression test following the specified procedure. List the readings obtained for each cylinder:**

   NOTE Make sure the person snapping the throttle open is ready to turn off the ignition switch if the throttle sticks open.

Cylinder	#1	#2	#3	#4	#5	#6	#7	#8
Idle (psi/kPa)								
Snap throttle (psi/kPa)								

a. Determine any necessary action(s):

6. Have your supervisor/instructor verify satisfactory completion of this procedure, any observations found, and any necessary action(s) recommended.

Performance Rating

CDX Tasksheet Number: C709

☐	☐	☐	☐	☐
0	1	2	3	4

Supervisor/instructor signature _____ Date _____

Time off_____

Time on_____

Total time_____

CDX Tasksheet Number: C395

1. **List all of the possible places where compression can leak out of a cylinder:**

2. Remove the appropriate spark plugs to test the cylinder with the lowest compression pressure.

3. **Bring that piston up to top dead center on the compression stroke and install the cylinder leakage tester. List the reading you obtained.**

   a. **Cylinder #:** _____
   b. **Cylinder leakage:** _____ %
   c. **Leaking from:** _____

4. **Perform this test on one other cylinder. List the reading you obtained. Before removing the cylinder leakage tester, call your supervisor/instructor over to verify the reading.**

   a. **Cylinder #:** _____
   b. **Cylinder leakage:** _____ %
   c. **Leaking from:** _____

5. **Determine any necessary action(s):**

6. Have your supervisor/instructor verify satisfactory completion of this procedure, any observations found, and any necessary action(s) recommended.

Performance Rating

CDX Tasksheet Number: C395

☐	☐	☐	☐	☐
0	1	2	3	4

Supervisor/instructor signature _____ Date _____

Engine Repair: Engine Removal

Student/intern information:

Name_____ Date_____ Class_____

Vehicle used for this activity:

Year _____ Make _____ Model_____

Odometer_____VIN_____

Learning Objective/Task	CDX Tasksheet Number	2013 MLR NATEF Reference Number; Priority Level	2013 AST NATEF Reference Number; Priority Level	2013 MAST NATEF Reference Number; Priority Level
• Remove and reinstall engine in an OBDII or newer vehicle; reconnect all attaching components and restore the vehicle to running condition.	C671		1A10; P-3	1A10; P-3

Recommended Resource Materials

- CDX Automotive program
- Technical service bulletins, shop manuals, and any other information applicable to the specific vehicle or components you are working on
- Class notes

Materials Required

- Vehicle
- Lift or jack and jack stands
- Fastener storage containers
- Drain pan(s)
- Engine hoist (crane)
- Manufacturer- or job-specific tools

Some Safety Issues to Consider

- This procedure may require cleaning the engine prior to inspection. If so, use the proper equipment and procedures to carry this out safely. Also, get your supervisor's/instructor's permission prior to cleaning.
- You will be working under the hood of a running vehicle. Keep your hands and fingers away from moving belts, fans, and other parts.
- Lifting equipment such as vehicle jacks and stands, vehicle hoists, and engine hoists are important tools that increase productivity and make the job easier. However, they can also cause severe injury or death if used improperly. Make sure you follow the manufacturer's operation procedures. Also, make sure you have your supervisor's/instructor's permission to use any particular type of lifting equipment.
- Comply with personal and environmental safety practices associated with clothing; eye protection; hand tools; power equipment; proper ventilation; and the handling, storage, and disposal of chemicals/materials in accordance with local, state, and federal safety and environmental regulations.

Performance Standard

0—No exposure: No information or practice provided during the program; complete training required

1—Exposure only: General information provided with no practice time; close supervision needed; additional training required

2—Limited practice: Has practiced job during training program; additional training required to develop skill

3—Moderately skilled: Has performed job independently during training program; limited additional training may be required

4—Skilled: Can perform job independently with no additional training

► **TASK** Remove and reinstall engine in an OBDII or newer vehicle; reconnect all attaching components and restore the vehicle to running condition.

AST
1A10

MAST
1A10

CDX Tasksheet Number: C671

1. Research the procedure and specifications for removing and installing the engine in the appropriate service information.

   a. **List the flat rate time for R&R engine:** _____ hr

   b. **List the flat rate time for R&R engine and O/H:** _____ hr

   c. **List any special tools required for this task:**

   d. **List the specified engine oil:** _____

   e. **List the engine oil capacity:** _____ qt/lt

   f. **List the specified coolant:** _____

   g. **List the cooling system capacity:** _____ qt/lt

   h. **List any precautions specific to replacing the engine in this vehicle:**

2. Following the specified procedure(s), prepare the vehicle for engine removal by properly locating it in the work stall, draining any appropriate fluids such as engine coolant and oil, and removing any body components such as the hood, inner fender(s), etc.

3. Following the specified procedure(s), remove the engine assembly from the vehicle.

4. **Inspect the assembly for any damaged components, fasteners, etc., and list your observation(s):**

5. **List the amount of time it took to remove the engine assembly:**
   _____ hr

6. Have your supervisor/instructor verify removal of the engine assembly. **Supervisor's/instructor's initials:** _____

   > **NOTE** If you are rebuilding the engine, continue on to the Cylinder Head Removal, Inspection, and Installation tasksheet. After completion of those tasks, return here to reinstall the engine assembly.

7. Following the specified procedure(s) and specifications, reinstall the engine into the engine compartment.

8. Reconnect all hoses, wiring, belts, cables, and components, being careful to install them in their proper places.

9. Refill the engine with the specified oil. Ensure that the oil filter is installed.

10. Refill the cooling system with the specified coolant and bleed any air from the system.

11. Check all other fluid levels such as power steering fluid and brake fluid. Top off as necessary.

12. Recheck that all fasteners are properly torqued.

13. Perform any other prestart procedures such as charging the vehicle's battery, priming the lubrication system, etc.

14. **List any specified break-in/start-up procedures:**

15. Have your supervisor/instructor verify that the engine is ready to start.
    Supervisor's/instructor's initials: _____

> **NOTE** It is good practice to have a fire extinguisher close by in case of a fire.

16. **Install the exhaust hose(s). Start the engine and check for proper oil pressure, leaks, and abnormal noises. If any problems arise, shut down the engine and repair any issues. List your observation(s):**

17. Verify the proper adjustment of any timing components, if applicable.

18. Continue the break-in/start-up procedure, being careful to monitor the engine temperature, oil pressure, and malfunction indicator lamp (MIL). Stop the engine if any issues arise.

19. **Once the initial break-in period is complete, shut down the engine and check for leaks, loose components, etc. List any observation(s):**

20. Have your supervisor/instructor verify proper engine operation. **Supervisor's/ instructor's initials:** _____

21. Reinstall any removed items such as the hood and inner fenders. Align as necessary.

22. Recheck the fluid levels and inspect for any leaks.

23. List the amount of time it took to install the engine assembly: _____ hr

24. With your instructor's permission, test drive the vehicle to verify correct operation. List your observation(s):

25. Have your supervisor/instructor verify satisfactory completion of this procedure, any observations found, and any necessary action(s) recommended.

Performance Rating

CDX Tasksheet Number: C671

0	1	2	3	4

Supervisor/instructor signature _____ Date _____

Engine Repair: Cylinder Head Removal, Inspection, and Installation

Student/intern information:

Name_____ Date_____ Class_____

Vehicle used for this activity:

Year_____ Make_____ Model_____

Odometer_____VIN_____

Time off_____

Time on_____

Total time_____

Learning Objective/Task	CDX Tasksheet Number	2013 MLR NATEF Reference Number; Priority Level	2013 AST NATEF Reference Number; Priority Level	2013 MAST NATEF Reference Number; Priority Level
• Remove, inspect, or replace crankshaft vibration damper (harmonic balancer).	C679		1C1; P-2	1C1; P-2
• Remove and replace timing belt; verify correct camshaft timing.	C899	1A5; P-1	1A6; P-1	1A6; P-1
• Inspect and replace camshaft and drive belt/chain (includes checking drive gear wear and backlash, endplay, sprocket and chain wear, overhead cam drive sprocket[s], drive belt[s], belt tension, tensioners, camshaft reluctor ring/tone-wheel, and variable valve timing components); verify correct camshaft timing.	C676		1B5; P-1	1B5; P-1
• Remove cylinder head; inspect gasket condition; install cylinder head and gasket; tighten according to manufacturer's specifications and procedures.	C673		1B1; P-1	1B1; P-1
• Clean and visually inspect a cylinder head for cracks; check gasket surface areas for warpage and surface finish; check passage condition.	C674		1B2; P-1	1B2; P-1

Materials Required

- Complete engine
- Harmonic balancer puller
- Harmonic balancer installation kit
- Head stand
- Head gasket set
- Torque wrench
- Torque angle gauge
- Gasket scraper (nonmetallic on aluminum and plastic surfaces)
- Some engines require a liquid gasket remover and chemical metal prep
- Straightedge, piece of glass, or granite comparator surface
- Feeler blade set
- Crack detection equipment (magna-flux for cast iron; Zyglo for aluminum)
- Blowgun/air nozzle
- Vehicle-specific tools

Some Safety Issues to Consider

- This procedure may require cleaning the engine prior to inspection. If so, use the proper equipment and procedures to carry this out safely. Also, get your supervisor's/instructor's permission prior to cleaning.
- Lifting equipment such as vehicle jacks and stands, vehicle hoists, and engine hoists are important tools that increase productivity and make the job easier. However, they can also cause severe injury or death if used improperly. Make sure you follow the manufacturer's operation procedures. Also, make sure you have your supervisor's/instructor's permission to use any particular type of lifting equipment.
- Cylinder heads can be heavy, so make sure you get help when removing and installing them.
- Compressed air can be very dangerous. Never blow it at someone. Never use it to remove dirt or dust from your skin or clothing. Never use it without an OSHA-approved nozzle.
- Comply with personal and environmental safety practices associated with clothing; eye protection; hand tools; power equipment; proper ventilation; and the handling, storage, and disposal of chemicals/materials in accordance with local, state, and federal safety and environmental regulations.

Performance Standard

0—No exposure: No information or practice provided during the program; complete training required

1—Exposure only: General information provided with no practice time; close supervision needed; additional training required

2—Limited practice: Has practiced job during training program; additional training required to develop skill

3—Moderately skilled: Has performed job independently during training program; limited additional training may be required

4—Skilled: Can perform job independently with no additional training

► **TASK** Remove, inspect, or replace crankshaft vibration damper (harmonic balancer).

AST 1C1   **MAST** 1C1

CDX Tasksheet Number: C679

1. **Research the procedure for removing and inspecting the crankshaft vibration damper in the appropriate service information.**

   a. **Specified crankshaft pulley bolt torque:** _____ **ft-lb/Nm**

   b. **List any special procedures or precautions related to the harmonic balancer:**

2. Following the specified procedure, remove the harmonic balancer.

3. **Following the specified procedure, inspect the harmonic balancer. List your observation(s):**

4. **Determine any necessary action(s):**

5. Have your supervisor/instructor verify removal of the harmonic balancer and your answers. **Supervisor/instructor:** _____

   > **NOTE** You may want to continue on with the next task at this point. If so, return to this task after reinstalling the timing components.

6. Following the specified procedure, reinstall the harmonic balancer.

7. Have your supervisor/instructor verify satisfactory completion of this procedure, any observations found, and any necessary action(s) recommended.

Performance Rating

CDX Tasksheet Number: C679

0	1	2	3	4

Supervisor/instructor signature _____ Date _____

▶ TASK Remove and replace timing belt; verify correct camshaft timing.

MLR 1A5   **AST** 1A6   **MAST** 1A6

Time off_____

Time on_____

Total time_____

CDX Tasksheet Number: C899

1. Research the procedure and specifications for inspecting and replacing the timing belt components in the appropriate service information.

    a. **List the recommended change interval for the timing belt:**
    _____ mi/km

    b. **List the flat rate time for removing and replacing the timing belt:**
    _____ hrs

    c. **What other components does the manufacturer recommend changing at the same time as the timing belt?**

    d. **List or print off and attach the steps for removing and replacing the timing belt:**

    i. **Supervisor's/instructor's initials verifying approval to remove this timing belt:** _____

2. With your instructor's permission, and following the specified steps, remove the timing belt.

3. **Inspect the belt, pulleys, tensioner, cam seals, and water pump. List your observations for each:**

4. **Have your instructor verify removal of the timing belt and your observations:**
_____

5. Following the specified procedure, reinstall the timing belt, making sure the timing marks are properly aligned and the belt is properly tensioned. Do not install the timing cover yet.

6. **Have your instructor verify installation of the timing belt and camshaft timing:**
   _____

7. Reassemble any removed components and belts being careful to properly tighten all fasteners and accessory drive belts.

8. When everything is back together, carefully turn the engine by hand (ignition key off) at least two complete turns to verify there isn't a piston-to-valve interference.

9. If the engine turns over properly, start the engine, verify it is running properly, and make any timing or other adjustments.

10. Have your supervisor/instructor verify satisfactory completion of this procedure, any observations found, and any necessary action(s) recommended.

Performance Rating

CDX Tasksheet Number: C899

0	1	2	3	4

Supervisor/instructor signature _____ Date _____

Inspect and replace camshaft and drive belt/chain (includes checking drive gear wear and backlash, endplay, sprocket and chain wear, overhead cam drive sprocket[s], drive belt[s], belt tension, tensioners, camshaft reluctor ring/tone-wheel, and variable valve timing components); verify correct camshaft timing.

| AST 1B5 | MAST 1B5 |

Time off_____

Time on_____

Total time_____

CDX Tasksheet Number: C676

1. **Research the procedure and specifications for inspecting and replacing the camshaft and timing components in the appropriate service information.**

    a. **Type of cam drive system used:** _____

    b. **Is this engine equipped with variable valve timing? Yes:** _____
    No: _____

    c. **Camshaft endplay:** _____ **in/mm**

    d. **Camshaft drive gear backlash, if equipped:** _____ **in/mm**

    e. **List or print off and attach to this sheet any precautions when performing this task:**

    f. **List or print off and attach to this sheet any measurement and torque specifications for this task:**

2. **Following the specified procedure, remove any timing belt/chain covers. Visually inspect the installed timing components, including belt/chain tensioner. List your observations:**

3. Following the specified procedure, disassemble the cam drive system. Clean all gasket surfaces.

4. **Inspect the condition of the following components, if equipped, and list your observations:**

    a. **Timing belt/chain:** _____

    b. **Sprockets:** _____

    c. **Belt/chain tensioners:** _____

    d. Camshaft endplay: _____ in/mm

    e. Camshaft drive-gear backlash: _____ in/mm

    f. Camshaft reluctor ring/tone-wheel: _____

    g. Crank and cam oil seals: _____

    h. Water pump: _____

    i. Variable valve timing components: _____

5. Determine any necessary action(s):

6. **Have your instructor verify removal of the timing components and your observations:** _____

7. Following the specified procedure, reinstall the timing components, making sure the timing marks are properly aligned and the belt or chain is properly tensioned. Do not install the timing cover yet.

8. **Have your instructor verify installation of the timing components and camshaft timing:** _____

9. Reassemble any removed components and belts, being careful to properly tighten all fasteners and accessory drive belts.

10. When everything is back together, carefully turn the engine by hand (ignition key off) at least two complete turns to verify there isn't a piston-to-valve interference.

11. If the engine turns over properly, start the engine, verify it is running properly, and make any timing or other adjustments.

12. Have your supervisor/instructor verify satisfactory completion of this procedure, any observations found, and any necessary action(s) recommended.

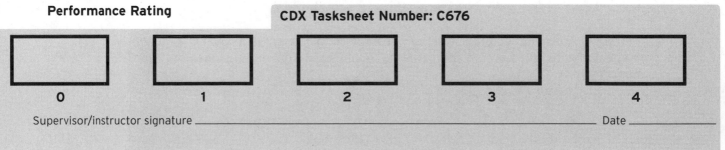

Performance Rating

CDX Tasksheet Number: C676

0	1	2	3	4

Supervisor/instructor signature _____ Date _____

▶ TASK Remove cylinder head; inspect gasket condition; install cylinder head and gasket; tighten according to manufacturer's specifications and procedures.

AST 1B1 **MAST** 1B1

Time off_____

Time on_____

Total time_____

CDX Tasksheet Number: C673

1. **Research the procedure and specifications for removing and installing the cylinder head(s) in the appropriate service information.**

    a. **Does this vehicle use TTY head bolts? Yes: _____ No: _____**

    b. **List or print off and attach to this sheet any special tools required for this task:**

    c. **List or print off and attach to this sheet any special precautions required for this task:**

    d. **List or print off and attach to this sheet the straightness specifications for the head surface:**

    e. **List or print off and attach to this sheet the surface finish requirements for the head surface:**

    f. **List or print off and attach to this sheet the torque procedure for the head bolts:**

g. **Draw or print off and attach to this sheet the torque sequence for the head bolts:**

2. Following the specified procedure, remove the cylinder head(s).

> **NOTE** Be very careful not to damage or scratch the head surface as this could cause a leak. Lay the head down on shop towels, and only use nonmetallic scrapers on aluminum or plastic surfaces.

3. **Inspect the old gasket(s) and list your observation(s):**

> **NOTE** While the head(s) is(are) removed from the engine, it makes sense to perform task C674: Clean and visually inspect a cylinder head for cracks; check gasket surface areas for warpage and surface finish; check passage condition. Please refer to page 134 for the completion of this task.

Total time

Time on

Time off

▶ **TASK** Clean and visually inspect a cylinder head for cracks; check gasket surface areas for warpage and surface finish; check passage condition.

AST 1B2 **MAST** 1B2

CDX Tasksheet Number: C674

1. Following the procedure in the service information, clean the head surfaces and prepare them for inspection.

> **NOTE** Be very careful not to damage or scratch the head surface as this could cause a leak. Lay the head down on shop towels, and only use nonmetallic scrapers on aluminum or plastic surfaces.

2. **Inspect the heads for signs of any cracks. This may involve magnafluxing or chemical crack detection. List the procedure you used and any observation(s):**

3. **Measure the gasket surfaces for warpage. List your measurements and observation(s):**

4. **Check the surface finish according to the manufacturer's procedure. List your observation(s):**

5. **Inspect the passages for blockage or leakage. List your observation(s):**

6. Have your supervisor/instructor verify satisfactory completion of this procedure, any observations found, and any necessary action(s) recommended.

Performance Rating

CDX Tasksheet Number: C674

0	1	2	3	4

Supervisor/instructor signature _____ Date _____

▶ CONTINUATION OF TASK {C673/1B1} Remove cylinder head; inspect gasket condition; install cylinder head and gasket; tighten according to manufacturer's specifications and procedures (from page 132).

AST 1B1 | **MAST** 1B1

CDX Tasksheet Number: C673

4. Following the procedure in the service information, install the head gasket(s) and cylinder head(s). Make sure you follow the specified procedure and sequence for tightening down the head bolts. Failure to do so could cause the gasket to fail.

5. Have your supervisor/instructor verify satisfactory completion of this procedure, any observations found, and any necessary action(s) recommended.

Performance Rating

CDX Tasksheet Number: C673

0	1	2	3	4

Supervisor/instructor signature _____ Date _____

Engine Repair: Cylinder Head Disassembly, Inspection, and Repair

Student/intern information:

Name_____ Date_____ Class_____

Vehicle used for this activity:

Year _____ Make _____ Model_____

Odometer_____ VIN_____

Time off_____

Time on_____

Total time_____

Learning Objective/Task	CDX Tasksheet Number	2013 MLR NATEF Reference Number; Priority Level	2013 AST NATEF Reference Number; Priority Level	2013 MAST NATEF Reference Number; Priority Level
• Inspect pushrods, rocker arms, rocker arm pivots, and shafts for wear, bending, cracks, looseness, and blocked oil passages (orifices); determine necessary action.	C021		1B3; P-2	1B3; P-2
• Inspect valve lifters; determine necessary action.	C722			1B12; P-2
• Inspect and/or measure camshaft for runout, journal wear, and lobe wear.	C724			1B13; P-2
• Inspect camshaft bearing surface for wear, damage, out-of-round, and alignment; determine necessary action.	C027			1B14; P-3
• Inspect valve springs for squareness and free height comparison; determine necessary action.	C718			1B7; P-3
• Inspect valve guides for wear; check valve stem-to-guide clearance; determine necessary action.	C719			1B9; P-3
• Inspect valves and valve seats; determine necessary action.	C720			1B10; P-3
• Check valve spring assembled height and valve stem height; determine necessary action.	C721			1B11; P-3
• Establish camshaft position sensor indexing.	C677		1B6; P-1	1B6; P-1
• Adjust valves (mechanical or hydraulic lifters).	C723	1B1; P-1	1B4; P-1	1B4; P-1

Recommended Resource Materials	Materials Required
• CDX Automotive program • Technical service bulletins, shop manuals, and any other information applicable to the specific vehicle or components you are working on • Class notes	• Straightedge or piece of glass • Feeler blades • Blow gun/air nozzle • Set of V-blocks • Valve spring tension gauge • Square • Machinist's rule • Installed height micrometer • Ball micrometers • Outside micrometers • Dial indicator

Some Safety Issues to Consider

- Engine castings and parts can have sharp edges. Be careful when handling them.
- Cleaning parts may bring you in contact with hazardous chemicals. Always wear the appropriate gloves and clothing when working with chemicals. Refer to the material safety data sheet (MSDS) for further information.
- Used engine oil contains cancer-causing agents. Always avoid oil contact with your hands. Always wash your hands after completing this task.
- Compressed air can be very dangerous. Never blow it at someone. Never use it to remove dirt or dust from your skin or clothing. Never use it without an OSHA-approved nozzle.
- Comply with personal and environmental safety practices associated with clothing; eye protection; hand tools; power equipment; proper ventilation; and the handling, storage, and disposal of chemicals/materials in accordance with local, state, and federal safety and environmental regulations.

Performance Standard

0—No exposure: No information or practice provided during the program; complete training required

1—Exposure only: General information provided with no practice time; close supervision needed; additional training required

2—Limited practice: Has practiced job during training program; additional training required to develop skill

3—Moderately skilled: Has performed job independently during training program; limited additional training may be required

4—Skilled: Can perform job independently with no additional training

> **TASK** Inspect pushrods, rocker arms, rocker arm pivots, and shafts for wear, bending, cracks, looseness, and blocked oil passages (orifices); determine necessary action.

AST 1B3　**MAST** 1B3

Time off_____

Time on_____

Total time_____

CDX Tasksheet Number: CO21

1. Research the procedure and specifications for disassembling and inspecting the pushrods, rocker arms, pivots, and shafts in the appropriate service information.

    a. **List, or print off and attach to this sheet, the procedure for inspecting these parts:**

2. Disassemble the rocker arm assemblies and clean them in a safe and environmentally approved way. This is commonly performed in a hot water spray machine.

3. Inspect the following parts:

    a. **Pushrods: Worn _____ Bent _____ Cracked _____ Blocked passages _____ OK _____ (Check any that apply)**
    b. **Rocker arms: Worn _____ Bent _____ Cracked _____ Blocked passages _____ OK _____ (Check any that apply)**
    c. **Rocker arm studs: Worn _____ Bent _____ Cracked _____ OK _____ (Check any that apply)**
    d. **Pivots/shafts: Worn _____ Bent _____ Cracked _____ Blocked passages _____ OK _____ (Check any that apply)**

4. **Determine any necessary action(s):**

5. Have your supervisor/instructor verify satisfactory completion of this procedure, any observations found, and any necessary action(s) recommended.

Performance Rating

CDX Tasksheet Number: CO21

0	1	2	3	4

Supervisor/instructor signature _____ Date _____

MAST
1B12

CDX Tasksheet Number: C722

1. Research the procedure and specifications for inspecting the valve lifters in the appropriate service information.

   a. **List the type of lifter this engine is equipped with:**
      Hydraulic _____ Solid _____

   b. **List, or print off and attach to this sheet, the inspection procedure and any specifications:**

2. **Inspect the valve lifters and list your observation(s):**

3. **Determine any necessary action(s):**

4. Have your supervisor/instructor verify satisfactory completion of this procedure, any observations found, and any necessary action(s) recommended.

Performance Rating

CDX Tasksheet Number: C722

0	1	2	3	4

Supervisor/instructor signature _____ Date _____

► **TASK** Inspect and/or measure camshaft for runout, journal wear, and lobe wear.

MAST
1B13

CDX Tasksheet Number: C724

1. Research the procedure and specifications for inspecting and measuring the camshaft in the appropriate service information.

    a. **Specified maximum camshaft journal runout:** _____ in/mm

    b. **Specified camshaft journal diameter:** _____ in/mm

    c. **Specified lobe lift**

        i. **Intake:** _____ in/mm

        ii. **Exhaust:** _____ in/mm

    d. **Specified maximum lobe wear:** _____ in/mm

2. **Visually inspect the condition of the cam lobes for excessive wear. List your observation(s):**

3. Following the specified procedure, measure the camshaft journal runout. **List the measurement. List which journals were supported and which one was measured.**

4. Following the specified procedure, measure the camshaft journal diameter. **List your measurements for each cam journal in the table below.**

Camshaft Journal	#1	#2	#3	#4	#5
Cam #1 (in/mm)					
Cam #2 (in/mm)					
Cam #3 (in/mm)					
Cam #4 (in/mm)					

5. **Calculate the maximum camshaft journal wear:** _____ in/mm

6. **Following the specified procedure, measure the cam lobe lift and list your measurements in the table below.**

	#1	#2	#3	#4	#5	#6	#7	#8
Intake lobes								
Exhaust Lobes								

7. **Calculate the maximum lobe wear.**

    a. **Intake:** _____ in/mm

    b. **Exhaust:** _____ in/mm

8. **Determine any necessary action(s):**

9. Have your supervisor/instructor verify satisfactory completion of this procedure, any observations found, and any necessary action(s) recommended.

Performance Rating

CDX Tasksheet Number: C724

0	1	2	3	4

Supervisor/instructor signature _____ Date _____

MAST
1B14

CDX Tasksheet Number: C027

> **NOTE** Perform this task only if the engine is an overhead cam design. If it is a cam-in-block design, the camshaft bearings are inspected during the Block Disassembly, Inspection, and Repair tasksheet.

1. Research the procedures and specifications for inspecting and measuring the camshaft bearings in the appropriate service information.

   a. **Specified camshaft bearing inside diameter:** _____ **in/mm**
   b. **Specified camshaft journal diameter:** _____ **in/mm**
   c. **Specified camshaft journal bearing clearance:** _____ **in/mm**

2. Measure the inside diameter of the camshaft bearings. **List your measurements in the table below.**

Camshaft Bearing	#1	#2	#3	#4	#5
Cam #1 (in/mm)					
Cam #2 (in/mm)					
Cam #3 (in/mm)					
Cam #4 (in/mm)					

3. Measure the diameter of the camshaft journals (or copy them from the previous task). **List your measurements in the table below.**

Camshaft Journal	#1	#2	#3	#4	#5
Cam #1 (in/mm)					
Cam #2 (in/mm)					
Cam #3 (in/mm)					
Cam #4 (in/mm)					

4. Calculate the camshaft journal bearing clearance. **List your measurements in the table below.**

Camshaft Journal	#1	#2	#3	#4	#5
Cam #1 (in/mm)					
Cam #2 (in/mm)					
Cam #3 (in/mm)					
Cam #4 (in/mm)					

5. Inspect the bearings and journals for evidence of damage, wear, and misalignment. **List your observation(s):**

6. Determine any necessary action(s):

7. Have your supervisor/instructor verify satisfactory completion of this procedure, any observations found, and any necessary action(s) recommended.

Performance Rating

CDX Tasksheet Number: C027

0	1	2	3	4

Supervisor/instructor signature _____ Date _____

Inspect valve springs for squareness and free height comparison; determine necessary action.

MAST
1B7

Time off_____

Time on_____

Total time_____

CDX Tasksheet Number: C718

1. Research the procedure and specifications for checking valve spring squareness and free height in the appropriate service information.

   a. List, or print off and attach to this sheet, the procedure for checking squareness:

   b. Specified valve spring free height

      i. Intake: _____ in/mm

      ii. Exhaust: _____ in/mm

   c. Specified valve spring installed height

      i. Intake: _____ in/mm

      ii. Exhaust: _____ in/mm

   d. Specified valve spring pressure at the specified installed height

      i. Intake: _____ lb/kg at
   _____ in/mm

      ii. Exhaust: _____ lb/kg at
   _____ in/mm

   e. Specified valve spring pressure at the specified valve open height

      i. Intake: _____ lb/kg at
   _____ in/mm

      ii. Exhaust: _____ lb/kg at
   _____ in/mm

   > **NOTE** You may want to measure and record the existing valve installed height and valve stem height before grinding the valves or machining the valve seats since specifications are not always available. Since some engines have nonadjustable valve trains, this is a critical measurement when reassembling the valve assemblies.

2. Disassemble the valve and valve spring assemblies, if not already done.

3. Check the valve springs for squareness using the protractor-head square. **List your observation(s):**

4. Measure the free height of each valve spring. **List your measurements in the table below.**

Valve Spring	#1	#2	#3	#4	#5	#6	#7	#8
Intake (in/mm)								
Exhaust (in/mm)								

5. Measure the valve spring pressure at the specified installed height. **List your measurements in the table below.**

Valve Spring	#1	#2	#3	#4	#5	#6	#7	#8
Intake (lb/kg)								
Exhaust (lb/kg)								

6. Measure the valve spring pressure at the specified valve open height. **List your measurements in the table below.**

Valve Spring	#1	#2	#3	#4	#5	#6	#7	#8
Intake (lb/kg)								
Exhaust (lb/kg)								

7. Determine any necessary action(s):

8. Have your supervisor/instructor verify satisfactory completion of this procedure, any observations found, and any necessary action(s) recommended.

Performance Rating

CDX Tasksheet Number: C718

☐ 0   ☐ 1   ☐ 2   ☐ 3   ☐ 4

Supervisor/instructor signature _____ Date _____

► **TASK** Inspect valve guides for wear; check valve stem-to-guide clearance; determine necessary action.

MAST
1B9

Time off_____

Time on_____

Total time_____

CDX Tasksheet Number: C719

1. Research the procedure and specifications for checking valve guides and clearance in the appropriate service information.

   a. **Specified valve guide clearance**

   i. **Intake:** _____ in/mm

   ii. **Exhaust:** _____ in/mm

   b. **Which method of determining valve guide clearance is recommended? Micrometer method / Dial indicator method (Circle one)**

2. Measure the intake valve guide inner diameter and the intake valve stem diameter; calculate the clearance (micrometer method) or measure the side-to-side play of the valve stem with a dial indicator (dial indicator method). **List your measurements in the table below.**

Intake Valve	#1	#2	#3	#4	#5	#6	#7	#8
Guide (in/mm)								
Valve (in/mm)								
Clearance (in/mm)								

3. Measure the exhaust valve guide inner diameter and the exhaust valve stem diameter, then calculate the clearance (micrometer method), or measure the side-to-side play of the valve stem with a dial indicator (dial indicator method). **List your measurements in the table below.**

Exhaust Valve	#1	#2	#3	#4	#5	#6	#7	#8
Guide (in/mm)								
Valve (in/mm)								
Clearance (in/mm)								

4. **Determine any necessary action(s):**

5. Have your supervisor/instructor verify satisfactory completion of this procedure, any observations found, and any necessary action(s) recommended.

Performance Rating

CDX Tasksheet Number: C719

0	1	2	3	4

Supervisor/instructor signature _____ Date _____

MAST
1B10

CDX Tasksheet Number: C720

1. Research the procedure and specifications for inspecting valves and valve seats in the appropriate service information.

    a. **Specified valve stem diameter**

        i. **Intake:** _____ in/mm

        ii. **Exhaust:** _____ in/mm

    b. **Specified valve margin thickness**

        i. **Intake:** _____ in/mm

        ii. **Exhaust:** _____ in/mm

    c. **Specified valve face angle**

        i. **Intake:** _____ degrees

        ii. **Exhaust:** _____ degrees

    d. **Specified valve seat angle**

        i. **Intake:** _____ degrees

        ii. **Exhaust:** _____ degrees

    e. **Specified valve seat width**

        i. **Intake:** _____ in/mm

        ii. **Exhaust:** _____ in/mm

    f. **List, or print off and attach to this sheet, the procedure for inspecting the valves and valve seats:**

2. Measure the valve stem diameter and check for taper. **List your measurements in the table below.**

Valve	#1	#2	#3	#4	#5	#6	#7	#8
Intake (in/mm)								
Exhaust (in/mm)								

3. Measure the valve margin thickness. **List your measurements in the table below.**

Valve	#1	#2	#3	#4	#5	#6	#7	#8
Intake (in/mm)								
Exhaust (in/mm)								

4. Measure the valve seat width. **List your measurements in the table below.**

Valve Seat	#1	#2	#3	#4	#5	#6	#7	#8
Intake (in/mm)								
Exhaust (in/mm)								

5. Inspect the valves and valve seats according to the manufacturer's procedure. **List your observation(s):**

6. **Determine any necessary action(s):**

7. Have your supervisor/instructor verify satisfactory completion of this procedure, any observations found, and any necessary action(s) recommended.

Performance Rating

CDX Tasksheet Number: C720

0	1	2	3	4

Supervisor/instructor signature _____ Date _____

► **TASK** Check valve spring assembled height and valve stem height; determine necessary action.

MAST
1B11

Time off_____

Time on_____

Total time_____

CDX Tasksheet Number: C721

1. Research the procedure and specifications in the appropriate service information for checking the following:

   a. **Specified valve stem height**

      i. **Intake:** _____ in/mm

      ii. **Exhaust:** _____ in/mm

   b. **Specified valve spring assembled height**

      i. **Intake:** _____ in/mm

      ii. **Exhaust:** _____ in/mm

   c. **List, or print off and attach to this sheet, the procedure for making these measurements:**

2. Perform this task only if the valves and valve seats are ready to be put back into service.

   > **NOTE** The valves are ready to be put back into service if they have been reground to meet specifications or if they have been replaced with new valves. This also applies for the valve seats. If you sent the heads out to be machined, the machinist should have ensured that these specifications were met.

3. Measure the valve stem height. **List your measurements in the table below.**

Valve	#1	#2	#3	#4	#5	#6	#7	#8
Intake (in/mm)								
Exhaust (in/mm)								

4. Measure the valve spring assembled height. **List your measurements in the table below.**

   > **NOTE** If the valve springs have been replaced with new ones, double-check the valve spring pressure to make sure they meet specifications. If you are reusing the existing valve springs and they passed this test earlier, continue on.

Valve	#1	#2	#3	#4	#5	#6	#7	#8
Intake (in/mm)								
Exhaust (in/mm)								

5. Determine any necessary action(s):

6. Have your supervisor/instructor verify satisfactory completion of this procedure, any observations found, and any necessary action(s) recommended.

> **NOTE** NATEF has not specified a task for reassembling the head(s). However, now would be a good time to do so. Follow the specified procedure to reassemble the head(s), but be sure to follow all the necessary precautions.

> **NOTE** Some overhead cam heads with bucket-style cam followers may need to have their valves adjusted at this point with the use of select fit shims. Check the service information to determine if this procedure is required for this engine. If so, adjust the valve at this time. Otherwise, valve adjustment will happen after the head and timing components have been installed.

Performance Rating

CDX Tasksheet Number: C721

0	1	2	3	4
☐	☐	☐	☐	☐

Supervisor/instructor signature _____ Date _____

AST 1B6   **MAST** 1B6

CDX Tasksheet Number: C677

> **NOTE** If not already done, install the timing components following the specified procedure, being careful to line up all timing marks. Also, ensure that all belts/chains are properly tensioned.

1. Research the procedure and specifications to establish camshaft position indexing in the appropriate service information.

    a. **List, or print off and attach to this sheet, the procedure for indexing the camshaft position sensor:**

2. Following the specified procedure, index the camshaft position sensor. **List your observation(s):**

3. Have your supervisor/instructor verify satisfactory completion of this procedure, any observations found, and any necessary action(s) recommended.

Performance Rating

CDX Tasksheet Number: C677

0	1	2	3	4

Supervisor/instructor signature _____ Date _____

MLR 1B1　**AST** 1B4　**MAST** 1B4

Time off_____

Time on_____

Total time_____

CDX Tasksheet Number: C723

1. On a vehicle with adjustable valves, research the procedure and specifications for adjusting the valves in the appropriate service information.

   a. **List the type of lifters this engine uses: Mechanical:** _____ **Hydraulic:** _____

   b. **How are the valves adjusted on this engine?**

   c. **Specified valve clearance**

      i. **Intake:** _____ **In/mm @** _____ **°F/°C**

      ii. **Exhaust:** _____ **in/mm @** _____ **°F/°C**

   d. **Valve adjustment locknut torque, if equipped:** _____ **ft-lb/Nm**

2. Following the specified procedure, adjust the valves to specification. **List your observation(s):**

3. **Determine any necessary action(s):**

4. Have your supervisor/instructor verify satisfactory completion of this procedure, any observations found, and any necessary action(s) recommended.

Performance Rating

CDX Tasksheet Number: C723

0	1	2	3	4

Supervisor/instructor signature _____ Date _____

Engine Repair: Block Disassembly, Inspection, and Repair

© 2015 Jones & Bartlett Learning, LLC, an Ascend Learning Company

Student/intern information:

Name _____ Date _____ Class _____

Vehicle used for this activity:

Year _____ Make _____ Model _____

Odometer _____ VIN _____

Time off _____

Time on _____

Total time _____

Learning Objective/Task	CDX Tasksheet Number	2013 MLR NATEF Reference Number; Priority Level	2013 AST NATEF Reference Number; Priority Level	2013 MAST NATEF Reference Number; Priority Level
• Disassemble engine block; clean and prepare components for inspection and reassembly.	C029			1C2; P-1
• Inspect engine block for visible cracks, passage condition, core and gallery plug condition, and surface warpage; determine necessary action.	C030			1C3; P-2
• Inspect and measure cylinder walls/sleeves for damage, wear, and ridges; determine necessary action.	C726			1C4; P-2
• Inspect and measure piston skirts and ring lands; determine necessary action.	C678			1C10; P-2
• Deglaze and clean cylinder walls.	C727			1C5; P-2
• Inspect and measure camshaft bearings for wear, damage, out-of-round, and alignment; determine necessary action.	C034			1C6; P-3
• Inspect auxiliary shaft(s) (balance, intermediate, idler, counterbalance, or silencer); inspect shaft(s) and support bearings for damage and wear; determine necessary action; reinstall and time.	C730			1C13; P-2

Recommended Resource Materials

- CDX Automotive program
- Technical service bulletins, shop manuals, and any other information applicable to the specific vehicle or components you are working on
- Class notes

Materials Required

- Complete engine, simulator, or vehicle
- Harmonic balance puller

Some Safety Issues to Consider

- Lifting equipment such as engine hoists are important tools that increase productivity and make the job easier. However, they can also cause severe injury or death if used improperly. Make sure you follow the manufacturer's operation procedures.

- If using an engine stand, make sure the engine stand is rated for the weight of the engine you are mounting on it. Also, use bolts with the proper strength and length. Severe injury could occur if the engine were to fall due to failure of the engine stand or bolts.
- Compressed air can be very dangerous. Never blow it at someone. Never use it to remove dirt or dust from your skin or clothing. Never use it without an OSHA-approved nozzle.
- Comply with personal and environmental safety practices associated with clothing; eye protection; hand tools; power equipment; proper ventilation; and the handling, storage, and disposal of chemicals/materials in accordance with local, state, and federal safety and environmental regulations.

Performance Standard

0—No exposure: No information or practice provided during the program; complete training required

1—Exposure only: General information provided with no practice time; close supervision needed; additional training required

2—Limited practice: Has practiced job during training program; additional training required to develop skill

3—Moderately skilled: Has performed job independently during training program; limited additional training may be required

4—Skilled: Can perform job independently with no additional training

Disassemble engine block; clean and prepare components for inspection and reassembly.

MAST
1C2

Time off_____

Time on_____

Total time_____

CDX Tasksheet Number: C029

1. Research the procedure and specifications for disassembling and inspecting the engine block in the appropriate service information.

   a. Print off the procedure for disassembling the block and attach it to this sheet.

   b. **List the specification for crankshaft end play:** _____ **in/mm**

> **NOTE** Make sure the engine stand is rated for the weight of the engine you are mounting on it. Also, use bolts with the proper strength and length. Severe injury could occur if the engine were to fall due to failure of the engine stand or bolts.

2. If not already completed, mount the engine block to an appropriate engine stand. This may require the removal of the flex plate or flywheel.

3. **Following the specified procedure, measure the crankshaft end play:** _____ **in/mm**

4. Disassemble the engine block assembly following the specified procedure. Be sure to label all parts to identify where they will be reinstalled. As the engine is being disassembled, visually inspect the parts for obvious damage. **List your observation(s):**

> **NOTE** Be very careful not to damage or scratch any aluminum sealing surfaces since doing so could cause a leak. Do not use metal scrapers, wire brushes, or power abrasive disks to clean aluminum or plastic surfaces.

5. Remove any gasket material still stuck to the sealing surfaces with an approved scraper.

6. Clean the parts in a safe and environmentally approved way. This is commonly performed in a hot water spray machine.

7. Visually inspect all parts. **List your observation(s):**

8. Have your supervisor/instructor verify satisfactory completion of this procedure, any observations found, and any necessary action(s) recommended.

Performance Rating

CDX Tasksheet Number: C029

0	1	2	3	4

Supervisor/instructor signature _____ Date _____

▶ TASK Inspect engine block for visible cracks, passage condition, core and gallery plug condition, and surface warpage; determine necessary action.

CDX Tasksheet Number: C030

1. Research the procedure and specifications for measuring the engine block for warpage in the appropriate service information.

   a. List the specification(s) for block deck warpage:

2. Following the specified procedure, carefully inspect the engine block for visible cracks (using magnaflux equipment or penetrating dyes). **List your observation(s):**

3. Inspect the condition of all passages. **List your observation(s):**

   NOTE Core plugs are normally replaced during engine overhaul, so you may want to remove them at this time. Also, make sure the gallery plugs are removed for the cleaning process.

4. Inspect the condition of core and gallery plugs. **List your observation(s):**

5. Inspect all sealing surfaces for damage. **List your observation(s):**

6. Determine any necessary action(s):

7. Have your supervisor/instructor verify satisfactory completion of this procedure, any observations found, and any necessary action(s) recommended.

Performance Rating

CDX Tasksheet Number: CO30

0	1	2	3	4

Supervisor/instructor signature _____ Date _____

► **TASK** Inspect and measure cylinder walls/sleeves for damage, wear, and ridges; determine necessary action.

MAST 1C4

CDX Tasksheet Number: C726

1. Research the procedures and specifications for inspecting and measuring the cylinder walls/sleeves in the appropriate service information.

    a. **Specified cylinder bore diameter:** _____ in/mm
    b. **Specified cylinder bore maximum out-of-round:** _____ in/mm
    c. **Specified cylinder bore maximum taper:** _____ in/mm

2. Following the specified procedure, carefully measure the diameter and the maximum out-of-round diameter for each cylinder bore. **List your measurements in the table below.**

Cylinder	#1	#2	#3	#4	#5	#6	#7	#8
Top (in/mm)								
Bottom (in/mm)								
Taper (in/mm)								
Out-of-round (in/mm)								

3. Following the specified procedure, carefully inspect the cylinder walls/sleeves for damage, wear, and ridges. **List your observation(s):**

4. **Determine any necessary action(s):**

5. Have your supervisor/instructor verify satisfactory completion of this procedure, any observations found, and any necessary action(s) recommended.

Performance Rating

CDX Tasksheet Number: C726

0	1	2	3	4

Supervisor/instructor signature _____ Date _____

Inspect and measure piston skirts and ring lands; determine necessary action.

MAST
1C10

Time off_____

Time on_____

Total time_____

CDX Tasksheet Number: C678

1. Research the procedures and specifications for inspecting and measuring the piston skirts and ring lands in the appropriate service information.

    a. Specified piston skirt diameter: _____ **in/mm**

    b. Specified piston ring groove width

       i. Compression (top): _____ **in/mm**

       ii. Compression (bottom): _____ **in/mm**

       iii. Oil: _____ **in/mm**

    c. Specified piston-to-cylinder clearance: _____ **in/mm**

2. Inspect the piston surfaces for obvious signs of damage. **List your observation(s):**

3. Following the specified procedure, carefully measure the diameter, the piston-to-cylinder clearance, and the piston ring groove width (for top compression, bottom compression, and oil rings). **List your measurements in the table below.**

Piston	#1	#2	#3	#4	#5	#6	#7	#8
Diameter (in/mm)								
Clearance (in/mm)								
Groove width (top) (in/mm)								
Groove width (bottom) (in/mm)								
Groove width (oil) (in/mm)								

4. **Are the pistons within specified tolerance?   Yes: _____   No: _____**

    a. Why or why not?

5. **Determine any necessary action(s):**

6. Have your supervisor/instructor verify satisfactory completion of this procedure, any observations found, and any necessary action(s) recommended.

Performance Rating

CDX Tasksheet Number: C678

0	1	2	3	4

Supervisor/instructor signature _____ Date _____

MAST
1C5

CDX Tasksheet Number: C727

> **NOTE** This task should be performed only on engines that are not going to be machined over-size. Have your supervisor approve this task based on the results of the previous tasks before you continue.

1. **Is this cylinder block a good candidate for the deglazing process?**
   Yes: _____ No: _____

2. **Do you have your supervisor's approval for this task? Yes: _____ No: _____**

3. Research the procedures and specifications for deglazing the cylinder walls.

   a. **Specified coarseness of stones/ball hone:** _____
   b. **Specified deglazing lubricant:** _____
   c. **Specified crosshatch angle/pattern:** _____
   d. **Specified cleaning process after deglazing:** _____

4. Following the specified procedure, carefully deglaze the cylinder walls using the appropriate honing/deglazing equipment.

5. Use the specified cleaning process to clean the cylinder walls and block.

6. Inspect the surface of the cylinders for proper deglazing finish. **List your observation(s):**

7. Have your supervisor/instructor verify satisfactory completion of this procedure, any observations found, and any necessary action(s) recommended.

Performance Rating

CDX Tasksheet Number: C727

0	1	2	3	4

Supervisor/instructor signature _____ Date _____

Inspect and measure camshaft bearings for wear, damage, out-of-round, and alignment; determine necessary action.

MAST
1C6

Time off_____

Time on_____

Total time_____

CDX Tasksheet Number: C034

> **NOTE** Perform this task only if the engine is a cam-in-block design. If it is an overhead cam design, the camshaft bearings are inspected during the Cylinder Head Disassembly, Inspection, and Repair tasksheet.

1. Research the procedures and specifications for inspecting and measuring the camshaft bearings in the appropriate service information.

   a. **Specified camshaft bearing inside diameter:** _____ in/mm
   b. **Specified camshaft journal diameter:** _____ in/mm
   c. **Specified camshaft journal bearing clearance:** _____ in/mm
   d. **Specified camshaft journal out-of-round (max):** _____ in/mm

2. Inspect the condition of the cam lobes for excessive wear or damage. **List your observation(s):**

3. Measure the **inside diameter of the camshaft bearings** and the **outside diameter of the cam journals**. Calculate the **bearing clearance** and measure the **maximum out-of-round reading** for each camshaft journal. **List your measurements in the table below.**

Cam Bearing or Journal	#1	#2	#3	#4	#5
Cam bearing diameter (in/mm)					
Cam journal diameter (in/mm)					
Bearing clearance (in/mm)					
Out-of-round (in/mm)					

4. Inspect the bearings and journals for evidence of damage, wear, and misalignment. **List your observation(s):**

5. **Determine any necessary action(s):**

6. Have your supervisor/instructor verify satisfactory completion of this procedure, any observations found, and any necessary action(s) recommended.

Performance Rating

CDX Tasksheet Number: CO34

0	1	2	3	4

Supervisor/instructor signature _____ Date _____

Inspect auxiliary shaft(s) (balance, intermediate, idler, counterbalance, or silencer); inspect shaft(s) and support bearings for damage and wear; determine necessary action; reinstall and time.

MAST
1C13

CDX Tasksheet Number: C730

1. Research the procedures and specifications to inspect any auxiliary shaft(s) and support bearings in the appropriate service information.

    a. List the type of shaft(s) this engine is equipped with:

    b. List any appropriate specification(s):

    c. List, or print off and attach to this sheet, the installation and timing procedure:

2. Inspect the auxiliary shaft(s) and support bearings. **List your observation(s):**

3. Determine any necessary action(s):

4. Have your supervisor/instructor check your answers.
   Supervisor/instructor initials: _____

5. Following the specified procedure, reinstall and time the auxiliary shaft(s).

6. Have your supervisor/instructor verify satisfactory completion of this procedure, any observations found, and any necessary action(s) recommended.

Performance Rating

CDX Tasksheet Number: C730

0	1	2	3	4

Supervisor/instructor signature _____ Date _____

Engine Repair: Crankshaft and Oil Pump Service

Student/intern information:

Name_____ Date_____ Class_____

Vehicle used for this activity:

Year_____ Make_____ Model_____

Odometer_____VIN_____

Time off_____

Time on_____

Total time_____

Learning Objective/Task	CDX Tasksheet Number	2013 MLR NATEF Reference Number; Priority Level	2013 AST NATEF Reference Number; Priority Level	2013 MAST NATEF Reference Number; Priority Level
• Inspect crankshaft for straightness, journal damage, keyway damage, thrust flange and sealing surface condition, and visual surface cracks; check oil passage condition; measure end play and journal wear; check crankshaft position sensor reluctor ring (where applicable); determine necessary action.	C728			1C7; P-1
• Inspect main and connecting rod bearings for damage and wear; determine necessary action.	C036			1C8; P-2
• Identify piston and bearing wear patterns that indicate connecting rod alignment and main bearing bore problems; determine necessary action.	C729			1C9; P-3
• Inspect oil pump gears or rotors, housing, pressure relief devices, and pump drive; perform necessary action.	C733			1D13; P-2

Materials Required

- Engine block, crankshaft, and oil pump
- Engine stand
- Dial indicator
- Straightedge and feeler blade set
- Inside and outside micrometer sets
- Dial bore gauge set

Some Safety Issues to Consider

- Compressed air can be very dangerous. Never blow it at someone. Never use it to remove dirt or dust from your skin or clothing. Never use it without an OSHA-approved nozzle.
- Make sure the engine stand is rated for the weight of the engine you are mounting on it. Also, use bolts with the proper strength and length. Severe injury could occur if the engine were to fall due to failure of the engine stand or bolts.

- Engine castings and parts can have sharp edges. Always exercise extreme caution when working around them. Also, the parts are relatively heavy and can cause serious pinching of fingers. Be careful when handling them.
- Comply with personal and environmental safety practices associated with clothing; eye protection; hand tools; power equipment; proper ventilation; and the handling, storage, and disposal of chemicals/materials in accordance with local, state, and federal safety and environmental regulations.

Performance Standard

0–No exposure: No information or practice provided during the program; complete training required

1–Exposure only: General information provided with no practice time; close supervision needed; additional training required

2–Limited practice: Has practiced job during training program; additional training required to develop skill

3–Moderately skilled: Has performed job independently during training program; limited additional training may be required

4–Skilled: Can perform job independently with no additional training

> **NOTE** In order to easily compare specifications to measurements, space has been provided in each of the sections below to write the specifications.

Inspect crankshaft for straightness, journal damage, keyway damage, thrust flange and sealing surface condition, and visual surface cracks; check oil passage condition; measure end play and journal wear; check crankshaft position sensor reluctor ring (where applicable); determine necessary action.

MAST
1C7

Time off_____

Time on_____

Total time_____

CDX Tasksheet Number: C728

1. Research the procedure and specifications for inspecting the crankshaft and related parts in the appropriate service information.

2. Following the specified procedure, measure the crankshaft run-out (straightness).

   a. **Specs:** _____ **in/mm**
   b. **Measurement:** _____ **in/mm**

3. Following the specified procedure, visually inspect the following for damage, wear, or cracks. **List your observations.**

   a. **Crankshaft main bearing journals: Worn _____ Damaged _____ Cracks _____ OK _____ (Check any that apply) Comments:**

   b. **Crankshaft rod bearing journals: Worn _____ Damaged _____ Cracks _____ OK _____ (Check any that apply) Comments:**

   c. **Crankshaft keyway: Worn _____ Damaged _____ Cracks _____ OK _____ (Check any that apply) Comments:**

   d. **Thrust flange: Worn _____ Damaged _____ Cracks _____ OK _____ (Check any that apply) Comments:**

   e. **Rear main bearing sealing surface: Worn _____ Damaged _____ Cracks _____ OK _____ (Check any that apply) Comments:**

f. Oil passages: Worn _____ Damaged _____ Cracks _____ OK _____
(Check any that apply) Comments:

g. Crankshaft position sensor reluctor ring: Worn _____ Damaged _____
Cracks _____ OK _____ (Check any that apply) Comments:

4. Following the specified procedure, measure the crankshaft main bearing journals.
List your measurements in the table below.

Journal	Specs	#1	#2	#3	#4	#5	#6
Diameter (in/mm)							
Out-of-round (in/mm)							
Taper (in/mm)							

5. Following the specified procedure, measure the crankshaft connecting rod journals.
List your measurements in the table below.

Journal	Specs	#1	#2	#3	#4	#5	#6	#7	#8
Diameter (in/mm)									
Out-of-round (in/mm)									
Taper (in/mm)									

6. **Determine any necessary action(s):**

7. Have your supervisor/instructor verify satisfactory completion of this procedure, any observations found, and any necessary action(s) recommended.

Performance Rating

CDX Tasksheet Number: C728

0	1	2	3	4

Supervisor/instructor signature _____ Date _____

▶ **TASK** Inspect main and connecting rod bearings for damage and wear; determine necessary action.

MAST
1C8

Time off_____

Time on_____

Total time_____

CDX Tasksheet Number: C036

1. Research the procedure and specifications for inspecting the main and connecting rod bearings in the appropriate service information.

   a. **List, or print off and attach to this sheet, the faults and wear patterns for the various bearing issues:**

2. Following the specified procedure, inspect the main and connecting rod bearings. **List your observations:**

3. **Determine any necessary action(s):**

4. Have your supervisor/instructor verify satisfactory completion of this procedure, any observations found, and any necessary action(s) recommended.

Performance Rating

CDX Tasksheet Number: C036

0	1	2	3	4

Supervisor/instructor signature _____ Date _____

▶ TASK Identify piston and bearing wear patterns that indicate connecting rod alignment and main bearing bore problems; determine necessary action.

MAST
1C9

Time off_____

Time on_____

Total time_____

CDX Tasksheet Number: C729

1. Research the procedure and specifications for inspecting the piston and bearing wear patterns in the appropriate service information.

    a. **List, or print off and attach to this sheet, the faults and wear patterns for the various connecting rod and main bearing bore issues:**

2. Following the specified procedure, visually inspect the pistons and bearings for abnormal wear patterns. **List your observations:**

3. **Determine any necessary action(s):**

4. Have your supervisor/instructor verify satisfactory completion of this procedure, any observations found, and any necessary action(s) recommended.

Performance Rating

CDX Tasksheet Number: C729

0	1	2	3	4

Supervisor/instructor signature _____ Date _____

© 2015 Jones & Bartlett Learning, LLC, an Ascend Learning Company

Engine Repair **179**

► **TASK** Inspect oil pump gears or rotors, housing, pressure relief devices, and pump drive; perform necessary action.

MAST
1D13

Time off_____

Time on_____

Total time_____

CDX Tasksheet Number: C733

1. Research the procedure and specifications to disassemble and inspect the oil pump in the appropriate service information.

    a. **Type of oil pump:** _____

    b. **Regulated oil pressure:** _____ psi/kPa

    c. **List, or print off and attach to this sheet, the specified clearances for this pump:**

2. Following the specified procedure, disassemble the pump and visually inspect the parts (including the pressure relief device and pump drive). **List your observation(s):**

3. Following the specified procedure, measure the pump clearances. **List your findings:**

4. **Determine any necessary action(s):**

5. Have your supervisor/instructor verify satisfactory completion of this procedure, any observations found, and any necessary action(s) recommended.

Performance Rating

CDX Tasksheet Number: C733

0	1	2	3	4

Supervisor/instructor signature _____ Date _____

Engine Repair: Assemble Engine Block

Student/intern information:

Name_____ Date_____ Class_____

Vehicle used for this activity:

Year _____ Make _____ Model_____

Odometer_____ VIN_____

Learning Objective/Task	CDX Tasksheet Number	2013 MLR NATEF Reference Number; Priority Level	2013 AST NATEF Reference Number; Priority Level	2013 MAST NATEF Reference Number; Priority Level
• Determine piston-to-bore clearance.	C597			1C11; P-2
• Inspect, measure, and install piston rings.	C040			1C12; P-2
• Assemble engine block.	C731			1C14; P-1

Time off_____

Time on_____

Total time_____

Materials Required

- Engine block, pistons, and piston rings
- Engine stand
- Feeler blade set
- Inside and outside micrometer sets
- Torque wrench
- Plastigauge®

Some Safety Issues to Consider

- Make sure the engine stand is rated for the weight of the engine you are mounting on it. Also, use bolts with the proper strength and length. Severe injury could occur if the engine were to fall due to failure of the engine stand or bolts.
- Engine castings and parts can have sharp edges. Always exercise extreme caution when working around them. Also, the parts are relatively heavy and can cause serious pinching of fingers. Be careful when handling them.
- Comply with personal and environmental safety practices associated with clothing; eye protection; hand tools; power equipment; proper ventilation; and the handling, storage, and disposal of chemicals/materials in accordance with local, state, and federal safety and environmental regulations.

Performance Standard

0—No exposure: No information or practice provided during the program; complete training required

1—Exposure only: General information provided with no practice time; close supervision needed; additional training required

2—Limited practice: Has practiced job during training program; additional training required to develop skill

3—Moderately skilled: Has performed job independently during training program; limited additional training may be required

4—Skilled: Can perform job independently with no additional training

MAST
1C11

CDX Tasksheet Number: C597

1. Research the procedure and specifications for determining the piston-to-bore clearance in the appropriate service information.

   a. **Specified piston-to-bore clearance:** _____ **in/mm**

2. Ensure the cylinder block is thoroughly cleaned according to the manufacturer's recommended procedure and is properly protected from rust and/or corrosion.

3. If the pistons have been replaced, follow the specified procedure to measure the piston-to-bore clearance for each piston and cylinder. **List your measurements in the table below.** If the bore and pistons are being reused, transfer the measurements from task C678, "Inspect and measure piston skirts and ring lands"; determine necessary action on page 165.

Cylinder	#1	#2	#3	#4	#5	#6	#7	#8
Piston-to-bore clearance (in/mm)								

4. **Is the piston-to-bore clearance within the specified tolerance?**
   Yes: _____ No: _____

5. Have your supervisor/instructor verify satisfactory completion of this procedure, any observations found, and any necessary action(s) recommended.

Performance Rating

CDX Tasksheet Number: C597

0	1	2	3	4

Supervisor/instructor signature _____ Date _____

MAST
1C12

CDX Tasksheet Number: CO40

1. Research the procedure and specifications for inspecting, measuring, and installing piston rings in the appropriate service information.

   a. Specified piston ring end gap

   i. **Top compression ring:** _____ in/mm

   ii. **Bottom compression ring:** _____ in/mm

   iii. **Oil ring:** _____ in/mm

   b. List the markings or ring configuration that determine which side of the ring goes up.

   i. **Top compression ring:** _____

   ii. **Bottom compression ring:** _____

   iii. **Oil ring:** _____

   c. Draw, or print off and attach to this sheet, the specified position of each piston ring gap when installed on the piston:

2. Following the specified procedure, measure the piston ring end gap for each cylinder. **List in the table below.**

Cylinder	#1	#2	#3	#4	#5	#6	#7	#8
Top compression ring (in/mm)								
Bottom compression ring (in/mm)								
Oil ring (in/mm)								

   a. Do all of the piston ring end gaps meet specifications?

   Yes: _____ **No:** _____

3. If the end gaps meet specifications, install piston rings on each piston. Be sure each ring is placed in the proper ring groove and is installed with the correct side up and in the correct orientation around the piston.

4. **Determine any necessary action(s):**

5. Have your supervisor/instructor verify satisfactory completion of this procedure, any observations found, and any necessary action(s) recommended.

Performance Rating

0	1	2	3	4

Supervisor/instructor signature _____ Date _____

MAST
1C14

Time off_____

Time on_____

Total time_____

CDX Tasksheet Number: C731

> **NOTE** Due to the differences in assembly procedures and specifications, it is recommended that the specified procedure and specifications be printed out and followed exactly.

> **NOTE** Most measurements were taken during the engine disassembly process to determine the necessary actions. Now that the engine is ready to be reassembled, all measurements need to be repeated to verify that parts are within their specified tolerances. Use the Engine Build Sheet on page 191 to record all of your measurements. When provided to customers, it lends a touch of professionalism to the job.

1. Reassemble the engine block following all manufacturer specifications and procedures. **List the specifications in the CDX Engine Build/Spec Sheet.** Be sure to verify the following information.

   a. Make sure the camshaft turns freely. If not, check for proper installation of the cam bearings.

   b. Check all oil gallery plugs, and make sure they are tightened/installed properly.

   c. Check all water jacket soft plugs for proper installation.

   d. Check crankshaft main journals for proper clearance, and record on the Engine Build/Spec Sheet.

   e. Check crankshaft end play, and record on the Engine Build/Spec Sheet.

   f. Clean and lubricate the cylinder walls. Lubricate the pistons and piston rings.

   g. Install the pistons with the rings in the proper orientation.

   h. Measure the connecting rod bearing clearance, and record on the Engine Build/Spec Sheet.

   i. Pack the oil pump with the proper lubricant and install the pump.

2. **Once the block is assembled, list any observation(s):**

3. Have your supervisor/instructor verify satisfactory completion of this procedure, any observations found, and any necessary action(s) recommended.

Performance Rating

CDX Tasksheet Number: C731

0	1	2	3	4

Supervisor/instructor signature _____ Date _____

NOTE Once the block is assembled, return to the Cylinder Head Disassembly, Inspection, and Repair tasksheet to continue with the installation of the cylinder heads and valve timing components.

Engine Build/Spec Sheet

Year _____ Make _____ Engine size _____

> **NOTE** Bolt Torque—Print out all bolt torque specifications and check them off as you torque each item. Record all measurements on the spec sheet for archival purposes.

Valve guide inside diameter		Valve spring seat pressure	
Valve stem diameter		Valve spring open pressure	
Valve stem clearance		Coil bind	
Valve adjustment intake		Cylinder head torque	
Valve adjustment exhaust		Camshaft cap torque	
Valve stem installed height		Cam bolt torque	

Piston Clearance

Piston	#1	#2	#3	#4	#5	#6	#7	#8
Cylinder bore								
Piston diameter								
Clearance								

Piston-to-valve clearance. Intake: _____ Exhaust: _____

Engine displacement: _____ (Bore^2) × 0.785 = _____ ×

_____ (Stroke) = _____ ci cylinder displacement × _____

(# of Cylinders) = _____ ci engine displacement

Ring Gap

Cylinder	#1	#2	#3	#4	#5	#6	#7	#8
#1 Compression ring								
#2 Compression ring								
Oil control ring								

Crankshaft Main Journal and Bearing Measurements

Main Bearing	#1	#2	#3	#4	#5	#6
Main bearings (inside diameter)						
Crankshaft mains (outside diameter)						
Clearance						
Plastigauge®						

Crankshaft end play: _____   Main cap torque: _____

Connecting Rod Journal and Bearing Measurements

Connecting Rod	#1	#2	#3	#4	#5	#6	#7	#8
Rod bearing (inside diameter)								
Rod journal (outside diameter)								
Clearance								
Plastigauge®								

Rod side clearance: _____   _____   _____   _____
Rod cap torque: _____   Wrist pin clearance: _____

Build Sheet Parts List

Gasket set brand/part number (PN) _____
Cylinder head brand/PN _____
Intake valve brand/PN _____
Exhaust valve brand/PN _____
Valve guides brand/PN _____
Valve springs brand/PN _____
Valve retainers brand/PN _____
Valve keepers brand/PN _____
Pistons brand/PN _____
Rings brand/PN _____
Crankshaft brand/PN _____
Main bearings brand/PN _____
Rod bearings brand/PN _____
Wrist pin bushings brand/PN _____
Oil pump brand/PN _____
Connecting rod brand/PN _____
Camshaft brand/PN _____
Camshaft duration at 0.050 lift _____
Camshaft centerline degrees _____
Lifters brand/PN _____
Cam bearings brand/PN _____
Timing set brand/PN _____
Intake manifold brand/PN _____

Notes:

Engine Repair: Miscellaneous In-Vehicle Engine Tasks

Student/intern information:

Name_____ Date_____ Class_____

Vehicle used for this activity:

Year _____ Make _____ Model_____

Odometer_____VIN_____

Time off_____

Time on_____

Total time_____

Learning Objective/Task	CDX Tasksheet Number	2013 MLR NATEF Reference Number; Priority Level	2013 AST NATEF Reference Number; Priority Level	2013 MAST NATEF Reference Number; Priority Level
• Install engine covers using gaskets, seals, and sealers as required.	C541	1A4; P-1	1A5; P-1	1A5; P-1
• Inspect, remove, and replace engine mounts.	C596		1A8; P-2	1A8; P-2
• Replace valve stem seals on an assembled engine; inspect valve spring retainers, locks/keepers, and valve lock/keeper grooves; determine necessary action.	C675			1B8; P-3

Materials Required

- Vehicle
- Gasket scraper (nonabrasive for aluminum and plastic surfaces)
- Seal pullers and installers
- Vehicle hoist
- Engine support or transmission jack
- Valve spring compressor
- Cylinder leakage tester

Some Safety Issues to Consider

- Lifting equipment such as engine hoists are important tools that increase productivity and make the job easier. However, they can also cause severe injury or death if used improperly. Make sure you follow the manufacturer's operation procedures.
- This procedure will require cleaning the components. Use the proper personal protective equipment for the chemicals and processes used.
- Engine castings and parts can have sharp edges. Always exercise extreme caution when working around them. Also, the parts are relatively heavy and can cause serious pinching of fingers. Be careful when handling them.
- Diagnosis of this fault may require test-driving the vehicle on the school grounds. Attempt this task only with full permission from your instructor and follow all the guidelines exactly.
- Comply with personal and environmental safety practices associated with clothing; eye protection; hand tools; power equipment; proper ventilation; and the handling, storage, and disposal of chemicals/materials in accordance with local, state, and federal safety and environmental regulations.

Performance Standard

0–No exposure: No information or practice provided during the program; complete training required

1–Exposure only: General information provided with no practice time; close supervision needed; additional training required

2–Limited practice: Has practiced job during training program; additional training required to develop skill

3–Moderately skilled: Has performed job independently during training program; limited additional training may be required

4–Skilled: Can perform job independently with no additional training

► **TASK** Install engine covers using gaskets, seals, and sealers as required.

Time off_____

Time on_____

CDX Tasksheet Number: C541

Total time_____

> **NOTE** This task may be completed as part of an engine rebuild or done separately on another vehicle.

1. **List the gaskets and/or seals you are installing:**

2. **Research the procedure and specifications for the gaskets and/or seals you are removing/installing in the appropriate service information.**

   a. **List the recommended sealant required for each gasket/seal, if needed:**

   b. **List or print off and attach to this sheet any torque specifications for the cover(s) you are removing:**

3. Following the specified procedure, remove the appropriate engine cover.

4. **Remove any seals and gasket material with the proper tools. Be careful not to gouge or damage the surfaces being cleaned. Also, prepare the sealing surfaces for cover reinstallation according to the service information. List your observation(s):**

5. Have your supervisor/instructor verify that the cover is ready to be reinstalled. **Supervisor's/instructor's initials:** _____

6. Reinstall the cover following the specified procedure. Torque all fasteners to the proper torque and check for any leakage.

7. Have your supervisor/instructor verify satisfactory completion of this procedure, any observations found, and any necessary action(s) recommended.

Performance Rating

CDX Tasksheet Number: C541

0	1	2	3	4

Supervisor/instructor signature _____ Date _____

► **TASK** Inspect, remove, and replace engine mounts.

AST 1A8 **MAST** 1A8

Time off_____

Time on_____

Total time_____

CDX Tasksheet Number: C596

1. Research the procedure to inspect and replace the engine mounts in the appropriate service information.

    a. List the type of engine mount this vehicle uses: _____

    b. List or print off and attach to this sheet the precautions for performing this task:

    c. List or print off and attach to this sheet the procedure for inspecting the engine mounts:

2. Following the specified procedure, inspect the engine mounts and list your observations:

3. Determine any necessary action(s):

4. Have your supervisor/instructor verify your answers and initial if correct.
   Supervisor's/instructor's initials: _____

5. With your instructor's permission, remove one or more engine mounts following the specified procedure. Inspect the removed engine mount(s) and list your observations:

6. Have your supervisor/instructor verify the removal of the mount.
   Supervisor's/instructor's initials: _____

7. Reinstall the engine mount(s) according to the specified procedure.

8. **Determine any necessary action(s):**

9. Have your supervisor/instructor verify satisfactory completion of this procedure, any observations found, and any necessary action(s) recommended.

Performance Rating

CDX Tasksheet Number: C596

☐	☐	☐	☐	☐
0	1	2	3	4

Supervisor/instructor signature _____ Date _____

▶ **TASK** Replace valve stem seals on an assembled engine; inspect valve spring retainers, locks/keepers, and valve lock/keeper grooves; determine necessary action.

MAST
1B8

Time off_____

Time on_____

Total time_____

CDX Tasksheet Number: C675

1. **Research the procedures and specifications for replacing the valve stem seals while the engine is installed in the vehicle in the appropriate service information.**

   a. **List, or print off and attach to this sheet, the precautions for performing this task:**

   b. **List the type of valve seals this engine is equipped with:** _____

   c. **List the flat rate time to perform this task:** _____ hr

   d. **List the special tools required to perform this task:**

2. Have your supervisor/instructor verify your answers and initial. **Supervisor/instructor's initials:** _____

3. Following the specified procedure, prepare the engine for removal of the valve spring keepers and retainer by removing the valve cover and rocker arm or cam follower (some engines may require removal of the cam).

4. With the valve firmly held in place with compressed air, tap the valve retainer with a hammer and socket to break the bond between the retainer and keepers. Tap in line with the valve stem; do not tap sideways because that could bend the valve stem.

5. Install the valve spring compressor and compress the valve spring. Remove the keepers; be sure not to let them fall into the engine. Remove the valve spring and retainer.

6. Check to see if there is a burr on the valve stem near the keeper groove. File it smooth if necessary. Remove the old valve seal. Install the new valve seal according to the specified procedure. This may include using a sleeve that fits over the valve stem to protect the valve seal during installation. Also lubricate the seal before installation. And make sure it is fully seated if it is of the positive seal type.

7. Reinstall the valve spring, retainer, and keepers. Be sure to seat the keepers fully in the valve stem groove.

8. Have your supervisor/instructor verify correct installation of the valve seals and springs. **Supervisor/instructor's initials:** _____

9. Reinstall the removed valve cover/s and other parts.

10. Start the engine and verify correct operation.

11. Have your supervisor/instructor verify satisfactory completion of this procedure, any observations found, and any necessary action/s recommended.

Performance Rating

CDX Tasksheet Number: C675

0	1	2	3	4

Supervisor/instructor signature _____ Date _____

Engine Repair: Lubrication System Service

Student/intern information:

Name_____ Date_____ Class_____

Vehicle used for this activity:

Year _____ Make _____ Model_____

Odometer_____VIN_____

Time off_____

Time on_____

Total time_____

Learning Objective/Task	CDX Tasksheet Number	2013 MLR NATEF Reference Number; Priority Level	2013 AST NATEF Reference Number; Priority Level	2013 MAST NATEF Reference Number; Priority Level
• Perform engine oil and filter change.	C737	1C5; P-1	1D10; P-1	1D10; P-1
• Perform oil pressure tests; determine necessary action.	C732		1D9; P-1	1D9; P-1
• Inspect, test, and replace oil temperature and pressure switches and sensors.	C736		1D12; P-2	1D12; P-2

Materials Required

- Vehicle or simulator
- Vehicle hoist
- Exhaust hose(s)
- Drain pan
- Wheel chocks
- Oil-change sticker
- Remote oil pressure gauge
- Oil pressure-sensor socket
- DVOM

Some Safety Issues to Consider

- Changing oil on a hot engine can lead to burns. Always be careful to avoid hot engine oil.
- Used engine oil contains cancer-causing agents. Always avoid oil contact with your hands. Always wash your hands after completing this task.
- Vehicle hoists are important tools that increase productivity and make the job easier. However, they can also cause severe injury or death if used improperly. Make sure you follow the hoist's and vehicle manufacturer's operation procedures. Also, make sure you have your supervisor's/instructor's permission to use a vehicle hoist.
- Comply with personal and environmental safety practices associated with clothing; eye protection; hand tools; power equipment; proper ventilation; and the handling, storage, and disposal of chemicals/materials in accordance with local, state, and federal safety and environmental regulations.

Performance Standard

0—No exposure: No information or practice provided during the program; complete training required

1—Exposure only: General information provided with no practice time; close supervision needed; additional training required

2—Limited practice: Has practiced job during training program; additional training required to develop skill

3—Moderately skilled: Has performed job independently during training program; limited additional training may be required

4—Skilled: Can perform job independently with no additional training

MLR
1C5

AST
1D10

MAST
1D10

Time off_____

Time on_____

Total time_____

CDX Tasksheet Number: C737

1. Research the following specifications/procedures for this vehicle in the appropriate service information.

    a. Oil capacity: _____ qt/lt

    b. Oil viscosity: _____

    c. API or other specified rating: _____

    d. Oil pan drain plug torque: _____ ft-lb/Nm

    e. Oil filter part number: _____

    f. List any special requirements/procedures for changing the oil and filter on this vehicle:

> **NOTE** Some vehicles have more than one oil drain plug and/or a special procedure for changing the filter.

---

    g. Determine that a new filter, and the proper oil, is available for this vehicle before proceeding.   Yes: _____ No: _____

2. Safely raise and secure the vehicle on a hoist.

> **NOTE** Removing the oil filler cap may allow the oil to drain faster.

---

3. Follow the specified procedure for draining the used oil and removing the old oil filter.

> **NOTE** The oil may be extremely hot. Be sure not to come into contact with the used oil.

---

    a. Is the drain plug gasket reusable? Yes: _____ No: _____

    b. Did the oil filter gasket come off with the oil filter? Yes: _____
       No: _____

    c. Have your instructor verify these answers by initialing here: _____

4. Once the used oil has been drained, follow the manufacturer's procedure for installing the new oil filter (oil the gasket) and reinstalling the drain plug (tighten to the specified torque).

5. Lower the vehicle.

6. Following the appropriate service information, add the proper amount of new oil.

7. Prepare to start the vehicle by applying the parking brake and placing exhaust hoses over the exhaust pipe(s). Start the vehicle and check for oil leaks. If oil leaks are found, shut off the engine immediately, locate the source of the leak, and inform your instructor. If no leaks are found, shut off the engine after a minute or two of running.

8. Let the engine oil drain back into the oil pan for a few minutes and then check to see that the oil is at the proper level. Add oil if necessary.

   a. **What is the final oil level?** _____

9. Dispose of the old oil and filter according to legislative guidelines (national, federal, state, and local).

10. Reset the maintenance reminder system if equipped, or fill out an oil-change reminder sticker and place it on the vehicle according to your shop's policy.

11. Have your supervisor/instructor verify satisfactory completion of this procedure, any observations found, and any necessary action(s) recommended.

Performance Rating

CDX Tasksheet Number: C737

0	1	2	3	4

Supervisor/instructor signature _____ Date _____

Perform oil pressure tests; determine necessary action.

Time off_____

Time on_____

Total time_____

CDX Tasksheet Number: C732

1. Research the following specifications/procedures for this vehicle in the appropriate service information.

    a. **Oil pressure specification(s):** _____

    b. **List or print off and attach to this sheet the procedure for performing the oil pressure test:**

2. Using the appropriate tools, remove the oil pressure switch/sensor from the engine block and install the mechanical oil pressure gauge fitting to the place where the switch was fitted. Place the gauge in a position where you can easily view it, but out of the way of any moving parts, exhaust pipes, etc.

3. Prepare to start the vehicle by applying the parking brake and placing exhaust hoses over the exhaust pipe(s).

4. **With a relatively cold engine, start the car and note the pressure gauge reading at idle:** _____ **psi/kPa**

5. **Increase the engine speed and watch the pressure gauge reading. Note the cold readings below.**

    a. **@ 1000 RPM:** _____ **psi/kPa**
    b. **@ 1500 RPM:** _____ **psi/kPa**
    c. **@ 2000 RPM:** _____ **psi/kPa**
    d. **@ 2500 RPM:** _____ **psi/kPa**

6. **Repeat the readings at a normal engine-operating temperature at idle:** _____ **psi/kPa. Note the hot readings here.**

    a. **@ 1000 RPM:** _____ **psi/kPa**
    b. **@ 1500 RPM:** _____ **psi/kPa**
    c. **@ 2000 RPM:** _____ **psi/kPa**
    d. **@ 2500 RPM:** _____ **psi/kPa**

7. **Do the readings meet the specifications? Yes:** _____ **No:** _____

8. **Determine any necessary action(s):**

9. Have your supervisor/instructor verify satisfactory completion of this procedure, any observations found, and any necessary action(s) recommended.

Performance Rating

CDX Tasksheet Number: C732

0	1	2	3	4

Supervisor/instructor signature _____ Date _____

▶ **TASK** Inspect, test, and replace oil temperature and pressure switches and sensors.

AST 1D12   MAST 1D12

CDX Tasksheet Number: C736

1. **Research the following specifications/procedures for this vehicle in the appropriate service information.**

   a. **Is this vehicle equipped with an oil temperature sensor?**
   Yes: _____ No: _____

   b. **Is this vehicle equipped with an oil pressure switch (warning light style)?**
   Yes: _____ No: _____

   c. **Is this vehicle equipped with an oil pressure-sending unit (gauge style)?**
   Yes: _____ No: _____

   d. **Is the vehicle equipped with an oil pressure sensor (PCM sensor style)?**
   Yes: _____ No: _____

   e. **List the specification(s) for each sensor/switch the vehicle is equipped with:**

   i. **Oil temperature sensor:**

   ii. **Oil pressure switch:**

   iii. **Oil pressure-sending unit:**

   iv. **Oil pressure sensor:**

2. **Following the appropriate service information procedure, test each switch/sensor (as equipped) and list your findings.**

   a. **Oil temperature sensor:**

b. Oil pressure switch:

c. Oil pressure-sending unit:

d. Oil pressure sensor:

3. Determine any necessary action(s):

4. Have your supervisor/instructor verify satisfactory completion of this procedure, any observations found, and any necessary action(s) recommended.

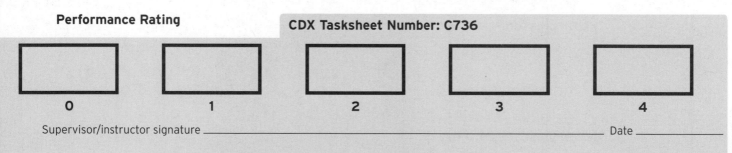

Performance Rating

CDX Tasksheet Number: C736

| 0 | 1 | 2 | 3 | 4 |

Supervisor/instructor signature _____ Date _____

Engine Repair: Cooling System Service

Student/intern information:

Name_____ Date_____ Class_____

Vehicle used for this activity:

Year _____ Make _____ Model_____

Odometer_____VIN_____

Learning Objective/Task	CDX Tasksheet Number	2013 MLR NATEF Reference Number; Priority Level	2013 AST NATEF Reference Number; Priority Level	2013 MAST NATEF Reference Number; Priority Level
• Perform cooling system pressure and dye tests to identify leaks; check coolant condition; inspect and test radiator, pressure cap, coolant recovery tank, and heater core; determine necessary action.	C578	1C1; P-1	1D1; P-1	1D1; P-1
• Inspect, replace, and adjust drive belts, tensioners, and pulleys; check pulley and belt alignment.	C734	1C2; P-1	1D3; P-1	1D3; P-1
• Inspect and replace engine cooling and heater system hoses.	NN10	N/A	N/A	N/A
• Remove, inspect, and replace thermostat and gasket/seal.	C735	1C3; P-1	1D7; P-1	1D7; P-1
• Inspect and test coolant; drain and recover coolant; flush and refill cooling system with recommended coolant; bleed air as required.	C050	1C4; P-1	1D4; P-1	1D4; P-1
• Inspect, remove, and replace water pump.	C680		1D5; P-2	1D5; P-2
• Remove and replace radiator.	C052		1D6; P-2	1D6; P-2
• Inspect and test fan(s) (electrical or mechanical), fan clutch, fan shroud, and air dams.	C053		1D8; P-1	1D8; P-1
• Inspect auxiliary coolers; determine necessary action.	C871		1D11; P-3	1D11; P-3
• Identify causes of engine overheating.	C598		1D2; P-1	1D2; P-1

Time off_____

Time on_____

Total time_____

Materials Required

- Vehicle or simulator
- Cooling system pressure tester
- Anti-freeze hydrometer (or refractometer)
- pH test strip or pH tester
- Infrared temperature gun
- DVOM
- Drain pan
- Gasket scraper

Some Safety Issues to Consider

- Only open the radiator cap (or any other part of the cooling system) when the engine is cool. Opening a radiator cap on a warm or hot engine could cause severe burns.
- Electric fans can turn on at any time. Keep hands and fingers away.
- Remove the ignition key and secure it so the vehicle can't be started. And if the vehicle is equipped with a push button start, keep the key at least 25 feet away from the vehicle.
- Keep away from moving belts and pulleys as they can severely injure or kill you.
- When running any vehicles in the shop, make sure you use the shop's exhaust ventilation system to discharge all exhaust gas safely outside.
- Comply with personal and environmental safety practices associated with clothing; eye protection; hand tools; power equipment; proper ventilation; and the handling, storage, and disposal of chemicals/materials in accordance with local, state, and federal safety and environmental regulations.

Performance Standard

0–No exposure: No information or practice provided during the program; complete training required

1–Exposure only: General information provided with no practice time; close supervision needed; additional training required

2–Limited practice: Has practiced job during training program; additional training required to develop skill

3–Moderately skilled: Has performed job independently during training program; limited additional training may be required

4–Skilled: Can perform job independently with no additional training

▶ **TASK** Perform cooling system pressure and dye tests to identify leaks; check coolant condition; inspect and test radiator, pressure cap, coolant recovery tank, and heater core; determine necessary action.

MLR 1C1   **AST** 1D1   **MAST** 1D1

CDX Tasksheet Number: C578

1. **Research the following specifications for this vehicle in the appropriate service information.**

   a. **Radiator cap pressure rating:** _____ psi/kPa
   b. **Cooling system capacity:** _____ qt/lt
   c. **Type of coolant:** _____
   d. **Specified pH:** _____

2. Cooling System Pressure Test: If the vehicle is cold or cool, and the engine is not running, remove the radiator cap. Top off the radiator with the correct type of coolant/water mix if it is not already full. Install the proper adapter on the cooling system access point. Pressurize the cooling system to the specified radiator cap pressure listed above (or a maximum of 2 psi higher). Make sure you leave the system pressurized for a minimum of 10 minutes while you inspect for coolant leaks.

   > **NOTE** Do not forget to check the heater core and the core plugs.

   a. **List any leaks found and any necessary action(s):**

3. Coolant Condition: Remove the pressure tester from the radiator. Fit the proper adapter on the tester so that you can check the radiator cap.

   a. **Pressure-test the cap and check it for the following information.**

      i. **At what pressure does it vent?** _____ psi/kPa
      ii. **At what pressure does it hold?** _____ psi/kPa
      iii. **Determine any necessary action(s):**

   b. **Use an anti-freeze hydrometer or refractometer to test the coolant's freezing and boiling points.**

      i. **Freezing point:** _____ °F/°C
      ii. **Boiling point:** _____ °F/°C

   c. **Use a pH test strip or a pH tester to determine the pH balance of the anti-freeze.**

     i. **pH reading:** _____

     ii. **Determine any necessary action(s):**

4. **Radiator, Recovery Tank, and Hoses: Inspect the radiator, recovery tank, and hoses for damage or broken/missing pieces. List your findings and any necessary action(s):**

5. Radiator Test: Reinstall the radiator cap on the radiator. Place the exhaust hose over the vehicle's exhaust pipe(s). Start the vehicle and allow the engine to warm up.

   a. Use the infrared temperature gun to measure the temperature across the radiator core. The temperature should show a steady cooling reading as you trace the core tubes from the hot side of the radiator to the cool side. Any tubes that are significantly cooler than the others indicate a plugged tube in the radiator.

   b. **List your observations and determine any necessary action(s):**

6. Have your supervisor/instructor verify satisfactory completion of this procedure, any observations found, and any necessary action(s) recommended.

Performance Rating

CDX Tasksheet Number: C578

0	1	2	3	4

Supervisor/instructor signature _____ Date _____

Inspect, replace, and adjust drive belts, tensioners, and pulleys; check pulley and belt alignment.

MLR	**AST**	**MAST**
1C2	1D3	1D3

Time off_____

Time on_____

Total time_____

CDX Tasksheet Number: C734

1. Locate "inspecting, adjusting and or replacing a generator (alternator) drive belts, pulleys, and tensioners; check pulley and belt alignment" in the appropriate service information for the vehicle you are working on.

    a. List the specified drive belt tension: _____

    b. List the faults to look for when inspecting drive belts, pulleys, and tensioners:

    c. Describe how to check the correct pulley and belt alignment:

    d. Locate the belt routing diagram, or draw a picture of the current routing arrangement:

2. **Remove the vehicle drive belt(s).**

3. **Inspect the vehicle drive belts, pulleys, and tensioners for faults. List your observations for the following parts:**

    a. Vehicle drive belt(s):

    b. Pulleys:

    c. Tensioner(s):

    d. Pulley/belt alignment:

4. **Have your instructor verify the removal of the belt(s) and the faults found. Supervisor's/instructor's initials:** _____

5. Reinstall the vehicle drive belts using the appropriate service information.

6. Re-tension the drive belt(s) using the appropriate service information.

7. Check for the correct pulley, tensioner, and drive belt alignment.

8. **Determine any necessary action(s):**

9. Have your supervisor/instructor verify satisfactory completion of this procedure, any observations found, and any necessary action(s) recommended.

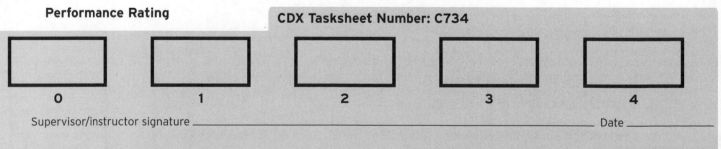

Performance Rating

CDX Tasksheet Number: C734

| 0 | 1 | 2 | 3 | 4 |

Supervisor/instructor signature _____ Date _____

Time off_____

Time on_____

Total time_____

CDX Tasksheet Number: NN10

1. **Visually inspect the external condition of all the hoses that carry coolant on the vehicle. Also, squeeze each hose and check for soft or brittle conditions. List your observations below.**

   a. **Radiator hose condition:**

   b. **Heater hose condition:**

   c. **Other hoses (bypass hoses, heated intake hoses, etc.):**

2. Drain an appropriate amount of coolant from the system to lower the coolant level below the level of the hose you are removing.

3. Remove the hose. Be careful not to damage the fitting it is connected to.

   > **NOTE** Do not twist the hose to loosen it from the radiator or heater core fittings. You could pull the fitting out of the core. Either carefully slide a tool between the fitting and the hose, or slit the hose on top of the fitting, being careful not to damage the fitting, and peel the hose off of the fitting.

4. **Inspect the inside of the hose. List your observation(s):**

5. Have your instructor verify the removal and the faults found.
   Supervisor's/instructor's initials: _____

6. Replace the hose with a new one, if needed. Be sure to properly route it.

7. Refill the system with the proper coolant; perform a pressure or vacuum test to check for leaks.

8. Apply the vehicle's parking brake and secure the vehicle with wheel chocks to prevent the vehicle from rolling. Also, place the exhaust hose over the exhaust pipe(s).

9. Start the engine and allow it to warm up to a normal operating temperature and recheck for leaks and proper coolant level.

10. Have your supervisor/instructor verify satisfactory completion of this procedure, any observations found, and any necessary action(s) recommended.

Performance Rating

CDX Tasksheet Number: NN10

0	1	2	3	4

Supervisor/instructor signature _____ Date _____

© 2015 Jones & Bartlett Learning, LLC, an Ascend Learning Company

▶ TASK Remove, inspect, and replace thermostat and gasket/seal.

MLR 1C3   **AST** 1D7   **MAST** 1D7

Time off_____

Time on_____

Total time_____

CDX Tasksheet Number: C735

1. **Research the thermostat replacement procedure for this vehicle in the appropriate service information.**

   a. **List any special procedures and/or tools to perform this task:**

   b. **List the thermostat housing bolt torque:** _____ **ft-lb/Nm**

2. **Look up the flat rate time for this task in a flat rate manual:** _____ **hr**

3. Drain enough coolant out of the radiator to lower the level below the thermostat. Save this to put back in the system when the task is finished. Keep it free of dirt and debris.

4. Follow the manufacturer's procedure and remove the thermostat.

5. Carefully scrape off any old gasket residue from the thermostat housing and mating surface. Be careful not to gouge the sealing surfaces.

6. Have your instructor verify removal of the thermostat. Supervisor's/instructor's initials: _____

   > **NOTE** Ask your supervisor/instructor whether or not to perform the next action before proceeding.

7. **Test the old thermostat in a pan of boiling water to see at what temperature it opens. Suspend the thermostat in a pan of heated water using a piece of wire. The thermostat should be fully immersed in water, but do not allow it to touch the side or bottom of the pan.**

   a. **List the temperature at which the thermostat started to open:** _____ **°F/°C**

   b. **List the temperature at which the thermostat was fully open:** _____ **°F/°C**

   c. **How far did the thermostat open?** _____ **in/mm**

   d. **Did the thermostat operate according to specifications?**
      Yes: _____ **No:** _____

8. Install a new thermostat and gasket/seal (or reinstall the old one if your instructor directed you to do so). Torque bolts to the proper torque.

   > **NOTE** Be careful when bolting down the thermostat housing. Make sure the thermostat is still in its recessed groove. Failure to do so will result in a broken housing and damaged thermostat. If in doubt, ask your supervisor/instructor.

9. Once the thermostat is installed, return the drained anti-freeze back into the system.

10. Follow the manufacturer's procedure to bleed any air from the cooling system.

11. Apply the vehicle's parking brake and secure the vehicle with wheel chocks to prevent the vehicle from rolling. Also, place the exhaust hose over the exhaust pipe(s).

12. Start the vehicle and check for any leaks or overheating. Immediately shut off the vehicle if a leak or overheating is found. Repair any leaks, or determine the reason for overheating if present.

13. Return the vehicle to its beginning condition and return any tools that you may have used to their proper locations.

14. Have your supervisor/instructor verify satisfactory completion of this procedure, any observations found, and any necessary action(s) recommended.

Performance Rating

CDX Tasksheet Number: C735

0	1	2	3	4

Supervisor/instructor signature _____ Date _____

▶ **TASK** Inspect and test coolant; drain and recover coolant; flush and refill cooling system with recommended coolant; bleed air as required.

MLR 1C4 | **AST** 1D4 | **MAST** 1D4

Time off_____

Time on_____

Total time_____

CDX Tasksheet Number: C050

1. **Research the following specifications/procedures for this vehicle in the appropriate service information.**

   a. **What is the cooling system capacity?** _____ qt/lt

   b. **What type of anti-freeze is required?** _____

   c. **List or print off and attach to this sheet the cooling system bleeding procedure:**

2. **Coolant Test:**

   a. **If the vehicle is cold or cool and not running, remove the radiator cap and test the coolant's freeze protection.**

      i. **What is the coolant's freeze protection point?** _____ °F/°C

   b. **List the coolant's boiling point:** _____ °F/°C at _____ psi/kPa

   c. **Test the coolant's pH reading:** _____

      i. **Is this within specification? Yes:** _____ **No:** _____

   d. **Determine any necessary action(s):**

3. Using the appropriate cooling system recycle/flush machine, flush and refill the cooling system with the correct amount of recommended anti-freeze. Properly recycle/dispose of any used coolant.

   a. **When this procedure is finished, retest the coolant's freeze protection:** _____ °F/°C

      i. **What is the coolant pH?** _____

      ii. **Is this within specification? Yes:** _____ **No:** _____

   b. Follow the manufacturer's procedure to bleed air out of the cooling system, if necessary.

   c. Place exhaust hoses on the vehicle's exhaust pipe(s) and wheel chocks to prevent the vehicle from moving. Start the vehicle and monitor the cooling system to make sure that the engine warms up properly and that the thermostat opens at the correct temperature. Also, check that the coolant is at the correct level.

© 2015 Jones & Bartlett Learning, LLC, an Ascend Learning Company

d. Determine any necessary action(s):

4. Return the vehicle to its beginning condition and return any tools that you may have used to their proper locations.

5. Have your supervisor/instructor verify satisfactory completion of this procedure, any observations found, and any necessary action(s) recommended.

Performance Rating

CDX Tasksheet Number: C050

☐	☐	☐	☐	☐
0	1	2	3	4

Supervisor/instructor signature _____ Date _____

AST 1D5   MAST 1D5

CDX Tasksheet Number: C680

1. **Research the following specifications/procedures for this vehicle in the appropriate service information.**

    a. **Water pump bolt torque:** _____ **ft-lb/Nm**

    b. **Type of anti-freeze:** _____

    c. **Draw or print off and attach to this sheet the belt routing diagram:**

2. Drain the coolant out of the radiator. In most situations, the coolant gets replaced/ recycled. If your instructor wants you to reuse the coolant, save it in a clean container and keep it free of dirt and debris.

3. Following the specified procedure, remove the water pump.

4. **Inspect the pump for signs of deterioration, leaks, and worn bearings. List your observations:**

5. Have your instructor verify the removal of the water pump.
   Supervisor's/instructor's initials: _____

6. Replace the water pump with a new water pump, if needed. Torque all fasteners to the proper torque.

7. Reinstall the removed coolant (or new coolant) into the radiator. Top off with the correct coolant, if needed.

8. Pressure test or vacuum test the cooling system to check for leaks. Repair any leaks found.

9. Apply the vehicle's parking brake or secure the vehicle with wheel chocks to prevent the vehicle from rolling. Also, place the exhaust hose over the exhaust pipe(s).

10. Start the vehicle and check for any leaks or overheating. Immediately shut off the vehicle if a leak or overheating is found. Repair any leaks, or determine the reason for overheating if present.

11. Return the vehicle to its beginning condition and return any tools that you may have used to their proper locations.

12. Have your supervisor/instructor verify satisfactory completion of this procedure, any observations found, and any necessary action(s) recommended.

Performance Rating

CDX Tasksheet Number: C680

0	1	2	3	4

Supervisor/instructor signature _____ Date _____

Time off_____

Time on_____

Total time_____

CDX Tasksheet Number: C052

1. **Research the following specifications/procedures for this vehicle in the appropriate service information.**

   a. **Cooling system capacity:** _____ qt/lt

   b. **Type of anti-freeze:** _____

2. Drain as much coolant from the vehicle as possible into a clean drain pan so that you can reuse the coolant. Also, place the drain pan so that dirt and other debris will not contaminate it while removing the radiator.

3. Follow the specified procedure to remove the radiator.

   > **NOTE** Be careful when removing the hoses from the radiator. You will need to slide a thin tool (such as a small screwdriver) carefully between the hose and the radiator fitting to loosen the hose, or slit the hose and carefully peel it off of the fitting. Failure to do this could cause damage to the radiator fitting.

4. **Inspect the radiator for any damage and list your observation(s):**

5. Have your instructor verify the removal of the radiator.
   Supervisor's/instructor's initials: _____

6. Reinstall the radiator following the specified procedure.

7. Reinstall the removed coolant into the radiator. Top off with the correct coolant, if needed.

8. Pressure test or vacuum test the cooling system to check for leaks. Repair any leaks found.

9. Apply the vehicle's parking brake or secure the vehicle with wheel chocks to prevent the vehicle from rolling. Also, place the exhaust hose over the exhaust pipe(s).

10. Start the vehicle and check for any leaks or overheating. Immediately shut off the vehicle if a leak or overheating is found. Repair any leaks, or determine the reason for overheating if present.

11. Have your supervisor/instructor verify satisfactory completion of this procedure, any observations found, and any necessary action(s) recommended.

Performance Rating

0	1	2	3	4

Supervisor/instructor signature _____ Date _____

Inspect and test fan(s) (electrical or mechanical), fan clutch, fan shroud, and air dams.

AST
1D8

MAST
1D8

Time off_____

Time on_____

Total time_____

CDX Tasksheet Number: C053

Mechanical Fans:

1. Research the fan inspection and testing procedure for this vehicle in the appropriate service information.

   a. List or print off and attach to this sheet the inspection and testing procedure for the fan system:

2. **Visually inspect the fan and fan clutch for damage or wear and list your observations:**

3. **Test the fan clutch according to the specified procedure and list your observations:**

4. **Determine any necessary action(s):**

Electric Fans:

1. Research the fan inspection and testing procedure for this vehicle in the appropriate service information.

   a. List or print off and attach to this sheet the inspection and testing procedure for the fan system:

   b. List the temperature at which the electric fan should turn on: _____ °F/°C

2. **Visually inspect the fan for damage or wear and list your observations:**

3. **Test the fan system according to the specified procedure and list your observations:**

4. **Determine any necessary action(s):**

Fan Shroud and Air Dam:

1. **Visually inspect the fan shroud and air dam for any damage, missing parts, or wear and list your observations:**

2. **Determine any necessary action(s):**

3. Return the vehicle to its beginning condition and return any tools that you may have used to their proper locations.

4. Have your supervisor/instructor verify satisfactory completion of this procedure, any observations found, and any necessary action(s) recommended.

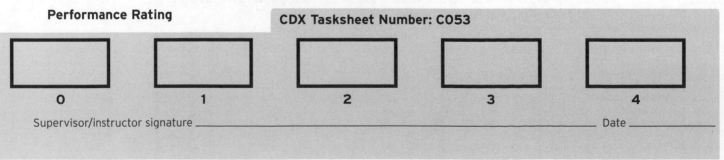

Performance Rating

CDX Tasksheet Number: C053

| 0 | 1 | 2 | 3 | 4 |

Supervisor/instructor signature _____ Date _____

AST 1D11 **MAST** 1D11

Time off_____

Time on_____

Total time_____

CDX Tasksheet Number: C871

1. Research the auxiliary cooler testing procedure for this vehicle in the appropriate service information. Normally, the coolers are located either in front of the radiator or as part of the cooler end of the radiator.

   a. **List the auxiliary cooler(s) this vehicle is equipped with (and the type: air-cooled, liquid cooled, etc.):**

   b. **List or print off and attach to this sheet the inspection and testing procedure for the cooler(s):**

2. **Closely examine the unit for leaks or damage that could develop into leaks under normal operating conditions. Make particular note of the condition of any tubes or hoses, and the condition of their fittings. List your test(s) and observation(s):**

3. **Determine any necessary action(s):**

4. Return the vehicle to its beginning condition and return any tools that you may have used to their proper locations.

5. Have your supervisor/instructor verify satisfactory completion of this procedure, any observations found, and any necessary action(s) recommended.

Performance Rating

CDX Tasksheet Number: C871

0	1	2	3	4

Supervisor/instructor signature _____ Date _____

AST 1D2 **MAST** 1D2

Time off_____

Time on_____

Total time_____

CDX Tasksheet Number: C598

Vehicle used for this activity:

Year _____ Make _____ Model_____

Odometer_____ VIN_____

1. **List the customer concern in relation to the overheating problem:**

2. **Research the particular concern in the appropriate service information and list the possible causes:**

3. **Inspect the cooling system and engine to determine the cause of the concern. List your tests and results:**

4. **Determine any necessary action(s) to correct the fault:**

5. Return the vehicle to its beginning condition and return any tools that you may have used to their proper locations.

6. Have your supervisor/instructor verify satisfactory completion of this procedure, any observations found, and any necessary action(s) recommended.

Performance Rating

CDX Tasksheet Number: C598

0	1	2	3	4

Supervisor/instructor signature _____ Date _____

Section A2:
Automatic Transmission and Transaxle

CONTENTS

Automatic Transmission and Transaxle: Vehicle, Customer, and Service Information

Student/intern information:

Name _____ Date _____ Class _____

Vehicle used for this activity:

Year _____ Make _____ Model _____

Odometer _____ VIN _____

Learning Objective/Task	CDX Tasksheet Number	2013 MLR NATEF Reference Number; Priority Level	2013 AST NATEF Reference Number; Priority Level	2013 MAST NATEF Reference Number; Priority Level
• Research applicable vehicle and service information, fluid type, vehicle service history, service precautions, and technical service bulletins.	C681	2A1; P-1	2A2; P-1	2A2; P-1
• Identify and interpret transmission/transaxle concern; differentiate between engine performance and transmission/transaxle concerns; determine necessary action.	C599		2A1; P-1	2A1; P-1
• Check fluid level in a transmission or a transaxle equipped with a dipstick.	C902	2A2; P-1	2A4; P-1	2A4; P-1
• Check fluid level in a transmission or a transaxle not equipped with a dipstick.	C903	2A3;P-1	2A5; P-1	2A5; P-1
• Check transmission fluid condition; check for leaks.	C904	2A4; P-2		
• Diagnose fluid loss and condition concerns; determine necessary action.	C682		2A3; P-1	2A3; P-1
• Drain and replace fluid and filter(s).	C907	2B4; P-1	2B4; P-1	2B4; P-1
• Describe the operational characteristics of a continuously variable transmission (CVT).	C606	2C1; P-3	2C4; P-3	2C4; P-3
• Describe the operational characteristics of a hybrid vehicle drive train.	C607	2C2; P-3	2C5; P-3	2C5; P-3
• Demonstrate use of 3 Cs (concern, cause, correction).	NN02	N/A	N/A	N/A

Time off _____

Time on _____

Total time _____

Materials Required

- Blank work order
- Vehicle with available service history records
- Depending on the type of concern, special diagnostic tools may be required. See your supervisor/instructor for instructions to identify what tools may be required.

Some Safety Issues to Consider

- This task may require test-driving the vehicle on the school grounds. Attempt this task only with full permission from your instructor and follow all the guidelines exactly.
- When running any vehicles in the shop, make sure you use the shop's exhaust ventilation system to discharge all exhaust gas safely outside.
- Lifting equipment such as vehicle jacks and stands, vehicle hoists, and engine hoists are important tools that increase productivity and make the job easier. However, they can also cause severe injury or death if used improperly. Make sure you follow the manufacturer's operation procedures. Also, make sure you have your supervisor's/instructor's permission to use any particular type of lifting equipment.
- Comply with personal and environmental safety practices associated with clothing; eye protection; hand tools; power equipment; proper ventilation; and the handling, storage, and disposal of chemicals/materials in accordance with local, state, and federal safety and environmental regulations.

Performance Standard

0—No exposure: No information or practice provided during the program; complete training required

1—Exposure only: General information provided with no practice time; close supervision needed; additional training required

2—Limited practice: Has practiced job during training program; additional training required to develop skill

3—Moderately skilled: Has performed job independently during training program; limited additional training may be required

4—Skilled: Can perform job independently with no additional training

Research applicable vehicle and service information,
fluid type, vehicle service history, service
precautions, and technical service bulletins.

MLR 2A1   **AST** 2A2   **MAST** 2A2

Time off_____

Time on_____

Total time_____

CDX Tasksheet Number: C681

1. Using the vehicle VIN for identification, use the appropriate source to access the vehicle's service history in relation to prior related transmission/transaxle work or customer concerns.

   a. List any transmission-related repairs/concerns, and their dates:

2. **List the specified type of fluid for this vehicle:** _____

3. Using the vehicle VIN for identification, access any relevant technical service bulletins for the particular vehicle you are working on in relation to any transmission/transaxle updates, precautions, or other service issues. **List any related service bulletins and their titles:**

4. Have your supervisor/instructor verify satisfactory completion of this procedure, any observations found, and any necessary action(s) recommended.

Performance Rating

CDX Tasksheet Number: C681

0	1	2	3	4

Supervisor/instructor signature _____ Date _____

Identify and interpret transmission/transaxle concern; differentiate between engine performance and transmission/transaxle concerns; determine necessary action.

AST 2A1   **MAST** 2A1

Time off_____

Time on_____

Total time_____

CDX Tasksheet Number: C599

1. Ask your instructor to assign you a vehicle that has a potential transmission/engine performance concern. **List the customer concern(s):**

2. Research the particular concern in the appropriate service manual.

    a. **List the possible causes:**

3. Inspect the vehicle to determine the cause of the concern (differentiate between engine performance and transmission/transaxle concerns).

    a. **List the steps you took and their results to determine the fault(s):**

4. **List the cause of the concern(s):**

5. **List the necessary action(s) to correct the fault(s):**

6. Have your supervisor/instructor verify satisfactory completion of this procedure, any observations found, and any necessary action(s) recommended.

Performance Rating

CDX Tasksheet Number: C599

0	1	2	3	4

Supervisor/instructor signature _____ Date _____

Check fluid level in a transmission or a transaxle equipped with a dipstick.

MLR 2A2 | **AST** 2A4 | **MAST** 2A4

Time off_____

Time on_____

Total time_____

CDX Tasksheet Number: C902

1. Research the procedure to check the transmission fluid level in the appropriate service information. **List the specified steps:**

2. Following the specified steps, check the transmission fluid level. **List level:**

3. Have your supervisor/instructor verify satisfactory completion of this procedure, any observations found, and any necessary action(s) recommended.

Performance Rating

CDX Tasksheet Number: C902

0	1	2	3	4

Supervisor/instructor signature _____ Date _____

Check fluid level in a transmission or a transaxle not equipped with a dipstick.

MLR	AST	MAST
2A3	2A5	2A5

Time off_____

Time on_____

Total time_____

CDX Tasksheet Number: C903

Vehicle used for this activity:

Year_____ Make_____ Model_____

Odometer_____ VIN _____

1. Research the procedure to check the transmission fluid level in a vehicle that doesn't use a transmission dipstick in the appropriate service information. **List the specified steps:**

2. Following the specified steps, check the transmission fluid level. **List level:**

3. Have your supervisor/instructor verify satisfactory completion of this procedure, any observations found, and any necessary action(s) recommended.

Performance Rating

CDX Tasksheet Number: C903

0	1	2	3	4

Supervisor/instructor signature _____ Date _____

CDX Tasksheet Number: C904

Vehicle used for this activity:

Year_____ Make_____ Model_____

Odometer_____ VIN _____

1. Place a few drops of transmission fluid from the transmission on a clean white paper towel. The transmission fluid should have a clean appearance on the towel. If the center portion of the fluid is dirty, the fluid is dirty. **List your observation(s):**

2. Smell the transmission fluid. Compare the smell of the fluid to a fresh sample of the correct fluid. **List your observation(s):**

3. Safely raise and support the vehicle on a hoist. Inspect the transmission for any fluid leaks. **List the source of any leaks:**

4. Have your supervisor/instructor verify satisfactory completion of this procedure, any observations found, and any necessary action(s) recommended.

Performance Rating

CDX Tasksheet Number: C904

0	1	2	3	4

Supervisor/instructor signature _____ Date _____

AST 2A3   **MAST** 2A3

Time off_____

Time on_____

Total time_____

CDX Tasksheet Number: C682

1. **List the automatic transmission fluid loss or condition concern:**

2. Safely raise and support the vehicle on a hoist. Inspect the transmission for any fluid leaks. **List the source of any leaks:**

3. Place a few drops of transmission fluid from the transmission on a clean white paper towel. The transmission fluid should have a clean appearance on the towel. If the center portion of the fluid is dirty, then the fluid is dirty. **List your observation(s):**

4. Smell the transmission fluid. Compare it to a fresh sample of the correct transmission fluid. **List your observation(s):**

5. If the fluid is in poor condition, ask your instructor if you should change the fluid and filter. If so, inspect the bottom of the pan once it is removed. **List your observation(s):**

6. **Determine any necessary actions to correct the fault(s):**

7. Have your supervisor/instructor verify satisfactory completion of this procedure, any observations found, and any necessary action(s) recommended.

Performance Rating

CDX Tasksheet Number: C682

0	1	2	3	4

Supervisor/instructor signature _____ Date _____

▶ TASK Drain and replace fluid and filter(s).

MLR 2B4 **AST** 2B4 **MAST** 2B4

Time off_____

Time on_____

CDX Tasksheet Number: C907

Vehicle used for this activity:

Year _____ Make _____ Model_____

Odometer_____ VIN_____

Total time_____

1. Research the specifications and procedure in the appropriate service information.

   a. **Transmission service interval:** _____ mi/km
   b. **Transmission fluid type:** _____
   c. **Transmission fluid capacity:** _____ qt/lt
   d. **Pan bolts torque:** _____ in-lb/ft-lb/Nm
   e. **Filter screw torque, if needed:** _____ in-lb/ft-lb/Nm
   f. **List the steps required to properly check the fluid level:**

2. Following the specified procedure, remove the transmission pan and filter (filter may be an external filter). Inspect any residue and debris in the bottom of the pan or stuck to the filter. **List your observations:**

3. **Determine any necessary action(s):**

4. Have your supervisor/instructor verify removal of the pan and filter. **Supervisor's/instructor's initials:** _____

5. Clean the pan, magnet, and gasket surfaces.

6. Following the specified procedure, install the filter, pan, gasket, initial amount of fluid, and any other removed components.

> **NOTE** Make sure you fill the transmission with the proper amount of the specified fluid. Most service information lists two fluid capacities: one for a drain and refill, and the second for an overhaul. Make sure you use the proper specification.

© 2015 Jones & Bartlett Learning, LLC, an Ascend Learning Company

7. Follow the specified procedure to circulate the fluid and bleed any air from the system. This usually involves moving the gear selector through each position and then checking the fluid level. Add fluid to bring the fluid to the proper level (do NOT overfill).

8. Verify the correct operation of the transmission. This may require a test drive. **Get your supervisor's/instructor's permission before performing this step, and list your observation(s):**

9. Have your supervisor/instructor verify satisfactory completion of this procedure, any observations found, and any necessary action(s) recommended.

Performance Rating

CDX Tasksheet Number: C907

0	1	2	3	4

Supervisor/instructor signature _____ Date _____

▶ **TASK** Describe the operational characteristics of a
continuously variable transmission (CVT).

MLR 2C1 **AST** 2C4 **MAST** 2C4

Time off_____

Time on_____

Total time_____

CDX Tasksheet Number: C606

Vehicle used for this activity:

Year_____ Make_____ Model_____

Odometer_____ VIN _____

1. Research the description and operation of a continuously variable transmission in the
   appropriate service information.

   a. **What type of CVT is this transmission?**_____

   b. **How does this CVT achieve reduction?**

   c. **How does this CVT achieve direct drive?**

   d. **How does this CVT achieve neutral?**

   e. **How does this CVT achieve reverse?**

f. **What type of fluid does this CVT use?** _____

g. **What is the fluid capacity?** _____ qt/lt

h. **What is the service interval for the transmission fluid?** _____ mi/km

i. Look up if there is a fluid condition monitor for the transmission. **What is the procedure to reset the fluid monitor?**

2. Have your supervisor/instructor verify satisfactory completion of this procedure, any observations found, and any necessary action(s) recommended.

Performance Rating

CDX Tasksheet Number: C606

0	1	2	3	4

Supervisor/instructor signature _____ Date _____

Describe the operational characteristics of a hybrid vehicle drive train.

MLR 2C2 **AST** 2C5 **MAST** 2C5

Time off_____

Time on_____

CDX Tasksheet Number: C607

Total time_____

1. Research the description and operation of a hybrid vehicle drive train in the appropriate service information.

   a. **What type of hybrid is this vehicle?**

   Series: _____ **Parallel:** _____ **Series-Parallel:** _____

   b. **Can this vehicle operate only on the internal combustion engine?**
   Yes: _____ **No:** _____

   c. **Describe the conditions when the internal combustion engine runs:**

   d. **Can this vehicle operate only on the electric motor?**
   Yes: _____ **No:** _____

   e. **Describe the conditions when the electric motor operates:**

   f. **Does this vehicle use regeneration?**
   Yes: _____ **No:** _____

   g. **Describe how regeneration operates in this vehicle:**

2. Have your supervisor/instructor verify satisfactory completion of this procedure, any observations found, and any necessary action(s) recommended.

Performance Rating

CDX Tasksheet Number: C607

0	1	2	3	4

Supervisor/instructor signature _____ Date _____

▶ **TASK** Demonstrate use of 3 Cs (concern, cause, and correction).

Additional Task

CDX Tasksheet Number: NN02

1. Using the following scenario, write up the 3 Cs as listed on most repair orders. Assume that the customer authorized the recommended repairs.

   A compact vehicle is brought to your shop with an automatic transaxle concern. The customer tells you that the transmission started slipping a couple of days ago, and it is getting worse. You road test the vehicle and notice that it is slipping in all gears when under moderate load. You pull the vehicle onto a rack and find the following:

   a. The vehicle has 122,000 miles on it, but is in good condition otherwise.
   b. The transmission fluid is dark and smells burnt. The fluid is about two pints too low, but topping it off does not stop the vehicle from slipping when it is stall-tested.
   c. The transmission-pan gasket and both axle seals are seeping heavily.
   d. With the pan removed, there is a lot of band and clutch material in the bottom, but very few metal filings.
   e. The transmission mount is torn.
   f. Both outer CV joint boots are badly cracked and just starting to leak grease, but the joints are still good.

   > **NOTE** Ask your instructor whether you should use a copy of the shop repair order or the 3 Cs here to record this information.

2. **Concern:**

3. **Cause:**

4. **Correction:**

5. Other recommended service:

6. Have your supervisor/instructor verify satisfactory completion of this task, and any necessary action(s) recommended.

Performance Rating

CDX Tasksheet Number: NN02

0	1	2	3	4
☐	☐	☐	☐	☐

Supervisor/instructor signature _____ Date _____

Automatic Transmission and Transaxle: Inspection and Testing

Student/intern information:

Name _____ Date _____ Class _____

Vehicle used for this activity:

Year _____ Make _____ Model _____

Odometer _____ VIN _____

Learning Objective/Task	CDX Tasksheet Number	2013 MLR NATEF Reference Number; Priority Level	2013 AST NATEF Reference Number; Priority Level	2013 MAST NATEF Reference Number; Priority Level
• Perform pressure tests (including transmissions/transaxles equipped with electronic pressure control); determine necessary action.	C740			2A6; P-1
• Perform stall test; determine necessary action.	C741		2A6; P-3	2A8; P-3
• Perform lock-up converter system tests; determine necessary action.	C063		2A7; P-3	2A9; P-3

Time off_____

Time on_____

Total time_____

Materials Required

- Vehicle with automatic transmission/transaxle and lock-up converter
- Vehicle hoist
- Flashlight or shop light
- Optional: fluorescent dye and ultraviolet light
- Transmission pressure gauge set
- Tachometer
- Scan tool
- DVOM/DMM

Some Safety Issues to Consider

- Vehicle hoists are important tools that increase productivity and make the job easier. However, they can also cause severe injury or death if used improperly. Make sure you follow the manufacturer's operation procedures. Also, make sure you have your supervisor's/instructor's permission to use a hoist.
- This procedure may require cleaning the transmission or axle assembly prior to inspection. If so, use the proper equipment and procedures to carry this out safely. Also, get your supervisor's/instructor's permission prior to cleaning.
- **Caution:** Stall testing for more than a few seconds can damage the transmission or other parts of the vehicle. It is also a hazardous task. Perform this task with the utmost care! Note that some manufacturers don't allow a stall test to be performed on their vehicles.

- When running any vehicles in the shop, make sure you use the shop's exhaust ventilation system to discharge all exhaust gas safely outside.
- Diagnosis of this fault may require test-driving the vehicle on the school grounds. Attempt this task only with full permission from your instructor and follow all the guidelines exactly.
- Comply with personal and environmental safety practices associated with clothing; eye protection; hand tools; power equipment; proper ventilation; and the handling, storage, and disposal of chemicals/materials in accordance with local, state, and federal safety and environmental regulations.

Performance Standard

0–No exposure: No information or practice provided during the program; complete training required

1–Exposure only: General information provided with no practice time; close supervision needed; additional training required

2–Limited practice: Has practiced job during training program; additional training required to develop skill

3–Moderately skilled: Has performed job independently during training program; limited additional training may be required

4–Skilled: Can perform job independently with no additional training

Perform pressure tests (including transmissions/transaxles equipped with electronic pressure control); determine necessary action.

MAST
2A6

Time off_____

Time on_____

Total time_____

CDX Tasksheet Number: C740

1. Research all applicable pressure specifications and test procedure(s) for this transmission in the appropriate service information.

   a. **Line pressure:** _____ psi/kPa
   b. **Governor pressure:** _____ psi/kPa
   c. **Throttle pressure:** _____ psi/kPa
   d. **Low-gear servo/clutch pressure:** _____ psi/kPa
   e. **Second-gear servo/clutch pressure:** _____ psi/kPa
   f. **Direct-clutch pressure:** _____ psi/kPa
   g. **Cooler-circuit pressure:** _____ psi/kPa
   h. **List any other pressure specifications off to the right side of the above specifications.**

2. Perform the applicable transmission-pressure tests. Be sure to follow the specified procedures. Note that a scan tool may need to be used on electronically controlled transmissions. List your observations below.

   a. **Line pressure:** _____ psi/kPa
   b. **Governor pressure:** _____ psi/kPa
   c. **Throttle pressure:** _____ psi/kPa
   d. **Low-gear servo/clutch pressure:** _____ psi/kPa
   e. **Second-gear servo/clutch pressure:** _____ psi/kPa
   f. **Direct-clutch pressure:** _____ psi/kPa
   g. **Cooler-circuit pressure:** _____ psi/kPa
   h. **List any other pressures off to the right side of the above readings.**

3. **Determine any necessary action(s):**

4. Have your supervisor/instructor verify satisfactory completion of this procedure, any observations found, and any necessary action(s) recommended.

Performance Rating

CDX Tasksheet Number: C740

0	1	2	3	4

Supervisor/instructor signature _____ Date _____

AST 2A6 **MAST** 2A8

Time off_____

Time on_____

CDX Tasksheet Number: C741

Total time_____

1. Research the specifications and procedures to stall test this transmission.

> **NOTE** Do not perform this test on a transmission if the line pressure is not up to specifications or further damage to the transmission could quickly result. Also, some manufacturers do not want their transmissions stall tested. And on vehicles with electronic throttle control, the PCM may not allow a stall test to be performed without a scan tool.

    a. **Does the manufacturer recommend a stall test? Yes: _____ No: _____**

    b. **Specified stall speed(s) _____**

    c. **List all precautions when performing the stall test:**

2. Perform the stall test. Be sure to follow all safety precautions. **List your observation(s):**

3. **Determine any necessary action(s):**

4. Have your supervisor/instructor verify satisfactory completion of this procedure, any observations found, and any necessary action(s) recommended.

Performance Rating

CDX Tasksheet Number: C741

0	1	2	3	4

Supervisor/instructor signature _____ Date _____

▶ **TASK** Perform lock-up converter system tests; determine necessary action.

AST 2A7 | MAST 2A9

Time off_____

Time on_____

Total time_____

CDX Tasksheet Number: C063

1. Research the specifications and procedure for testing the lock-up converter.

   a. **Lock-up converter solenoid resistance:** _____ **ohms**

   b. **List or print off and attach to this sheet the procedure for testing the lock-up converter:**

   c. **Ask your instructor where you are to perform the lock-up converter test: Road test:** _____ **Vehicle hoist:** _____

2. Have your supervisor/instructor approve your answers. **Supervisor's/instructor's initials:** _____

3. Perform the lock-up converter performance test.

   a. Prepare the vehicle for this test by following the specified procedure.

   b. Test the operation of the lock-up converter system following your instructor's directions. **List your observation(s):**

4. Perform the lock-up converter pinpoint test.

   a. Test for the proper electrical signal at the lock-up converter solenoid connector following the specified procedure. **List your observation(s):**

   b. **Measure the electrical continuity/resistance of the solenoid:** _____ **ohms**

5. **Determine any necessary action(s):**

6. Have your supervisor/instructor verify satisfactory completion of this procedure, any observations found, and any necessary action(s) recommended.

Performance Rating

CDX Tasksheet Number: C063

0	1	2	3	4

Supervisor/instructor signature _____ Date _____

Automatic Transmission and Transaxle: Diagnosis

© 2015 Jones & Bartlett Learning, LLC, an Ascend Learning Company

Student/intern information:

Name _____ Date _____ Class _____

Vehicle used for this activity:

Year _____ Make _____ Model_____

Odometer_____VIN_____

Time off_____

Time on_____

Total time_____

Learning Objective/Task	CDX Tasksheet Number	2013 MLR NATEF Reference Number; Priority Level	2013 AST NATEF Reference Number; Priority Level	2013 MAST NATEF Reference Number; Priority Level
• Diagnose electronic transmission/ transaxle control systems using appropriate test equipment and service information.	C600			2A11; P-1
• Inspect, test, adjust, repair, or replace electrical/electronic components and circuits including computers, solenoids, sensors, relays, terminals, connectors, switches, and harnesses.	C601		2B3; P-1	2B3; P-1
• Diagnose transmission/transaxle gear reduction/multiplication concerns using driving, driven, and held-member (power flow) principles.	C066		2A8; P-1	2A10; P-1
• Diagnose pressure concerns in a transmission using hydraulic principles (Pascal's Law).	C747		2A9; P-2	2A12; P-2
• Diagnose noise and vibration concerns; determine necessary action.	C743			2A7; P-2

Materials Required

- Vehicle with automatic transmission/transaxle
- Vehicle hoist
- Transmission pressure gauge set
- Tachometer
- Scan tool
- DVOM/DMM

Some Safety Issues to Consider

- Vehicle hoists are important tools that increase productivity and make the job easier. However, they can also cause severe injury or death if used improperly. Make sure you follow the manufacturer's operation procedures. Also, make sure you have your supervisor's/instructor's permission to use a hoist.

- When running any vehicles in the shop, make sure you use the shop's exhaust ventilation system to discharge all exhaust gas safely outside.
- Diagnosis of this fault may require test-driving the vehicle on the school grounds. Attempt this task only with full permission from your instructor and follow all the guidelines exactly.
- Always wear the correct protective eyewear and clothing, and use the appropriate safety equipment, as well as fender covers, seat protectors, and floor mat protectors.
- Comply with personal and environmental safety practices associated with clothing; eye protection; hand tools; power equipment; proper ventilation; and the handling, storage, and disposal of chemicals/materials in accordance with local, state, and federal safety and environmental regulations.

Performance Standard

0–No exposure: No information or practice provided during the program; complete training required

1–Exposure only: General information provided with no practice time; close supervision needed; additional training required

2–Limited practice: Has practiced job during training program; additional training required to develop skill

3–Moderately skilled: Has performed job independently during training program; limited additional training may be required

4–Skilled: Can perform job independently with no additional training

MAST
2A11

Time off_____

Time on_____

Total time_____

CDX Tasksheet Number: C600

1. **List the customer concern related to an electronic control system issue:**

2. Connect an appropriate scan tool to the data link connector (DLC). **Retrieve and list any transmission-related codes:**

3. Research the specifications and procedures for diagnosing the code(s).
   a. **List the possible cause(s) of the code(s):**

   b. **List or print off and attach to this sheet the procedure for diagnosing the code(s):**

4. Perform the diagnostic tests following the specified procedure using the appropriate test equipment.
   a. **List your tests and test results:**

b. List the test equipment you used to diagnose this concern:

5. Determine any necessary action(s) to correct the fault:

6. Have your supervisor/instructor verify satisfactory completion of this procedure, any observations found, and any necessary action(s) recommended.

Performance Rating

CDX Tasksheet Number: C600

0	1	2	3	4

Supervisor/instructor signature _____ Date _____

Inspect, test, adjust, repair, or replace electrical/electronic components and circuits, including computers, solenoids, sensors, relays, terminals, connectors, switches, and harnesses.

Time off_____

Time on_____

Total time_____

AST	MAST
2B3	2B3

CDX Tasksheet Number: C601

1. Research the specifications and procedures for inspecting, testing, adjusting, and replacing the electrical/electronic components and sensors.

   a. List or print off and attach to this sheet the procedure for inspecting, testing, adjusting, and replacing these components:

   b. List any specified precautions:

2. **Inspect the following components for proper operation and list your observations.**

   a. **Computer:**

   b. **Solenoids/relays:**

   c. **Sensors/switches:**

   d. **Terminals/connectors/harnesses:**

3. Ask your instructor which components you should replace.

   a. **Computer: Yes: _____ No: _____**
   b. **Solenoids/relays: Yes: _____ No: _____**
   c. **Sensors/switches: Yes: _____ No: _____**
   d. **Terminals/connectors/harnesses: Yes: _____ No: _____**

4. Remove the appropriate component(s) following the specified procedure. **List your observation(s):**

5. Have your supervisor/instructor verify removal and your observations. **Supervisor's/instructor's initials:** _____

6. Replace each component following the specified procedure.

7. Adjust each component following the specified procedure.

8. Have your supervisor/instructor verify satisfactory completion of this procedure, any observations found, and any necessary action(s) recommended.

Performance Rating

CDX Tasksheet Number: C601

0	1	2	3	4

Supervisor/instructor signature _____ Date _____

Diagnose transmission/transaxle gear reduction/multiplication concerns using driving, driven, and held-member (power flow) principles.

AST 2A8 | **MAST** 2A10

Time off_____

Time on_____

Total time_____

CDX Tasksheet Number: C066

Vehicle used for this activity:

Year _____ Make _____ Model_____

Odometer_____ VIN_____

1. **List the customer concern:**

2. Research the particular transmission/transaxle concern in the appropriate service information, including power flow charts and driving, driven, and held-member charts.

   a. **List the possible cause(s) of the concern:**

   b. **List or print off and attach to this sheet the procedure for diagnosing the concern:**

3. Perform the diagnostic tests following the specified procedure.

   a. **List your tests and test results:**

b. Describe how you used the diagnostic charts to diagnose the concern:

4. **Determine any necessary action(s) to correct the fault:**

5. Have your supervisor/instructor verify satisfactory completion of this procedure, any observations found, and any necessary action(s) recommended.

Performance Rating

CDX Tasksheet Number: CO66

0	1	2	3	4

Supervisor/instructor signature _____ Date _____

Time off_____

Time on_____

Total time_____

CDX Tasksheet Number: C747

Vehicle used for this activity:

Year _____ Make _____ Model _____

Odometer _____ VIN _____

1. **List the transmission/transaxle pressure-related concern:**

2. Research the concern in the appropriate service information.

   a. **List the possible cause(s) of the concern:**

   b. **List (or print off and attach) any specified transmission pressures:**

3. **Write out Pascal's Law in your own words:**

4. **Describe how you will use Pascal's Law to help you diagnose this concern:**

5. Perform the appropriate pressure tests and list your observation(s):

6. Determine any necessary action(s) to correct the fault:

7. Have your supervisor/instructor verify satisfactory completion of this procedure, any observations found, and any necessary action(s) recommended.

Performance Rating

CDX Tasksheet Number: C747

0	1	2	3	4

Supervisor/instructor signature _____ Date _____

► **TASK** Diagnose noise and vibration concerns; determine necessary action.

CDX Tasksheet Number: C743

Vehicle Used for this activity:

Year _____ Make _____ Model_____

Odometer_____ VIN_____

1. **List the transmission-noise and vibration-related concern:**

2. Research the concern in the appropriate service information.
   a. **List the possible cause(s) of the concern:**

   b. **List or print off and attach to this sheet the specified procedure for diagnosing the concern:**

3. **Perform the appropriate tests, following the specified procedure. List your observation(s):**

4. **List the cause(s) of the concern:**

5. Determine any necessary action(s) to correct the fault:

6. Have your supervisor/instructor verify satisfactory completion of this procedure, any observations found, and any necessary action(s) recommended.

Performance Rating

CDX Tasksheet Number: C743

0	1	2	3	4

Supervisor/instructor signature _____ Date _____

Automatic Transmission and Transaxle: Maintenance and Repair

Student/intern information:

Name_____ Date_____ Class_____

Vehicle used for this activity:

Year _____ Make _____ Model_____

Odometer_____VIN_____

Learning Objective/Task	CDX Tasksheet Number	2013 MLR NATEF Reference Number; Priority Level	2013 AST NATEF Reference Number; Priority Level	2013 MAST NATEF Reference Number; Priority Level
• Inspect, adjust, and replace external manual-valve shift linkage, transmission-range sensor/switch, and park/neutral position switch.	C683	2B1; P-2	2B1; P-2	2B1; P-2
• Inspect for leakage at external seals, gaskets, and bushings.	C905	2B2; P-2		
• Inspect for leakage; replace external seals, gaskets, and bushings.	C748		2B2; P-2	2B2; P-2
• Inspect, replace, and align powertrain mounts.	C602	2B3; P-2	2B5; P-2	2B5; P-2

Time off_____

Time on_____

Total time_____

Materials Required

- Vehicle with automatic transmission/transaxle
- Vehicle hoist
- Scan tool
- DVOM/DMM
- Floor jack
- Drain pan
- Torque wrench
- Specified filter and fluid
- DVOM

Some Safety Issues to Consider

- Vehicle hoists are important tools that increase productivity and make the job easier. However, they can also cause severe injury or death if used improperly. Make sure you follow the manufacturer's operation procedures. Also, make sure you have your supervisor's/instructor's permission to use a hoist.
- When running any vehicles in the shop, make sure you use the shop's exhaust ventilation system to discharge all exhaust gas safely outside.
- Diagnosis of this fault may require test-driving the vehicle on the school grounds. Attempt this task only with full permission from your instructor and follow all the guidelines exactly.

- This procedure may require cleaning the transmission or axle assembly prior to inspection. If so, use the proper equipment and procedures to carry this out safely. Also, get your supervisor's/instructor's permission prior to cleaning.
- Comply with personal and environmental safety practices associated with clothing; eye protection; hand tools; power equipment; proper ventilation; and the handling, storage, and disposal of chemicals/materials in accordance with local, state, and federal safety and environmental regulations.

Performance Standard

0—No exposure: No information or practice provided during the program; complete training required

1—Exposure only: General information provided with no practice time; close supervision needed; additional training required

2—Limited practice: Has practiced job during training program; additional training required to develop skill

3—Moderately skilled: Has performed job independently during training program; limited additional training may be required

4—Skilled: Can perform job independently with no additional training

MLR 2B1 | **AST** 2B1 | **MAST** 2B1

Time off_____

Time on_____

Total time_____

CDX Tasksheet Number: C683

1. Research the specifications and procedures for inspecting, adjusting, and replacing the manual valve shift linkage, transmission range sensor/switch, and park/neutral position switch in the appropriate service information.

   a. **List or print off and attach to this sheet the procedure for inspecting, adjusting, and replacing these components:**

   b. **List any specified precautions:**

2. Inspect the following components for proper operation. **List your observations.**

   a. **Manual-valve shift linkage:**

   b. **Transmission-range sensor/switch:**

   c. **Park/neutral position switch:**

3. **Ask your instructor which components you should replace.**
   a. Manual valve shift linkage: Yes: _____ No: _____
   b. Transmission-range sensor/switch: Yes: _____ No: _____
   c. Park/neutral position switch: Yes: _____ No: _____

4. Remove the appropriate component(s) following the specified procedure. **List your observation(s):**

5. Have your supervisor/instructor verify removal. **Supervisor's/instructor's initials:**
_____

6. Replace each component following the specified procedure.

7. Adjust each component following the specified procedure.

8. Have your supervisor/instructor verify satisfactory completion of this procedure, any observations found, and any necessary action(s) recommended.

Performance Rating

CDX Tasksheet Number: C683

☐	☐	☐	☐	☐
0	1	2	3	4

Supervisor/instructor signature _____ Date _____

CDX Tasksheet Number: C905

Vehicle used for this activity:

Year _____ Make _____ Model_____

Odometer_____ VIN_____

Time off_____

Time on_____

Total time_____

1. Safely raise and support the vehicle on a hoist.

2. Inspect the transmission/transaxle seals and gaskets for leaks.

   a. List each external seal, gasket, and bushing; and identify the source of any leak(s):

3. Have your supervisor/instructor verify satisfactory completion of this procedure, any observations found, and any necessary action(s) recommended.

Performance Rating

CDX Tasksheet Number: C905

0	1	2	3	4

Supervisor/instructor signature _____ Date _____

AST
2B2

MAST
2B2

Time off_____

Time on_____

Total time_____

CDX Tasksheet Number: C748

Vehicle used for this activity:

Year _____ Make _____ Model_____

Odometer_____ VIN_____

1. Safely raise and support the vehicle on a hoist.

2. Inspect the transmission/transaxle seals and gaskets for leaks.

   a. **List each external seal, gasket, and bushing; and identify the source of any leak(s):**

3. With your instructor's permission, replace any leaking seals or gaskets. **List the parts replaced and your observations:**

4. Have your supervisor/instructor verify satisfactory completion of this procedure, any observations found, and any necessary action(s) recommended.

Performance Rating

CDX Tasksheet Number: C748

0	1	2	3	4

Supervisor/instructor signature _____ Date _____

Inspect, replace, and align powertrain mounts.

MLR 2B3   **AST** 2B5   **MAST** 2B5

Time off_____

Time on_____

Total time_____

CDX Tasksheet Number: C602

Vehicle used for this activity:

Year_____ Make _____ Model_____

Odometer_____ VIN _____

1. Research the procedure to inspect, replace, and align the powertrain mounts in the appropriate service information.

   a. **List the type of mount(s) this vehicle uses:** _____

   b. **List or print off and attach to this sheet the procedure for inspecting the mount(s):**

   c. **List or print off and attach to this sheet the precautions for performing this task:**

2. **Following the specified procedure, inspect each of the powertrain mounts, and list your observations:**

3. **Determine any necessary action(s):**

4. Have your supervisor/instructor verify your answers. **Supervisor/instructor initials:** _____

5. **With your supervisor/instructor's permission, remove one or more powertrain mounts following the specified procedure. Inspect the removed mount(s) and list your observations:**

6. Have your supervisor/instructor verify the removal of the mount. **Supervisor/instructor initials:** _____

7. Reinstall and align the powertrain mount(s) according to the specified procedure.

8. **Determine any necessary action(s):**

9. Have your supervisor/instructor verify satisfactory completion of this procedure, any observations found, and any necessary action(s) recommended.

Performance Rating

CDX Tasksheet Number: C602

0	1	2	3	4

Supervisor/instructor signature _____ Date _____

Automatic Transmission and Transaxle: Transmission Removal and Replacement

Student/intern information:

Name_____ Date_____ Class_____

Vehicle used for this activity:

Year _____ Make _____ Model_____

Odometer_____VIN_____

Learning Objective/Task	CDX Tasksheet Number	2013 MLR NATEF Reference Number; Priority Level	2013 AST NATEF Reference Number; Priority Level	2013 MAST NATEF Reference Number; Priority Level
• Remove and reinstall transmission/transaxle and torque converter; inspect engine core plugs, rear crankshaft seal, dowel pins, dowel pinholes, and mating surfaces.	C604		2C1; P-1	2C1; P-1
• Inspect converter flex (drive) plate, converter-attaching bolts, converter pilot, converter pump-drive surfaces, converter endplay, and crankshaft pilot bore.	C605		2C2; P-1	2C2; P-1
• Inspect, leak test, and flush or replace transmission/transaxle oil cooler, lines, and fittings.	C749		2C3; P-2	2C3; P-2
• Measure transmission/transaxle end play or preload; determine necessary action.	C689			2C11; P-1

Time off_____

Time on_____

Total time_____

Materials Required

- Vehicle with automatic transmission/transaxle
- Vehicle hoist
- Transmission jack
- Dial indicator
- Drain pan
- Cooler flushing equipment
- Torque wrench
- Manufacturer or job specific special tools.

Some Safety Issues to Consider

- Vehicle hoists are important tools that increase productivity and make the job easier. However, they can also cause severe injury or death if used improperly. Make sure you follow the manufacturer's operation procedures. Also, make sure you have your supervisor's/instructor's permission to use a hoist.
- When running any vehicles in the shop, make sure you use the shop's exhaust ventilation system to discharge all exhaust gas safely outside.
- Diagnosis of this fault may require test-driving the vehicle on the school grounds. Attempt this task only with full permission from your instructor and follow all the guidelines exactly.

- This procedure may require cleaning the transmission or axle assembly prior to inspection. If so, use the proper equipment and procedures to carry this out safely. Also, get your supervisor's/instructor's permission prior to cleaning.
- Automotive transmissions/transaxles are heavy. Make sure they are secured to the transmission jack during removal and installation.
- Comply with personal and environmental safety practices associated with clothing; eye protection; hand tools; power equipment; proper ventilation; and the handling, storage, and disposal of chemicals/materials in accordance with local, state, and federal safety and environmental regulations.

Performance Standard

0—No exposure: No information or practice provided during the program; complete training required

1—Exposure only: General information provided with no practice time; close supervision needed; additional training required

2—Limited practice: Has practiced job during training program; additional training required to develop skill

3—Moderately skilled: Has performed job independently during training program; limited additional training may be required

4—Skilled: Can perform job independently with no additional training

Remove and reinstall transmission/transaxle and torque converter; inspect engine core plugs, rear crankshaft seal, dowel pins, dowel pinholes, and mating surfaces.

AST 2C1 **MAST** 2C1

CDX Tasksheet Number: C604

1. Research the following torque specifications and transmission/transaxle removal and installation procedure in the appropriate service information.

   a. **Flex plate-to-crankshaft bolt torque:** _____ **ft-lb/Nm**
   b. **Torque converter-to-flex plate bolt torque:** _____ **ft-lb/Nm**
   c. **Transmission-to-block bolt torque:** _____ **ft-lb/Nm**
   d. **Transmission fluid type:** _____
   e. **Transmission fluid capacity:** _____ **qt/lt**
   f. **List or print off and attach to this sheet the procedure for removing and installing the transmission/transaxle:**

2. Following the specified procedure, remove the transmission/transaxle from the vehicle.

3. **Inspect the following components and list your observations.**
   a. **Engine core plugs:**

   b. **Rear crankshaft seal:**

   c. **Dowel pins and holes:**

   d. **Engine and bell-housing mating surfaces:**

4. Have your supervisor/instructor verify your observations. **Supervisor's/instructor's initials:**_____

> **NOTE** At this time, you may want to overhaul the transmission/transaxle or perform other tasks such as inspecting/replacing the torque converter or flushing the transmission/transaxle cooler lines. Once any related tasks are completed and it is time to reinstall the transmission/transaxle, return to this page to complete the task and have it signed off.

5. Prepare the transmission to be reinstalled. Ensure that the torque converter is fully engaged in the transmission. Failure to do so may cause severe damage to the transmission/transaxle and the converter.

6. Have your instructor check that the convertor is installed properly. **Supervisor's/instructor's initials:** _____

7. Position all wires, hoses, and tubes out of the way and in their specified positions. Secure them temporarily if necessary.

> **NOTE** It is easy for wires and hoses to fall down and get pinched between the engine and bell housing. This will cause electrical issues in the vehicle as well as alignment issues with the transmission.

8. Following the specified procedure, reinstall the transmission/transaxle. Be sure to tighten all fasteners to the proper torque.

9. Refill the transmission/transaxle to the proper level.

10. Check that all cooler lines, electrical wires, linkages, and other removed components are properly installed and adjusted.

11. Have your instructor verify that the vehicle is ready to be started. **Supervisor's/instructor's initials:** _____

12. Place exhaust hose(s) over the exhaust pipe(s) and set the parking brake.

13. Start the vehicle and move the transmission selector through each gear. Check the transmission fluid level and top off as necessary.

14. **Check for leaks, loose parts, or anything that isn't right with the transmission and the related parts. List your observation(s):**

15. **With your supervisor's/instructor's permission, test drive the vehicle to ensure the transmission operates correctly. List your observations:**

16. Double check your work and verify that there are no leaks and that everything is back in its proper place. List your observations:

17. Have your supervisor/instructor verify satisfactory completion of this procedure, any observations found, and any necessary action(s) recommended.

Performance Rating

0	1	2	3	4

Supervisor/instructor signature _____ Date _____

▶ **TASK** Inspect converter flex (drive) plate, converter-attaching bolts, converter pilot, converter pump-drive surfaces, converter endplay, and crankshaft pilot bore.

AST 2C2   **MAST** 2C2

CDX Tasksheet Number: C605

1. Research the procedure and specifications for inspecting the torque converter, flex plate, and crankshaft pilot bore.

   a. **Torque converter-to-flex plate bolt torque:** _____ **ft-lb/Nm**

   b. **Flex plate-to-crankshaft bolt torque:** _____ **ft-lb/Nm**

   c. **Converter endplay:** _____ **in/mm**

   d. **Converter pilot diameter, if specified:** _____ **in/mm**

   e. **Crankshaft pilot bore, if specified:** _____ **in/mm**

2. Following the specified procedure, inspect each of the listed items below.
   List your observations.

   a. **Flex plate (cracks, warpage, elongated holes, starter ring-gear wear, etc.):**

   b. **Converter-attaching bolts (worn, stretched, rounded heads, etc.):**

   c. **Converter pilot (gouges, excessive rust, etc.):**

   d. **Crankshaft pilot bore (gouges, excessive rust, etc.):**

   e. **Converter pump-drive surface (wear, nicks, burrs, etc.):**

   f. **Converter endplay:** _____ **in/mm**

3. **Determine any necessary action(s):**

4. Have your supervisor/instructor verify satisfactory completion of this procedure, any observations found, and any necessary action(s) recommended.

Performance Rating

CDX Tasksheet Number: C605

0	1	2	3	4

Supervisor/instructor signature _____ Date _____

Inspect, leak test, and flush or replace transmission/
transaxle oil cooler, lines, and fittings.

AST
2C3

MAST
2C3

Time off_____

Time on_____

Total time_____

CDX Tasksheet Number: C749

1. Research the procedure to inspect, test, flush, and replace the cooler lines and fittings.

   a. **List or print off and attach to this sheet the steps to test, flush, and replace the cooler lines:**

2. Following the specified procedure, perform the following tasks. **List your observations**.

   a. **Inspect the cooler, lines, and fittings for damage or wear:**

   b. **Test the cooler, lines, and fittings for leaks:**

   c. **Flush or replace the cooler and lines:**

3. Have your supervisor/instructor verify satisfactory completion of this procedure, any observations found, and any necessary action(s) recommended.

Performance Rating

CDX Tasksheet Number: C749

0	1	2	3	4

Supervisor/instructor signature _____ Date _____

MAST
2C11

Time off_____

Time on_____

Total time_____

CDX Tasksheet Number: C689

1. Research the procedure and specifications to measure the end play or preload.

    a. **Specified end play or preload:** _____

    b. **List, or print off and attach to this sheet, the steps to perform the end play or preload measurement:**

    c. **How is the end play or preload adjusted on this transmission/transaxle?**

2. **Following the specified procedure, measure the end play or preload:** _____

3. **Determine any necessary action/s:**

4. Have your supervisor/instructor verify satisfactory completion of this procedure, any observations found, and any necessary action/s recommended.

Performance Rating

CDX Tasksheet Number: C689

0	1	2	3	4

Supervisor/instructor signature _____ Date _____

Automatic Transmission and Transaxle: Transmission Disassembly and Inspection

Student/intern information:

Name _____ Date _____ Class _____

Vehicle used for this activity:

Year _____ Make _____ Model _____

Odometer _____ VIN _____

Learning Objective/Task	CDX Tasksheet Number	2013 MLR NATEF Reference Number; Priority Level	2013 AST NATEF Reference Number; Priority Level	2013 MAST NATEF Reference Number; Priority Level
• Disassemble, clean, and inspect transmission/transaxle.	C684			2C6; P-2
• Inspect, measure, and reseal oil pump assembly and components.	C688			2C10; P-2
• Inspect and measure planetary gear assembly components; determine necessary action.	C752			2C15; P-2
• Inspect bushings; determine necessary action.	C751			2C14; P-2
• Inspect, measure, and replace thrust washers and bearings.	C750			2C12; P-2
• Inspect roller and sprag clutch, races, rollers, sprags, springs, cages, and retainers; determine necessary action.	C759			2C22; P-2
• Inspect oil delivery circuits, including seal rings, ring grooves, and sealing surface areas, feed pipes, orifices, and check valves/balls.	C690			2C13; P-2
• Inspect case bores, passages, bushings, vents, and mating surfaces; determine necessary action.	C753			2C16; P-2
• Inspect servo and accumulator bores, pistons, seals, pins, springs, and retainers; determine necessary action.	C686			2C8; P-2
• Inspect clutch drum, piston, check balls, springs, retainers, seals, and friction and pressure plates, bands, and drums; determine necessary action.	C756			2C19; P-2
• Measure clutch pack clearance; determine necessary action.	C757			2C20; P-1
• Air test operation of clutch and servo assemblies.	C758			2C21; P-1
• Inspect, measure, clean, and replace valve body (includes surfaces, bores, springs, valves, sleeves, retainers, brackets, check valves/balls, screens, spacers, and gaskets).	C685			2C7; P-2

Time off _____

Time on _____

Total time _____

• Diagnose and inspect transaxle drive, link chains, sprockets, gears, bearings, and bushings; perform necessary action.	C754			2C17; P-2
• Inspect, measure, repair, adjust, or replace transaxle final drive components.	C755			2C18; P-2

Materials Required

- Transmission/transaxle
- Snap ring pliers
- Dial indicator
- Feeler blades
- Straightedge
- Approved air nozzle
- Manufacturer-specific tools

Some Safety Issues to Consider

- Castings and machined parts may have sharp edges. Handle these parts with care.
- Many transmission parts are round and can easily roll off of tables and carts. Be sure to place them in a secure manner to prevent component damage or personal injury from falling objects.
- Compressed air can be very dangerous if applied to broken skin or body cavities. Always use approved air nozzles, and never point them at yourself or another person.
- Transmissions, transaxles, and their component assemblies are heavy and can slip easily. Work safely, get help, and do not overextend your abilities.
- Comply with personal and environmental safety practices associated with clothing; eye protection; hand tools; power equipment; proper ventilation; and the handling, storage, and disposal of chemicals/materials in accordance with local, state, and federal safety and environmental regulations.

Performance Standard

0—No exposure: No information or practice provided during the program; complete training required

1—Exposure only: General information provided with no practice time; close supervision needed; additional training required

2—Limited practice: Has practiced job during training program; additional training required to develop skill

3—Moderately skilled: Has performed job independently during training program; limited additional training may be required

4—Skilled: Can perform job independently with no additional training

MAST
2C6

Time off_____

Time on_____

Total time_____

CDX Tasksheet Number: C684

1. Research the disassembly and inspection procedures in the appropriate service information.

    a. **List any precautions for performing this task:**

    b. **List any special tools required to perform this task:**

2. Following the specified procedure, disassemble the transmission/transaxle into its unit components, ensuring that you note their location and orientation. Make notes or take pictures as appropriate. Also, lay them out in a logical manner to facilitate reassembly.

    NOTE Round objects such as clutch drums, ball bearings, roller bearings, and bushings can roll off of the work table if not secured, causing personal injury. This could also lead to damage or loss of the components. Always lay round objects on their side when possible, or store them in a work tray to prevent rolling.

3. Clean the components according to the specified procedure. Make sure you relocate them in the same logical sequence as before

4. Perform a preliminary visual inspection of the components. This is an initial inspection designed to identify major issues with the transmis-sion/transaxle. Further inspection of the subunits will occur later. **List your observations for each main assembly:**

5. Have your supervisor/instructor verify satisfactory completion of this procedure, any observations found, and any necessary action(s) recom-mended.

Performance Rating

CDX Tasksheet Number: C684

0	1	2	3	4
☐	☐	☐	☐	☐

Supervisor/instructor signature _____ Date _____

Time off_____

Time on_____

CDX Tasksheet Number: C688

Total time_____

1. Research the procedure for disassembling and inspecting the oil pump in the appropriate service information.

   a. **Type of pump (gerotor, crescent, vane, etc.):** _____

   b. **List, or print off and attach to this sheet, the clearance specifications for this pump:**

   c. **Pump housing bolt torque:** _____ **ft-lb/Nm**
   d. **Pump-to-case bolt torque:** _____ **ft-lb/Nm**

2. Following the specified procedure, disassemble the oil pump. Be sure not to damage any of the surfaces or parts.

   > **NOTE** You may need to scribe a mark on the pump halves so that you can reassemble the pump in the proper orientation. Refer to the service information to see if this is the case. Also be careful not to damage any of the wear surfaces with a scribe. Use a nondamaging method of marking the components.

3. Measure the specified clearances. **List your readings:**

4. **Determine any necessary action(s):**

5. Have your supervisor/instructor verify disassembly.
   Supervisor/instructor's initials: _____

6. Following the specified procedure, reassemble the oil pump. Be sure to prelubricate the oil pump and replace any seals and bushings as necessary. **List your observations:**

7. Have your supervisor/instructor verify satisfactory completion of this procedure, any observations found, and any necessary action(s) recommended.

Performance Rating

CDX Tasksheet Number: C688

0	1	2	3	4

Supervisor/instructor signature _____ Date _____

▶ **TASK** Inspect and measure planetary gear assembly components;
determine necessary action.

CDX Tasksheet Number: C752

Time off_____

Time on_____

Total time_____

1. Research the procedure for inspecting and measuring the planetary gear(s) in the
   appropriate service information.

   a. **Type of planetary gear (Simpson, Ravigneaux, etc.):** _____

   b. **List, or print off and attach to this sheet, the clearance and other specifi-
      cations for the planetary gear(s):**

2. Following the specified procedure, perform any planetary gear assembly measurements. **List your observations:**

3. Visually inspect the planetary gear assemblies (including the sun gear, ring gear,
   planetary gears, thrust washers, and carrier assembly) for wear or damage. **List your
   observations:**

4. **Determine any necessary action(s):**

5. Have your supervisor/instructor verify satisfactory completion of this procedure, any observations found, and any necessary action(s) recommended.

Performance Rating

CDX Tasksheet Number: C752

0	1	2	3	4

Supervisor/instructor signature _____ Date _____

MAST
2C14

CDX Tasksheet Number: C751

1. Research the procedure and any specifications for inspecting the bushings in the appropriate service information.

    a. **List the name and any specifications for each bushing:**

2. Following the specified procedure, inspect and/or measure each bushing. **List your observations:**

3. **Determine any necessary action(s):**

4. Have your supervisor/instructor verify satisfactory completion of this procedure, any observations found, and any necessary action(s) recommended.

Performance Rating

CDX Tasksheet Number: C751

0	1	2	3	4

Supervisor/instructor signature _____ Date _____

MAST
2C12

Time off_____

Time on_____

CDX Tasksheet Number: C750

Total time_____

1. Research the procedure and specifications for inspecting, measuring, and replacing thrust washers and bearings in the appropriate service information.

   a. **List the name and specified thickness for each thrust washer and thrust bearing:**

   b. **Which thrust washer(s) or thrust bearing(s) is the selective fit for obtaining the proper gear train end play?**

2. Following the specified procedure, inspect and/or measure each thrust washer and thrust bearing. **List your observations:**

3. **Determine any necessary action(s):**

4. Have your supervisor/instructor verify satisfactory completion of this procedure, any observations found, and any necessary action(s) recommended.

Performance Rating

CDX Tasksheet Number: C750

0	1	2	3	4

Supervisor/instructor signature _____ Date _____

Inspect roller and sprag clutch, races, rollers, sprags, springs, cages, and retainers; determine necessary action.

MAST
2C22

Time off_____

Time on_____

Total time_____

CDX Tasksheet Number: C759

1. Research the procedure and any specifications for inspecting the roller or sprag clutch assemblies in the appropriate service information.

   a. **List the device that each roller or sprag clutch holds:**

   b. **List, or print off and attach to this sheet, any inspection procedures for these components:**

2. Following the specified procedure, inspect each roller and sprag clutch (including races, rollers, sprags, springs, cages, and retainers). **List your observations:**

3. **Determine any necessary action(s):**

4. Have your supervisor/instructor verify satisfactory completion of this procedure, any observations found, and any necessary action(s) recommended.

Performance Rating

CDX Tasksheet Number: C759

0	1	2	3	4

Supervisor/instructor signature _____ Date _____

Inspect oil delivery circuits, including seal rings, ring grooves, and sealing surface areas, feed pipes, orifices, and check valves/balls.

MAST
2C13

Time off_____

Time on_____

Total time_____

CDX Tasksheet Number: C690

1. Research the procedure and any specifications for inspecting the oil delivery circuits, including seal rings, ring grooves, and sealing surface areas; feed pipes; orifices; and check valves/balls.

   a. List any specifications for the above components:

2. Following the specified procedure, inspect the oil delivery circuits (including the components above). **List your observations:**

3. **Determine any necessary action(s):**

4. Have your supervisor/instructor verify satisfactory completion of this procedure, any observations found, and any necessary action(s) recommended.

Performance Rating

CDX Tasksheet Number: C690

0	1	2	3	4

Supervisor/instructor signature _____ Date _____

Inspect case bores, passages, bushings, vents, and mating surfaces; determine necessary action.

MAST
2C16

Time off_____

Time on_____

Total time_____

CDX Tasksheet Number: C753

1. Research the procedure and any specifications for inspecting case bores, passages, bushings, vents, and mating surfaces.

   a. **List any specifications for the above components:**

2. Following the specified procedure, inspect case bores, passages, bushings, vents, and mating surfaces. **List your observations:**

3. **Determine any necessary action(s):**

4. Have your supervisor/instructor verify satisfactory completion of this procedure, any observations found, and any necessary action(s) recommended.

Performance Rating

CDX Tasksheet Number: C753

0	1	2	3	4

Supervisor/instructor signature _____ Date _____

Inspect servo and accumulator bores, pistons, seals, pins, springs, and retainers; determine necessary action.

Time off_____

Time on_____

Total time_____

CDX Tasksheet Number: C686

1. Research the procedure and any specifications for inspecting servo and accumulator bores, pistons, seals, pins, springs, and retainers.

   a. **List any specifications for the above components:**

2. If not already completed, disassemble each servo and accumulator.

3. Following the specified procedure, inspect servo and accumulator bores, pistons, seals, pins, springs, and retainers. **List your observations:**

4. **Determine any necessary action(s):**

5. Have your supervisor/instructor verify satisfactory completion of this procedure, any observations found, and any necessary action(s) recommended.

Performance Rating

CDX Tasksheet Number: C686

0	1	2	3	4

Supervisor/instructor signature _____ Date _____

Inspect clutch drum, piston, check balls, springs, retainers, seals, and friction and pressure plates, bands, and drums; determine necessary action.

MAST
2C19

Time off_____

Time on_____

Total time_____

CDX Tasksheet Number: C756

1. Research the procedure and specifications for inspecting the clutch drum, piston, check balls, springs, retainers, seals, and friction and pressure plates for each clutch.

   a. **In the table below, list the name of each clutch this transmission/transaxle is equipped with and the number of steel plates and friction plates it contains.**

Name of Clutch	Number of Steel Plates	Number of Friction Plates

   b. **List, or print off and attach to this sheet, any specifications related to the clutch drum, piston, check balls, springs, retainers, seals, and friction and pressure plates:**

   c. Research the procedure and specifications for inspecting the bands and drums.

   i. **List each band and the gear(s) each band is applied in:**

ii. **List any specifications for each band and drum:**

2. Following the specified procedure, disassemble and inspect the components for each clutch assembly. **List your observations for each clutch:**

3. Following the specified procedure, inspect each band and drum for wear or damage. **List your observations:**

4. **Determine any necessary action(s):**

5. Have your supervisor/instructor verify satisfactory completion of this procedure, any observations found, and any necessary action(s) recommended.

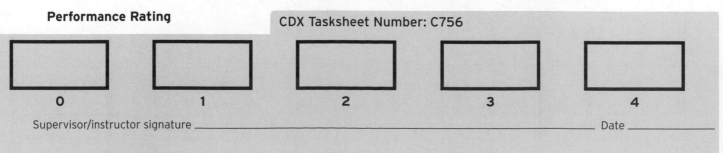

Performance Rating

CDX Tasksheet Number: C756

| 0 | 1 | 2 | 3 | 4 |

Supervisor/instructor signature _____ Date _____

MAST
2C20

CDX Tasksheet Number: C757

1. Research the procedure and specifications for measuring clutch pack clearance in the appropriate service information.

   a. **List the specified clutch pack clearance for each clutch in the table below.**

Name of Clutch	Specified Clearance (in/mm)

   b. **List how each clutch pack clearance is adjusted on this transmission/ transaxle:**

2. If not already completed, reassemble each clutch following the specified procedure.

3. Following the specified procedure, measure the clutch pack clearance for each clutch. **List your measurements in the table below.**

Name of Clutch	Specified Clearance (in/mm)

   4. **Determine any necessary action(s):**

5. Have your supervisor/instructor verify satisfactory completion of this procedure, any observations found, and any necessary action(s) recom-mended.

Performance Rating

CDX Tasksheet Number: C757

☐	☐	☐	☐	☐
0	1	2	3	4

Supervisor/instructor signature _____ Date _____

MAST
2C21

Time off_____

Time on_____

Total time_____

> **NOTE** Most clutch assemblies can usually be air tested outside of the transmission once they are completely assembled with the clutch pack. Therefore, now would be a good time to perform that task for each self-contained clutch pack. Servos, which operate bands, must usually be tested with the gear train and bands installed. You may have to come back to this task for supervisor/instructor sign-off when it is appropriate to air test any servos during the assembly of the transmission/transaxle.

1. Research the procedure for air testing each clutch and servo assembly.

   a. **List any special tools needed for this procedure:**

2. Following the specified procedure, air test each clutch assembly. **List your observations for each one in the table below.**

Name of Clutch	Observations

3. Have your supervisor/instructor verify the above results. **Supervisor/instructor's initials:** _____

4. Once the transmission/transaxle is assembled far enough to air test the servos, test each one following the specified procedure. **List your observations in the table below.**

Name of Servo	Observations

a. Determine any necessary action(s):

5. Have your supervisor/instructor verify satisfactory completion of this procedure, any observations found, and any necessary action(s) recommended.

Performance Rating

CDX Tasksheet Number: C758

0	1	2	3	4

Supervisor/instructor signature _____ Date _____

Inspect, measure, clean, and replace valve body (includes surfaces, bores, springs, valves, sleeves, retainers, brackets, check valves/balls, screens, spacers, and gaskets).

MAST
2C7

Time off_____

Time on_____

Total time_____

CDX Tasksheet Number: C685

1. Research the procedure and specifications to inspect, measure, clean, and replace the valve body.

   a. **List, or print off and attach to this sheet, any precautions for this task:**

   b. **List, or print off and attach to this sheet, any specifications related to this task:**

   c. **List, or print off and attach to this sheet, the torque specifications for the valve body bolts, screws, and fasteners:**

2. Following the specified procedure, disassemble, clean, measure, and inspect the valve body components. **List your observations for each.**

   a. **Valve body and plate surfaces:**

   b. **Bores, valves, and sleeves:**

c. **Springs:**

d. **Retainers, spacers, and brackets:**

e. **Check valves and check balls:**

f. **Gaskets and screens:**

3. Have your supervisor/instructor verify disassembly of the valve body.
Supervisor/instructor's initials: _____

4. Following the specified procedure, reassemble the valve body. Be careful to install all valves, springs, check balls, and gaskets in the proper orientation. Also, be sure to torque all fasteners in the correct sequence and to the proper torque.

5. Have your supervisor/instructor verify satisfactory completion of this procedure, any observations found, and any necessary action(s) recommended.

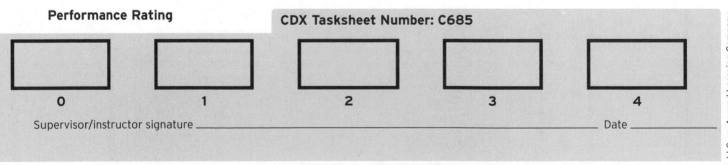

Performance Rating

CDX Tasksheet Number: C685

0	1	2	3	4

Supervisor/instructor signature _____ Date _____

MAST
2C17

CDX Tasksheet Number: C754

1. Research the procedure and specifications to inspect the transaxle drive, link chains, sprockets, gears, bearings, and bushings.

    a. **List, or print off and attach to this sheet, any precautions for this task:**

    b. **List, or print off and attach to this sheet, any specifications related to this task:**

2. Following the specified procedure, inspect the following components. **List your observations.**

    a. **Link chains:**

    b. **Sprockets:**

    c. **Gears:**

    d. **Bearings:**

e. Bushings:

3. Determine any necessary action(s):

4. Have your supervisor/instructor verify satisfactory completion of this procedure, any observations found, and any necessary action(s) recommended.

Performance Rating

CDX Tasksheet Number: C754

0	1	2	3	4

Supervisor/instructor signature _____ Date _____

▶ TASK Inspect, measure, repair, adjust, or replace transaxle final drive components.

MAST
2C18

Time off_____

Time on_____

Total time_____

CDX Tasksheet Number: C755

1. Research the procedure and specifications to inspect, measure, repair, adjust, or replace transaxle final drive components.

   a. **List, or print off and attach to this sheet, any precautions for this task:**

   b. **List any special tools required to complete this task:**

   c. **List, or print off and attach to this sheet, any specifications related to this task:**

2. Following the specified procedure, inspect, measure, repair, adjust, or replace the following components. **List your observations.**

   a. **Link chains:**

   b. **Sprockets:**

c. Gears:

d. Bearings:

e. Bushings:

3. **Determine any necessary action(s):**

4. Have your supervisor/instructor verify satisfactory completion of this procedure, any observations found, and any necessary action(s) recommended.

Performance Rating

CDX Tasksheet Number: C755

0	1	2	3	4

Supervisor/instructor signature _____ Date _____

Automatic Transmission and Transaxle:
Assemble Transmission

Student/intern information:

Name _____ Date _____ Class _____

Vehicle used for this activity:

Year _____ Make _____ Model _____

Odometer _____ VIN _____

Learning Objective/Task	CDX Tasksheet Number	2013 MLR NATEF Reference Number; Priority Level	2013 AST NATEF Reference Number; Priority Level	2013 MAST NATEF Reference Number; Priority Level
• Assemble transmission/transaxle.	C083			2C9; P-2
• Install and seat torque converter to engage drive/splines.	N/A	N/A	N/A	N/A

Time off_____

Time on_____

Total time_____

Materials Required

- Transmission/transaxle
- Torque wrenches of appropriate size
- Feeler blades
- Approved air nozzle
- Dial indicator
- Specified assembly lubricant
- Manufacturer-specific tools

Some Safety Issues to Consider

- Castings and machined parts may have sharp edges. Handle these parts with care.
- Many transmission parts are round and can easily roll off of tables and carts. Be sure to place them in a secure manner to prevent component damage or personal injury from falling objects.
- Compressed air can be very dangerous if applied to broken skin or body cavities. Always use approved air nozzles, and never point them at yourself or another person.
- Transmissions, transaxles, and their component assemblies are heavy and can slip easily. Work safely, get help, and do not overextend your abilities.
- Comply with personal and environmental safety practices associated with clothing; eye protection; hand tools; power equipment; proper ventilation; and the handling, storage, and disposal of chemicals/materials in accordance with local, state, and federal safety and environmental regulations.

Performance Standard

0–No exposure: No information or practice provided during the program; complete training required

1–Exposure only: General information provided with no practice time; close supervision needed; additional training required

2–Limited practice: Has practiced job during training program; additional training required to develop skill

3–Moderately skilled: Has performed job independently during training program; limited additional training may be required

4–Skilled: Can perform job independently with no additional training

Time off_____

Time on_____

Total time_____

CDX Tasksheet Number: C083

1. Research the reassembly procedure for this transmission/transaxle in the appropriate service information.

   a. List the specified assembly lubricant: _____

   b. List the special tools required to perform this task:

   c. Transmission/transaxle end play: _____ **in/mm**

   > **NOTE** All of the component assemblies should already be properly reassembled. If they are not, reassemble them according to the specified procedures as listed in previous tasks. Ensure that they meet all specifications.

2. **Following the specified procedure, reassemble the transmission, making sure all components are seated properly. Perform all specified checks along the way. List your observations:**

3. Once the transmission/transaxle gear train and pump are fully installed, adjust any bands if necessary.

   a. Air check each servo and clutch. List each clutch and servo and your observations:

> **NOTE** Your instructor may want to approve the servo air check from task C758, "Air test operation of clutch and servo assemblies," after you perform it here.

    b. Measure the gear train end play: _____ in/mm

4. Following the specified procedure, reinstall the valve body, linkage, filter, and pan(s).

5. Complete any other specified procedures related to the assembly process.

6. Have your supervisor/instructor verify satisfactory completion of this procedure, any observations found, and any necessary action(s) recommended.

Performance Rating

CDX Tasksheet Number: C083

0	**1**	**2**	**3**	**4**

Supervisor/instructor signature _____ Date _____

Time off_____

Time on_____

Total time_____

CDX Tasksheet Number: N/A

1. Research the procedure for installing and seating the torque converter in the appropriate service information.

   a. **Some transmissions list a specification and procedure for measuring the installed depth of the torque converter. If this is true for this transmission/transaxle, list, or print off and attach to this sheet, the procedure and specification for this procedure:**

   b. **Transmissions/transaxles without torque converter depth specifications can usually be installed by carefully counting the engagement of each component as the torque converter is installed. For example, on many transmissions, you would expect to feel the stator support, input shaft, and pump drive each engage as you install the converter. If you do not feel all three components engage, remove the converter, recheck the positioning of each item, and retry to install and seat the converter. List the components that need to engage for the converter to be fully seated:**

2. **Following the specified procedure, install and seat the torque converter. Perform any measurements or count the number of engagements as they occur. List your observations:**

3. Have your supervisor/instructor verify satisfactory completion of this procedure, any observations found, and any necessary action(s) recommended.

Performance Rating

CDX Tasksheet Number: N/A

0	1	2	3	4
☐	☐	☐	☐	☐

Supervisor/instructor signature _____ Date _____

Section A3:
Manual Drive Train and Axles

CONTENTS

Manual Drive Train and Axles: Vehicle, Customer, and Service Information

Student/intern information:

Name _____ Date _____ Class _____

Vehicle used for this activity:

Year _____ Make _____ Model _____

Odometer _____ VIN _____

Learning Objective/Task	CDX Tasksheet Number	2013 MLR NATEF Reference Number; Priority Level	2013 AST NATEF Reference Number; Priority Level	2013 MAST NATEF Reference Number; Priority Level
• Research applicable vehicle and service information, fluid type, vehicle service history, service precautions, and technical service bulletins.	C102	3A1; P-1	3A2; P-1	3A2; P-1
• Identify and interpret drive train concern; determine necessary action.	C101		3A1; P-1	3A1; P-1
• Describe the operational characteristics of an electronically controlled manual transmission/transaxle.	C611	3C1; P-3	3C2; P-3	3C2; P-3
• Demonstrate use of 3 Cs (concern, cause, and correction).	NN03	N/A	N/A	N/A

Time off _____

Time on _____

Total time _____

Materials Required

- Blank work order
- Vehicle with available service history records
- Depending on the type of concern, special diagnostic tools may be required. See your supervisor/instructor for instructions to identify what tools may be required.

Some Safety Issues to Consider

- Diagnosis of this fault may require test-driving the vehicle on the school grounds. Attempt this task only with full permission from your instructor and follow all the guidelines exactly.

- When running any vehicles in the shop, make sure you use the shop's exhaust ventilation system to discharge all exhaust gas safely outside.

- Lifting equipment such as vehicle jacks and stands, vehicle hoists, and engine hoists are important tools that increase productivity and make the job easier. However, they can also cause severe injury or death if used improperly. Make sure you follow the manufacturer's operation procedures. Also, make sure you have your supervisor's/instructor's permission to use any particular type of lifting equipment.

- Comply with personal and environmental safety practices associated with clothing; eye protection; hand tools; power equipment; proper ventilation; and the handling, storage, and disposal of chemicals/materials in accordance with local, state, and federal safety and environmental regulations.

Performance Standard

0—No exposure: No information or practice provided during the program; complete training required

1—Exposure only: General information provided with no practice time; close supervision needed; additional training required

2—Limited practice: Has practiced job during training program; additional training required to develop skill

3—Moderately skilled: Has performed job independently during training program; limited additional training may be required

4—Skilled: Can perform job independently with no additional training

Research applicable vehicle and service information, fluid type, vehicle service history, service precautions, and technical service bulletins.

MLR 3A1   **AST** 3A2   **MAST** 3A2

Time off_____

Time on_____

Total time_____

CDX Tasksheet Number: C102

1. Using the vehicle VIN for identification, use the appropriate source to access the vehicle's service history in relation to prior related drive train system work or customer concerns.

   a. **List any related repairs/concerns, and their dates:**

2. **List the specified type of transmission fluid for this vehicle:** _____

3. **Using the vehicle VIN for identification, access any relevant technical service bulletins for the particular vehicle you are working on in relation to any drive train system updates, precautions, or other service issues. List any related service bulletins:**

4. Have your supervisor/instructor verify satisfactory completion of this procedure, any observations found, and any necessary action(s) recommended.

Performance Rating

CDX Tasksheet Number: C102

0	1	2	3	4

Supervisor/instructor signature _____ Date _____

AST 3A1 **MAST** 3A1

CDX Tasksheet Number: C101

1. **List the customer's transmission-related concern(s):**

2. **Research the particular concern in the appropriate service information. List the possible causes:**

3. **Inspect the vehicle to determine the cause of the concern. List the steps you took to determine the fault(s):**

4. **List the cause of the concern(s):**

5. **List the necessary action(s) to correct the fault(s):**

6. Have your supervisor/instructor verify satisfactory completion of this procedure, any observations found, and any necessary action(s) recommended.

Performance Rating

CDX Tasksheet Number: C101

0	1	2	3	4

Supervisor/instructor signature _____ Date _____

Describe the operational characteristics of an electronically controlled manual transmission/transaxle.

MLR	AST	MAST
3C1	3C2	3C2

CDX Tasksheet Number: C611

Vehicle used for this activity:

Year _____ Make _____ Model _____

Odometer _____ VIN _____

1. Research the description and operation of an electronically controlled manual transmission/transaxle in the appropriate service information.

   a. How many forward speeds does this transmission have?

   b. How do the electronics interface with the transmission to control the transmission?

   c. How does this transmission achieve neutral?

   d. What type of fluid does this transmission use? _____
   e. What is the fluid capacity? _____ **qt/lt**
   f. What type of clutch(es) does this transmission use?

2. Have your supervisor/instructor verify satisfactory completion of this procedure, any observations found, and any necessary action(s) recommended.

Performance Rating

CDX Tasksheet Number: C611

0	1	2	3	4

Supervisor/instructor signature _____ Date _____

Demonstrate use of 3 Cs (concern, cause, and correction).

CDX Tasksheet Number: N/A

1. Using the following scenario, write up the 3 Cs as listed on most repair orders. Assume that the customer authorized the recommended repairs.
    A late model half-ton pickup truck is brought to your shop with a manual transaxle concern. The customer tells you that the transmission started slipping a couple of days ago after his brother used it to haul several loads of gravel. You road test the vehicle and notice that it is slipping in all gears when under a moderate load. Also, the clutch pedal seems softer than normal, and there is a burning smell when you get back to the shop. You pull the vehicle onto a rack, and find the following:

    a. The vehicle has 91,000 miles on it, but otherwise is in good condition.
    b. The transmission fluid is full and looks good.
    c. The slave cylinder is seeping brake fluid slightly from the dust boot, and the clutch master cylinder fluid level is a bit low.
    d. With the clutch inspection cover removed, there is a lot of clutch material and the burning smell is very strong.
    e. The rear shocks are leaking badly past the shaft seal.

    > **NOTE** Ask your instructor whether you should use a copy of the shop repair order or the 3 Cs below to record this information.

2. **Concern:**

3. **Cause:**

4. **Correction:**

5. **Other recommended service:**

6. Have your supervisor/instructor verify satisfactory completion of this procedure, any observations found, and any necessary action(s) recommended.

Performance Rating

CDX Tasksheet Number: NN03

0	1	2	3	4

Supervisor/instructor signature _____ Date _____

Manual Drive Train and Axles: Transmission/Transaxle Maintenance

Student/intern information:

Name _____ Date _____ Class _____

Vehicle used for this activity:

Year _____ Make _____ Model _____

Odometer _____ VIN _____

Learning Objective/Task	CDX Tasksheet Number	2013 MLR NATEF Reference Number; Priority Level	2013 AST NATEF Reference Number; Priority Level	2013 MAST NATEF Reference Number; Priority Level
• Check fluid condition; check for leaks.	C901	3A3; P-1		
• Check fluid condition; check for leaks; determine necessary action.	C691		3A3; P-1	3A3; P-1
• Drain and refill manual transmission/transaxle and final drive unit.	C105	3A2; P-1	3A4; P-1	3A4; P-1

Time off _____

Time on _____

Total time _____

Materials Required

- Vehicle with manual transmission/transaxle
- Vehicle hoist
- Drain pan
- Flashlight or shop light
- Fluorescent dye and ultraviolet light (optional)
- Specified fluid

Some Safety Issues to Consider

- Vehicle hoists are important tools that increase productivity and make the job easier. However, they can also cause severe injury or death if used improperly. Make sure you follow the manufacturer's operation procedures. Also, make sure you have your supervisor's/instructor's permission to use any particular type of lifting equipment.
- When running any vehicles in the shop, make sure you use the shop's exhaust ventilation system to discharge all exhaust gas safely outside.
- This procedure may require cleaning the engine prior to inspection. If so, use the proper equipment and procedures to carry this out safely. Also, get your supervisor's/instructor's permission prior to cleaning.
- Comply with personal and environmental safety practices associated with clothing; eye protection; hand tools; power equipment; proper ventilation; and the handling, storage, and disposal of chemicals/materials in accordance with local, state, and federal safety and environmental regulations.

Performance Standard

0—No exposure: No information or practice provided during the program; complete training required

1—Exposure only: General information provided with no practice time; close supervision needed; additional training required

2—Limited practice: Has practiced job during training program; additional training required to develop skill

3—Moderately skilled: Has performed job independently during training program; limited additional training may be required

4—Skilled: Can perform job independently with no additional training

▶ **TASK** Check fluid condition; check for leaks.

Time off_____

Time on_____

Total time_____

CDX Tasksheet Number: C901

1. List the transmission designation for this vehicle: _____

2. Research the following specifications for this vehicle in the appropriate service information.

   a. **Fluid type:** _____
   b. **Fluid capacity:** _____ qt/lt
   c. **How is the fluid level checked?**

3. Safely raise and secure the vehicle on a hoist.

4. **Following the specified procedure, check the fluid level and list your observation(s):**

5. **Inspect the condition of the fluid. Look for contaminants, metal shavings, and degraded fluid condition. List your observation(s):**

6. Inspect the transmission/transaxle assembly for leaks.

   a. **Identify and list the source of any leak(s):**

7. Have your supervisor/instructor verify satisfactory completion of this procedure, any observations found, and any necessary action(s) recommended.

Performance Rating

CDX Tasksheet Number: C901

0	1	2	3	4

Supervisor/instructor signature _____ Date _____

Check fluid condition; check for leaks; determine necessary action.

AST 3A3   **MAST** 3A3

Time off_____

Time on_____

Total time_____

CDX Tasksheet Number: C691

1. **List the transmission designation for this vehicle:** _____

2. Research the following specifications for this vehicle in the appropriate service information.

   a. **Fluid type:** _____
   b. **Fluid capacity:** _____ **qt/lt**
   c. **How is the fluid level checked?**

3. Safely raise and secure the vehicle on a hoist.

4. **Following the specified procedure, check the fluid level and list your observation(s):**

5. **Inspect the condition of the fluid. Look for contaminants, metal shavings, and degraded fluid condition. List your observation(s):**

6. Inspect the transmission/transaxle assembly for leaks.

   a. **Identify and list the source of any leak(s):**

7. **Determine any necessary action(s):**

8. Have your supervisor/instructor verify satisfactory completion of this procedure, any observations found, and any necessary action(s) recommended.

Performance Rating

CDX Tasksheet Number: C691

0	1	2	3	4

Supervisor/instructor signature _____ Date _____

Drain and fill manual transmission/transaxle and final drive unit.

MLR 3A2   **AST** 3A4   **MAST** 3A4

Time off_____

Time on_____

Total time_____

CDX Tasksheet Number: C105

1. Research the following specifications and procedure in the appropriate service information.

   a. **Transmission/transaxle service interval:** _____ **km/mi**

   b. **Transmission/transaxle fluid type:** _____

   c. **Transmission/transaxle fluid capacity:** _____ **qt/lt**

   d. **Final drive service interval:** _____ **km/mi**

   e. **Final drive fluid type:** _____

   f. **Final drive fluid capacity:** _____ **qt/lt**

2. **Following the specified procedure, drain the transmission/transaxle fluid into a clean drain pan. Inspect any residue and debris in the bottom of the drain pan. List your observations:**

3. **Determine any necessary action(s):**

4. **Drain the final drive unit (if separate from the transmission) into a clean drain pan. Inspect any residue and debris in the bottom of the drain pan. List your observations:**

5. Have your supervisor/instructor verify fluid removal and your answers. **Supervisor's/instructor's initials:** _____

6. **Following the specified procedure, refill the transmission/transaxle and final drive unit. Replace all fill plugs and tighten them to the proper torque. List your observations:**

7. Have your supervisor/instructor verify satisfactory completion of this procedure, any observations found, and any necessary action(s) recommended.

Performance Rating

CDX Tasksheet Number: C105

0	1	2	3	4

Supervisor/instructor signature _____ Date _____

Manual Drive Train and Axles: Clutch Maintenance

Student/intern information:

Name _____ Date _____ Class _____

Vehicle used for this activity:

Year _____ Make _____ Model_____

Odometer_____VIN_____

Learning Objective/Task	CDX Tasksheet Number	2013 MLR NATEF Reference Number; Priority Level	2013 AST NATEF Reference Number; Priority Level	2013 MAST NATEF Reference Number; Priority Level
• Inspect clutch pedal linkage, cables, automatic adjuster mechanisms, brackets, bushings, pivots, and springs; perform necessary action.	C107		3B2; P-1	3B2; P-1
• Check and adjust clutch master cylinder fluid level.	C908	3B1; P-1	3B5	
• Check for system leaks.	C909	3B2; P-1		
• Check and adjust clutch master cylinder fluid level; check for leaks.	C938		3B5; P-1	3B5; P-1
• Bleed clutch hydraulic system.	C111		3B4; P-1	3B4; P-1

Time off_____

Time on_____

Total time_____

Materials Required

- Vehicle with manual transmission/transaxle
- Vehicle hoist
- Flashlight or shop light
- Ruler
- Brake/clutch bleeding kit
- Drain pan
- Line or flare wrench set
- Specified fluid

Some Safety Issues to Consider

- Vehicle hoists are important tools that increase productivity and make the job easier. However, they can also cause severe injury or death if used improperly. Make sure you follow the manufacturer's operation procedures. Also, make sure you have your supervisor's/instructor's permission to use any particular type of lifting equipment.
- When running any vehicles in the shop, make sure you use the shop's exhaust ventilation system to discharge all exhaust gas safely outside.
- Diagnosis of this fault may require test-driving the vehicle on the school grounds. Attempt this task only with full permission from your instructor and follow all the guidelines exactly.
- Brake fluid can damage painted surfaces. Avoid spills and splashes, and rinse off with water immediately.

- Comply with personal and environmental safety practices associated with clothing; eye protection; hand tools; power equipment; proper ventilation; and the handling, storage, and disposal of chemicals/materials in accordance with local, state, and federal safety and environmental regulations.

Performance Standard

0—No exposure: No information or practice provided during the program; complete training required

1—Exposure only: General information provided with no practice time; close supervision needed; additional training required

2—Limited practice: Has practiced job during training program; additional training required to develop skill

3—Moderately skilled: Has performed job independently during training program; limited additional training may be required

4—Skilled: Can perform job independently with no additional training

Inspect clutch pedal linkage, cables, automatic adjuster mechanisms, brackets, bushings, pivots, and springs; perform necessary action.

AST 3B2 **MAST** 3B2

Time off_____

Time on_____

Total time_____

CDX Tasksheet Number: C107

1. Research the procedure and specifications for inspecting and adjusting the clutch linkage in the appropriate service information.

     a. **Clutch pedal height:** _____ in/mm
     b. **Clutch pedal free play:** _____ in/mm
     c. **Is this an adjustable clutch? Yes:** _____ **No:** _____
     d. **If yes, how is it adjusted?**

2. **Following the specified procedure, inspect the following parts for damage, wear, or missing components. List your observations for each.**

     a. **Clutch pedal linkage:**

     b. **Cable(s):**

     c. **Automatic adjuster mechanism, if equipped:**

     d. **Brackets:**

     e. **Bushings/guides/pivots:**

f. Springs:

3. **Measure the clutch pedal height:** _____ **in/mm**

4. **Measure the clutch pedal free play:** _____ **in/mm**

5. **Determine any necessary action(s):**

6. Have your supervisor/instructor verify your answers.
   Supervisor's/instructor's initials: _____

7. **Perform any necessary action(s) and list your observations:**

8. Have your supervisor/instructor verify satisfactory completion of this procedure, any observations found, and any necessary action(s) recommended.

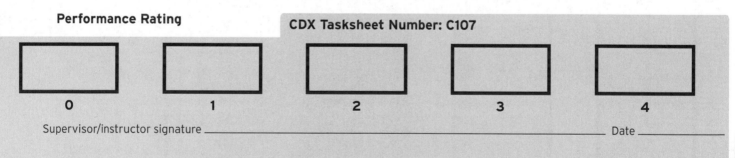

Performance Rating

CDX Tasksheet Number: C107

| 0 | 1 | 2 | 3 | 4 |

Supervisor/instructor signature _____ Date _____

Check and adjust clutch master cylinder fluid level.

MLR
3B1

Time off_____

Time on_____

Total time_____

CDX Tasksheet Number: C908

1. Research the procedure and specifications for checking and adjusting the master cylinder fluid level in the appropriate service information.

   a. **Specified clutch master cylinder fluid:** _____

   b. **Specified clutch master cylinder fluid replacement interval:**
   _____ **mi/km/mo**

2. **Check the clutch master cylinder fluid level and condition.**
   List your observations:

3. Have your supervisor/instructor verify satisfactory completion of this procedure, any observations found, and any necessary action(s) recommended.

Performance Rating

CDX Tasksheet Number: C908

0	1	2	3	4

Supervisor/instructor signature _____ Date _____

Time off_____

Time on_____

Total time_____

CDX Tasksheet Number: C909

1. **Inspect the following clutch hydraulic system components for leaks. List your observations:**

    a. **Clutch master cylinder:**

    b. **Clutch slave cylinder (look under the dust boot):**

    c. **Hydraulic clutch lines and hoses:**

2. Have your supervisor/instructor verify satisfactory completion of this procedure, any observations found, and any necessary action(s) recommended.

Performance Rating

CDX Tasksheet Number: C909

0	1	2	3	4

Supervisor/instructor signature _____ Date _____

Check and adjust clutch master cylinder fluid level; check for leaks.

AST 3B5 · **MAST** 3B5

Time off _____

Time on _____

Total time _____

CDX Tasksheet Number: C938

1. Research the procedure and specifications for checking and adjusting the master cylinder fluid level in the appropriate service information.

   a. **Specified clutch master cylinder fluid:** _____

   b. **Specified clutch master cylinder fluid replacement interval:**
   _____ **mi/km/mo**

2. **Check the clutch master cylinder fluid level and condition.**
   List your observations:

3. **Inspect the following clutch hydraulic system components for leaks.**
   List your observations:

   a. **Clutch master cylinder:**

   b. **Clutch slave cylinder (look under the dust boot):**

   c. **Hydraulic clutch lines and hoses:**

4. Have your supervisor/instructor verify satisfactory completion of this procedure, any observations found, and any necessary action(s) recommended.

Performance Rating

CDX Tasksheet Number: C938

| 0 | 1 | 2 | 3 | 4 |

Supervisor/instructor signature _____ Date _____

AST	MAST
3B4	3B4

Time off_____

Time on_____

Total time_____

CDX Tasksheet Number: C111

Vehicle used for this activity:

Year _____ Make _____ Model_____

Odometer_____ VIN_____

1. Research the procedure and specifications for bleeding the clutch hydraulic system in the appropriate service information.

   a. Specified fluid: _____

   b. List or print off and attach to this sheet the steps to bleed the system:

   c. List any special tools needed for this task:

2. **Following the specified procedure, inspect the following parts for damage, wear, or missing components. List your observations for each.**

   a. Clutch master cylinder:

   b. Clutch slave cylinder:

   c. Lines (steel or plastic):

d. Hoses (flexible):

3. **Following the specified procedure, bleed the hydraulic clutch system, being careful not to run the reservoir low. List your observation(s):**

4. Have your supervisor/instructor verify satisfactory completion of this procedure, any observations found, and any necessary action(s) recommended.

Performance Rating

CDX Tasksheet Number: C111

0	1	2	3	4

Supervisor/instructor signature _____ Date _____

Manual Drive Train and Axles: Clutch Diagnosis and Repair

Student/intern information:

Name _____ Date _____ Class _____

Vehicle used for this activity:

Year _____ Make _____ Model_____

Odometer_____ VIN_____

Learning Objective/Task	CDX Tasksheet Number	2013 MLR NATEF Reference Number; Priority Level	2013 AST NATEF Reference Number; Priority Level	2013 MAST NATEF Reference Number; Priority Level
• Diagnose clutch noise, binding, slippage, pulsation, and chatter; determine necessary action.	C106		3B1; P-1	3B1; P-1
• Remove and reinstall transmission/transaxle.	NN13	N/A	N/A	N/A
• Measure flywheel runout and crankshaft end play; determine necessary action.	C848		3B7; P-2	3B7; P-2
• Inspect flywheel and ring gear for wear and cracks; determine necessary action.	C847		3B6; P-1	3B6; P-1
• Inspect engine block, core plugs, rear main engine oil seal, clutch (bell) housing, transmission/transaxle case mating surfaces, and alignment dowels; determine necessary action.	NN14	N/A	N/A	N/A
• Inspect and replace clutch pressure plate assembly, clutch disc, release (throw-out) bearing and linkage, and pilot bearing/bushing (as applicable).	C608		3B3; P-1	3B3; P-1

Time off_____

Time on_____

Total time_____

Materials Required

- Vehicle with manual transmission/transaxle
- Vehicle hoist
- Transmission jack
- Flashlight or shop light
- Dial indicator
- Flywheel wrench (holding tool)
- 1/8" to 3/16" pin punch
- Clutch alignment tool
- Torque wrench

Some Safety Issues to Consider

- Only students who have their supervisor's/instructor's direct permission should perform this task due to the safety concerns involved.

- Diagnosis of this fault may require test-driving the vehicle on the school grounds. Attempt this task only with full permission from your instructor and follow all the guidelines exactly.

- **Caution**: Clutch dust may contain asbestos, which has been determined to cause cancer when inhaled or ingested. Treat all clutch dust as if it contains asbestos and use OSHA-approved asbestos removal equipment. DO NOT allow clutch dust to become airborne by using anything that would disturb the dust. Also, wear protective gloves during this procedure and dispose of or clean them in an approved manner.

- Vehicle hoists are important tools that increase productivity and make the job easier. However, they can also cause severe injury or death if used improperly. Make sure you follow the manufacturer's operation procedures. Also, make sure you have your supervisor's/instructor's permission to use any particular type of lifting equipment.

- Comply with personal and environmental safety practices associated with clothing; eye protection; hand tools; power equipment; proper ventilation; and the handling, storage, and disposal of chemicals/materials in accordance with local, state, and federal safety and environmental regulations.

Performance Standard

0—No exposure: No information or practice provided during the program; complete training required

1—Exposure only: General information provided with no practice time; close supervision needed; additional training required

2—Limited practice: Has practiced job during training program; additional training required to develop skill

3—Moderately skilled: Has performed job independently during training program; limited additional training may be required

4—Skilled: Can perform job independently with no additional training

Diagnose clutch noise, binding, slippage, pulsation, and chatter; determine necessary action.

AST 3B1 **MAST** 3B1

Time off_____

Time on_____

Total time_____

CDX Tasksheet Number: C106

1. List the customer concern(s) related to the conditions listed above:

2. If your instructor approves, test-drive the vehicle to verify the concern. List your observation(s):

> **NOTE** If the clutch is spongy, you may need to do some preliminary checks such as checking the level of fluid in the hydraulic clutch master cylinder before test-driving the vehicle.

3. Research the concern in the appropriate service information. List or print off and attach to this sheet the possible causes:

   a. List or print off and attach to this sheet the steps to diagnose this concern:

4. **Following the specified procedure, diagnose the cause of the customer concern. List your steps and the results obtained:**

5. **Determine any necessary action(s) to correct the fault:**

6. Have your supervisor/instructor verify satisfactory completion of this procedure, any observations found, and any necessary action(s) recommended.

Performance Rating

CDX Tasksheet Number: C106

0	1	2	3	4

Supervisor/instructor signature _____ Date _____

CDX Tasksheet Number: NN13

1. Research the procedure and specifications for removing and installing the transmission/transaxle in the appropriate service information.

    a. **Transmission fluid type:** _____

    b. **Transmission fluid capacity:** _____ **qt/lt**

    c. **Bell housing-to-block torque:** _____ **ft-lb/Nm**

    d. **Clutch free play:** _____ **in/mm**

    e. **List or print off and attach to this sheet the procedure for removing and installing the transmission/transaxle:**

2. **Following the specified procedure, remove the transmission/transaxle from the vehicle. List your observations:**

3. Have your supervisor/instructor verify removal of the transmission/transaxle from the vehicle and initial below.

    a. **Supervisor's/instructor's initials:** _____

> **NOTE** At this time, you may want to overhaul the transmission/transaxle or perform other tasks such as inspecting/replacing the clutch assembly or replacing the rear crankshaft main seal. Once any related tasks are completed and it is time to reinstall the transmission/transaxle, return to this page to complete the task and have it signed off.

4. Prepare the transmission to be reinstalled. Ensure that the release (throw-out) bearing and clutch fork are properly installed and the clutch disc is centered in the pressure plate. If specified, lubricate the pilot bushing/bearing.

5. Position all wires, hoses, and tubes out of the way and in their specified positions. Secure them temporarily if necessary.

> **NOTE** It is easy for wires and hoses to fall down and get pinched between the engine and bell housing. This will cause electrical issues in the vehicle as well as alignment issues with the transmission.

6. Following the specified procedure, reinstall the transmission/transaxle. Be sure to tighten all fasteners to the proper torque.

7. If the vehicle is equipped with a cable or linkage style clutch release system, reinstall and adjust it for the proper free play. If equipped with a hydraulic clutch, reinstall the slave cylinder and bleed and/or adjust it if necessary.

8. Refill the transmission/transaxle to the proper level with the specified fluid.

9. Check that all electrical wires, linkages, drive/axle shafts and other removed components are properly installed and adjusted.

10. Have your supervisor/instructor verify that the vehicle is ready to be test-driven and initial below.

   a. Supervisor's/instructor's initials: _____

11. Place exhaust hose(s) over the exhaust pipe(s) and set the parking brake. Make sure no one is standing in front of or behind the vehicle.

12. Start the vehicle and check the action of the clutch and gear shift linkage. If the clutch disengages so that the gearshift can select gears and engages at the correct height and everything is working properly, take the vehicle for a test-drive to confirm proper operation of the clutch and transmission. **List your observations:**

13. After the test-drive, raise the vehicle on a hoist and double-check your work. Verify that there are no leaks, loose fasteners, or misrouted components. Verify proper clutch adjustment. **List your observations:**

14. Have your supervisor/instructor verify satisfactory completion of this procedure, any observations found, and any necessary action(s) recommended.

Performance Rating

CDX Tasksheet Number: NN13

0	1	2	3	4

Supervisor/instructor signature _____ Date _____

▶ **TASK** Measure flywheel runout and crankshaft end play; determine necessary action.

AST 3B7   MAST 3B7

Time off_____

Time on_____

Total time_____

CDX Tasksheet Number: C848

1. Research the specifications and procedure for measuring flywheel runout and crankshaft end play in the appropriate service information.

    a. **Flywheel runout:** _____ **in/mm**
    b. **Crankshaft end play:** _____ **in/mm**

2. **If not already completed, following the specified procedure, remove the transmission/transaxle. List any observations:**

3. Following the specified procedure, remove the pressure plate and clutch disc.

    NOTE It is good practice to remove the pressure plate bolts evenly. This requires backing each bolt out a turn or two at a time to avoid warping the pressure plate. Also, have an assistant hold the pressure plate and clutch disc when they get close to becoming loose to avoid dropping them on the floor and damaging them or injuring your feet.

4. Clean up any debris using an approved method for disposing of hazardous dust.

5. **Following the specified procedure, measure the following.**

    a. **Flywheel runout:** _____ **in/mm**
    b. **Crankshaft end play:** _____ **in/mm**

6. **Determine any necessary action(s):**

7. Have your supervisor/instructor verify satisfactory completion of this procedure, any observations found, and any necessary action(s) recommended.

Performance Rating

CDX Tasksheet Number: C848

0	1	2	3	4

Supervisor/instructor signature _____ Date _____

▶ **TASK** Inspect flywheel and ring gear for wear and cracks; determine necessary action.

AST 3B6   MAST 3B6

CDX Tasksheet Number: C847

1. **Research the procedure for inspecting the flywheel and ring gear in the appropriate service information. List any specifications or specific instructions for inspection:**

2. **Inspect the flywheel for wear and cracks. List your observations:**

3. **Inspect the ring gear for wear, chipped teeth, and cracks. List your observations:**

> **NOTE** It is common for the ring gear teeth to be worn in a pattern. For example, a 4-cylinder engine will have greater wear every 180°, a 6-cylinder engine every 120°, and an 8-cylinder engine every 90°. Therefore, be sure to inspect all of the teeth, not just a few of them.

4. **Determine any necessary action(s):**

5. **Have your supervisor/instructor verify satisfactory completion of this procedure, any observations found, and any necessary action(s) recommended.**

Performance Rating

CDX Tasksheet Number: C847

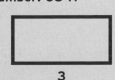
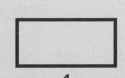

| 0 | 1 | 2 | 3 | 4 |

Supervisor/instructor signature _____ Date _____

Inspect engine block, core plugs, rear main engine oil seal, clutch (bell) housing, transmission/transaxle case mating surfaces, and alignment dowels; determine necessary action.

Additional Task

Time off_____

Time on_____

Total time_____

CDX Tasksheet Number: NN14

1. **Research the procedure for inspecting the items listed above. List any specifications or specific instructions for inspection:**

2. Remove the flywheel if it is not already removed.

3. **Inspect each of the following and list your observations.**

   a. **Engine block:**

   b. **Core plugs (Test their integrity by tapping on them lightly with a punch.):**

   c. **Rear main oil seal:**

   d. **Clutch (bell) housing:**

   e. **Transmission/transaxle case mating surfaces:**

    f. **Alignment dowels:**

4. **Determine any necessary action(s):**

5. Have your supervisor/instructor verify satisfactory completion of this procedure, any observations found, and any necessary action(s) recommended.

Performance Rating

CDX Tasksheet Number: NN14

0	1	2	3	4

Supervisor/instructor signature _____ Date _____

Inspect and replace clutch pressure plate assembly, clutch disc, release (throw-out) bearing and linkage, and pilot bearing/bushing (as applicable).

AST 3B3 **MAST** 3B3

Time off_____

Time on_____

Total time_____

CDX Tasksheet Number: C608

1. Research the procedure and any specifications for inspecting the clutch assembly.

   a. List any specifications or specific instructions for inspection:

   b. Flywheel-to-crankshaft bolt torque: _____ **ft-lb/Nm**

      i. Threadlock required: Yes: _____ **No:** _____

   c. Pressure plate-to-flywheel bolt torque: _____ **ft-lb/Nm**

   d. Pilot bushing/bearing lubricant, if applicable: _____

2. **Inspect each of the following and list your observations.**

   a. Pressure plate assembly:

   b. Clutch disc:

   c. Release (throw-out) bearing and linkage:

   d. Pilot bearing/bushing:

3. **Determine any necessary action(s):**

4. Have your supervisor/instructor verify your observations and recommendations and initial below.

   a. **Supervisor's/instructor's initials:** _____

5. With your instructor's permission, replace any worn parts with new/remanufactured components.

6. Following the specified procedure, install the pilot bushing/bearing, if removed. Lubricate it with the specified lubricant, if applicable.

7. Following the specified procedure, install the flywheel. Be sure to torque the flywheel bolts.

8. Following the specified procedure, install the clutch disc and pressure plate. Use an appropriate clutch alignment tool to ensure proper positioning of the clutch disc.

> **NOTE** The pressure plate bolts should be tightened down evenly. This is usually done by tightening each bolt a turn or two, one at a time, until the pressure plate is evenly seated on the flywheel surface. Then, torque each bolt according to the specified torque and sequence.

9. Install the release (throw-out) bearing and linkage.

10. **List any observation(s):**

11. Have your supervisor/instructor verify satisfactory completion of this procedure, any observations found, and any necessary action(s) recommended.

Performance Rating

CDX Tasksheet Number: C608

0	1	2	3	4

Supervisor/instructor signature _____ Date _____

Manual Drive Train and Axles: Transmission/Transaxle Diagnosis

© 2015 Jones & Bartlett Learning, LLC, an Ascend Learning Company

Student/intern information:

Name _____ Date _____ Class _____

Vehicle used for this activity:

Year _____ Make _____ Model_____

Odometer_____ VIN_____

Learning Objective/Task	CDX Tasksheet Number	2013 MLR NATEF Reference Number; Priority Level	2013 AST NATEF Reference Number; Priority Level	2013 MAST NATEF Reference Number; Priority Level
• Diagnose noise concerns through the application of transmission/transaxle powerflow principles.	C609			3C3; P-2
• Diagnose hard shifting and jumping out of gear concerns; determine necessary action.	C693			3C4; P-2
• Diagnose transaxle final drive assembly noise and vibration concerns; determine necessary action.	C887			3C5; P-3

Time off_____

Time on_____

Total time_____

Materials Required

- Vehicle(s) with specific concern(s)
- Vehicle hoist
- Powerflow flowcharts
- Stethoscope
- Job-specific tools
- Manufacturer-specific tools

Some Safety Issues to Consider

- Vehicle hoists are important tools that increase productivity and make the job easier. However, they can also cause severe injury or death if used improperly. Make sure you follow the manufacturer's operation procedures. Also, make sure you have your supervisor's/instructor's permission to use any particular type of lifting equipment.
- When running any vehicles in the shop, make sure you use the shop's exhaust ventilation system to discharge all exhaust gas safely outside.
- Diagnosis of this fault may require test-driving the vehicle on the school grounds. Attempt this task only with full permission from your instructor and follow all the guidelines exactly.
- Castings and machined parts may have sharp edges. Handle these parts with care.
- Comply with personal and environmental safety practices associated with clothing; eye protection; hand tools; power equipment; proper ventilation; and the handling, storage, and disposal of chemicals/materials in accordance with local, state, and federal safety and environmental regulations.

Performance Standard

0–No exposure: No information or practice provided during the program; complete training required

1–Exposure only: General information provided with no practice time; close supervision needed; additional training required

2–Limited practice: Has practiced job during training program; additional training required to develop skill

3–Moderately skilled: Has performed job independently during training program; limited additional training may be required

4–Skilled: Can perform job independently with no additional training

MAST
3C3

Time off_____

Time on_____

Total time_____

CDX Tasksheet Number: C609

1. **List the transmission/transaxle noise-related customer concern:**

2. **Research the concern in the appropriate service information and list the possible causes:**

3. **Following the specified procedure, use powerflow flowcharts to identify the cause of the noise concern. List your tests and observations:**

4. **List the cause of the noise concern:**

5. **Determine any necessary action(s) to correct the fault:**

6. Have your supervisor/instructor verify satisfactory completion of this procedure, any observations found, and any necessary action(s) recommended.

Performance Rating

CDX Tasksheet Number: C609

0	1	2	3	4

Supervisor/instructor signature _____ Date _____

Diagnose hard shifting and jumping out of gear concerns; determine necessary action.

MAST
3C4

Time off_____

Time on_____

Total time_____

CDX Tasksheet Number: C693

Vehicle used for this activity:

Year _____ Make _____ Model _____

Odometer _____ VIN _____

1. **List the hard shifting or jumping out of gear customer concern:**

2. **Research the concern in the appropriate service information and list the possible causes:**

3. **Following the specified procedure, diagnose the fault. List your tests and observations:**

4. **List the cause of the hard shifting or jumping out of gear concern:**

5. **Determine any necessary action(s) to correct the fault:**

6. **Have your supervisor/instructor verify satisfactory completion of this procedure, any observations found, and any necessary action(s) recommended.**

Performance Rating

CDX Tasksheet Number: C693

0	1	2	3	4

Supervisor/instructor signature _____ Date _____

Diagnose transaxle final drive assembly noise and vibration concerns; determine necessary action.

MAST
3C5

Time off_____

Time on_____

Total time_____

CDX Tasksheet Number: C887

Vehicle used for this activity:

Year _____ Make _____ Model_____

Odometer_____ VIN_____

1. **List the final drive noise or vibration customer concern:**

2. **Research the concern in the appropriate service information and list the possible causes:**

3. **Following the specified procedure, diagnose the fault. List your tests and observations:**

4. **List the cause of the noise or vibration concern:**

5. **Determine any necessary action(s) to correct the fault:**

6. Have your supervisor/instructor verify satisfactory completion of this procedure, any observations found, and any necessary action(s) recommended.

Performance Rating

CDX Tasksheet Number: C887

0	1	2	3	4

Supervisor/instructor signature _____ Date _____

Manual Drive Train and Axles: Transmission/Transaxle Repair

Student/intern information:

Name_____ Date_____ Class_____

Vehicle used for this activity:

Year _____ Make _____ Model_____

Odometer_____VIN_____

Learning Objective/Task	CDX Tasksheet Number	2013 MLR NATEF Reference Number; Priority Level	2013 AST NATEF Reference Number; Priority Level	2013 MAST NATEF Reference Number; Priority Level
• Inspect, adjust, and reinstall shift linkages, brackets, bushings, cables, pivots, and levers.	C768		3C1; P-2	3C1; P-2

Time off_____

Time on_____

Total time_____

Materials Required

- Vehicle/simulator
- Parts trays
- Manufacturer-specific tools

Some Safety Issues to Consider

- Castings and machined parts may have sharp edges. Handle these parts with care.
- Comply with personal and environmental safety practices associated with clothing; eye protection; hand tools; power equipment; proper ventilation; and the handling, storage, and disposal of chemicals/materials in accordance with local, state, and federal safety and environmental regulations.

Performance Standard

0–No exposure: No information or practice provided during the program; complete training required

1–Exposure only: General information provided with no practice time; close supervision needed; additional training required

2–Limited practice: Has practiced job during training program; additional training required to develop skill

3–Moderately skilled: Has performed job independently during training program; limited additional training may be required

4–Skilled: Can perform job independently with no additional training

AST 3C1 | **MAST** 3C1

Time off_____

Time on_____

Total time_____

CDX Tasksheet Number: C768

1. Research the procedure and specifications for inspecting, adjusting, and installing shift linkages in the appropriate service information.

   a. **List or print off and attach to this sheet the procedure for adjusting the shift linkages, if applicable:**

2. **Following the specified procedure, inspect the shift linkage components. List your observations for each component.**

   a. **Shift linkages:**

   b. **Brackets:**

   c. **Bushings:**

   d. **Cables:**

     e. **Pivots:**

     f. **Levers:**

3. **Following the specified procedure, adjust each shift linkage. List your observations:**

4. Have your supervisor/instructor verify satisfactory completion of this procedure, any observations found, and any necessary action(s) recommended.

Performance Rating

CDX Tasksheet Number: C768

0	1	2	3	4

Supervisor/instructor signature _____ Date _____

Manual Drive Train and Axles: Drive Shaft, Half Shaft, Universal, and Constant-Velocity Joint Diagnosis and Repair

Student/intern information:

Name _____ Date _____ Class _____

Vehicle used for this activity:

Year _____ Make _____ Model _____

Odometer _____ VIN _____

<table>
<tr><th>Learning Objective/Task</th><th>CDX Tasksheet Number</th><th>2013 MLR NATEF Reference Number; Priority Level</th><th>2013 AST NATEF Reference Number; Priority Level</th><th>2013 MAST NATEF Reference Number; Priority Leve</th></tr>
<tr><td>Diagnose constant-velocity (CV) joint noise and vibration concerns; determine necessary action.</td><td>C132</td><td></td><td>3D1; P-1</td><td>3D1; P-1</td></tr>
<tr><td>Inspect, service, and replace shafts, yokes, boots, and universal/CV joints.</td><td>C849</td><td>3D2; P-2</td><td>3D4; P-1</td><td>3D4; P-1</td></tr>
<tr><td>Inspect, remove, and replace front wheel drive (FWD) bearings, hubs, and seals.</td><td>C134</td><td>3D1; P-2</td><td>3D3; P-1</td><td>3D3; P-1</td></tr>
<tr><td>Diagnose universal joint noise and vibration concerns; perform necessary action.</td><td>C133</td><td></td><td>3D2; P-2</td><td>3D2; P-2</td></tr>
<tr><td>Check shaft balance and phasing; measure shaft runout; measure and adjust driveline angles.</td><td>C779</td><td></td><td>3D5; P-2</td><td>3D5; P-2</td></tr>
</table>

Time off _____

Time on _____

Total time _____

Materials Required

- Vehicle hoist
- Dial indicator
- Driveline angle gauge
- Hydraulic press
- U-joint press or equivalent
- Torque wrench
- Manufacturer-specific tools

Some Safety Issues to Consider

- Diagnosis of this fault may require test-driving the vehicle on the school grounds. Attempt this task only with full permission from your instructor and follow all the guidelines exactly.
- Vehicle hoists are important tools that increase productivity and make the job easier. However, they can also cause severe injury or death if used improperly. Make sure you follow the manufacturer's operation procedures. Also, make sure you have your supervisor's/instructor's permission to use any particular type of lifting equipment.

- Lug nuts must always be tightened to the proper torque. Always use a properly calibrated torque wrench.
- CV joints may contain grease made with lead, which can be harmful to your health. Avoid getting it on your skin and hands. Wash your hands thoroughly before eating.
- Comply with personal and environmental safety practices associated with clothing; eye protection; hand tools; power equipment; proper ventilation; and the handling, storage, and disposal of chemicals/materials in accordance with local, state, and federal safety and environmental regulations

Performance Standard

0—No exposure: No information or practice provided during the program; complete training required

1—Exposure only: General information provided with no practice time; close supervision needed; additional training required

2—Limited practice: Has practiced job during training program; additional training required to develop skill

3—Moderately skilled: Has performed job independently during training program; limited additional training may be required

4—Skilled: Can perform job independently with no additional training

Diagnose constant-velocity (CV) joint noise and vibration concerns; determine necessary action.

AST 3D1   **MAST** 3D1

Time off_____

Time on_____

Total time_____

CDX Tasksheet Number: C132

1. **List the CV-related customer concern:**

2. With your instructor's permission, test-drive the vehicle in an open area on a firm surface. Turn the steering wheel to its maximum lock position and drive smoothly in a tight circle. Listen for a distinctive clicking or knocking noise coming from one or more corners of the vehicle. **List your observations:**

3. Repeat step 2, turning the steering wheel in the other direction while driving in a tight circle. **List your observations:**

4. Safely raise and secure the vehicle on a hoist and visually inspect the CV joint boots for splits and tears, or signs of grease leakage from the boot or joint housing. **List your observations:**

5. Check for excessive play or binding in the inboard and outboard CV joints. **List your observations:**

6. **Determine any necessary action(s):**

7. Have your supervisor/instructor verify satisfactory completion of this procedure, any observations found, and any necessary action(s) recommended.

Performance Rating

CDX Tasksheet Number: C132

0	1	2	3	4

Supervisor/instructor signature _____ Date _____

▶ **TASK** Inspect, service, and replace shafts, yokes, boots, and universal/CV joints.

MLR 3D2 **AST** 3D4 **MAST** 3D4

Time off_____

Time on_____

Total time_____

CDX Tasksheet Number: C849

1. Research the procedure and specifications to inspect, service, and replace shafts, yokes, boots, and universal/CV joints in the appropriate service information.

    a. **List any special tools required to perform this task:**

    b. **List any specific precautions when performing this task:**

    c. **List or print off and attach to this sheet the procedure for servicing universal/CV joints, shafts, and boots:**

2. **If not already done, safely raise and support the vehicle on a hoist and inspect the half shafts and boots. List your observations:**

3. Following the specified procedure, remove the worn half shaft(s).

4. With your instructor's permission, disassemble the half shaft(s) following the specified procedure.

5. **Clean and inspect all parts. List your observations for each.**

    a. **Shaft(s):**

    b. **Yoke(s):**

   c. Boots (and clamps):

   d. CV joint(s) (including any balls or rollers):

6. Determine any necessary action(s):

7. Have your supervisor/instructor verify disassembly and your observations.
Supervisor's/instructor's initials: _____

> **NOTE** You may want to continue on with the next task once the half shaft(s) are reassembled and removed. If so, return here to complete this task once you are ready to reinstall the half shaft(s).

8. Perform any necessary actions to service the half shaft(s) and reinstall them in the vehicle following the specified procedure. **List your observations:**

> **NOTE** Be sure to tighten all fasteners to the proper torque.

9. Have your supervisor/instructor verify satisfactory completion of this procedure, any observations found, and any necessary action(s) recommended.

Performance Rating

CDX Tasksheet Number: C849

0	1	2	3	4

Supervisor/instructor signature _____ Date _____

Inspect, remove, and replace front wheel drive (FWD) bearings, hubs, and seals.

Time off_____

Time on_____

Total time_____

CDX Tasksheet Number: C134

1. Research the procedure and specifications for removing and replacing the FWD wheel bearing, hub, and seals in the appropriate service information.

   a. List any special tools required to perform this task:

   b. List any specific precautions when performing this task:

   c. List or print off and attach to this sheet the procedure for replacing the wheel bearing, seal, and hub:

2. If not already done, safely raise and support the vehicle on a hoist and remove the wheel bearing following the specified procedure.

3. Inspect the bearing, shaft, and hub for damage or wear. **List your observations:**

4. **Determine any necessary action(s):**

5. Have your supervisor/instructor verify removal and your observations. **Supervisor's/instructor's initials:** _____

6. Following the specified procedure, replace the wheel bearing, seal, and hub. Make sure the bearing is fully seated and retained in the hub. **List your observations:**

> **NOTE** Be sure to tighten all fasteners to the proper torque.

7. Have your supervisor/instructor verify satisfactory completion of this procedure, any observations found, and any necessary action(s) recommended.

Performance Rating

CDX Tasksheet Number: C134

0	1	2	3	4

Supervisor/instructor signature _____ Date _____

► TASK Diagnose universal joint noise and vibration concerns; perform necessary action.

AST 3D2 **MAST** 3D2

Time off_____

Time on_____

Total time_____

CDX Tasksheet Number: C133

Vehicle used for this activity:

Year _____ Make _____ Model _____

Odometer _____ VIN _____

1. **List the universal joint-related customer concern:**

2. With your instructor's permission, test-drive the vehicle in an open area on a firm surface. Listen for a distinctive squeaking noise or clunking sound coming from under the vehicle, which is usually worse at low speeds. Universal joints can also cause a vibration at low speeds due to intermittent binding, or at higher speeds due to causing the drive shaft to be located off center. **List your observations:**

3. Safely raise and secure the vehicle on a hoist and inspect the universal joints for looseness, wear, and damage. **List your observations:**

   NOTE Make sure the parking brake is not applied and the transmission is in neutral. This will allow you to turn the drive shaft to check it for play and binding in various positions.

4. **Determine any necessary action(s):**

5. Have your supervisor/instructor verify your observations and diagnosis.
   Supervisor's/instructor's initials: _____

© 2015 Jones & Bartlett Learning, LLC, an Ascend Learning Company

6. Perform any necessary action(s) following the specified procedure.
List your observations:

NOTE Be sure to tighten all fasteners to the proper torque.

---

7. Have your supervisor/instructor verify satisfactory completion of this procedure, any observations found, and any necessary action(s) recommended.

Performance Rating

CDX Tasksheet Number: C133

0	1	2	3	4

Supervisor/instructor signature _____ Date _____

Check shaft balance and phasing; measure shaft runout; measure and adjust driveline angles.

AST
3D5

MAST
3D5

Time off_____

Time on_____

Total time_____

CDX Tasksheet Number: C779

Vehicle used for this activity:

Year _____ Make _____ Model_____

Odometer_____ VIN_____

1. Research the procedure and specifications for inspecting, measuring, and adjusting the driveline balance, phasing, and angles in the appropriate service information.

   a. List any special tools required to perform this task:

   b. List any specific precautions when performing this task:

   c. List any specifications for balance, phasing, runout, and driveline angles:

   d. List or print off and attach to this sheet the procedure for inspecting, measuring, and adjusting the driveline balance, phasing, and angles:

2. Safely raise and secure the vehicle on a hoist. Make sure the parking brake is released and the transmission is in neutral.

3. Check the drive shaft for phasing. List your observation(s):

4. Measure drive shaft runout: _____ in/mm

5. Measure driveline angles.

    a. Front: _____ degrees

    b. Center (if specified): _____ degrees

    c. Rear: _____ degrees

6. Check the drive shaft for balance. List your observation(s):

7. Determine any necessary action(s):

8. Have your supervisor/instructor verify satisfactory completion of this procedure, any observations found, and any necessary action(s) recommended.

Performance Rating

CDX Tasksheet Number: C779

0	1	2	3	4

Supervisor/instructor signature _____ Date _____

Manual Drive Train and Axles: Drive Axle Diagnosis and Repair
Ring and Pinion Gears and Differential Case Assembly

Student/intern information:

Name _____ Date _____ Class _____

Vehicle used for this activity:

Year _____ Make _____ Model _____

Odometer _____ VIN _____

Learning Objective/Task	CDX Tasksheet Number	2013 MLR NATEF Reference Number; Priority Level	2013 AST NATEF Reference Number; Priority Level	2013 MAST NATEF Reference Number; Priority Level
• Check and adjust differential housing fluid level.	C911	3E2; P-1	3E1:2; P-1	3E1:2; P-1
• Drain and refill differential housing.	C912	3E3; P-1	3E1:3; P-1	3E1:3; P-1
• Clean and inspect differential housing; check for leaks; inspect housing vent.	C785	3E1, P-2	3E1:1, P-2	3E1:1, P-2
• Inspect and replace companion flange and pinion seal; measure companion flange runout.	C889		3E1:4; P-2	3E1:5; P-2
• Diagnose noise and vibration concerns; determine necessary action.	C138			3E1:4; P-2
• Inspect ring gear and measure runout; determine necessary action.	C780			3E1:6; P-3
• Remove, inspect, and reinstall drive pinion and ring gear, spacers, sleeves, and bearings.	C890			3E1:7; P-3
• Disassemble, inspect, measure, and adjust or replace differential pinion gears (spiders), shaft, side gears, side bearings, thrust washers, and case.	C147			3E1:12; P-3
• Measure and adjust drive pinion depth.	C781			3E1:8; P-3
• Measure and adjust drive pinion bearing preload.	C782			3E1:9; P-3
• Reassemble and reinstall differential case assembly; measure runout; determine necessary action.	C148			3E1:13; P-3
• Measure and adjust side bearing preload and ring and pinion gear total backlash and backlash variation on a differential carrier assembly (threaded cup or shim types).	C145			3E1:10; P-3
• Check ring and pinion tooth contact patterns; perform necessary action.	C783			3E1:11; P-3

Time off_____

Time on_____

Total time_____

Some Safety Issues to Consider

- Vehicle hoists are important tools that increase productivity and make the job easier. However, they can also cause severe injury or death if used improperly. Make sure you follow the manufacturer's operation procedures. Also, make sure you have your supervisor's/instructor's permission to use any particular type of lifting equipment.
- When running any vehicles in the shop, make sure you use the shop's exhaust ventilation system to discharge all exhaust gas safely outside.
- Diagnosis of this fault may require test-driving the vehicle on the school grounds. Attempt this task only with full permission from your instructor and follow all the guidelines exactly.
- Castings and machined parts may have sharp edges. Handle these parts with care.
- Comply with personal and environmental safety practices associated with clothing; eye protection; hand tools; power equipment; proper ventilation; and the handling, storage, and disposal of chemicals/materials in accordance with local, state, and federal safety and environmental regulations.

Performance Standard

0–No exposure: No information or practice provided during the program; complete training required

1–Exposure only: General information provided with no practice time; close supervision needed; additional training required

2–Limited practice: Has practiced job during training program; additional training required to develop skill

3–Moderately skilled: Has performed job independently during training program; limited additional training may be required

4–Skilled: Can perform job independently with no additional training

MLR 3E2 **AST** 3E1:2 **MAST** 3E1:2

Time off_____

Time on_____

Total time_____

CDX Tasksheet Number: C911

1. List the drive axle designation for this vehicle: _____

2. Research the following specifications for this vehicle in the appropriate service information.

   a. Fluid type: _____

   b. Fluid capacity: _____ qt/lt

   c. How is the fluid level checked?

   d. Are any additives required? Yes: _____ No: _____

      i. If yes, what additive? _____

3. Safely raise and secure the vehicle on a hoist.

4. **Check the fluid level and adjust as necessary with the proper fluid. List your observation(s):**

5. Inspect the drive axle assembly for leaks.

   a. **Identify and list the source of any leak(s):**

6. **Inspect the condition of the fluid. Look for contaminants, metal shavings, and degraded fluid condition. List your observation(s):**

7. **Determine any necessary action(s):**

8. Have your supervisor/instructor verify satisfactory completion of this procedure, any observations found, and any necessary action(s) recommended.

Performance Rating

CDX Tasksheet Number: C911

0	1	2	3	4

Supervisor/instructor signature _____ Date _____

► **TASK** Drain and refill differential housing.

Time off_____

Time on_____

Total time_____

CDX Tasksheet Number: C912

Vehicle used for this activity:

Year _____ Make _____ Model_____

Odometer_____ VIN_____

1. **Research the following specifications for this vehicle in the appropriate service information.**

   a. **Fluid type:**_____

   b. **Fluid capacity:** _____ qt/lt

   c. **Differential fluid service interval:** _____ mi/km

   d. **How is fluid drained from this differential housing?**

2. Safely raise and secure the vehicle on a hoist.

3. **Following the specified procedure, drain the fluid from the differential housing. List your observations:**

4. Have your supervisor/instructor verify removal of the fluid, and your observations. **Supervisor's/instructor initials:** _____

5. Replace the drain plug or rear cover making sure the plug or bolts are tightened properly.

6. Fill the differential housing to the proper level with the specified lubricant.

   NOTE Some differentials require special additives. Always check the service information to determine the proper fluid or additives.

7. Have your supervisor/instructor verify satisfactory completion of this procedure, any observations found, and any necessary action(s) recommended.

Performance Rating

CDX Tasksheet Number: C912

0	1	2	3	4

Supervisor/instructor signature _____ Date _____

Clean and inspect differential housing; check for leaks; inspect housing vent.

MLR
3E1

AST
3E1:1

MAST
3E1:1

Time off_____

Time on_____

Total time_____

CDX Tasksheet Number: C785

Vehicle used for this activity:

Year _____ Make _____ Model_____

Odometer_____ VIN_____

1. **Research the procedure and specifications for cleaning and inspecting the differential housing and vent in the appropriate service information.**

   a. **Specified lubricant and/or additive:** _____
   b. **Differential lubricant capacity:** _____ qt/lt
   c. **Differential fluid service interval:** _____ mi/km
   d. **How is the lubricant level checked in this vehicle?**

2. Safely raise and secure the vehicle on a hoist.

3. **Inspect the differential housing for leaks or damage. List your observation(s):**

4. Following the specified procedure, drain the differential housing into a clean drain pan. Inspect any residue and debris in the bottom of the drain pan and the differential housing. **List your observation(s):**

5. Inspect the vent and make sure it is clear of any obstructions, and connected to its vent hose if equipped. **List your observations:**

6. **Determine any necessary action(s):**

7. Have your supervisor/instructor verify your answers.
   Supervisor's/instructor's initials: _____

8. **Following the specified procedure, refill the differential housing to the proper level with the specified lubricant and/or additive. Replace all fill and drain plugs and tighten them to the proper torque. List your observation(s):**

9. Have your supervisor/instructor verify satisfactory completion of this procedure, any observations found, and any necessary action(s) recommended.

Performance Rating

CDX Tasksheet Number: C785

0	1	2	3	4

Supervisor/instructor signature _____ Date _____

Inspect and replace companion flange and pinion seal; measure companion flange runout.

Time off_____

Time on_____

Total time_____

CDX Tasksheet Number: C889

Vehicle used for this activity:

Year _____ Make _____ Model_____

Odometer_____ VIN_____

1. Research the procedure and specifications for inspecting and replacing the companion flange and pinion seal in the appropriate service information.

   a. **Maximum allowable companion flange runout (if specified):** _____ in/mm
   b. **Companion flange nut torque:** _____ ft-lb/Nm
   c. **Drive shaft-to-drive axle bolt torque:** _____ ft-lb/Nm

2. Safely raise and secure the vehicle on a hoist.

3. Perform an initial visual inspection of the companion flange and pinion seal. **List your observation(s):**

4. Following the specified procedure, remove the drive shaft.

5. **Measure the companion flange runout, if possible:** _____ in/mm

6. Following the specified procedure, remove the companion flange and pinion seal. Inspect the following components for damage or wear.

   a. **Companion flange:**

   b. **Pinion seal:**

   c. **Pinion shaft sealing surface:**

7. Determine any necessary action(s):

8. Have your supervisor/instructor verify removal and your observations.
Supervisor's/instructor's initials: _____

> **NOTE** If you are tasked with disassembling the drive axle assembly, continue on with the following tasks and return here when you are ready to reinstall the pinion seal and companion flange.

9. Following the specified procedure, replace the pinion seal and companion flange. Be sure to properly tighten the companion flange nut. Once torqued, check the turning effort required to rotate the companion flange. **List your observation(s):**

10. Re-measure the companion flange runout: _____ **in/mm**

    a. If the runout is not within specifications, inform your instructor.

11. Reinstall the drive shaft and any other removed components. Torque all fasteners to specifications.

12. Have your supervisor/instructor verify satisfactory completion of this procedure, any observations found, and any necessary action(s) recommended.

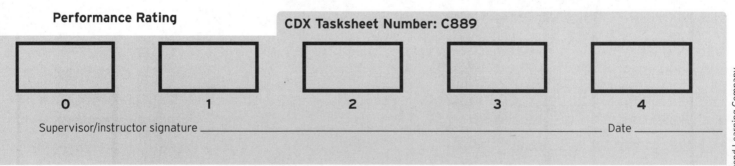

Performance Rating

CDX Tasksheet Number: C889

0	1	2	3	4

Supervisor/instructor signature _____ Date _____

Time off_____

Time on_____

Total time_____

CDX Tasksheet Number: C138

1. **List the drive axle noise and vibration-related customer concern:**

2. Research the concern in the appropriate service information.

    a. **List the possible causes of the concern:**

    b. **List, or print off and attach to this sheet, the specified procedure for diagnosing the concern:**

3. Perform the appropriate tests, following the specified procedure.
   List your observation/s:

4. **List the cause of the concern:**

5. **Determine any necessary action/s to correct the fault:**

6. Have your supervisor/instructor verify satisfactory completion of this procedure, any observations found, and any necessary action/s recommended.

Performance Rating

CDX Tasksheet Number: C138

0	1	2	3	4

Supervisor/instructor signature _____ Date _____

► **TASK** Inspect ring gear and measure runout; determine necessary action.

MAST
3E1:6

Time off_____

Time on_____

Total time_____

CDX Tasksheet Number: C780

Vehicle used for this activity:

Year _____ Make _____ Model_____

Odometer_____ VIN_____

1. Research the procedure and specifications for inspecting and measuring ring gear runout in the appropriate service information.

   a. **Maximum allowable ring gear runout: _____ in/mm**
   b. **Type of drive axle: Integral / Unitized or Removable Carrier (Circle one)**
   c. **Does this vehicle have a removable rear differential cover? Yes / No (Circle one)**

2. Following the specified procedure, remove the appropriate components to gain access to the ring gear assembly.

3. **Visually inspect the ring gear for wear and damage. List your observation/s:**

4. **Using a dial indicator, measure the ring gear runout: _____ in/mm**

5. **Determine any necessary action/s:**

6. Have your supervisor/instructor verify satisfactory completion of this procedure, any observations found, and any necessary action/s recommended.

Performance Rating

CDX Tasksheet Number: C780

0	1	2	3	4

Supervisor/instructor signature _____ Date _____

▶ **TASK** Remove, inspect, and reinstall drive pinion and ring gear,
spacers, sleeves, and bearings.

MAST
3E1:7

CDX Tasksheet Number: C890

1. Research the procedure and specifications for removing, inspecting, and reinstalling the drive pinion and ring gear in the appropriate service information.

   a. **Ring gear bolt torque:** _____ **ft-lb/Nm**

   b. **List any special tools required for this task:**

   c. **List, or print off and attach to this sheet, the steps to perform this task:**

2. Following the specified procedure, remove the drive pinion and ring gear.

3. Inspect the following components for wear or damage. **List your observations for each.**

   a. **Drive pinion:**

   b. **Ring gear:**

   c. **Spacers and sleeves:**

   d. **Bearings:**

4. Determine any necessary action/s:

5. Have your supervisor/instructor verify satisfactory completion of this procedure, any observations found, and any necessary action/s recommended.

Performance Rating

CDX Tasksheet Number: C890

☐	☐	☐	☐	☐
0	1	2	3	4

Supervisor/instructor signature _____ Date _____

CDX Tasksheet Number: C147

1. Research the procedure and specifications for disassembling, inspecting, measuring, and replacing the differential gears and associated parts.

    a. List any measurements or specifications for this task:

    b. List any special tools required for this task:

    c. List, or print off and attach to this sheet, the steps for performing this task:

2. Following the specified procedure, disassemble the differential pinion gears and associated parts.

3. Inspect and measure the following parts. List your observations for each.

    a. Differential pinion gears:

    b. Shaft:

    c. Side gears:

d. Side bearings:

e. Thrust washers:

f. Case:

4. Determine any necessary action/s:

5. Have your supervisor/instructor verify satisfactory completion of this procedure, any observations found, and any necessary action/s recommended.

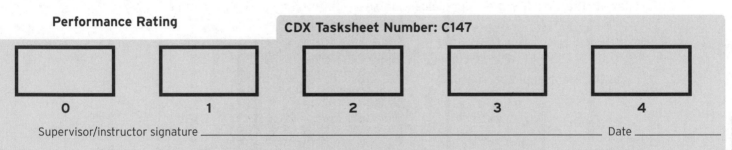

Performance Rating

CDX Tasksheet Number: C147

| 0 | 1 | 2 | 3 | 4 |

Supervisor/instructor signature _____ Date _____

MAST
3E1:8

Time off_____

Time on_____

Total time_____

CDX Tasksheet Number: C781

1. Research the procedure and specifications for measuring and adjusting drive pinion depth in the appropriate service information.

   a. **Specified drive pinion depth:** _____ **in/mm**

   b. **How is the drive pinion depth adjusted on this drive axle?**

   c. **List any special tools required for this task:**

   d. **List, or print off and attach to this sheet, the steps to perform this task:**

2. **Following the specified procedure, measure the drive pinion depth:** _____ **in/mm**

   a. Is this within specifications? **Yes:** _____ **No:** _____

3. If outside of specifications, adjust the drive pinion depth.

   a. **Final measurement:** _____ **in/mm**

4. Have your supervisor/instructor verify satisfactory completion of this procedure, any observations found, and any necessary action/s recommended.

Performance Rating

CDX Tasksheet Number: C781

0	1	2	3	4

Supervisor/instructor signature _____ Date _____

MAST
3E1:9

Time off_____

Time on_____

CDX Tasksheet Number: C782

Total time_____

1. Research the procedure and specifications for measuring and adjusting drive pinion preload in the appropriate service information.

    a. **Specified drive pinion preload:** _____ **in-lb/Nm**
    b. **How is the drive pinion preload adjusted on this drive axle?**

    c. **List any special tools required for this task:**

2. Following the specified procedure, measure the drive pinion preload: _____ **in-lb/Nm**

    a. Is this within specifications? **Yes:** _____ **No:** _____

3. If outside of specifications, adjust the drive pinion preload.

    a. **Final measurement:** _____ **in-lb/Nm**

4. Have your supervisor/instructor verify satisfactory completion of this procedure, any observations found, and any necessary action/s recommended.

Performance Rating

CDX Tasksheet Number: C782

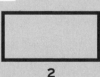 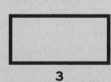 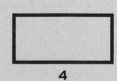

| 0 | 1 | 2 | 3 | 4 |

Supervisor/instructor signature _____ Date _____

Reassemble and reinstall differential case assembly;
measure runout; determine necessary action.

MAST
3E1:13

Time off_____

Time on_____

Total time_____

CDX Tasksheet Number: C148

1. Research the procedure and specifications for reassembling the differential case assembly in the appropriate service information.

    a. Specified maximum differential case runout: _____ **in/mm**
    b. **List, or print off and attach to this sheet, any other specifications for this task:**

2. Following the specified procedure, reassemble and reinstall the differential case assembly.

3. Measure the differential case runout: _____ **in/mm**

4. **Determine any necessary action/s:**

5. Have your supervisor/instructor verify satisfactory completion of this procedure, any observations found, and any necessary action/s recommended.

Performance Rating

CDX Tasksheet Number: C148

| 0 | 1 | 2 | 3 | 4 |

Supervisor/instructor signature _____ Date _____

Measure and adjust side bearing preload and ring and pinion gear total backlash and backlash variation on a differential carrier assembly (threaded cup or shim types).

MAST
3E1:10

Time off_____

Time on_____

Total time_____

CDX Tasksheet Number: C145

1. Research the procedure and specifications to measure and adjust backlash on a differential carrier assembly in the appropriate service information.

    a. **Side bearing preload:** _____ **in-lb/Nm**
    b. **Ring and pinion gear total backlash:** _____ **in/mm**
    c. **Backlash variation:** _____ **in/mm**
    d. **List, or print off and attach to this sheet, the steps to perform this task:**

2. **Following the specified procedure, perform the following measurements.**

    a. **Side bearing preload:** _____ **in-lb/Nm**
    b. **Ring and pinion gear total backlash:** _____ **in/mm**
    c. **Backlash variation:** _____ **in/mm**

3. **Determine any necessary action/s:**

4. If outside of specifications, adjust the preload and backlash. List your final measurements.

    a. **Side bearing preload:** _____ **in-lb/Nm**
    b. **Ring and pinion gear total backlash:** _____ **in/mm**
    c. **Backlash variation:** _____ **in/mm**

5. Have your supervisor/instructor verify satisfactory completion of this procedure, any observations found, and any necessary action/s recommended.

Performance Rating

CDX Tasksheet Number: C145

0	1	2	3	4

Supervisor/instructor signature _____ Date _____

Check ring and pinion tooth contact patterns; perform necessary action.

MAST
3E1:11

Time off_____

Time on_____

Total time_____

CDX Tasksheet Number: C783

1. Research the procedure and specifications to check and correct ring and pinion gear tooth patterns in the appropriate service information.

   a. **Draw, or print off and attach to this sheet, the correct ring and pinion gear tooth pattern for both the drive and coast sides:**

2. **Following the specified procedure, check the ring and pinion gear tooth patterns. List your observations:**

3. **Determine any necessary action/s:**

4. Have your supervisor/instructor verify your observations. **Supervisor/instructor's initials:** _____

5. **Perform any necessary action/s. List your observation/s:**

6. **Do the patterns meet specifications? Yes:** _____ **No:** _____

7. Have your supervisor/instructor verify satisfactory completion of this procedure, any observations found, and any necessary action/s recommended.

Performance Rating

CDX Tasksheet Number: C783

0	1	2	3	4

Supervisor/instructor signature _____ Date _____

Limited Slip Differential

Student/intern information:

Name _____ Date _____ Class _____

Vehicle used for this activity:

Year _____ Make _____ Model_____

Odometer_____ VIN_____

Learning Objective/Task	CDX Tasksheet Number	2013 MLR NATEF Reference Number; Priority Level	2013 AST NATEF Reference Number; Priority Level	2013 MAST NATEF Reference Number; Priority Level
• Diagnose noise, slippage, and chatter concerns; determine necessary action.	C784			3E2:1; P-3
• Measure rotating torque; determine necessary action.	C786			3E2:2; P-3

Time off_____

Time on_____

Total time_____

Materials Required

- Drive axle with limited slip differential
- Specified lubricant and/or additive
- Drain pan
- Torque wrenches
- Manufacturer-specific tools

Some Safety Issues to Consider

- Vehicle hoists are important tools that increase productivity and make the job easier. However, they can also cause severe injury or death if used improperly. Make sure you follow the manufacturer's operation procedures. Also, make sure you have your supervisor's/instructor's permission to use any particular type of lifting equipment.
- When running any vehicles in the shop, make sure you use the shop's exhaust ventilation system to discharge all exhaust gas safely outside.
- Diagnosis of this fault may require test-driving the vehicle on the school grounds. Attempt this task only with full permission from your instructor and follow all the guidelines exactly.
- Castings and machined parts may have sharp edges. Handle these parts with care.
- Comply with personal and environmental safety practices associated with clothing; eye protection; hand tools; power equipment; proper ventilation; and the handling, storage, and disposal of chemicals/materials in accordance with local, state, and federal safety and environmental regulations.

Performance Standard

0—No exposure: No information or practice provided during the program; complete training required

1—Exposure only: General information provided with no practice time; close supervision needed; additional training required

2—Limited practice: Has practiced job during training program; additional training required to develop skill

3—Moderately skilled: Has performed job independently during training program; limited additional training may be required

4—Skilled: Can perform job independently with no additional training

Diagnose noise, slippage, and chatter concerns; determine necessary action.

MAST
3E2:1

CDX Tasksheet Number: C784

1. **List the limited slip differential customer concern:**

2. **Research the procedure and specifications to diagnose noise, slipping, and chatter concerns in the appropriate service information.**

   a. **List or print off and attach to this sheet the steps to diagnose this concern:**

   b. **List the specified lubricant and/or additive:** _____

3. **Following the specified procedure, diagnose the customer concern. List your tests and results:**

4. **List the cause(s) of the concern:**

5. **List the necessary action(s) to correct the concern:**

6. **Have your supervisor/instructor verify satisfactory completion of this procedure, any observations found, and any necessary action(s) recommended.**

Performance Rating

CDX Tasksheet Number: C784

0	1	2	3	4

Supervisor/instructor signature _____ Date _____

MAST
3E2:2

CDX Tasksheet Number: C786

1. Research the procedure and specifications for measuring the rotating torque on the limited slip differential in the appropriate service information.

   a. **Specified breakaway torque:** _____ **ft-lb/Nm**
   b. **List, or print off and attach to this sheet, the steps for measuring the rotating torque:**

2. **Following the specified procedure, measure the rotating torque:** _____ **ft-lb/Nm**

   a. **Is this within specifications? Yes / No (Circle one)**

3. **Determine any necessary action/s:**

4. Have your supervisor/instructor verify satisfactory completion of this procedure, any observations found, and any necessary action/s recommended.

Performance Rating

CDX Tasksheet Number: C786

0	1	2	3	4

Supervisor/instructor signature _____ Date _____

Drive Axle Shaft

Student/intern information:

Name _____ Date _____ Class _____

Vehicle used for this activity:

Year _____ Make _____ Model _____

Odometer _____ VIN _____

Learning Objective/Task	CDX Tasksheet Number	2013 MLR NATEF Reference Number; Priority Level	2013 AST NATEF Reference Number; Priority Level	2013 MAST NATEF Reference Number; Priority Level
• Diagnose drive axle shafts, bearings, and seals for noise, vibration, and fluid leakage concerns; determine necessary action.	C153			3E3:5; P-2
• Inspect and replace drive axle wheel studs.	C154	3E1:1; P-2	3E2:1; P-1	3E3:1; P-1
• Measure drive axle flange runout and shaft end play; determine necessary action.	C850		3E2:4; P-2	3E3:4; P-2
• Remove and replace drive axle shafts.	C155		3E2:2; P-1	3E3:2; P-1
• Inspect and replace drive axle shaft seals, bearings, and retainers.	C156		3E2:3; P-2	3E3:3; P-2

Time off _____

Time on _____

Total time _____

Materials Required

- Dial indicator
- Stethoscope
- Hydraulic press
- Seal puller
- Torque wrenches
- Manufacturer-specific tools

Some Safety Issues to Consider

- Diagnosis of this fault may require test-driving the vehicle on the school grounds. Attempt this task only with full permission from your instructor and follow all the guidelines exactly.
- Vehicle hoists are important tools that increase productivity and make the job easier. However, they can also cause severe injury or death if used improperly. Make sure you follow the manufacturer's operation procedures. Also, make sure you have your supervisor's/instructor's permission to use any particular type of lifting equipment.
- Lug nuts must always be tightened to the proper torque. Always use a properly calibrated torque wrench.
- This task may require you to run the vehicle on the hoist. Attempt this only with your instructor's permission.
- Comply with personal and environmental safety practices associated with clothing; eye protection; hand tools; power equipment; proper ventilation; and the handling, storage, and disposal of chemicals/materials in accordance with local, state, and federal safety and environmental regulations.

Performance Standard

0—No exposure: No information or practice provided during the program; complete training required

1—Exposure only: General information provided with no practice time; close supervision needed; additional training required

2—Limited practice: Has practiced job during training program; additional training required to develop skill

3—Moderately skilled: Has performed job independently during training program; limited additional training may be required

4—Skilled: Can perform job independently with no additional training

▶ **TASK** Diagnose drive axle shafts, bearings, and seals for noise, vibration, and fluid leakage concerns; determine necessary action.

MAST
3E3:5

Time off_____

Time on_____

Total time_____

CDX Tasksheet Number: C153

1. **List the customer concern:**

2. With your instructor's permission, test-drive the vehicle in an open area with minimal noise on a smooth road surface. Listen for excessive noise while gradually increasing speed. **List your observation(s):**

> **NOTE** A worn wheel bearing will usually make noise in a manner proportional to speed. When you are traveling at a speed that is making the noise, it is good practice to put the vehicle in neutral and allow the vehicle to coast. If the wheel bearing(s) is (are) worn, this will cause no considerable difference in sound. Also, try different transmission gears to rule out transmission- and clutch-related noises.

3. Safely raise and secure the vehicle on a hoist.

4. Perform a visual inspection for obvious damage or leaks, paying particular attention to the brake backing plates and center differential. **List your observation(s):**

5. With your instructor's permission, run the vehicle in gear on the hoist while listening to the wheel bearings with a stethoscope. Make sure the vehicle is very secure on the hoist. **List your observation(s):**

6. **Determine any necessary action(s):**

7. Have your supervisor/instructor verify satisfactory completion of this procedure, any observations found, and any necessary action(s) recommended.

Performance Rating

0	1	2	3	4

Supervisor/instructor signature _____ Date _____

Inspect and replace drive axle shaft wheel studs.

MLR	AST	MAST
3E1:1	3E2:1	3E3:1

Time off_____

Time on_____

Total time_____

CDX Tasksheet Number: C154

Vehicle used for this activity:

Year _____ Make _____ Model_____

Odometer_____ VIN_____

1. Research the procedure and specifications for replacing the axle shaft wheel studs in the appropriate service information.

    a. There are generally two standard procedures for replacing wheel studs. One is to remove the hub from the vehicle and use a hydraulic press to remove and install the studs. The other is to use a hammer to drive out the old stud, and then use washers and the flat side of the lug nut to draw the new stud into the hub. **Which method does the service information describe for this vehicle?**

    b. **List any special tools or procedures for this task:**

    c. **Lug nut torque: _____ ft-lb/Nm**

2. Safely raise and secure the vehicle on a hoist.

3. Remove the wheel assembly and inspect the lug nuts and wheel studs. **List your observations and any necessary actions:**

4. Have your supervisor/instructor verify your observations. **Supervisor's/instructor's initials: _____**

5. Remove the damaged wheel stud(s) from the hub. **Supervisor's/instructor's initials: _____**

6. Install the new wheel stud(s) in the hub, following all service information instructions.

7. Have your supervisor/instructor verify satisfactory completion of this procedure, any observations found, and any necessary action(s) recommended.

Performance Rating

CDX Tasksheet Number: C154

0	1	2	3	4

Supervisor/instructor signature _____ Date _____

▶ TASK Measure drive axle flange runout and shaft end play; determine necessary action.

AST 3E2:4 **MAST** 3E3:4

Time off_____

Time on_____

Total time_____

CDX Tasksheet Number: C850

Vehicle used for this activity:

Year _____ Make _____ Model_____

Odometer_____ VIN_____

1. Research the procedure and specifications for measuring the drive axle flange and shaft end play in the appropriate service information.

   a. **Maximum specified axle flange runout:** _____ **in/mm**
   b. **Specified axle shaft end play:** _____ **in/mm**

2. Perform an initial visual inspection of the axle flange. **List your observation(s):**

3. **Following the specified procedure, measure the axle flange runout:** _____ **in/mm**

4. **Following the specified procedure, measure the axle shaft end play:** _____ **in/mm**

5. **Determine any necessary action(s):**

6. Have your supervisor/instructor verify satisfactory completion of this procedure, any observations found, and any necessary action(s) recommended.

Performance Rating

CDX Tasksheet Number: C850

0	1	2	3	4

Supervisor/instructor signature _____ Date _____

© 2015 Jones & Bartlett Learning, LLC, an Ascend Learning Company

AST 3E2:2   **MAST** 3E3:2

Time off_____

Time on_____

Total time_____

CDX Tasksheet Number: C155

Vehicle used for this activity:

Year _____ Make _____ Model _____

Odometer _____ VIN _____

1. Research the procedure and specifications for replacing the drive axle shafts in the appropriate service information.

   a. **Specified retainer bolt torque, if equipped:** _____ **ft-lb/Nm**

   b. **List or print off and attach to this sheet the steps to replace the axle shaft:**

2. **Following the specified procedure, remove the axle shaft. List your observation(s):**

3. Have your supervisor/instructor verify removal and your observations. Supervisor's/ instructor's initials: _____

   > **NOTE** You may want to skip ahead to the next task while the axle shaft is removed. Return here once that task is completed to reinstall the axle shaft.

4. Following the specified procedure, reinstall the axle shaft. Be sure to tighten all fasteners to the specified torque. **List your observation(s):**

5. Have your supervisor/instructor verify satisfactory completion of this procedure, any observations found, and any necessary action(s) recommended.

Performance Rating

CDX Tasksheet Number: C155

0	1	2	3	4

Supervisor/instructor signature _____ Date _____

► **TASK** Inspect and replace drive axle shaft seals, bearings, and retainers.

AST 3E2:3 | MAST 3E3:3

Time off_____

Time on_____

Total time_____

CDX Tasksheet Number: C156

Vehicle used for this activity:

Year _____ Make _____ Model_____

Odometer_____ VIN_____

1. Research the procedure and specifications for inspecting and replacing the seals, bearings, and retainers in the appropriate service information.

   a. List or print off and attach to this sheet the steps for performing this task:

2. **Following the specified procedure, inspect each component and list your observations.**

   a. Seal(s):

   b. Bearing(s):

   c. Retainer(s):

3. **Remove the bearing(s), seal(s), and retainer(s). List your observations:**

4. Have your supervisor/instructor verify removal and your observations. **Supervisor's/instructor's initials: _____**

5. Reinstall the bearing(s), seal(s), and retainer(s). **List your observations:**

6. Have your supervisor/instructor verify satisfactory completion of this procedure, any observations found, and any necessary action(s) recommended.

Performance Rating

CDX Tasksheet Number: C156

0	1	2	3	4

Supervisor/instructor signature _____ Date _____

Manual Drive Train and Axles: Four-Wheel Drive/All-Wheel Drive Component Diagnosis and Repair

---

Student/intern information:

Name _____ Date _____ Class _____

Vehicle used for this activity:

Year _____ Make _____ Model _____

Odometer _____ VIN _____

Learning Objective/Task	CDX Tasksheet Number	2013 MLR NATEF Reference Number; Priority Level	2013 AST NATEF Reference Number; Priority Level	2013 MAST NATEF Reference Number; Priority Level
• Diagnose noise, vibration, and unusual steering concerns; determine necessary action.	C787			3F5; P-3
• Inspect, adjust, and repair shifting controls (mechanical, electrical, and vacuum), bushings, mounts, levers, and brackets.	C788		3F1; P-3	3F1; P-3
• Disassemble, service, and reassemble transfer case and components.	C875			3F7; P-3
• Inspect front-wheel bearings and locking hubs.	C913	3F1; P-3		
• Inspect front-wheel bearings and locking hubs; perform necessary action.	C876		3F2; P-3	3F2; P-3
• Check for leaks at drive assembly seals and vents; check lube level.	C914	3F2; P-2	3F3; P-3	3F3; P-3
• Diagnose, test, adjust, and replace electrical/electronic components of four-wheel drive systems.	C878			3F6; P-3
• Identify concerns related to variations in tire circumference and/or final drive ratios.	C613		3F4; P-3	3F4; P-3

Time off_____

Time on_____

Total time_____

Materials Required

- 4WD/AWD-equipped vehicle
- Stethoscope
- Transmission jack
- Seal puller
- Wheel-bearing socket set
- Specified wheel-bearing grease
- Torque wrenches
- Tape measure
- DVOM
- Manufacturer-specific tools

Some Safety Issues to Consider

- Vehicle hoists are important tools that increase productivity and make the job easier. However, they can also cause severe injury or death if used improperly. Make sure you follow the manufacturer's operation procedures. Also, make sure you have your supervisor's/instructor's permission to use any particular type of lifting equipment.
- When running any vehicles in the shop, make sure you use the shop's exhaust ventilation system to discharge all exhaust gas safely outside.
- Diagnosis of this fault may require test-driving the vehicle on the school grounds. Attempt this task only with full permission from your instructor and follow all the guidelines exactly.
- Castings and machined parts may have sharp edges. Handle these parts with care.
- Comply with personal and environmental safety practices associated with clothing; eye protection; hand tools; power equipment; proper ventilation; and the handling, storage, and disposal of chemicals/materials in accordance with local, state, and federal safety and environmental regulations.

Performance Standard

0–No exposure: No information or practice provided during the program; complete training required

1–Exposure only: General information provided with no practice time; close supervision needed; additional training required

2–Limited practice: Has practiced job during training program; additional training required to develop skill

3–Moderately skilled: Has performed job independently during training program; limited additional training may be required

4–Skilled: Can perform job independently with no additional training

► **TASK** Diagnose noise, vibration, and unusual steering concerns; determine necessary action.

MAST
3F5

Time off_____

Time on_____

Total time_____

CDX Tasksheet Number: C787

1. List the 4-wheel drive/all-wheel drive steering-related customer concern:

2. Research the concern in the appropriate service information and list the possible causes:

3. Following the specified procedure, diagnose the fault. List your tests and observations:

4. List the cause of the noise, vibration, or steering concern:

5. Determine any necessary action(s) to correct the fault:

6. Have your supervisor/instructor verify satisfactory completion of this procedure, any observations found, and any necessary action(s) recommended.

Performance Rating

CDX Tasksheet Number: C787

0	1	2	3	4

Supervisor/instructor signature _____ Date _____

▶ **TASK** Inspect, adjust, and repair shifting controls (mechanical, electrical, and vacuum), bushings, mounts, levers, and brackets.

AST 3F1   MAST 3F1

CDX Tasksheet Number: C788

1. Research the procedure and specifications for inspecting, adjusting, and repairing the shifting controls in the appropriate service information.

   a. What type of controls does this vehicle use? _____

   b. List or print off and attach to this sheet the steps to inspect and adjust the four-wheel drive shift controls:

2. Safely raise and support the vehicle on a hoist and inspect the following. List your observations for each.

   a. Linkage:

   b. Bushings:

   c. Mounts:

   d. Levers:

   e. Brackets:

f. Electric controls (if equipped):

g. Vacuum controls (if equipped):

3. Determine any necessary action(s):

4. Have your supervisor/instructor verify satisfactory completion of this procedure, any observations found, and any necessary action(s) recommended.

Performance Rating

CDX Tasksheet Number: C788

0	1	2	3	4

Supervisor/instructor signature _____ Date _____

► **TASK** Disassemble, service, and reassemble transfer case and components.

MAST
3F7

Time off_____

Time on_____

Total time_____

CDX Tasksheet Number: C875

1. Research the procedure and specifications for disassembling, servicing, and reassembling the transfer case in the appropriate service information.

   a. List any special tools required for this task:

   b. List the flat rate time for this task: _____ hr

   c. List or print off and attach to this sheet the steps to disassemble and reassemble the transfer case:

2. Following the specified procedure, disassemble the transfer case.

   > **NOTE** It is good practice to lay out the components on a workbench or parts tray in a logical manner to facilitate reassembly.

3. **Following the specified procedure, inspect the components for wear or damage. List your observations:**

4. **Determine any necessary action(s):**

5. Have your supervisor/instructor verify disassembly and observations.
   Supervisor's/instructor's initials: _____

6. **Following the specified procedure, service the transfer case components and list your actions:**

7. Have your supervisor/instructor verify that the transfer case is ready to be reassembled and initial below.

   a. Supervisor's/instructor's initials: _____

8. Following the specified procedure, reassemble the transfer case. Be sure to tighten all fasteners to the proper torque. **List your observations:**

9. Have your supervisor/instructor verify satisfactory completion of this procedure, any observations found, and any necessary action(s) recommended.

Performance Rating

CDX Tasksheet Number: C875

0	1	2	3	4

Supervisor/instructor signature _____ Date _____

Time off_____

Time on_____

CDX Tasksheet Number: C913

Total time_____

1. Research the procedure and specifications for servicing the wheel bearings and locking hubs in the appropriate service information.

   a. **List the specified wheel-bearing lubricant:** _____

   b. **List or print off and attach to this sheet the procedure for adjusting the wheel bearings:**

2. Safely raise and support the vehicle on a hoist or jack stands.

3. Following the specified procedure, remove the locking hub(s) and wheel bearings (inner and outer). **List your observation(s):**

4. Following the specified procedure, disassemble the locking hub(s). Clean all parts in an environmentally safe way and re-inspect each components. **List your observation(s):**

> **NOTE** There are various views on whether a wheel bearing should be cleaned with solvents, as it could leave solvent-laden grease in the bearing. See your instructor or the service information for the recommended procedure for cleaning and packing wheel bearings.

5. **Determine any necessary action(s):**

6. Have your supervisor/instructor verify satisfactory completion of this procedure, any observations found, and any necessary action(s) recommended.

Performance Rating

CDX Tasksheet Number: C913

0	1	2	3	4

Supervisor/instructor signature _____ Date _____

▶ TASK Inspect front-wheel bearings and locking hubs; perform necessary action.

AST 3F2   **MAST** 3F2

Time off_____

Time on_____

Total time_____

CDX Tasksheet Number: C876

1. Research the procedure and specifications for servicing the wheel bearings and locking hubs in the appropriate service information.

   a. **List the specified wheel-bearing lubricant:** _____

   b. **List or print off and attach to this sheet the procedure for adjusting the wheel bearings:**

2. Safely raise and support the vehicle on a hoist or jack stands.

3. Following the specified procedure, remove the locking hub(s) and wheel bearings (inner and outer). **List your observation(s):**

4. Following the specified procedure, disassemble the locking hub(s). Clean all parts in an environmentally safe way and re-inspect each component. **List your observation(s):**

> **NOTE** There are various views on whether a wheel bearing should be cleaned with solvents, as it could leave solvent-laden grease in the bearing. See your instructor or the service information for the recommended procedure for cleaning and packing wheel bearings.

5. **Determine any necessary action(s):**

6. Have your supervisor/instructor verify disassembly and observations. **Supervisor's/instructor's initials:** _____

7. Following the specified procedure, repack the wheel bearings and lubricate the locking hub components.

© 2015 Jones & Bartlett Learning, LLC, an Ascend Learning Company

Manual Drive Train and Axles   461

8. Following the specified procedure, reassemble the wheel bearings. Make sure you properly adjust the wheel bearings.

> **NOTE** Most wheel bearings require a three-step adjustment procedure. First, apply a large initial torque to the wheel-bearing adjustment nut to seat the wheel bearings. Second, back off the adjustment nut. Third, readjust with a much smaller torque to provide the proper bearing preload. Do not leave the bearings torqued to the higher torque or damage to the bearings will result. Also, remember to use a new cotter pin if that is the method used to retain the adjustment nut.

9. Have your supervisor/instructor verify correct bearing adjustment. Supervisor's/instructor's initials: _____

10. Following the specified procedure, reassemble the locking hubs. **List your observation(s):**

11. Have your supervisor/instructor verify satisfactory completion of this procedure, any observations found, and any necessary action(s) recommended.

Performance Rating

CDX Tasksheet Number: C876

| 0 | 1 | 2 | 3 | 4 |

Supervisor/instructor signature _____ Date _____

► **TASK** Check for leaks at drive assembly seals and vents; check lube level.

Time off_____

Time on_____

Total time_____

CDX Tasksheet Number: C914

1. Research the procedure and specifications for this task in the appropriate service information.

    a. List the specified lube for the drive axle: _____

2. Following the specified procedure, perform a visual inspection of the drive assembly seals and vents. **List your observation(s) for each.**

    a. Drive assembly seals:

    b. Vents:

3. **Following the specified procedure, check the level of the lubricant. List your observations:**

4. **Determine any necessary action(s):**

5. Have your supervisor/instructor verify satisfactory completion of this procedure, any observations found, and any necessary action(s) recommended.

Performance Rating

CDX Tasksheet Number: C914

0	1	2	3	4

Supervisor/instructor signature _____ Date _____

▶ **TASK** Diagnose, test, adjust, and replace electrical/electronic components of four-wheel drive systems.

MAST
3F6

Time off_____

Time on_____

Total time_____

CDX Tasksheet Number: C878

Vehicle used for this activity:

Year _____ Make _____ Model _____

Odometer _____ VIN _____

1. **List the related customer concern:**

2. **Research the possible cause(s) of the concern in the appropriate service information. List the possible cause(s):**

3. **Following the specified procedure, diagnose the cause of the concern. List your tests and observation(s):**

4. **List the cause of the concern:**

5. **Determine any necessary action(s) to correct the fault:**

6. Have your supervisor/instructor verify satisfactory completion of this procedure, any observations found, and any necessary action(s) recommended.

Performance Rating

CDX Tasksheet Number: C878

0	1	2	3	4

Supervisor/instructor signature _____ Date _____

Identify concerns related to variations in tire
circumference and/or final drive ratios.

AST
3F4

MAST
3F4

Time off_____

Time on_____

Total time_____

CDX Tasksheet Number: C613

1. Research the effects of variations in tire circumference and final drive ratios on the operation of a four-wheel drive/all-wheel drive vehicle in the appropriate service information.

2. **What would the customer concern be for a 4-wheel drive/all-wheel drive vehicle equipped with different size tires?**

3. **What would the customer concern be for a vehicle equipped with different final drive ratios?**

4. **Set the tire pressure to the specified pressure. Measure the tire circumference for each tire and list below:**

    a. **Left front tire circumference:** _____ in/mm
    b. **Right front tire circumference:** _____ in/mm
    c. **Right rear tire circumference:** _____ in/mm
    d. **Left rear tire circumference:** _____ in/mm

5. **How much difference in circumference is generally allowable?** _____ in/mm

6. **Determine the final drive ratios for each axle assembly:**

    a. **Rear axle ratio:** _____
    b. **Front axle ratio:** _____

7. **Determine any necessary action(s):**

8. Have your supervisor/instructor verify satisfactory completion of this procedure, any observations found, and any necessary action(s) recommended.

Performance Rating

CDX Tasksheet Number: C613

0	1	2	3	4

Supervisor/instructor signature _____ Date _____

Section A4: Suspension and Steering Systems

CONTENTS

Suspension and Steering Systems: Vehicle, Customer, and Service Information

Student/intern information:

Name _____ Date _____ Class _____

Vehicle used for this activity:

Year _____ Make _____ Model _____

Odometer _____ VIN _____

Learning Objective/Task	CDX Tasksheet Number	2013 MLR NATEF Reference Number; Priority Level	2013 AST NATEF Reference Number; Priority Level	2013 MAST NATEF Reference Number; Priority Level
• Research applicable vehicle and service information, such as suspension and steering system operation, vehicle service history, service precautions, and technical service bulletins.	C166	4A1; P-1	4A1; P-1	4A1; P-1
• Identify and interpret suspension and steering system concerns; determine necessary action.	C851			4A2; P-1
• Demonstrate use of 3 Cs (concern, cause, correction)	NN04	N/A	N/A	N/A

Time off _____

Time on _____

Total time _____

Materials Required

- Blank work order
- Vehicle with available service history records
- Depending on the type of concern, special diagnostic tools may be required. See your supervisor/instructor for instructions to identify what tools may be required.

Some Safety Issues to Consider

- Diagnosis of this fault may require test-driving the vehicle on the school grounds. Attempt this task only with full permission from your instructor and follow all the guidelines exactly.
- When running any vehicles in the shop, make sure you use the shop's exhaust ventilation system to discharge all exhaust gas safely outside.
- Lifting equipment such as vehicle jacks and stands, vehicle hoists, and engine hoists are important tools that increase productivity and make the job easier. However, they can also cause severe injury or death if used improperly. Make sure you follow the manufacturer's operation procedures. Also, make sure you have your supervisor's/instructor's permission to use any particular type of lifting equipment.
- Comply with personal and environmental safety practices associated with clothing; eye protection; hand tools; power equipment; proper ventilation; and the handling, storage, and disposal of chemicals/materials in accordance with local, state, and federal safety and environmental regulations.

Performance Standard

0—No exposure: No information or practice provided during the program; complete training required

1—Exposure only: General information provided with no practice time; close supervision needed; additional training required

2—Limited practice: Has practiced job during training program; additional training required to develop skill

3—Moderately skilled: Has performed job independently during training program; limited additional training may be required

4—Skilled: Can perform job independently with no additional training

Research applicable vehicle and service information, such as suspension and steering system operation, vehicle service history, service precautions, and technical service bulletins.

MLR	AST	MAST
4A1	4A1	4A1

Time off_____

Time on_____

Total time_____

CDX Tasksheet Number: C166

1. Using the VIN for identification, use the appropriate source to access the vehicle's service history in relation to prior related suspension and steering system work or customer concerns.

   a. List any related steering and suspension system repairs/concerns and their dates:

2. Using the VIN for identification, access any relevant technical service bulletins for the particular vehicle you are working on in relation to steering and suspension updates or other service issues.

   a. List any steering and suspension system-related service bulletins and their titles:

3. **Research the type of front and rear suspension used on this vehicle and list here:**

4. **Research the type of steering system used on this vehicle and list here:**

5. Have your supervisor/instructor verify satisfactory completion of this procedure, any observations found, and any necessary action(s) recommended.

Performance Rating

CDX Tasksheet Number: C166

☐	☐	☐	☐	☐
0	1	2	3	4

Supervisor/instructor signature _____ Date _____

Identify and interpret suspension and steering system concerns; determine necessary action.

MAST
4A2

CDX Tasksheet Number: C851

1. **List the customer concern:**

2. Research the particular concern in the appropriate service information.

    a. **List the possible causes:**

3. Inspect the steering and suspension system to determine the cause of the concern. **List the steps you took to determine the fault:**

4. **List the cause of the concern:**

5. **List the necessary action(s) to correct this fault:**

6. Have your supervisor/instructor verify satisfactory completion of this procedure, any observations found, and any necessary action(s) recommended.

Performance Rating

CDX Tasksheet Number: C851

0	1	2	3	4

Supervisor/instructor signature _____ Date _____

Time off_____

Time on_____

Total time_____

CDX Tasksheet Number: NN04

1. Using the following scenario, write up the 3 Cs as listed on most repair orders. Assume that the customer authorized the recommended repairs.

A vehicle is brought to your shop with a steering or suspension concern. The customer tells you that the vehicle has been pulling to the right ever since he hit a big pothole on a recent trip. The vehicle also has a vibration that is very noticeable when driving and is getting worse. He would like an estimate before the end of the day, because he will be leaving on a two-week vacation in the morning, and he would like the vehicle repaired while he is away. You test-drive the vehicle to verify the concerns, pull the vehicle up on the alignment hoist, and find the following:

a. The tires are only a few months old, but the right front tire has broken belts as evidenced by the bulge in one edge.
b. The right front wheel has a bent flange.
c. The wheel alignment machine shows improper toe-out on turns that, upon further inspection, are shown to be caused by a bent right front steering arm on the steering knuckle.
d. The rear struts are excessively worn and don't dampen like they should.
e. The vehicle is about 1000 miles past its scheduled oil and filter change.
f. The serpentine belt is showing excessive wear.

> **NOTE** Ask your instructor if you should use the shop's repair order to complete this task, or the 3 Cs listed here.

2. **Concern/complaint:**

3. **Cause:**

4. **Correction:**

5. Other recommended service:

6. Have your supervisor/instructor verify satisfactory completion of this procedure, any observations found, and any necessary action(s) recommended.

Performance Rating

CDX Tasksheet Number: NN04

0	1	2	3	4

Supervisor/instructor signature _____ Date _____

Suspension and Steering Systems: Wheel and Tire Maintenance

Student/intern information:

Name _____ Date _____ Class _____

Vehicle used for this activity:

Year _____ Make _____ Model _____

Odometer _____ VIN _____

Learning Objective/Task	CDX Tasksheet Number	2013 MLR NATEF Reference Number; Priority Level	2013 AST NATEF Reference Number; Priority Level	2013 MAST NATEF Reference Number; Priority Level
• Inspect tire condition; identify tire wear patterns; check for correct size and application (load and speed ratings) and adjust air pressure; determine necessary action.	C619	4D1; P-1	4F1; P-1	4F1; P-1
• Rotate tires according to manufacturer's recommendations.	C222	4D2; P-1	4F3; P-1	4F3; P-1
• Dismount, inspect, and remount tire on wheel; balance wheel and tire assembly (static and dynamic).	C620	4D3; P-1	4F6; P-1	4F6; P-1
• Demonstrate knowledge of steps required to remove and replace sensors in a tire-pressure monitoring system.	C936	4D8; P-2	4F11; P-1	4F11; P-1
• Dismount, inspect, and remount tire on wheel equipped with tire-pressure monitoring system sensor.	C621	4D4; P-2	4F7; P-2	4F7; P-2

Time off_____

Time on_____

Total time_____

Materials Required

- Worn tire assigned by supervisor/instructor
- Tread-depth gauge
- Tire-pressure gauge
- Tire inflator
- Tire valve core tool
- Wheel weight hammer
- Vehicle hoist
- Lug wrench (or impact wrench with appropriate impact socket)
- Torque wrench and appropriate socket
- Tire mounting and balancing equipment
- Depending on the type of concern, special diagnostic tools may be required. See your supervisor/instructor for instructions to identify what tools may be required.

Some Safety Issues to Consider

- Worn or damaged tires may have steel cords sticking out of the tire. These wires are very sharp and will severely cut you. Do not rub your hand across a tire without checking first for exposed cords.
- Vehicle hoists are important tools that increase productivity and make the job easier. However, they also can cause severe injury or death if used improperly. Make sure you follow the hoist and vehicle manufacturer's operation procedures. Also make sure you have your supervisor's/instructor's permission to use a vehicle hoist.
- Compressed air can be very dangerous. Never blow it at someone. Never use it to remove dirt or dust from your skin or clothing. Never use it without an OSHA-approved nozzle.
- Over-inflating tires could cause the tire to explode with great force. Never exceed the maximum tire pressure for the tire you are working on. Use a tire cage when inflating a tire that has been removed from a rim or repaired.
- Tires, even if they have good tread, only have a safe life of 6–10 years depending on type, condition, and environment. Check your state and local regulations about the age that tires should be replaced, and do not repair/service a tire older than that.
- Lug nuts must always be torqued to the proper torque. Always use a properly calibrated torque wrench. Never use an impact wrench to tighten lug nuts. This could cause the wheel to come loose and fall off if under-tightened. Or, if over-tightened, the lug studs might get damaged which could also cause the wheel to fall off the vehicle. It could also cause the brake rotors to become warped.
- Comply with personal and environmental safety practices associated with clothing; eye protection; hand tools; power equipment; proper ventilation; and the handling, storage, and disposal of chemicals/materials in accordance with local, state, and federal safety and environmental regulations.

Performance Standard

0–No exposure: No information or practice provided during the program; complete training required

1–Exposure only: General information provided with no practice time; close supervision needed; additional training required

2–Limited practice: Has practiced job during training program; additional training required to develop skill

3–Moderately skilled: Has performed job independently during training program; limited additional training may be required

4–Skilled: Can perform job independently with no additional training

▶ TASK Inspect tire condition; identify tire wear patterns; check for correct size and application (load and speed ratings) and adjust air pressure; determine necessary action.

MLR	AST	MAST
4D1	4F1	4F1

Time off_____

Time on_____

Total time_____

CDX Tasksheet Number: C619

1. Research tread wear patterns in the appropriate information.

2. Research the following tire specifications on the vehicle's tire decal and on the sidewall of the tire itself:

   a. **Tire decal (usually located on the vehicle door, door pillar, or glove box lid):**
   Recommended tire designation: _____
   Maximum load on front axle: _____ lb/kg
   Maximum load on rear axle: _____ lb/kg
   Required tire speed rating: _____
   Maximum speed for this rating: _____ mph/kph
   Recommended tire pressure: Front: _____ psi/kPa
   Rear: _____ psi/kPa

   b. **Information on sidewall of tire:**
   Tire designation: _____
   Maximum load: _____ lb/kg
   Speed rating: _____ **Speed tire is safe for:** _____ mph/kph
   Maximum tire pressure: _____ psi/kPa
   Tread wear rating: _____
   Traction rating: _____
   Temperature rating: _____
   DOT date of manufacture code: _____ **Age of tire today:** __ (yrs/mos)

3. **On the most-worn tire, measure the tread depth across the tire tread and list your measurements below:**

   a. Tread depth (inside of tread): _____ in/mm
   b. Tread depth (center of tread): _____ in/mm
   c. Tread depth (outside of tread): _____ in/mm

4. **Check to make sure there are no exposed steel cords. Carefully run your hand across the tread and feel for a feathered condition. Also, run your hand in line with the tread to feel for lumps and bulges.**

   a. Is the tire feathered? Yes: _____ No: _____
   b. Are there any bulges? Yes: _____ No: _____

5. **Based on your observations and measurements, determine what, if any, wear patterns exist and list them here:**

6. **Measure the pressure in the tire(s) and record it here:** _____ psi/kPa

7. **If the tire is not at the correct pressure, increase or decrease pressure.**

   a. **Record final pressure:** _____ **psi/kPa**

8. **Determine any necessary action(s):**

9. Have your supervisor/instructor verify satisfactory completion of this procedure, any observations found, and any necessary action(s) recommended.

Performance Rating

CDX Tasksheet Number: C619

0	1	2	3	4

Supervisor/instructor signature _____ Date _____

Rotate tires according to manufacturer's recommendations.

Time off_____

Time on_____

Total time_____

CDX Tasksheet Number: C222

1. Research the following specifications in the appropriate service information.

> **NOTE** Vehicles equipped with a tire-pressure monitoring system (TPMS) may need the system reset after rotating the tires. Verify that you have all the necessary tools and manufacturer's procedure prior to removing the wheels on these vehicles.

    a. Is this vehicle equipped with TPMS? Yes: _____ No: _____

        i. If yes, do you have the specified tools and procedures to reset the TPMS system? Yes: _____ No: _____

    b. Lug nut torque: _____ ft-lbs/Nm

    c. Manufacturer's recommended tire rotation pattern. **Draw diagram below.**

    d. Manufacturer's recommended lug nut torque sequence. **Draw diagram below.**

2. Remove the wheel/tire assemblies from the vehicle.

> **NOTE** When removing hubcaps and wheels, please store them in such a manner so as not to damage the visible side of the hubcap or wheel. Laying them face down will cause them to become scratched and damaged. Also, store the lug nuts so they will not get lost or kicked.

3. Have your supervisor/instructor verify removal.
    Supervisor's/instructor's initials: _____

4. Rotate the tires according to the manufacturer's recommendation. As part of this procedure, check the tire pressure. If a tire is found to be under-inflated, check the tire for a leak. If a leak is found, notify your supervisor/instructor for further directions. Also, inspect each tire for nails or other foreign objects. Notify your supervisor/instructor if a problem is found. **List your observations:**

5. Torque the lug nuts to manufacturer's specifications in the specified sequence.

   a. **Record torque:** _____ **ft-lbs/Nm**

6. Reset TPMS if necessary. Follow manufacturer's procedure.

7. Reinstall hubcaps, if equipped. Make sure they are fully seated to prevent them from falling off while driving. If in doubt, ask your supervisor/instructor.

8. Have your supervisor/instructor verify satisfactory completion of this procedure, any observations found, and any necessary action(s) recommended.

Performance Rating

CDX Tasksheet Number: C222

0	1	2	3	4

Supervisor/instructor signature _____ Date _____

Dismount, inspect, and remount tire on wheel; balance wheel and tire assembly (static and dynamic).

MLR 4D3   **AST** 4F6   **MAST** 4F6

Time off_____

Time on_____

Total time_____

CDX Tasksheet Number: C620

> **NOTE** Verify that this wheel is NOT equipped with TPMS.

1. **List the customer concern, if any:**

2. Prepare the vehicle and remove the wheel concerned.

3. Inspect the outer surface of the entire wheel and tire assembly. **List your observations:**

4. Using the correct procedure, dismount the tire from the wheel.

5. Inspect the inside of the tire, the tire bead, the inside of the rim, and the valve stem. **List your observations:**

6. Have your supervisor/instructor verify removal.
   Supervisor's/instructor's initials: _____

7. Remount tire on the wheel using the correct equipment and procedure.

8. **Balance wheel and tire assembly (static and dynamic) and draw a diagram of the position and size of the weights:**

9. Determine any necessary action(s):

10. Have your supervisor/instructor verify satisfactory completion of this procedure, any observations found, and any necessary action(s) recommended.

Performance Rating

CDX Tasksheet Number: C620

0	1	2	3	4

Supervisor/instructor signature _____ Date _____

► **TASK** Demonstrate knowledge of steps required to remove and replace sensors in a tire-pressure monitoring system.

MLR	AST	MAST
4D8	4F11	4F11

Time off_____

Time on_____

Total time_____

CDX Tasksheet Number: C936

1. Research the procedure for replacing TPMS sensors on at least 3 vehicles (1 domestic car, 1 imported car, and 1 all-wheel drive vehicle) in the appropriate service information.

   a. Vehicle year, make, and model: _____

      i. **Summarize the steps to replace the TPMS sensor:**

      ii. **List any precautions when replacing the TPMS sensor:**

   b. Vehicle year, make, and model: _____

      i. **Summarize the steps to replace the TPMS sensor:**

      ii. **List any precautions when replacing the TPMS sensor:**

   c. Vehicle year, make, and model: _____

      i. **Summarize the steps to replace the TPMS sensor:**

ii. List any precautions when replacing the TPMS sensor:

2. Have your supervisor/instructor verify satisfactory completion of this procedure, any observations found, and any necessary action(s) recommended.

Performance Rating

CDX Tasksheet Number: C936

0	1	2	3	4

Supervisor/instructor signature _____ Date _____

▶ TASK Dismount, inspect, and remount tire on wheel equipped with tire-pressure monitoring system sensor.

MLR 4D4 **AST** 4F7 **MAST** 4F7

Time off_____

Time on_____

Total time_____

CDX Tasksheet Number: C621

Vehicle used for this activity:

Year _____ Make _____ Model _____

Odometer _____ VIN _____

1. **List the customer concern, if any:**

2. Research the following in the appropriate service information:

   a. Tire removal/installation on TPMS-equipped vehicles. **List the proper positioning of the wheel on the tire machine when removing the tire:**

   b. TPMS maintenance needs and service. **List any maintenance that can be performed on the TPMS sensors:**

   c. TPMS reset procedure, if necessary. **List the steps to reset the TPMS sensors:**

3. Prepare the vehicle and remove the wheel concerned.

4. Inspect the outer surface of the entire wheel and tire assembly. **List your observations:**

5. Using the correct procedure, dismount the tire from the wheel. Be careful not to damage the TPMS sensor.

6. **Inspect the inside of the tire, the tire bead, the inside of the rim, the valve stem, and the TPMS sensor. List your observations:**

7. Have your supervisor/instructor verify removal.
   Supervisor's/instructor's initials: _____

8. **Perform any needed maintenance/service on the TPMS system. List your actions:**

9. Remount tire on wheel using the correct equipment and procedure. Be careful not to damage the TPMS sensor.

10. Balance wheel and tire assembly, if necessary, and draw a diagram of the position and size of the weights:

11. Reinstall wheel/tire assembly on the vehicle and torque lug nuts to the proper torque in the proper sequence.

12. **If necessary, reset the TPMS according to the specified procedure. List your observations:**

13. **Determine any necessary action(s):**

14. Have your supervisor/instructor verify satisfactory completion of this procedure, any observations found, and any necessary action(s) recommended.

Performance Rating

0	1	2	3	4

Supervisor/instructor signature _____ Date _____

Suspension and Steering Systems: Wheel and Tire Diagnosis

Student/intern information:

Name _____ Date _____ Class _____

Vehicle used for this activity:

Year _____ Make _____ Model _____

Odometer _____ VIN _____

Learning Objective/Task	CDX Tasksheet Number	2013 MLR NATEF Reference Number; Priority Level	2013 AST NATEF Reference Number; Priority Level	2013 MAST NATEF Reference Number; Priority Level
• Inspect tire and wheel assembly for air loss; perform necessary action.	C580	4D5; P-1	4F8; P-1	4F8; P-1
• Repair tire using internal patch.	C552	4D6; P-1	4F9; P-1	4F9; P-1
• Measure wheel, tire, axle flange, and hub runout; determine necessary action.	C701		4F4; P-2	4F4; P-2
• Identify and test tire pressure monitoring systems (indirect and direct) for operation; verify operation of instrument panel lamps.	C935	4D7; P-2	4F10; P-2	
• Identify and test tire-pressure monitoring system (indirect and direct) for operation; calibrate system; verify operation of instrument panel lamps.	C937			4F10; P-2
• Diagnose wheel/tire vibration, shimmy, and noise; determine necessary action.	C855		4F2; P-2	4F2; P-2
• Diagnose tire pull problems; determine necessary action.	C796		4F5; P-2	4F5; P-2

Time off_____

Time on_____

Total time_____

Materials Required

- Leaky tire assigned by supervisor/instructor
- Tire-pressure gauge
- Tire inflator
- Tire valve core tool
- Vehicle hoist or floor jack and jack stand(s)
- Lug wrench (or impact wrench with appropriate impact socket)
- Tire dunk tank or soapy water in a spray bottle
- Torque wrench and appropriate socket
- Tire patching tools and supplies
- Dial indicator
- Depending on the type of concern, special diagnostic tools may be required. See your supervisor/instructor for instructions to identify what tools may be required.

Some Safety Issues to Consider

- Worn or damaged tires may have steel cords sticking out of the tire. These wires are very sharp and will severely cut you. Do not rub your hand across a tire without checking first for exposed cords.
- Vehicle hoists are important tools that increase productivity and make the job easier. However, they also can cause severe injury or death if used improperly. Make sure you follow the hoist and vehicle manufacturer's operation procedures. Also make sure you have your supervisor's/instructor's permission to use a vehicle hoist.
- Compressed air can be very dangerous. Never blow it at someone. Never use it to remove dirt or dust from your skin or clothing. Never use it without an OSHA-approved nozzle.
- Over-inflating tires could cause the tire to explode with great force. Never exceed the maximum tire pressure for the tire you are working on. Use a tire cage when inflating a tire that has been removed from a rim or repaired.
- Lug nuts must always be torqued to the proper torque. Always use a properly calibrated torque wrench. Never use an impact wrench to tighten lug nuts. This could cause the wheel to come loose and fall off if under-tightened. Or, if over-tightened, the lug studs might get damaged which could also cause the wheel to fall off the vehicle. It could also cause the brake rotors to become warped.
- Comply with personal and environmental safety practices associated with clothing; eye protection; hand tools; power equipment; proper ventilation; and the handling, storage, and disposal of chemicals/materials in accordance with local, state, and federal safety and environmental regulations.

Performance Standard

0—No exposure: No information or practice provided during the program; complete training required

1—Exposure only: General information provided with no practice time; close supervision needed; additional training required

2—Limited practice: Has practiced job during training program; additional training required to develop skill

3—Moderately skilled: Has performed job independently during training program; limited additional training may be required

4—Skilled: Can perform job independently with no additional training

► **TASK** Inspect tire and wheel assembly for air loss; perform necessary action.

MLR	AST	MAST
4D5	4F8	4F8

Time off_____

Time on_____

Total time_____

CDX Tasksheet Number: C580

1. Research the following specifications in the appropriate service information.

   a. **Lug nut torque:** _____ **ft-lbs/Nm**

   b. **Is this vehicle equipped with TPMS? Yes:** _____ **No:** _____

   c. **If yes, do you have the specified tools and procedures to reset the TPMS system? Yes:** _____ **No:** _____

2. Remove wheel/tire assembly from vehicle and check it for any leaks using soapy water or a dunk tank. **List your observations:**

> **NOTE** When removing hubcaps and wheels, please store them in such a manner as not to damage the visible side of the hubcap or wheel. Laying them face down will cause them to become scratched and damaged. Also store the lug nuts so they will not get lost or kicked.

3. Mark the position of all wheel weights and the valve stem on the tire with a tire crayon. This is so you can reinstall the tire and weights on the wheel in the same position so rebalancing is unnecessary.

4. Using the correct procedure, dismount the tire from the wheel. Be careful not to damage the TPMS, if equipped.

5. **Inspect the wheel and tire for any damage, rust, or other defects and list them here:**

6. **Are the defects repairable? Yes:** _____ **No:** _____

7. Have your supervisor/instructor verify your observations, and ask permission to make any repairs. **Supervisor's/instructor initials:** _____

8. With supervisor/instructor approval, repair all defects found.

> **NOTE** If the tire has a leak that can be repaired with an integrated plug-patch or internal patch, skip ahead to task C552: Repair tire using internal patch, and return here once the task has been completed.

9. Remount the tire on the wheel, positioning the tire and weights in their original positions on the wheel to restore existing tire balance.

10. Recheck the wheel/tire assembly for leaks. If there are none, reinstall it on the vehicle and torque the lug nuts to the proper specification and in the proper sequence.

11. Have your supervisor/instructor verify satisfactory completion of this procedure, any observations found, and any necessary action(s) recommended.

Performance Rating

CDX Tasksheet Number: C580

0	1	2	3	4

Supervisor/instructor signature _____ Date _____

▶ **TASK** Repair tire using internal patch.

Time off_____

Time on_____

Total time_____

CDX Tasksheet Number: C552

1. Inspect the tire for remaining tread life and ensure that any repair undertaken will meet all legislative requirements.

   a. **Measure the minimum tread depth:** _____ in/mm
   b. **Is the tread depth above the legal limit? Yes:** _____ **No:** _____
   c. **Is the hole within the repairable zone of the tread?**
      Yes: _____ **No:** _____
   d. **Is the diameter of the hole within patching limits? Yes:** _____
      No: _____
   e. **What type of internal patch are you using? Standard internal patch:**
      _____ **Integrated plug patch:** _____

2. Using a recommended method, prepare the tire for repair, (perform all steps except applying glue and the patch). **List your steps and observations here:**

3. Have your instructor verify the proper preparation for the patch.
   Supervisor's/Instructor initials: _____

4. Determine any necessary action(s), and undertake the repair by applying the glue and patch in accordance with the manufacturer's recommendations and process (most tire patch glues MUST be allowed to fully dry before applying the patch).

5. Have your supervisor/instructor verify satisfactory completion of this procedure, any observations found, and any necessary action(s) recommended.

Performance Rating

CDX Tasksheet Number: C552

0	1	2	3	4

Supervisor/instructor signature _____ Date _____

Measure wheel, tire, axle flange, and hub runout; determine necessary action.

AST
4F4

MAST
4F4

Time off_____

Time on_____

Total time_____

CDX Tasksheet Number: C701

Vehicle used for this activity:

Year _____ Make _____ Model_____

Odometer_____ VIN_____

1. **List the customer concern; if applicable:**

2. Research the procedure for measuring tire, wheel, and hub runout in the appropriate service information. **List the following specifications:**

   a. **Tire pressure:** _____ psi/kPa
   b. **Tire designation:** _____
   c. **Maximum tire runout:** _____ in/mm
   d. **Maximum wheel runout:** _____ in/mm
   e. **Maximum axle flange/hub runout:** _____ in/mm

3. Check and adjust the tire pressures according to specifications.

4. **Inspect each tire and list its designation:**

   a. **LF tire:**_____
   b. **RF tire:**_____
   c. **RR tire:**_____
   d. **LR tire:**_____
   e. **Does each tire meet the manufacturer's recommendations?**
      Yes: _____ No: _____

5. Properly raise the front of the vehicle and support it securely.

6. **Following the manufacturer's procedure, measure runout of the following:**

   a. **LF tire:** _____ in/mm
   b. **RF tire:** _____ in/mm
   c. **LF wheel:** _____ in/mm
   d. **RF wheel:** _____ in/mm
   e. **LF hub:** _____ in/mm
   f. **RF hub:** _____ in/mm

7. **Determine any necessary action(s):**

8. Have your supervisor/instructor verify satisfactory completion of this procedure, any observations found, and any necessary action(s) recommended.

Performance Rating

CDX Tasksheet Number: C701

0	1	2	3	4

Supervisor/instructor signature _____ Date _____

Identify and test tire pressure monitoring systems (indirect and direct) for operation; verify operation of instrument panel lamps. **MLR** **AST**
4D7   4F10

Time off_____

Time on_____

Total time_____

CDX Tasksheet Number: C935

Vehicle used for this activity:

Year _____ Make _____ Model_____

Odometer_____ VIN_____

1. Research the TPMS system in the appropriate service information.

    a. **Choose the type of TMPS system: Indirect: _____ Direct: _____**

    b. **List how the instrument panel warning lamps should behave if the system is operating normally:**

    c. **List how the instrument panel warning lamps should behave if the system is NOT operating normally:**

2. **Describe how an indirect TPMS system detects a tire with low tire pressure:**

3. **Describe how a direct TPMS system detects a tire with low tire pressure:**

4. Check the operation of the TPMS warning lamp and list your observations:

5. Have your supervisor/instructor verify satisfactory completion of this procedure, any observations found, and any necessary action(s) recommended.

Performance Rating

0	1	2	3	4

Supervisor/instructor signature _____ Date _____

Identify and test tire-pressure monitoring system
(indirect and direct) for operation; calibrate system;
verify operation of instrument panel lamps.

MAST
4F10

CDX Tasksheet Number: C937

Vehicle used for this activity:

Year _____ Make _____ Model_____

Odometer_____ VIN_____

1. Research the TPMS system in the appropriate service information.

    a. **Choose the type of TMPS system: Indirect: _____ Direct: _____**

    b. **List or print off and attach to this sheet the process for calibrating the TPMS system:**

    c. **List how the instrument panel warning lamps should behave if the system is operating normally:**

    d. **List how the instrument panel warning lamps should behave if the system is NOT operating normally:**

2. **Describe how an indirect TPMS system detects a tire with low tire pressure:**

3. **Describe how a direct TPMS system detects a tire with low tire pressure:**

4. Check the operation of the TPMS warning lamp and list your observations:

5. Swap the two front-wheel assemblies and calibrate the TPMS system in accordance with the manufacturer's instructions. List your steps and observations here:

6. Have your supervisor/instructor verify satisfactory completion of this procedure, any observations found, and any necessary action(s) recommended.

Performance Rating

CDX Tasksheet Number: C937

0	1	2	3	4

Supervisor/instructor signature _____ Date _____

▶ TASK Diagnose wheel/tire vibration, shimmy, and noise; determine necessary action.

Time off_____

Time on_____

Total time_____

CDX Tasksheet Number: C855

Vehicle used for this activity:

Year _____ Make _____ Model_____

Odometer_____ VIN_____

1. **List the wheel/tire-related customer concern(s):**

2. Research the concern in the appropriate service information and any technical service bulletins that may apply.

   a. **List any applicable service bulletins:**

   b. **List or print off and attach to this sheet the procedure for diagnosing the concern:**

3. **With the supervisor's/instructor's permission, test-drive the vehicle. Listen and feel for any unusual noises and vibrations. List your observations:**

4. **Using the recommended procedure, inspect and diagnose any vibration, shimmy, or noise concerns. List your tests and results here:**

5. List the cause of the concern:

6. Determine any necessary action(s) to correct the fault:

7. Have your supervisor/instructor verify satisfactory completion of this procedure, any observations found, and any necessary action(s) recommended.

Performance Rating

CDX Tasksheet Number: C855

0	1	2	3	4

Supervisor/instructor signature _____ Date _____

Diagnose tire pull problems; determine necessary action.

AST
4F5

MAST
4F5

Time off_____

Time on_____

Total time_____

CDX Tasksheet Number: C796

Vehicle used for this activity:

Year _____ Make _____ Model_____

Odometer_____ VIN_____

1. **List the tire pull-related customer concern(s):**

2. Research the configuration of this vehicle in the appropriate service information and any technical service bulletins that may apply.

    a. **List any applicable service bulletins and their titles:**

    b. **List or print off and attach to this sheet the procedure for diagnosing the concern:**

3. With the supervisor's/instructor's permission, test-drive the vehicle. Check for any tire pull problems. **List your observations:**

4. **Using the recommended procedure, inspect and diagnose any tire pull problems. List your tests and results here:**

5. **List the cause of the concern:**

6. **Determine any necessary action(s) to correct the fault:**

7. Have your supervisor/instructor verify satisfactory completion of this procedure, any observations found, and any necessary action(s) recommended.

Performance Rating

CDX Tasksheet Number: C796

0	1	2	3	4

Supervisor/instructor signature _____ Date _____

Suspension and Steering Systems: Power Steering Pump Maintenance and Service

Student/intern information:

Name _____ Date _____ Class _____

Vehicle used for this activity:

Year _____ Make _____ Model _____

Odometer _____ VIN _____

© 2015 Jones & Bartlett Learning, LLC, an Ascend Learning Company

Time off _____

Time on _____

Total time _____

Learning Objective/Task	CDX Tasksheet Number	2013 MLR NATEF Reference Number; Priority Level	2013 AST NATEF Reference Number; Priority Level	2013 MAST NATEF Reference Number; Priority Level
• Determine proper power steering fluid type; inspect fluid level and condition.	C177	4B2; P-1	4B9; P-1	4B9; P-1
• Replace power steering pump filter(s).	C182	N/A	N/A	N/A
• Flush, fill, and bleed power steering system.	C178	4B3; P-2	4B10; P-2	4B10; P-2
• Remove, inspect, replace, and adjust power steering pump belt.	C180	4B5; P-1	4B12; P-1	4B12; P-1
• Inspect for power steering fluid leakage; determine necessary action.	C179	4B4; P-1	4B11; P-1	4B11; P-1
• Inspect and replace power steering hoses and fittings.	C183	4B6; P-2	4B15; P-2	4B15; P-2
• Remove and reinstall power steering pump.	C181		4B13; P-2	4B13; P-2
• Remove and reinstall press-fit power steering pump pulley; check pulley and belt alignment.	C699		4B14; P-2	4B14; P-2

Materials Required

- Vehicle or simulator, equipped with power steering
- Correct power steering fluid
- White piece of paper
- Power steering flush machine or drain pan
- Funnel
- Belt-tension gauge
- Power steering
- pump pulley remover/installer tool
- Depending on the type of concern, special diagnostic tools may be required. See your supervisor/instructor for instructions to identify what tools may be required.

Some Safety Issues to Consider

- You will be working under the hood of a running vehicle. Keep your hands and fingers away from moving belts, fans, and other parts.
- When running any vehicles in the shop, make sure you use the shop's exhaust ventilation system to discharge all exhaust gas safely outside.
- Lifting equipment such as vehicle jacks and stands, vehicle hoists, and engine hoists are important tools that increase productivity and make the job easier. However, they can also cause severe injury or death if used improperly. Make sure you follow the manufacturer's operation procedures. Also make sure you have your supervisor's/instructor's permission to use any particular type of lifting equipment.
- Caution must be exercised when working around the power steering pump, especially if the vehicle has been driven recently or the engine is at operating temperature. The power steering fluid can be extremely hot and can burn if it comes in contact with unprotected skin. When operating the power steering system, it can be under high hydraulic pressure.
- Comply with personal and environmental safety practices associated with clothing; eye protection; hand tools; power equipment; proper ventilation; and the handling, storage, and disposal of chemicals/materials in accordance with local, state, and federal safety and environmental regulations.

Performance Standard

0—No exposure: No information or practice provided during the program; complete training required

1—Exposure only: General information provided with no practice time; close supervision needed; additional training required

2—Limited practice: Has practiced job during training program; additional training required to develop skill

3—Moderately skilled: Has performed job independently during training program; limited additional training may be required

4—Skilled: Can perform job independently with no additional training

Determine proper power steering fluid type; inspect fluid level and condition.

Time off_____

Time on_____

Total time_____

CDX Tasksheet Number: C177

1. Research specified power steering fluid for this vehicle using the appropriate service information.

   a. **Specified fluid:** _____

   b. **When should the fluid be checked? Hot:** _____ **Cold:** _____
   Either: _____

   c. **If the service information lists a procedure for flushing the power steering fluid, list the main steps (you can paraphrase, or print off the procedure):**

2. Follow the manufacturer's procedure to check the fluid level.

   > **NOTE** If power steering fluid is below the minimum level, it could mean there is a leak in the system. Investigate this possibility and report it to your supervisor/instructor.

3. Locate the power steering-fluid reservoir.

   a. **List the level of the power steering fluid:** _____

4. **Place a small amount of the fluid from the reservoir on a white piece of paper and describe its condition:**

5. **Determine any necessary action(s):**

6. Have your supervisor/instructor verify satisfactory completion of this procedure, any observations found, and any necessary action(s) recommended.

Performance Rating

CDX Tasksheet Number: C177

0	1	2	3	4

Supervisor/instructor signature _____ Date _____

▶ **TASK** Replace power steering pump filter(s).

Time off_____

Time on_____

Total time_____

CDX Tasksheet Number: C182

Vehicle used for this activity:

Year _____ Make _____ Model_____

Odometer_____ VIN_____

1. Research the vehicle you are working on to determine if it has a power steering pump filter.

   a. **List the location of the filter:** _____
   b. **Recommended change interval:** _____
   c. **Specified fluid:** _____
   d. **Flat-rate time to change the filter:** _____ hrs

2. Following the specified procedure, remove the filter and inspect any hoses or fittings for cracks and damage. **List your observations:**

3. Have your instructor verify removal and your observations. **Supervisor's/instructor initials:** _____

4. Following the specified procedure, install the new filter.

5. Top off the reservoir with the correct fluid and check for proper operation.

6. Have your supervisor/instructor verify satisfactory completion of this procedure, any observations found, and any necessary action(s) recommended.

Performance Rating

CDX Tasksheet Number: C182

0	1	2	3	4

Supervisor/instructor signature _____ Date _____

MLR 4B3   **AST** 4B10   **MAST** 4B10

Time off_____

Time on_____

Total time_____

CDX Tasksheet Number: C178

1. Follow the specified procedure to flush the power steering fluid. **If no procedure is specified, ask your supervisor/instructor to approve the following procedure**: _____

   a. With the engine off, place a drain pan under the power steering pump return hose and out of the way of the fan or other moving parts.

   b. Remove the return hose from the power steering pump. Place the return hose in the drain pan. Plug the return line fitting in the power steering pump with an appropriate plug or cap.

   c. Fill the reservoir to the proper level with new fluid. Have an assistant start the engine and slowly turn the steering wheel to flush out the old fluid. At the same time, continue to add fluid to the reservoir (with the funnel) to keep it approximately full. Continue this until clean fluid comes out of the return line and then turn off the vehicle.

   d. Reinstall the return line and fill the reservoir to the proper level.

   e. Start the vehicle again and turn the steering wheel a few times from lock to lock. Check the fluid level and top off as necessary.

   f. If a buzzing noise is heard, there is probably air trapped in the system. In this case, turn off the engine, raise the front wheels off the ground (support the vehicle on jack stands or a hoist), and turn the wheels from lock to lock with the engine off. Do this several times. Check the fluid level and top off if necessary. Lower the vehicle. Restart the engine and listen and feel for proper operation. Repeat if necessary.

   g. Properly dispose of the old power steering fluid.

   h. **List your observations:**

2. Have your supervisor/instructor verify satisfactory completion of this procedure, any observations found, and any necessary action(s) recommended.

Performance Rating

CDX Tasksheet Number: C178

0	1	2	3	4

Supervisor/instructor signature _____ Date _____

▶ TASK Remove, inspect, replace, and adjust power steering pump belt.

MLR	AST	MAST
4B5	4B12	4B12

CDX Tasksheet Number: C180

1. **Using the service information, list the following:**

   a. **Type of power steering fluid:** _____

   b. **Type of belt: V-belt:** _____ **Serpentine belt:** _____
      Toothed belt: _____

   c. **Belt-adjustment mechanism: Manual:** _____ **Automatic:** _____

   d. **Belt tension, if specified:** _____

   e. **Draw or print off and attach to this sheet the belt-routing diagram:**

2. Following the recommended procedure, loosen the adjustment mechanism and remove the power steering pump drive belt.

3. Examine the belt for cracks, splints, frayed surfaces, and distorted configurations (including stretching). **Record your observation(s):**

4. Examine the drive pulleys for any damage. **Record your observation(s):**

5. Have your supervisor/instructor verify removal. **Supervisor's/instructor's initials:** _____

   > **NOTE** You may want to skip ahead and perform the next task C181: Remove and install power steering pump while you have the belt removed. If so, return to this point when you are ready to reinstall the drive belt.

6. Following the specified procedure, replace the drive belt.

7. **Check the drive belt alignment in relation to the drive pulleys. List your observation(s):**

8. Adjust the drive belt tension to the shop manufacturer's specifications (on the manually adjusted system).

   a. **Measure the belt tension:** _____

9. Check the fluid level in the power steering reservoir. Top off with the proper fluid, if necessary.

10. Start the engine and turn the steering wheel from lock to lock. Check for the following:

    a. **Binding: Yes:** _____ **No:** _____
    b. **Excessive steering effort: Yes:** _____ **No:** _____
    c. **Uneven steering effort: Yes:** _____ **No:** _____

11. Turn the engine off.

12. **Re-measure the drive belt tension and list here:** _____

13. Have your supervisor/instructor verify satisfactory completion of this procedure, any observations found, and any necessary action(s) recommended.

Performance Rating

CDX Tasksheet Number: C180

| 0 | 1 | 2 | 3 | 4 |

Supervisor/instructor signature _____ Date _____

► **TASK** Inspect for power steering fluid leakage; determine necessary action.

MLR	AST	MAST
4B4	4B11	4B11

CDX Tasksheet Number: C179

Vehicle used for this activity:

Year _____ Make _____ Model _____

Odometer _____ VIN _____

> **NOTE** If the vehicle's engine assembly is coated with leaking fluids and road dirt, you may need to pressure wash the engine compartment before inspecting for leaks. Get your instructor's permission before performing a cleaning operation.

> **NOTE** Some very small leaks, or leaks in engines that have a lot of accumulated residue, may be best diagnosed with the use of a fluorescent dye and ultraviolet light. Check with your instructor if this vehicle is a good candidate for that procedure. If so, follow the dye check equipment manufacturer's instructions for performing this test.

1. Using a good light, inspect under the hood for any power steering fluid leaks. Inspect the reservoir, pump (including shaft seal), hoses, and fittings. **List your observation(s):**

> **NOTE** Remember that gravity tends to pull any leaking fluid down. You may need to identify the highest point of the leak to locate the source.

2. Safely raise and support the vehicle on the hoist.

3. Inspect the power steering pump, hoses, and gear box for leaks. **Identify and list the source(s) of any leak(s):**

4. **Determine necessary action(s):**

5. Have your supervisor/instructor verify satisfactory completion of this procedure, any observations found, and any necessary action(s) recommended.

Performance Rating

CDX Tasksheet Number: C179

0	1	2	3	4

Supervisor/instructor signature _____ Date _____

MLR 4B6 · **AST** 4B15 · **MAST** 4B15

Time off_____

Time on_____

Total time_____

CDX Tasksheet Number: C183

1. Research the procedure to remove and install the power steering hoses and fittings. **List the steps or print off the procedure:**

2. Following the specified procedure, drain the power steering fluid into a clean container for proper disposal according to environmental guidelines and regulations.

3. Disconnect power steering hoses from both the power steering pump and the power steering box or rack. Plug any exposed fittings to prevent entry of dirt or debris.

4. Disconnect any retaining clips.

5. Remove power steering hoses from the vehicle and place on your workbench.

6. Examine the flexible hoses for cracks, splits, chafed surfaces, and distorted configurations (including hardening and loss of flexibility). **List your observation(s):**

7. Examine any steel tubes and fittings, check for heat damage, splits, kinking, damaged threads, or restrictions. **List your observation(s):**

8. Have your supervisor/instructor verify removal. **Supervisor's/instructor's initials:** _____

9. Following the specified procedure, reinstall the power steering hoses being careful not to cross-thread any fittings or damage any hoses or tubes.

10. Have your supervisor/instructor verify satisfactory completion of this procedure, any observations found, and any necessary action(s) recommended.

Performance Rating

CDX Tasksheet Number: C183

0	1	2	3	4

Supervisor/instructor signature _____ Date _____

AST 4B13   **MAST** 4B13

Time off_____

Time on_____

Total time_____

CDX Tasksheet Number: C181

1. Research the procedure to remove and install the power steering pump. **List the steps or print off the procedure:**

2. Following the specified procedure, remove the power steering pump being careful not to damage any fittings or hoses. Also, pay close attention to the positioning of any brackets and spacers.

3. Inspect the pump and pulley. **List your observation(s):**

4. Have your supervisor/instructor verify removal. **Supervisor's/instructor's initials:** _____

NOTE You may want to skip ahead and perform the next task C699: Remove and reinstall press-fit power steering pump pulley; check pulley and belt alignment while you have the pump removed. If so, return to this point when you are ready to reinstall the pump.

5. Following the specified procedure, reinstall the power steering pump. Be careful to properly align all brackets, fittings, and hoses. Also, tighten all fasteners to their specified torque.

6. Have your supervisor/instructor verify satisfactory completion of this procedure, any observations found, and any necessary action(s) recommended.

NOTE Return to step 6 of task C180: Remove, inspect, replace, and adjust power steering pump belt to complete that task.

Performance Rating

CDX Tasksheet Number: C181

0	1	2	3	4

Supervisor/instructor signature _____ Date _____

▶ **TASK** Remove and reinstall press-fit power steering pump pulley; check pulley and belt alignment.

AST 4B14 **MAST** 4B14

CDX Tasksheet Number: C699

1. Research the procedure to remove and install the power steering pump pulley in the appropriate service information. **List the steps or print off the procedure:**

2. Using the appropriate tools, remove the press-fit power steering pump drive pulley from the drive shaft and inspect the pulley for any damage. **List your observation(s):**

3. Inspect the pump drive shaft and shaft seal for any damage. **List your observation(s):**

4. Have your supervisor/instructor verify removal. **Supervisor's/instructor's initials:** _____

5. Reinstall the press-fit drive pulley on the power steering pump using the appropriate tool(s).

> **NOTE** Return to task **C180: Remove, inspect, replace, and adjust power steering pump belt** step 6 to complete that task.

6. Have your supervisor/instructor verify satisfactory completion of this procedure, any observations found, and any necessary action(s) recommended.

Performance Rating

CDX Tasksheet Number: C699

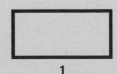 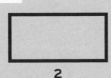 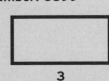

| 0 | 1 | 2 | 3 | 4 |

Supervisor/instructor signature _____ Date _____

Suspension and Steering Systems: Steering Gear Service

Student/intern information:

Name _____ Date _____ Class _____

Vehicle used for this activity:

Year _____ Make _____ Model _____

Odometer _____ VIN _____

Time off_____

Time on_____

Total time_____

Learning Objective/Task	CDX Tasksheet Number	2013 MLR NATEF Reference Number; Priority Level	2013 AST NATEF Reference Number; Priority Level	2013 MAST NATEF Reference Number; Priority Level
• Inspect rack and pinion steering gear inner tie rod ends (sockets) and bellows boots.	C933	4B1; P-1		
• Inspect rack and pinion steering gear inner tie rod ends (sockets) and bellows boots; replace as necessary.	C883		4B8; P-2	4B8; P-2
• Remove and replace rack and pinion steering gear; inspect mounting bushings and brackets.	C882		4B7; P-2	4B7; P-2

Materials Required

- Vehicle hoist
- Vehicle with rack and pinion steering gear system
- Inner tie rod socket removal tool
- Depending on the type of concern, special diagnostic tools may be required. See your supervisor/instructor for instructions to identify what tools may be required.

Some Safety Issues to Consider

- Lifting equipment such as vehicle jacks and stands, vehicle hoists, and engine hoists are important tools that increase productivity and make the job easier. However, they can also cause severe injury or death if used improperly. Make sure you follow the manufacturer's operation procedures. Also, make sure you have your supervisor's/instructor's permission to use any particular type of lifting equipment.
- Comply with personal and environmental safety practices associated with clothing; eye protection; hand tools; power equipment; proper ventilation; and the handling, storage, and disposal of chemicals/materials in accordance with local, state, and federal safety and environmental regulations.

Performance Standard

0—No exposure: No information or practice provided during the program; complete training required

1—Exposure only: General information provided with no practice time; close supervision needed; additional training required

2—Limited practice: Has practiced job during training program; additional training required to develop skill

3—Moderately skilled: Has performed job independently during training program; limited additional training may be required

4—Skilled: Can perform job independently with no additional training

Inspect rack and pinion steering gear inner tie rod ends
(sockets) and bellows boots.

Time off_____

Time on_____

Total time_____

CDX Tasksheet Number: C993

1. Research the inspection procedure for the inner tie rod ends (sockets) and bellows boots in the appropriate service information. **List any precautions:**

2. Following the specified procedure, inspect the inner tie rod ends (sockets) and bellows boots. **List your observation(s):**

   a. **Inner tie rod ends:**

   b. **Belows boots:**

3. Have your supervisor/instructor verify satisfactory completion of this procedure, any observations found, and any necessary action(s) recommended.

Performance Rating

CDX Tasksheet Number: C993

0	1	2	3	4

Supervisor/instructor signature _____ Date _____

▶ TASK Inspect rack and pinion steering gear inner tie rod ends (sockets) and bellows boots; replace as necessary.

AST 4B8 **MAST** 4B8

Time off_____

Time on_____

Total time_____

CDX Tasksheet Number: C883

1. Following the service information procedure, inspect the tie rod ends (sockets) and bellows boots. **List your observation(s):**

2. **Determine which inner tie rod end your supervisor/instructor would like you to remove:**

3. Remove the bellows boot to gain access to the inner tie rod.

4. Following the service information procedure, extend the rack (by turning the pinion shaft) to expose the locking nut of the inner tie rod socket. Using the appropriate tools, loosen the inner tie rod socket and unscrew the tie rod end.

5. **Inspect the components and list your observations:**

6. Have your supervisor/instructor verify removal. **Supervisor's/instructor's initials:** _____

7. Following the service information procedure, reassemble the inner tie rod socket and torque to the manufacturer's specifications.

8. Have your supervisor/instructor verify proper torque. **Supervisor's/instructor's initials:** _____

9. Reassemble the bellows boot and secure it according to the manufacturer's procedure.

10. Have your supervisor/instructor verify satisfactory completion of this procedure, any observations found, and any necessary action(s) recommended.

Performance Rating

CDX Tasksheet Number: C883

0	1	2	3	4

Supervisor/instructor signature _____ Date _____

Remove and replace rack and pinion steering gear; inspect mounting bushings and brackets.

AST 4B7   **MAST** 4B7

Time off_____

Time on_____

Total time_____

CDX Tasksheet Number: C882

1. Research the following procedures and specifications in the appropriate service information.

   a. **R & R rack and pinion flat rate time:** _____ hrs
   b. **R & R inner tie rod end (either side) flat rate time:** _____ hrs
   c. **Type of power steering fluid:** _____
   d. Rack and pinion steering gear removal. **List the main steps (you can paraphrase or print off the procedure):**

2. Start the engine and straighten the wheels. Turn the engine off and lock the steering column. This will keep the clock spring centered.

3. Follow the service information procedure to remove the rack and pinion steering gear. Be careful not to damage any lines, tubes, or fittings. Plug any lines or fittings to prevent entry of dirt or debris.

4. **Inspect the condition of the mounting bushings and brackets. List your observations:**

   a. Have your **supervisor/instructor** verify removal. **Supervisor's/Instructor's Initials** _____

   > NOTE You may want to skip to task **C883: Inspect rack and pinion steering gear inner tie rod ends (sockets) and bellows boots; replace as necessary**. This task will be much easier to perform with the rack and pinion removed from the vehicle. If so, return to this point when you are ready to reinstall the rack and pinion.

5. Follow the service information procedure to reinstall the rack and pinion steering gear. Be careful not to damage any lines, tubes, or fittings. Also, unless the manufacturer directs otherwise, make sure the rack is centered in its travel so that the clock spring will be indexed to the rack.

6. Torque all fasteners and fittings.

7. Check the fluid level in the power steering reservoir. Top off with the proper fluid.

8. Start the engine and bleed any air from the power steering system. Top off fluid as necessary.

9. **With the engine running, turn the steering wheel from lock to lock. Check for the following:**

    a. **Binding:** Yes: _____ No: _____

    b. **Excessive steering effort:** Yes: _____ No: _____

    c. **Uneven steering effort:** Yes: _____ No: _____

10. Have your supervisor/instructor verify satisfactory completion of this procedure, any observations found, and any necessary action(s) recommended.

Performance Rating

CDX Tasksheet Number: C882

0	1	2	3	4
☐	☐	☐	☐	☐

Supervisor/instructor signature _____ Date _____

Suspension and Steering Systems: Steering Linkage Service

Student/intern information:

Name _____ Date _____ Class _____

Vehicle used for this activity:

Year _____ Make _____ Model _____

Odometer _____ VIN _____

Time off _____

Time on _____

Total time _____

Learning Objective/Task	CDX Tasksheet Number	2013 MLR NATEF Reference Number; Priority Level	2013 AST NATEF Reference Number; Priority Level	2013 MAST NATEF Reference Number; Priority Level
• Inspect pitman arm, relay (centerlink/intermediate) rod, idler arm and mountings, and steering linkage damper.	C918	4B7; P-1		
• Inspect tie rod ends (sockets), tie rod sleeves, and clamps.	C916	4B8; P-1		
• Inspect and replace pitman arm, relay (centerlink/intermediate) rod, idler arm and mountings, and steering linkage damper.	C184		4B16; P-2	4B16; P-2
• Inspect, replace, and adjust tie rod ends (sockets), tie rod sleeves, and clamps.	C185		4B17; P-1	4B17; P-1

Materials Required

- Vehicle hoist
- Vehicle with recirculating ball steering gear system
- Pitman arm puller
- Depending on the type of concern, special diagnostic tools may be required. See your supervisor/instructor for instructions to identify what tools may be required.

Some Safety Issues to Consider

- Lifting equipment such as vehicle jacks and stands, vehicle hoists, and engine hoists are important tools that increase productivity and make the job easier. However, they can also cause severe injury or death if used improperly. Make sure you follow the manufacturer's operation procedures. Also, make sure you have your supervisor's/instructor's permission to use any particular type of lifting equipment.
- Comply with personal and environmental safety practices associated with clothing; eye protection; hand tools; power equipment; proper ventilation; and the handling, storage, and disposal of chemicals/materials in accordance with local, state, and federal safety and environmental regulations.

Performance Standard

0—No exposure: No information or practice provided during the program; complete training required

1—Exposure only: General information provided with no practice time; close supervision needed; additional training required

2—Limited practice: Has practiced job during training program; additional training required to develop skill

3—Moderately skilled: Has performed job independently during training program; limited additional training may be required

4—Skilled: Can perform job independently with no additional training

Inspect pitman arm, relay (centerlink/intermediate) rod, idler arm and mountings, and steering linkage damper.

MLR
4B7

Time off_____

Time on_____

Total time_____

CDX Tasksheet Number: C918

1. Research the following specifications and procedures in the appropriate service information.

   a. **Pitman arm locking nut torque:** _____ **ft-lbs/Nm**

   b. **Tie rod nut torque:** _____ **ft-lbs/Nm**

   c. **Maximum allowable play in each of the steering linkage joints:**

2. Safely lift and support the vehicle according to the procedure listed in the service information.

3. **Follow the manufacturer's procedure and inspect the steering system parts listed. List your observation(s):**

   a. **Pitman arm:**

   b. **Relay (centerlink/intermediate) rod:**

   c. **Idler arm and mountings:**

   d. **Steering linkage damper, if equipped:**

   e. **Tie rod ends:**

    f. Tie rod sleeves and clamps:

4. Determine any necessary actions:

5. Have your supervisor/instructor verify satisfactory completion of this procedure, any observations found, and any necessary action(s) recommended.

Performance Rating

CDX Tasksheet Number: C918

0	1	2	3	4

Supervisor/instructor signature _____ Date _____

MLR
4B8

Time off_____

Time on_____

Total time_____

CDX Tasksheet Number: C916

1. Research the following specifications and procedures in the appropriate service information.

    a. Maximum allowable play in the tie rod ends:

2. Safely lift and support the vehicle according to the specified procedure listed in the service information.

3. Follow the manufacturer's procedure and inspect the steering system parts listed. **List your observation(s):**

    a. Tie rod ends:

    b. Tie rod sleeves and clamps:

4. **Determine any necessary actions:**

5. Have your supervisor/instructor verify satisfactory completion of this procedure, any observations found, and any necessary action(s) recommended.

Performance Rating

CDX Tasksheet Number: C916

0	1	2	3	4

Supervisor/instructor signature _____ Date _____

► **TASK** Inspect and replace pitman arm, relay (centerlink/
intermediate) rod, idler arm and mountings, and
steering linkage damper.

AST 4B16 **MAST** 4B16

Time off_____
Time on_____
Total time_____

CDX Tasksheet Number: C184

> **NOTE** Completion of this task also satisfies task C916 above: Inspect pitman arm,
> relay (centerlink/intermediate) rod, idler arm and mountings, and steering linkage
> damper. MLR:4B8 Have your instructor sign off this task at the same time.

1. Research the following specifications and procedures in the appropriate service
   information.

   a. **Maximum allowable play in each of the steering linkage joints:**

2. Lift and support the vehicle according to the procedure listed in the service
   information.

3. Follow the manufacturer's procedure and inspect the steering system parts listed.
   List your observation(s):

   a. **Pitman arm:**

   b. **Relay (centerlink/intermediate) rod:**

   c. **Idler arm and mountings:**

   d. **Steering linkage damper, if equipped:**

    e. **Tie rod ends:**

    f. **Tie rod sleeves and clamps:**

4. Following the manufacturer's procedure, mark the location of the pitman arm shaft and pitman arm splines. Disconnect the pitman arm from the relay (centerlink/intermediate) rod steering linkage.

5. Remove the pitman arm-retaining nut and, using the manufacturer's recommended removal tool, remove the pitman arm.

6. If the vehicle is fitted with a steering damper, remove the steering damper and place it on your workbench.

7. Disconnect the relay (centerlink/intermediate) rod steering linkage.

8. Remove idler arm assembly.

9. Remove tie rod ends from steering knuckles.

> **NOTE** The use of a pickle fork will damage the dust boots. Only use this tool on joints you will be replacing. On joints you will be reusing, try the hammer method to break the joint free. See your instructor for details.

10. Loosen the tie rod adjusting sleeve clamp bolts. Remove tie rod ends from sleeves.

> **NOTE** Count the number of turns as you back out each tie rod from its sleeve so you can reinstall it in approximately the same position. This will assist in making the wheel alignment easier to perform.

11. **Inspect all components and list your observations:**

12. Have your supervisor/instructor verify removal. **Supervisor's/instructor's initials: _____**

13. Reassemble all components following the manufacturer's recommended procedure, being sure to torque all fasteners and secure all joints with new cotter pins (or other approved method).

   a. List the torque you tightened the tie rod nuts to: _____ ft-lb/Nm
   b. List the torque you tightened the tie rod adjusting sleeve nuts to: _____ ft-lb/Nm
   c. Did you replace all removed cotter pins with new cotter pins? Yes: _____ No: _____

14 Start the vehicle and check for binding or improper steering operation. List your observations:

NOTE Before this vehicle can be driven, it MUST have a wheel alignment performed. Failure to do so means this is an unsafe vehicle, which could result in substantial injury or even death.

15. Have your supervisor/instructor verify satisfactory completion of this procedure, any observations found, and any necessary action(s) recommended.

Performance Rating

CDX Tasksheet Number: C184

0	1	2	3	4

Supervisor/instructor signature _____ Date _____

Inspect, replace, and adjust tie rod ends (sockets), tie rod sleeves, and clamps.

AST 4B17 **MAST** 4B17

Time off_____

Time on_____

Total time_____

CDX Tasksheet Number: C185

> **NOTE** Completion of this task also satisfies task C920 above: Inspect tie rod ends (sockets), tie rod sleeves, and clamps. MLR:4B9 Have your instructor sign off this task at the same time.

1. Research the following specifications and procedures in the appropriate service information.

   a. **Maximum allowable play in the tie rod ends:**

2. Lift and support the vehicle according to the procedure listed in the service information.

3. Follow the manufacturer's procedure and inspect the steering system parts listed. **List your observation(s):**

   a. **Tie rod ends:**

   b. **Tie rod sleeves and clamps:**

4. **Determine any necessary actions:**

5. Remove tie rod ends from steering knuckles.

> **NOTE** The use of a pickle fork will damage the dust boots. Only use this tool on joints you will be replacing. On joints you will be reusing, try the hammer method to break the joint free. See your instructor for details.

6. Loosen the tie rod adjusting sleeve clamp bolts. Remove tie rod ends from sleeves.

> **NOTE** Count the number of turns as you back out each tie rod from its sleeve so you can reinstall it in approximately the same position. This will assist in making the wheel alignment easier to perform.

7. **Inspect all components and list your observations:**

8. Have your supervisor/instructor verify removal. **Supervisor's/instructor's initials:** _____

9. Reassemble all components following the manufacturer's specified procedure, being sure to torque all fasteners and secure all joints with new cotter pins (or other approved method).
    a. **List the torque you tightened the tie rod nuts to:** _____ **ft-lb/Nm**
    b. **List the torque you tightened the tie rod adjusting sleeve nuts to:** _____ **ft-lb/Nm**
    c. **Did you replace all removed cotter pins with new cotter pins? Yes:** _____ **No:** _____

10. Start the vehicle and check for binding or improper steering operation. List your observations:

> **NOTE** Before this vehicle can be driven, it MUST have a wheel alignment performed. Failure to do so means this is an unsafe vehicle which could result in substantial injury or even death.

11. Have your supervisor/instructor verify satisfactory completion of this procedure, any observations found, and any necessary action(s) recommended.

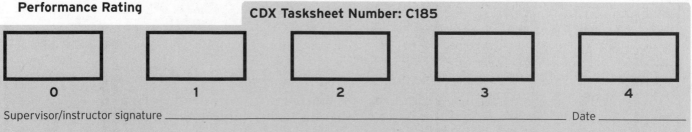

Performance Rating

CDX Tasksheet Number: C185

0	1	2	3	4

Supervisor/instructor signature _____ Date _____

Suspension and Steering Systems: Steering Gear Diagnosis

Student/intern information:

Name _____ Date _____ Class _____

Vehicle used for this activity:

Year _____ Make _____ Model_____

Odometer_____VIN_____

Learning Objective/Task	CDX Tasksheet Number	2013 MLR NATEF Reference Number; Priority Level	2013 AST NATEF Reference Number; Priority Level	2013 MAST NATEF Reference Number; Priority Level
• Diagnose power steering gear (non-rack and pinion) binding, uneven turning effort, looseness, hard steering, and noise concerns; determine necessary action.	C884		4B4; P-2	4B4; P-2
• Diagnose power steering gear (rack and pinion) binding, uneven turning effort, looseness, hard steering, and noise concerns; determine necessary action.	C880		4B5; P-2	4B5; P-2

Time off_____

Time on_____

Total time_____

Materials Required

- Vehicle hoist
- Vehicle with rack and pinion steering gear system concern
- Vehicle with non-rack and pinion steering gear system concern
- Depending on the type of concern, special diagnostic tools may be required. See your supervisor/instructor for instructions to identify what tools may be required.

Some Safety Issues to Consider

- Diagnosis of this fault may require test-driving the vehicle on the school grounds. Attempt this task only with full permission from your instructor and follow all the guidelines exactly.
- You will be working under the hood of a running vehicle. Keep your hands and fingers away from moving belts, fans, and other parts.
- When running any vehicles in the shop, make sure you use the shop's exhaust ventilation system to discharge all exhaust gas safely outside.
- Lifting equipment such as vehicle jacks and stands, vehicle hoists, and engine hoists are important tools that increase productivity and make the job easier. However, they can also cause severe injury or death if used improperly. Make sure you follow the manufacturer's operation procedures. Also, make sure you have your supervisor's/instructor's permission to use any particular type of lifting equipment.
- Comply with personal and environmental safety practices associated with clothing; eye protection; hand tools; power equipment; proper ventilation; and the handling, storage, and disposal of chemicals/materials in accordance with local, state, and federal safety and environmental regulations.

Performance Standard

0—No exposure: No information or practice provided during the program; complete training required

1—Exposure only: General information provided with no practice time; close supervision needed; additional training required

2—Limited practice: Has practiced job during training program; additional training required to develop skill

3—Moderately skilled: Has performed job independently during training program; limited additional training may be required

4—Skilled: Can perform job independently with no additional training

► **TASK** Diagnose power steering gear (non-rack and pinion) binding, uneven turning effort, looseness, hard steering, and noise concerns; determine necessary action.

AST	MAST
4B4	4B4

CDX Tasksheet Number: C884

1. **List the power steering system-related customer concern:**

2. **Verify the concern and list your observations here:**

3. Research the possible causes for this concern in the appropriate service information.

    a. **List or print off and attach to this sheet the possible causes:**

    b. **List or print off and attach to this sheet the procedure for diagnosing the concern:**

4. Follow the specified procedure to diagnose the concern. **List your tests and results here:**

5. **List the cause of the concern:**

6. **Determine any necessary action(s) to correct the fault:**

7. Have your supervisor/instructor verify satisfactory completion of this procedure, any observations found, and any necessary action(s) recommended.

Performance Rating

CDX Tasksheet Number: C884

0	1	2	3	4

Supervisor/instructor signature _____ Date _____

Diagnose power steering gear (rack and pinion) binding, uneven turning effort, looseness, hard steering, and noise concerns; determine necessary action.

AST 4B5 **MAST** 4B5

Time off_____

Time on_____

Total time_____

CDX Tasksheet Number: C880

Vehicle used for this activity:

Year _____ Make _____ Model_____

Odometer_____ VIN_____

1. **List the power steering system-related customer concern:**

2. **Verify the concern and list your observations here:**

3. Research the possible causes for this concern in the appropriate service information.

    a. **List or print off and attach to this sheet the possible causes:**

    b. **List or print off and attach to this sheet the procedure for diagnosing the concern:**

4. Follow the specified procedure to diagnose the concern. **List your tests and results here:**

5. List the cause of the concern:

6. Determine any necessary action(s) to correct the fault:

7. Have your supervisor/instructor verify satisfactory completion of this procedure, any observations found, and any necessary action(s) recommended.

Performance Rating

CDX Tasksheet Number: C880

0	1	2	3	4

Supervisor/instructor signature _____ Date _____

Suspension and Steering Systems: Steering Column Service

Student/intern information:

Name _____ Date _____ Class _____

Vehicle used for this activity:

Year _____ Make _____ Model _____

Odometer _____ VIN _____

Time off _____

Time on _____

Total time _____

Learning Objective/Task	CDX Tasksheet Number	2013 MLR NATEF Reference Number; Priority Level	2013 AST NATEF Reference Number; Priority Level	2013 MAST NATEF Reference Number; Priority Level
• Disable and enable supplemental restraint system (SRS).	C168	4A2; P-1	4B1; P-1	4B1; P-1
• Remove and replace steering wheel; center/time supplemental restraint system (SRS) coil (clock spring).	C169		4B2; P-1	4B2; P-1
• Inspect steering shaft universal joint(s), flexible coupling(s), collapsible column, lock cylinder mechanism, and steering wheel; perform necessary action.	C173		4B6; P-2	4B6; P-2
• Diagnose steering column noises, looseness, and binding concerns (including tilt mechanisms); determine necessary action.	C170		4B3; P-2	4B3; P-2

Materials Required

- Vehicle fitted with supplemental restraint system (SRS)
- Steering wheel puller
- Manufacturer- and job-specific tools
- Masking tape

Some Safety Issues to Consider

- Working on the airbag system can be very dangerous. Consult the service information for the vehicle you are working on and ensure all safety precautions are followed.
- Accidental deployment of the airbag system could happen if you inadvertently probe the wrong wire. Most manufacturers use yellow-colored wiring to denote wiring for the airbag system. Always be aware of the system/circuit you are working on.
- Comply with personal and environmental safety practices associated with clothing; eye protection; hand tools; power equipment; proper ventilation; and the handling, storage, and disposal of chemicals/materials in accordance with local, state, and federal safety and environmental regulations.

Performance Standard

0–No exposure: No information or practice provided during the program; complete training required

1–Exposure only: General information provided with no practice time; close supervision needed; additional training required

2–Limited practice: Has practiced job during training program; additional training required to develop skill

3–Moderately skilled: Has performed job independently during training program; limited additional training may be required

4–Skilled: Can perform job independently with no additional training

► **TASK** Disable and enable supplemental restraint system (SRS).

MLR 4A2 **AST** 4B1 **MAST** 4B1

CDX Tasksheet Number: C168

1. Locate "disable vehicle SRS system" in the appropriate service information for the vehicle you are working on.

    a. **List or print off and attach to this sheet the safety precautions to be taken when disabling the SRS system:**

    b. **List or print off and attach to this sheet the steps to disable the SRS system:**

    c. **List or print off and attach to this sheet the steps to enable the SRS system:**

2. Have your supervisor/instructor verify your listed procedures. **Supervisor's/ instructor's initials:** _____

3. Disarm the SRS system.

4. Have your supervisor/instructor verify that the SRS is disabled. **Supervisor's/ instructor's initials:** _____

> **NOTE** You may want to consider skipping to task C169: Remove and replace steering wheel; center/time supplemental restraint system (SRS) coil (clock spring) since it requires disabling the SRS. Return to this step when you complete that task and re-enable the SRS.

5. Following the specified procedure, enable the vehicle's SRS.

6. Have your supervisor/instructor verify satisfactory completion of this procedure, any observations found, and any necessary action(s) recommended.

Performance Rating

CDX Tasksheet Number: C168

0	1	2	3	4

Supervisor/instructor signature _____ Date _____

▶ **TASK** Remove and replace steering wheel; center/time supplemental
restraint system (SRS) coil (clock spring).

AST 4B2   **MAST** 4B2

Time off_____

Time on_____

Total time_____

CDX Tasksheet Number: C169

1. Locate "remove and replace steering wheel" and "center/time SRS clock spring" procedures in the appropriate service information.

   a. **List or print off and attach to this sheet the procedures for removing and replacing the steering wheel:**

   b. **List or print off and attach to this sheet the procedure to center/time the SRS clock spring:**

2. Have your supervisor/instructor verify your listed procedures. **Supervisor's/ instructor's initials:** _____

3. Following the specified procedures and precautions, remove the steering wheel.

4. Following the specified procedures and precautions, remove the clock spring.

5. **Inspect the components and list your observation(s):**

6. Have your supervisor/instructor verify the removal of these components. **Supervisor's/instructor's initials:** _____

7. Reassemble the steering column. Be sure to follow all manufacturer-recommended procedures and precautions.

   NOTE Return to task step 5 of C168: Disable and enable supplemental restraint system (SRS) to enable the SRS.

8. Have your supervisor/instructor verify satisfactory completion of this procedure, any observations found, and any necessary action(s) recommended.

Performance Rating

CDX Tasksheet Number: C169

0	1	2	3	4

Supervisor/instructor signature _____ Date _____

▶ TASK Inspect steering shaft universal joint(s), flexible coupling(s), collapsible column, lock cylinder mechanism, and steering wheel; perform necessary action.

AST 4B6 **MAST** 4B6

Time off_____

Time on_____

Total time_____

CDX Tasksheet Number: C173

1. If the vehicle is fitted with an SRS, disable it according to the manufacturer's procedure and precautions.

2. Safely raise and support the vehicle so the tires are a few inches off the floor.

3. With the steering column lock activated, try to turn the steering wheel from side to side.

   a. **Is the locking mechanism working? Yes: _____ No: _____**
   b. **List your observation(s):**

4. With the engine ignition key in the "off" position, ensure the steering lock is not engaged and have an assistant rock the steering wheel from side to side (just enough to move the road wheels slightly). While the steering wheel is being rocked, check for any wear or looseness in the shaft universal joint(s) or flexible coupling(s).

   a. **List your observation(s):**

5. Following the specified procedure, check that the steering column collapsible action has not been compromised.

   a. **List your observation(s):**

6. **Check the steering wheel for the following and list any observation(s):**

   a. **Looseness on the steering shaft:**

   b. **Structural damage:**

   c. **SRS airbag is intact and has appropriate pad/cover:**

   d. **Size and appropriateness for the make and model of the vehicle (refer to the service information):**

7. Have your supervisor/instructor verify your observations. **Supervisor's/instructor's initials:** _____

8. **Perform any necessary action(s) and list them here:**

9. Following the specified procedure, enable the SRS.

10. Have your supervisor/instructor verify satisfactory completion of this procedure, any observations found, and any necessary action(s) recommended.

Performance Rating

CDX Tasksheet Number: C173

0	1	2	3	4

Supervisor/instructor signature _____ Date _____

Diagnose steering column noises, looseness, and binding concerns (including tilt mechanisms); determine necessary action.

CDX Tasksheet Number: C170

Vehicle used for this activity:

Year _____ Make _____ Model_____

Odometer_____ VIN_____

1. **List the steering column-related customer concern:**

2. **Verify the concern and list your observations here:**

3. Research the possible causes for this concern in the appropriate service information.

   a. **List or print off and attach to this sheet the possible causes:**

   b. **List or print off and attach to this sheet the procedure for diagnosing the concern:**

   c. **List the precautions when working on this steering column:**

4. **Follow the specified procedure to diagnose the concern. List your tests and results here:**

5. **List the cause of the concern:**

6. **Determine any necessary action(s) to correct this fault:**

7. Have your supervisor/instructor verify satisfactory completion of this procedure, any observations found, and any necessary action(s) recommended.

Performance Rating

CDX Tasksheet Number: C170

0	1	2	3	4

Supervisor/instructor signature _____ Date _____

Suspension and Steering Systems: Front Suspension Service—Long and Short Arm

Student/intern information:

Name _____ Date _____ Class _____

Vehicle used for this activity:

Year _____ Make _____ Model _____

Odometer _____ VIN _____

Learning Objective/Task	CDX Tasksheet Number	2013 MLR NATEF Reference Number; Priority Level	2013 AST NATEF Reference Number; Priority Level	2013 MAST NATEF Reference Number; Priority Level
• Inspect and replace front stabilizer bar (sway bar) bushings, brackets, and links.	C925	4B15; P-1		
• Inspect suspension system coil springs and spring insulators (silencers).	C923	4B13; P-1		
• Inspect upper- and lower-control arms, bushings, and shafts.	C920	4B9; P-1		
• Inspect and replace rebound and jounce bumpers.	C919	4B10; P-1		
• Inspect upper- and lower-ball joints (with or without wear indicators).	C922	4B12; P-1		
• Inspect, remove, and install front stabilizer bar (sway bar) bushings, brackets, and links.	C793		4C9; P-3	4C9; P-3
• Inspect, remove, and install short- and long-arm suspension system coil springs and spring insulators.	C193		4C7; P-3	4C7; P-3
• Inspect, remove, and install steering knuckle assemblies.	C192		4C6; P-3	4C6; P-3
• Remove, inspect, and install upper- and lower-control arms, bushings, shafts, and rebound bumpers.	C790		4C3; P-3	4C3; P-3
• Inspect, remove, and install strut rods and bushings.	C791		4C4: P-3	4C4: P-3
• Inspect, remove, and install upper- and/or lower-ball joints (with or without wear indicators).	C792		4C5; P-2	4C5; P-2

Time off_____

Time on_____

Total time_____

- Vehicle equipped with short- and long-arm suspension
- Dial indicator
- Spring compressor
- Ball Joint press
- Torque wrench
- Manufacturer- and job-specific tools
- Grease gun with specified grease

Some Safety Issues to Consider

- Lifting equipment such as vehicle jacks and stands, vehicle hoists, and engine hoists are important tools that increase productivity and make the job easier. However, they can also cause severe injury or death if used improperly. Make sure you follow the manufacturer's operation procedures. Also, make sure you have your supervisor's/instructor's permission to use any particular type of lifting equipment.
- Some suspension systems are electronically controlled, and can raise or lower without notice. Please familiarize yourself with the manufacturer's safety precautions related to these procedures.
- Vehicle springs store a lot of energy, which, if released improperly, can cause injury or death. Please familiarize yourself with the manufacturer's safety precautions related to these procedures.
- Comply with personal and environmental safety practices associated with clothing; eye protection; hand tools; power equipment; proper ventilation; and the handling, storage, and disposal of chemicals/materials in accordance with local, state, and federal safety and environmental regulations.

Performance Standard

0–No exposure: No information or practice provided during the program; complete training required

1–Exposure only: General information provided with no practice time; close supervision needed; additional training required

2–Limited practice: Has practiced job during training program; additional training required to develop skill

3–Moderately skilled: Has performed job independently during training program; limited additional training may be required

4–Skilled: Can perform job independently with no additional training

► TASK Inspect and replace front stabilizer bar (sway bar) bushings, brackets, and links.

Time off_____

Time on_____

Total time_____

CDX Tasksheet Number: C925

1. Research the disassembly and inspection procedure for the stabilizer bar, bushings, brackets, and links in the appropriate service information.

   a. List any precautions:

   b. List or print off and attach to this sheet the steps to disassemble the stabilizer bar system.

2. Safely raise and support the vehicle.

3. Following the instructions and all the safety precautions outlined in the service information, inspect the stabilizer bar, bushings, and links. **List your observation(s):**

   a. Stabilizer bar:

   b. Bushing(s):

   c. Link(s):

4. Following the instructions and all the safety precautions outlined in the service information, dismantle, clean, and re-inspect the stabilizer bar, bushings, and links. **List your observation(s):**

   a. Stabilizer bar:

b. Bushing(s):

c. Link(s):

5. **Determine any necessary action(s):**

6. Have your supervisor/instructor verify disassembly and your observations. **Supervisor's/instructor's initials:** _____

7. Following the specified procedure, reassemble the stabilizer bar, bushings, and links. **List your observations:**

8. Have your supervisor/instructor verify satisfactory completion of this procedure, any observations found, and any necessary action(s) recommended.

Performance Rating

CDX Tasksheet Number: C925

0	1	2	3	4

Supervisor/instructor signature _____ Date _____

CDX Tasksheet Number: C923

1. Research the inspection procedure for the coil springs and spring insulators in the appropriate service information.

   a. **List or print off and attach to this sheet the steps to inspect the coil springs and insulators:**

2. Following the instructions and all the safety precautions outlined in the service information, inspect the coil spring and spring insulators. **List your observation(s):**

   a. **Coil spring:**

   b. **Spring insulators:**

3. **Determine any necessary action(s):**

4. Have your supervisor/instructor verify satisfactory completion of this procedure, any observations found, and any necessary action(s) recommended.

Performance Rating

CDX Tasksheet Number: C923

0	1	2	3	4

Supervisor/instructor signature _____ Date _____

CDX Tasksheet Number: C920

1. Research the inspection procedure for the upper- and lower-control arms, bushings, and shafts in the appropriate service information.

    a. **List any precautions:**

    b. **List or print off and attach to this sheet the steps to inspect the control arms:**

2. **Following the specified procedure outlined in the service information, inspect the upper- and lower-control arms, bushings and shafts. List your observation(s):**

    a. **Upper-control arm:**

    b. **Lower-control arm:**

    c. **Bushings:**

    d. **Shafts:**

3. **Determine any necessary action(s):**

4. Have your supervisor/instructor verify satisfactory completion of this procedure, any observations found, and any necessary action(s) recommended.

Performance Rating

CDX Tasksheet Number: C920

0	1	2	3	4

Supervisor/instructor signature _____ Date _____

MLR
4B10

Time off _____

Time on _____

CDX Tasksheet Number: C919

Total time _____

1. Research the inspection and replacement procedure for any rebound and jounce bumpers in the appropriate service information.

   a. **List or print off and attach to this sheet the steps to inspect and replace any rebound and jounce bumpers:**

2. **Following the specified procedure outlined in the service information, inspect the rebound and jounce bumpers. List your observation(s):**

   a. **Rebound bumpers:**

   b. **Jounce bumpers:**

3. **Determine any necessary action(s):**

4. Following the specified procedure, remove at least one rebound or jounce bumper. **List your observations:**

5. Have your supervisor/instructor verify removal and your observations. **Supervisor's/ instructor's initials:** _____

6. Following the specified procedure, reinstall the rebound or jounce bumper.

7. Have your supervisor/instructor verify satisfactory completion of this procedure, any observations found, and any necessary action(s) recommended.

Performance Rating

CDX Tasksheet Number: C919

0	1	2	3	4

Supervisor/instructor signature _____ Date _____

CDX Tasksheet Number: C922

Time off _____

Time on _____

Total time _____

1. Research the inspection procedure for the upper- and/or lower-ball joints in the appropriate service information.

   a. Maximum allowable play in the lower-ball joint: _____ in/mm

   b. Maximum allowable play in the upper-ball joint; if applicable: _____ in/mm

   c. Which ball joint is the load-bearing ball joint? Lower: _____ Upper: _____

   d. List or print off and attach to this sheet the steps to inspect the lower- and/or upper-ball joints:

2. **Following the specified procedure outlined in the service information, measure the play in the lower- and/or upper-ball joints. List your observation(s):**

   a. Measure the play in the lower-ball joint: LF: _____ in/mm RF: _____ in/mm

   b. Measure the play in the upper-ball joint: LF: _____ in/mm RF: _____ in/mm

3. **Determine any necessary action(s):**

4. Have your supervisor/instructor verify satisfactory completion of this procedure, any observations found, and any necessary action(s) recommended.

Performance Rating

CDX Tasksheet Number: C922

0	1	2	3	4

Supervisor/instructor signature _____ Date _____

Inspect, remove, and install front stabilizer bar (sway bar) bushings, brackets, and links.

AST 4C9   **MAST** 4C9

Time off_____

Time on_____

Total time_____

CDX Tasksheet Number: C793

1. Research the disassembly and inspection procedure for the stabilizer bar, bushings, brackets, and links in the appropriate service information.

   a. **List any precautions:**

   b. **List or print off and attach to this sheet the steps to disassemble the stabilizer bar system.**

2. Safely raise and support the vehicle.

3. **Following the specified procedure outlined in the service information, inspect, dismantle, clean, and re-inspect the stabilizer bar, bushings, and links. List your observation(s):**

   a. **Stabilizer bar:**

   b. **Bushing(s):**

   c. **Link(s):**

4. **Determine any necessary action(s):**

   The rest of this task is completed by performing the remainder of the tasks, and can be signed off at the end of this tasksheet. Please refer to page 588 for the completion of this task.

Inspect, remove, and install short- and long-arm suspension system coil springs and spring insulators.

AST 4C7   **MAST** 4C7

Time off_____

Time on_____

Total time_____

CDX Tasksheet Number: C193

1. Research the removal and inspection procedure for the coil springs and spring insulators in the appropriate service information.

    a. **List any precautions:**

    b. **List or print off and attach to this sheet the steps to remove the coil springs.**

2. Have your supervisor/instructor verify your listed precautions and procedures. **Supervisor's/instructor's initials:** _____

3. Following the specified procedure outlined in the service information, inspect, remove, clean, and re-inspect the coil spring and spring insulators. **List your observation(s):**

    a. **Coil spring:**

    b. **Spring insulators:**

4. **Determine any necessary action(s):**

    The rest of this task is completed by performing the remainder of the tasks, and can be signed off at the end of this tasksheet. Please refer to page 587 for the completion of this task.

CDX Tasksheet Number: C192

1. Research the removal and inspection procedure for the steering knuckle assembly in the appropriate service information.

   a. **List any precautions:**

   b. **List or print off and attach to this sheet the steps to remove the steering knuckle assembly.**

2. Following the specified procedure outlined in the service information, inspect, remove, clean, and re-inspect the steering knuckle assembly. **List your observation(s):**

   a. **Steering knuckle:**

3. **Determine any necessary action(s):**

The rest of this task is completed by performing the remainder of the tasks, and can be signed off at the end of this tasksheet. Please refer to page 588 for the completion of this task.

Remove, inspect, and install upper- and lower-control arms, bushings, shafts, and rebound bumpers.

AST 4C3 **MAST** 4C3

Time off_____

Time on_____

CDX Tasksheet Number: C790

Total time_____

1. Research the removal and inspection procedure for the upper- and lower-control arms, bushings, shafts, and rebound bumpers in the appropriate service information.

    a. List any precautions:

    b. List or print off and attach to this sheet the steps to remove the control arms.

2. Following the specified procedure outlined in the service information, inspect, remove, clean, and re-inspect the upper- and lower-control arms, bushings, shafts, and rebound bumpers. **List your observation(s):**

    a. Upper-control arm:

    b. Lower-control arm:

    c. Bushings:

    d. Shafts:

    e. Rebound bumper(s):

3. **Determine any necessary action(s):**

The rest of this task is completed by performing the remainder of the tasks, and can be signed off at the end of this tasksheet. Please refer to page 587 for the completion of this task.

Time off_____

Time on_____

Total time_____

CDX Tasksheet Number: C791

1. Research the inspection and disassembly procedure for the strut rods and bushings in the appropriate service information.

   a. **List any precautions:**

   b. **List or print off and attach to this sheet the steps to inspect and disassemble the strut rods and bushings:**

2. Following the specified procedure outlined in the service information, remove the strut rods and bushings from the vehicle. **List your observation(s):**

   a. **Strut rod:**

   b. **Bushings:**

3. **Determine any necessary action(s):**

   The rest of this task is completed by performing the remainder of the tasks, and can be signed off at the end of this tasksheet. Please refer to page 587 for the completion of this task.

► **TASK**   Inspect, remove, and install upper- and/or lower-ball joints
(with or without wear indicators).

AST **4C5**   **MAST 4C5**

Time off_____

Time on_____

Total time_____

CDX Tasksheet Number: C792

1. Research the inspection and disassembly procedure for the upper- and/or lower-ball joints in the appropriate service information.

> **NOTE** The ball joints play was measured during Task C922, prior to disassembling the suspension system. Transfer the appropriate readings from that tasksheet, and continue on step 1f. If you are performing this task individually, begin with step 1.

   a. **Maximum allowable play in the lower-ball joint:** _____ **in/mm**

   b. **Maximum allowable play in the upper-ball joint; if applicable:** _____ **in/mm**

   c. **Which ball joint is the load-bearing ball joint? Lower:** _____
   Upper: _____

   d. **List any precautions:**

   e. **List or print off and attach to this sheet the steps to inspect the lower- and/or upper-ball joints.**

   f. **List or print off and attach to this sheet the steps to disassemble the lower- and/or upper-ball joints.**

2. Following the specified procedure, measure the play in the lower and/or upper ball joint(s). **List your observation(s):**

   a. **Measure the play in the lower ball joint: Left** _____ **in/mm**
   Right: _____ **in/mm**

   b. **Measure the play in the upper ball joints: Left:** _____ **in/mm**
   Right: _____ **in/mm.**

3. Following the specified procedure, remove, clean, and re-inspect the lower-and/or upper-ball joints. **List your observation(s):**

4. **Determine any necessary action(s):**

5. Have your instructor verify the removal of all suspension components and check your observations and necessary actions. Get permission to reassemble the assembly.
Supervisor's/instructor's initials: _____

> **NOTE** At this time, replace/reinstall all removed suspension components following the manufacturer's procedures and precautions. Be sure to tighten all fasteners to their specified torque and replace any retaining devices such as cotter pins (with new ones) and nylon locking nuts. Be careful to route all wires, hoses, and tubes in their original factory position.

6. Inspect the reassembled suspension unit for any loose fasteners, improperly installed components, etc. **List your observations here:**

7. Determine any necessary action(s):

8. Have your supervisor/instructor verify satisfactory completion of this procedure, any observations found, and any necessary action(s) recommended.

Performance Rating

CDX Tasksheet Number: C792

0	1	2	3	4

Supervisor/instructor signature _____ Date _____

▶ TASK **CONTINUATION OF TASK** C791/4C4: Inspect, remove, and install strut rods and bushings (from page 583).

Time off_____

Time on_____

CDX Tasksheet Number: C791

5. Have your supervisor/instructor verify satisfactory completion of this procedure, any observations found, and any necessary action(s) recommended.

Total time_____

Performance Rating

CDX Tasksheet Number: C791

| 0 | 1 | 2 | 3 | 4 |

Supervisor/instructor signature _____ Date _____

▶ TASK **CONTINUATION OF TASK** C790/4C3: Remove, inspect, and install upper- and lower-control arms, bushings, shafts, and rebound bumpers (from page 581).

Time off_____

Time on_____

CDX Tasksheet Number: C709

4. Have your supervisor/instructor verify satisfactory completion of this procedure, any observations found, and any necessary action(s) recommended.

Total time_____

Performance Rating

CDX Tasksheet Number: C709

| 0 | 1 | 2 | 3 | 4 |

Supervisor/instructor signature _____ Date _____

▶ TASK **CONTINUATION OF TASK** C193/4C7: Inspect, remove, and install short- and long-arm suspension system coil springs and spring insulators (from page 577).

Time off_____

Time on_____

CDX Tasksheet Number: C193

6. Have your supervisor/instructor verify satisfactory completion of this procedure, any observations found, and any necessary action(s) recommended.

Total time_____

Performance Rating

CDX Tasksheet Number: C193

| 0 | 1 | 2 | 3 | 4 |

Supervisor/instructor signature _____ Date _____

Total time

Time on

Time off

▶ **TASK** **CONTINUATION OF TASK** C192/4C6: Inspect, remove, and install steering knuckle assemblies (from page 579).

CDX Tasksheet Number: C192

4. Have your supervisor/instructor verify satisfactory completion of this procedure, any observations found, and any necessary action(s) recommended.

Performance Rating

CDX Tasksheet Number: C192

0	1	2	3	4

Supervisor/instructor signature _____ Date _____

Total time

Time on

Time off

▶ **TASK** **CONTINUATION OF TASK** C793/4C9: Inspect, remove, and install front stabilizer bar (sway bar) bushings, brackets, and links (from page 575).

CDX Tasksheet Number: C793

5. Have your supervisor/instructor verify satisfactory completion of this procedure, any observations found, and any necessary action(s) recommended.

Performance Rating

CDX Tasksheet Number: C793

0	1	2	3	4

Supervisor/instructor signature _____ Date _____

Suspension and Steering Systems: Front Suspension Service–Strut and Torsion Bar

Student/intern information:

Name _____ Date _____ Class _____

Vehicle used for this activity:

Year _____ Make _____ Model _____

Odometer _____ VIN _____

Learning Objective/Task	CDX Tasksheet Number	2013 MLR NATEF Reference Number; Priority Level	2013 AST NATEF Reference Number; Priority Level	2013 MAST NATEF Reference Number; Priority Level
• Inspect strut cartridge or assembly.	C926	4B16; P-1		
• Inspect front-strut bearing and mount.	C927	4B17; P-1		
• Inspect track bar, strut rods/radius arms, and related mounts and bush-ings.	C921	4B11; P-1		
• Inspect suspension system torsion bars and mounts.	C924	4B14; P-1		
• Inspect, remove, and install strut cartridge or assembly, strut coil spring, insulators (silencers), and upper-strut bearing mount.	C794		4C10; P-3	4C10; P-3
• Inspect, remove, and install track bar, strut rods/radius arms, and related mounts and bushings.	C934		4C11; P-3	4C11; P-3
• Inspect, remove, and install torsion bars and mounts.	C194		4C8; P-3	4C8; P-3

Materials Required

- Vehicle equipped with strut suspension
- Vehicle with torsion bar suspension
- Strut compressor
- Torque wrench
- Manufacturer- and job-specific tools

Some Safety Issues to Consider

- Lifting equipment such as vehicle jacks and stands, vehicle hoists, and engine hoists are important tools that increase productivity and make the job easier. However, they can also cause severe injury or death if used improperly. Make sure you follow the manufacturer's operation procedures. Also, make sure you have your supervisor's/instructor's permission to use any particular type of lifting equipment.
- Some suspension systems are electronically controlled, and can raise or lower without notice. Please familiarize yourself with the manufacturer's safety precautions related to these procedures.
- Vehicle springs store a lot of energy, which, if released improperly, can cause injury or death. Please familiarize yourself with the manufacturer's safety precautions related to these procedures.
- Comply with personal and environmental safety practices associated with clothing; eye protection; hand tools; power equipment; proper ventilation; and the handling, storage, and disposal of chemicals/materials in accordance with local, state, and federal safety and environmental regulations.

Performance Standard

0—No exposure: No information or practice provided during the program; complete training required

1—Exposure only: General information provided with no practice time; close supervision needed; additional training required

2—Limited practice: Has practiced job during training program; additional training required to develop skill

3—Moderately skilled: Has performed job independently during training program; limited additional training may be required

4—Skilled: Can perform job independently with no additional training

MLR
4B16

Time off_____

Time on_____

Total time_____

CDX Tasksheet Number: C926

1. Research the inspection procedure for the strut cartridge or assembly in the appropriate service information.

   a. **List any precautions:**

   b. **List or print off and attach to this sheet the steps to inspect the strut assembly:**

2. Following the specified procedure outlined in the service information, inspect the struts on the vehicle. **List your observations:**

3. **Determine any necessary action(s):**

4. Have your supervisor/instructor verify satisfactory completion of this procedure, any observations found, and any necessary action(s) recommended.

Performance Rating

CDX Tasksheet Number: C926

0	1	2	3	4

Supervisor/instructor signature _____ Date _____

Time off_____

Time on_____

Total time_____

CDX Tasksheet Number: C927

1. Research the inspection procedure for the strut bearings and mounts in the appropriate service information.

   a. **List any precautions:**

   b. **List or print off and attach to this sheet the steps to inspect the strut bearings and mounts:**

2. Following the specified procedure outlined in the service information, inspect the strut bearings and mounts on the vehicle. **List your observations:**

   a. **Strut bearings:**

   b. **Mounts:**

3. **Determine any necessary action(s):**

4. Have your supervisor/instructor verify satisfactory completion of this procedure, any observations found, and any necessary action(s) recommended.

Performance Rating

CDX Tasksheet Number: C927

0	1	2	3	4

Supervisor/instructor signature _____ Date _____

Inspect track bar, strut rods/radius arms, and related mounts and bushings.

MLR
4B11

Time off_____

Time on_____

Total time_____

CDX Tasksheet Number: C921

1. Research the inspection procedure for the track bar, strut rods/radius arms, mounts, and bushings in the appropriate service information.

   a. **List or print off and attach to this sheet the steps to inspect the track bar, strut rods/radius arms, mounts and bushings:**

2. Following the specified procedure outlined in the service information, inspect the track bars, strut rods/radius arms, mounts, and bushings. **List your observation(s):**

   a. **Track bars:**

   b. **Strut rods/radius arms:**

   c. **Mounts:**

   d. **Bushings:**

3. **Determine any necessary action(s):**

4. Have your supervisor/instructor verify satisfactory completion of this procedure, any observations found, and any necessary action(s) recommended.

Performance Rating

CDX Tasksheet Number: C921

0	1	2	3	4

Supervisor/instructor signature _____ Date _____

Inspect suspension system torsion bars and mounts.

MLR
4B14

Time off_____

Time on_____

Total time_____

CDX Tasksheet Number: C924

Vehicle used for this activity:

Year_____ Make_____ Model_____

Odometer_____ VIN _____

1. Research the inspection procedure for the torsion bars and mounts in the appropriate service information.

   a. List any precautions:

   b. List or print off and attach to this sheet the steps to inspect the torsion bar:

   c. Specified ride height: _____

2. Have your supervisor/instructor verify your answers.
   Supervisor's/instructor's initials: _____

3. Measure and record vehicle ride height. **Note your findings here:**

4. Following the specified procedure, inspect each torsion bar and mount. **List your observations:**

5. **Determine any necessary action(s):**

6. Have your supervisor/instructor verify satisfactory completion of this procedure, any observations found, and any necessary action(s) recommended.

Performance Rating

CDX Tasksheet Number: C924

0	1	2	3	4

Supervisor/instructor signature _____ Date _____

Inspect, remove, and install strut cartridge or assembly, strut coil spring, insulators (silencers), and upper-strut bearing mount.

AST 4C10   **MAST** 4C10

Time off_____

Time on_____

Total time_____

CDX Tasksheet Number: C794

1. Research the disassembly and inspection procedure for the strut cartridge or assembly, strut coil spring, insulators (silencers), and upper-strut bearing mount in the appropriate service information.

    a. List any precautions:

    b. List or print off and attach to this sheet the steps to inspect, remove, and disassemble the strut assembly:

2. Have your supervisor/instructor verify your listed precautions and procedures. **Supervisor's/instructor's initials:** _____

3. Safely raise and support the vehicle.

4. Following the specified procedure outlined in the service information, inspect the struts on the vehicle. **List your observations:**

5. Following the specified procedure, remove the strut assembly from the vehicle.

    NOTE On some vehicles, it makes sense to mark the position of the adjustable components so they can be reinstalled into their original positions.

6. Following the specified procedure outlined in the service information, disassemble the strut. Improperly removing the spring can cause severe injury or death.

7. Clean and inspect the strut cartridge or assembly, strut coil spring, insulators (silencers), and upper-strut bearing mount. **List your observation(s):**

    a. Strut cartridge or assembly:

    b. Strut coil spring:

    c. Spring insulators:

    d. Upper-strut bearing mount:

8. **Determine any necessary action(s):**

> **NOTE** You may be able to continue on with the next task C791: Inspect, remove, and install strut rods and bushings while you have the strut removed. If so, return to this point once you have that task completed.

9. Have your instructor verify the removal and disassembly of the strut, and check your observations and necessary actions. Get permission to reassemble the strut. **Supervisor's/instructor's initials:** _____

10. Reassemble the strut according to the manufacturer's procedure and precautions. Be careful when compressing and installing the spring as it can cause severe injury or death if installed improperly.

11. Reinstall the strut into the vehicle. Be sure to tighten all fasteners to their specified torque and replace any retaining devices such as cotter pins and nylon locking nuts. Be careful to route all wires, hoses, and tubes in their original factory positions.

12. Inspect the reassembled strut assembly for any loose fasteners, improperly installed components, etc. **List your observations here:**

13. Have your supervisor/instructor verify satisfactory completion of this procedure, any observations found, and any necessary action(s) recommended.

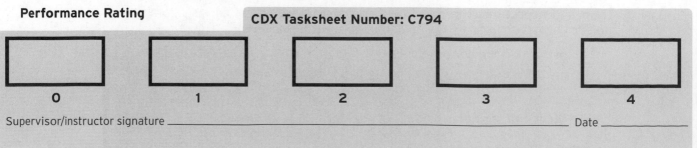

Performance Rating

CDX Tasksheet Number: C794

| 0 | 1 | 2 | 3 | 4 |

Supervisor/instructor signature _____ Date _____

▶ **TASK** Inspect, remove, and install track bar, strut rods/radius arms, and related mounts and bushings.

AST 4C11 **MAST** 4C11

CDX Tasksheet Number: C934

1. Research the inspection and disassembly procedure for the track bars, strut rods/radius arms, mounts, and bushings in the appropriate service information.

   a. **List or print off and attach to this sheet the steps to inspect and disassemble the track bars, strut rods/radius arms, mounts, and bushings:**

2. Following the specified procedure outlined in the service information, remove the track bars, strut rods/radius arms, mounts, and bush-ings from the vehicle. **List your observation(s):**

   a. **Track bars:**

   b. **Strut rod/radius arms:**

   c. **Mounts:**

   d. **Bushings:**

3. **Determine any necessary action(s):**

4. Have your instructor verify the removal and disassembly of the track bars, strut rod/radius arms, mounts, and bushings, and check your observa-tions and necessary actions. Also, have your instructor sign off on the disassembly of the strut in the previous task. **Supervisor's/instructor's initials:** _____

5. Reassemble the strut rods, mounts, and bushings according to the manufacturer's procedure and precautions.

> **NOTE** Return to step 6 of task C794: Inspect, remove, and install strut cartridge or assembly, strut coil spring, insulators (si-lencers), and upper-strut bearing mount.

6. Have your supervisor/instructor verify satisfactory completion of this procedure, any observations found, and any necessary action(s) recommended.

Performance Rating

CDX Tasksheet Number: C934

| 0 | 1 | 2 | 3 | 4 |

Supervisor/instructor signature _____ Date _____

CDX Tasksheet Number: C194

Vehicle used for this activity:

Year_____ Make_____ Model_____

Odometer_____ VIN _____

1. Research the disassembly and inspection procedure for the torsion bars and mounts in the appropriate service information.

   a. List any precautions:

   b. List or print off and attach to this sheet the steps to remove the torsion bar:

   c. List the flat rate time to remove and install one torsion bar: _____ **hrs**
   d. Specified ride height: _____

2. Have your supervisor/instructor verify your answers.
   Supervisor's/instructor's initials: _____

3. **Measure and record vehicle ride height. Note your findings here:**

4. Safely raise and support the vehicle.

5. Following the specified procedure outlined in the service information, remove one torsion bar from the vehicle. **List your observation(s):**

   a. Torsion bar:

   b. Mounts:

   c. Height-adjustment mechanism:

   d. Bushing(s):

6. Determine any necessary action(s):

7. Have your instructor verify the removal and disassembly of the torsion bar, and check your observations and necessary actions.
Supervisor's/instructor's initials: _____

8. Reinstall the torsion bar according to the manufacturer's procedure and precautions. Be careful when installing and compressing the spring as it can cause severe injury or death if installed improperly.

9. Torque all retaining bolts to the manufacturer's specifications.

10. Following the manufacturer's procedure, adjust the ride height of the vehicle to meet specifications.

11. Inspect the suspension for any loose fasteners, improperly installed components, etc.
List your observations here:

12. **Determine any necessary action(s):**

13. Have your supervisor/instructor verify satisfactory completion of this procedure, any observations found, and any necessary action(s) recommended.

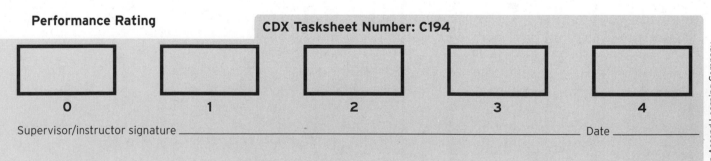

Performance Rating

CDX Tasksheet Number: C194

| 0 | 1 | 2 | 3 | 4 |

Supervisor/instructor signature _____ Date _____

Suspension and Steering Systems: Front-Suspension Diagnosis

Student/intern information:

Name _____ Date _____ Class _____

Vehicle used for this activity:

Year _____ Make _____ Model_____

Odometer_____VIN_____

Learning Objective/Task	CDX Tasksheet Number	2013 MLR NATEF Reference Number; Priority Level	2013 AST NATEF Reference Number; Priority Level	2013 MAST NATEF Reference Number; Priority Level
• Diagnose short- and long-arm suspension system noises, body sway, and uneven ride-height concerns; determine necessary action.	C852		4C1; P-1	4C1; P-1
• Diagnose strut suspension system noises, body sway, and uneven ride-height concerns; determine necessary action.	C853		4C2; P-1	4C2; P-1

Time off_____

Time on_____

Total time_____

Materials Required

- Vehicle hoist
- Vehicle with short- and long-arm suspension system concern
- Vehicle with strut suspension system concern
- Depending on the type of concern, special diagnostic tools may be required. See your supervisor/instructor for instructions to identify what tools may be required.

Some Safety Issues to Consider

- When running any vehicles in the shop, make sure you use the shop's exhaust ventilation system to discharge all exhaust gas safely outside.
- Lifting equipment such as vehicle jacks and stands, vehicle hoists, and engine hoists are important tools that increase productivity and make the job easier. However, they can also cause severe injury or death if used improperly. Make sure you follow the manufacturer's operation procedures. Also, make sure you have your supervisor's/instructor's permission to use any particular type of lifting equipment.
- Vehicle springs store a lot of energy, which, if released improperly, can cause injury or death. Please familiarize yourself with the manufacturer's safety precautions related to these procedures.
- Some suspension systems are electronically controlled and can raise or lower without notice. Please familiarize yourself with the manufacturer's safety precautions related to these procedures.
- Comply with personal and environmental safety practices associated with clothing; eye protection; hand tools; power equipment; proper ventilation; and the handling, storage, and disposal of chemicals/materials in accordance with local, state, and federal safety and environmental regulations.

Performance Standard

0—No exposure: No information or practice provided during the program; complete training required

1—Exposure only: General information provided with no practice time; close supervision needed; additional training required

2—Limited practice: Has practiced job during training program; additional training required to develop skill

3—Moderately skilled: Has performed job independently during training program; limited additional training may be required

4—Skilled: Can perform job independently with no additional training

▶ TASK Diagnose short- and long-arm suspension system noises, body sway, and uneven ride-height concerns; determine necessary action.

AST 4C1 **MAST** 4C1

Time off_____

Time on_____

Total time_____

CDX Tasksheet Number: C852

1. **List the short- and long-arm suspension system–related customer concern:**

2. **Verify the concern and list your observations here:**

3. Research the possible causes for this concern in the appropriate service information:

   a. **List or print off and attach to this sheet the possible causes:**

   b. **List or print off and attach to this sheet the procedure for diagnosing the concern:**

4. **Follow the service-specified procedure to diagnose the concern. List your tests and results here:**

5. **List the cause of the concern:**

6. **Determine any necessary action(s) to correct the fault:**

7. Have your supervisor/instructor verify satisfactory completion of this procedure, any observations found, and any necessary action(s) recommended.

Performance Rating

CDX Tasksheet Number: C852

0	1	2	3	4

Supervisor/instructor signature _____ Date _____

Diagnose strut suspension system noises, body sway, and uneven ride-height concerns; determine necessary action.

AST 4C2 **MAST** 4C2

Time off_____

Time on_____

Total time_____

CDX Tasksheet Number: C853

Vehicle used for this activity:

Year _____ Make _____ Model_____

Odometer_____ VIN_____

1. **List the strut suspension system-related customer concern:**

2. **Verify the concern and list your observations here:**

3. Research the possible causes for this concern in the appropriate service information.

   a. **List or print off and attach to this sheet the possible causes:**

   b. **List or print off and attach to this sheet the procedure for diagnosing the concern:**

4. **Follow the specified procedure to diagnose the concern. List your tests and results here:**

5. List the cause of the concern:

6. Determine any necessary action(s) to correct the fault:

7. Have your supervisor/instructor verify satisfactory completion of this procedure, any observations found, and any necessary action(s) recommended.

Performance Rating

CDX Tasksheet Number: C853

0	1	2	3	4

Supervisor/instructor signature _____ Date _____

Suspension and Steering Systems: Rear Suspension Service

Student/intern information:

Name _____ Date _____ Class _____

Vehicle used for this activity:

Year _____ Make _____ Model _____

Odometer _____ VIN _____

Learning Objective/Task	CDX Tasksheet Number	2013 MLR NATEF Reference Number; Priority Level	2013 AST NATEF Reference Number; Priority Level	2013 MAST NATEF Reference Number; Priority Level
• Inspect, remove, and replace shock absorbers; inspect mounts and bushings.	C202	4B20; P-1	4D1; P-1	4D1; P-1
• Inspect rear suspension system lateral links/arms (track bars), control (trailing) arms.	C928	4B18; P-1		
• Inspect rear suspension system leaf spring(s), spring insulators (silencers), shackles, brackets, bushings, center pins/bolts, and mounts.	C929	4B19; P-1		
• Inspect rear suspension system leaf spring(s), bushings, center pins/bolts, and mounts.	C854		4C12; P-1	4C12; P-1
• Remove, inspect, and service or replace front and rear wheel bearings.	C203		4D2; P-1	4D2; P-1

Time off_____

Time on_____

Total time_____

Materials Required

- Vehicle with hydraulic shock absorbers and leaf springs
- Vehicle lifting equipment
- Safety stands
- Manufacturer- and job-specific tools
- Specified wheel-bearing grease
- New cotter pin(s), depending on application

Some Safety Issues to Consider

- Vehicle hoists are important tools that increase productivity and make the job easier. However, they also can cause severe injury or death if used improperly. Make sure you follow the hoist and vehicle manufacturer's operation procedures. Also make sure you have your supervisor's/instructor's permission to use a vehicle hoist.
- Shock absorbers may be the primary fastening device for holding the suspension, or axle assembly, in the vehicle. Be sure to support the suspension with the appropriate safety stands.
- Some shock absorbers are pressurized with nitrogen gas. Keep your fingers from being pinched by an expanding shock absorber.

- Some shock absorbers have overload springs attached to them. Be careful not to accidentally release the spring. Serious pinching could occur.
- Some shock absorbers are electronically controlled and can extend or retract without notice. Please familiarize yourself with the manufacturer's safety precautions related to these procedures.
- Always wear the correct protective eyewear and clothing, and use the appropriate safety equipment, as well as fender covers, seat protectors, and floor mat protectors.
- Make sure you understand and observe all legislative and personal safety procedures when carrying out practical assignments. If you are unsure of what these are, ask your supervisor/instructor.

Performance Standard
0–No exposure: No information or practice provided during the program; complete training required
1–Exposure only: General information provided with no practice time; close supervision needed; additional training required
2–Limited practice: Has practiced job during training program; additional training required to develop skill
3–Moderately skilled: Has performed job independently during training program; limited additional training may be required
4–Skilled: Can perform job independently with no additional training

MLR	AST	MAST
4B20	4D1	4D1

CDX Tasksheet Number: C202

1. Research the shock absorber removal and installation procedure in the appropriate service information. Follow all directions.

    a. **Shock absorber fastener torque:** _____ **ft-lbs/Nm**

    b. **List the flat rate time for this job:** _____ **hrs**

2. Carefully bounce check the shock absorbers by pushing on each corner of the bumpers. Let go at the bottom of the travel and observe how many oscillations it takes for the vehicle to come to a stop. **List your observations:**

3. Safely raise and support the vehicle on a hoist. Check to see that the vehicle is secure on the hoist, and then remove the shock absorbers following the service information procedures.

> **NOTE** Be sure to support the suspension, or axle assembly, with safety stands before removing the shocks.

4. **Inspect the shock absorbers, rubber bushings (bushes), and mounts and list your observations:**

    a. **Shock absorbers:**

    b. **Rubber bushings (bushes):**

    c. **Shock mounts:**

5. Determine any necessary action(s):

6. Have your supervisor/instructor verify the removal and your observations.
   Supervisor's/instructor's initials: _____

7. Reinstall the shock absorbers according to the specified procedure. Be sure to torque all fasteners properly.

8. Have your supervisor/instructor verify satisfactory completion of this procedure, any observations found, and any necessary action(s) recommended.

Performance Rating

CDX Tasksheet Number: C202

0	1	2	3	4

Supervisor/instructor signature _____ Date _____

Inspect rear suspension system lateral links/arms (track bars), control (trailing) arms.

MLR
4B18

Time off_____

Time on_____

Total time_____

CDX Tasksheet Number: C928

1. Research the inspection procedure for the rear suspension lateral links/arms (track bars), control (trailing) arms in the appropriate service information.

   a. **List or print off and attach to this sheet the steps to inspect the rear suspension lateral links/arms (track bars), control (trailing) arms:**

2. Following the specified procedure, inspect the rear suspension lateral links/arms (track bars), control (trailing) arms. **List your observation(s):**

   a. **Lateral links/arms (track bars):**

   b. **Control (trailing) arms:**

3. **Determine any necessary action(s):**

4. Have your supervisor/instructor verify satisfactory completion of this procedure, any observations found, and any necessary action(s) recommended.

Performance Rating

CDX Tasksheet Number: C928

0	1	2	3	4

Supervisor/instructor signature _____ Date _____

Inspect rear suspension system leaf spring(s), spring insulators (silencers), shackles, brackets, bushings, center pins/bolts, and mounts.

MLR
4B19

Time off_____

Time on_____

Total time_____

CDX Tasksheet Number: C929

Vehicle used for this activity:

Year _____ Make _____ Model_____

Odometer_____ VIN_____

1. Research the leaf-spring inspection procedure in the appropriate service information. Follow all directions.

    a. U-bolt torque: _____ **ft-lbs/Nm**

    b. Shackle bolt torque: _____ **ft-lbs/Nm**

2. Safely raise and support the vehicle. Support the axle assembly with safety stands.

3. **Following the specified procedure, inspect and record the condition of each of the following:**

    a. Rear-shackle bushings:

    b. Front-shackle bushings:

    c. Spring-leaf insulators:

    d. U-bolts and nuts:

    e. Rubber-bump stops:

f. Spring shackles and plates:

g. Leaf-spring pack:

4. **Determine any necessary action(s):**

5. Have your supervisor/instructor verify satisfactory completion of this procedure, any observations found, and any necessary action(s) recommended.

Performance Rating

0	1	2	3	4

Supervisor/instructor signature _____ Date _____

Inspect rear suspension system leaf spring(s), bushings, center pins/bolts, and mounts.

AST
4C12

MAST
4C12

Time off_____

Time on_____

Total time_____

CDX Tasksheet Number: C854

Vehicle used for this activity:

Year _____ Make _____ Model_____

Odometer_____ VIN_____

1. Research the leaf-spring inspection procedure in the appropriate service information. Follow all directions.

    a. **U-bolt torque:** _____ ft-lbs/Nm
    b. **Shackle bolt torque:** _____ ft-lbs/Nm

2. Safely raise and support the vehicle. Support the axle assembly with safety stands.

3. **Following the specified procedure, inspect and record the condition of each of the following:**

    a. **Rear-shackle bushings:**

    b. **Front-shackle bushings:**

    c. **Spring-leaf insulators:**

    d. **U-bolts and nuts:**

    e. **Rubber-bump stops:**

    f. Spring shackles and plates:

    g. Leaf-spring pack:

4. Determine any necessary action(s):

5. Have your supervisor/instructor verify satisfactory completion of this procedure, any observations found, and any necessary action(s) recommended.

Performance Rating

CDX Tasksheet Number: C854

0	1	2	3	4

Supervisor/instructor signature _____ Date _____

Remove, inspect, and service or replace front- and rear-wheel bearings.

Time off_____

Time on_____

Total time_____

CDX Tasksheet Number: C203

Vehicle used for this activity:

Year _____ Make _____ Model _____

Odometer _____ VIN _____

1. **Which wheel bearing are you servicing?** _____

2. **What type of bearing is this vehicle equipped with? Serviceable:** _____ **Sealed:** _____

3. Research the wheel-bearing removal, service, and installation procedure in the appropriate service information. Follow all directions.

    a. **List the bearing adjustment procedure, if applicable:**

    b. **Specified wheel-bearing grease:** _____
    c. **Lug nut torque:** _____ **ft-lbs/Nm**
    d. **List the flat rate time for this job:** _____ **hrs**

4. Safely raise and support the vehicle.

5. Following the specified procedure, dismantle, clean, and inspect wheel bearing and race. **List your observation(s):**

    a. **Wheel bearing:**

    b. **Race:**

    c. **Spindle:**

d. Hub:

e. Grease seal:

f. Are these parts serviceable? Yes: _____ **No:** _____

6. Determine any necessary action(s):

7. Have your supervisor/instructor verify the removal and your observations. **Supervisor's/instructor's initials:** _____

8. Repack (if applicable) the wheel bearings with the specified grease.

9. Following the specified procedure, reinstall and adjust the wheel-bearing assembly. Before locking the adjustment nut, have your supervisor/instructor verify the wheel-bearing adjustment. **Supervisor's/instructor's initials:** _____

10. Following the specified procedure, lock the wheel-bearing adjustment nut with the specified retaining device. Always replace disposable devices such as cotter pins with new parts.

11. Return the vehicle to its beginning condition and clean and return any tools that you may have used to their proper locations.

12. Have your supervisor/instructor verify satisfactory completion of this procedure, any observations found, and any necessary action(s) recommended.

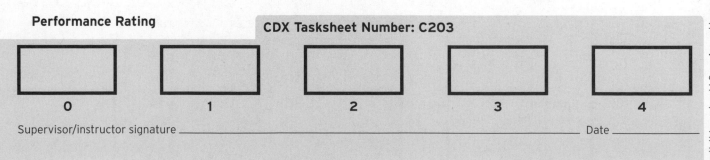

Performance Rating

CDX Tasksheet Number: C203

| 0 | 1 | 2 | 3 | 4 |

Supervisor/instructor signature _____ Date _____

Suspension and Steering Systems:
Electronically Controlled Steering and Suspension Service

Student/intern information:

Name _____ Date _____ Class _____

Vehicle used for this activity:

Year _____ Make _____ Model _____

Odometer _____ VIN _____

Time off_____

Time on_____

Total time_____

Learning Objective/Task	CDX Tasksheet Number	2013 MLR NATEF Reference Number; Priority Level	2013 AST NATEF Reference Number; Priority Level	2013 MAST NATEF Reference Number; Priority Level
• Inspect electric power-assisted steering.	C700	4B21; P-3	4C19; P-3	4C20; P-3
• Test and diagnose components of electronically controlled steering systems using a scan tool; determine necessary action.	C186			4B19; P-3
• Describe the function of the power steering pressure switch.	C931	4B23; P-3	4D3; P-3	4D3; P-3
• Identify hybrid vehicle power steering system electrical circuits and safety precautions.	C551	4B22; P-2	4B18; P-2	4B19; P-2

Materials Required

- Vehicle with electronically controlled steering system
- Scan tool
- DMM/DVOM
- Manufacturer- and job-specific tools

Some Safety Issues to Consider

- Diagnosis of this fault may require test-driving the vehicle on the school grounds. Attempt this task only with full permission from your instructor and follow all guidelines and policies exactly.
- Lifting equipment such as vehicle jacks and stands, vehicle hoists, and engine hoists are important tools that increase productivity and make the job easier. However, they can also cause severe injury or death if used improperly. Make sure you follow the manufacturer's operation procedures. Also, make sure you have your supervisor's/instructor's permission to use any particular type of lifting equipment.
- Vehicle springs store a lot of energy, which, if released improperly, can cause injury or death. Please familiarize yourself with the manufacturer's safety precautions related to these procedures.
- Some suspension systems are electronically controlled, and can raise or lower without notice. Please familiarize yourself with the manufacturer's safety precautions related to these procedures.

• Comply with personal and environmental safety practices associated with clothing; eye protection; hand tools; power equipment; proper ventilation; and the handling, storage, and disposal of chemicals/materials in accordance with local, state, and federal safety and environmental regulations.

Performance Standard

0—No exposure: No information or practice provided during the program; complete training required

1—Exposure only: General information provided with no practice time; close supervision needed; additional training required

2—Limited practice: Has practiced job during training program; additional training required to develop skill

3—Moderately skilled: Has performed job independently during training program; limited additional training may be required

4—Skilled: Can perform job independently with no additional training

MLR 4B21 | **AST** 4B19 | **MAST** 4B20

Time off_____

Time on_____

Total time_____

CDX Tasksheet Number: C700

1. Research the electric power-assisted steering system in the appropriate service information for the vehicle you are working on.

   a. Read the "description and operation" section.
   b. Read the "testing and diagnosis" section.
   c. **List any precautions mentioned:**

2. **Following the specified procedure, inspect the electric-power steering system. List your observation(s):**

3. **Determine any necessary action(s):**

4. Have your supervisor/instructor verify satisfactory completion of this procedure, any observations found, and any necessary action(s) recommended.

Performance Rating

CDX Tasksheet Number: C700

0	1	2	3	4

Supervisor/instructor signature _____ Date _____

Test and diagnose components of electronically controlled steering systems using a scan tool; determine necessary action.

MAST
4B18

Time off_____

Time on_____

Total time_____

CDX Tasksheet Number: C816

Vehicle used for this activity:

Year _____ Make _____ Model_____

Odometer_____ VIN_____

1. **List the electronically controlled steering system-related customer concern:**

2. **Verify the concern and list your observations:**

3. **Retrieve any DTCs with a scan tool and list those DTCs:**

4. Research the possible causes for this concern in the appropriate service information.

   a. **List or print off and attach to this sheet the possible causes:**

   b. **List or print off and attach to this sheet the procedure for diagnosing the concern:**

5. **Follow the specified procedure to diagnose the concern. List your tests and results:**

6. List the cause of the concern:

7. Determine any necessary action(s) to correct the fault:

8. Have your supervisor/instructor verify satisfactory completion of this procedure, any observations found, and any necessary action(s) recommended.

Performance Rating

CDX Tasksheet Number: C816

0	1	2	3	4

Supervisor/instructor signature _____ Date _____

MLR 4B23   **AST** 4D3   **MAST** 4D3

Time off_____

Time on_____

Total time_____

CDX Tasksheet Number: C931

Vehicle used for this activity:

Year _____ Make _____ Model_____

Odometer_____ VIN_____

1. Research the function of the power steering pressure switch in the appropriate service information.

   a. **Describe, in your own words, the function of the power steering pressure switch:**

2. Have your supervisor/instructor verify satisfactory completion of your answers.

Performance Rating

CDX Tasksheet Number: C931

0	1	2	3	4

Supervisor/instructor signature _____ Date _____

Identify hybrid vehicle power steering system electrical circuits and safety precautions.

MLR 4B22   **AST** 4B18   **MAST** 4B19

Time off_____

Time on_____

CDX Tasksheet Number: C551

Vehicle used for this activity:

Year _____ Make _____ Model_____

Odometer_____ VIN_____

Total time_____

1. Research the location and safety precautions for the power steering system the vehicle is equipped with in the appropriate service information.

   a. **List the voltage that the power steering system operates at:** _____ V
   b. **List any safety precautions when working on or around the power steering systems and circuits:**

2. **What color wires are used on the hybrid vehicle power steering system electrical circuits?**

3. On the vehicle, locate and point out the power steering electrical circuits and components to your instructor.

4. Have your supervisor/instructor verify satisfactory completion of your answers.

Performance Rating

CDX Tasksheet Number: C551

0	1	2	3	4

Supervisor/instructor signature _____ Date _____

Suspension and Steering Systems:
Wheel Alignment Diagnosis, Adjustment, and Repair

Student/intern information:

Name _____ Date _____ Class _____

Vehicle used for this activity:

Year _____ Make _____ Model _____

Odometer _____ VIN _____

Learning Objective/Task	CDX Tasksheet Number	2013 MLR NATEF Reference Number; Priority Level	2013 AST NATEF Reference Number; Priority Level	2013 MAST NATEF Reference Number; Priority Level
• Diagnose vehicle wander, drift, pull, hard steering, bump steer, memory steer, torque steer, and steering return concerns; determine necessary action.	C206		4E1; P-1	4E1; P-1
• Perform prealignment inspection and measure vehicle ride height; determine necessary action.	C939	4C1; P-1		
• Perform prealignment inspection and measure vehicle ride height; perform necessary action.	C617		4E2; P-1	4E2; P-1
• Prepare vehicle for wheel alignment on the alignment machine; perform four-wheel alignment by checking and adjusting front- and rear-wheel caster, camber, and toe as required; center steering wheel.	C618		4E3; P-1	4E3; P-1
• Check toe-out-on-turns (turning radius); determine necessary action.	C213		4E4; P-2	4E4; P-2
• Check SAI (steering axis inclination) and included angle; determine necessary action.	C214		4E5; P-2	4E5; P-2
• Check rear-wheel thrust angle; determine necessary action.	C216		4E6; P-1	4E6; P-1
• Check for front-wheel setback; determine necessary action.	C217		4E7; P-2	4E7; P-2
• Check front- and/or rear-cradle (subframe) alignment; determine nec-essary action.	C795		4E8; P-3	4E8; P-3
• Reset steering angle sensor.	C940		4E9; P-2	4E9; P-2

Time off _____

Time on _____

Total time _____

Materials Required

- Vehicle with alignment concern
- Tire-pressure gauge and inflator
- Tape measure
- Wheel-alignment machine
- Manufacturer- or job-specific tools

Some Safety Issues to Consider

- Diagnosis of this fault may require test-driving the vehicle on the school grounds. Attempt this task only with full permission from your instructor and follow all guidelines and policies exactly.
- Lifting equipment such as vehicle jacks and stands, vehicle hoists, and engine hoists are important tools that increase productivity and make the job easier. However, they can also cause severe injury or death if used improperly. Make sure you follow the manufacturer's operation procedures. Also, make sure you have your supervisor's/instructor's permission to use any particular type of lifting equipment.
- Vehicle springs store a lot of energy, which, if released improperly, can cause injury or death. Please familiarize yourself with the manufacturer's safety precautions related to these procedures.
- Some suspension systems are electronically controlled, and can raise or lower without notice. Please familiarize yourself with the manufacturer's safety precautions related to these procedures.
- Comply with personal and environmental safety practices associated with clothing; eye protection; hand tools; power equipment; proper ventilation; and the handling, storage, and disposal of chemicals/materials in accordance with local, state, and federal safety and environmental regulations.

Performance Standard

0—No exposure: No information or practice provided during the program; complete training required

1—Exposure only: General information provided with no practice time; close supervision needed; additional training required

2—Limited practice: Has practiced job during training program; additional training required to develop skill

3—Moderately skilled: Has performed job independently during training program; limited additional training may be required

4—Skilled: Can perform job independently with no additional training

Diagnose vehicle wander, drift, pull, hard steering, bump steer, memory steer, torque steer, and steering return concerns; determine necessary action.

AST 4E1 **MAST** 4E1

Time off_____

Time on_____

Total time_____

CDX Tasksheet Number: C206

1. **List the wheel alignment-related customer concern:**

2. **Verify the concern and list your observations here:**

3. Research the possible causes for this concern in the appropriate service information.

    a. **List or print off and attach to this sheet the possible causes:**

    b. **List or print off and attach to this sheet the procedure for diagnosing the concern:**

    The rest of this task is completed by performing the remainder of the tasks, and can be signed off at the end of this tasksheet. Please refer to page 653 for the completion of this task.

Perform prealignment inspection and measure vehicle ride height; determine necessary action.

Time off_____

Time on_____

Total time_____

CDX Tasksheet Number: C939

1. Research the prealignment process for this vehicle in the appropriate service information.

   a. List the ride-height specifications:

   b. Can the ride height be manually adjusted on this vehicle?
   Yes: _____ No: _____

   i. If yes, what is the specified adjustment procedure?

   c. List the specified tire size: _____

   d. List the specified tire pressure(s): _____ **psi/kPa**

   e. List any other manufacturer-specified checks:

2. Following the specified procedure, inspect the vehicle.

   a. Is the vehicle abnormally loaded? Yes: _____ **No:** _____

   b. Are the specified tires installed on the vehicle? Yes: _____
   No: _____

   c. List the condition and wear of each tire as you inflate the tires to proper pressure:
   Left front: (Initial psi): _____ **psi; Condition:** _____
   Right front: (Initial psi): _____ **psi; Condition:** _____
   Right rear: (Initial psi): _____ **psi; Condition:** _____
   Left rear: (Initial psi): _____ **psi; Condition:** _____

   d. Does the vehicle meet the specified ride height?
   Yes: _____ No: _____

   e. List the results of other specified checks:

3. Determine any necessary action(s):

4. **Does the vehicle meet the prealignment inspection requirements for an alignment? Yes: _____ No: _____**

5. Have your supervisor/instructor verify satisfactory completion of this procedure, any observations found, and any necessary action(s) recommended.

Performance Rating

CDX Tasksheet Number: C939

0	1	2	3	4

Supervisor/instructor signature _____ Date _____

▶ **TASK** Perform prealignment inspection and measure vehicle ride height; perform necessary action.

AST 4E2   **MAST** 4E2

Time off_____

Time on_____

Total time_____

CDX Tasksheet Number: C617

1. Research the prealignment process for this vehicle in the appropriate service information.

   a. **List the ride-height specifications:**

   b. **Can the ride height be manually adjusted on this vehicle?**
      Yes: _____ No: _____

      i. **If yes, what is the specified adjustment procedure?**

   c. **List the specified tire size:** _____

   d. **List the specified tire pressure(s):** _____ **psi/kPa**

   e. **List any other manufacturer-specified checks:**

2. Following the specified procedure, inspect the vehicle.

   a. **Is the vehicle abnormally loaded? Yes: _____ No: _____**

   b. **Are the specified tires installed on the vehicle?**
      Yes: _____ No: _____

   c. **List the condition and wear of each tire as you inflate the tires to proper pressure:**

   Left front: (Initial psi): _____ psi; Condition:_____
   Right front: (Initial psi): _____ psi; Condition:_____
   Right rear: (Initial psi): _____ psi; Condition:_____
   Left rear: (Initial psi): _____ psi; Condition:_____

   d. **Does the vehicle meet the specified ride height?**
      Yes: _____ No: _____

   e. **List the results of other specified checks:**

3. **Perform any necessary action(s) and list your results:**

4. **Does the vehicle meet the prealignment inspection requirements for an alignment? Yes: _____ No: _____**

5. Have your supervisor/instructor verify satisfactory completion of this procedure, any observations found, and any necessary action(s) recommended.

Performance Rating

CDX Tasksheet Number: C617

0	1	2	3	4

Supervisor/instructor signature _____ Date _____

Prepare vehicle for wheel alignment on the alignment machine; perform four-wheel alignment by checking and adjusting front- and rear-wheel caster, camber, and toe as required; center steering wheel.

AST 4E3   **MAST** 4E3

CDX Tasksheet Number: C618

1. Prepare the vehicle for wheel alignment on the alignment machine.

2. **Perform four-wheel alignment measurements and list the following readings:**
   Front wheels:
   a. **Caster: LF:** _____ **RF:** _____ **Specs:** _____
   b. **Cross caster: Measured:** _____ **Specs:** _____
   c. **Camber: LF:** _____ **RF:** _____ **Specs:** _____
   d. **Cross camber: Measured:** _____ **Specs:** _____
   e. **Toe: LF:** _____ **RF:** _____ **Specs:** _____
   f. **Total toe: Measured:** _____ **Specs:** _____

   Rear wheels:
   g. **Caster: LF:** _____ **RF:** _____
      Specs: _____
   h. **Cross caster: Measured:** _____ **Specs:** _____
   i. **Camber: LF:** _____ **RF:** _____ **Specs:** _____
   j. **Cross camber: Measured:** _____ **Specs:** _____
   k. **Toe: LF:** _____ **RF:** _____ **Specs:** _____
   l. **Total toe: Measured:** _____ **Specs:** _____

3. **Determine any necessary action(s):**

   It will be more efficient if you perform the remainder of the measurement tasks before making any further adjustments to the caster, camber, and toe as those measurements may identify additional service or repair needs. The rest of this task is completed by performing the remainder of the tasks, and can be signed off at the end of this tasksheet. Please refer to page 651 for the completion of this task.

Check toe-out-on-turns (turning radius); determine necessary action.

AST
4E4

MAST
4E4

Time off_____

Time on_____

Total time_____

CDX Tasksheet Number: C213

1. **Following the manufacturer's procedure, measure toe-out-on-turns.**
   a. **LF wheel set at:** _____ **degrees**
   b. **RF wheel measures:** _____ **degrees**
   c. **RF wheel set at:** _____ **degrees**
   d. **LF wheel measures:** _____ **degrees**

2. **Determine any necessary action(s):**

The rest of this task is completed by performing the remainder of the tasks, and can be signed off at the end of this tasksheet. Please refer to page 651 for the completion of this task.

Check SAI (steering axis inclination) and included angle; determine necessary action.

AST 4E5 **MAST** 4E5

Time off_____

Time on_____

Total time_____

CDX Tasksheet Number: C214

1. **Following the manufacturer's procedure, measure SAI (steering axis inclination) and included angle.**
   a. **SAI: LF:** _____ **Specs:** _____
   b. **SAI: RF:** _____ **Specs:** _____
   c. **Included angle: LF:** _____ **Specs:** _____
   d. **Included angle: RF:** _____ **Specs:** _____

2. **Determine any necessary action(s):**

The rest of this task is completed by performing the remainder of the tasks, and can be signed off at the end of this tasksheet. Please refer to page 652 for the completion of this task.

Check rear-wheel thrust angle; determine necessary action.

AST 4E6 | **MAST** 4E6

Time off_____

Time on_____

CDX Tasksheet Number: C216

1. **Following the manufacturer's procedure, measure the rear-wheel thrust angle.**
   a. **Manufacturer's specifications:** _____
   b. **Measured thrust angle:** _____

Total time_____

2. **Determine any necessary action(s):**

The rest of this task is completed by performing the remainder of the tasks, and can be signed off at the end of this tasksheet. Please refer to page 652 for the completion of this task.

Time off_____

Time on_____

Total time_____

CDX Tasksheet Number: C217

1. **Following the manufacturer's procedure, check for front-wheel setback.**
   a. **Manufacturer's specifications:** _____
   b. **Measured setback:** _____

2. **Determine any necessary action(s):**

3. Have your supervisor/instructor verify all of your measurements and necessary actions for all of the previous tasks. Get permission to perform the necessary action(s). **Supervisor's/instructor's initials:** _____

4. Perform all of the adjustments necessary for a four-wheel alignment as listed in the previous tasks.

5. When finished, remeasure all alignment angles to make sure they are within specifications.

6. **List or print off and attach to this sheet the post-alignment measurements. Front wheels:**
   a. **Caster: LF:** _____ **RF:** _____ **Specs:** _____
   b. **Cross caster: Measured:** _____ **Specs:** _____
   c. **Camber: LF:** _____ **RF:** _____ **Specs:** _____
   d. **Cross camber: Measured:** _____ **Specs:** _____
   e. **Toe: LF:** _____ **RF:** _____ **Specs:** _____
   f. **Total toe: Measured:** _____ **Specs:** _____

   Rear wheels:
   a. **Caster: LF:** _____ **RF:** _____ **Specs:** _____
   b. **Cross caster: Measured:** _____ **Specs:** _____
   c. **Camber: LF:** _____ **RF:** _____ **Specs:** _____
   d. **Cross camber: Measured:** _____ **Specs:** _____
   e. **Toe: LF:** _____ **RF:** _____ **Specs:** _____
   f. **Total toe: Measured:** _____ **Specs:** _____

   Toe-out-on-turns:
   a. **LF wheel set at:** _____ **degrees**
   b. **RF wheel measures:** _____ **degrees**
   c. **RF wheel set at:** _____ **degrees**
   d. **LF wheel measures:** _____ **degrees**

7. **SAI:** _____ **degrees**

8. **Included angle:** _____ **degrees**

9. **Rear-wheel thrust angle:** _____ **degrees**

10. List the measurement(s) for front-wheel setback: _____

11. Is the steering wheel centered? Yes: _____ No: _____

12. Do all the angles meet the manufacturer's specifications?
    Yes: _____ No: _____

13. Determine any further necessary action(s), such as resetting the steering angle sensor:

14. **Inspect the vehicle for any loose or missing fasteners or improper repairs. List your observation(s):**

15. Have your supervisor/instructor verify satisfactory completion of this procedure, any observations found, and any necessary action(s) recommended.

Performance Rating

CDX Tasksheet Number: C217

0	1	2	3	4

Supervisor/instructor signature _____ Date _____

CONTINUATION OF TASK C618/4E3: Prepare vehicle for wheel alignment on the alignment machine; perform four-wheel alignment by checking and adjusting front- and rear-wheel caster, camber, and toe as required; center steering wheel (from page 641).

Time off_____

Time on_____

Total time_____

CDX Tasksheet Number: C618

4. Have your supervisor/instructor verify satisfactory completion of this procedure, any observations found, and any necessary action(s) recommended.

Performance Rating

CDX Tasksheet Number: C618

0	1	2	3	4

Supervisor/instructor signature _____ Date _____

▶ TASK **CONTINUATION OF TASK** C213/4E4: Check toe-out-on-turns (turning radius); determine necessary action (from page 643).

Time off_____

Time on_____

Total time_____

CDX Tasksheet Number: C213

3. Have your supervisor/instructor verify satisfactory completion of this procedure, any observations found, and any necessary action(s) recommended.

Performance Rating

CDX Tasksheet Number: C213

0	1	2	3	4

Supervisor/instructor signature _____ Date _____

▶ **TASK** **CONTINUATION OF TASK** C214/4E5: Check SAI (steering axis inclination) and included angle; determine necessary action (from page 645).

CDX Tasksheet Number: C214

3. Have your supervisor/instructor verify satisfactory completion of this procedure, any observations found, and any necessary action(s) recommended.

Performance Rating

CDX Tasksheet Number: C214

0	1	2	3	4

Supervisor/instructor signature _____ Date _____

▶ **TASK** **CONTINUATION OF TASK** C216/4E6: Check rear-wheel thrust angle; determine necessary action (from page 647).

CDX Tasksheet Number: C216

3. Have your supervisor/instructor verify satisfactory completion of this procedure, any observations found, and any necessary action(s) recommended.

Performance Rating

CDX Tasksheet Number: C216

0	1	2	3	4

Supervisor/instructor signature _____ Date _____

CONTINUATION OF TASK C206/4E1: Diagnose vehicle wander, drift, pull, hard steering, bump steer, memory steer, torque steer, and steering return concerns; determine necessary action (from page 635).

Time off_____

Time on_____

Total time_____

CDX Tasksheet Number: C206

4. **Reflecting back over these tasks, complete the 3Cs, which you stated previously.**

   a. **List the customer concern(s):**

   b. **List the cause(s) of the concern(s):**

   c. **List the action(s) necessary to correct the fault(s):**

5. Have your supervisor/instructor verify satisfactory completion of this procedure, any observations found, and any necessary action(s) recommended.

Performance Rating

CDX Tasksheet Number: C206

0	1	2	3	4

Supervisor/instructor signature _____ Date _____

Check front- and/or rear-cradle (subframe) alignment; determine necessary action.

AST 4E8 **MAST** 4E8

Time off _____

Time on _____

Total time _____

CDX Tasksheet Number: C795

Vehicle used for this activity:

Year _____ Make _____ Model _____

Odometer _____ VIN _____

1. **Following the manufacturer's procedure, check front- and rear-cradle alignment.**

    a. **Manufacturer's specifications:**

    b. **Measured cradle alignment:**

2. **Determine any necessary action(s):**

3. Have your supervisor/instructor verify satisfactory completion of this procedure, any observations found, and any necessary action(s) recommended.

Performance Rating

CDX Tasksheet Number: C795

| 0 | 1 | 2 | 3 | 4 |

Supervisor/instructor signature _____ Date _____

AST
4E9

MAST
4E9

Time off_____

Time on_____

Total time_____

CDX Tasksheet Number: C940

1. Research the steering angle sensor reset procedure for this vehicle in the appropriate service information.

   a. **List, or print out and attach, the steps to reset the sensor:**

   b. **List any special tools required for this procedure:**

2. **If possible, list the current steering angle:** _____

3. Following the specified procedure, reset the steering angle sensor.
   List any observation(s):

4. **List the final steering angle:** _____

5. Have your supervisor/instructor verify satisfactory completion of this procedure, any observations found, and any necessary action(s) recommended.

Performance Rating

CDX Tasksheet Number: C940

0	1	2	3	4

Supervisor/instructor signature _____ Date _____

Section A5: Brakes

CONTENTS

Brakes: Vehicle, Customer, and Service Information

Student/intern information:

Name_____ Date_____ Class_____

Vehicle used for this activity:

Year_____ Make_____ Model_____

Odometer_____VIN_____

Learning Objective/Task	CDX Tasksheet Number	2013 MLR NATEF Reference Number; Priority Level	2013 AST NATEF Reference Number; Priority Level	2013 MAST NATEF Reference Number; Priority Level
• Research applicable vehicle and service information, vehicle service history, service precautions, and technical service bulletins.	C230	5A1; P-1	5A2; P-1	5A2; P-1
• Identify and interpret brake system concerns; determine necessary action.	C229		5A1; P-1	5A1; P-1
• Describe procedure for performing a road test to check brake system operation, including an anti-lock brake system (ABS).	C944	5A2; P-1	5A3; P-1	5A3; P-1
• Demonstrate use of 3 Cs (concern, cause, and correction).	NN05	N/A	N/A	N/A

Time off_____

Time on_____

Total time_____

Materials Required

- Blank work order
- Vehicle with available service history records
- Depending on the type of concern, special diagnostic tools may be required. See your supervisor/instructor for instructions to identify what tools may be required.

Some Safety Issues to Consider

- If you need to start the vehicle, you should ensure that the parking brake is firmly applied; if necessary, use wheel chocks to prevent the vehicle from moving when the vehicle is started to verify the completion of these tasks.
- Diagnosis of this fault may require test-driving the vehicle on the school grounds. Attempt this task only with full permission from your supervisor/instructor and follow all the guidelines exactly.
- Lifting equipment such as vehicle jacks and stands, vehicle hoists, and engine hoists are important tools that increase productivity and make the job easier. However, they can also cause severe injury or death if used improperly. Make sure you follow the manufacturer's operation procedures. Also make sure you have your supervisor's/instructor's permission to use any particular type of lifting equipment.
- **Caution:** Most types of brake fluid are harmful to painted surfaces. Be sure to prevent brake fluid from coming into contact with a vehicle's paint. Use fender covers to minimize this risk and be sure to wipe up any spilled brake fluid immediately with a wet rag.

- **Caution:** Brake dust may contain asbestos, which has been determined to cause cancer when inhaled or ingested. Treat all brake dust as if it contains asbestos and use OSHA-approved asbestos removal equipment. Do not allow brake dust to become airborne by using anything that would disturb the dust. Also, wear protective gloves during this procedure and dispose of or clean them in an approved manner.
- Comply with personal and environmental safety practices associated with clothing; eye protection; hand tools; power equipment; proper ventilation; and the handling, storage, and disposal of chemicals/materials in accordance with local, state, and federal safety and environmental regulations.

Performance Standard

0—No exposure: No information or practice provided during the program; complete training required

1—Exposure only: General information provided with no practice time; close supervision needed; additional training required

2—Limited practice: Has practiced job during training program; additional training required to develop skill

3—Moderately skilled: Has performed job independently during training program; limited additional training may be required

4—Skilled: Can perform job independently with no additional training

Research applicable vehicle and service information, vehicle service history, service precautions, and technical service bulletins.

MLR
5A1 **AST**
5A2 **MAST**
5A2

Time off_____

Time on_____

Total time_____

CDX Tasksheet Number: C230

1. Using the VIN for identification, use the appropriate source to access the vehicle's service history in relation to prior braking system work or customer concerns.

   a. List any related repairs/concerns, and their dates:

   b. List any service precautions related to brake system diagnosis and repair:

2. **Using the VIN for identification, access any relevant technical service bulletins for the particular vehicle you are working on in relation to braking system updates or other service issues. List related TSBs and their description(s):**

3. Have your supervisor/instructor verify satisfactory completion of this procedure, any observations found, and any necessary action(s) recommended.

Performance Rating

CDX Tasksheet Number: C230

0	1	2	3	4

Supervisor/instructor signature _____ Date _____

Identify and interpret brake system concerns; determine necessary action.

AST 5A1 — **MAST** 5A1

Time off_____

Time on_____

Total time_____

CDX Tasksheet Number: C229

1. **List the customer concern:**

2. Research the particular concern in the appropriate service information.

   a. **List the possible causes:**

3. **Inspect the braking system to determine the cause of the concern, and list the steps you took to determine the fault:**

4. **List the cause of the concern/complaint:**

5. **List the necessary action(s) to correct this fault:**

6. Have your supervisor/instructor verify satisfactory completion of this procedure, any observations found, and any necessary action(s) recommended.

Performance Rating

CDX Tasksheet Number: C229

0	1	2	3	4

Supervisor/instructor signature _____ Date _____

Describe procedure for performing a road test to check brake system operation, including an anti-lock brake system (ABS).

MLR 5A2   **AST** 5A3   **MAST** 5A3

Time off_____

Time on_____

Total time_____

CDX Tasksheet Number: C944

1. **Research the shop policies for performing a road test to check brake system operation. List the shop policies:**

2. **List the precautions that should be taken before road testing brakes:**

3. **List the precautions that should be taken during road testing of brakes, including testing of the ABS:**

4. Have your supervisor/instructor verify satisfactory completion of this procedure, any observations found, and any necessary action(s) recommended.

Performance Rating

CDX Tasksheet Number: C944

0	1	2	3	4

Supervisor/instructor signature _____ Date _____

▶ **TASK** Demonstrate use of 3 Cs (concern, cause, and correction).

Additional Task

Time off_____

Time on_____

Total time_____

CDX Tasksheet Number: NN05

1. Using the following scenario, write up the 3 Cs as listed on most repair orders. Assume that the customer authorized the recommended repairs.

    A vehicle is brought to your shop with a brake concern. The customer tells you that the brakes make a grinding noise that comes from the front wheels when the brakes are applied. The vehicle has been doing this for about two weeks, but the customer was too busy to bring the car in for repairs. You remove the wheels, inspect all of the brakes, and find the following:

    a. The brake pads on the left front are worn down to metal and have scored the rotor badly. The rotor is worn down to the point that it is .043 of an inch under the minimum specified thickness.

    b. The right side brake pads are worn well below minimum specifications but have not worn down to metal. The rotor is about .040 of an inch thicker than the minimum thickness specified.

    c. Both front calipers appear to be original and the pistons do not move as freely as they should; the brake fluid is very dark and dirty.

    d. The rear brake shoes are in like-new condition, but wet with brake fluid. Both

    > **NOTE** Ask your instructor whether you should use a copy of the shop repair order, or the 3 Cs here, to record this information.

2. **Concern/complaint:**

3. **Cause:**

4. **Correction:**

5. **Other recommended service:**

6. Have your supervisor/instructor verify satisfactory completion of this procedure, any observations found, and any necessary action(s) recommended.

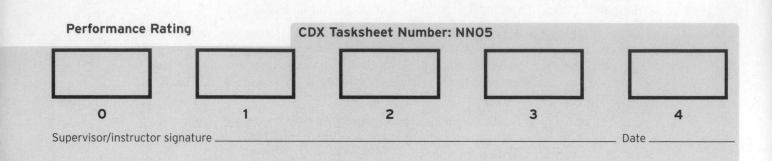

Performance Rating

CDX Tasksheet Number: NN05

| 0 | 1 | 2 | 3 | 4 |

Supervisor/instructor signature _____ Date _____

Brakes: Brake Fluid Testing and Maintenance

Student/intern information:

Name_____ Date_____ Class_____

Vehicle used for this activity:

Year_____ Make_____ Model_____

Odometer_____VIN_____

Learning Objective/Task	CDX Tasksheet Number	2013 MLR NATEF Reference Number; Priority Level	2013 AST NATEF Reference Number; Priority Level	2013 MAST NATEF Reference Number; Priority Level
• Select, handle, store, and fill brake fluids to proper levels.	C239	5B4; P-1	5B9; P-1	5B9; P-1
• Test brake fluid for contamination.	C625	5B7; P-1	5B13; P-1	5B13; P-1
• Bleed and/or flush brake system.	C705	5B6; P-1	5B12; P-1	5B12; P-1

Time off_____

Time on_____

Total time_____

Materials Required

- Vehicle or brake system simulator
- Specified brake fluid
- DVOM or brake fluid tester/test strip
- Brake bleeder wrenches
- Suction gun or brake fluid removal device
- Brake bleeder

Some Safety Issues to Consider

- **Caution:** Most types of brake fluid are harmful to painted surfaces. Be sure to prevent brake fluid from coming into contact with a vehicle's paint. Use fender covers to minimize this risk and be sure to wipe up any spilled brake fluid immediately with a wet rag.
- Do not mix DOT 5 brake fluid with a DOT 3 or 4 glycol-based fluid. They are incompatible.
- If you need to start the vehicle, you should ensure that the parking brake is firmly applied. If necessary, use wheel chocks to prevent the vehicle from moving when the vehicle is started to verify the completion of these tasks.
- Before moving a vehicle that has had any brake system or hydraulic system repairs, make sure the brake pedal is firm. If not, do not move the vehicle.
- When running any vehicles in the shop, make sure you use the shop's exhaust ventilation system to discharge all exhaust gas safely outside.
- Completion of this task may require test-driving the vehicle on the school grounds. Attempt this task only with full permission from your supervisor/instructor and follow all the guidelines exactly.
- Comply with personal and environmental safety practices associated with clothing; eye protection; hand tools; power equipment; proper ventilation; and the handling, storage, and disposal of chemicals/materials in accordance with local, state, and federal safety and environmental regulations.

Performance Standard

0—No exposure: No information or practice provided during the program; complete training required

1—Exposure only: General information provided with no practice time; close supervision needed; additional training required

2—Limited practice: Has practiced job during training program; additional training required to develop skill

3—Moderately skilled: Has performed job independently during training program; limited additional training may be required

4—Skilled: Can perform job independently with no additional training

Select, handle, store, and fill brake fluids
to proper levels.

Time off_____

Time on_____

Total time_____

CDX Tasksheet Number: C239

1. Research the specified brake fluid and the bleeding/flushing procedure for this
   vehicle using the appropriate service information.

   a. **Specified fluid:** _____

   b. **Bleeding/flushing sequence:** _____

   c. **Bleeding/flushing precautions:**

2. Locate the master cylinder reservoir.

   a. **List the level of the brake fluid:** _____

   > **NOTE** If the brake fluid is below the minimum level, it could mean there is a leak
   > in the system or the disc brake pads are worn. Investigate these possibilities and
   > report them to your supervisor/instructor.

3. If appropriate, add the appropriate type of brake fluid to the master cylinder reservoir
   to bring it to the full mark.

4. **Knowledge Check: What precautions should be taken when brake fluid is stored?**

5. **Knowledge Check: List the different types of brake fluid available:**

6. Have your supervisor/instructor verify satisfactory completion of this procedure,
   any observations found, and any necessary action(s) recommended.

Performance Rating

CDX Tasksheet Number: C239

0	1	2	3	4

Supervisor/instructor signature _____ Date _____

MLR 5B7   **AST** 5B13   **MAST** 5B13

Time off_____

Time on_____

Total time_____

CDX Tasksheet Number: C625

1. Test the fluid using one of the following procedures:

   a. DVOM–Galvanic Reaction Test

   i. Remove the master cylinder cap.
   ii. Set the DVOM to DC volts.
   iii. Place the red voltmeter lead in the reservoir brake fluid.
   iv. Place the black lead on the metal housing of the master cylinder.
   v. List the voltage reading obtained: _____ **V**

   > **NOTE** If reading is above .3V, this indicates a galvanic reaction and means there is an unacceptable level of moisture in the brake fluid.

   Determine any necessary actions:

   b. Brake Fluid Tester

   i. Follow the directions for the tester you have and test the brake fluid.
   ii. List your findings:

   c. Brake Fluid Test Strip

   i. Follow the directions for the test strip you have and test the brake fluid.
   ii. List your findings:

2. Have your supervisor/instructor verify satisfactory completion of this procedure, any observations found, and any necessary action(s) recommended.

Performance Rating

CDX Tasksheet Number: C625

0	1	2	3	4

Supervisor/instructor signature _____ Date _____

MLR 5B6 **AST** 5B12 **MAST** 5B12

Time off_____

Time on_____

Total time_____

CDX Tasksheet Number: C705

1. **Which method of bleeding/flushing will you use?** _____

2. **In what order will you be bleeding the brakes?** _____

3. Remove all old brake fluid from the master cylinder reservoir using the suction gun. Dispose of the fluid properly.

4. Refill the master cylinder reservoir using the specified brake fluid.

5. Using the appropriate equipment, bleed/flush each brake assembly until clean fluid comes out, making sure you keep the master cylinder reservoir from running low on fluid. Carefully tighten the bleeder screw and replace the bleeder screw dust cap when each wheel assembly is finished.

    a. **List the condition of the removed fluid:**

6. **Start the engine and apply the brakes to make sure the pedal is still firm. List the pedal feel:** _____

7. Refill the master cylinder reservoir to the proper level.

8. **List any necessary action(s):**

9. Return the vehicle to its beginning condition and return any tools you used to their proper locations.

10. Have your supervisor/instructor verify satisfactory completion of this procedure, any observations found, and any necessary action(s) recommended.

Performance Rating

CDX Tasksheet Number: C705

0	1	2	3	4

Supervisor/instructor signature _____ Date _____

Brakes: Master Cylinder Testing and Service

Student/intern information:

Name_____ Date_____ Class_____

Vehicle used for this activity:

Year _____ Make _____ Model_____

Odometer_____VIN_____

Learning Objective/Task	CDX Tasksheet Number	2013 MLR NATEF Reference Number; Priority Level	2013 AST NATEF Reference Number; Priority Level	2013 MAST NATEF Reference Number; Priority Level
• Measure brake pedal height, travel, and free play (as applicable); determine necessary action.	C622	5B1; P-1	5B2; P-1	5B2; P-1
• Check master cylinder for external leaks and proper operation.	C946	5B2; P-1		
• Check master cylinder for internal/external leaks and proper operation; determine necessary action.	C704		5B3; P-1	5B3; P-1
• Remove, bench bleed, and reinstall master cylinder.	C235		5B4; P-1	5B4; P-1
• Measure and adjust master cylinder pushrod length.	C556		5E5; P-3	5E5; P-3

Time off_____

Time on_____

Total time_____

Materials Required

- Depending on the type of concern, special diagnostic tools may be required. See your supervisor/instructor for instructions to identify what tools may be required.
- Tape measure
- Vehicle or simulator
- Work light and shop rag
- Line wrenches

Some Safety Issues to Consider

- If you need to start the vehicle, you should ensure that the parking brake is firmly applied; if necessary, use wheel chocks to prevent the vehicle from moving when the vehicle is started to verify the completion of these tasks.
- When running any vehicles in the shop, make sure you use the shop's exhaust ventilation system to discharge all exhaust gas safely outside.
- Only students who have their supervisor's/instructor's direct permission should perform this task due to the safety concerns involved.
- Diagnosis of this fault may require test-driving the vehicle on the school grounds. Attempt this task only with full permission from your supervisor/instructor and follow all the guidelines exactly.

- **Caution:** Most types of brake fluid are harmful to painted surfaces. Be sure to prevent brake fluid from coming into contact with a vehicle's paint. Use fender covers to minimize this risk and be sure to wipe up any spilled brake fluid immediately with a wet rag.
- Comply with personal and environmental safety practices associated with clothing; eye protection; hand tools; power equipment; proper ventilation; and the handling, storage, and disposal of chemicals/materials in accordance with local, state, and federal safety and environmental regulations.

Performance Standard

0–No exposure: No information or practice provided during the program; complete training required

1–Exposure only: General information provided with no practice time; close supervision needed; additional training required

2–Limited practice: Has practiced job during training program; additional training required to develop skill

3–Moderately skilled: Has performed job independently during training program; limited additional training may be required

4–Skilled: Can perform job independently with no additional training

Measure brake pedal height, travel, and free play
(as applicable); determine necessary action.

Time off_____

Time on_____

Total time_____

CDX Tasksheet Number: C622

1. Research the description and operation of the brake system for this vehicle in
    the appropriate service information. Also research the master cylinder diagnostic
    procedure and removal/installation procedures. Check off the systems in the list
    below that this vehicle is equipped with:

    a. **Power assist: Yes:** _____ **No:** _____

    b. **ABS: Yes:** _____ **No:** _____

    c. **Four-wheel ABS: Yes:** _____ **No:** _____

    d. **Rear-wheel ABS: Yes:** _____ **No:** _____

    e. **Traction control: Yes:** _____ **No:** _____

    f. **Front-/rear-split hydraulic system: Yes:** _____ **No:** _____

    g. **Diagonal-split hydraulic system: Yes:** _____ **No:** _____

    h. **Brake pedal height:** _____ **in/mm**

    i. **Brake pedal free play:** _____ **in/mm**

    j. **Brake pedal reserve height:** _____ **in/mm**

2. Brake pedal height

    a. **Following the service procedure, measure the brake pedal height. Record
        your readings here:** _____ **in/mm**

    b. **Within specifications? Yes:** _____ **No:** _____

    c. **If not as specified, determine any necessary actions:**

3. Reserve pedal height/pedal travel

    a. **Following the service procedure, start the vehicle and apply the brake
        pedal with moderate foot pressure. Measure the reserve pedal height/
        pedal travel and record the measurement:** _____ **in/mm**

    b. **If not as specified, determine any necessary actions:**

4. Brake pedal free play

    a. **Following the service procedure, measure the brake pedal free play and
        record the measurement here:** _____ **in/mm**

    b. **Within specifications? Yes:** _____ **No:** _____

    c. **If not as specified, determine any necessary actions:**

5. Have your supervisor/instructor verify satisfactory completion of this procedure, any observations found, and any necessary action(s) recommended.

Performance Rating

0	1	2	3	4

Supervisor/instructor signature _____ Date _____

Check master cylinder for external leaks and proper operation.

Time off_____

Time on_____

Total time_____

CDX Tasksheet Number: C946

1. Research the description and operation of the master cylinder for this vehicle in the appropriate service information.

2. Inspect the master cylinder for external leaks.

   a. **Check the brake fluid level in the reservoir. Record your reading here:** _____

   b. Inspect the master cylinder for obvious signs of leakage. Be sure to check all brake line fittings, sensor connections, reservoir seal(s), and the areas at the rear of the master cylinder near the seal. Also check the inside of the vacuum hose to the power booster.

   > **NOTE** If fluid is found on the inside of the hose, the rear seal in the master cylinder may be leaking fluid into the booster.

   c. **List your observations:**

2. Check the master cylinder for proper operation.

   a. Start the vehicle, apply the brake pedal beginning with a very light pressure, and gradually increasing the pressure. The brake pedal should hold its position with very little travel beyond its applied height. If the pedal continues to sink, the system may have an external or internal leak. Do this test several times with various pedal pressures and time elements. Be sure you hold foot pressure on the system for at least one minute.

   b. **List your observations:**

3. Have your supervisor/instructor verify satisfactory completion of this procedure, any observations found, and any necessary action(s) recommended.

Performance Rating

CDX Tasksheet Number: C946

0	1	2	3	4

Supervisor/instructor signature _____ Date _____

▶ **TASK** Check master cylinder for internal/external leaks
and proper operation; determine necessary action.

AST 5B3   MAST 5B3

Time off_____

Time on_____

Total time_____

CDX Tasksheet Number: C704

1. Research the description and operation of the brake system for this vehicle in the appropriate service information. Also research the master cylinder diagnostic procedure and removal/installation procedures.

   a. **Master cylinder pushrod length:** _____ **in/mm**
   b. **Master cylinder nut/bolt torque:** _____ **ft/lb or Nm**

2. Inspect the master cylinder for external leaks.

   a. **Check the brake fluid level in the reservoir.**
      Record your reading here: _____
   b. Inspect the master cylinder for obvious signs of leakage. Be sure to check all brake line fittings, sensor connections, reservoir seal(s), and the areas at the rear of the master cylinder near the seal. Also check the inside of the vacuum hose to the power booster.

   > **NOTE** If fluid is found on the inside of the hose, the rear seal in the master cylinder may be leaking fluid into the booster.

   c. **List your observations:**

2. Check the master cylinder for proper operation.

   a. Start the vehicle, apply the brake pedal beginning with a very light pressure, and gradually increasing the pressure. The brake pedal should hold its position with very little travel beyond its applied height. If the pedal continues to sink, the system may have an external or internal leak. Do this test several times with various pedal pressures and time elements. Be sure you hold foot pressure on the system for at least one minute.
   b. **List your observations:**

3. Inspect the master cylinder for internal leaks.

   a. Remove the master cylinder reservoir cap.
   b. Have an assistant apply the brake pedal firmly and hold it. Watch the fluid in the reservoir; it should have an initial spurt of fluid from each of the two compensating ports as the brake pedal is first moved.

> **NOTE** The brake fluid level should not rise in the reservoir as the brake pedal is held down. If it does, this indicates an internal leak in one or more of the master cylinder seals and it will need to be serviced. On quick take-up type master cylinders, the quick take-up valve vents excess fluid to the rear half of the reservoir.

    c. List your observations:

4. Determine any necessary action(s):

5. Have your supervisor/instructor verify satisfactory completion of this procedure, any observations found, and any necessary action(s) recommended.

Performance Rating

CDX Tasksheet Number: C704

0	1	2	3	4

Supervisor/instructor signature _____ Date _____

Time off_____

Time on_____

Total time_____

CDX Tasksheet Number: C235

1. Following the specified procedure, perform the following steps to remove the master cylinder.

   a. If the master cylinder is being replaced with a new or rebuilt unit, compare the new unit to the old one to verify that it is the correct replacement. If not, inform your supervisor/instructor.

   b. Use a suction gun to remove as much brake fluid from the master cylinder reservoir as possible. Do not drip brake fluid on any painted surface of the vehicle.

   > **NOTE** Be careful to avoid getting brake fluid on any painted surface of the vehicle.

   c. Using flare nut or line wrenches, loosen the brake line fittings. Also use the double wrench method of loosening the fittings if fitted with an adapter. Place a rag under the fittings to catch any leaking brake fluid.

   d. Unbolt the master cylinder from the power booster and remove the master cylinder, being careful to avoid getting brake fluid on any painted surface of the vehicle.

   The rest of this task is performed at the end of the master cylinder service. Please refer to page 691 for the completion of this task.

AST 5E5   **MAST** 5E5

Time off_____

Time on_____

Total time_____

CDX Tasksheet Number: C556

1. Research the specifications and procedure for measuring and adjusting pushrod length in the appropriate service information.

    a. **Master cylinder pushrod length:** _____ in/mm
    b. **Master cylinder nut/bolt torque:** _____ ft/lb or Nm

2. Measure the pushrod length according to the manufacturer's procedure.

    a. **List measurement here:** _____ in/mm

3. **Determine any necessary action(s): Knowledge Check: What would be the customer concern if the pushrod length were too long and caused the master cylinder piston seal to cover one or both of the compensating ports? List your answer.**

4. **Knowledge Check: What would be the customer concern if the pushrod length were substantially shorter than specifications? List your answer.**

5. Have your supervisor/instructor verify satisfactory completion of this procedure, any observations found, and any necessary action(s) recommended.

Performance Rating

CDX Tasksheet Number: C556

0	1	2	3	4

Supervisor/instructor signature _____ Date _____

CONTINUATION OF TASK {C235/5B4} Remove,
bench bleed, and reinstall master cylinder (from page 687).

AST
5B4

MAST
5B4

Time off_____

Time on_____

Total time_____

CDX Tasksheet Number: C235

2. Bench bleed the master cylinder.

3. Install the master cylinder, being careful not to cross-thread the fittings.

> **NOTE** It is good practice to start the fittings by finger before the bolts holding the master cylinder in place are tightened. This helps prevent cross-threading of the fittings in the master cylinder, especially on aluminum master cylinders.

4. Bleed any remaining air from the hydraulic brake system.

5. Verify the correct brake pedal travel and feel.

6. Return the vehicle to its beginning condition and return any tools you used to their proper locations.

7. Have your supervisor/instructor verify satisfactory completion of this procedure, any observations found, and any necessary action(s) recommended.

Performance Rating

CDX Tasksheet Number: C235

0	1	2	3	4

Supervisor/instructor signature _____ Date _____

Brakes: Brake Lines and Hoses Inspection and Repair

Student/intern information:

Name_____ Date_____ Class_____

Vehicle used for this activity:

Year _____ Make _____ Model_____

Odometer_____VIN_____

© 2015 Jones & Bartlett Learning, LLC, an Ascend Learning Company

Learning Objective/Task	CDX Tasksheet Number	2013 MLR NATEF Reference Number; Priority Level	2013 AST NATEF Reference Number; Priority Level	2013 MAST NATEF Reference Number; Priority Level
• Inspect brake lines, flexible hoses, and fittings for leaks, dents, kinks, rust, cracks, bulging, wear, and loose fittings and supports; determine necessary action.	C237	5B3; P-1	5B6; P-1	5B6; P-1
• Replace brake lines, hoses, fittings, and supports.	C623		5B7; P-2	5B7; P-2
• Fabricate brake lines using proper material and flaring procedures (double flare and ISO types).	C624		5B8; P-2	5B8; P-2

Time off_____

Time on_____

Total time_____

Materials Required

- Vehicle or brake system simulator
- Vehicle hoist
- Flare nut wrenches
- Flaring tool set of the correct type
- Brake tubing to flare
- Specified brake fluid

Some Safety Issues to Consider

- If you need to start the vehicle, you should ensure that the parking brake is firmly applied; if necessary, use wheel chocks to prevent the vehicle from moving when the vehicle is started to verify the completion of these tasks.
- When running any vehicles in the shop, make sure you use the shop's exhaust ventilation system to discharge all exhaust gas safely outside.
- Only students who have their supervisor's/instructor's direct permission should perform this task due to the safety concerns involved.
- Diagnosis of this fault may require test-driving the vehicle on the school grounds. Attempt this task only with full permission from your supervisor/instructor and follow all the guidelines exactly.
- Comply with personal and environmental safety practices associated with clothing; eye protection; hand tools; power equipment; proper ventilation; and the handling, storage, and disposal of chemicals/materials in accordance with local, state, and federal safety and environmental regulations.

Performance Standard

0—No exposure: No information or practice provided during the program; complete training required

1—Exposure only: General information provided with no practice time; close supervision needed; additional training required

2—Limited practice: Has practiced job during training program; additional training required to develop skill

3—Moderately skilled: Has performed job independently during training program; limited additional training may be required

4—Skilled: Can perform job independently with no additional training

Inspect brake lines, flexible hoses, and fittings for leaks, dents, kinks, rust, cracks, bulging, wear, and loose fittings and supports; determine necessary action.

MLR	AST	MAST
5B3	5B6	5B6

Time off_____

Time on_____

Total time_____

CDX Tasksheet Number: C237

1. Safely raise and secure the vehicle on the hoist, then trace all brake lines from the master cylinder to each wheel's brake assembly. **Inspect the steel brake lines for the following defects and list each defect's location and cause:**

   a. Leaks:

   b. Dents:

   c. Kinks:

   d. Rust:

   e. Cracks:

   f. Wear:

   g. Loose fittings or supports:

2. **Inspect all flexible brake lines for the following defects and list each defect's location and cause:**

   a. Cracks:

b. Bulging:

c. Wear:

d. Loose fittings or supports:

3. Determine any necessary action(s):

4. Have your supervisor/instructor verify satisfactory completion of this procedure, any observations found, and any necessary action(s) recommended.

Performance Rating

CDX Tasksheet Number: C237

0	1	2	3	4

Supervisor/instructor signature _____ Date _____

AST 5B7 **MAST** 5B7

Time off_____

Time on_____

Total time_____

CDX Tasksheet Number: C623

1. Safely raise and secure the vehicle on the hoist and, where appropriate, drain the brake line of fluid and safely dispose of it.

   NOTE You may be able to use a brake pedal depressor to hold down the brake pedal slightly. This will close off the compensating ports in the master cylinder and therefore minimize the amount of fluid draining out of the system. Just remember that the brake lights will stay on continuously while the pedal is depressed.

2. Carefully remove (using flare nut wrenches) any brake lines, hoses, fittings, and supports that are to be replaced.

3. **Have your instructor initial to verify removal:** _____

4. Replace any removed flexible hoses, fittings, and supports in accordance with the service manual procedure.

   NOTE Be sure to properly route the lines and tighten adequately.

5. Fill the master cylinder reservoir with the specified fluid.

6. Bleed the system in accordance with the recommended procedure.

7. **Test the system for leaks and integrity. List your observations:**

8. Have your supervisor/instructor verify satisfactory completion of this procedure, any observations found, and any necessary action(s) recommended.

Performance Rating

CDX Tasksheet Number: C623

0	1	2	3	4

Supervisor/instructor signature _____ Date _____

► **TASK** Fabricate brake lines using proper material and flaring procedures (double flare and ISO types).

Time off_____

Time on_____

Total time_____

CDX Tasksheet Number: C624

1. Safely raise and secure the vehicle on the hoist and, where appropriate, drain the brake line of fluid and safely dispose of it.

> **NOTE** You may be able to use a brake pedal depressor to hold down the brake pedal slightly. This will close off the compensating ports in the master cylinder and therefore minimize the amount of fluid draining out of the system. Just remember that the brake lights will stay on continuously while the pedal is depressed.

2. Carefully remove (using flare nut wrenches) any brake lines and supports that are to be replaced. **List the type of flare used on this brake line:**

3. Fabricate (using the correct equipment and procedure) any brake lines that are to be replaced using proper material and flaring procedures (double flare and ISO types). The old ones can be used for patterns in this regard.

4. **List the type of tube material used:** _____

5. Have your instructor inspect the flare. **Supervisor's/Instructor's initials:** _____

6. Replace any removed brake lines, fittings, and supports in accordance with the service information procedure.

> **NOTE** Be sure to route the lines properly and tighten adequately.

7. Fill the master cylinder reservoir with the specified fluid.

8. Bleed the system in accordance with the recommended procedure.

9. **Test the system for leaks and integrity. List your observations:**

10. Have your supervisor/instructor verify satisfactory completion of this procedure, any observations found, and any necessary action(s) recommended.

Performance Rating

CDX Tasksheet Number: C624

☐   ☐   ☐   ☐   ☐

0   1   2   3   4

Supervisor/instructor signature _____ Date _____

Brakes: Disc Brake Inspection, Maintenance, and Service

Student/intern information:

Name_____ Date_____ Class_____

Vehicle used for this activity:

Year_____ Make_____ Model_____

Odometer_____ VIN_____

Learning Objective/Task	CDX Tasksheet Number	2013 MLR NATEF Reference Number; Priority Level	2013 AST NATEF Reference Number; Priority Level	2013 MAST NATEF Reference Number; Priority Level
• Diagnose poor stopping, noise, vibration, pulling, grabbing, dragging, or pulsation concerns; determine necessary action.	C708		5D1; P-1	5D1; P-1
• Remove and clean caliper assembly; inspect for leaks and damage/wear to caliper housing; determine necessary action.	C802	5D1; P-1	5D2; P-1	5D2; P-1
• Clean and inspect caliper mounting and slides/pins for proper operation, wear, and damage; determine necessary action.	C803	5D2; P-1	5D3; P-1	5D3; P-1
• Check brake pad wear indicator; determine necessary action.	C632	5D10; P-2	5D11; P-2	5D11; P-2
• Remove, inspect, and replace pads and retaining hardware; determine necessary action.	C627	5D3; P-1	5D4; P-1	5D4; P-1
• Reassemble, lubricate, and reinstall seat pads and caliper, pads, and related hardware; inspect for leaks.	C805	5D4; P-1	5D5; P-1	5D5; P-1
• Install wheel and torque lug nuts, and make final checks and adjustments.	C251	N/A	N/A	N/A
• Retract and readjust caliper piston on an integrated parking brake system.	C631	5D9; P-3	5D10; P-3	5D10; P-3
• Describe the importance of operating vehicle to burnish/break in replacement brake pads according to manufacturer's recommendations.	C948	5D11; P-1	5D12; P-1	5D12; P-1

Time off_____

Time on_____

Total time_____

Some Safety Issues to Consider

- If you need to start the vehicle, you should ensure that the parking brake is firmly applied; if necessary, use wheel chocks to prevent the vehicle from moving when the vehicle is started to verify the completion of these tasks.
- When running any vehicles in the shop, make sure you use the shop's exhaust ventilation system to discharge all exhaust gas safely outside.
- Only students who have their supervisor's/instructor's direct permission should perform this task due to the safety concerns involved.
- Diagnosis of this fault and verification of repairs may require test driving the vehicle on the school grounds. Attempt this task only with full permission from your supervisor/instructor and follow all the guidelines exactly.
- Vehicle hoists are important tools that increase productivity and make the job easier. However, they can also cause severe injury or death if used improperly. Make sure you follow the hoist's and vehicle manufacturers' operation procedures. Also make sure you have your supervisor's/ instructor's permission to use a vehicle hoist.
- **Caution:** Brake dust may contain asbestos, which has been determined to cause cancer when inhaled or ingested. Treat all brake dust as if it contains asbestos and use OSHA-approved asbestos removal equipment. Do not allow brake dust to become airborne by using anything that would disturb the dust. Also, wear protective gloves during this procedure and dispose of or clean them in an approved manner.
- **Caution:** Most types of brake fluid are harmful to painted surfaces. Be sure to prevent brake fluid from coming in contact with a vehicle's paint. Use fender covers to minimize this risk and be sure to wipe up any spilled brake fluid immediately with a wet rag.
- Comply with personal and environmental safety practices associated with clothing; eye protection; hand tools; power equipment; proper ventilation; and the handling, storage, and disposal of chemicals/materials in accordance with local, state, and federal safety and environmental regulations.

Performance Standard

0–No exposure: No information or practice provided during the program; complete training required

1–Exposure only: General information provided with no practice time; close supervision needed; additional training required

2–Limited practice: Has practiced job during training program; additional training required to develop skill

3–Moderately skilled: Has performed job independently during training program; limited additional training may be required

4–Skilled: Can perform job independently with no additional training

Diagnose poor stopping, noise, vibration, pulling, grabbing, dragging, or pulsation concerns; determine necessary action. **AST** 5D1 **MAST** 5D1

Time off_____

Time on_____

Total time_____

1. **List the brake-related customer complaints/concerns:**

2. Research the description and operation of the brake system for this vehicle in the appropriate service information. Also, research the disc brake diagnostic procedure and removal/installation procedures.

   a. **List the possible cause(s) of the complaint/concern:**

   b. **Minimum brake pad thickness:** _____ in/mm
   c. **Caliper bore-to-piston clearance (maximum):** _____ in/mm
   d. **List specified caliper slide lubricant:** _____
   e. **Caliper bolt torque:** _____ ft-lb/Nm
   f. **Lug nut torque:** _____ ft-lb/Nm
   g. **Draw the lug nut torque pattern for this vehicle:**

3. With instructor permission, test-drive the vehicle to verify the complaint.

   NOTE Be sure to follow all shop policies regarding test drives.

   a. **List your observations:**

   The rest of this task is performed at the end of the disc brake service. Please refer to page 717 for the completion of this task.

Remove and clean caliper assembly; inspect for leaks and damage/wear to caliper housing; determine necessary action.

MLR	AST	MAST
5D1	5D2	5D2

Time off_____

Time on_____

Total time_____

CDX Tasksheet Number: C802

1. Raise the vehicle and support it properly. Remove the wheel and tire assembly.

2. Break loose or open the bleeder screw (then close it) to ensure that it is not seized in place and is able to open. Failure to find this out now could waste a lot of time later trying to repair a bleeder screw that has broken off, if it is seized. Also, if replacing the caliper, it is good practice to bleed all of the old brake fluid out of the brake system at this time, so that old brake fluid isn't run though the new caliper.

3. Remove the caliper assembly from its mountings, following the specified procedure. If removing the caliper completely, be careful not to lose the two copper sealing rings when removing the brake line, if applicable.

4. **Inspect the caliper for leaks or damage, being careful to avoid dislodging brake dust, which may contain asbestos. List your observations:**

    a. **Leaks:**

    b. **Damage/wear:**

5. Following the specified procedure, clean the caliper assembly.

6. **Based on your observations, determine any necessary action(s):**

7. Have your supervisor/instructor verify satisfactory completion of this procedure, any observations found, and any necessary action(s) recommended.

Performance Rating

CDX Tasksheet Number: C802

0	1	2	3	4

Supervisor/instructor signature _____ Date _____

► **TASK** Clean and inspect caliper mounting and slides/pins for proper operation, wear, and damage; determine necessary action.

MLR
5D2 **AST** 5D3 **MAST** 5D3

CDX Tasksheet Number: C803

1. Following the specified procedure, clean the caliper mounts and slides/pins.

2. Inspect the caliper mounts, slides/pins, and any threads for operation, wear, and damage. **List your observations:**

   a. **Operation:**
   b. **Wear:**
   c. **Damage:**

3. **Based on your observations, determine any necessary action(s):**

4. Have your supervisor/instructor verify satisfactory completion of this procedure, any observations found, and any necessary action(s) recommended.

Performance Rating

CDX Tasksheet Number: C803

0	1	2	3	4

Supervisor/instructor signature _____ Date _____

MLR 5D10 | **AST** 5D11 | **MAST** 5D11

Time off_____

Time on_____

Total time_____

CDX Tasksheet Number: C632

1. **List what type of wear indicator system this vehicle uses:**

2. Check the brake pad-wear indicator. How much brake pad thickness remains until the indicator contacts the surface of the rotor?

   Note your measurement: _____ **in/mm**

3. **Determine any necessary action(s):**

4. Have your supervisor/instructor verify satisfactory completion of this procedure, any observations found, and any necessary action(s) recommended.

Performance Rating

CDX Tasksheet Number: C632

0	1	2	3	4

Supervisor/instructor signature _____ Date _____

▶ TASK Remove, inspect, and replace pads and retaining hardware; determine necessary action.

MLR 5D3　**AST** 5D4　**MAST** 5D4

Time off_____

Time on_____

Total time_____

CDX Tasksheet Number: C627

1. Remove and inspect pads and retaining hardware in accordance with the correct procedure.

2. **Measure the remaining brake pad thickness:** _____ **in/mm**

3. **Inspect the brake pads and retaining hardware. List condition(s) found:**

4. **Determine any necessary action(s):**

5. Have your supervisor/instructor verify satisfactory completion of this procedure, any observations found, and any necessary action(s) recommended.

Performance Rating

CDX Tasksheet Number: C627

0	1	2	3	4

Supervisor/instructor signature _____ Date _____

NOTE Because you have the rotor exposed, go to the "Rotor Inspection and Service" tasksheet and complete the tasks listed there. This will save you time and effort. Return to this tasksheet and pick up here once you are done with the rotor.

© 2015 Jones & Bartlett Learning, LLC, an Ascend Learning Company

Reassemble, lubricate, and reinstall seat pads, and caliper, pads, and related hardware; inspect for leaks.

MLR 5D4 **AST** 5D5 **MAST** 5D5

Time off_____

Time on_____

Total time_____

CDX Tasksheet Number: C805

1. Make sure the rotor has been properly installed on the hub/spindle.

2. Reassemble the pads, hardware, and caliper on caliper mounts using the specified lubricant.

   NOTE Torque all bolts to specified torque.

4. If removed, reinstall the brake line fittings using two copper washers (if equipped). Place one between the brake line fitting and the head of the banjo bolt and the other between the brake line fitting and the caliper.

   NOTE Before performing the next step, ensure that all brake assemblies are completely reassembled, including all brake drums. This will prevent damage to wheel cylinders, brake shoes, and pads.

5. Seat the pads by applying the brake pedal several times. This will force the brake caliper pistons to adjust to the proper clearance for proper brake application.

   NOTE Failure to perform this step could lead to no brake application when the vehicle is first moved.

6. If the brake pedal is spongy, you will need to bleed the brakes of any trapped air in the system. See the appropriate CDX tasksheet for guidance.

7. **If the brake pedal is firm and does not sink over time, there could still be a small leak that would cause a brake failure at some point in time. Inspect the system for any brake fluid leaks, no matter how small; if found, inform your supervisor/ instructor.**

   a. **Are there any leaks in the system? Yes:** _____ **No:** _____
   b. **If yes, where?**

8. Have your supervisor/instructor verify satisfactory completion of this procedure, any observations found, and any necessary action(s) recommended.

Performance Rating

CDX Tasksheet Number: C805

0	1	2	3	4

Supervisor/instructor signature _____ Date _____

Install wheel and torque lug nuts, and make final checks and adjustments.

Additional Task

Time off_____

Time on_____

Total time_____

CDX Tasksheet Number: C251

1. Install the wheel(s), place lug nuts on the studs with the proper side facing the wheel, and torque all of them to the proper torque.

> **NOTE** The lug nut contact face MUST match the contact face in the wheel. If the wheel contact face is tapered, the lug nut contact face MUST also be tapered to match. If the contact face in the wheel is flat, the contact face of the lug nut MUST be flat. If in doubt about which way the lug nuts should face, ask your instructor.

2. Reinstall any wheel covers that have been removed.

3. **Check to see that the brake master cylinder contains the proper amount of brake fluid:**

    a. **Is it at the proper level? Yes:** _____ **No:** _____
    b. **If no, refill to the proper level with the proper fluid.**

4. **Check the brake hoses and calipers for any leaks or loose fasteners. Verify that the brake hoses are not kinked or in the wrong position.**

    a. **Are there any leaks? Yes:** _____ **No:** _____
    b. **Are all fasteners tightened/torqued properly? Yes:** _____
       No: _____
    c. **Are the brake lines/hoses secure and routed correctly? Yes:** _____
       No: _____

5. Place any/all core parts in their original box(es) and return them to the appropriate place in the shop.

6. Ask your supervisor/instructor if you are now expected to test-drive the vehicle. If so, you must be licensed and approved to carry out this task and you must follow all relevant school/shop policies and other guidelines. Failure to do so may result in severe injury or death. **Supervisor's/instructor's initials:** _____

7. Have your supervisor/instructor verify satisfactory completion of this procedure, any observations found, and any necessary action(s) recommended.

Performance Rating

CDX Tasksheet Number: N/A

0	1	2	3	4

Supervisor/instructor signature _____ Date _____

CONTINUATION OF TASK {C708/5D1}: Diagnose poor stopping, noise, vibration, pulling, grabbing, dragging, or pulsation concerns; determine necessary action (from page 703).

AST
5D1

MAST
5D1

Time off_____

Time on_____

Total time_____

CDX Tasksheet Number: C708

4. **Reflecting back on this job, list the cause(s) of the customer concerns as listed at the beginning of this tasksheet:**

5. **Document the correction(s) required to fix the customer concern:**

6. **Did you repair the vehicle? Yes:** _____ **No:** _____

7. **List any additional necessary action(s):**

8. Return the vehicle to its beginning condition and return any tools you used to their proper locations.

9. Have your supervisor/instructor verify satisfactory completion of this procedure, any observations found, and any necessary action(s) recommended.

Performance Rating

CDX Tasksheet Number: C708

0	1	2	3	4

Supervisor/instructor signature _____ Date _____

Retract and readjust caliper piston on an integrated parking brake system.

Time off_____

Time on_____

Total time_____

CDX Tasksheet Number: C631

1. Research the proper method of retracting and readjusting the caliper piston on an integrated parking brake system in the appropriate service information. **List any precautions below.**

2. **Following the recommended process, retract the caliper piston. Instructor initials:** _____

3. **Reinstall the caliper and readjust the caliper piston. Instructor initials:** _____

4. **Determine any necessary action(s):**

5. Have your supervisor/instructor verify satisfactory completion of this procedure, any observations found, and any necessary action(s) recommended.

Performance Rating

CDX Tasksheet Number: C631

0	1	2	3	4

Supervisor/instructor signature _____ Date _____

Describe the importance of operating vehicle to burnish/break in replacement brake pads according to manufacturer's recommendations.

MLR	AST	MAST
5D11	5D12	5D12

Time off_____

Time on_____

Total time_____

CDX Tasksheet Number: C948

1. Research the brake pad burnishing/break in process for the vehicle you are working on, in the appropriate service information. **List the process here (or print off and attach to this sheet):**

2. **Describe in your own words why it is important to properly burnish/break in brake pads after installation:**

3. Have your supervisor/instructor verify satisfactory completion of this procedure, any observations found, and any necessary action(s) recommended.

Performance Rating

CDX Tasksheet Number: C948

0	1	2	3	4

Supervisor/instructor signature _____ Date _____

Brakes: Rotor Inspection and Service

© 2015 Jones & Bartlett Learning, LLC, an Ascend Learning Company

Student/intern information:

Name_____ Date_____ Class_____

Vehicle used for this activity:

Year_____ Make_____ Model_____

Odometer_____VIN_____

Learning Objective/Task	CDX Tasksheet Number	2013 MLR NATEF Reference Number; Priority Level	2013 AST NATEF Reference Number; Priority Level	2013 MAST NATEF Reference Number; Priority Level
• Clean and inspect rotor and measure rotor thickness, thickness variation, and lateral runout; determine necessary action.	C628	5D5; P-1	5D6; P-1	5D6; P-1
• Remove and reinstall rotor.	C806	5D6; P-1	5D7; P-1	5D7; P-1
• Refinish rotor off vehicle; measure final rotor thickness and compare with specifications.	C630	5D8; P-1	5D9; P-1	5D9; P-1
• Refinish rotor on vehicle; measure final rotor thickness and compare with specifications.	C629	5D7; P-1	5D8; P-1	5D8; P-1
• Inspect and replace wheel studs.	C274	5F6; P-1	5F7; P-1	5F8; P-1

Time off_____

Time on_____

Total time_____

Materials Required

- Vehicle or simulator with disc brake concern
- Vehicle lifting equipment
- Asbestos removal equipment
- Torque wrench/es
- Micrometer
- Dial indicator
- Off-car brake lathe
- On-car brake lathe
- Hydraulic press or hammer and flat washers

Some Safety Issues to Consider

- Vehicle hoists are important tools that increase productivity and make the job easier. However, they can also cause severe injury or death if used improperly. Make sure you follow the hoist's and vehicle manufacturers' operation procedures. Also make sure you have your supervisor's/instructor's permission to use a vehicle hoist.
- **Caution:** Brake dust may contain asbestos, which has been determined to cause cancer when inhaled or ingested. Treat all brake dust as if it contains asbestos and use OSHA-approved asbestos removal equipment. Do not allow brake dust to become airborne by using anything

that would disturb the dust. Also, wear protective gloves during this procedure and dispose of or clean them in an approved manner.

- **Caution:** Most types of brake fluid are harmful to painted surfaces. Be sure to prevent brake fluid from coming into contact with a vehicle's paint. Use fender covers to minimize this risk and be sure to wipe up any spilled brake fluid immediately with a wet rag.
- Only students who have their supervisor's/instructor's direct permission should perform this task due to the safety concerns involved.
- Brake lathes are very powerful. Follow all manufacturer instructions when setting up and operating a brake lathe.
- On-car brake lathes typically spin both rotors/wheels on an axle. Make sure the opposite rotor/wheel is free to spin and people stay away from it while refinishing the other rotor.
- Diagnosis of this fault, or verification after repair, may require test-driving the vehicle on the school grounds. Attempt this task only with full permission from your supervisor/instructor and follow all the guidelines exactly.
- Comply with personal and environmental safety practices associated with clothing; eye protection; hand tools; power equipment; proper ventilation; and the handling, storage, and disposal of chemicals/materials in accordance with local, state, and federal safety and environmental regulations.

Performance Standard

0—No exposure: No information or practice provided during the program; complete training required

1—Exposure only: General information provided with no practice time; close supervision needed; additional training required

2—Limited practice: Has practiced job during training program; additional training required to develop skill

3—Moderately skilled: Has performed job independently during training program; limited additional training may be required

4—Skilled: Can perform job independently with no additional training

► **TASK** Clean and inspect rotor and measure rotor thickness, thickness variation, and lateral runout; determine necessary action.

MLR 5D5 | **AST 5D6** | **MAST 5D6**

Time off_____

Time on_____

Total time_____

CDX Tasksheet Number: C628

1. Research rotor inspection, refinishing, removal, and installation procedure in the appropriate service information. Follow all directions.

    a. **Minimum rotor thickness:** _____ in/mm
    b. **Maximum thickness variation:** _____ in/mm
    c. **Maximum lateral runout:** _____ in/mm

2. If you haven't already done so, remove the caliper assembly, brake pads, and any hardware following the manufacturer's procedure.

3. Clean the rotor with approved asbestos removal equipment.

4. **Inspect/measure the rotor for the following:**

    a. **Hard spots/hot spots: Yes:** _____ **No:** _____
    b. **Cracks: Yes:** _____ **No:** _____
    c. **Rotor thickness:** _____ in/mm
    d. **Thickness variation (maximum variation) (check in 6-8 places):** _____ in/mm
    e. **Lateral runout:** _____ in/mm
    f. **Is the rotor machinable? Yes:** _____ **No:** _____

5. **Determine any necessary action(s):**

6. Have your supervisor/instructor verify satisfactory completion of this procedure, any observations found, and any necessary action(s) recommended.

Performance Rating

CDX Tasksheet Number: C628

0	1	2	3	4

Supervisor/instructor signature _____ Date _____

> **NOTE** If you are refinishing this rotor on the vehicle, skip down to task C629/ MLR 5D7 and AST/MAST 5D8. Refinish rotor on vehicle; measure final rotor thickness and compare with specifications. If you are refinishing this rotor off the vehicle, continue on to the next task

© 2015 Jones & Bartlett Learning, LLC, an Ascend Learning Company

MLR 5D6 **AST** 5D7 **MAST** 5D7

Time off_____

Time on_____

Total time_____

CDX Tasksheet Number: C806

1. Remove the rotor following the specified procedure.

2. Now would be a good time to inspect the rotor, if you haven't already, and consider refinishing it. Ask your supervisor/instructor if you are to inspect and/or refinish the rotor. If so, proceed to task C630/5D8/9 below.

3. **If you are to reinstall this rotor, have your supervisor/instructor confirm removal. Supervisor's/instructor's initials:** _____

   The rest of this task is performed at the end of the rotor service. Please refer to page 733 for the completion of this task.

Refinish rotor off vehicle; measure final rotor thickness and compare with specifications.

MLR	AST	MAST
5D8	5D9	5D9

CDX Tasksheet Number: C630

1. Mount the rotor on the brake lathe following the manufacturer's procedure and set it up, ready to make a cut (but don't yet).

2. **Measure or list the existing rotor thickness:** _____ in/mm

3. **Have your instructor verify proper set-up and initial here:** _____

4. **Using the correct procedure, refinish the brake rotor to within allowable tolerances.**

5. **Give the rotor a non-directional finish using sandpaper or an appropriate sanding wheel.**

6. **Measure the refinished rotor thickness:** _____ in/mm

7. **Calculate the amount of material that was removed:** _____ in/mm

8. **Is the rotor fit for return to service? Yes:** _____ **No:** _____

9. **Determine any necessary action(s):**

10. Have your supervisor/instructor verify satisfactory completion of this procedure, any observations found, and any necessary action(s) recommended.

> **NOTE** If the rotor is serviceable, skip down to task C806/5D6/5D7: Remove and reinstall rotor.

Performance Rating

CDX Tasksheet Number: C630

0	1	2	3	4

Supervisor/instructor signature _____ Date _____

▶ **TASK** Refinish rotor on vehicle; measure final rotor thickness and compare with specifications.

MLR 5D7   AST 5D8   MAST 5D8

Time off_____

Time on_____

Total time_____

CDX Tasksheet Number: C629

1. Set up the on-car brake lathe following the manufacturer's procedure, ready to make a cut (but don't yet).

2. **Measure or list the existing rotor thickness:** _____ **in/mm**

3. **Have your instructor verify proper setup and initial here:** _____

4. Using the correct procedure, refinish the brake rotor to within allowable tolerances. If necessary, give the rotor a non-directional finish using sandpaper or a sanding disc.

5. **Measure the refinished rotor thickness:** _____ **in/mm**

6. **Calculate the amount of material that was removed:** _____ **in/mm**

7. **Is the rotor fit for return to service? Yes:** _____ **No:** _____

8. **Determine any necessary action(s):**

> **NOTE** If the rotor is serviceable, skip down to task C806/5D6/5D7: Remove and reinstall rotor.

9. Have your supervisor/instructor verify satisfactory completion of this procedure, any observations found, and any necessary action(s) recommended.

Performance Rating

CDX Tasksheet Number: C629

0	1	2	3	4

Supervisor/instructor signature _____ Date _____

MLR	AST	MAST
5D6	5D7	5D7

Time off_____

Time on_____

Total time_____

CDX Tasksheet Number: C806

4. When appropriate (most likely after refinishing), reinstall the rotor according to the manufacturer's recommendations.

5. If you had to remove the wheel bearing during disassembly, have your supervisor/instructor verify proper adjustment of the bearings.

    a. **Supervisor's/instructor's initials:** _____

6. Have your supervisor/instructor verify satisfactory completion of this procedure, any observations found, and any necessary action(s) recommended.

> **NOTE** If you came to this tasksheet from the "Disc Brake Inspection and Service" tasksheet, return to that tasksheet and continue where you left off.

Performance Rating

CDX Tasksheet Number: C806

0	1	2	3	4

Supervisor/instructor signature _____ Date _____

MLR 5F6 **AST** 5F7 **MAST** 5F8

Time off _____

Time on _____

Total time _____

CDX Tasksheet Number: C274

1. Research the wheel stud removal and installation procedure in the appropriate service manual. Follow all directions carefully.

   a. There are generally two standard procedures for replacing wheel studs. One is to remove the hub from the vehicle and use a hydraulic press to remove and install the studs. The other is to use a hammer to drive out the old stud, then use washers and the flat side of the lug nut to draw the new stud into the hub. Which method does the service manual describe for this vehicle?

   _____

   b. **List any special tools or procedures for this task:**

   c. **Lug nut torque:** _____ **ft-lbs/Nm**

2. Safely raise the vehicle on a hoist. Check to see that the vehicle is secure on the hoist.

3. Remove the wheel assembly and inspect the lug nuts and wheel studs. **List your observations and any necessary actions:**

4. Have your supervisor/instructor verify your observations. **Supervisor/instructor's initials:** _____

5. Remove the damaged wheel stud/s from the hub, being careful to follow the specified procedure. **List your observations:**

6. Have your supervisor/instructor verify removal. **Supervisor/instructor's initials:** _____

7. **Install a new wheel stud/s in the hub, following the specified procedure. Make sure the stud is fully seated in the hub. List your observations:**

8. Have your supervisor/instructor verify the installation. **Supervisor/instructor's initials:** _____

> NOTE If you came to this tasksheet from the "Disc Brake Inspection and Service" tasksheet, return to that tasksheet and continue where you left off.

9. Reinstall the hub on the vehicle if it was removed. Reinstall the wheel assembly. Torque lug nuts to proper torque.

10. Have your supervisor/instructor verify satisfactory completion of this procedure, any observations found, and any necessary action/s recommended.

Performance Rating

CDX Tasksheet Number: C274

0	1	2	3	4

Supervisor/instructor signature _____ Date _____

Brakes: Drum Brake Inspection, Maintenance, and Service

Student/intern information:

Name_____ Date_____ Class_____

Vehicle used for this activity:

Year _____ Make _____ Model_____

Odometer_____VIN_____

Time off_____

Time on_____

Total time_____

Learning Objective/Task	CDX Tasksheet Number	2013 MLR NATEF Reference Number; Priority Level	2013 AST NATEF Reference Number; Priority Level	2013 MAST NATEF Reference Number; Priority Level
• Diagnose poor stopping, noise, vibration, pulling, grabbing, dragging, or pedal pulsation concerns; determine necessary action.	C706		5C1; P-1	5C1; P-1
• Remove, clean, inspect, and measure brake drum diameter; determine necessary action.	C800	5C1; P-1	5C2; P-1	5C2; P-1
• Refinish brake drum and measure final drum diameter; compare to specifications.	C626	5C2; P-1	5C3; P-1	5C3; P-1
• Remove, clean, and inspect brake shoes, springs, pins, clips, levers, adjusters/self-adjusters, other related brake hardware, and backing support plates; lubricate and reassemble.	C248	5C3; P-1	5C4; P-1	5C4; P-1
• Inspect wheel cylinders for leaks and proper operation; remove and replace as needed.	C707	5C4; P-2	5C5; P-2	5C5; P-2
• Pre-adjust brake shoes and parking brake; install brake drums or drum/hub assemblies and wheel bearings; make final checks and adjustments.	C801	5C5; P-2	5C6; P-2	5C6; P-2
• Install wheel and torque lug nuts.	C251	5A3; P-1	5A4; P-1	5A4; P-1

Materials Required

- Vehicle or simulator with drum brakes
- Vehicle lifting equipment
- Asbestos removal equipment
- Drum brake micrometer
- Brake Lathe
- Brake spring tools
- Micrometer or dial caliper
- Flare nut wrench to fit brake line fitting
- Brake spoon
- Lubriplate

Some Safety Issues to Consider

- Diagnosis of this fault may require test-driving the vehicle on the school grounds or on a hoist, both of which carry severe risks. Attempt this task only with full permission from your supervisor/instructor and follow all the guidelines exactly.
- **Caution:** Brake dust may contain asbestos, which has been determined to cause cancer when inhaled or ingested. Treat all brake dust as if it contains asbestos and use OSHA-approved asbestos removal equipment. Do not allow brake dust to become airborne by using anything that would disturb the dust. Also, wear protective gloves during this procedure and dispose of or clean them in an approved manner.
- Brake springs can fly off with much force. Always wear safety glasses, and grip the springs firmly when removing and installing them.
- Brake lathes are very powerful. Follow all manufacturer instructions when setting up and operating a brake lathe.
- Lifting equipment such as vehicle jacks and stands, vehicle hoists, and engine hoists are important tools that increase productivity and make the job easier. However, they can also cause severe injury or death if used improperly. Make sure you follow the manufacturer's operation procedures. Also make sure you have your supervisor's/instructor's permission to use any particular type of lifting equipment.
- Comply with personal and environmental safety practices associated with clothing; eye protection; hand tools; power equipment; proper ventilation; and the handling, storage, and disposal of chemicals/materials in accordance with local, state, and federal safety and environmental regulations.

Performance Standard

0—No exposure: No information or practice provided during the program; complete training required

1—Exposure only: General information provided with no practice time; close supervision needed; additional training required

2—Limited practice: Has practiced job during training program; additional training required to develop skill

3—Moderately skilled: Has performed job independently during training program; limited additional training may be required

4—Skilled: Can perform job independently with no additional training

Diagnose poor stopping, noise, vibration, pulling, grabbing, dragging, or pedal pulsation concerns; determine necessary action.

AST 5C1 **MAST** 5C1

Time off_____

Time on_____

Total time_____

CDX Tasksheet Number: C706

1. **List the drum brake-related customer complaint/concern:**

2. Research the description and operation of the brake system for this vehicle in the appropriate service information. Also research the drum brake diagnostic procedure and removal/installation procedures.

   a. **List the possible cause(s) of the complaint/concern:**

3. With instructor permission, test-drive the vehicle to verify the concern. Be sure to follow all shop policies regarding test drives. **List your observations:**

   The rest of this task is performed at the end of the drum brake service. Please refer to page 755 for the completion of this task.

▶ **TASK** Remove, clean, inspect, and measure brake drum
diameter; determine necessary action.

MLR 5C1 **AST** 5C2 **MAST** 5C2

Time off_____

Time on_____

Total time_____

CDX Tasksheet Number: C800

1. Research the description and operation of the brake system for this vehicle in the appropriate service information. Also research the drum brake removal/installation procedures.

    a. **Maximum drum diameter:** _____ **in/mm**

    b. **Maximum drum out-of-round:** _____ **in/mm**

    c. **Minimum lining thickness: (Primary)** _____ **in/mm;**
       (Secondary) _____ **in/mm**

    d. **Parking brake adjustment specification:** _____

    e. **Lug nut torque:** _____ **ft-lb/Nm**

       i. **Draw lug nut-torque pattern:**

2. Remove the brake drum following the specified procedure, being careful not to disturb any brake dust. Clean the brake drum using equipment/procedures for dealing with asbestos/dust.

3. Inspect the drum.

    a. **Measure and record the diameter:** _____ **in/mm**

    b. **Measure and record the amount of out-of-round:** _____ **in/mm**

> **NOTE** Measure in at least three places equally spaced around the drum.

    c. **Hot spots? Yes:** _____ **No:** _____

    d. **Cracks? Yes:** _____ **No:** _____

    e. **Other defects? List if found:**

4. **Based on your observations/measurements, determine any necessary action(s):**

5. Have your supervisor/instructor verify satisfactory completion of this procedure, any observations found, and any necessary action(s) recommended.

© 2015 Jones & Bartlett Learning, LLC, an Ascend Learning Company

Performance Rating

CDX Tasksheet Number: C800

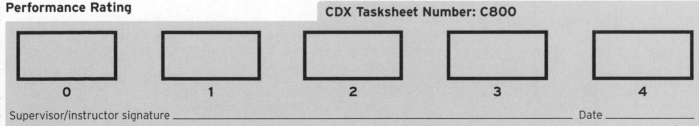

| 0 | 1 | 2 | 3 | 4 |

Supervisor/instructor signature _____ Date _____

▶ **TASK** Refinish brake drum and measure final drum diameter; compare to specifications.

Time off_____

Time on_____

Total time_____

CDX Tasksheet Number: C626

1. Mount the brake drum on the brake lathe following the brake lathe manufacturer's procedure, and set it up for a cut, BUT DON'T MAKE A CUT!

2. Have your instructor verify proper set-up. **Supervisor/Instructor initials:** _____

3. Using the correct equipment and procedure, refinish the brake drum to within allowable tolerances.

4. **Measure the final drum diameter and note your measurement here:** _____ in/mm

5. **Calculate the amount of material removed by the refinishing process:** _____ in/mm

6. **Does the drum meet specifications to be safely put back into service?**
   Yes: _____ **No:** _____

   a. **Why or why not?**

7. Have your supervisor/instructor verify satisfactory completion of this procedure, any observations found, and any necessary action(s) recommended.

Performance Rating

CDX Tasksheet Number: C626

0	1	2	3	4

Supervisor/instructor signature _____ Date _____

Remove, clean, and inspect brake shoes, springs, pins, clips, levers, adjusters/self-adjusters, other related brake hardware, and backing support plates; lubricate and reassemble.

MLR	AST	MAST
5C3	5C4	5C4

CDX Tasksheet Number: C248

1. Clean brake shoes, hardware, and backing plates using equipment and procedures for dealing with asbestos/dust.

2. Disassemble the brake shoes and hardware from the backing plate, being careful not to lose any parts and remembering how they go back together.

    a. **Measure lining thickness: (Primary)** _____ **in/mm;**
       (Secondary) _____ **in/mm**

    b. **Inspect and clean hardware:**

       i. **Springs:**

          Damaged: _____ **Missing:** _____
          Weak: _____ **Okay:** _____

       ii. **Pins:**

          Damaged: _____ **Missing:** _____
          Okay: _____

       iii. **Levers and adjusters:**

          Damaged: _____ **Missing:** _____
          Okay: _____

       iv. **Backing plate:**

          Damaged: _____ **Worn:** _____
          Okay: _____

       v. **Other hardware:**

          Damaged: _____ **Missing:** _____
          Okay: _____

3. **Determine any necessary action(s):**

4. Have your instructor initial to verify condition of hardware: _____

The rest of this task is performed at the end of the drum brake service. Please refer to page 749 for the completion of this task.

MLR
5C4

AST
5C5

MAST
5C5

Time off_____

Time on_____

Total time_____

CDX Tasksheet Number: C707

1. Inspect the wheel cylinder for leaks or damages dust boots. **List your observations:**

2. Place one thumb in each end of the wheel cylinder. Try to move both pistons side-to-side. This will indicate whether the pistons are stuck in their bores. **List your observations:**

3. Remove the wheel cylinder following the specified procedure.

   NOTE To prevent twisting the brake line, it is common practice to loosen the brake line fitting before unbolting the wheel cylinder from the backing plate.

4. Ask your instructor if you should disassemble the wheel cylinder. If no, skip to step #4. If yes, disassemble, clean, and inspect the wheel cylinder for damage, wear, or missing pieces.

   a. **Bore:**
      Damaged: _____ Okay: _____

   b. **Pistons:**
      Damaged: _____ Missing: _____
      Okay: _____

   c. **Seals:**
      Damaged: _____ Missing: _____
      Okay: _____

   d. **Dust boots:**
      Damaged: _____ Missing: _____
      Okay: _____

   e. **Spring(s):**
      Damaged: _____ Missing: _____
      Okay: _____

5. **List any necessary action(s):**

6. Have your supervisor/instructor inspect the removed or disassembled wheel cylinder and determine whether it should be rebuilt, replaced with new, or reinstalled:

   a. Rebuild: _____ Replace: _____ Reinstall: _____
   (Choose one, then instructor initial) _____

   b. If rebuilding the wheel cylinder, use new seals, dust boots, springs and expanders.

7. Reinstall the wheel cylinder on the backing plate.

NOTE It is usually best to start the brake line fitting into the wheel cylinder before bolting the cylinder down. This will allow the threads of the brake line fitting to align with the threads in the wheel cylinder, helping to prevent cross-threading of the parts.

---

8. Have your supervisor/instructor verify satisfactory completion of this procedure, any observations found, and any necessary action(s) recommended.

Performance Rating

CDX Tasksheet Number: C707

0	1	2	3	4

Supervisor/instructor signature _____ Date _____

CONTINUATION OF TASK C248/5C4 Remove, clean, and inspect brake shoes, springs, pins, clips, levers, adjusters/self-adjusters, other related brake hardware, and backing support plates; lubricate and reassemble (from page 745).

MLR	AST	MAST
5C3	5C4	5C4

Time off_____

Time on_____

Total time_____

CDX Tasksheet Number: C248

> **NOTE** Many vehicles use a primary shoe toward the front of the vehicle and a secondary shoe toward the rear of the vehicle. Refer to the manufacturer's procedure to install the shoes, springs, and hardware correctly.

5. Following the manufacturer's procedure, lightly lubricate the support pads on the backing plate and reassemble the brake assembly (shoes, springs, hardware, etc.).

> **NOTE** The brake shoe support pads on the backing plate require a thin film of the proper lubricant applied to their contact surface. This will reduce the wear on the backing plate as the side of the brake shoe rubs against the backing plate as the brakes are operated. Lubriplate (or in some cases, antiseize) is commonly used for this purpose. Just make sure that it only goes on light enough so you can see through it. If too much lubricant is used, it can contaminate the brake linings, which can cause the brakes to grab.

6. **Are the springs seated correctly? Yes:** _____ **No:** _____

7. **Does the self-adjuster operate properly? Yes:** _____ **No:** _____

8. **List any necessary action(s):**

9. Have your supervisor/instructor verify satisfactory completion of this procedure, any observations found, and any necessary action(s) recommended.

Performance Rating

CDX Tasksheet Number: C248

0	1	2	3	4

Supervisor/instructor signature _____ Date _____

▶ **TASK** Pre-adjust brake shoes and parking brake; install brake drums or drum/hub assemblies and wheel bearings; make final checks and adjustments.

MLR	AST	MAST
5C5	5C6	5C6

Time off_____

Time on_____

Total time_____

CDX Tasksheet Number: C801

1. Following the specified procedure, pre-adjust the brake shoes and parking brake.

2. If this vehicle uses serviceable wheel bearings, see the "Wheel Bearing Service" (page 783) tasksheet and clean, inspect, service, reinstall, and adjust them according to manufacturer's procedure.

3. Install the brake drum.

   a. **Does the brake drum turn without excessive drag? Yes:** _____
      No: _____
   b. **If equipped with adjustable wheel bearings, are they adjusted properly?**
      Yes: _____ **No:** _____

> **NOTE** The brakes may need air bled out of the wheel cylinders if they were removed from the vehicle. If they were, consider bleeding all wheel cylinders once all drums and calipers are back in place. Failure to have all drums and calipers installed could cause damage to the wheel cylinders, calipers, brake shoes, and pads. Ask your instructor if you are unclear about this.

4. Check to see that the brake master cylinder has the proper amount of brake fluid in it.

   a. **Is it at the proper level? Yes:** _____ **No:** _____
      i. **If no, refill with the proper fluid.**

5. **Start the engine and apply the brake pedal (only when all drums and calipers are installed). List brake pedal feel:**

6. **Shut off the engine and check wheel cylinders and brake line fittings for signs of leakage. List your observations:**

7. Have your supervisor/instructor verify satisfactory completion of this procedure, any observations found, and any necessary action(s) recommended.

Performance Rating

CDX Tasksheet Number: C801

0	1	2	3	4

Supervisor/instructor signature _____ Date _____

MLR	**AST**	**MAST**
5A3	5A4	5A4

Time off_____

Time on_____

Total time_____

CDX Tasksheet Number: C251

1. Install the wheel(s), place lug nuts on studs with the proper side facing the wheel, and torque them to proper torque in the specified sequence.

> **NOTE** The lug nut contact face MUST match the contact face in the wheel. If the wheel contact face is tapered, the lug nut contact face MUST also be tapered to match. If the contact face in the wheel is flat, the contact face of the lug nut MUST be flat. If in doubt about which way the lug nuts should face, ask your instructor.

2. **To what torque did you tighten the lug nuts?** _____ **ft-lb/Nm**

3. Reinstall any wheel covers that have been removed.

4. Have your supervisor/instructor feel brake pedal application and determine whether a test drive is necessary to final adjust the brakes and verify satisfactory operation of brakes.

Performance Rating

CDX Tasksheet Number: C251

0	1	2	3	4

Supervisor/instructor signature _____ Date _____

CONTINUATION OF TASK {C706/5C1} Diagnose poor stopping, noise, vibration, pulling, grabbing, dragging, or pedal pulsation concerns; determine necessary action (from page 739).

AST
5C1

MAST
5C1

Time off_____

Time on_____

Total time_____

CDX Tasksheet Number: C706

4. Reflecting back on this job, list the causes of the customer concern as listed at the beginning of this tasksheet:

5. Document the correction(s) required to correct the customer concern:

6. **Did you repair the vehicle? Yes:** _____ **No:** _____

7. **List any additional necessary action(s):**

8. Have your supervisor/instructor verify satisfactory completion of this procedure, any observations found, and any necessary action(s) recommended.

Performance Rating

CDX Tasksheet Number: C706

0	1	2	3	4

Supervisor/instructor signature _____ Date _____

Brakes: Parking Brake Inspection and Service

Student/intern information:

Name _____ Date _____ Class _____

Vehicle used for this activity:

Year _____ Make _____ Model _____

Odometer _____ VIN _____

Learning Objective/Task	CDX Tasksheet Number	2013 MLR NATEF Reference Number; Priority Level	2013 AST NATEF Reference Number; Priority Level	2013 MAST NATEF Reference Number; Priority Level
• Check parking brake cables and components for wear, binding, and corrosion; clean, lubricate, adjust, or replace as needed.	C811	5F2; P-2	5F3; P-2	5F3; P-2
• Check parking brake operation and indicator light system operation; determine necessary action.	C633	5F3; P-1	5F4; P-1	5F4; P-1

Time off_____

Time on_____

Total time_____

Materials Required
- Vehicle or brake system simulator
- Vehicle hoist
- Lubricant suitable for parking brake cables (see service information)

Some Safety Issues to Consider
- If you need to start the vehicle, you should ensure that the parking brake is firmly applied; if necessary, use wheel chocks to prevent the vehicle from moving when the vehicle is started to verify the completion of these tasks.
- When running any vehicles in the shop, make sure you use the shop's exhaust ventilation system to discharge all exhaust gas safely outside.
- Only students who have their supervisor's/instructor's direct permission should perform this task due to the safety concerns involved.
- Vehicle hoists are important tools that increase productivity and make the job easier. However, they also can cause severe injury or death if used improperly. Make sure you follow the hoist's and vehicle manufacturers' operation procedures. Also make sure you have your supervisor's/instructor's permission to use a vehicle hoist.
- **Caution:** Brake dust may contain asbestos, which has been determined to cause cancer when inhaled or ingested. Treat all brake dust as if it contains asbestos and use OSHA-approved asbestos removal equipment. Do not allow brake dust to become airborne by using anything that would disturb the dust. Also, wear protective gloves during this procedure and dispose of or clean them in an approved manner.
- Comply with personal and environmental safety practices associated with clothing; eye protection; hand tools; power equipment; proper ventilation; and the handling, storage, and disposal of chemicals/materials in accordance ith local, state, and federal safety and environmental regulations.

Performance Standard

0–No exposure: No information or practice provided during the program; complete training required

1–Exposure only: General information provided with no practice time; close supervision needed; additional training required

2–Limited practice: Has practiced job during training program; additional training required to develop skill

3–Moderately skilled: Has performed job independently during training program; limited additional training may be required

4–Skilled: Can perform job independently with no additional training

Check parking brake cables and components for wear, binding, and corrosion; clean, lubricate, adjust, or replace as needed.

MLR 5F2 **AST** 5F3 **MAST** 5F3

Time off_____

Time on_____

Total time_____

CDX Tasksheet Number: C811

1. **Research the following specifications for this vehicle in the appropriate service information.**

   a. **Specified parking brake cable lubricant:** _____
   b. **Parking brake adjustment:** _____

2. **Safely raise and support the vehicle on the hoist. Trace all parking brake cables to each wheel's brake assembly. Inspect the cables for the following defects and list the location and cause of the defect(s):**

   a. **Wear:** _____
   b. **Rusting:** _____
   c. **Binding:** _____
   d. **Corrosion:** _____

3. **Clean, lubricate, or replace cables as necessary and list the actions performed:**

4. Check the parking brake adjustment (this could be counting clicks of the ratchet assembly). **List your observations:**

5. If the parking brake needs adjustment, perform that now.

6. Have your supervisor/instructor verify satisfactory completion of this procedure, any observations found, and any necessary action(s) recommended.

Performance Rating

CDX Tasksheet Number: C811

0	1	2	3	4

Supervisor/instructor signature _____ Date _____

Check parking brake operation and indicator light
system operation; determine necessary action.

MLR 5F3 **AST** 5F4 **MAST** 5F4

Time off_____

Time on_____

Total time_____

CDX Tasksheet Number: C633

1. Verify that the parking brake is adjusted properly. If necessary, adjust it, being sure to follow the manufacturer's procedure.

2. Check the parking brake indicator light by turning the ignition key to the run position (do not start the engine) and observing the brake-warning lamp on the dash. Apply and release the parking brake.

    a. List your observations:

    > **NOTE** If the parking brake light did not go off, check the level of brake fluid in the master cylinder reservoir. If low, top up with the specified brake fluid. If it still is on, research the diagnostic procedure in the service information.

4. Apply the parking brake. Ensure that no people, tools, or equipment are in front of or behind the vehicle. With instructor permission, start the vehicle and verify that the parking brake properly holds the vehicle when placed in drive and reverse.

    > **NOTE** Use extreme caution when performing this test. If the vehicle moves, stop.

    a. Does the parking brake hold the vehicle? Yes: _____ No: _____

5. **Determine necessary action(s):**

6. Have your supervisor/instructor verify satisfactory completion of this procedure, any observations found, and any necessary action(s) recommended.

Performance Rating

CDX Tasksheet Number: C633

0	1	2	3	4

Supervisor/instructor signature _____ Date _____

Brakes: Power Booster Inspection

Student/intern information:

Name_____ Date_____ Class_____

Vehicle used for this activity:

Year _____ Make _____ Model_____

Odometer_____VIN_____

Learning Objective/Task	CDX Tasksheet Number	2013 MLR NATEF Reference Number; Priority Level	2013 AST NATEF Reference Number; Priority Level	2013 MAST NATEF Reference Number; Priority Level
• Check brake pedal travel with, and without, engine running to verify proper power booster operation.	C807	5E1; P-2	5E1; P-2	5E1; P-2
• Check vacuum supply (manifold or auxiliary pump) to vacuum-type power booster.	C808	5E2; P-1	5E2; P-1	5E2; P-1
• Inspect the vacuum-type power booster unit for leaks; inspect the check valve for proper operation; determine necessary action.	C809		5E3; P-1	5E3; P-1
• Inspect and test the hydraulically assisted power brake system for leaks and proper operation; determine necessary action.	C581		5E4; P-3	5E4; P-3

Time off_____

Time on_____

Total time_____

Materials Required

- Vehicle or brake system simulator
- Vacuum gauge
- Listening device (electronic stethoscope or length of 3/4-inch heater hose)

Some Safety Issues to Consider

- If you need to start the vehicle, you should ensure that the parking brake is firmly applied; if necessary, use wheel chocks to prevent the vehicle from moving when the vehicle is started to verify the completion of these tasks.
- Only students who have a valid driver's license and their supervisor's/instructor's direct permission should perform this task due to the safety concerns involved.
- When running any vehicles in the shop, make sure you use the shop's exhaust ventilation system to discharge all exhaust gas safely outside.
- Comply with personal and environmental safety practices associated with clothing; eye protection; hand tools; power equipment; proper ventilation; and the handling, storage, and disposal of chemicals/materials in accordance with local, state, and federal safety and environmental regulations.

Performance Standard

0—No exposure: No information or practice provided during the program; complete training required

1—Exposure only: General information provided with no practice time; close supervision needed; additional training required

2—Limited practice: Has practiced job during training program; additional training required to develop skill

3—Moderately skilled: Has performed job independently during training program; limited additional training may be required

4—Skilled: Can perform job independently with no additional training

▶ TASK Check brake pedal travel with, and without, engine running to verify proper power booster operation.

MLR 5E1 **AST** 5E1 **MAST** 5E1

Time off_____

Time on_____

Total time_____

CDX Tasksheet Number: C807

1. Research the power booster description, operation, and testing procedure in the appropriate service information.

   a. **Type of vacuum supply used: Manifold:** _____
      Auxiliary pump: _____
   b. **Minimum vacuum at power booster:** _____ **in.hg**
   c. **Minimum time power booster should hold vacuum:** _____ **minutes**

2. Test the ability of the power booster to provide assist.

   a. Without starting the vehicle, depress the brake pedal several times. This removes any vacuum from the brake booster. Hold moderate foot pressure on the brake pedal and start the engine.

      i. **List the brake pedal action:**

      ii. **Is the power booster working properly? Yes:** _____
          No: _____

   b. If the power booster is not working properly, follow the service manual procedure to determine the cause. **List any necessary action(s):**

3. Test the ability of the power booster to hold a vacuum.

   a. Without starting the vehicle, depress the brake pedal several times. This removes all vacuum from the brake booster and allows you to feel the brakes without vacuum assist.

      i. **Approximately how far down does the brake pedal go with moderate foot pressure w/o assist?** _____ **in/mm**

   b. With your foot off the brake pedal, start the engine, wait a few seconds, and depress the brake pedal once. This allows you to feel the brakes with power assist. This is how the brake pedal should respond if the power booster is holding vacuum properly.

      i. **Approximately how far down does the brake pedal travel with moderate foot pressure with assist?** _____ **in/mm**

   c. Remove your foot from the brake pedal, turn off the engine, and wait the specified time the power booster should hold vacuum listed above.

d. After waiting the designated time, and without starting the vehicle, depress the brake pedal once and observe whether the brake pedal travel was the same as in step 3b, indicating the power booster is holding vacuum.
List your observations:

e. If the brake pedal responded as in step 3b, no further inspection of the booster is needed.
f. If the brake pedal responded as if it had no vacuum assist (as in 3a), the power booster has a leak, which will need to be diagnosed.

4. Have your supervisor/instructor verify satisfactory completion of this procedure, any observations found, and any necessary action(s) recommended.

Performance Rating

CDX Tasksheet Number: C807

☐	☐	☐	☐	☐
0	1	2	3	4

Supervisor/instructor signature _____ Date _____

► **TASK** Check vacuum supply (manifold or auxiliary pump) to vacuum-type power booster.

Time off_____

Time on_____

Total time_____

CDX Tasksheet Number: C808

1. Following the specified procedure with the engine running, check the vacuum supply at the brake power booster.

    a. **List the vacuum reading obtained:** _____

2. **Does this meet the specification requirements for this vehicle?**
   Yes: _____**No:** _____

    a. **If no, determine the cause(s) of the low vacuum reading and list the condition(s) found.**

> **NOTE** This could be caused by a leak in the system or an engine mechanical/tune-up problem if manifold vacuum is used. Find the specific cause.

4. **Determine necessary action(s):**

5. Remove the vacuum gauge and reinstall the check valve in the booster.

6. Have your supervisor/instructor verify satisfactory completion of this procedure, any observations found, and any necessary action(s) recommended.

Performance Rating

CDX Tasksheet Number: C808

0	1	2	3	4

Supervisor/instructor signature _____ Date _____

Inspect the vacuum-type power booster unit for leaks; inspect the check valve for proper operation; determine necessary action.

AST 5E3 **MAST** 5E3

Time off_____

Time on_____

Total time_____

CDX Tasksheet Number: C809

1. Test the ability of the power booster to hold a vacuum.

   a. Without starting the vehicle, depress the brake pedal several times with moderate pressure.

   b. **After the vacuum has bled off, approximately how far down does the brake pedal go? _____ in/mm**

   > **NOTE** This removes any vacuum from the brake booster and allows you to feel the brakes without vacuum assist.

2. Start the engine, wait a few seconds, and depress the brake pedal once.

   > **NOTE** This allows you to feel the brakes with vacuum assist. This is how the brake pedal should respond if the vacuum booster is holding a vacuum properly.

   a. **Approximately how far down does the brake pedal go now? _____ in/mm**

3. Let off the brakes, turn off the engine, and wait the specified time the power booster should hold a vacuum listed previously.

4. After waiting the designated time and without starting the vehicle, depress the brake pedal once.

   a. **Does the brake pedal feel the same as in step 2? Yes: _____ No: _____**

5. If yes, the power booster and check valve are capable of holding a vacuum, which means the system doesn't have an external vacuum leak (it may still have an internal leak).

6. If no, the brake pedal responded as if it had no vacuum assist. Start the vehicle and do the following:

   a. Use the electronic stethoscope or the heater hose to listen for vacuum leaks around the outside of the power booster.

   b. **Listen under the dash at the power booster control valve assembly. List observations found:**

7. Inspect the check valve for proper operation.

   a. **Carefully remove the check valve from the power booster, leaving it inserted in the vacuum hose. Start the vehicle and feel whether air is being** drawn through the check valve. If it is, this indicates that the valve is not plugged or stuck closed. List observations found:

b. **Reinsert the check valve into the power booster and allow the engine to run for 30 seconds to evacuate the booster. Turn off the engine, wait for the specified minimum time that the power booster should hold a vacuum (listed previously), and then remove the check valve from the booster. There should be a large rush of air into the booster. If there is, the check valve is holding a vacuum and is okay. List observations found:**

8. Perform an internal leak test.

a. **Start the engine and let it idle. Apply the brake pedal with moderately firm pressure (20-30 lb) and hold it steady. Without moving your foot, shut off the engine and observe the pedal for approximately one minute. If it stays steady, there are no internal leaks. If the pedal rises, there is an internal leak in either the diaphragm or control valve. List observations found:**

9. **Based on your observations, determine any necessary actions:**

10. Return the vehicle to its beginning condition and return any tools you used to their proper locations.

11. Have your supervisor/instructor verify satisfactory completion of this procedure, any observations found, and any necessary action(s) recommended.

Performance Rating

CDX Tasksheet Number: C809

0	1	2	3	4

Supervisor/instructor signature _____ Date _____

Inspect and test the hydraulically assisted power brake system for leaks and proper operation; determine necessary action.

AST 5E4 **MAST** 5E4

Time off_____

Time on_____

Total time_____

CDX Tasksheet Number: C581

Vehicle used for this activity:

Year _____ Make _____ Model_____

Odometer_____ VIN_____

1. Performance Test: Begin with the vehicle engine off. Apply and release the brake pedal 5 or 6 times to discharge the accumulator.

    a. Hold the brake pedal down with moderately firm pressure (20–30 lb).

    b. Start the engine and observe the brake pedal. If it drops an inch or two, the booster is providing boost. If it does not drop, check the power steering pump belt and power steering pump system. **List observations found:**

> **NOTE** If they are in good condition, consult the service information for further diagnosis.

2. Accumulator Leak Test: Start the engine, apply the brake pedal, and note the pedal feel and applied height.

    a. Release the brake pedal, turn off the engine, and wait at least 10 minutes.

    b. Apply the brake pedal with moderately firm pressure (20–30 lb). **List observations found:**

    c. Apply the pedal several more times with the same moderately firm pressure. Each application should result in a higher pedal as the accumulator pressure is released from the booster. If it did, then there are no substantial leaks in the system. If it didn't hold pressure, you will need to perform manufacturer specified tests to determine what is causing the loss in pressure. **Determine any necessary action(s):**

3. Have your supervisor/instructor verify satisfactory completion of this procedure, any observations found, and any necessary action(s) recommended.

Performance Rating

CDX Tasksheet Number: C581

0	1	2	3	4

Supervisor/instructor signature _____ Date _____

Brakes: Hydraulic System Diagnosis and Service

Student/intern information:

Name_____ Date_____ Class_____

Vehicle used for this activity:

Year _____ Make _____ Model_____

Odometer_____VIN_____

Learning Objective/Task	CDX Tasksheet Number	2013 MLR NATEF Reference Number; Priority Level	2013 AST NATEF Reference Number; Priority Level	2013 MAST NATEF Reference Number; Priority Level
• Diagnose pressure concerns in the brake system using hydraulic principles (Pascal's Law).	C894		5B1; P-1	5B1; P-1

Time off_____

Time on_____

Total time_____

Materials Required

• Technical service manuals and any other information applicable to the specific activity you are undertaking

Some Safety Issues to Consider

• Although you will not be working on a vehicle, remember that if you had to apply some of the theories contained within this exercise, you should observe all appropriate safety measures when working on a vehicle.
• Comply with personal and environmental safety practices associated with clothing; eye protection; hand tools; power equipment; proper ventilation; and the handling, storage, and disposal of chemicals/materials in accordance with local, state, and federal safety and environmental regulations.

Performance Standard

0—No exposure: No information or practice provided during the program; complete training required

1—Exposure only: General information provided with no practice time; close supervision needed; additional training required

2—Limited practice: Has practiced job during training program; additional training required to develop skill

3—Moderately skilled: Has performed job independently during training program; limited additional training may be required

4—Skilled: Can perform job independently with no additional training

AST 5B1   **MAST** 5B1

Time off_____

Time on_____

Total time_____

CDX Tasksheet Number: C894

1. Have your supervisor/instructor assign you a vehicle found in the service information (you don't need the actual vehicle for this task). Write the details of that vehicle at the top of this page.

2. **Write out Pascal's Law here:**

3. Research the description and operation of the vehicle assigned in the appropriate service manual.

4. Using Pascal's Law and the service manual, answer the following questions:

   a. **While braking, how would the vehicle react with a missing left rear wheel cylinder piston seal or caliper seal?**

   b. **While braking, how would the vehicle react with a completely blocked left front flexible brake line?**

   c. **While braking, how would the vehicle react with a torn primary piston pressure seal in the master cylinder?**

5. Have your supervisor/instructor verify satisfactory completion of this procedure, any observations found, and any necessary action(s) recommended.

Performance Rating

CDX Tasksheet Number: C894

0	1	2	3	4

Supervisor/instructor signature _____ Date _____

Student/intern information:

Name_____ Date_____ Class_____

Vehicle used for this activity:

Year _____ Make _____ Model_____

Odometer_____ VIN_____

Learning Objective/Task	CDX Tasksheet Number	2013 MLR NATEF Reference Number; Priority Level	2013 AST NATEF Reference Number; Priority Level	2013 MAST NATEF Reference Number; Priority Level
• Diagnose poor stopping, pulling or dragging concerns caused by malfunctions in the hydraulic system; determine necessary action.	C236		5B5; P-1	5B5; P-1

Some Safety Issues to Consider

• Diagnosis of this fault may require test-driving the vehicle on the school grounds or on a hoist, both of which carry severe risks. Attempt this task only with full permission from your supervisor/instructor and follow all the guidelines exactly.

• **Caution:** Brake dust may contain asbestos, which has been determined to cause cancer when inhaled or ingested. Treat all brake dust as if it contains asbestos and use OSHA-approved asbestos removal equipment. Do not allow brake dust to become airborne by using anything that would disturb the dust. Also, wear protective gloves during this procedure and dispose of or clean them in an approved manner.

• Lifting equipment such as vehicle jacks and stands, vehicle hoists, and engine hoists are important tools that increase productivity and make the job easier. However, they can also cause severe injury or death if used improperly. Make sure you follow the manufacturer's operation procedures. Also make sure you have your supervisor's/instructor's permission to use any particular type of lifting equipment.

• Comply with personal and environmental safety practices associated with clothing; eye protection; hand tools; power equipment; proper ventilation; and the handling, storage, and disposal of chemicals/materials in accordance with local, state, and federal safety and environmental regulations.

Performance Standard

0—No exposure: No information or practice provided during the program; complete training required

1—Exposure only: General information provided with no practice time; close supervision needed; additional training required

2—Limited practice: Has practiced job during training program; additional training required to develop skill

3—Moderately skilled: Has performed job independently during training program; limited additional training may be required

4—Skilled: Can perform job independently with no additional training

Diagnose poor stopping, pulling, or dragging concerns caused by malfunctions in the hydraulic system; determine necessary action.

AST 5B5 **MAST** 5B5

CDX Tasksheet Number: C236

1. **List the brake-related (hydraulic system) customer complaint or concern:**

2. **Research the particular concern in the appropriate service ingormation. List the possible cause(s):**

3. With instructor permission, test-drive the vehicle to verify the concern.

   NOTE Be sure to follow all shop policies regarding test drives.

   a. **List your observations:**

4. **Follow the specified procedure to inspect and diagnose the problem. Document the steps you took to determine the cause, and the results of those steps, in the space below:**

5. **List the root cause(s) of the concern(s):**

6. **Determine any necessary action(s):**

7. Have your supervisor/instructor verify satisfactory completion of this procedure, any observations found, and any necessary action(s) recommended.

Performance Rating

CDX Tasksheet Number: C236

0	1	2	3	4

Supervisor/instructor signature _____ Date _____

Brakes: Wheel Bearing Inspection, Maintenance, and Service

© 2015 Jones & Bartlett Learning, LLC, an Ascend Learning Company

Student/intern information:

Name_____ Date_____ Class_____

Vehicle used for this activity:

Year_____ Make_____ Model_____

Odometer_____VIN_____

Learning Objective/Task	CDX Tasksheet Number	2013 MLR NATEF Reference Number; Priority Level	2013 AST NATEF Reference Number; Priority Level	2013 MAST NATEF Reference Number; Priority Level
• Remove, clean, inspect, repack, and install wheel bearings; replace seals; install hub and adjust bearings.	C810	5F1; P-1	5F2; P-1	5F2; P-1
• Replace wheel bearing and race.	C273	5F5; P-2	5F6; P-2	5F6; P-2
• Remove and reinstall sealed wheel-bearing assembly.	C275		5F8; P-2	5F7; P-2
• Diagnose wheel bearing noises, wheel shimmy, and vibration concerns; determine necessary action.	C267		5F1; P-3	5F1; P-3

Time off_____

Time on_____

Total time_____

Materials Required

- Vehicle or simulator with serviceable and sealed wheel bearings
- Inch-pound torque wrench
- Ft-lb or Nm torque wrench
- Hammer and brass (or soft) punch
- Specified bearing grease
- Bearing packer (optional)
- New cotter pin/s (if needed)
- Stethoscope

Some Safety Issues to Consider

- Lifting equipment such as vehicle jacks and stands, vehicle hoists, and engine hoists are important tools that increase productivity and make the job easier. However, they can also cause severe injury or death if used improperly. Make sure you follow the manufacturer's operation procedures. Also make sure you have your supervisor's/instructor's permission to use any particular type of lifting equipment.
- **Caution:** Brake dust may contain asbestos, which has been determined to cause cancer when inhaled or ingested. Treat all brake dust as if it contains asbestos and use OSHA-approved asbestos removal equipment. Do not allow brake dust to become airborne by using anything that would disturb the dust. Also, wear protective gloves during this procedure and dispose of or clean them in an approved manner.

- This procedure may require the removal of one or more cotter pin(s). Always replace the removed ones with new ones. Failure to do so could cause a component to come unfastened and cause serious injury or death.
- Comply with personal and environmental safety practices associated with clothing; eye protection; hand tools; power equipment; proper ventilation; and the handling, storage, and disposal of chemicals/materials in accordance with local, state, and federal safety and environmental regulations.

Performance Standard

0–No exposure: No information or practice provided during the program; complete training required

1–Exposure only: General information provided with no practice time; close supervision needed; additional training required

2–Limited practice: Has practiced job during training program; additional training required to develop skill

3–Moderately skilled: Has performed job independently during training program; limited additional training may be required

4–Skilled: Can perform job independently with no additional training

Remove, clean, inspect, repack, and install wheel
bearings; replace seals; install hub and
adjust bearings.

MLR	AST	MAST
5F1	5F2	5F2

CDX Tasksheet Number: C716

1. Research the wheel bearing disassembly, cleaning, inspection, repacking, and
   installation procedure in the appropriate service information and list the following
   specifications:

   a. **Specified wheel bearing grease:** _____

   b. **Steps for adjusting the wheel bearing:**

   c. **Spindle nut final torque, if specified:** _____ **in-lb:** _____
      ft-lb: _____ **Nm:** _____

2. Remove the wheel bearings from one wheel assembly, following the specified
   procedure. Be sure to use the appropriate brake dust removal system to properly
   remove and dispose of any brake dust. Clean and inspect the wheel bearings and
   race. Also clean and inspect the spindle. **List your observations:**

3. Show your supervisor/instructor the wheel bearings and races.
   Supervisor's/instructor's initials: _____

   > **NOTE** It may make sense to perform the next task, C273: Replace wheel bearing
   > and race, at this time. Ask your instructor.

4. Repack the wheel bearings with the proper grease. Install the inner bearing in the
   race and replace the old grease seal with a new one (being careful to not damage it).

5. Reinstall the hub and outer bearing onto the spindle.

6. Adjust the wheel bearing preload, or torque spindle nut (depending on application),
   according to the specified procedure.

   > **NOTE** Most adjustable wheel bearings require a fairly heavy torque to seat the
   > bearings (example: 25 ft-lb) and a lighter torque to preload the bearing (example:
   > 20 in-lb). Failure to loosen the bearing and preload it to the lower torque will result
   > in burned-up bearings.

7. Have your instructor verify the wheel bearing adjustment.
   Supervisor's/instructor's initials: _____

8. Install a new cotter pin or secure the spindle nut, according to the specified procedure.

9. Have your supervisor/instructor verify satisfactory completion of this procedure, any observations found, and any necessary action(s) recommended.

Performance Rating

CDX Tasksheet Number: C716

0	1	2	3	4

Supervisor/instructor signature _____ Date _____

MLR
5F5
AST
5F6
MAST
5F6

Time off_____

Time on_____

Total time_____

CDX Tasksheet Number: C273

1. **Research the wheel bearing and race disassembly and installation procedure in the appropriate service information and list the following specifications:**

   a. **Specified wheel bearing grease:** _____

   b. **Steps for adjusting the wheel bearing:**

   c. **Spindle nut final torque, if specified:** _____ ft-lb/Nm

2. Using a hammer and soft punch, carefully drive the race from the hub. Avoid scarring the surface of the hub with the punch and hammer.

3. **Clean and inspect the wheel bearings and race. List your observations:**

4. Show your supervisor/instructor the wheel bearing and race.
   Supervisor's/instructor's initials: _____

5. Unless your supervisor/instructor directs you otherwise, replace the wheel bearing and race with new ones, following the specified procedure. Make sure the race is fully seated in the hub.

6. Repack the wheel bearings with the proper grease. Install the inner bearing in the race and replace the old grease seal with a new one.

7. Reinstall the hub and outer bearing onto the spindle.

8. Install the thrust washer and adjustment nut on the spindle. Adjust the wheel bearing preload, or torque spindle nut (depending on application), according to the specified procedure. **Supervisor's/instructor's initials:** _____

9. Install a new cotter pin, or secure the spindle nut, according to the specified procedure.

10. Have your supervisor/instructor verify satisfactory completion of this procedure, any observations found, and any necessary action(s) recommended.

Performance Rating

CDX Tasksheet Number: C273

0	1	2	3	4

Supervisor/instructor signature _____ Date _____

AST
5F8

MAST
5F7

Time off_____

Time on_____

Total time_____

CDX Tasksheet Number: C275

1. **Research the sealed wheel-bearing assembly removal and installation procedure in the appropriate service information.**

    a. **Hub bolt torque:** _____ **ft/lbs or Nm**
    b. **Axle nut torque (if equipped):** _____ **ft/lbs or Nm**

2. Remove the sealed wheel bearing assembly from the vehicle, following the specified procedure.

3. Show your supervisor/instructor the wheel bearing assembly. **Supervisor's/ instructor's initials:** _____

4. Replace or reinstall the wheel bearing assembly, again following the specified procedure. Be sure to properly torque all fasteners and replace any removed cotter pins with new cotter pins.

5. Have your supervisor/instructor verify satisfactory completion of this procedure, any observations found, and any necessary action(s) recommended.

Performance Rating

CDX Tasksheet Number: C275

0	1	2	3	4

Supervisor/instructor signature _____ Date _____

AST 5F1 **MAST** 5F1

Time off_____

Time on_____

Total time_____

CDX Tasksheet Number: C267

Vehicle used for this activity:

Year _____ Make _____ Model_____

Odometer_____ VIN_____

1. **List the customer concern/complaint regarding a wheel-bearing issue:**

2. Research possible causes of the concern in the appropriate service information. **List possible causes:**

3. Follow the specified procedure for determining the cause of the complaint/concern. Depending on the actual fault, this could require many steps. **List the steps you took to determine the fault:**

4. **List the cause of the concern/complaint:**

5. **List the necessary action(s) to correct this fault:**

6. Have your supervisor/instructor verify satisfactory completion of this procedure, any observations found, and any necessary action(s) recommended.

Performance Rating

CDX Tasksheet Number: C267

0	1	2	3	4

Supervisor/instructor signature _____ Date _____

Brakes: Brake Warning Light and Stop Light Inspection and Service

Student/intern information:

Name_____ Date_____ Class_____

Vehicle used for this activity:

Year _____ Make _____ Model_____

Odometer_____VIN_____

Learning Objective/Task	CDX Tasksheet Number	2013 MLR NATEF Reference Number; Priority Level	2013 AST NATEF Reference Number; Priority Level	2013 MAST NATEF Reference Number; Priority Level
• Check operation of brake stop light system; determine necessary action.	C272	5F4; P-1	5F5; P-1	5F5; P-1
• Identify components of brake warning light system.	C947	5B5; P-3	5B11; P-2	5B11; P-2
• Inspect, test, and/or replace components of brake warning light system.	C242		5B10; P-3	5B10; P-3

Time off_____

Time on_____

Total time_____

Materials Required

- Vehicle
- Student assistant
- Test light/multimeter if diagnosis is required

Some Safety Issues to Consider

- Accidental deployment of the airbag system could happen if you inadvertently probe the wrong wire. Most manufacturers use yellow-colored wiring to denote wiring for the airbag system. Always be aware of the system/circuit you are working on.
- **Caution:** Most types of brake fluid are harmful to painted surfaces. Be sure to prevent brake fluid from coming into contact with a vehicle's paint. Use fender covers to minimize this risk and be sure to wipe up any spilled brake fluid immediately with a wet rag.
- Comply with personal and environmental safety practices associated with clothing; eye protection; hand tools; power equipment; proper ventilation; and the handling, storage, and disposal of chemicals/materials in accordance with local, state, and federal safety and environmental regulations.

Performance Standard

0—No exposure: No information or practice provided during the program; complete training required

1—Exposure only: General information provided with no practice time; close supervision needed; additional training required

2—Limited practice: Has practiced job during training program; additional training required to develop skill

3—Moderately skilled: Has performed job independently during training program; limited additional training may be required

4—Skilled: Can perform job independently with no additional training

► **TASK** Check operation of brake stop light system; determine necessary action.

MLR 5F4　**AST** 5F5　**MAST** 5F5

Time off_____

Time on_____

Total time_____

CDX Tasksheet Number: C272

1. Research the correct brake light bulb number(s) in the appropriate service information.

   a. **Specified brake lamp bulb number:** _____

   b. **High-mounted stop light bulb number, if equipped with replaceable bulbs:**
   _____

2. Locate the wiring diagram for the brake warning light system. **List below the name of each switch that can illuminate the brake warning light:**

3. Have another student step on the brake pedal while you observe the reaction of the brake lights (including the high-mounted stop light, if equipped). **List your observation(s):**

4. If the brake lights do not work properly, check simple things like individual bulbs to see if individual lights are out. If all of the brake lights are out, check the brake circuit fuse. **List your findings:**

5. **Determine any necessary action(s):**

6. Have your supervisor/instructor verify satisfactory completion of this procedure, any observations found, and any necessary action(s) recommended.

Performance Rating

CDX Tasksheet Number: C272

0	1	2	3	4

Supervisor/instructor signature _____ Date _____

MLR	AST	MAST
5B5	5B11	5B11

CDX Tasksheet Number: C947

1. **On the appropriate wiring diagram, locate each switch that activates the brake warning light. List those switches here:**

2. Locate all of the brake warning light switches on the vehicle/simulator. Be prepared to point them out to your supervisor/instructor.

   a. Point out the location of the switches to your supervisor/instructor.

3. Have your supervisor/instructor verify satisfactory completion of this procedure, any observations found, and any necessary action(s) recommended.

Performance Rating

CDX Tasksheet Number: C947

0	1	2	3	4

Supervisor/instructor signature _____ Date _____

AST 5B10 **MAST** 5B10

Time off_____

Time on_____

Total time_____

CDX Tasksheet Number: C242

1. Locate all of the brake warning light switches on the vehicle/simulator. Be prepared to point them out to your supervisor/instructor. Select one of the switches to demonstrate the proper testing procedure. **List which switch you are testing:**

2. Research the diagnosis procedure for the switch being tested.

3. **Perform the tests on the designated switch and list the steps you took and the results for each:**

4. **Determine any necessary action(s):**

5. Have your supervisor/instructor verify satisfactory completion of this procedure, any observations found, and any necessary action(s) recommended.

Performance Rating

CDX Tasksheet Number: C242

0	1	2	3	4

Supervisor/instructor signature _____ Date _____

Brakes: Electronic Brake Control Maintenance and Service

Student/intern information:

Name_____ Date_____ Class_____

Vehicle used for this activity:

Year_____ Make_____ Model_____

Odometer_____VIN_____

Learning Objective/Task	CDX Tasksheet Number	2013 MLR NATEF Reference Number; Priority Level	2013 AST NATEF Reference Number; Priority Level	2013 MAST NATEF Reference Number; Priority Level
• Identify traction control/vehicle stability control system components.	C857	5G1; P-3	5G2; P-3	5G2; P-3
• Identify and inspect electronic brake control system components; determine necessary action.	C634		5G1; P-1	5G1; P-1
• Describe the operation of a regenerative braking system.	C950	5G2; P-3	5G3; P-3	5G3; P-3

Time off_____

Time on_____

Total time_____

Materials Required

- Vehicle with traction control
- Vehicle hoist to see some of the components that are located under the vehicle
- DMM/DVOM
- Lab scope

Some Safety Issues to Consider

- Diagnosis of this fault may require test-driving the vehicle on the school grounds or on a hoist, both of which carry severe risks. Attempt this task only with full permission from your supervisor/instructor and follow all the guidelines exactly.
- Anti-lock brake systems store brake fluid under tremendous pressure that can cause severe injury, even when the engine is not running. Always refer to the service manual to determine how to depressurize the system safely whenever working on it.
- **Caution:** Most types of brake fluid are harmful to painted surfaces. Be sure to prevent brake fluid from coming into contact with a vehicle's paint. Use fender covers to minimize this risk and be sure to wipe up any spilled brake fluid immediately with a wet rag.
- Comply with personal and environmental safety practices associated with clothing; eye protection; hand tools; power equipment; proper ventilation; and the handling, storage, and disposal of chemicals/materials in accordance with local, state, and federal safety and environmental regulations.

Performance Standard

0—No exposure: No information or practice provided during the program; complete training required

1—Exposure only: General information provided with no practice time; close supervision needed; additional training required

2—Limited practice: Has practiced job during training program; additional training required to develop skill

3—Moderately skilled: Has performed job independently during training program; limited additional training may be required

4—Skilled: Can perform job independently with no additional training

Identify traction control/vehicle stability control
system components.

MLR 5G1 | **AST** 5G2 | **MAST** 5G2

Time off_____

Time on_____

Total time_____

CDX Tasksheet Number: C857

1. Research the traction/vehicle stability control system description, theory of
   operation, and testing procedures for this vehicle in the appropriate service
   information.

2. **Which of the following components are used in this traction control system?**

   a. **Wheel speed sensors at each wheel: Yes:** _____ **No:** _____
   b. **ABS hydraulic control unit: Yes:** _____ **No:** _____
   c. **Electronically controlled throttle body: Yes:** _____ **No:** _____
   d. **ABS control module: Yes:** _____ **No:** _____
   e. **Yaw sensor: Yes:** _____ **No:** _____
   f. **Other (please specify):** _____

3. Locate the previously listed components of the traction/vehicle stability control
   system on the vehicle. Once you have located all of them, point them out to your
   supervisor/instructor.

4. Have your supervisor/instructor verify satisfactory completion of this procedure, any
   observations found, and any necessary action(s) recommended.

Performance Rating

CDX Tasksheet Number: C857

0	1	2	3	4

Supervisor/instructor signature _____ Date _____

Identify and inspect electronic brake control system components; determine necessary action.

AST 5G1 | **MAST** 5G1

Time off_____

Time on_____

Total time_____

CDX Tasksheet Number: C634

1. Research the electronic brake control system description, theory of operation, and testing procedures for this vehicle in the appropriate service information.

   a. List the main components in the electronic brake control system:

   b. List the type of wheel speed sensor used: _____
   c. Wheel speed sensor resistance (if inductive style): _____ ohms

2. Inspect the wheel speed sensors for integrity and condition.

   a. Wheel speed sensor resistance: (if inductive style)
      Left front: _____ ohms
      Right front: _____ ohms
      Left rear: _____ ohms
      Right rear: _____ ohms

   b. Wheel Speed Sensor Lab Scope Pattern: Sketch the lab scope pattern of one wheel speed sensor while the wheel is turning.

3. **Do the wheel speed sensors meet specifications? Yes:** _____ **No:** _____

4. Have your supervisor/instructor verify satisfactory completion of this procedure, any observations found, and any necessary action(s) recommended.

Performance Rating

CDX Tasksheet Number: C634

0	1	2	3	4

Supervisor/instructor signature _____ Date _____

Describe the operation of a regenerative braking system.

MLR 5G2 | **AST** 5G3 | **MAST** 5G3

Time off_____

Time on_____

Total time_____

CDX Tasksheet Number: C950

1. Research the operation of a regenerative braking system on a vehicle equipped with this system in the appropriate service information.

   a. **In your own words, write out a summary of how the system operates:**

2. Have your supervisor/instructor verify satisfactory completion of this procedure, any observations found, and any necessary action(s) recommended.

Performance Rating

CDX Tasksheet Number: C950

0	1	2	3	4

Supervisor/instructor signature _____ Date _____

Brakes: Electronic Brake Control Hydraulic Service

Student/intern information:

Name_____ Date_____ Class_____

Vehicle used for this activity:

Year _____ Make _____ Model_____

Odometer_____VIN_____

Learning Objective/Task	CDX Tasksheet Number	2013 MLR NATEF Reference Number; Priority Level	2013 AST NATEF Reference Number; Priority Level	2013 MAST NATEF Reference Number; Priority Level
• Depressurize high-pressure components of the electronic brake control system.	C812			5G6; P-3
• Bleed the electronic brake control system hydraulic circuits.	C637			5G7; P-1

Time off_____

Time on_____

Total time_____

Materials Required

- Vehicle or simulator with ABS
- Depending on the type of concern, special diagnostic tools may be required. See your supervisor/instructor for instructions to identify what tools may be required.

Some Safety Issues to Consider

- Anti-lock brake systems store brake fluid under tremendous pressure that can cause severe injury, even when the engine is not running. Always refer to the service manual to determine how to depressurize the system safely whenever working on it.
- If you need to start the vehicle, you should ensure that the parking brake is firmly applied; if necessary, use wheel chocks to prevent the vehicle from moving when the vehicle is started to verify the completion of these tasks.
- When running any vehicles in the shop, make sure you use the shop's exhaust ventilation system to discharge all exhaust gas safely outside.
- Only students who have their supervisor's/instructor's direct permission should perform this task due to the safety concerns involved.
- Diagnosis of this fault may require test-driving the vehicle on the school grounds. Attempt this task only with full permission from your supervisor/instructor and follow all the guidelines exactly.
- Comply with personal and environmental safety practices associated with clothing; eye protection; hand tools; power equipment; proper ventilation; and the handling, storage, and disposal of chemicals/materials in accordance with local, state, and federal safety and environmental regulations.

Performance Standard

0—No exposure: No information or practice provided during the program; complete training required

1—Exposure only: General information provided with no practice time; close supervision needed; additional training required

2—Limited practice: Has practiced job during training program; additional training required to develop skill

3—Moderately skilled: Has performed job independently during training program; limited additional training may be required

4—Skilled: Can perform job independently with no additional training

▶ **TASK** Depressurize high-pressure components of the electronic brake control system.

MAST
5G6

Time off_____

Time on_____

Total time_____

CDX Tasksheet Number: C812

1. Research the procedure to depressurize the high-pressure components of the ABS system in the appropriate service information. **List the steps to perform this task:**

2. Perform the steps necessary to depressurize the ABS system, being careful to follow the specified procedure. **Determine any necessary action(s):**

3. Have your supervisor/instructor verify satisfactory completion of this procedure, any observations found, and any necessary action(s) recommended.

Performance Rating

CDX Tasksheet Number: C812

0	1	2	3	4

Supervisor/instructor signature _____ Date _____

MAST
5G7

Time off_____

Time on_____

Total time_____

CDX Tasksheet Number: C637

1. **Research the correct procedure to bleed the system in the appropriate service information. List the steps here:**

2. Using the identified procedure and equipment, bleed the electronic brake control system hydraulic circuits.

3. **Determine any necessary action(s):**

4. Have your supervisor/instructor verify satisfactory completion of this procedure, any observations found, and any necessary action(s) recommended.

Performance Rating

CDX Tasksheet Number: C637

0	1	2	3	4

Supervisor/instructor signature _____ Date _____

Brakes: Electronic Brake Control Diagnosis

Student/intern information:

Name_____ Date_____ Class_____

Vehicle used for this activity:

Year _____ Make _____ Model_____

Odometer_____VIN_____

Learning Objective/Task	CDX Tasksheet Number	2013 MLR NATEF Reference Number; Priority Level	2013 AST NATEF Reference Number; Priority Level	2013 MAST NATEF Reference Number; Priority Level
• Diagnose poor stopping, wheel lock-up, abnormal pedal feel, unwanted application, and noise concerns associated with the electronic brake control system; determine necessary action.	C635			5G4; P-2
• Diagnose electronic brake control system electronic control(s) and components by retrieving diagnostic trouble codes, and/or using recommended test equipment; determine necessary action.	C636			5G5; P-2
• Test, diagnose, and service electronic brake control system speed sensors (digital and analog), toothed ring (tone wheel), and circuits using a graphing multimeter (GMM)/digital storage oscilloscope (DSO) (includes output signal, resistance, shorts to voltage/ground, and frequency data).	C639			5G8; P-2
• Diagnose electronic brake control system braking concerns caused by vehicle modifications (tire size, curb height, final drive ratio, etc.).	C813			5G9; P-2

Time off_____

Time on_____

Total time_____

Materials Required

- DVOM
- GMM/DSO
- Scan Tool
- Depending on the type of concern, special diagnostic tools may be required. See your supervisor/instructor for instructions to identify what tools may be required.

Some Safety Issues to Consider

- If you need to start the vehicle, you should ensure that the parking brake is firmly applied; if necessary, use wheel chocks to prevent the vehicle from moving when the vehicle is started to verify the completion of this task.
- When running any vehicles in the shop, make sure you use the shop's exhaust ventilation system to discharge all exhaust gas safely outside.

- Only students who have their supervisor/instructor's direct permission should perform these tasks due to the safety concerns involved.
- Diagnosis of this fault may require test driving the vehicle on the school grounds. Attempt this task only with full permission from your instructor and follow all the guidelines exactly.
- Comply with personal and environmental safety practices associated with clothing; eye protection; hand tools; power equipment; proper ventilation; and the handling, storage, and disposal of chemicals/materials in accordance with local, state, and federal safety and environmental regulations.

Performance Standard

0—No exposure: No information or practice provided during the program; complete training required

1—Exposure only: General information provided with no practice time; close supervision needed; additional training required

2—Limited practice: Has practiced job during training program; additional training required to develop skill

3—Moderately skilled: Has performed job independently during training program; limited additional training may be required

4—Skilled: Can perform job independently with no additional training

© 2015 Jones & Bartlett Learning, LLC, an Ascend Learning Company

▶ TASK Diagnose poor stopping, wheel lock-up, abnormal pedal feel, unwanted application, and noise concerns associated with the electronic brake control system; determine necessary action.

MAST
5G4

Time off_____

Time on_____

Total time_____

CDX Tasksheet Number: C635

1. **List the ABS brake-related customer complaint/concern:**

2. Research the particular concern in the appropriate service Information. **List the possible causes:**

3. Test the vehicle and diagnose poor stopping, wheel lock-up, abnormal pedal feel, unwanted application, and noise concerns associated with the electronic brake control system. **List your tests and the results:**

4. **List the cause of the concern:**

5. **Determine any necessary action/s to correct the fault:**

6. Have your supervisor/instructor verify satisfactory completion of this procedure, any observations found, and any necessary action/s recommended.

Performance Rating

CDX Tasksheet Number: C635

0	1	2	3	4

Supervisor/instructor signature _____ Date _____

Diagnose electronic brake control system electronic control(s) and components by retrieving diagnostic trouble codes, and/or using recommended test equipment; determine necessary action.

MAST
5G5

Time off_____

Time on_____

Total time_____

CDX Tasksheet Number: C636

1. **List the ABS brake-related customer complaint/concern:**

2. Research the particular concern in the appropriate service Information. **List the possible causes:**

3. Use a scan tool to retrieve diagnostic trouble codes. **List any codes and their descriptions:**

4. Diagnose the electronic brake control system electronic control/s and the system components. **List your tests and the results:**

5. **List the cause of the concern:**

6. **Determine any necessary action/s to correct the fault:**

7. Have your supervisor/instructor verify satisfactory completion of this procedure, any observations found, and any necessary action/s recommended.

Performance Rating

CDX Tasksheet Number: C636

0	1	2	3	4

Supervisor/instructor signature _____ Date _____

▶ TASK Test, diagnose, and service electronic brake control system speed sensors (digital and analog), toothed ring (tone wheel), and circuits using a graphing multimeter (GMM)/digital storage oscilloscope (DSO) (includes output signal, resistance, shorts to voltage/ground, and frequency data).

MAST
5G8

Time off_____

Time on_____

Total time_____

CDX Tasksheet Number: C639

1. **List the ABS brake-related customer complaint/concern:**

2. Research the particular concern in the appropriate service Information.
   List the possible causes:

3. **Carry out the tests using a graphing multimeter (GMM) or digital storage oscilloscope (DSO) and list your results. The tests should include:**
   a. **Output signal:** _____
   b. **Resistance:** _____
   c. **Shorts to voltage/ground:** _____
   d. **Frequency data:** _____

4. **Note your conclusions here:**

5. **Determine any necessary action/s to correct the fault:**

6. Have your supervisor/instructor verify satisfactory completion of this procedure, any observations found, and any necessary action/s recommended.

Performance Rating

CDX Tasksheet Number: C639

0	1	2	3	4

Supervisor/instructor signature _____ Date _____

Diagnose electronic brake control system braking concerns caused by vehicle modifications (tire size, curb height, final drive ratio, etc.).

MAST
5G9

Time off_____

Time on_____

Total time_____

CDX Tasksheet Number: C813

1. **List the ABS brake-related customer complaint/concern (caused by vehicle modifications):**

2. Research the particular concern in the appropriate service information. **List the possible cause/s:**

3. Following the specified procedure, diagnose the electronic brake control concern (caused by vehicle modifications). **List your tests and the results:**

4. **List the root cause of the problem:**

6. **Determine any necessary action/s to correct the fault:**

7. Have your supervisor/instructor verify satisfactory completion of this procedure, any observations found, and any necessary action/s recommended.

Performance Rating

CDX Tasksheet Number: C813

0	1	2	3	4

Supervisor/instructor signature _____ Date _____

Section A6: Electrical/Electronic Systems

CONTENTS

Electrical/Electronic Systems: Vehicle, Customer, and Service Information

Student/intern information:

Name _____ Date _____ Class _____

Vehicle used for this activity:

Year _____ Make _____ Model _____

Odometer _____ VIN _____

Learning Objective/Task	CDX Tasksheet Number	2013 MLR NATEF Reference Number; Priority Level	2013 AST NATEF Reference Number; Priority Level	2013 MAST NATEF Reference Number; Priority Level
• Research applicable vehicle and service information, vehicle service history, service precautions, and technical service bulletins.	C286	6A1; P-1	6A1; P-1	6A1; P-1
• Demonstrate knowledge of electrical/electronic series, parallel, and series-parallel circuits using principles of electricity (Ohm's Law).	C951	6A2; P-1	6A2; P-1	6A2; P-1
• Demonstrate the use of 3 Cs (concern, cause, and correction).	NN06	N/A	N/A	N/A

Time off _____

Time on _____

Total time _____

Materials Required

- Vehicle with available service history records
- Technical Service Bulletins

Some Safety Issues to Consider

- Comply with personal and environmental safety practices associated with clothing; eye protection; hand tools; power equipment; proper ventilation; and the handling, storage, and disposal of chemicals/materials in accordance with local, state, and federal safety and environmental regulations.

Performance Standard

0—No exposure: No information or practice provided during the program; complete training required

1—Exposure only: General information provided with no practice time; close supervision needed; additional training required

2—Limited practice: Has practiced job during training program; additional training required to develop skill

3—Moderately skilled: Has performed job independently during training program; limited additional training may be required

4—Skilled: Can perform job independently with no additional training

▶ TASK Research applicable vehicle and service information, vehicle service history, service precautions, and technical service bulletins.

MLR 6A1 **AST** 6A1 **MAST** 6A1

CDX Tasksheet Number: C286

1. Using the VIN for identification, use the appropriate source to access the vehicle's service history in relation to prior electrical system work or customer concerns.

    a. List any related repairs/concerns, and their dates:

2. Using the VIN for identification, access any relevant technical service bulletins for the particular vehicle you are working on in relation to electrical system updates or other service issues.

    a. List any related service bulletins and their titles:

3. **Research the operation of the headlights.**

    a. Are they protected by a fuse? Yes: _____ No: _____
    b. Are they protected by a circuit breaker? Yes: _____ No: _____
    c. Do they use a relay? Yes: _____ No: _____

4. Have your supervisor/instructor verify satisfactory completion of this procedure, any observations found, and any necessary action(s) recommended.

Performance Rating

CDX Tasksheet Number: C286

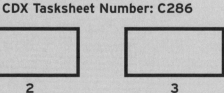 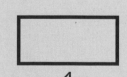

| 0 | 1 | 2 | 3 | 4 |

Supervisor/instructor signature _____ Date _____

Demonstrate knowledge of electrical/electronic series, parallel, and series-parallel circuits using principles of electricity (Ohm's Law).

MLR
6A2 | AST
6A2 | MAST
6A2

Time off_____

Time on_____

Total time_____

CDX Tasksheet Number: C951

> **NOTE** Use Ohm's Law to solve the circuit information in this task.

1. Series Circuit: Circuit Voltage = 12 volts, R1 = 3 ohms, R2 = 9 ohms

    a. Draw this circuit in the space below:

    b. Total circuit resistance: _____ **ohms**
    c. Total circuit current flow: _____ **amps**
    d. Voltage drop across R1: _____ **volts**
    e. Voltage drop across R2: _____ **volts**
    f. Current flow through R1: _____ **amps**
    g. Current flow through R2: _____ **amps**

2. Parallel Circuit: Circuit voltage = 12 volts and Branch 1, R1 = 2 ohms and Branch 2, R2 = 4 ohms

    a. Draw this circuit in the space below:

    b. Total circuit resistance: _____ **ohms**
    (Hint: Rt = R1 x R2/R1 + R2)
    c. Total circuit current flow: _____ **amps**
    d. Voltage drop across R1: _____ **volts**
    e. Voltage drop across R2: _____ **volts**
    f. Current flow through R1: _____ **amps**
    g. Current flow through R2: _____ **amps**

3. Series-Parallel Circuit: Circuit voltage = 12 volts, R1 = 2 ohms is in series with the parallel circuit of R2 = 3 ohms and R3 = 3 ohms

    a. **Draw this circuit in the space below:**

    b. **Total resistance of the parallel circuit:** _____ **ohms**

    c. **Total circuit resistance:** _____ **ohms**

    d. **Total circuit current flow:** _____ **amps**

    e. **Voltage drop across R1:** _____ **volts**

    f. **Voltage drop across R2 and R3:** _____ **volts**

    g. **Current flow through R2:** _____ **amps**

    h. **Current flow through R3:** _____ **amps**

4. Have your supervisor/instructor verify satisfactory completion of this procedure, any observations found, and any necessary action(s) recommended.

Performance Rating

CDX Tasksheet Number: C951

0	1	2	3	4
☐	☐	☐	☐	☐

Supervisor/instructor signature _____ Date _____

Time off_____

Time on_____

Total time_____

CDX Tasksheet Number: NN06

1. Using the following scenario, write up the 3 Cs as listed on most repair orders. Assume that the customer authorized the recommended repairs.

   A vehicle is brought to your shop with an electrical concern. The customer tells you that the battery has been going dead for the last few days, but jump starting it would allow him to drive the vehicle. He also said he replaced the battery with a new one, but that didn't solve the problem. You inspect the vehicle and find the following:

   a. The alternator puts out less than half of the current flow at which it is rated. A check of the diodes show shorted diodes, causing a key-off battery drain.
   b. The battery appears to be new and, once charged, passes the capacity test.
   c. The serpentine drive belt appears old, glazed, and excessively cracked.
   d. The starter draw test shows that the starter is drawing the specified amperage; it sounds normal when cranking the engine.
   e. The right front low beam headlamp is burned out.
   f. The battery hold-down is missing.

   NOTE Ask your instructor whether you should use a copy of the shop repair order or the 3 Cs below to record this information.

2. **Concern/complaint:**

3. **Cause:**

4. **Correction:**

5. **Other recommended service:**

6. Have your supervisor/instructor verify satisfactory completion of this procedure, any observations found, and any necessary action/s recommended.

Performance Rating

CDX Tasksheet Number: NN06

0	1	2	3	4
☐	☐	☐	☐	☐

Supervisor/instructor signature _____ Date _____

Electrical/Electronic Systems: Battery Diagnosis and Service

Student/intern information:

Name _____ Date _____ Class _____

Vehicle used for this activity:

Year _____ Make _____ Model_____

Odometer_____VIN_____

Time off_____

Time on_____

Total time_____

Learning Objective/Task	CDX Tasksheet Number	2013 MLR NATEF Reference Number; Priority Level	2013 AST NATEF Reference Number; Priority Level	2013 MAST NATEF Reference Number; Priority Level
• Perform battery state-of-charge test; determine necessary action.	C302	6B1; P-1	6B1; P-1	6B1; P-1
• Confirm proper battery capacity for vehicle application; perform battery capacity test; determine necessary action.	C818	6B2; P-1	6B2; P-1	6B2; P-1
• Identify electronic modules, security systems, radios, and other accessories that require reinitialization or code entry after reconnecting the vehicle battery.	C645	6B8; P-1	6B8; P-1	6B8; P-1
• Maintain or restore electronic memory functions.	C304	6B3; P-1	6B3; P-1	6B3; P-1
• Inspect and clean battery; fill battery cells; check battery cables, connectors, clamps, and hold-downs.	C644	6B4; P-1	6B4; P-1	6B4; P-1
• Perform slow/fast battery charge according to manufacturer's instructions.	C819	6B5; P-1	6B5; P-1	6B5; P-1
• Jump-start vehicle using jumper cables and a booster battery or an auxiliary power supply.	C820	6B6; P-1	6B6; P-1	6B6; P-1
• Measure key-off battery drain (parasitic draw).	C954	6A8; P-1		
• Diagnose the cause(s) of excessive key-off battery drain (parasitic draw); determine necessary action.	C817		6A8; P-1	6A8; P-1
• Chesney Parasitic Load test	NN12	N/A	N/A	N/A

Some Safety Issues to Consider

- Be cautious around electricity. High voltage (enough to injure or kill you) is present on many vehicles. Ignition systems, hybrid vehicles, and 42-volt electrical systems are just a few hazards to be careful of.
- Accidental deployment of the airbag system could happen if you inadvertently probe the wrong wire. Most manufacturers use yellow-colored wiring to denote wiring for the airbag system. Always be aware of the system/circuit you are working on.
- Use extreme caution when working around batteries. Immediately remove any electrolyte that may come into contact with you. Electrolyte is a mixture of sulfuric acid and water. Please consult with the shop safety and emergency procedures when working with or around batteries.
- Batteries give off hydrogen gas during charging and discharging. Never use an open flame, torch, or grinder near a battery.
- Comply with personal and environmental safety practices associated with clothing; eye protection; hand tools; power equipment; proper ventilation; and the handling, storage, and disposal of chemicals/materials in accordance with local, state, and federal safety and environmental regulations.

Performance Standard

0–No exposure: No information or practice provided during the program; complete training required

1–Exposure only: General information provided with no practice time; close supervision needed; additional training required

2–Limited practice: Has practiced job during training program; additional training required to develop skill

3–Moderately skilled: Has performed job independently during training program; limited additional training may be required

4–Skilled: Can perform job independently with no additional training

► **TASK** Perform battery state-of-charge test; determine necessary action.

MLR
6B1

AST
6B1

MAST
6B1

Time off_____

Time on_____

Total time_____

CDX Tasksheet Number: C302

1. Research the following specifications for this vehicle in the appropriate service information.

    a. **Specified battery capacity:** _____ **cold cranking amps (CCA)**
    b. **Group size, if specified**: _____ **BCI group**

> **NOTE** Check with your supervisor/instructor which of the following tests you are to perform, or whether you should perform all of them.

2. Perform a Specific Gravity Test. The battery must have removable vent caps.

    a. Locate and review the "Specific Gravity State of Charge Test" in the appropriate service information.
    b. Clean the top of the battery.

> **NOTE** This must be done prior to the removal of the vent caps.

    c. Remove the vent caps.
    d. Verify that the electrolyte level is high enough above the cells to fill the hydrometer.
    e. Draw enough electrolyte from a cell so the float is suspended. Determine the specific gravity reading and return the electrolyte into the cell. Repeat this for each cell and record your readings below. Be sure to compensate for temperature if you are using a hydrometer that is not automatically temperature compensated.

        Cell #1: _____
        Cell #2: _____
        Cell #3: _____
        Cell #4: _____
        Cell #5: _____
        Cell #6: _____

    f. **Calculate the maximum difference between the cell readings:** _____
    g. **What is the maximum allowable difference in cell readings:** _____
    h. **Compare the readings to the information in the service information, and list the state of charge:** _____ **%**
        i. Clean the hydrometer and tools.

3. Perform an Open Circuit Voltage Test. This test is for maintenance-free or non-vented batteries.

    a. Locate and review the "Open Circuit Voltage Test" in the service Information.
    b. Make sure the engine is off and the battery is stabilized. If the battery has just been recharged, you must remove the surface charge. Wait at least 5 minutes after removing the surface charge before measuring the open circuit voltage. Please follow the manufacturer's recommendations closely.

   c. Prepare the digital volt/ohm meter (DVOM) to measure voltage.

   d. Place the red lead on the positive post/terminal and the black lead on the negative post/terminal.

   e. What is the measured voltage (open-circuit voltage) of the battery?
   _____ volts

   f. The table below represents the open-circuit voltage of the battery. Please select the battery's percent of charge as it relates to the voltage measured.

Voltage	Percent Charge
12.6 or greater	100
12.4-12.6	75-100
12.2-12.4	50-75
12.0-12.2	25-50
11.7-12.0	0-25
0.0-11.7	0; no charge

4. Perform a Conductance Test.

   a. Review the process for performing a battery conductance test.

   b. Connect the conductance tester to the battery terminals (some testers require the removal of the battery cable for accuracy).

   c. Follow the prompts on the conductance tester for the type and CCAs of the battery being tested.

   d. Start the conductance test.

   e. List the state of charge (usually a % of charge): _____ %

   f. Record the available CCAs listed on the conductance tester: _____

5. Determine any necessary action(s):

6. Have your supervisor/instructor verify satisfactory completion of this procedure, any observations found, and any necessary action(s) recommended.

Performance Rating

CDX Tasksheet Number: C302

☐	☐	☐	☐	☐
0	1	2	3	4

Supervisor/instructor signature _____ Date _____

▶ **TASK** Confirm proper battery capacity for vehicle application; perform battery capacity test; determine necessary action.

MLR 6B2 **AST** 6B2 **MAST** 6B2

Time off_____

Time on_____

Total time_____

CDX Tasksheet Number: C818

> **NOTE** The battery capacity test is also known as a load test or battery performance test. Follow all directions of the manufacturer whose tool you are using to load test the battery.

1. **Research the specifications and procedures for testing the battery in the appropriate service information.**

   a. **What is the specified battery capacity for the vehicle you are working on?** _____ **CCA**

   b. **What type of battery is specified for this battery?**
   Flooded cell: _____ **AGM:** _____ **Other (list):** _____

2. **Inspect the battery and find its listed capacity rating:** _____

3. **Does this battery meet the specified CCA requirements for this vehicle?**
   Yes: _____ **No:** _____

4. **Determine the following load test variables for this battery:**

   a. **Required load test amps:** _____ **amps**

   b. **Required load test time (some testers are automatic):** _____ **seconds**

4. Connect the load tester as directed by the equipment manufacturer. Make sure the tester clamps are secure on the battery terminals, and the inductive amps clamp is around the proper cable.

5. **Load-test the battery. What was the battery minimum voltage (at the end of the load test time)?** _____ **volts**

6. **Did the battery pass the load test? Yes:** _____ **No:** _____

7. **If a battery fails the load test, what should be done next?**

8. **Determine any necessary action(s):**

9. Have your supervisor/instructor verify satisfactory completion of this procedure, any observations found, and any necessary action(s) recommended.

Performance Rating

0	1	2	3	4

Supervisor/instructor signature _____ Date _____

Identify electronic modules, security systems, radios, and other accessories that require reinitialization or code entry after reconnecting the vehicle battery.

MLR 6B8 **AST** 6B8 **MAST** 6B8

Time off_____

Time on_____

Total time_____

CDX Tasksheet Number: C645

1. Research the components that require reinitialization or code entry on the vehicle you are working on after reconnecting the battery. **List those components here:**

2. **List the correct process for reinitialization or code entry for each of the components listed above:**

3. Have your supervisor/instructor verify satisfactory completion of this procedure, any observations found, and any necessary action(s) recommended.

Performance Rating

CDX Tasksheet Number: C645

0	1	2	3	4

Supervisor/instructor signature _____ Date _____

MLR *AST* *MAST*
6B3   6B3   6B3

Time off_____

Time on_____

Total time_____

CDX Tasksheet Number: C304

1. Research the maintaining or restoring of electronic memory functions for this vehicle in the appropriate service information. Please follow all directions, and note that some vehicle electronic devices REQUIRE specific codes for reinitialization. If you don't have those codes available, do NOT disconnect the battery

> **NOTE** Some manufacturers require the use of tools that help maintain memories, such as radios, adaptive strategies, etc. The use of these tools can minimize down time in restoring electronic memories lost when a battery is disconnected. In some cases, the use of a "memory minder," which is basically a battery that plugs into the 12V accessory socket or the data link connector, can be utilized. In all cases, follow the manufacturer's instructions.

2. Restore electronic memory functions.

    a. **Change the vehicle's radio pre-set frequencies of the FM (1) stations and list those resets here:**

       1._____ 2._____ 3._____ 4._____

    b. With NO memory minder installed, disconnect the negative battery terminal for at least 15 seconds.

    c. Reconnect the negative battery terminal, and tighten properly.

    d. **Check the radio pre-sets. Did they change? Yes:_____**
       No:_____

       i. **Why or why not?**

    f. Restore the frequencies, as per manufacturer recommendations, to the stations noted in step 2a.

    g. **What would you have to do to restore the vehicle's PCM adaptive learning memory if it is erased?**

3. Maintain the electronic memory functions

    a. Reset the radio pre-sets to the same stations you did before.

    b. Install a memory minder to maintain electrical power in the system.

c. Disconnect the negative battery terminal for at least 1 minute.

d. Check the radio pre-sets. Did they change? Yes: _____ No: _____

    i. Why or why not?

e. Under this scenario, what happens to the vehicle's PCM adaptive learning memory if the battery is disconnected?

4. What did you learn?

5. Have your supervisor/instructor verify satisfactory completion of this procedure, any observations found, and any necessary action(s) recommended.

Performance Rating

CDX Tasksheet Number: C304

| 0 | 1 | 2 | 3 | 4 |

Supervisor/instructor signature _____ Date _____

▶ **TASK** Inspect and clean battery; fill battery cells; check battery cables, connectors, clamps, and hold-downs.

MLR 6B4 | **AST** 6B4 | **MAST** 6B4

Time off_____

Time on_____

Total time_____

CDX Tasksheet Number: C644

1. On the vehicle that was assigned to you by your supervisor/instructor, and following all steps listed in the service information, disconnect the negative battery terminal and move it out of the way so it cannot touch the terminal, or spring back against it. (Consider using a memory minder.)

2. Disconnect the positive battery terminal and move it out of the way. Place a glove or other insulating material over the end of the battery cable to prevent shorting out the memory minder.

3. Remove the battery hold-down so that the battery is sitting in the battery tray or box.

4. Remove the battery from the battery tray.

5. **Inspect the battery hold-down hardware and the battery tray. List your observations:**

6. Clean the battery, battery terminals, battery tray, and hold-down hardware with a suitable cleaner or by mixing baking soda and water.

> **NOTE** The consistency of the baking soda and water should be like a thin paste. The use of a small brush will help the cleaning process.

7. Rinse the components with lots of clean water. Wipe the components dry with some paper towels.

> **NOTE** DO NOT USE COMPRESSED AIR! It can blow acid around.

8. Clean the battery terminals and posts with a battery terminal cleaner.

9. Check the battery electrolyte level. This can be done only on non-maintenance-free batteries. If the level is low, add only distilled water to the proper level.

   a. Have your supervisor/instructor check your work.
   Supervisor's/instructor's initials: _____

10. Install the battery and hold-down hardware, and reconnect the cables as outlined in the service information.

11. Install a battery terminal protective spray onto the battery terminals.

12. **Determine any necessary action(s):**

13. Have your supervisor/instructor verify satisfactory completion of this procedure, any observations found, and any necessary action(s) recommended.

Performance Rating

CDX Tasksheet Number: C644

0	1	2	3	4

Supervisor/instructor signature _____ Date _____

Perform slow/fast battery charge according to manufacturer's instructions.

MLR
6B5

AST
6B5

MAST
6B5

Time off_____

Time on_____

Total time_____

CDX Tasksheet Number: C819

> **NOTE** Recharging a battery differs from manufacturer to manufacturer. It is important that you follow the recharging steps recommended by the manufacturer of the battery that is assigned to you.

1. Research slow and/or fast battery charging for this vehicle battery in the appropriate service information. Follow all directions. If no directions are given, use the following information:

   It is best to disconnect the negative battery terminal when charging a battery. Consider using a memory minder to maintain the memories on electronic control modules.

   The ideal rate for charging a battery can be found by dividing the battery's CCA by 70.

   To find the maximum charging rate for fast charging a battery, divide the battery's CCA by 40.

   The faster a battery is charged, the shorter its life.

   Do not exceed: 15.5V on a flooded cell battery; 14.8V on an AGM battery; or 14.3V on a gel cell battery.

2. **List the steps for recharging this battery:**

3. **What method is recommended for recharging the battery?**
   Slow charge: _____ Fast charge: _____

   a. Have your supervisor/instructor verify the steps above.
   Supervisor's/instructor's initials: _____

4. **Charge the battery according to the manufacturer's recommendations.**
   a. **How long did the battery charge? _____ time**
   b. **What was the highest amperage reading during charging? _____ amps**
   c. **What was the lowest amperage reading during charging? _____ amps**
   d. **What was the highest voltage during charging? _____ volts**
   e. **How did you determine the battery was fully charged?**

5. **Determine any necessary action(s):**

6. Have your supervisor/instructor verify satisfactory completion of this procedure, any observations found, and any necessary action(s) recommended.

Performance Rating

0	1	2	3	4
□	□	□	□	□

Supervisor/instructor signature _____ Date _____

Jump-start vehicle using jumper cables and a booster
battery or an auxiliary power supply.

MLR 6B6   **AST** 6B6   **MAST** 6B6

Time off_____

Time on_____

Total time_____

CDX Tasksheet Number: C820

1. **Research "starting a vehicle with a dead battery" or "jump starting procedures" in the appropriate service information for the vehicle you are working on. List the steps as outlined in the service information.**

   NOTE Caution: Some vehicle manufacturers prohibit jump-starting of their vehicles. If this is the case, inform your supervisor/instructor.

   NOTE Follow these steps *exactly*!

2. **Why is the last connection away from the battery, preferably on an unpainted solid metal component connected to the engine block?**

3. Have your supervisor/instructor verify your answers.
   Supervisor's/Instructor's Initials: _____

4. Connect the jumper cables as outlined in the service information or connect the auxiliary power supply (jump box) as was outlined in the service information.

5. Start the engine.

6. Remove the cables in the reverse order as they were installed.

7. Have your supervisor/instructor verify satisfactory completion of this procedure, any observations found, and any necessary action(s) recommended.

Performance Rating

CDX Tasksheet Number: C820

0	1	2	3	4

Supervisor/instructor signature _____ Date _____

Time off_____

Time on_____

Total time_____

CDX Tasksheet Number: C954

> **NOTE** Be sure to follow the correct steps for connecting your DVOM to check for amperage/current flow. Have your supervisor/instructor check your connections. Improper connection of the DVOM may damage your meter.

1. Research key-off battery drain (parasitic drain) checks in the appropriate service information.
   a. List the maximum allowable key-off battery drain (parasitic drain) for the vehicle/simulator that has been assigned to you. **What is the maximum allowable drain?** _____ **mA**
   b. **What is the specified time for the last module to go to sleep?** _____ **sec/min**

2. **List the appropriate steps to measure the key-off battery drain (parasitic drain):**

3. Using the steps listed, measure the key-off battery drain (parasitic drain):
   a. **What is the actual drain?** _____ **mA**
   b. **Is this reading within specifications? Yes:** _____ **No:** _____

4. **Is the reading within specifications? Yes:** _____ **No:** _____

5. Have your supervisor/instructor verify satisfactory completion of this procedure, any observations found, and any necessary action(s) recommended.

Performance Rating

CDX Tasksheet Number: C954

0	1	2	3	4

Supervisor/instructor signature _____ Date _____

Diagnose the cause(s) of excessive key-off battery drain (parasitic draw); determine necessary action.

CDX Tasksheet Number: C817

> **NOTE** Be sure to follow the correct steps for connecting your DVOM to check for amperage/current flow. Have your supervisor/instructor check your connections. Improper connection of the DVOM may damage your meter.

1. Research key-off battery drain (parasitic drain) checks in the appropriate service information.

   a. List the maximum allowable key-off battery drain (parasitic drain) for the vehicle/simulator that has been assigned to you. **What is the maximum allowable drain? _____ mA**

   b. **What is the specified time for the last module to go to sleep? _____ sec/min**

2. **List the appropriate steps to measure the key-off battery drain (parasitic drain):**

3. Using the steps listed, measure the key off battery drain (parasitic drain):

   a. **What is the actual drain? _____ mA**

   b. **Is this reading within specifications? Yes: _____ No: _____**

      i. If no, identify the faulty circuit by pulling and replacing fuses one at a time. Watch the amps reading on the meter to see if it drops. If it drops substantially, you will want to investigate that circuit further, by disconnecting the loads and tracing the wires.

4. If pulling the fuses does not identify the faulty circuit, disconnect unfused wires one at a time, such as the alternator output wire and the ignition switch feed wire.

5. **List the steps you took to diagnose the cause of the parasitic draw and their results:**

6. **Determine any necessary action(s):**

7. **What would the customer concern be that would require you to perform this test?**

8. Have your supervisor/instructor verify satisfactory completion of this procedure, any observations found, and any necessary action(s) recommended.

Performance Rating

CDX Tasksheet Number: C817

0	1	2	3	4

Supervisor/instructor signature _____ Date _____

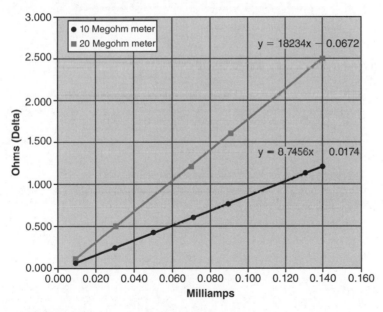

Time off_____

Time on_____

Total time_____

CDX Tasksheet Number: NN12

1. **Determine what the impedance of the DVOM is. List the impedance:**
   _____ **megohms (meter impedance)**

2. Set the DVOM to ohms and touch the leads together. This is the delta reading. **List the reading:** _____ **ohms (Delta)**

   Note: if the meter has a delta adjustment feature, press it so that the meter reads 0 ohms when the leads are touching. You won't have to worry about the delta reading in this case.

3. With the car off, and all doors closed, wait 30 seconds and then place the ohmmeter's black lead on the negative battery terminal and the red lead on the alternator case.

4. Read the ohmmeter and subtract the delta reading given previously. **List the reading:** _____ **ohms (minus delta reading)**

5. Compare this reading to the Chesney Parasitic Load Test Graph. **Approximately how many amps are draining?** _____ **mA**

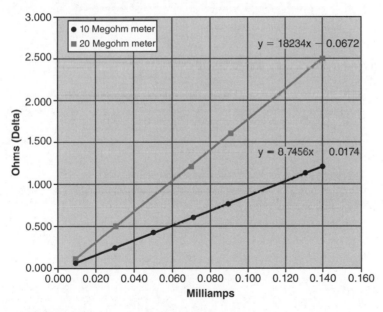

6. **Is the reading within specifications? Yes:** _____ **No:** _____

7. Open the driver's door and insure at least one dome light is on.

8. Place the black ohmmeter lead on the battery negative and the red lead on the alternator case.

9. Read the ohmmeter and subtract the delta reading given previously. **List the reading:** _____ **ohms (minus delta reading)**

10. Compare this reading to the Chesney Parasitic Load Test graph. **Approximately how many amps are draining?** _____ **mA**

11. Have your supervisor/instructor verify satisfactory completion of this procedure, any observations found, and any necessary action(s) recommended

Performance Rating

CDX Tasksheet Number: NN12

☐	☐	☐	☐	☐
0	1	2	3	4

Supervisor/instructor signature _____ Date _____

Electrical/Electronic Systems: Starting System Diagnosis and Repair

Student/intern information:

Name _____ Date _____ Class _____

Vehicle used for this activity:

Year _____ Make _____ Model_____

Odometer_____VIN_____

Learning Objective/Task	CDX Tasksheet Number	2013 MLR NATEF Reference Number; Priority Level	2013 AST NATEF Reference Number; Priority Level	2013 MAST NATEF Reference Number; Priority Level
• Perform starter current draw tests; determine necessary action.	C309	6C1; P-1	6C1; P-1	6C1; P-1
• Perform starter circuit voltage drop tests; determine necessary action.	C310	6C2; P-1	6C2; P-1	6C2; P-1
• Inspect and test switches, connectors, and wires of starter control circuits; perform necessary action.	C313	6C5; P-2	6C5; P-2	6C5; P-2
• Inspect and test starter relays and solenoids; determine necessary action.	C311	6C3; P-2	6C3; P-2	6C3; P-2
• Remove and install starter in a vehicle.	C312	6C4; P-1	6C4; P-1	6C4; P-1
• Differentiate between electrical and engine mechanical problems that cause a slow-crank or a no-crank condition.	C314		6C6; P-2	6C6; P-2

Time off_____

Time on_____

Total time_____

Materials Required

- Vehicle or simulator
- Starting and/or charging system tester
- Digital volt ohm meter (DVOM)
- Test light
- Fused jumper wire/s
- Floor jack and stands or vehicle hoist (preferred)

Some Safety Issues to Consider

- Be cautious around electricity. High voltage (enough to injure or kill you) is present on many vehicles. Ignition systems, hybrid vehicles, and 42-volt electrical systems are just a few hazards to be careful of.
- Accidental deployment of the airbag system could happen if you inadvertently probe the wrong wire. Most manufacturers use yellow-colored wiring to denote wiring for the airbag system. Always be aware of the system/circuit you are working on.
- Use extreme caution when working around batteries. Immediately remove any electrolyte that may come into contact with you. Electrolyte is a mixture of sulfuric acid and water. Please consult with the shop safety and emergency procedures when working with or around batteries.

- Never exceed 16 volts when charging a 12-volt battery. Overheating and explosion hazards are greatly increased.
- Disconnect the battery before using wrenches or sockets to remove wires from the starter or solenoid to prevent short circuits and fires.
- Starter motors are heavy, always use another person to hold the starter while it is being removed and installed.
- Be careful when cranking engines while working under the hood. Keep away from moving belts, pulleys, and other parts.
- Comply with personal and environmental safety practices associated with clothing; eye protection; hand tools; power equipment; proper ventilation; and the handling, storage, and disposal of chemicals/materials in accordance ith local, state, and federal safety and environmental regulations.

Performance Standard

0–No exposure: No information or practice provided during the program; complete training required

1–Exposure only: General information provided with no practice time; close supervision needed; additional training required

2–Limited practice: Has practiced job during training program; additional training required to develop skill

3–Moderately skilled: Has performed job independently during training program; limited additional training may be required

4–Skilled: Can perform job independently with no additional training

Perform starter current draw tests; determine necessary action.

MLR 6C1   **AST** 6C1   **MAST** 6C1

Time off_____

Time on_____

Total time_____

CDX Tasksheet Number: C309

1. Research the specifications and procedures for performing starting system tests and repairs.

    a. **List the starter current draw specs:** _____ **amps at** _____ **volts (if listed)**

2. Connect the starting system tester as outlined in the appropriate service information.

3. This test will require either the fuel system or ignition system to be disabled. Please follow the manufacturer's recommendations for disabling one of these two systems.

4. **Identify below which system was disabled and the steps you took to do this:**

5. Have your supervisor/instructor check your connections and how you disabled the fuel or ignition system(s).

    a. **Supervisor's/instructor's initials:** _____

6. **Conduct the Starter Draw Test.**

    a. **What was the current draw during the first second or two?** _____ **amps**
    b. **What was the final current draw (after three or four seconds)?** _____ **amps**
    c. **What was the lowest voltage during the test?** _____ **volts**

7. Compare your results to the manufacturer's specifications. **List your observations:**

8. **Determine any necessary action(s):**

9. Have your supervisor/instructor verify satisfactory completion of this procedure, any observations found, and any necessary action(s) recommended.

Performance Rating

0	1	2	3	4

Supervisor/instructor signature _____ Date _____

MLR 6C2   **AST** 6C2   **MAST** 6C2

Time off_____

Time on_____

Total time_____

CDX Tasksheet Number: C310

1. Research the specifications and procedures for performing the starter circuit voltage drop tests in the appropriate service informaation.

   a. **What is the maximum starter circuit (high current cables) voltage drop specification(s) for this test?**

   i. **Positive side:** _____ **volts**

   ii. **Negative (ground) side, if specified:** _____ **volts**

2. Disable the vehicle's fuel or ignition system so it will not start.

3. Conduct the Starter Circuit Voltage Drop Test–Positive/Feed Side (heavy positive battery cable, not the control circuit).

   a. **List the voltmeter connection points in the circuit:**

   DVOM black lead: _____

   DVOM red lead: _____

   b. Conduct the Starter Circuit Voltage Drop Test:

   What is the voltage drop on the positive side? _____ **volts**

   Is this reading within specifications? Yes: _____ **No:** _____

4. Conduct the Starter Circuit Voltage Drop Test–Ground Side.

   a. **List the voltmeter connection points in the circuit:**

   DVOM black lead: _____

   DVOM red lead: _____

   b. Conduct the Starter Circuit Voltage Drop Test:

   What is the voltage drop on the negative side? _____ **volts**

   Is this reading within specifications? Yes: _____ **No:** _____

5. **Determine any necessary action(s):**

6. Have your supervisor/instructor verify satisfactory completion of this procedure, any observations found, and any necessary action(s) recommended.

Performance Rating

CDX Tasksheet Number: C310

0	1	2	3	4

Supervisor/instructor signature _____ Date _____

MLR	AST	MAST
6C5	6C5	6C5

Time off_____

Time on_____

Total time_____

CDX Tasksheet Number: C313

1. Refering to the appropriate service information, draw a diagram of the starter control circuit (small wires) from battery positive terminal to the starter. **On the diagram, list the components the current goes through to get to the starter.**

    a. **List the maximum specified voltage drop across the starter relay/solenoid contacts: _____ volts**

2. **Write a short description of how the starter control circuit operates to enable the starter to crank the engine:**

3. Disable the vehicle's fuel or ignition system so it will not start.

4. Conduct the Starter Control Circuit Voltage Drop Test–Positive Side.

    a. List the voltmeter connection points in the circuit:

    DVOM black lead: _____

    DVOM red lead: _____

    b. Conduct the Starter Control Circuit Voltage Drop Test:

    What is the voltage drop on the positive side? _____ volts

    Is this reading within specifications? Yes: _____ No: _____

    i. **If no, refer to the service information for further tests. List those tests and their results:**

5. Determine any necessary action(s):

6. Have your supervisor/instructor verify satisfactory completion of this procedure, any observations found, and any necessary action(s) recommended.

Performance Rating

CDX Tasksheet Number: C313

0	1	2	3	4

Supervisor/instructor signature _____ Date _____

MLR 6C3 | **AST** 6C3 | **MAST** 6C3

Time off_____

Time on_____

Total time_____

CDX Tasksheet Number: C311

1. Research the procedure and specifications for testing starter relays and solenoids in the appropriate service information.

   a. **What is this vehicle's starting system equipped with?**
      Starter Solenoid _____; Starter Relay _____; Both _____

   b. **List the resistance of the starter solenoid windings:**
      Pull in: _____ ohms; hold in: _____ ohms

   c. **List the specified resistance of the starter relay winding: _____ ohms**

2. Disable the vehicle's fuel or ignition system so it will not start.

3. Following the manufacturer's test procedure, list the voltmeter connection points in the circuit to test the voltage drop across the relay or solenoid contacts.

   a. **DVOM red lead:** _____

   b. **DVOM black lead:** _____

4. Conduct the Starter Relay/Solenoid Voltage Drop Test.

   a. **List the voltage drop:** _____ volts

   b. **Is this reading within specifications? Yes:** _____ **No:** _____

5. Measure the resistance of the starter solenoid windings:

   a. **Pull in:** _____ ohms

   b. **Hold in:** _____ ohms

6. **Measure the resistance of the starter relay winding:** _____ ohms

7. **Determine any necessary actions:**

8. Have your supervisor/instructor verify satisfactory completion of this procedure, any observations found, and any necessary action(s) recommended.

Performance Rating

CDX Tasksheet Number: C311

☐	☐	☐	☐	☐
0	1	2	3	4

Supervisor/instructor signature _____ Date _____

MLR 6C4 **AST** 6C4 **MAST** 6C4

Time off_____

Time on_____

Total time_____

CDX Tasksheet Number: C312

1. Research the procedure and specifications for removing and installing the starter in the appropriate service information.

   a. **List the specified starter mounting bolt torque:** _____ **ft-lb/Nm**

   b. **List the first step that should be performed prior to lifting the vehicle to remove the starter:**

2. Remove the starter following the manufacturer's procedure.

   a. Have your supervisor/instructor verify the starter removal.
   Supervisor's/instructor's initials: _____

3. Inspect the gear teeth on the flywheel ring gear all the way around by turning the crankshaft by hand (ignition key "Off"). **List your observations:**

4. Install the starter following the manufacturer's procedures.

5. Restore the fuel system/ignition system to its proper operating condition. Start the vehicle and verify proper vehicle operation.

6. Have your supervisor/instructor verify satisfactory completion of this procedure, any observations found, and any necessary action(s) recommended.

Performance Rating

CDX Tasksheet Number: C312

0	1	2	3	4

Supervisor/instructor signature _____ Date _____

Differentiate between electrical and engine mechanical problems that cause a slow-crank or no-crank condition.

AST 6C6 **MAST** 6C6

Time off_____

Time on_____

Total time_____

CDX Tasksheet Number: C314

Vehicle used for this activity:

Year _____ Make _____ Model_____

Odometer_____ VIN_____

1. Locate a no-crank or slow-crank starting system symptom chart in the appropriate service information for the vehicle you are working on.

   a. Research the repair procedures for the condition of the vehicle, as outlined in the service information, for the vehicle assigned to you.

2. Most vehicles can be tested using the following procedure to determine whether the vehicle is experiencing an electrical or mechanical problem: Turn on the headlights and try to start the engine while listening to the starter and watching the headlights. Place a check mark next to the condition below that happened during this test.

   a. **No starter noises and the headlights stayed at the same intensity:** _____

   > **NOTE** This fault is likely an electrical fault in the starter itself or the control circuit to the starter.

   b. **Loud single click when the key is turned to "crank" and headlights don't dim, or only dim slightly.** _____

   > **NOTE** This fault is likely an electrical fault caused by solenoid contacts or starter motor brushes that are excessively worn.

   c. **Loud repeated clicking "machine guns" when the key is turned to "crank":** _____

   > **NOTE** This fault is likely an electrical fault that may be caused by high resistance in the starter feed cable, a short circuit in the main starter feed cable after the starter relay, or the hold-in windings in the solenoid are open.

   d. **The starter engages and tries to crank, or cranks the engine slowly and the headlights went substantially dim:** _____

   > **NOTE** This fault could be an electrical fault or a mechanical fault. It may be caused by a discharged or weak battery, a shorted or dragging starter motor, or an engine that is mechanically bound up, such as from a hydro-locked cylinder, spun main bearing, or seized accessory drive on the engine. Turn the engine over by hand to determine if It is caused by a mechanical condition.

e. The engine cranks substantially faster than normal: _____

> **NOTE** This fault is likely a mechanical fault caused by low compression due to a broken or slipped timing belt/chain, bent valves, or piston rings that are not sealing.

3. **Diagnose the problem based on these conditions. List the steps you took to diagnose the problem and the results you obtained:**

4. **Determine any necessary actions:**

5. Have your supervisor/instructor verify satisfactory completion of this procedure, any observations found, and any necessary action(s) recommended.

Performance Rating

CDX Tasksheet Number: C314

0	1	2	3	4

Supervisor/instructor signature _____ Date _____

Electrical/Electronic Systems: Charging System Diagnosis and Repair

Student/intern information:

Name _____ Date _____ Class _____

Vehicle used for this activity:

Year _____ Make _____ Model _____

Odometer _____ VIN _____

Learning Objective/Task	CDX Tasksheet Number	2013 MLR NATEF Reference Number; Priority Level	2013 AST NATEF Reference Number; Priority Level	2013 MAST NATEF Reference Number; Priority Level
• Inspect, adjust, or replace generator (alternator) drive belts; check pulleys and tensioners for wear; check pulley and belt alignment.	C317	6D2; P-1	6D3; P-1	6D3; P-1
• Perform charging system output test; determine necessary action.	C315	6D1; P-1	6D1; P-1	6D1; P-1
• Perform charging circuit voltage drop tests; determine necessary action.	C319	6D4; P-1	6D5; P-1	6D5; P-1
• Remove, inspect, and reinstall generator (alternator).	C318	6D3; P-1	6D4; P-1	6D4; P-1
• Diagnose (troubleshoot) charging system for the cause of undercharge, no-charge, and overcharge conditions.	C316		6D2; P-1	6D2; P-1

Time off _____

Time on _____

Total time _____

Materials Required

- Vehicle/simulator
- Belt tension measuring device
- Charging system tester
- Tachometer, either hand-held or the vehicle's tachometer, if equipped
- Digital voltmeter
- Exhaust hose/s and wheel chocks

Some Safety Issues to Consider

- If you need to start the vehicle, you should ensure that the parking brake is firmly applied; if necessary, use wheel chocks to prevent the vehicle from moving when the vehicle is started to verify the completion of these tasks.
- When running any vehicles in the shop, make sure you use the shop's exhaust ventilation system to discharge all exhaust gas safely outside.
- Only students who have their supervisor's/instructor's direct permission should perform this task due to the safety concerns involved.

- Diagnosis of this fault may require test-driving the vehicle on the school grounds or on a hoist, both of which carry severe risks. Attempt this task only with full permission from your supervisor/instructor and follow all the guidelines exactly.
- Use extreme caution when working around batteries. Immediately remove any electrolyte that may come into contact with you. Electrolyte is a mixture of sulfuric acid and water. Please consult with the shop safety and emergency procedures when working with or around batteries
- Never exceed 16 volts when charging a 12-volt battery. Overheating and explosion hazards are greatly increased.
- Be cautious around electricity. High voltage (enough to injure or kill you) is present on many vehicles. Ignition systems, hybrid vehicles, and 42-volt electrical systems are just a few hazards to be careful of.
- Accidental deployment of the airbag system could happen if you inadvertently probe the wrong wire. Most manufacturers use yellow-colored wiring to denote wiring for the airbag system. Always be aware of the system/circuit you are working on.
- Comply with personal and environmental safety practices associated with clothing; eye protection; hand tools; power equipment; proper ventilation; and the handling, storage, and disposal of chemicals/materials in accordance ith local, state, and federal safety and environmental regulations.

Performance Standard

0–No exposure: No information or practice provided during the program; complete training required

1–Exposure only: General information provided with no practice time; close supervision needed; additional training required

2–Limited practice: Has practiced job during training program; additional training required to develop skill

3–Moderately skilled: Has performed job independently during training program; limited additional training may be required

4–Skilled: Can perform job independently with no additional training

Inspect, adjust, or replace generator (alternator) drive belts; check pulleys and tensioners for wear; check pulley and belt alignment.

Time off_____

Time on_____

Total time_____

CDX Tasksheet Number: C317

1. Locate "inspecting, adjusting, and/or replacing generator (alternator) drive belts, pulleys, and tensioners; check pulley and belt alignment" in the appropriate service information for the vehicle you are working on.

     a. **List the specified generator (alternator) drive belt tension:**

     _____

     b. **List the faults to look for when inspecting drive belts, pulleys, and tensioners:**

     c. **Describe how to check correct pulley and belt alignment:**

     d. **Locate the belt routing diagram or draw a picture of the current routing arrangement.**

2. Install the fender covers.

3. Remove the vehicle drive belt(s).

4. Inspect the vehicle drive belts, pulleys, and tensioners for faults. **List your observations for the following:**

     a. **Vehicle drive belt(s):**

b. Pulleys:

c. Tensioners:

d. Pulley/belt alignment:

5. Have your instructor verify removal of belt(s) and faults found: _____

6. Reinstall the vehicle drive belts using the appropriate service information.

7. Re-tension the drive belt(s) using the appropriate service information.

8. Check for correct pulley, tensioner, and drive belt alignment.

9. Have your supervisor/instructor verify satisfactory completion of this procedure, any observations found, and any necessary action(s) recommended.

Performance Rating

CDX Tasksheet Number: C317

0	1	2	3	4

Supervisor/instructor signature _____ Date _____

► **TASK** Perform charging system output test; determine necessary action.

MLR 6D1 AST 6D1 MAST 6D1

Time off_____

Time on_____

Total time_____

CDX Tasksheet Number: C315

1. Research "performing a charging system output test" in the appropriate service information for the vehicle you are working on. **What is the specified charging system output?** _____ **amps at** _____ **volts at** _____ **rpm**

2. Install the fender covers, exhaust hose(s), and wheel chocks, and set the parking brake.

3. Connect the charging system tester as outlined in the appropriate service information.

   a. Heavy red lead to the battery positive terminal
   b. Heavy black lead to the battery negative terminal
   c. Green/Black amps clamp around alternator output wire (facing the correct direction)

4. Have your supervisor/instructor verify your test procedure and connections. **Supervisor's/instructor's initials:** _____

5. Conduct the charging system output test. **List the measured results at the maximum output:** _____ **amps at** _____ **volts at** _____ **engine rpm**

6. Compare your results to the manufacturer's specifications. **List your observations:**

7. **Determine any necessary action(s):**

8. Have your supervisor/instructor verify satisfactory completion of this procedure, any observations found, and any necessary action(s) recommended.

Performance Rating

CDX Tasksheet Number: C315

0	1	2	3	4
□	□	□	□	□

Supervisor/instructor signature _____ Date _____

© 2015 Jones & Bartlett Learning, LLC, an Ascend Learning Company

Perform charging circuit voltage drop tests; determine necessary action.

Time off_____

Time on_____

Total time_____

CDX Tasksheet Number: C319

1. Research the procedure and specifications for performing the charging circuit voltage drop tests in the appropriate service information.

    a. **List the maximum allowable voltage drop (generator output terminal to battery positive post):** _____ **volts**

    b. **List the maximum allowable voltage drop (generator housing to battery negative post):** _____ **volts**

2. Install the fender covers, exhaust hose(s), and wheel chocks, and set the parking brake.

3. Connect the DVOM as outlined in the appropriate service information.

    a. List the points that each voltmeter test lead should be connected to, to test the voltage drop between the output terminal of the alternator and the positive post of the battery:

    i. **DVOM black lead:** _____

    ii. **DVOM red lead:** _____

    b. List the points that each voltmeter test lead should be connected to, to test the voltage drop between the housing of the alternator and the negative post of the battery:

    i. **DVOM black lead:** _____

    ii. **DVOM red lead:** _____

4. Have your supervisor/instructor verify your test procedure and connections. **Supervisor's/instructor's initials:** _____

5. Conduct the charging system voltage drop test. **List the measured results:**

    a. **Voltage drop between the alternator output terminal and battery positive post is:** _____ **V at:** _____ **A**

    b. **Voltage drop between the alternator housing and battery negative post is:** _____ **V at:** _____ **A**

6. Compare your results to the manufacturer's specifications. **List your observations:**

7. **Determine any necessary action(s):**

8. Have your supervisor/instructor verify satisfactory completion of this procedure, any observations found, and any necessary action(s) recommended.

Performance Rating

CDX Tasksheet Number: C319

0	1	2	3	4

Supervisor/instructor signature _____ Date _____

MLR	AST	MAST
6D3	6D4	6D4

Time off_____

Time on_____

Total time_____

CDX Tasksheet Number: C318

1. Research the procedure for removing, inspecting and installing a generator (alternator) in the appropriate service information. **List any precautions:**

2. Disconnect battery negative terminal (consider using a battery minder while doing this task).

3. Remove the generator (alternator) as per the service information.

4. Inspect the generator (alternator) as per the service procedure. **List any faults or defects found:**

   a. **Determine any necessary action(s):**

5. Have your supervisor/instructor verify removal of generator (alternator). **Supervisor's/instructor's initials:** _____

6. Install the generator (alternator) as per the service information and properly tension the belt(s).

7. Start the engine to make sure everything is operating correctly. **List your observations:**

8. Have your supervisor/instructor verify satisfactory completion of this procedure, any observations found, and any necessary action(s) recommended.

Performance Rating

CDX Tasksheet Number: C318

0	1	2	3	4

Supervisor/instructor signature _____ Date _____

© 2015 Jones & Bartlett Learning, LLC, an Ascend Learning Company

AST 6D2 **MAST** 6D2

Time off_____

Time on_____

Total time_____

CDX Tasksheet Number: C316

1. Research the following specifications in the appropriate service information for the vehicle assigned.

> **NOTE** Some charging systems use variable charging modes depending on the conditions present, such as battery temperature, driving condition, etc. Make sure you follow the manufacturer's specified testing procedures when testing these systems.

    a. Rated output for the alternator being tested: _____ **amps**

    b. Regulated voltage: _____ **volts**

    c. How is the alternator full fielded on this vehicle?

2. Install the exhaust hose(s) and wheel chocks, and set the parking brake.

3. Connect the charging system tester as outlined in the appropriate service information.

4. Test the maximum current output of the alternator. **List reading here:** _____ **amps**

5. Using the diode/stator setting or AC ripple setting, test the integrity of the diodes and stator. **List the results:**

6. Conduct the charging system regulated voltage test. Do this by measuring the maximum voltage that the charging system achieves while the engine runs at approximately 1500 rpm and waiting until the voltage doesn't rise any further. Do NOT allow the voltage to exceed 16 volts. **Regulated voltage:** _____ **V**

7. Compare your results to the manufacturer's specifications. **List your observations:**

8. Determine any necessary action(s):

9. Have your supervisor/instructor verify satisfactory completion of this procedure, any observations found, and any necessary action(s) recommended.

Performance Rating

CDX Tasksheet Number: C316

0	1	2	3	4

Supervisor/instructor signature _____ Date _____

Electrical/Electronic Systems: Lighting System Diagnosis and Repair

Student/intern information:

Name _____ Date _____ Class _____

Vehicle used for this activity:

Year _____ Make _____ Model _____

Odometer _____ VIN _____

Learning Objective/Task	CDX Tasksheet Number	2013 MLR NATEF Reference Number; Priority Level	2013 AST NATEF Reference Number; Priority Level	2013 MAST NATEF Reference Number; Priority Level
• Identify system voltage and safety precautions associated with high-intensity discharge headlights.	C564	6E3; P-2	6E4; P-2	6E4; P-2
• Inspect interior and exterior lamps and sockets including headlights and auxiliary lights (fog lights/driving lights); replace as needed.	C956	6E1; P-1	6E2; P-1	6E2; P-1
• Aim headlights.	C321	6E2; P-2	6E3; P-2	6E3; P-2
• Diagnose (troubleshoot) the cause of brighter-than-normal, intermittent, dim, or no-light operation; determine necessary action.	C320		6E1; P-1	6E1; P-1

Time off_____

Time on _____

Total time_____

Materials Required

- Vehicle or simulator equipped with HID headlights
- DMM/DVOM
- Test light
- Headlight aligner or approved method

Some Safety Issues to Consider

- Be cautious around electricity. High voltage (enough to injure or kill you) is present on many vehicles. Ignition systems, hybrid vehicles, high-intensity discharge headlights, and 42-volt electrical systems are just a few to be careful of.
- Wear lightweight leather-type gloves when removing small light bulbs as they can shatter, severely cutting fingers and tendons.
- Comply with personal and environmental safety practices associated with clothing; eye protection; hand tools; power equipment; proper ventilation; and the handling, storage, and disposal of chemicals/materials in accordance ith local, state, and federal safety and environmental regulations.

Performance Standard

0–No exposure: No information or practice provided during the program; complete training required

1–Exposure only: General information provided with no practice time; close supervision needed; additional training required

2–Limited practice: Has practiced job during training program; additional training required to develop skill

3–Moderately skilled: Has performed job independently during training program; limited additional training may be required

4–Skilled: Can perform job independently with no additional training

Identify system voltage and safety precautions associated with high-intensity discharge headlights.

MLR 6E3   **AST** 6E4   **MAST** 6E4

Time off_____

Time on_____

Total time_____

CDX Tasksheet Number: C564

1. Using appropriate service information, identify system voltage and safety precautions associated with high-intensity discharge (HID) headlights.

    a. HID lamp voltage: _____ **volts**

    b. List the safety precautions required when working on HID system:

2. Have your supervisor/instructor verify satisfactory completion of this task.

Performance Rating

CDX Tasksheet Number: C564

0	1	2	3	4
☐	☐	☐	☐	☐

Supervisor/instructor signature _____ Date _____

▶ **TASK** Inspect interior and exterior lamps and sockets including headlights and auxiliary lights (fog lights/driving lights); replace as needed.

MLR	AST	MAST
6E1	6E2	6E2

Time off_____

Time on_____

Total time_____

CDX Tasksheet Number: C956

1. Inspect the operation of the following interior lights (vehicles have different arrangements, so find as many as possible). **List your observations for each light listed:**

   a. **Dome:** _____

   b. **Map:** _____

   c. **Dash:** _____

   d. **Kick panel:** _____

   e. **Glove box:** _____

   f. **Vanity mirror:** _____

   g. **Rear passenger:** _____

   h. **Other:** _____

2. Inspect the operation of the following exterior lights (vehicles have different arrangements, so find as many as possible):

   a. **Rear tail:** _____

   b. **License:** _____

   c. **Rear-side marker:** _____

   d. **Brake:** _____

   e. **Center high-mount stoplight:** _____

   f. **Back-up:** _____

   g. **Front park:** _____

   h. **Front-side marker:** _____

   i. **Low beam:** _____

   j. **High beam:** _____

   k. **Fog:** _____

   l. **Driving:** _____

   m. **Cornering:** _____

   n. **Clearance:** _____

   o. **Under-hood:** _____

   p. **Trunk:** _____

   q. **Other:** _____

3. Ask your instructor which bulbs he/she would like you to remove. **List them here:**

4. **List the name of the light and the bulb number for each bulb you removed:**

5. Inspect/clean the sockets for each bulb you removed.

6. Ask your supervisor/instructor if you should apply dielectric grease to the socket of the bulb you have removed.

7. Reinstall the bulb into the socket and reinstall any other pieces that were removed to gain access to the bulb.

8. Have your supervisor/instructor verify satisfactory completion of this procedure.

Performance Rating

CDX Tasksheet Number: C956

0	1	2	3	4

Supervisor/instructor signature _____ Date _____

MLR | AST | MAST
6E2 | 6E3 | 6E3

Time off_____

Time on_____

CDX Tasksheet Number: C321

Total time_____

1. Research the headlamp or exterior lighting section in the appropriate service information for the vehicle you are working on.

   a. **Type of headlights vehicle is equipped with:** _____
   b. **High-beam bulb number:** _____
   c. **Low-beam bulb number:** _____

2. Research the headlamp aiming process in the appropriate service information for the vehicle you are working on. **List (or print off and attach) the steps that are required to aim these headlamps:**

> **NOTE** Do not touch the bulb with your fingers. Some bulbs will fail prematurely due to the oils from your skin.

3. Aim the headlamps following the specified procedure.

4. **List any challenges you had performing this task:**

5. Have your supervisor/instructor verify satisfactory completion of this procedure.

Performance Rating

CDX Tasksheet Number: C321

0	1	2	3	4

Supervisor/instructor signature _____ Date _____

► **TASK** Diagnose (troubleshoot) the cause of brighter-than-normal, intermittent, dim, or no-light operation; determine necessary action.

AST
6E1

MAST
6E1

Time off_____

Time on_____

Total time_____

CDX Tasksheet Number: C320

Vehicle used for this activity:

Year _____ Make _____ Model_____

Odometer_____ VIN_____

1. **List the customer complaint/concern regarding the lighting system fault:**

2. If the lights are dim or do not operate, go to step 3. If the lights are too bright, go to step 9.

3. Research the affected lighting system troubleshooting section and the wiring diagram(s) in the appropriate service information for the vehicle you are working on.

4. **Turn on the affected light(s), measure the battery voltage, and list it here:** _____ **volts**

5. Measure the voltage across the power and ground at the light (light illuminated). **List the voltage:** _____ **volts**

    a. **Calculate the total voltage drop in the circuit and list it here:** _____ **volt drop**
    b. **Is the voltage drop excessive?** Yes: _____ No: _____
    c. If yes, go to step 7. If no, go to step 6.

6. Inspect the bulb and connections for any faults (wrong bulb, corroded, or loose connection). **List your observations:**

7. Measure the voltage drop from the battery positive post to the input terminal of the light.

    a. **List the voltage drop:** _____ volts
    b. **Is this within specifications?** Yes: _____ No: _____
    c. **Determine any necessary action(s):**

8. Measure the voltage drop from the bulb ground to the battery negative post.

    a. List the voltage drop: _____ **volts**

    b. Is this within specifications?   Yes: _____ **No:** _____

    c. Determine any necessary action(s):

9. Install exhaust hose(s) and wheel chocks, and set the parking brake. Start the vehicle.

10. Measure the charging system voltage at the battery, with the engine running at 1500 rpm: _____ **volts**

    a. Is this within specification?   Yes: _____ **No:** _____

> **NOTE** If the battery voltage is too high, you will need to perform charging system checks to determine the cause of the overcharge.

11. List your observations:

12. Determine any necessary action(s):

13. Have your supervisor/instructor verify satisfactory completion of this procedure, any observations found, and any necessary action(s) recommended.

Performance Rating

CDX Tasksheet Number: C320

0	1	2	3	4
□	□	□	□	□

Supervisor/instructor signature _____ Date _____

Electrical/Electronic Systems: Fundamentals

© 2015 Jones & Bartlett Learning, LLC, an Ascend Learning Company

Student/intern information:

Name _____ Date _____ Class _____

Vehicle used for this activity:

Year _____ Make _____ Model_____

Odometer_____VIN_____

Time off_____

Time on _____

Total time_____

Learning Objective/Task	CDX Tasksheet Number	2013 MLR NATEF Reference Number; Priority Level	2013 AST NATEF Reference Number; Priority Level	2013 MAST NATEF Reference Number; Priority Level
• Use wiring diagrams to trace electrical/electronic circuits.	C289	6A3; P-1	6A7; P-1	6A7; P-1
• Use wiring diagrams during the diagnosis (troubleshooting) of electrical/electronic circuit problems.	C952	N/A	6A7; P-1	6A7; P-1
• Demonstrate the proper use of a digital multimeter (DMM) when measuring source voltage, voltage drop (including grounds), current flow, and resistance.	C641	6A4; P-1	6A3; P-1	6A3; P-1
• Check operation of electrical circuits with a test light.	C291	6A6; P-2	6A5; P-2	6A5; P-2
• Check operation of electrical circuits with fused jumper wires.	C295	6A7; P-2	6A6; P-2	6A6; P-2
• Inspect and test fusible links, circuit breakers, and fuses; determine necessary action.	C298	6A9; P-1	6A9; P-1	6A9; P-1
• Demonstrate knowledge of the causes and effects from shorts, grounds, opens, and resistance problems in electrical/electronic circuits.	C296	6A5; P-1	6A4; P-1	6A4; P-1
• Inspect and test switches, connectors, relays, solenoid solid-state devices, and wires of electrical/electronic circuits; determine necessary action.	C299		6A10; P-1	6A10; P-1
• Check electrical/electronic circuit waveforms; interpret readings and determine needed repairs.	C642			6A14; P-2

Some Safety Issues to Consider

- Comply with personal and environmental safety practices associated with clothing; eye protection; hand tools; power equipment; proper ventilation; and the handling, storage, and disposal of chemicals/materials in accordance ith local, state, and federal safety and environmental regulations.

Performance Standard

0—No exposure: No information or practice provided during the program; complete training required

1—Exposure only: General information provided with no practice time; close supervision needed; additional training required

2—Limited practice: Has practiced job during training program; additional training required to develop skill

3—Moderately skilled: Has performed job independently during training program; limited additional training may be required

4—Skilled: Can perform job independently with no additional training

Time off_____

Time on_____

Total time_____

CDX Tasksheet Number: C289

1. Ask your instructor for a wiring diagram, or have him/her assign a circuit for you to print a wiring diagram of. If you instructor has no preference, print off a wiring diagram of a port fuel injection circuit from a vehicle less than 10 years old.

2. Using a red crayon or highlighter, trace all of the wires that are connected directly to power.

3. Using an orange crayon or highlighter, trace all of the wires that are switched to power.

4. Using a green crayon or highlighter, trace all of the wires that are connected directly to ground.

5. Using a yellow crayon or highlighter, trace all of the wires that are switched to ground.

6. Using a blue crayon or highlighter, trace all of the wires that are variable wires, such as sensor outputs.

7. If any wires switch polarity (such as a power window motor), trace those wires with alternating orange and yellow.

8. Have your supervisor/instructor verify satisfactory completion of this procedure.

Performance Rating

CDX Tasksheet Number: C289

0	1	2	3	4
☐	☐	☐	☐	☐

Supervisor/instructor signature _____ Date _____

Use wiring diagrams during the diagnosis (troubleshooting) of electrical/electronic circuit problems.

Time off_____

Time on_____

Total time_____

CDX Tasksheet Number: C952

> **NOTE** This task requires diagnosis of an electrical problem. Please ask your instructor/supervisor to assign you a vehicle that qualifies for this task and several that follow.

1. **List the customer concern/complaint:**

2. **Which electrical circuit(s) are involved?**

3. **How many circuit protection devices are there in this circuit?** _____

   a. **List the circuit protection devices in this circuit:**

   b. **List the circuit control devices in this circuit:**

   c. **Which side of the load(s) is controlled?**

4. Diagnose the fault and list each test and its result:

5. Determine any necessary actions:

6. Have your supervisor/instructor verify satisfactory completion of this procedure, any observations found, and any necessary action(s) recommended.

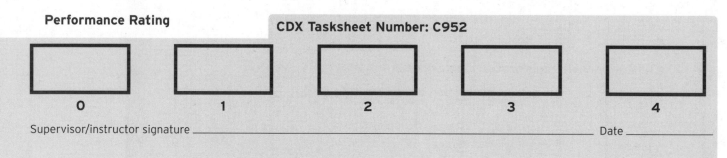

Performance Rating

CDX Tasksheet Number: C952

| 0 | 1 | 2 | 3 | 4 |

Supervisor/instructor signature _____ Date _____

NOTE Continue with the diagnosis of the electrical fault from the previous task.

► **TASK** Demonstrate the proper use of a digital multimeter (DMM) when measuring source voltage, voltage drop (including grounds), current flow, and resistance.

MLR 6A4   **AST** 6A3   **MAST** 6A3

Time off_____

Time on_____

Total time_____

CDX Tasksheet Number: C641

> **NOTE** This task is best performed on either the CDX DVOM simulator, a physical simulator, or a bugged vehicle.

1. Ask your instructor what lighting circuit he/she would like you to perform the following meter readings on. **List circuit here:**

2. Using the appropriate wiring diagram as a reference and a DMM, determine the following:

   a. **Measured source voltage (at battery):** _____ **volts**
   b. **Measured voltage drop (positive side of circuit):** _____ **volts**
   c. **Measured voltage drop (negative side of circuit):** _____ **volts**
   d. **Measured resistance of light:** _____ **ohms**
   e. **Measured current flow through light:** _____ **amps**

3. **Were any of the readings out of specification? Yes:** _____ **No:** _____

   a. **List your observations:**

4. Have your supervisor/instructor verify satisfactory completion of this procedure and any observations found.

Performance Rating

CDX Tasksheet Number: C641

0	1	2	3	4

Supervisor/instructor signature _____ Date _____

MLR 6A6 **AST** 6A5 **MAST** 6A5

Time off_____

Time on_____

CDX Tasksheet Number: C291

Total time_____

1. Test for proper operation of the test light by connecting it across the vehicle's battery terminals.

   a. Connect the clip end (negative) of the test light to the negative battery terminal.

   b. Touch the probe end of the test light to the positive battery terminal. The test light should light.

   c. Did the test light operate correctly? Yes: _____ No: _____

   > NOTE Please notify your supervisor/instructor if the test light did not operate correctly.

2. Using the wiring diagram for the left tail lamp/parking light circuit of the assigned vehicle, identify the wire color for both the power (voltage) and ground (negative) wire.

   i. Power (positive): _____

   ii. Ground (negative): _____

3. Using the appropriate tools, remove the taillight assembly and disconnect the tail lamp connector. The headlamp switch should be set to "Off."

   a. Visually locate the power and ground wires, as described in step 2a.

   b. Turn the headlamp switch to the "Park" position.

   e. Connect the clip end of the test light to an unpainted metal surface that is a good ground.

   f. Touch the test light probe to the positive wire of the vehicle harness tail lamp connector cavity.

   i. Did the test light come on? Yes: _____ No: _____

   ii. Please explain your results:

   g. With the test light probe still connected to the positive wire, test the ground wire by removing the clip end of the test light and touching it to the ground wire of the tail lamp connector cavity, being careful not to cause a short circuit by touching the clip to the probe. The light should come on if there is a good ground.

   i. Did the light come on? Yes: _____ No: _____

3. **Based on your observations, determine any necessary action(s):**

4. Have your supervisor/instructor verify satisfactory completion of this procedure, any observations found, and any necessary action(s) recommended.

Performance Rating

CDX Tasksheet Number: C291

☐	☐	☐	☐	☐
0	1	2	3	4

Supervisor/instructor signature _____ Date _____

MLR 6A7 | **AST** 6A6 | **MAST** 6A6

Time off_____

Time on_____

Total time_____

CDX Tasksheet Number: C295

> **NOTE** Using a jumper wire to bypass components can cause damage if performed incorrectly. Never bypass the load in any circuit. Normally it is acceptable to bypass switches and some speed controlling resistors. If in doubt, ask your instructor.

1. Ask your instructor to assign you a vehicle equipped with an electric cooling fan controlled by a relay.

2. Research the wiring diagram for the cooling fan circuit. **Draw a diagram of that circuit.**

3. Locate the cooling fan relay.

4. **Draw a diagram of the relay socket and label each terminal with where the wire comes from, or goes to.**

5. Label the diagram with the two points to which you believe the jumper wires should be placed.

6. Apply the parking brake and make sure the vehicle is in park or neutral.

7. Ask your instructor to verify your answers and where you plan to place the fused jumper wire. Have him/her watch you during the next portion of this task to ensure no damage is done to the vehicle's electrical system.

   a. **Supervisor's/instructor's initials:** _____

8. Turn the ignition switch to the run position, but do not start the vehicle (Key On, Engine Off - KOEO).

9. Use the fused jumper wire to activate the relay by jumping the terminals that connect to the relay contacts.

   a. **List your observation(s):**

10. Determine any necessary action(s):

11. Have your supervisor/instructor verify satisfactory completion of this procedure, any observations found, and any necessary action(s) recommended.

Performance Rating

CDX Tasksheet Number: C295

0	1	2	3	4

Supervisor/instructor signature _____ Date _____

MLR 6A9   **AST** 6A9   **MAST** 6A9

Time off_____

Time on_____

Total time_____

CDX Tasksheet Number: C298

1. Using the appropriate service information, locate the fuse panel(s) for the vehicle/ simulator you are assigned to.

   a. List the locations of the fuse panel(s) and circuit protection devices for this vehicle/simulator:

2. Use a test light to test each fuse and circuit breaker in one of the fuse boxes. **List any circuit protection devices that are defective (open).**

   NOTE Circuit protection devices normally do not wear out. If a circuit protection device is found to be faulty, too much current was/is present. You should determine the reason for the fault.

3. **What is the rating (size) of the failed circuit protection device?** _____ **amps**

4. **Is the correct size fuse installed? Yes:** _____ **No:** _____

5. Determine the cause for the circuit protection device to fail. **List your tests and results below.**

6. **Determine any necessary action(s):**

7. Have your supervisor/instructor verify satisfactory completion of this procedure, any observations found, and any necessary action(s) recommended.

Performance Rating

CDX Tasksheet Number: C298

0	1	2	3	4

Supervisor/instructor signature _____ Date _____

Demonstrate knowledge of the causes and effects from shorts, grounds, opens, and resistance problems in electrical/electronic circuits.

MLR 6A5 | **AST** 6A4 | **MAST** 6A4

Time off_____

Time on_____

Total time_____

CDX Tasksheet Number: C296

1. Define "short circuit":

2. Define "short to ground":

3. Define "short to power":

4. Define "open circuit":

5. Define "high resistance":

6. List at least two examples of short circuits:

7. List at least two examples of grounded circuits:

8. List at least two examples of open circuits:

9. List at least two examples of high resistance in a circuit:

10. What are the effects of a short circuit in a load?

11. What are the effects on a circuit with an open circuit?

12. What are the effects on a circuit with high resistance?

13. Have your supervisor/instructor verify satisfactory completion of your answers in steps 1-12.

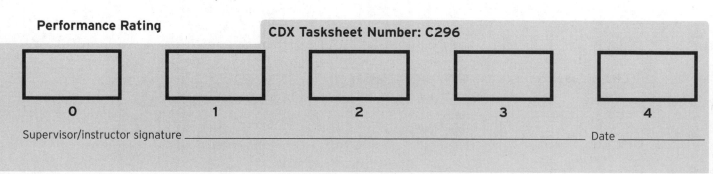

Performance Rating

CDX Tasksheet Number: C296

| 0 | 1 | 2 | 3 | 4 |

Supervisor/instructor signature _____ Date _____

Inspect and test switches, connectors, relays, solenoid solid-state devices, and wires of electrical/electronic circuits; determine necessary action.

AST 6A10 **MAST** 6A10

Time off_____

Time on_____

Total time_____

CDX Tasksheet Number: C299

Vehicle used for this activity:

Year _____ Make _____ Model_____

Odometer_____ VIN_____

1. **Ask your instructor which of the above components you should inspect and test. List here:** _____

2. Locate the wiring diagram for the component that you are testing. Determine the purpose and operation of the suspected component. (Understanding how a component is designed to operate within a circuit will make it easier to diagnose.)

   a. **Write a short description of the purpose and operation of the suspected component.**

   b. **Using the appropriate service information, list (or print off) the main steps necessary for testing the component:**

   c. **What is the rating (size) of the circuit protection device for this circuit?** _____ **amps**

3. **Carry out the suggested diagnostic procedure. List your tests and results:**

4. **Determine any necessary action(s):**

5. Have your supervisor/instructor verify satisfactory completion of this procedure, any observations found, and any necessary action(s) recommended.

Performance Rating

CDX Tasksheet Number: C299

0	1	2	3	4

Supervisor/instructor signature _____ Date _____

▶ **TASK** Check electrical/electronic circuit waveforms; interpret
readings and determine needed repairs.

MAST
6A14

Time off_____

Time on_____

Total time_____

CDX Tasksheet Number: C642

Vehicle used for this activity:

Year _____ Make _____ Model_____

Odometer_____ VIN_____

1. **List the two most common types of electrical waveforms and describe how each of them differ:**

2. Research various sensors for the vehicle you have been given.

    a. **List at least two sensors that give an analog signal:**

    b. **List at least two sensors that give a digital signal:**

3. Connect a lab scope to at least one analog sensor. **Test the sensor, draw a diagram of the waveform, and list the name of the analog sensor:**

4. Connect a lab scope to at least one digital sensor. **Test the sensor, draw a diagram of the waveform, and list the name of the digital sensor:**

5. Do these waveforms meet the manufacturer's specifications?
Yes: _____ No: _____

6. Determine any necessary action(s):

7. Have your supervisor/instructor verify satisfactory completion of this procedure, any observations found, and any necessary action(s) recommended.

Performance Rating

CDX Tasksheet Number: C642

0	1	2	3	4

Supervisor/instructor signature _____ Date _____

Electrical/Electronic Systems: Wire Repair

Student/intern information:

Name _____ Date _____ Class _____

Vehicle used for this activity:

Year _____ Make _____ Model _____

Odometer _____ VIN _____

Learning Objective/Task	CDX Tasksheet Number	2013 MLR NATEF Reference Number; Priority Level	2013 AST NATEF Reference Number; Priority Level	2013 MAST NATEF Reference Number; Priority Level
• Replace electrical connectors and terminal ends.	C643	6A11; P-1	6A11; P-1	6A11; P-1
• Perform solder repair of electrical wiring.	C301	6A10; P-1	6A13; P-1	6A13; P-1
• Repair wiring harness.	C955		6A12; P-3	6A12; P-3
• Repair wiring harness (including CAN/BUS systems).	C559			6A15; P-1

Time off _____

Time on _____

Total time _____

Materials Required

- Wiring harness (on or off the car)
- Terminal removal tool
- Wire stripper/crimper tool
- New replacement terminal
- Soldering iron
- 60/40 rosin core solder
- Heat shrink tube or electrical tape
- Wire strippers
- Heat gun, if using shrink tube

Some Safety Issues to Consider

- **Terminal picks can be sharp. Be careful when using them so they don't slip and stab you.**
- **Always strip wires in a direction pointing away from you so the stripper doesn't slip and hit you in the face.**
- **Soldering irons get, and stay, extremely hot so always pick them up only by the handle.**
- **Solder is extremely hot when molten. Prevent it from dripping onto your skin or clothing.**
- Comply with personal and environmental safety practices associated with clothing; eye protection; hand tools; power equipment; proper ventilation; and the handling, storage, and disposal of chemicals/materials in accordance ith local, state, and federal safety and environmental regulations.

Performance Standard

0—No exposure: No information or practice provided during the program; complete training required

1—Exposure only: General information provided with no practice time; close supervision needed; additional training required

2—Limited practice: Has practiced job during training program; additional training required to develop skill

3—Moderately skilled: Has performed job independently during training program; limited additional training may be required

4—Skilled: Can perform job independently with no additional training

MLR
6A11

AST
6A11

MAST
6A11

Time off_____

Time on_____

CDX Tasksheet Number: C643

Total time_____

1. Ask your instructor to assign a wiring harness for you to perform this task on.

2. Use the terminal removal tool to release the terminal(s) from the connector.

   a. With your instructor's approval, cut off one terminal to be replaced.
   b. Have your instructor verify removal of connector and terminal.
      Supervisor's/instructor's initials: _____

3. Use the wire stripper to remove the proper length of wire insulation.

4. Follow the service information to crimp the new terminal on the wire.

5. Reinsert the terminals into the connector so the terminal locks into place.

6. Have your supervisor/instructor verify satisfactory completion of this procedure, any observations found, and any necessary action(s) recommended.

Performance Rating

CDX Tasksheet Number: C643

0	1	2	3	4

Supervisor/instructor signature _____ Date _____

Time off_____

Time on_____

Total time_____

CDX Tasksheet Number: C301

> **NOTE** Use only rosin core solder for wiring repair. The use of acid core solder will result in corrosion, thereby causing high resistance in the circuit.

1. Obtain a segment of wire (6-8 inches [15 cm] in length is sufficient) and solder from your supervisor/instructor.

2. Prepare the wire ends for soldering. Remove about 1/2 inch (1 cm) of insulation at each end. If you are using heat shrink tube to cover your solder repair, now is the time to install the correct length and size.

3. Overlap the stripped ends of wire, twisting them tightly to create a secure mechanical joint.

   a. Have your supervisor/instructor check this joint prior to soldering.
   Supervisor's/instructor's initials: _____

4. Clean and tin the tip of the soldering iron if needed.

5. Heat the wire joint with the soldering iron.

> **NOTE** If the soldering iron is properly tinned, apply solder to the joint, not to the tip of the soldering iron. (Sometimes you may need to melt a small amount of solder to fill the gap between the tip and the wire joint to transfer heat to the wire more effectively.) When holding the solder against the wire joint, you will notice the solder begin to flow into the wires. Stop as soon as you notice the wires slightly and evenly coated with solder. Do not apply too much solder or heat.

   a. Have your supervisor/instructor check your solder joint.
   Supervisor's/instructor's initials: _____

6. Cover the repair area with the heat shrink tube that was installed in step 2 or electrical tape.

> **NOTE** Heat the shrink tube with a heat gun. Do not use an open flame and do not overheat the tube.

7. Have your supervisor/instructor verify satisfactory completion of this procedure.

Performance Rating

CDX Tasksheet Number: C301

0	1	2	3	4

Supervisor/instructor signature _____ Date _____

AST
6A12

MAST
6A12

Time off_____

Time on_____

CDX Tasksheet Number: C955

Total time_____

1. Ask your instructor to assign a wiring harness for you to perform this task on.

2. **List the steps to properly repair a damaged wire in a standard harness:**

3. **What type of solder is used to solder wires?** _____

4. With your instructor's permission, cut one wire in the wiring harness.

   a. Have your instructor verify the cut wire. **Supervisor's/instructor's initials:** _____

5. Perform the repair, being careful to solder properly, and avoid damaging any of the surrounding wires.

6. **What did you use to insulate the soldered joint?** _____

7. Have your supervisor/instructor verify satisfactory completion of this procedure, any observations found, and any necessary action(s) recommended.

Performance Rating

CDX Tasksheet Number: C955

0	1	2	3	4

Supervisor/instructor signature _____ Date _____

CDX Tasksheet Number: C559

1. Ask your instructor to assign a CAN/BUS wiring harness for you to perform this task on.

2. **Research the proper steps to repair the CAN/BUS wiring harness in the appropriate service information.**

   a. **List the steps to properly repair the CAN/BUS wiring:**

3. With your instructor's permission, cut one wire of the CAN/BUS system.

   a. Have your instructor verify the cut wire and repair procedure.
   Supervisor's/instructor's initials: _____

4. Perform the repair, being careful to follow all of the steps of the specified procedure.

5. **What did you do to prevent electrical noise from affecting the repaired wires once they are back in service?**

6. **How did you insulate the soldered joint?** _____

7. Have your supervisor/instructor verify satisfactory completion of this procedure, any observations found, and any necessary action(s) recommended.

Performance Rating

CDX Tasksheet Number: C559

0	1	2	3	4

Supervisor/instructor signature _____ Date _____

Electrical/Electronic Systems: Horn and Wiper/Washer Diagnosis and Repair

Student/intern information:

Name _____ Date _____ Class _____

Vehicle used for this activity:

Year _____ Make _____ Model _____

Odometer _____ VIN _____

Learning Objective/Task	CDX Tasksheet Number	2013 MLR NATEF Reference Number; Priority Level	2013 AST NATEF Reference Number; Priority Level	2013 MAST NATEF Reference Number; Priority Level
• Diagnose (troubleshoot) incorrect horn operation; perform necessary action.	C327		6G1; P-1	6G1; P-1
• Verify windshield wiper and washer operation; replace wiper blades.	C958	6F5; P-1	6H10; P-1	6H10; P-1
• Diagnose (troubleshoot) incorrect windshield washer problems; perform necessary action.	C329		6G3; P-2	6G3; P-2
• Diagnose (troubleshoot) causes of incorrect wiper operation; diagnose wiper speed control and park problems; perform necessary action.	C328		6G2; P-1	6G2; P-1

Time off _____

Time on _____

Total time _____

Materials Required

- Vehicle/simulator with inoperative horn
- Vehicle with inoperative washer/wipers
- Digital volt ohm meter (DVOM)
- Test light
- Fused jumper wire/s
- Fender cover

Some Safety Issues to Consider

- Windshield wiper motors can be very powerful. Use caution around operating wipers and linkage.
- Place a large folded-up towel or cloth fender cover on the windshield where the wiper would hit if the wiper slipped. The wiper hold-down spring is very stiff and can cause the wiper to break the windshield if allowed to slam back in place.
- Only operate the windshield wipers with water or washer solution on the windshield. Otherwise you could burn out the wiper motor.
- Comply with personal and environmental safety practices associated with clothing; eye protection; hand tools; power equipment; proper ventilation; and the handling, storage, and disposal of chemicals/materials in accordance ith local, state, and federal safety and environmental regulations.

Performance Standard

0—No exposure: No information or practice provided during the program; complete training required

1—Exposure only: General information provided with no practice time; close supervision needed; additional training required

2—Limited practice: Has practiced job during training program; additional training required to develop skill

3—Moderately skilled: Has performed job independently during training program; limited additional training may be required

4—Skilled: Can perform job independently with no additional training

CDX Tasksheet Number: C327

1. Locate "diagnosis of vehicle horn" and the wiring diagram in the appropriate service information for the vehicle you are working on.

   a. List the procedure for diagnosing the vehicle's horn circuit (or attach diagnosis printout):

3. Following the specified procedure, diagnose any faults in the vehicle horn circuit.

   a. List the tests you performed and their results:

4. **List the cause of the horn circuit fault:**

5. **Determine any necessary action(s):**

6. Have your supervisor/instructor verify satisfactory completion of this procedure, any observations found, and any necessary action(s) recommended.

Performance Rating

CDX Tasksheet Number: C327

0	1	2	3	4

Supervisor/instructor signature _____ Date _____

▶ **TASK** Verify windshield wiper and washer operation; replace wiper blades.

Time off_____

Time on_____

CDX Tasksheet Number: C958

Total time_____

1. Operate the windshield washer and observe the spray pattern. **Are the patterns appropriate? Yes:** _____ **No:** _____

2. If the washer works properly, operate the windshield wipers on each speed and verify proper operation. **List your observations for each speed:**

3. **If the wipers are equipped with a delay feature, operate that (with water on the windshield) mode in a few positions. List your observations:**

4. Place a large folded-up towel or cloth fender cover on the windshield where the wiper would hit it.

5. Remove the wiper blade from the wiper arm, being careful not to break any locking tabs.

6. **Have your instructor verify removal. Supervisor's/instructor's initials:** _____

> **NOTE** Also ask your instructor if he/she would like you to remove the wiper insert from the blade, and do so if requested.

7. **Determine any necessary action(s):**

8. Have your supervisor/instructor verify satisfactory completion of this procedure, any observations found, and any necessary action(s) recommended.

Performance Rating

CDX Tasksheet Number: C958

0	1	2	3	4

Supervisor/instructor signature _____ Date _____

Diagnose (troubleshoot) incorrect windshield washer problems; perform necessary action.

AST 6G3 **MAST** 6G3

Time off_____

Time on_____

Total time_____

CDX Tasksheet Number: C329

Vehicle used for this activity:

Year _____ Make _____ Model_____

Odometer_____ VIN_____

1. Locate "diagnosis of vehicle windshield washer system" and the wiring diagram in the appropriate service information for the vehicle you are working on.

   a. List the procedure for diagnosing the vehicle windshield washer system (or attach diagnosis printout):

3. Following the specified procedure, diagnose the fault in the windshield washer system.

   a. List the tests you performed and their results:

4. **List the cause of the windshield washer system fault:**

5. **Perform any necessary action(s) and list them here:**

6. Have your supervisor/instructor verify satisfactory completion of this procedure, any observations found, and any necessary action(s) recommended.

Performance Rating

CDX Tasksheet Number: C329

0	1	2	3	4

Supervisor/instructor signature _____ Date _____

▶ TASK Diagnose (troubleshoot) causes of incorrect wiper operation; diagnose wiper speed control and park problems; perform necessary action.

AST 6G2 **MAST** 6G2

Time off _____

Time on _____

Total time _____

CDX Tasksheet Number: C328

Vehicle used for this activity:

Year _____ Make _____ Model _____

Odometer _____ VIN _____

1. Locate "diagnosis of vehicle wiper system" and the wiring diagram in the appropriate service information for the vehicle you are working on.

   a. **List the procedure for diagnosing the windshield wiper system, including speed control and park problems (or attach diagnosis printout):**

3. Using the appropriate service information, diagnose faults in the vehicle windshield wiper system.

   a. **List the tests you performed and their results:**

4. **List the cause of the windshield wiper system fault:**

5. **Perform any necessary action(s) and list here:**

6. Have your supervisor/instructor verify satisfactory completion of this procedure, any observations found, and any necessary action(s) recommended.

Performance Rating

CDX Tasksheet Number: C328

0	1	2	3	4

Supervisor/instructor signature _____ Date _____

Electrical/Electronic Systems: Gauges, Warning Devices, and Driver Information Systems Diagnosis and Repair

Student/intern information:

Name _____ Date _____ Class _____

Vehicle used for this activity:

Year _____ Make _____ Model _____

Odometer _____ VIN _____

Learning Objective/Task	CDX Tasksheet Number	2013 MLR NATEF Reference Number; Priority Level	2013 AST NATEF Reference Number; Priority Level	2013 MAST NATEF Reference Number; Priority Level
• Verify operation of instrument panel gauges and warning/indicator lights; reset maintenance indicators.	C957	6F4; P-1	6H9; P-1	6H9; P-1
• Inspect and test gauges and gauge sending units for cause of abnormal gauge readings; determine necessary action.	C646		6F1; P-2	6F1; P-2
• Diagnose (troubleshoot) the cause of incorrect operation of warning devices and other driver information systems; determine necessary action.	C325		6F2; P-2	6F2; P-2

Time off_____

Time on_____

Total time_____

Materials Required

- Vehicle or simulator
- Depending on the type of concern, special diagnostic tools may be required. See your supervisor/instructor for instructions to identify what tools may be required.
- DMM/DVOM

Some Safety Issues to Consider

- If you need to start the vehicle, you should ensure that the parking brake is firmly applied; if necessary, use wheel chocks to prevent the vehicle from moving when the vehicle is started to verify the completion of these tasks.
- When running any vehicles in the shop, make sure you use the shop's exhaust ventilation system to discharge all exhaust gas safely outside.
- Only students who have their supervisor's/instructor's direct permission should perform this task due to the safety concerns involved.
- Diagnosis of this fault may require test-driving the vehicle on the school grounds. Attempt this task only with full permission from your instructor and follow all the guidelines exactly.
- Comply with personal and environmental safety practices associated with clothing; eye protection; hand tools; power equipment; proper ventilation; and the handling, storage, and disposal of chemicals/materials in accordance ith local, state, and federal safety and environmental regulations.

Performance Standard

0—No exposure: No information or practice provided during the program; complete training required

1—Exposure only: General information provided with no practice time; close supervision needed; additional training required

2—Limited practice: Has practiced job during training program; additional training required to develop skill

3—Moderately skilled: Has performed job independently during training program; limited additional training may be required

4—Skilled: Can perform job independently with no additional training

Verify operation of instrument panel gauges and warning/indicator lights; reset maintenance indicators.

Time off_____

Time on_____

Total time_____

CDX Tasksheet Number: C957

1. Research the operation of instrument panel gauges/indicator lights and the procedure for resetting the maintenance indicators in the service information. **List each of the maintenance indicators and the reset procedure:**

2. **Turn the ignition switch to the run position (Key On, Engine Off - KOEO). List the status of each gauge/indicator:**

3. **Start the engine and allow it to run for a few minutes. List the status of each gauge/indicator:**

4. **List any gauges/indicators that are showing a fault and the fault indicated:**

5. Have your supervisor/instructor verify satisfactory completion of this procedure, any observations found, and any necessary action(s) recommended.

Performance Rating

CDX Tasksheet Number: C957

0	1	2	3	4

Supervisor/instructor signature _____ Date _____

Inspect and test gauges and gauge sending units for cause of abnormal gauge readings; determine necessary action.

AST
6F1

MAST
6F1

Time off_____

Time on_____

Total time_____

CDX Tasksheet Number: C646

1. **List the customer concern/complaint regarding abnormal gauge readings:**

2. Research the particular complaint/concern in the appropriate service information. **List the possible causes:**

    a. **List any relevant gauge or sending unit specifications:**

3. Diagnose the cause of the concern/complaint using the service information and wiring diagrams. **List your tests and their results:**

4. **List the cause of the concern/complaint:**

5. **Determine any necessary action(s) to correct the fault:**

6. Have your supervisor/instructor verify satisfactory completion of this procedure, any observations found, and any necessary action(s) recommended.

Performance Rating

CDX Tasksheet Number: C646

0	1	2	3	4

Supervisor/instructor signature _____ Date _____

Diagnose (troubleshoot) the cause of incorrect operation of warning devices and other driver information systems; determine necessary action.

AST
6F2

MAST
6F2

CDX Tasksheet Number: C325

Vehicle used for this activity:

Year _____ Make _____ Model_____

Odometer_____ VIN_____

1. **List the customer concern/complaint regarding incorrect operation of warning devices and other driver information systems:**

2. Research the particular complaint/concern in the appropriate service information. **List the possible causes:**

   a. **List any relevant specifications:**

3. Diagnose the cause of the concern/complaint using the service information and wiring diagrams. **List your tests and their results:**

4. **List the cause of the concern/complaint:**

5. Determine any necessary action(s) to correct the fault:

6. Have your supervisor/instructor verify satisfactory completion of this procedure, any observations found, and any necessary action(s) recommended.

Performance Rating

CDX Tasksheet Number: C325

0	1	2	3	4

Supervisor/instructor signature _____ Date _____

Electrical/Electronic Systems: Accessories Diagnosis and Repair

Student/intern information:

Name _____ Date _____ Class _____

Vehicle used for this activity:

Year _____ Make _____ Model _____

Odometer _____ VIN _____

Time off _____

Time on _____

Total time _____

Learning Objective/Task	CDX Tasksheet Number	2013 MLR NATEF Reference Number; Priority Level	2013 AST NATEF Reference Number; Priority Level	2013 MAST NATEF Reference Number; Priority Level
• Diagnose (troubleshoot) incorrect operation of motor-driven accessory circuits; determine necessary action.	C330		6H1; P-2	6H1; P-2
• Describe the operation of keyless-entry/remote-start systems.	C648	6F3; P-3	6H8; P-3	6H8; P-3
• Diagnose (troubleshoot) incorrect electric lock operation (including remote keyless entry); determine necessary action.	C647		6H2; P-2	6H2; P-2
• Diagnose (troubleshoot) incorrect operation of cruise control systems; determine necessary action.	C333		6H3; P-3	6H3; P-3

Materials Required

- Vehicle/simulator with appropriate fault for each task
- DMM/DVOM
- Test light
- Fused jumper wire/s
- Possible special tools depending on the fault

Some Safety Issues to Consider

- Motor-driven systems contain rotating and moving parts. Be careful to ensure that clothing, your body, and tools are kept clear of moving parts.
- Be cautious around electricity. High voltage (enough to injure or kill you) is present on many vehicles. Ignition systems, hybrid vehicles, and 42-volt electrical systems are just a few hazards to be careful of.
- Accidental deployment of the airbag system could happen if you inadvertently probe the wrong wire. Most manufacturers use yellow-colored wiring to denote wiring for the airbag system. Always be aware of the system/circuit you are working on.
- Only students who have a valid driver's license and their supervisor's/instructor's direct permission should perform these tasks due to the safety concerns involved.

- Comply with personal and environmental safety practices associated with clothing; eye protection; hand tools; power equipment; proper ventilation; and the handling, storage, and disposal of chemicals/materials in accordance ith local, state, and federal safety and environmental regulations.

Performance Standard

0–No exposure: No information or practice provided during the program; complete training required

1–Exposure only: General information provided with no practice time; close supervision needed; additional training required

2–Limited practice: Has practiced job during training program; additional training required to develop skill

3–Moderately skilled: Has performed job independently during training program; limited additional training may be required

4–Skilled: Can perform job independently with no additional training

AST 6H1 | **MAST** 6H1

Time off_____

Time on_____

Total time_____

CDX Tasksheet Number: C330

1. Ask your instructor to assign a vehicle with a fault in a motor-driven accessory circuit. List the circuit:

2. **List the customer concern/complaint:**

3. Locate the diagnosis section and the wiring diagram for the motor-driven fault in the appropriate service information for the vehicle you are working on. **Briefly describe the diagnostic procedure for this vehicle's motor-driven accessory circuit (or attach diagnosis printout):**

4. Following the specified procedure, diagnose faults in the motor-driven accessory circuit. **List your tests and their results:**

5. **List the cause of the customer concern/complaint:**

6. **Determine any necessary action(s) to correct the fault:**

7. Have your supervisor/instructor verify satisfactory completion of this procedure, any observations found, and any necessary action(s) recommended.

Performance Rating

CDX Tasksheet Number: C330

☐	☐	☐	☐	☐
0	1	2	3	4

Supervisor/instructor signature _____ Date _____

▶ **TASK** Describe the operation of keyless-entry/remote-start systems.

MLR 6F3 **AST** 6H8 **MAST** 6H8

Time off_____

Time on_____

Total time_____

CDX Tasksheet Number: C648

1. Research the operation of the keyless-entry/remote-start system in the service information on a vehicle equipped with these features.

    a. Summarize the operation of the keyless-entry system:

    b. Summarize the operation of the remote-start system:

2. Have your supervisor/instructor verify your answers.

Performance Rating

CDX Tasksheet Number: C648

0	1	2	3	4

Supervisor/instructor signature _____ Date _____

© 2015 Jones & Bartlett Learning, LLC, an Ascend Learning Company

Diagnose (troubleshoot) incorrect electric lock operation (including remote keyless entry); determine necessary action.

AST 6H2   **MAST** 6H2

Time off_____

Time on_____

Total time_____

CDX Tasksheet Number: C647

1. Ask your instructor to assign a vehicle with a fault in an electric lock system.

2. **List the customer concern/complaint:**

3. Locate the diagnosis section and the wiring diagram for the electric lock system fault in the appropriate service information for the vehicle you are working on. **Briefly describe the diagnostic procedure for this vehicle's electric lock system (or attach diagnosis printout):**

4. Following the specified procedure, diagnose faults in the electric lock system. **List your tests and their results:**

5. **List the cause of the customer concern/complaint:**

6. **Determine any necessary action(s) to correct the fault:**

7. Have your supervisor/instructor verify satisfactory completion of this procedure, any observations found, and any necessary action(s) recommended.

Performance Rating

CDX Tasksheet Number: C647

0	1	2	3	4

Supervisor/instructor signature _____ Date _____

▶ TASK Diagnose (troubleshoot) incorrect operation of cruise control systems; determine necessary action.

AST 6H3 **MAST** 6H3

Time off_____

Time on_____

Total time_____

CDX Tasksheet Number: C333

1. Ask your instructor to assign a vehicle with a fault in the cruise control system.

2. **List the customer concern/complaint:**

3. Locate the diagnosis section and the wiring diagram for the cruise control system fault in the appropriate service information for the vehicle you are working on. **Briefly describe the diagnostic procedure for this vehicle's cruise control system (or attach diagnosis printout):**

4. Following the specified procedure, diagnose faults in the cruise control system. **List your tests and their results:**

5. **List the cause of the customer concern/complaint:**

6. **Determine any necessary action(s) to correct the fault:**

7. Have your supervisor/instructor verify satisfactory completion of this procedure, any observations found, and any necessary action(s) recommended.

Performance Rating

CDX Tasksheet Number: C333

0	1	2	3	4

Supervisor/instructor signature _____ Date _____

Accessories Diagnosis and Repair (cont.)

Student/intern information:

Name _____ Date _____ Class _____

Vehicle used for this activity:

Year _____ Make _____ Model _____

Odometer_____ VIN_____

Learning Objective/Task	CDX Tasksheet Number	2013 MLR NATEF Reference Number; Priority Level	2013 AST NATEF Reference Number; Priority Level	2013 MAST NATEF Reference Number; Priority Level
• Disable and enable the airbag system for vehicle service; verify indicator lamp operation.	C335	6F1; P-1	6H5; P-1	6H5; P-1
• Diagnose (troubleshoot) supplemental restraint system (SRS) problems; determine necessary action.	C861		6H4; P-2	6H4; P-2
• Remove and reinstall the door panel.	C337	6F2; P-1	6H6; P-1	6H6; P-1
• Diagnose (troubleshoot) radio static and weak, intermittent, or no radio reception; determine necessary action.	C336			6H11; P-3

Time off_____

Time on_____

Total time_____

Materials Required

- Vehicle/simulator with appropriate fault for each task
- Vehicle diagnostic scan tool
- DMM/DVOM
- Test light
- Door panel tools
- Manufacturer or job specific tools depending on the fault

Some Safety Issues to Consider

- Be cautious around electricity. High voltage (enough to injure or kill you) is present on many vehicles. Ignition systems, hybrid vehicles, and 42-volt electrical systems are just a few hazards to be careful of.
- Working on the airbag system can be very dangerous. Consult the shop manual for the vehicle you are working on and ensure all safety precautions are followed.
- Accidental deployment of the airbag system could happen if you inadvertently probe the wrong wire. Most manufacturers use yellow-colored wiring to denote wiring for the airbag system. Always be aware of the system/circuit you are working on.
- Only students who have their supervisor's/instructor's direct permission should perform these tasks due to the safety concerns involved.
- Always wear the correct protective eyewear and clothing, and use the appropriate safety equipment, as well as fender covers, seat protectors, and floor mat protectors.
- Make sure you understand and observe all legislative and personal safety procedures when carrying out practical assignments. If you are unsure of what these are, ask your supervisor/instructor.

Performance Standard

0—No exposure: No information or practice provided during the program; complete training required

1—Exposure only: General information provided with no practice time; close supervision needed; additional training required

2—Limited practice: Has practiced job during training program; additional training required to develop skill

3—Moderately skilled: Has performed job independently during training program; limited additional training may be required

4—Skilled: Can perform job independently with no additional training

Disable and enable the airbag system for vehicle service; verify indicator lamp operation.

MLR 6F1 | **AST** 6H5 | **MAST** 6H5

Time off_____

Time on_____

Total time_____

CDX Tasksheet Number: C335

1. Locate "disabling/enabling vehicle airbag system" in the appropriate service information for the vehicle you are working on.

   a. **List the safety precautions to be taken when disabling/enabling the airbag system for the vehicle you are working on:**

   b. **Describe the disabling/enabling procedure for the vehicle airbag system for the vehicle you are working on:**

   c. Have your supervisor/instructor verify your listed procedure. **Supervisor's/ instructor's initials:** _____

2. Disable the vehicle's airbag system. **Supervisor's/instructor's initials:** _____

3. Enable the vehicle's airbag system: **Supervisor's/instructor's initials:** _____

4. **What would happen if a technician were leaning over the steering wheel when the driver's side airbag activated?**

5. Have your supervisor/instructor verify satisfactory completion of this procedure, any observations found, and any necessary action(s) recommended.

Performance Rating

CDX Tasksheet Number: C335

0	1	2	3	4

Supervisor/instructor signature _____ Date _____

Diagnose (troubleshoot) supplemental restraint system (SRS) problems; determine necessary action.

AST 6H4 **MAST** 6H4

Time off_____

Time on_____

Total time_____

CDX Tasksheet Number: C861

Vehicle used for this activity:

Year _____ Make _____ Model_____

Odometer_____ VIN_____

1. **Locate "diagnosis of vehicle supplemental restraint systems" in the appropriate service information for the vehicle you are working on.**

   a. **List the safety precautions to be taken when working on the SRS for the vehicle you are working on:**

   b. **Briefly describe the main components of the SRS for the vehicle you are working on:**

   c. **Briefly describe the diagnostic procedure for this vehicle's SRS (or print and attach copy):**

   i. Have your supervisor/instructor verify your listed procedure. **Supervisor's/ instructor's initials: _____**

2. Following the specified procedure, diagnose faults in the vehicle SRS. **List your tests and their results:**

3. List the cause of the customer concern/complaint:

4. Determine any necessary action(s) to correct the customer concern/complaint:

5. Have your supervisor/instructor verify satisfactory completion of this procedure, any observations found, and any necessary action(s) recommended.

Performance Rating

CDX Tasksheet Number: C861

0	1	2	3	4

Supervisor/instructor signature _____ Date _____

MLR	AST	MAST
6F2	6H6	6H6

Time off_____

Time on_____

Total time_____

CDX Tasksheet Number: C337

Vehicle used for this activity:

Year _____ Make _____ Model_____

Odometer_____ VIN_____

1. Research the removal and installation procedure for the vehicle's door panel in the appropriate service information.

    a. **List the procedures and tools required to perform this task (or print and attach copy):**

    i. Have your supervisor/instructor verify the above steps. **Supervisor's/ instructor's initials:** _____

2. Remove the door panel as per the manufacturer's procedures. **List any observations:**

    a. Have your supervisor/instructor verify the door panel removal. **Supervisor's/ instructor's initials:** _____

3. Install the door panel as per the manufacturer's procedures.

4. **List any difficulties you had in performing this task:**

5. Have your supervisor/instructor verify satisfactory completion of this procedure, any observations found, and any necessary action(s) recommended.

Performance Rating

CDX Tasksheet Number: C337

0	1	2	3	4

Supervisor/instructor signature _____ Date _____

Diagnose (troubleshoot) radio static and weak, intermittent, or no radio reception; determine necessary action.

MAST
6H11

Time off_____

Time on_____

Total time_____

CDX Tasksheet Number: C336

Vehicle used for this activity:

Year _____ Make _____ Model_____

Odometer_____ VIN_____

1. Ask your instructor to assign a vehicle with a fault in the radio or entertainment system.

2. **List the customer concern/complaint:**

3. Locate "diagnosis of radio static and weak, intermittent, or no radio reception" in the appropriate service information for the vehicle you are working on. **Briefly describe the diagnostic procedure for the radio (or attach diagnosis printout):**

4. Following the specified procedure, diagnose radio static and weak, intermittent, or no radio reception. **List your tests and their results:**

5. **List the cause of the customer concern/complaint:**

6. **Determine any necessary action(s) to correct the customer concern/complaint:**

7. Have your supervisor/instructor verify satisfactory completion of this procedure, any observations found, and any necessary action(s) recommended.

Performance Rating

0	1	2	3	4

Supervisor/instructor signature _____ Date _____

Accessories Diagnosis and Repair (cont.)

Student/intern information:

Name _____ Date _____ Class _____

Vehicle used for this activity:

Year _____ Make _____ Model_____

Odometer_____ VIN _____

Learning Objective/Task	CDX Tasksheet Number	2013 MLR NATEF Reference Number; Priority Level	2013 AST NATEF Reference Number; Priority Level	2013 MAST NATEF Reference Number; Priority Level
• Diagnose (troubleshoot) body electronic system circuits using a scan tool; determine necessary action.	C338			6H12; P-3
• Check for module communication errors (including CAN/BUS systems) using a scan tool.	C821		6H7; P-2	6H7; P-2
• Diagnose the cause(s) of false, intermittent, or no operation of anti-theft systems.	C340			6H13; P-3
• Describe the process for software transfers, software updates, or flash reprogramming on electronic modules.	C649			6H14; P-3

Time off_____

Time on_____

Total time_____

Materials Required

- Vehicle/simulator with appropriate fault for each task
- Vehicle diagnostic scan tool
- DMM/DVOM
- Manufacturer or job specific tools depending on the fault

Some Safety Issues to Consider

- Be cautious around electricity. High voltage (enough to injure or kill you) is present on many vehicles. Ignition systems, hybrid vehicles, and 42-volt electrical systems are just a few hazards to be careful of.
- Accidental deployment of the airbag system could happen if you inadvertently probe the wrong wire. Most manufacturers use yellow-colored wiring to denote wiring for the airbag system. Always be aware of the system/circuit you are working on.
- Only students who have a valid driver's license and their supervisor's/instructor's direct permission should perform these tasks due to the safety concerns involved.
- If you need to start the vehicle you should ensure that the parking brake is firmly applied; if necessary, use wheel chocks to prevent the vehicle from moving when the vehicle is started to verify the completion of this task.
- When running any vehicles in the shop, make sure you use the shop's exhaust ventilation system to discharge all exhaust gas safely outside.
- Always wear the correct protective eyewear and clothing, and use the appropriate safety equipment, as well as fender covers, seat protectors, and floor mat protectors.
- Make sure you understand and observe all legislative and personal safety procedures when carrying out practical assignments. If you are unsure of what these are, ask your supervisor/instructor.

Performance Standard

0—No exposure: No information or practice provided during the program; complete training required

1—Exposure only: General information provided with no practice time; close supervision needed; additional training required

2—Limited practice: Has practiced job during training program; additional training required to develop skill

3—Moderately skilled: Has performed job independently during training program; limited additional training may be required

4—Skilled: Can perform job independently with no additional training

▶ **TASK** Diagnose (troubleshoot) body electronic system circuits using a scan tool; determine necessary action.

MAST
6H12

Time off_____

Time on_____

Total time_____

CDX Tasksheet Number: C338

1. Locate "diagnosis of body electronic systems with a scan tool' in the appropriate service information for the vehicle you are working on.

   a. **List the safety precautions to be taken when working on the body electronic systems:**

   b. **List the diagnostic procedures for the body electronic systems (or print and attach copy):**

2. **Check for any DTCs (diagnostic trouble codes) in the BCM (body control module) and list them and their descriptions here:**

3. Following the specified procedure, diagnose faults in the body electronic system. **List your tests and observations:**

4. **Determine any necessary action(s) to correct the fault:**

5. Have your supervisor/instructor verify satisfactory completion of this procedure, any observations found, and any necessary action(s) recommended.

Performance Rating

CDX Tasksheet Number: C338

0	1	2	3	4

Supervisor/instructor signature _____ Date _____

Check for module communication (including CAN/BUS systems) errors using a scan tool.

Time off_____

Time on_____

Total time_____

CDX Tasksheet Number: C821

Vehicle used for this activity:

Year _____ Make _____ Model_____

Odometer_____ VIN_____

1. Locate "diagnosis of CAN/BUS module communication errors" in the appropriate service information for the vehicle you are working on.

   a. List the safety precautions to be taken when working on the CAN/BUS system:

   b. List the diagnostic procedures for diagnosing the CAN/BUS system (or print and attach copy):

2. Check for any DTCs (diagnostic trouble codes) in the CAN/BUS system. **List the codes and descriptions here:**

3. Following the specified procedure, diagnose faults in the CAN/BUS system. **List your test and observations:**

4. Determine any necessary action(s) to correct the fault:

5. Have your supervisor/instructor verify satisfactory completion of this procedure, any observations found, and any necessary action(s) recommended.

Performance Rating

CDX Tasksheet Number: C821

0	1	2	3	4

Supervisor/instructor signature _____ Date _____

▶ **TASK** Diagnose the cause(s) of false, intermittent, or no operation of anti-theft systems.

MAST
6H13

CDX Tasksheet Number: C340

Vehicle used for this activity:

Year _____ Make _____ Model_____

Odometer_____ VIN_____

1. Locate "false, intermittent, or no operation of anti-theft systems" in the appropriate service information for the vehicle you are working on.

   a. **List the safety precautions to be taken when working on the anti-theft system:**

   b. **List the diagnostic procedures for the anti-theft system (or print and attach copy):**

2. Check for any DTCs in the anti-theft system. **List the DTCs and their descriptions here:**

3. Following the specified procedure, diagnose faults in the anti-theft system. **List your tests and observations:**

4. **Determine any necessary action(s) to correct the fault:**

5. Have your supervisor/instructor verify satisfactory completion of this procedure, any observations found, and any necessary action(s) recommended.

Performance Rating

CDX Tasksheet Number: C340

0	1	2	3	4

Supervisor/instructor signature _____ Date _____

▶ **TASK** Describe the process for software transfers, software updates, or flash reprogramming on electronic modules.

MAST
6H14

CDX Tasksheet Number: C649

Vehicle used for this activity:

Year _____ Make _____ Model _____

Odometer _____ VIN _____

1. **List the customer concern(s) related to software updates or the need for reprogramming electronic modules:**

2. **Verify the concern and list your observations including any codes, their descriptions, or any TSBs:**

3. Research the correct method to perform software transfers, software updates, or flash reprogramming on electronic modules in appropriate service information.

   a. **List any precautions here:**

   b. **List the steps needed to reprogram the electronic module (or print and attach):**

   c. **Have your instructor verify your process:** _____

4. Perform software transfers, software updates, or flash reprogramming on electronic modules.

5. Determine any necessary action(s):

6. Have your supervisor/instructor verify satisfactory completion of this procedure, any observations found, and any necessary action(s) recommended.

Performance Rating

CDX Tasksheet Number: C649

0	1	2	3	4

Supervisor/instructor signature _____ Date _____

Electrical/Electronic Systems: Hybrid Electrical Safety

Student/intern information:

Name _____ Date _____ Class _____

Vehicle used for this activity:

Year _____ Make _____ Model _____

Odometer _____ VIN _____

Learning Objective/Task	CDX Tasksheet Number	2013 MLR NATEF Reference Number; Priority Level	2013 AST NATEF Reference Number; Priority Level	2013 MAST NATEF Reference Number; Priority Level
• Identify high-voltage circuits of electric or hybrid-electric vehicle and related safety precautions.	C561	6B7:P-3	6B7; P-3	6B7; P-3
• Identify hybrid vehicle auxiliary (12V) battery service, repair, and test procedures.	C874	6B9; P-3	6B9; P-3	6B9; P-3

Time off _____

Time on _____

Total time _____

Materials Required

- Hybrid or electric vehicle
- Certified and tested, high voltage electrical gloves.
- Depending on the type of concern, special diagnostic tools may be required. See your supervisor/instructor for instructions to identify what tools may be required.

Some Safety Issues to Consider

- Hybrid and electric vehicles are especially dangerous due to their extremely high DC voltage and current (high enough to kill you). In many dealerships, only fully trained master technicians are allowed to work on hybrid and electric vehicles. Follow all manufacturer procedures exactly, and wear all required personal protective equipment at all times when working around these vehicles.
- **Always wear high-voltage personal protective equipment when working around high-voltage sources, components, and wires.**
- Only students who have their supervisor's/instructor's direct permission should perform this task due to the safety concerns involved.
- Use extreme caution when working around batteries. Immediately remove any electrolyte that may come into contact with you. Electrolyte is a mixture of sulfuric acid and water. Please consult with the shop safety and emergency procedures when working with or around batteries.
- Comply with personal and environmental safety practices associated with clothing; eye protection; hand tools; power equipment; proper ventilation; and the handling, storage, and disposal of chemicals/materials in accordance ith local, state, and federal safety and environmental regulations.

Performance Standard

0–No exposure: No information or practice provided during the program; complete training required

1–Exposure only: General information provided with no practice time; close supervision needed; additional training required

2–Limited practice: Has practiced job during training program; additional training required to develop skill

3–Moderately skilled: Has performed job independently during training program; limited additional training may be required

4–Skilled: Can perform job independently with no additional training

Identify high-voltage circuits of electric or hybrid-electric vehicle and related safety precautions.

MLR 6B7 **AST** 6B7 **MAST** 6B7

Time off_____

Time on_____

Total time_____

CDX Tasksheet Number: C561

1. Research the safety precautions for all high-voltage circuits and methods of identifying those circuits on the hybrid or electric vehicle.

   a. List the systems that use or create high voltage:

   b. List any safety precautions when working on or around these systems and circuits:

2. Locate and point out, on the vehicle, the high-voltage circuits and components to your instructor.

3. Have your supervisor/instructor verify satisfactory completion of this procedure, any observations found, and any necessary action(s) recommended.

Performance Rating

CDX Tasksheet Number: C561

0	1	2	3	4

Supervisor/instructor signature _____ Date _____

Identify hybrid vehicle auxiliary (12V) battery service, repair, and test procedures.

MLR 6B9   **AST** 6B9   **MAST** 6B9

Time off_____

Time on_____

Total time_____

CDX Tasksheet Number: C874

1. Research the hybrid vehicle auxiliary (12V) battery service, repair, and test procedures in the appropriate service information.

   a. **Does this vehicle use a 12V auxiliary battery? Yes:** _____
      No: _____

   b. **List any special testing, service, or repair procedures related to the 12V auxiliary battery:**

2. **If you performed any tests, services, or repairs on the 12V auxiliary battery, list all tests or service performed and any results:**

3. **Determine any necessary action(s):**

4. Have your supervisor/instructor verify satisfactory completion of this procedure, any observations found, and any necessary action(s) recommended.

Performance Rating

CDX Tasksheet Number: C874

0	1	2	3	4

Supervisor/instructor signature _____ Date _____

Section A7: HVAC

CONTENTS

HVAC: Vehicle, Customer, and Service Information

Student/intern information:

Name _____ Date _____ Class _____

Vehicle used for this activity:

Year _____ Make _____ Model _____

Odometer _____ VIN _____

Learning Objective/Task	CDX Tasksheet Number	2013 MLR NATEF Reference Number; Priority Level	2013 AST NATEF Reference Number; Priority Level	2013 MAST NATEF Reference Number; Priority Level
• Research applicable vehicle and service information, vehicle service history, service precautions, and technical service bulletins.	C342	7A1; P-1	7A2; P-1	7A2; P-1
• Identify and interpret heating and air conditioning problems; determine necessary action.	C341		7A1; P-1	7A1; P-1
• Identify hybrid vehicle A/C system electrical circuits and the service/safety precautions.	C827	7B2; P-2	7B4; P-2	7B4; P-2
• Demonstrate use of the 3 Cs (concern, cause, and correction).	NN07	N/A	N/A	N/A

Time off _____

Time on _____

Total time _____

Materials Required

- Blank work order
- Vehicle with available service history records
- Thermometer or temperature gun
- DVOM
- Depending on the type of concern, special diagnostic tools may be required. See your supervisor/instructor for instructions to identify what tools may be required.

Some Safety Issues to Consider

- Diagnosis of this fault may require test-driving the vehicle on the school grounds. Attempt this task only with full permission from your instructor and follow all the guidelines exactly.
- When running any vehicles in the shop, make sure you use the shop's exhaust ventilation system to discharge all exhaust gas safely outside.
- Extreme caution must be exercised when working around rotating components.
- Refrigerant can cause serious damage if it comes in contact with a person's unprotected skin and eyes.
- When operating, the air conditioning system is normally subject to very high pressure in the system. Extreme caution must be exercised when working on an operating system.
- Comply with personal and environmental safety practices associated with clothing; eye protection; hand tools; power equipment; proper ventilation; and the handling, storage, and disposal of chemicals/materials in accordance with local, state, and federal safety and environmental regulations.

Performance Standard

0—**No exposure:** No information or practice provided during the program; complete training required

1—**Exposure only:** General information provided with no practice time; close supervision needed; additional training required

2—**Limited practice:** Has practiced job during training program; additional training required to develop skill

3—**Moderately skilled:** Has performed job independently during training program; limited additional training may be required

4—**Skilled:** Can perform job independently with no additional training

▶ **TASK** Research applicable vehicle and service information, vehicle service history, service precautions, and technical service bulletins.

MLR 7A1 **AST** 7A2 **MAST** 7A2

Time off_____

Time on_____

Total time_____

CDX Tasksheet Number: C342

1. Using the VIN for identification, use the appropriate source to access the vehicle's service history in relation to prior related HVAC system work or customer concerns.

   a. List any related repairs/concerns and their dates:

2. Research the HVAC system description and operation in the appropriate service information.

   a. Specified refrigerant: _____

   b. Refrigerant capacity: _____ lb/kg

   c. Specified lubricant: _____

   d. Lubricant capacity: _____ oz/mL

   e. List the specified service precautions when servicing this system:

3. Using the VIN for identification, access any relevant technical service bulletins for the particular vehicle on which you are working in relation to any related HVAC issues.

   a. List any related service bulletins and their titles:

4. Have your supervisor/instructor verify satisfactory completion of this procedure, any observations found, and any necessary action(s) recommended.

Performance Rating

CDX Tasksheet Number: C342

0	1	2	3	4

Supervisor/instructor signature _____ Date _____

AST 7A1 **MAST** 7A1

CDX Tasksheet Number: C341

1. List the customer's heating and air conditioning-related concern(s):

2. Research the particular concern in the appropriate service information.

   a. **List the possible causes:**

3. Inspect the vehicle to determine the cause of the concern.

   a. **List the steps you took to determine the fault(s):**

4. **List the cause of the concern(s):**

5. **List the necessary action(s) to correct the fault(s):**

6. Have your supervisor/instructor verify satisfactory completion of this procedure, any observations found, and any necessary action(s) recommended.

Performance Rating

0	1	2	3	4

Supervisor/instructor signature _____ Date _____

▶ **TASK** Identify hybrid vehicle A/C system electrical circuits and the service/safety precautions.

MLR 7B2 — **AST** 7B4 — **MAST** 7B4

Time off_____

Time on_____

Total time_____

CDX Tasksheet Number: C827

Vehicle used for this activity:

Year _____ Make _____ Model_____

Odometer_____ VIN_____

1. Research the description and operation of a hybrid vehicle A/C system in the appropriate service information.

   a. What powers the A/C compressor (prime mover)?

   b. Does the manufacturer use a special designation for the A/C system electrical circuits? Yes: _____ No: _____

   i. If yes, what is it?

   c. List the voltage(s) that the A/C system electrical circuits operate on:

   d. How is the A/C compressor driven? V belt: _____ Serpentine belt:_____ Direct drive: _____ Other (specify below)

   i. Specified refrigerant: _____
   ii. Refrigerant capacity: _____ lb/kg
   iii. Specified lubricant: _____
   iv. Lubricant capacity: _____ oz/mL
   v. List the specified safety precautions when servicing this system:

2. Have your supervisor/instructor verify satisfactory completion of this procedure, any observations found, and any necessary action(s) recommended.

Performance Rating

CDX Tasksheet Number: C827

0	1	2	3	4

Supervisor/instructor signature _____ Date _____

Demonstrate use of the 3 Cs: concern, cause, and correction.

CDX Tasksheet Number: NN07

1. Using the following scenario, write up the 3 Cs as listed on most repair orders. Assume that the customer authorized the recommended repairs.

    A late model vehicle with 114,000 miles and equipped with an expansion-valve style HVAC system is brought into your shop with an A/C concern. The customer tells you that the A/C has not worked for the past several days. You perform a preliminary check and notice that the compressor clutch does not engage when moving the A/C controls to maximum cold with the A/C fan on high. Further testing shows the following:

    a. Normal static pressure in the system
    b. An open compressor clutch winding
    c. A dirty cabin air filter
    d. An excessively cracked engine serpentine belt
    e. A lightly leaking water pump seal
    f. A coolant freeze point of 20°F (−6°C)

    > **NOTE** Ask your instructor whether you should use a copy of the shop repair order or the 3 Cs below to record this information.

2. Concern:

3. Cause:

4. Correction:

5. Other recommended service:

6. Have your supervisor/instructor verify satisfactory completion of this procedure, any observations found, and any necessary action(s) recommended

Performance Rating

CDX Tasksheet Number: NN07

0	1	2	3	4
☐	☐	☐	☐	☐

Supervisor/instructor signature _____ Date _____

HVAC: Preliminary Testing

Student/intern information:

Name _____ Date _____ Class _____

Vehicle used for this activity:

Year _____ Make _____ Model_____

Odometer_____VIN_____

Learning Objective/Task	CDX Tasksheet Number	2013 MLR NATEF Reference Number; Priority Level	2013 AST NATEF Reference Number; Priority Level	2013 MAST NATEF Reference Number; Priority Level
• Performance test A/C system; identify problems.	C824		7A3; P-1	7A3; P-1
• Identify abnormal operating noises in the A/C system; determine necessary action.	C825		7A4; P-2	7A4; P-2
• Inspect A/C condenser for airflow restrictions; determine necessary action.	C959	7B3; P-1		
• Inspect A/C condenser for airflow restrictions; perform necessary action.	C356		7B7; P-1	7B7; P-1
• Inspect A/C evaporator for airflow restrictions; perform necessary action.	N/A	N/A	N/A	N/A
• Inspect evaporator housing water drain; perform necessary action.	C830		7B10; P-1	7B10; P-1
• Identify the source of A/C system odors.	C655	7D2; P-2	7D7; P-2	7D7; P-2

Time off_____

Time on_____

Total time_____

Materials Required

- Appropriate air conditioning manifold gauge set including service hoses
- Air conditioning service station recovery/recycling equipment as necessary
- Auxiliary fan for condenser (if needed)
- Appropriate thermometers
- Infrared temperature gun/thermocouple
- Anemometer
- Stethoscope
- Scan tool

Some Safety Issues to Consider

- Refrigerant can cause serious damage if it comes in contact with a person's unprotected skin and eyes.
- When operating, the air conditioning system is normally subject to very high pressure in the system. Extreme caution must be exercised when working on an operating system.
- Extreme caution must be exercised when working around rotating components.

- When running any vehicles in the shop, make sure you use the shop's exhaust ventilation system to discharge all exhaust gas safely outside.
- Diagnosis of this fault may require test-driving the vehicle on the school grounds. Attempt this task only with full permission from your instructor and follow all the guidelines exactly.
- Comply with personal and environmental safety practices associated with clothing; eye protection; hand tools; power equipment; proper ventilation; and the handling, storage, and disposal of chemicals/materials in accordance with local, state, and federal safety and environmental regulations.

Performance Standard

0–No exposure: No information or practice provided during the program; complete training required

1–Exposure only: General information provided with no practice time; close supervision needed; additional training required

2–Limited practice: Has practiced job during training program; additional training required to develop skill

3–Moderately skilled: Has performed job independently during training program; limited additional training may be required

4–Skilled: Can perform job independently with no additional training

CDX Tasksheet Number: C824

1. Research the procedure and specifications for performance testing the A/C system in the appropriate service information.

   a. **List or print off and attach to this sheet the steps to performance test the system:**

   b. **List or print off and attach to this sheet any specifications that the system should meet:**

2. **Following the specified procedure, carry out the performance test on the system. List the following readings:**

   > NOTE Use an auxiliary fan for additional condenser airflow if conditions warrant.

   a. **Engine RPM:** _____
   b. **Is the compressor clutch cycle time appropriate? Yes:** _____ **No:** _____
   c. **Ambient air temperature:** _____ **°F/°C**
   d. **A/C duct air temperature:** _____ **°F/°C**
   e. **Difference between ambient temp and A/C duct temp:** _____**°F/°C**

3. **Did the A/C system pass the performance test? Yes:** _____ **No:** _____

4. **Determine any necessary action(s):**

5. Have your supervisor/instructor verify satisfactory completion of this procedure, any observations found, and any necessary action(s) recommended.

Performance Rating

CDX Tasksheet Number: C824

0	1	2	3	4

Supervisor/instructor signature _____ Date _____

▶ TASK Identify abnormal operating noises in the A/C system; determine necessary action.

AST 7A4 **MAST** 7A4

Time off_____

Time on_____

Total time_____

CDX Tasksheet Number: C825

Vehicle used for this activity:

Year _____ Make _____ Model_____

Odometer_____ VIN_____

1. **List the A/C noise-related concern:**

2. **Start the vehicle and operate the A/C system to verify the noise concern. Try to determine the location of the noise. List your observation(s):**

3. Research the possible cause(s) and testing procedures in the appropriate service information.

   a. **List any possible cause(s):**

   b. **List or print off and attach to this sheet the steps for identifying the cause of the concern:**

4. Following the specified procedure, identify the cause of the concern. **List your test(s) and results:**

5. List the cause(s) of the concern:

6. Determine any necessary action(s) to correct the fault:

7. Have your supervisor/instructor verify satisfactory completion of this procedure, any observations found, and any necessary action(s) recommended.

Performance Rating

CDX Tasksheet Number: C825

0	1	2	3	4

Supervisor/instructor signature _____ Date _____

Inspect A/C condenser for airflow restrictions; determine necessary action.

MLR 7B3

CDX Tasksheet Number: C959

Vehicle used for this activity:

Year _____ Make _____ Model_____

Odometer_____ VIN_____

1. Research the procedure and specifications for inspecting the A/C condenser for airflow restrictions in the appropriate service information.

    a. List or print off and attach to this sheet any steps to perform this task:

    b. Specified condenser airflow: _____ **ft/min**

2. Following the specified procedure, inspect both sides of the A/C condenser for damage or blockage to the airflow. **List your observation(s):**

3. **Following the specified procedure, use the anemometer to measure the condenser airflow on the side of the condenser away from the fan:** _____ **ft/min**

    NOTE Be extra careful when performing this task.

4. **Determine any necessary action(s):**

5. Have your supervisor/instructor verify satisfactory completion of this procedure, any observations found, and any necessary action(s) recommended.

Performance Rating

CDX Tasksheet Number: C959

0	1	2	3	4

Supervisor/instructor signature _____ Date _____

Inspect A/C condenser for airflow restrictions; perform
necessary action.

AST 7B7   **MAST** 7B7

Time off_____

Time on_____

CDX Tasksheet Number: C356

Total time_____

Vehicle used for this activity:

Year _____ Make _____ Model_____

Odometer_____ VIN_____

1. Research the procedure and specifications for inspecting the A/C condenser for airflow restrictions in the appropriate service information.

   a. List or print off and attach to this sheet any steps to perform this task:

   b. Specified condenser airflow: _____ **ft/min**

2. Following the specified procedure, inspect both sides of the A/C condenser for damage or blockage to the airflow. **List your observation(s):**

3. **Following the specified procedure, use the anemometer to measure the condenser airflow:** _____ **ft/min**

4. **Determine any necessary action(s):**

5. Have your supervisor/instructor verify your observations and recommendations and initial below. **Supervisor's/instructor's initials:** _____

6. **Perform any necessary actions and list your observation(s):**

7. Have your supervisor/instructor verify satisfactory completion of this procedure, any observations found, and any necessary action(s) recommended.

Performance Rating

CDX Tasksheet Number: C356

0	1	2	3	4

Supervisor/instructor signature _____ Date _____

Inspect evaporator housing water drain; perform necessary action.

AST **MAST**
7B10   7B10

CDX Tasksheet Number: C830

1. Research the procedure for inspecting and cleaning the evaporator housing water drain in the appropriate service information.

   a. List or print off and attach to this sheet the steps to perform this task:

2. **Following the specified procedure, inspect the evaporator housing water drain. List your observation(s):**

3. Have your supervisor/instructor verify your observations.
   Supervisor's/instructor's initials: _____

4. **Perform any necessary action(s) and list your observation(s):**

5. Have your supervisor/instructor verify satisfactory completion of this procedure, any observations found, and any necessary action(s) recommended.

Performance Rating

CDX Tasksheet Number: C830

0	1	2	3	4

Supervisor/instructor signature _____ Date _____

MLR 7D2 **AST** 7D7 **MAST** 7D7

Time off_____

Time on_____

CDX Tasksheet Number: C655

Vehicle used for this activity:

Year _____ Make _____ Model_____

Odometer_____ VIN_____

Total time_____

1. **List the A/C system odor-related customer concern:**

2. Verify the concern by running the A/C system through all operating conditions. **List your observation(s):**

3. Research the procedure to identify the odor concern in the appropriate service information.

    a. **List the possible cause(s) of the concern:**

    b. **List, or print off and attach to this sheet, the steps to identify the source of the odor: (If no procedure is given, operate the system in each of the various functions, and see when the smell is the strongest.)**

4. **Following the specified procedure, inspect the A/C system to identify the cause of the odor. List your steps and results:**

5. **List the cause of the concern:**

6. **Determine any necessary action(s) to correct the fault:**

7. Have your supervisor/instructor verify satisfactory completion of this procedure, any observations found, and any necessary action(s) recommended.

Performance Rating

CDX Tasksheet Number: C655

0	1	2	3	4

Supervisor/instructor signature _____ Date _____

HVAC: Refrigerant Recovery, Recycling, and Handling

Student/intern information:

Name _____ Date _____ Class _____

Vehicle used for this activity:

Year _____ Make _____ Model_____

Odometer_____VIN_____

Learning Objective/Task	CDX Tasksheet Number	2013 MLR NATEF Reference Number; Priority Level	2013 AST NATEF Reference Number; Priority Level	2013 MAST NATEF Reference Number; Priority Level
• Identify refrigerant type; select and connect proper gauge set; record temperature and pressure readings.	C650		7A5; P-1	7A5; P-1
• Leak test A/C system; determine necessary action.	C347		7A6; P-1	7A6; P-1
• Identify and recover A/C system refrigerant.	C836		7E2; P-1	7E2; P-1
• Recycle, label, and store refrigerant.	C657		7E3; P-1	7E3; P-1
• Determine recommended oil and oil capacity for system application.	C652		7A8; P-1	7A8; P-1
• Inspect the condition of refrigerant oil removed from the system; determine necessary action.	C651		7A7; P-2	7A7; P-2
• Determine the need for an additional A/C system filter; perform necessary action.	C863		7B5; P-3	7B5; P-3

Time off_____

Time on_____

Total time_____

Materials Required

- Refrigerant identifier
- Appropriate air conditioning manifold gauge set including service hoses
- Infrared temp gun or AC thermometer
- Air conditioning service station recovery/recycling equipment as necessary
- Refrigerant detecting equipment
- Specified refrigerant oil

Some Safety Issues to Consider

- Refrigerant can cause serious damage if it comes in contact with a person's unprotected skin and eyes.
- When operating, the air conditioning system is normally subject to very high pressure in the system. Extreme caution must be exercised when working on an operating system.
- Extreme caution must be exercised when working around rotating components.

- When running any vehicles in the shop, make sure you use the shop's exhaust ventilation system to discharge all exhaust gas safely outside.
- Comply with personal and environmental safety practices associated with clothing; eye protection; hand tools; power equipment; proper ventilation; and the handling, storage, and disposal of chemicals/materials in accordance with local, state, and federal safety and environmental regulations.

Performance Standard

0—No exposure: No information or practice provided during the program; complete training required

1—Exposure only: General information provided with no practice time; close supervision needed; additional training required

2—Limited practice: Has practiced job during training program; additional training required to develop skill

3—Moderately skilled: Has performed job independently during training program; limited additional training may be required

4—Skilled: Can perform job independently with no additional training

© 2015 Jones & Bartlett Learning, LLC, an Ascend Learning Company

► **TASK** Identify refrigerant type; select and connect proper
gauge set; record temperature and pressure readings.

AST **MAST**
7A5 **7A5**

CDX Tasksheet Number: C650

1. Research the description, operation, and testing procedure for the A/C system in the appropriate service information.

   a. **Specified refrigerant type:** _____

   b. **Specified testing RPM (engine):** _____

   c. **Does this vehicle require auxiliary condenser airflow for testing?**
      Yes: _____ **No:** _____

   d. **Specified high side-pressure range:** _____ **psi/kPa**

   e. **Specified low side-pressure range:** _____ **psi/kPa**

   f. **Specified air duct temperature range:** _____ **°F/°C**

2. **Following the specified procedure, identify the refrigerant type:** _____

3. Obtain the proper gauge set and connect it to the A/C system service ports.

4. **Following the specified procedure, record the operating temperature and pressure readings below.**

   > **NOTE** Use an auxiliary fan for additional condenser airflow if conditions warrant.

   a. **Engine tested at:** _____ **RPM**

   b. **High side-pressure range:** _____ **psi/kPa**

   c. **Low side-pressure range:** _____ **psi/kPa**

   d. **Ambient air temperature:** _____ **°F/°C**

   e. **A/C duct air temperature:** _____ **°F/°C**

   f. **Difference between ambient temp and A/C duct temp:** _____ **°F/°C**

5. **Does the A/C system perform according to specifications?**
   Yes: _____ **No:** _____

6. Have your supervisor/instructor verify satisfactory completion of this procedure, any observations found, and any necessary action(s) recommended.

Performance Rating

CDX Tasksheet Number: C650

0	1	2	3	4

Supervisor/instructor signature _____ Date _____

AST
7A6

MAST
7A6

Time off_____

Time on_____

Total time_____

CDX Tasksheet Number: C347

1. Research the A/C leak detection procedure in the appropriate service information.

     a. **List the leak detection method you will use:**

2. Following the specified procedure, leak test the A/C system, including the evaporator, condenser, compressor, and all fittings and hoses.

     a. **List your observation(s):**

3. **Determine any necessary action(s):**

4. Have your supervisor/instructor verify satisfactory completion of this procedure, any observations found, and any necessary action(s) recommended.

Performance Rating

CDX Tasksheet Number: C347

0	1	2	3	4

Supervisor/instructor signature _____ Date _____

▶ **TASK** Identify and recover A/C system refrigerant.

AST 7E2 **MAST** 7E2

CDX Tasksheet Number: C836

1. Research the procedure and specifications to identify and recover refrigerant in the appropriate service information.

   a. **Specified type of refrigerant:** _____

   b. **Specified capacity of refrigerant:** _____ lb/kg

   c. **List the method you will use to identify the type of refrigerant installed in the A/C system:**

2. **Following the specified procedure, identify the existing refrigerant in the A/C system.**

   a. **Type identified:** _____

   b. **Is this the specified refrigerant? Yes:** _____ **No:** _____

   c. **Determine any necessary action(s):**

3. Following the specified procedure, recover the refrigerant installed in the A/C system.

   a. **How much refrigerant was recovered from the system?** _____ lb/kg

   b. **How much oil was recovered, if any?** _____ oz/mL

   c. **Are these the specified amounts? Yes:** _____ **No:** _____

   d. **Determine any necessary action(s):**

4. Have your supervisor/instructor verify satisfactory completion of this procedure, any observations found, and any necessary action(s) recommended.

Performance Rating

CDX Tasksheet Number: C836

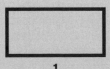 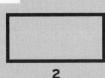 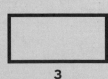

| 0 | 1 | 2 | 3 | 4 |

Supervisor/instructor signature _____ Date _____

Time off_____

Time on_____

Total time_____

CDX Tasksheet Number: C657

1. Research the procedure and specifications for this task in the appropriate service information.

   a. **List the type of refrigerant you are working with:** _____

   b. **List the container color code for the specified refrigerant:** _____

   c. **What does a bottle with a yellow top and a gray bottom indicate?**

   d. **List or print off and attach to this sheet the steps to recycle the refrigerant:**

   e. **What are the labeling requirements for this refrigerant?**

   f. **What are the requirements for safely storing this refrigerant?**

   g. **Using the proper refrigerant PT (pressure/temperature) chart, record the specified reading for today's ambient temperature: _____ psi/kPa**

2. Following the specified procedure, recycle the refrigerant. **List your observations:**

3. Following the specified procedure, ensure that the refrigerant is properly labeled. **List your observations:**

4. Following the specified procedure, properly store the refrigerant. **List your observations:**

5. Following the specified procedure, check for non-condensable gases. **List your observations:**

6. Have your supervisor/instructor verify satisfactory completion of this procedure, any observations found, and any necessary action(s) recommended.

Performance Rating

CDX Tasksheet Number: C657

0	1	2	3	4

Supervisor/instructor signature _____ Date _____

Determine recommended oil and oil capacity for system application.

AST 7A8 | MAST 7A8

Time off_____

Time on_____

Total time_____

CDX Tasksheet Number: C652

1. Research the following specifications in the appropriate service information.
   a. **Specified refrigerant oil:** _____
   b. **Specified refrigerant oil capacity:** _____ **oz/mL**

2. Have your supervisor/instructor verify satisfactory completion of this procedure, any observations found, and any necessary action(s) recommended.

Performance Rating

CDX Tasksheet Number: C652

0	1	2	3	4

Supervisor/instructor signature _____ Date _____

Inspect the condition of refrigerant oil removed from
the system; determine necessary action.

AST
7A7

MAST
7A7

Time off_____

Time on_____

Total time_____

CDX Tasksheet Number: C651

1. Research the procedure for inspecting the condition of the refrigerant oil in the appropriate service information.

   a. **List or print off and attach to this sheet the steps to inspect the refrigerant oil:**

2. Following the specified procedure, inspect the condition of the refrigerant oil. **List your observation(s):**

3. **Determine any necessary action(s):**

4. Have your supervisor/instructor verify satisfactory completion of this procedure, any observations found, and any necessary action(s) recommended.

Performance Rating

CDX Tasksheet Number: C651

0	1	2	3	4

Supervisor/instructor signature _____ Date _____

Determine the need for an additional A/C system filter; perform necessary action.

AST 7B5   **MAST** 7B5

Time off_____

Time on_____

Total time_____

CDX Tasksheet Number: C863

1. Research the conditions that require the need for an additional A/C system filter in the appropriate service information.

    a. List the conditions that require an additional filter(s):

    b. List the specified location(s) for the filter(s):

2. Following the specified procedure, inspect the system to see if an additional filter(s) is (are) needed. **List your observation(s):**

3. **Determine any necessary action(s):**

4. Have your supervisor/instructor verify your observations. **Supervisor's/instructor's initials:** _____

5. **Following the specified procedure, install the additional filter(s), if necessary. List your observation(s):**

6. Have your supervisor/instructor verify satisfactory completion of this procedure, any observations found, and any necessary action(s) recommended.

Performance Rating

CDX Tasksheet Number: C863

0	1	2	3	4

Supervisor/instructor signature _____ Date _____

HVAC: Refrigeration System Component Diagnosis and Repair

Student/intern information:

Name _____ Date _____ Class _____

Vehicle used for this activity:

Year _____ Make _____ Model _____

Odometer _____ VIN _____

Learning Objective/Task	CDX Tasksheet Number	2013 MLR NATEF Reference Number; Priority Level	2013 AST NATEF Reference Number; Priority Level	2013 MAST NATEF Reference Number; Priority Level
• Inspect and replace A/C compressor drive belts, pulleys, and tensioners; determine necessary action.	C653	7B1; P-1	7B1; P-1	7B1; P-1
• Inspect, test, and/or replace A/C compressor clutch components and/or assembly; check compressor clutch air gap; adjust as needed.	C654		7B2; P-2	7B2; P-2
• Remove, inspect, and reinstall A/C compressor and mountings; determine required oil quantity.	C826		7B3; P-2	7B3; P-2
• Remove and inspect A/C system mufflers, hoses, lines, fittings, O-rings, seals, and service valves; perform necessary action.	C355		7B6; P-2	7B6; P-2
• Remove, inspect, and reinstall receiver/drier or accumulator/drier; determine recommended oil quantity.	C829		7B8; P-2	7B8; P-2
• Remove, inspect, and install expansion valve or orifice (expansion) tube.	C873		7B9; P-1	7B9; P-1
• Evacuate and charge A/C system; add refrigerant oil as required.	C658		7E4; P-1	7E4; P-1
• Perform correct use and maintenance of refrigerant handling equipment according to equipment manufacturer's standards.	C656		7E1; P-1	7E1; P-1
• Determine procedure to remove and reinstall evaporator; determine required oil quantity.	C831		7B11; P-2	
• Remove, inspect, and reinstall condenser; determine required oil quantity.	C832			7B13; P-2

Time off_____

Time on_____

Total time_____

Materials Required

- Appropriate air conditioning manifold gauge set including service hoses
- Air conditioning service station and recovery/recycling equipment as necessary
- Refrigerant leak detecting equipment
- Refrigerant identifier
- Appropriate thermometers
- Feeler gauge set
- Clutch removal and installer tools
- Belt tension gauge
- Infrared temperature gun/thermocouple
- Anemometer
- DVOM
- Clean measuring container for refrigerant oil
- Specified refrigerant oil
- Specified vacuum pump oil

Some Safety Issues to Consider

- Refrigerant can cause serious damage if it comes in contact with a person's unprotected skin and eyes.
- When operating, the air conditioning system is normally subject to very high pressure in the system. Extreme caution must be exercised when working on an operating system.
- Extreme caution must be exercised when working around rotating components.
- When running any vehicles in the shop, make sure you use the shop's exhaust ventilation system to discharge all exhaust gas safely outside.
- Diagnosis of this fault may require test-driving the vehicle on the school grounds. Attempt this task only with full permission from your instructor and follow all the guidelines exactly.
- Vehicle hoists are important tools that increase productivity and make the job easier. However, they can also cause severe injury or death if used improperly. Make sure you follow the manufacturer's operation procedures.
- Comply with personal and environmental safety practices associated with clothing; eye protection; hand tools; power equipment; proper ventilation; and the handling, storage, and disposal of chemicals/materials in accordance with local, state, and federal safety and environmental regulations.

Performance Standard

0—No exposure: No information or practice provided during the program; complete training required

1—Exposure only: General information provided with no practice time; close supervision needed; additional training required

2—Limited practice: Has practiced job during training program; additional training required to develop skill

3—Moderately skilled: Has performed job independently during training program; limited additional training may be required

4—Skilled: Can perform job independently with no additional training

Inspect and replace A/C compressor drive belts, pulleys, and tensioners; determine necessary action.

MLR	AST	MAST
7B1	7B1	7B1

Time off_____

Time on_____

Total time_____

CDX Tasksheet Number: C653

1. Research the procedure and specifications to inspect and replace drive belts, pulleys, and tensioners in the appropriate service information.

   a. **List the specified drive belt tension:** _____ **lb/kg**

   b. **List the faults to look for when inspecting drive belts, pulleys, and tensioners:**

   c. **Describe how to check correct pulley and belt alignment:**

   d. **Locate the belt routing diagram, or draw a picture of the current routing arrangement below:**

2. Following the specified procedure, remove the A/C drive belt(s).

3. Inspect vehicle drive belts, pulleys, and tensioners for faults. **List your observations for the following components.**

   a. **Vehicle drive belt(s):**

   b. **Pulleys:**

   c. Tensioner(s):

   d. Pulley/belt alignment:

4. Determine any necessary action(s):

5. Have your supervisor/instructor verify belt removal.

   Supervisor's/instructor's initials: _____

> **NOTE** You may want to continue on to the next task while the belts are removed. If so, return here when you are ready to reinstall the drive belt(s).

6. Following the specified procedure, reinstall the drive belt(s). Be sure to tension them properly.

7. Recheck for correct pulley, tensioner, and belt alignment. List your observation(s):

8. Have your supervisor/instructor verify satisfactory completion of this procedure, any observations found, and any necessary action(s) recommended.

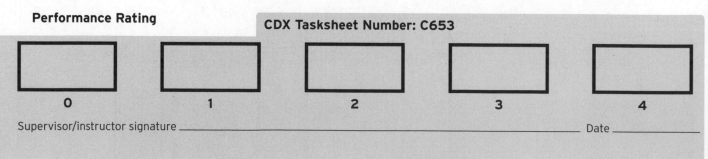

Performance Rating

CDX Tasksheet Number: C653

0	1	2	3	4

Supervisor/instructor signature _____ Date _____

Inspect, test, and/or replace A/C compressor clutch components and /or assembly; check compressor clutch air gap; adjust as needed.

AST
7B2

MAST
7B2

CDX Tasksheet Number: C654

Vehicle used for this activity:

Year _____ Make _____ Model _____

Odometer _____ VIN _____

1. Research the procedure and specifications to inspect, test, and replace the A/C compressor clutch components in the appropriate service information.

   a. **Specified compressor clutch coil resistance:** _____ **ohm**
   b. **Specified compressor clutch air gap:** _____ **in/mm**
   c. **Specified flat rate time to replace the compressor clutch:** _____ **hr**

2. Following the specified procedure, measure the resistance of the compressor clutch coil.

   a. **Measured clutch coil resistance:** _____ **ohm**

3. Following the specified procedure, measure the compressor clutch air gap.

   a. **Measured clutch air gap:** _____ **in/mm**

4. **Determine any necessary action(s):**

5. Have your supervisor/instructor verify your measurements. **Supervisor's/ instructor's initials:** _____

6. If approved by your instructor, remove the A/C compressor clutch components following the specified procedure.

7. Have your supervisor/instructor verify removal of the clutch components. **Supervisor's/instructor's initials:** _____

8. **Following the specified procedure, reinstall the A/C clutch components. Be sure that the air gap is properly adjusted. List your observation(s):**

9. Have your supervisor/instructor verify satisfactory completion of this procedure, any observations found, and any necessary action(s) recommended.

Performance Rating

CDX Tasksheet Number: C654

0	1	2	3	4

Supervisor/instructor signature _____ Date _____

Remove, inspect, and reinstall A/C compressor and mountings; determine required oil quantity.

AST 7B3 | **MAST** 7B3

Time off _____

Time on _____

Total time _____

CDX Tasksheet Number: C826

Vehicle used for this activity:

Year _____ Make _____ Model _____

Odometer _____ VIN _____

1. Research the procedure and specifications to remove, inspect, and reinstall the A/C compressor in the appropriate service information.

   a. **Specified refrigerant oil type:** _____
   b. **Specified refrigerant oil quantity to add during replacement of the compressor:** _____ oz/mL
   c. **List or print off and attach to this sheet the steps to remove, inspect, and reinstall the compressor:**

2. Following the specified procedure, remove the A/C compressor from the vehicle.

3. Following the specified procedure, drain the refrigerant oil from the compressor into a clean measuring container.

   a. **List the quantity of oil drained:** _____ oz/mL

4. Following the specified procedure, inspect the A/C compressor and mountings. **List your observations:**

5. **Determine any necessary action(s):**

6. Have your supervisor/instructor verify removal and your observations. **Supervisor's/instructor's initials:** _____

7. Following the specified procedure, reinstall the A/C compressor. Be sure to add the proper quantity and type of new refrigerant oil.

   a. **List the quantity of oil added to the compressor:** _____ oz/mL

8. Have your supervisor/instructor verify satisfactory completion of this procedure, any observations found, and any necessary action(s) recommended.

Performance Rating

CDX Tasksheet Number: C826

0	1	2	3	4

Supervisor/instructor signature _____ Date _____

Remove and inspect A/C system mufflers, hoses, lines, fittings, O-rings, seals, and service valves; perform necessary action.

AST 7B6 **MAST** 7B6

Time off_____

Time on_____

Total time_____

CDX Tasksheet Number: C355

Vehicle used for this activity:

Year _____ Make _____ Model_____

Odometer_____ VIN_____

1. Research the procedures and specifications for removing and inspecting the above A/C components in the appropriate service information.

   a. **List or print off and attach to this sheet the procedure and specifications for inspecting these components:**

2. Following the specified procedure, remove the following A/C system components. **Inspect each one and list your observations below.**

   a. **Muffler (if equipped):**

   b. **Hoses and lines:**

   c. **Fittings, O-rings, and seals:**

   d. **Service valves:**

3. **Determine any necessary action(s):**

4. Have your supervisor/instructor verify removal and observations. **Supervisor's/instructor's initials:** _____

5. Perform any necessary actions and list your observation(s):

6. Have your supervisor/instructor verify satisfactory completion of this procedure, any observations found, and any necessary action(s) recommended.

Performance Rating

CDX Tasksheet Number: C355

| 0 | 1 | 2 | 3 | 4 |

Supervisor/instructor signature _____ Date _____

Remove, inspect, and reinstall receiver/drier or accumulator/drier; determine recommended oil quantity.

AST 7B8 **MAST** 7B8

CDX Tasksheet Number: C829

Vehicle used for this activity:

Year _____ Make _____ Model_____

Odometer_____ VIN _____

1. Research the procedure and specifications for removing, inspecting, and reinstalling the receiver/drier or accumulator/drier in the appropriate service information.

   a. **Specified refrigerant oil type:** _____

   b. **Specified refrigerant oil quantity to add during replacement of the receiver/drier:** _____ oz/mL

   c. **List or print off and attach to this sheet the steps to remove, inspect, and reinstall the receiver/drier:**

2. Following the specified procedure, remove the receiver/drier or accumulator/drier from the vehicle.

3. Following the specified procedure, drain the refrigerant oil from the receiver/drier or accumulator/drier into a clean measuring container.

   a. **List the quantity of oil drained:** _____ oz/mL

4. Following the specified procedure, inspect the receiver/drier or accumulator/drier. **List your observation(s):**

5. **Determine any necessary action(s):**

6. Have your supervisor/instructor verify removal and your observations. **Supervisor's/instructor's initials:** _____

7. Following the specified procedure, reinstall the receiver/drier or accumulator/drier. Be sure to add the proper quantity and type of new refrigerant oil.

   a. **List the quantity of oil added to the receiver/drier or accumulator/drier:** _____ oz/mL

8. Have your supervisor/instructor verify satisfactory completion of this procedure, any observations found, and any necessary action(s) recommended.

Performance Rating

CDX Tasksheet Number: C829

| 0 | 1 | 2 | 3 | 4 |

Supervisor/instructor signature _____ Date _____

▶ **TASK** Remove, inspect, and install expansion valve or orifice (expansion) tube.

Time off_____

Time on_____

Total time_____

CDX Tasksheet Number: C873

Vehicle used for this activity:

Year _____ Make _____ Model_____

Odometer_____ VIN_____

1. Research the procedure and specifications for removing, inspecting, and installing the expansion valve or orifice tube in the appropriate service information.

   a. **List any precautions for this task:**

   b. **List the specified orifice tube color or expansion valve tonnage:** _____
   c. **Does the manufacturer allow interchange of orifice colors or expansion valve tonnage? Yes:** _____ **No:** _____
   d. **List or print off and attach to this sheet the steps to perform this task:**

2. Following the specified procedure, remove the expansion valve or orifice tube.

   a. **List the orifice tube color or expansion valve tonnage:** _____

3. Inspect the expansion valve or orifice tube for proper operation or debris. **List your observation(s):**

4. **Determine any necessary action(s):**

5. Have your supervisor/instructor verify removal and your observations. **Supervisor's/ instructor's initials:** _____

6. Reinstall the expansion valve or orifice tube. **List your observation(s):**

7. Have your supervisor/instructor verify satisfactory completion of this procedure, any observations found, and any necessary action(s) recommended.

Performance Rating

| 0 | 1 | 2 | 3 | 4 |

Supervisor/instructor signature _____ Date _____

▶ **TASK** Evacuate and charge A/C system; add refrigerant oil as required.

AST **MAST**
7E4 7E4

Time off_____

Time on_____

Total time_____

CDX Tasksheet Number: C658

1. Research the procedure and specifications for evacuating and charging the A/C system in the appropriate service information.

   a. **Specified type of refrigerant:** _____
   b. **Specified capacity of refrigerant:** _____ **lb/kg**
   c. **Specified refrigerant oil:** _____
   d. **Specified refrigerant oil capacity:** _____ **oz/mL**

   > **NOTE** Refrigerant oil capacity is only applicable in case of a system flush.

   e. **If you are recharging the system using the high side service port, list the specified time for the low side pressure to reach specifications:** _____ **seconds**

   > **NOTE** In the absence of a specified time, a good rule of thumb to remember is that the low side pressure should reach 0 psi within 7 seconds if the expansion valve or orifice tube is not restricted.

2. Following the specified procedure, evacuate the A/C system.

   a. **Inches of mercury attained:** _____
   b. **Microns attained:** _____

3. Have your supervisor/instructor verify the reading. Supervisor's/instructor's initials: _____

4. Following the specified procedure, add the refrigerant oil to the system, if needed.

   a. **List the amount of oil you added to the system:** _____ **oz/mL**

5. Following the specified procedure, charge the A/C system.

   a. **List the amount of refrigerant you installed:** _____ **lb/kg**
   b. **Did the low side pressure rise within the specified time?**
      Yes: _____ **No:** _____

6. **Is equalizing the refrigerant hoses necessary? Yes:** _____ **No:** _____

7. Start the engine and operate the A/C system.

8. Is the system operating properly? **List your observations including pressures and temperatures:**

9. **Determine any necessary action(s):**

10. Have your supervisor/instructor verify satisfactory completion of this procedure, any observations found, and any necessary action(s) recommended.

Performance Rating

CDX Tasksheet Number: C658

0	1	2	3	4

Supervisor/instructor signature _____ Date _____

Perform correct use and maintenance of refrigerant handling
equipment according to equipment manufacturer's standards. **AST** 7E1 **MAST** 7E1

CDX Tasksheet Number: C656

Vehicle used for this activity:

Year _____ Make _____ Model _____

Odometer_____ VIN_____

1. Research the operation and maintenance of the refrigerant handling equipment in
   the appropriate operator's manual.

   a. **List the manufacturer of the refrigerant handling equipment:** _____

   b. **List the functions this equipment is capable of performing:**

   c. **List any required maintenance tasks and the service intervals for this
      equipment:**

   d. **List any special precautions when using the refrigerant handling equipment:**

   e. Review the steps to correctly use the refrigerant handling equipment.

   f. **List the current EPA machine standards.**
      i. **For recovery-only machines:**

      ii. **For recycling machines:**

2. Following the specified procedure, demonstrate the correct use of the refrigerant handling equipment.

    a. Recovery

      Amount of refrigerant recovered: _____ **lb/kg**

      Amount of oil recovered, if any: _____ **oz/mL**

    b. Evacuate

      Inches of mercury attained: _____

      Microns attained: _____

    c. Oil inject

      Amount of oil injected: _____ **oz/mL**

    d. Recharge

      Amount of refrigerant charged: _____ **lb/kg**

3. **Determine any necessary action(s):**

4. Have your supervisor/instructor verify the correct use. Supervisor's/instructor's initials**:** _____

5. Following the specified procedure, perform the recommended maintenance on the refrigerant handling equipment.

    a. Test the vacuum pump for proper operation.

      Inches of mercury attained: _____

      Microns attained: _____

    b. Change the vacuum oil.

      Type of oil required: _____

      Quantity of oil required: _____ **oz/mL**

      Condition of oil drained:

    c. Perform a leak test on the machine using specified equipment.

      Equipment used to perform this test:

Results:

    d. **Change the recovery filter.**

       List the filter part number: _____

    e. **Charge the machine with refrigerant.**

       List the quantity charged: _____ **lb/kg**

6. **Determine any necessary action(s):**

7. Have your supervisor/instructor verify satisfactory completion of this procedure, any observations found, and any necessary action(s) recommended.

Performance Rating

0	1	2	3	4

Supervisor/instructor signature _____ Date _____

Determine procedure to remove and reinstall evaporator; determine required oil quantity.

AST
7B11

Time off_____

Time on_____

Total time_____

CDX Tasksheet Number: C831

1. Research the procedure and specifications for removing, inspecting, and reinstalling the evaporator in the appropriate service information.

   a. **Specified refrigerant oil type:** _____

   b. **Specified refrigerant oil quantity to add during replacement of the evaporator:** _____ oz/mL

   c. **Flat rate time to R&R the evaporator:** _____ hr

   d. **List, or print off and attach to this sheet, the steps to remove, inspect, and reinstall the evaporator:**

2. Have your supervisor/instructor verify satisfactory completion of this procedure, any observations found, and any necessary action/s recommended.

Performance Rating

CDX Tasksheet Number: C831

0	1	2	3	4

Supervisor/instructor signature _____ Date _____

Remove, inspect, and reinstall condenser; determine required oil quantity.

MAST
7B13

Time off_____

Time on_____

Total time_____

CDX Tasksheet Number: C832

1. Research the procedure and specifications for removing, inspecting, and reinstalling the condenser in the appropriate service information.

   a. Specified refrigerant oil type: _____

   b. Specified refrigerant oil quantity to add during replacement of the condenser: _____ **oz/mL**

   c. Flat rate time to R&R the condenser: _____ **hr**

   d. List, or print off and attach to this sheet, the steps to remove, inspect, and reinstall the condenser:

2. Before proceeding, have your instructor check your answers and obtain his or her permission to remove the condenser on this vehicle. **Supervisor/instructor's initials:** _____

3. Following the specified procedure, remove the condenser from the vehicle.

4. Following the specified procedure, drain the refrigerant oil from the condenser into a clean measuring container.

   a. List the quantity of oil drained: _____ **oz/mL**

5. Following the specified procedure, inspect the condenser and mountings. **List your observation/s:**

6. **Determine any necessary action/s:**

7. Have your supervisor/instructor verify removal and your observations and initial below. **Supervisor/instructor's initials:** _____

8. Following the specified procedure, reinstall the condenser. Be sure to add the proper quantity and type of new refrigerant oil.

   a. List the quantity of oil added to the condenser: _____ oz/mL

9. Have your supervisor/instructor verify satisfactory completion of this procedure, any observations found, and any necessary action/s recommended.

Performance Rating

CDX Tasksheet Number: C832

0	1	2	3	4

Supervisor/instructor signature _____ Date _____

HVAC: Heating, Ventilation, and Engine Cooling Systems Diagnosis and Repair

Student/intern information:

Name _____ Date _____ Class _____

Vehicle used for this activity:

Year _____ Make _____ Model _____

Odometer _____ VIN _____

Learning Objective/Task	CDX Tasksheet Number	2013 MLR NATEF Reference Number; Priority Level	2013 AST NATEF Reference Number; Priority Level	2013 MAST NATEF Reference Number; Priority Level
• Diagnose temperature control problems in the heater/ventilation system; determine necessary action.	C362			7C3; P-2
• Inspect engine cooling and heater system hoses; perform necessary action.	C364	7C1; P-1	7C1; P-1	7C1; P-1
• Inspect and test heater control valve(s); perform necessary action.	C370		7C2; P-2	7C2; P-2
• Inspect and test A/C-heater blower motors, resistors, switches, relays, wiring, and protection devices; perform necessary action.	C373		7D1; P-1	7D1; P-1
• Determine procedure to remove, inspect, and reinstall heater core.	C864		7C3; P-2	7C4; P-2

Time off_____

Time on_____

Total time_____

Materials Required

- Vehicle or simulator
- Cooling system pressure tester
- Infrared temperature gun
- DVOM
- Drain pan
- Hose slitter

Some Safety Issues to Consider

- Open the radiator cap (or any other part of the cooling system) only with the engine cold. Opening a radiator cap on a warm or hot engine could cause severe burns.
- Electric fans can turn on at any time. Keep hands and fingers away.
- When running any vehicles in the shop, make sure you use the shop's exhaust ventilation system to discharge all exhaust gas safely outside.
- Extreme caution must be exercised when working around rotating components.
- A hose slitter is handy for removing hoses from radiators and heater cores without damaging the metal tubes, but can cut you if not used carefully.

- Refrigerant can cause serious damage if it comes in contact with a person's unprotected skin and eyes.
- When operating, the air conditioning system is normally subject to very high pressure in the system. Extreme caution must be exercised when working on an operating system.
- Comply with personal and environmental safety practices associated with clothing; eye protection; hand tools; power equipment; proper ventilation; and the handling, storage, and disposal of chemicals/materials in accordance with local, state, and federal safety and environmental regulations.

Performance Standard

0—No exposure: No information or practice provided during the program; complete training required

1—Exposure only: General information provided with no practice time; close supervision needed; additional training required

2—Limited practice: Has practiced job during training program; additional training required to develop skill

3—Moderately skilled: Has performed job independently during training program; limited additional training may be required

4—Skilled: Can perform job independently with no additional training

MAST
7C3

Time off_____

Time on_____

Total time_____

CDX Tasksheet Number: C362

1. **List the heater/ventilation-related customer concern:**

2. Research the customer concern in the appropriate service information. **List the possible causes:**

3. Following the specified procedure, diagnose the customer concern. **List your tests and observations:**

4. **List the cause of the customer concern:**

5. **Determine any necessary action(s) to correct the fault:**

6. Have your supervisor/instructor verify satisfactory completion of this procedure, any observations found, and any necessary action(s) recommended.

Performance Rating

CDX Tasksheet Number: C362

0	1	2	3	4

Supervisor/instructor signature _____ Date _____

Inspect engine cooling and heater system hoses; perform necessary action.

MLR 7C1 | **AST** 7C1 | **MAST** 7C1

Time off_____

Time on_____

Total time_____

CDX Tasksheet Number: C364

Vehicle used for this activity:

Year _____ Make _____ Model _____

Odometer _____ VIN _____

1. Research the procedure and specifications for inspecting and replacing cooling system hoses and belts in the appropriate service information.

   a. **Specified change interval for radiator hoses:** _____ miles/months
   b. **Specified change interval for heater hoses:** _____ miles/months
   c. **Describe what to look for when inspecting cooling system hoses:**

2. Inspect the cooling and heater system hoses. **List your observations:**

3. Using a cooling system pressure tester, pressurize the cooling system to the specified radiator cap pressure. Inspect the cooling system for leaks. **List your observations:**

4. Have your supervisor/instructor verify your observations. **Supervisor's/instructor's initials:** _____

5. **Perform any necessary actions and list your observation(s):**

6. Have your supervisor/instructor verify satisfactory completion of this procedure, any observations found, and any necessary action(s) recommended.

Performance Rating

CDX Tasksheet Number: C364

0	1	2	3	4

Supervisor/instructor signature _____ Date _____

Inspect and test heater control valve(s); perform necessary action.

AST 7C2 **MAST** 7C2

CDX Tasksheet Number: C370

Vehicle used for this activity:

Year _____ Make _____ Model_____

Odometer_____ VIN_____

1. Research the procedure and specifications for inspecting and testing the heater control valve(s) in the appropriate service information.

   a. **Specified type of heater control valve(s): Cable: _____ Vacuum: _____ Electric: _____**

   b. **What does the temperature adjusting mechanism regulate? Coolant: _____ Air: _____**

2. Following the specified procedure, inspect and test the heater control valve(s). **List your tests and observation(s):**

3. **Determine any necessary action(s):**

4. Have your supervisor/instructor verify satisfactory completion of this procedure, any observations found, and any necessary action(s) recommended.

Performance Rating

CDX Tasksheet Number: C370

0	1	2	3	4

Supervisor/instructor signature _____ Date _____

Inspect and test A/C-heater blower, motors, resistors, switches, relays, wiring, and protection devices; perform necessary action.

Time off_____

Time on_____

Total time_____

CDX Tasksheet Number: C373

Vehicle used for this activity:

Year _____ Make _____ Model_____

Odometer_____ VIN_____

1. Research the procedure and specifications to inspect and test the electrical components of the A/C system in the appropriate service information.

    a. **Specified resistance of the blower motor:** _____ ohms

    b. **Specified resistance of the blower motor resistors**

    Resistance on the highest resisted speed: _____ ohm

    Resistance on medium-high resisted speed: _____ ohm

    Resistance on medium-low resisted speed: _____ ohm

    Resistance on the lowest resisted speed: _____ ohm

    c. **List all the protection devices for the blower motor circuit:**

2. Following the specified procedure, inspect and test the following devices. **List your observations below.**

    a. **Blower motor:**

    b. **Blower motor resistors:**

    c. **Appropriate switches:**

    d. **Appropriate relays:**

    e. Appropriate circuit protection devices:

    f. Appropriate wiring harness:

3. Determine any necessary action(s):

4. Have your supervisor/instructor verify satisfactory completion of this procedure, any observations found, and any necessary action(s) recommended.

Performance Rating

CDX Tasksheet Number: C373

0	1	2	3	4

Supervisor/instructor signature _____ Date _____

AST 7C3 **MAST** 7C4

Time off_____

Time on_____

Total time_____

CDX Tasksheet Number: C864

Vehicle used for this activity:

Year _____ Make _____ Model_____

Odometer_____ VIN_____

1. Research the procedure and specifications for inspecting and replacing the heater core in the appropriate service information.

   a. **List the flat rate time for removing and replacing the heater core:** _____ hr

   b. **Does this task require evacuation of the A/C refrigerant? Yes** _____ **No** _____

   c. **List, or print off and attach to this sheet, the steps to remove and replace the heater core:**

2. **List, or print off and attach to this sheet, the steps to inspect the heater core:**

3. Have your supervisor/instructor verify satisfactory completion of this procedure, any observations found, and any necessary action/s recommended.

Performance Rating

CDX Tasksheet Number: C864

0	1	2	3	4

Supervisor/instructor signature _____ Date _____

HVAC: Operating Systems and Related Controls Diagnosis and Repair

Student/intern information:

Name _____ Date _____ Class _____

Vehicle used for this activity:

Year _____ Make _____ Model _____

Odometer _____ VIN _____

Learning Objective/Task	CDX Tasksheet Number	2013 MLR NATEF Reference Number; Priority Level	2013 AST NATEF Reference Number; Priority Level	2013 MAST NATEF Reference Number; Priority Level
• Check operation of automatic or semi-automatic heating, ventilation, and A/C (HVAC) control systems; determine necessary action.	C866		7D8; P-2	7D8; P-2
• Using a scan tool, observe and record related HVAC data and trouble codes.	C566		7A9; P-3	7A9; P-3
• Diagnose A/C system conditions that cause the protection devices (pressure, thermal, and PCM) to interrupt system operation; determine necessary action.	C350			7B11; P-2
• Diagnose A/C compressor clutch control systems; determine necessary action.	C374		7D2; P-2	7D2; P-2
• Diagnose malfunctions in the vacuum, mechanical, and electrical components and controls of the heating, ventilation, and A/C (HVAC) system; determine necessary action.	C835		7D3; P-2	7D3; P-2
• Inspect and test A/C-heater control panel assembly; determine necessary action.	C376		7D4; P-3	7D4; P-3
• Inspect and test A/C-heater control cables, motors, and linkages; perform necessary action.	C865		7D5; P-3	7D5; P-3
• Inspect A/C-heater ducts, doors, hoses, cabin filters, and outlets; perform necessary action.	C378	7D1; P-1	7D6; P-3	7D6; P-3

Time off_____

Time on_____

Total time_____

- Appropriate air conditioning manifold gauge set including service hoses
- Air conditioning service station and recovery/recycling equipment as necessary
- Refrigerant leak detecting equipment
- Refrigerant identifier
- Appropriate thermometers
- Infrared temperature gun/thermocouple
- DVOM
- Hand vacuum pump

Some Safety Issues to Consider

- Refrigerant can cause serious damage if it comes in contact with a person's unprotected skin and eyes.
- When operating, the air conditioning system is normally subject to very high pressure in the system. Extreme caution must be exercised when working on an operating system.
- Extreme caution must be exercised when working around rotating components.
- When running any vehicles in the shop, make sure you use the shop's exhaust ventilation system to discharge all exhaust gas safely outside.
- Diagnosis of this fault may require test-driving the vehicle on the school grounds. Attempt this task only with full permission from your instructor and follow all the guidelines exactly.
- Comply with personal and environmental safety practices associated with clothing; eye protection; hand tools; power equipment; proper ventilation; and the handling, storage, and disposal of chemicals/materials in accordance with local, state, and federal safety and environmental regulations.

Performance Standard

0—No exposure: No information or practice provided during the program; complete training required

1—Exposure only: General information provided with no practice time; close supervision needed; additional training required

2—Limited practice: Has practiced job during training program; additional training required to develop skill

3—Moderately skilled: Has performed job independently during training program; limited additional training may be required

4—Skilled: Can perform job independently with no additional training

Check operation of automatic or semi-automatic heating, ventilation, and A/C (HVAC) control systems; determine necessary action.

AST **MAST**
7D8   7D8

Time off_____

Time on_____

Total time_____

CDX Tasksheet Number: C866

Vehicle used for this activity:

Year _____ Make _____ Model_____

Odometer_____ VIN_____

1. Research the description and operation of the HVAC climate control system in the appropriate service information.

   a. **Is this system a full-authority climate control system? Yes:** _____
      No: _____

   b. **If equipped, how do you test the evaporator thermistors?**

   c. **If equipped, how do you test the three-wire A/C pressure sensors?**

   d. **If equipped, how do you access the trouble codes on this vehicle?**

   e. **How is the heater controlled? Heater control valve:** _____
      Blend door: _____

   f. **Research the steps to test the operation of the climate control system:**

2. Following the specified procedure, test the operation of the climate control system.
   List your steps and the results:

3. **Determine any necessary action(s):**

4. Have your supervisor/instructor verify satisfactory completion of this procedure, any observations found, and any necessary action(s) recommended.

Performance Rating

0	1	2	3	4

Supervisor/instructor signature _____ Date _____

Using a scan tool, observe and record related HVAC data and trouble codes.

AST 7A9   **MAST** 7A9

Time off_____

Time on_____

CDX Tasksheet Number: C566

Vehicle used for this activity:

Year _____ Make _____ Model_____

Odometer_____ VIN_____

Total time_____

1. **List the HVAC-related customer concern:**

2. Start the vehicle and operate the A/C system to verify the concern. **List your observation(s):**

3. **Following the specified procedure, connect a scan tool to the vehicle. Obtain and record the following information.**

   a. **HVAC-related trouble code(s) and their description(s):**

   b. **HVAC-related data (list at least three readings and their descriptions):**

4. Have your supervisor/instructor verify satisfactory completion of this procedure, any observations found, and any necessary action(s) recommended.

Performance Rating

CDX Tasksheet Number: C566

0	1	2	3	4

Supervisor/instructor signature _____ Date _____

Diagnose A/C system conditions that cause the protection devices (pressure, thermal, and PCM) to interrupt system operation; determine necessary action.

MAST
7B11

CDX Tasksheet Number: C350

1. **List the A/C system protection device-related customer concern:**

2. Research the possible cause(s) and testing procedures in the appropriate service information.

   a. **List any possible cause(s):**

   b. **List or print off and attach to this sheet the steps for identifying the cause of the concern:**

3. **Following the specified procedure, identify the cause of the concern. List your test(s) and results:**

4. **List the cause of the concern:**

5. **Determine any necessary action(s) to correct the fault:**

6. Have your supervisor/instructor verify satisfactory completion of this procedure, any observations found, and any necessary action(s) recommended.

Performance Rating

CDX Tasksheet Number: C350

0	1	2	3	4

Supervisor/instructor signature _____ Date _____

Diagnose A/C compressor clutch control systems; determine necessary action.

AST 7D2   **MAST** 7D2

Time off_____

Time on_____

Total time_____

CDX Tasksheet Number: C374

Vehicle used for this activity:

Year _____ Make _____ Model _____

Odometer _____ VIN _____

1. Research the procedure and specifications to inspect and test the electrical components of the A/C compressor clutch control system in the appropriate service information.

   a. **Specified resistance of the clutch winding:** _____ **ohms**

   b. **A/C cycling switch specifications (if equipped)**

      Off pressure: _____ **psi/kPa**

      On pressure: _____ **psi/kPa**

   c. **A/C thermoswitch specifications (if equipped)**

      Off temperature: _____ **°F/°C**

      On temperature: _____ **°F/°C**

   d. **A/C duct temperature specifications:** _____ **°F/°C**

   e. **A/C high-pressure cut-out switch specifications**

      Off pressure: _____ **psi/kPa**

      On pressure: _____ **psi/kPa**

   f. **A/C low pressure cut-out switch (non-cycling) (if equipped)**

      Off pressure: _____ **psi/kPa**

      On pressure: _____ **psi/kPa**

   g. **A/C compressor clutch relay specifications (if equipped)**

      Relay winding resistance: _____ **ohm**

      Maximum allowable voltage drop across relay contacts: _____ **volt**

   h. **List all the fuses and/or fusible links for the A/C compressor clutch circuit:**

   i. **Does the compressor clutch share a fuse with the blower circuit?**
      Yes: _____ **No:** _____

2. Following the specified procedure, activate the A/C system.

   a. **Does the compressor clutch engage?** **Yes:** _____ **No:** _____

   b. **If yes, continue on to step 3. If no, skip to step 5.**

   _____

3. List your observations below.

   a. **A/C cycling switch readings (if equipped)**

      Off pressure: _____ **psi/kPa**

      On pressure: _____ **psi/kPa**

b. **A/C thermoswitch readings (if equipped)**

Off temperature: _____ °F/°C

On temperature: _____ °F/°C

c. **A/C duct temperature:** _____ °F/°C

d. A/C high pressure cut-out switch readings (may require condenser airflow blockage to test). **(DUE TO THE SAFETY IMPLICATIONS, ONLY PERFORM THIS TEST IF APPROVED BY YOUR SUPERVISOR/INSTRUCTOR)**

Off pressure: _____ psi/kPa

On pressure: _____ psi/kPa

e. **Determine any necessary action(s):**

4. Have your supervisor/instructor verify the readings. Supervisor's/instructor's initials: _____

> **NOTE** If your instructor signed off on this step, skip to the final check off.

5. If the clutch does not engage, install a gauge set and check for minimum refrigerant pressure. If pressure is insufficient, check for refrigerant leaks, then retest after repair. If pressure is sufficient, measure the voltage applied to the compressor clutch winding.

a. **Applied voltage to the compressor clutch:** _____ volt

b. **Compressor clutch winding resistance:** _____ ohm

c. **A/C compressor clutch relay readings**

Relay winding resistance: _____ ohm

Voltage at the relay contact input terminal: _____ volt

Voltage drop across relay contacts (A/C on): _____ volt

d. **Describe the circuit protection device(s) condition:**

6. **Determine any necessary action(s):**

> **NOTE** If repairs are made, return to step 3 and retest.

7. Have your supervisor/instructor verify satisfactory completion of this procedure, any observations found, and any necessary action(s) recommended.

Performance Rating

| 0 | 1 | 2 | 3 | 4 |

Supervisor/instructor signature _____ Date _____

Diagnose malfunctions in the vacuum, mechanical, and electrical
components and controls of the heating, ventilation, and
A/C (HVAC) system; determine necessary action.

Time off_____

Time on_____

Total time_____

CDX Tasksheet Number: C835

Vehicle used for this activity:

Year _____ Make _____ Model_____

Odometer_____ VIN_____

1. **List the vacuum, mechanical, or electrical controls-related HVAC customer concern:**

2. **Verify the concern by operating each of the HVAC vacuum, mechanical, and electrical controls through their range and list your observation(s):**

3. Research the procedure, specifications, and wiring diagrams for diagnosing the concern in the appropriate service information.

   a. **List the possible faults:**

   b. **List or print off and attach to this sheet the steps to diagnose the fault:**

4. **Following the specified procedure, diagnose the concern. List your tests and the results:**

5. List the cause of the concern:

6. Determine any necessary action(s) to correct the fault:

7. Have your supervisor/instructor verify satisfactory completion of this procedure, any observations found, and any necessary action(s) recommended.

Performance Rating

CDX Tasksheet Number: C835

0	1	2	3	4

Supervisor/instructor signature _____ Date _____

▶ **TASK** Inspect and test A/C-heater control panel assembly; determine necessary action.

CDX Tasksheet Number: C376

AST 7D4   **MAST** 7D4

Time off_____

Time on_____

Total time_____

Vehicle used for this activity:

Year _____ Make _____ Model_____

Odometer_____ VIN_____

1. **List the A/C-heater control panel-related HVAC customer concern:**

2. **Verify the concern by operating each of the control panel controls through their range and list your observation(s):**

3. Research the procedure and specifications for inspecting and testing the A/C-heater control panel in the appropriate service information.

   a. **What kind of controls is this vehicle equipped with?**_____
   _____

   b. **List or print off and attach to this sheet the steps to inspect and test the control panel:**

4. **Following the specified procedure, inspect and test the control panel. List your tests and results:**

5. List the cause of the concern:

6. Determine any necessary action(s) to correct the fault:

7. Have your supervisor/instructor verify satisfactory completion of this procedure, any observations found, and any necessary action(s) recommended.

Performance Rating

CDX Tasksheet Number: C376

0	1	2	3	4

Supervisor/instructor signature _____ Date _____

Inspect and test A/C-heater control cables, motors, and linkages; perform necessary action.

AST 7D5 | **MAST** 7D5

Time off_____

Time on_____

Total time_____

CDX Tasksheet Number: C865

Vehicle used for this activity:

Year _____ Make _____ Model_____

Odometer_____ VIN_____

1. Research the procedures and specifications to inspect and test the control cables, motors, and linkages in the appropriate service information.

    a. **List any precautions for this task:**

    b. **List or print off and attach to this sheet any procedures and specifications for this task:**

2. Verify the operation of all A/C control cables, motors, and linkages. **List your observation(s):**

3. Following the specified procedure, inspect and test the cables, motors, and linkages. **List your tests and results:**

4. **Determine any necessary action(s):**

5. Have your supervisor/instructor verify satisfactory completion of this procedure, any observations found, and any necessary action(s) recommended.

Performance Rating

CDX Tasksheet Number: C865

0	1	2	3	4

Supervisor/instructor signature _____ Date _____

Inspect A/C-heater ducts, doors, hoses, cabin filters, and outlets; perform necessary action.

MLR 7D1 **AST** 7D6 **MAST** 7D6

Time off_____

Time on_____

Total time_____

CDX Tasksheet Number: C378

Vehicle used for this activity:

Year _____ Make _____ Model_____

Odometer_____ VIN_____

1. Research the procedure and specifications for inspecting the above components in the appropriate service information.

    a. **Is this vehicle equipped with a cabin air filter? Yes: _____ No: _____**
    b. **What is the recommended replacement interval for the cabin air filter?**
    _____ **mi/km/mo**

2. Following the specified procedure, inspect the following components.
   List your observations below.

    a. **Ducts:**

    b. **Doors:**

    c. **Hoses:**

    d. **Cabin filter(s):**

    e. Outlets:

3. Determine any necessary action(s):

4. Have your supervisor/instructor verify satisfactory completion of this procedure, any observations found, and any necessary action(s) recommended.

Performance Rating

0	1	2	3	4

Supervisor/instructor signature _____ Date _____

Section A8:
Engine Performance

CONTENTS

Engine Performance: Vehicle, Customer, and Service Information

Student/intern information:

Name _____ Date _____ Class _____

Vehicle used for this activity:

Year _____ Make _____ Model _____

Odometer _____ VIN _____

Learning Objective/Task	CDX Tasksheet Number	2013 MLR NATEF Reference Number; Priority Level	2013 AST NATEF Reference Number; Priority Level	2013 MAST NATEF Reference Number; Priority Level
• Research applicable vehicle and service information, vehicle service history, service precautions, and technical service bulletins.	C387	8A1; P-1	8A2; P-1	8A2; P-1
• Demonstrate use of 3 Cs (concern, cause, and correction).	NN08	N/A	N/A	N/A
• Identify and interpret engine performance concern; determine necessary action.	C386		8A1; P-1	8A1, P-1

Time off _____

Time on _____

Total time _____

Materials Required

- Blank work order
- Vehicle with available service history records
- Depending on the type of concern, special diagnostic tools may be required. See your supervisor/instructor for instructions to identify what tools may be required.

Some Safety Issues to Consider

- Diagnosis of this fault may require test-driving the vehicle on the school grounds or on a hoist, both of which carry severe risks. Attempt this task only with full permission from your supervisor/instructor and follow all the guidelines exactly.
- When running any vehicles in the shop, make sure you use the shop's exhaust ventilation system to discharge all exhaust gas safely outside.
- Because the vehicle will be running for an extended amount of time, make sure the vehicle cannot move or roll by applying the parking brake and using wheel chocks.
- You will be working under the hood of a running vehicle. Keep your hands and fingers away from moving belts, fans, and other parts.

- This task may require working with liquid fuel. Prevent serious burns or fires by keeping open flame or any other source of ignition far away.
- Comply with personal and environmental safety practices associated with clothing; eye protection; hand tools; power equipment; proper ventilation; and the handling, storage, and disposal of chemicals/materials in accordance with local, state, and federal safety and environmental regulations.

Performance Standard

0—No exposure: No information or practice provided during the program; complete training required

1—Exposure only: General information provided with no practice time; close supervision needed; additional training required

2—Limited practice: Has practiced job during training program; additional training required to develop skill

3—Moderately skilled: Has performed job independently during training program; limited additional training may be required

4—Skilled: Can perform job independently with no additional training

Research applicable vehicle and service information, vehicle service history, service precautions, and technical service bulletins.

MLR	AST	MAST
8A1	8A2	8A2

Time off_____

Time on_____

Total time_____

CDX Tasksheet Number: C387

1. Using the VIN for identification, use the appropriate source to access the vehicle's service history in relation to prior related engine management work or customer concerns.

   a. **List any related repairs/concerns, and their dates:**

2. Using the VIN for identification, access any relevant technical service bulletins for the particular vehicle you are working on in relation to engine management updates or other service issues.

   a. **List any related service bulletins (bulletin number and title):**

3. Have your supervisor/instructor verify satisfactory completion of this procedure, any observations found, and any necessary action(s) recommended.

Performance Rating

CDX Tasksheet Number: C387

0	1	2	3	4

Supervisor/instructor signature _____ Date _____

▶ **TASK** Demonstrate use of 3 Cs (concern, cause, and correction).

Additional Task

Time off_____

Time on_____

Total time_____

CDX Tasksheet Number: NN08

1. Using the following scenario, write up the 3 Cs as listed on most repair orders. Assume that the customer authorized the recommended repairs.

   A vehicle has been brought to your shop with an engine performance/driveability concern. The customer tells you that the vehicle used to run rough only when accelerating up a hill but now it is running rough when accelerating even lightly. The MIL light also blinks when the engine is running rough. The customer thought it was bad gas, but after that tank ran out, the customer refilled it with good gas from a very reputable station and it still runs rough even after using half a tank. The customer authorizes your shop to perform a diagnosis and you find the following:

   a. P0305—Engine misfire on cylinder #5.
   b. #5 spark plug boot is leaking high voltage to the cylinder head under light load.
   c. All of the spark plugs are moderately worn.
   d. All of the spark plug wires are original. The vehicle is about 8 years old and has nearly 100,000 miles on it.
   e. Cylinder relative compression is within specifications.
   f. The air filter is dirty.
   g. The oil change is almost 1000 miles and 2 months overdue.
   h. The oil seals and gaskets look to be in good shape with no leaks.
   i. The water pump seal is starting to seep coolant and the coolant is a bit dirty.
   j. The belts look like they have been replaced recently.

   > **NOTE** Ask your instructor whether you should use a copy of the shop repair order or the 3Cs below to record this information.

2. **Concern/complaint:**

3. **Cause:**

4. **Correction:**

5. Other recommended service:

6. Have your supervisor/instructor verify satisfactory completion of this procedure, any observations found, and any necessary action(s) recommended.

Performance Rating

CDX Tasksheet Number: NN08

0	1	2	3	4

Supervisor/instructor signature _____ Date _____

Identify and interpret engine performance concern;
determine necessary action.

AST 8A1   **MAST** 8A1

Time off_____

Time on_____

Total time_____

CDX Tasksheet Number: C386

1. **List the customer concern:**

2. Research the particular concern in the appropriate service information.

    a. **List the possible causes:**

3. Inspect the engine and management system to determine the cause of the concern.

    a. **List the steps you took to determine the fault and the result for each step:**

4. **List the cause of the concern/complaint:**

5. **List the necessary action(s) to correct this fault:**

6. Have your supervisor/instructor verify satisfactory completion of this procedure, any observations found, and any necessary action(s) recommended.

Performance Rating

CDX Tasksheet Number: C386

0	1	2	3	4

Supervisor/instructor signature _____ Date _____

Engine Performance: Mechanical Engine Testing

Student/intern information:

Name _____ Date _____ Class _____

Vehicle used for this activity:

Year _____ Make _____ Model _____

Odometer _____ VIN _____

Learning Objective/Task	CDX Tasksheet Number	2013 MLR NATEF Reference Number; Priority Level	2013 AST NATEF Reference Number; Priority Level	2013 MAST NATEF Reference Number; Priority Level
• Perform cranking sound diagnosis.	NN09	N/A	N/A	N/A
• Perform engine absolute (vacuum/boost) manifold pressure tests; determine necessary action.	C392	8A2; P-1	8A5; P-1	8A5; P-1
• Perform cylinder power balance test; determine necessary action.	C393	8A3; P-1	8A6; P-2	8A6; P-2
• Perform cylinder cranking and running compression tests; determine necessary action.	C709	8A4; P-1	8A7; P-1	8A7; P-1
• Perform cylinder leakage test; determine necessary action.	C395	8A5; P-1	8A8; P-1	8A8; P-1
• Diagnose abnormal engine noise or vibration concerns; determine necessary action.	C390		8A3; P-3	8A3; P-3

Time off_____

Time on_____

Total time_____

Materials Required
- Vehicle or simulator
- Vacuum gauge
- Tachometer (handheld if vehicle is not equipped with an in-dash tachometer)
- Appropriate tool to disable cylinders (scan tool, insulated pliers, etc.)
- Compression tester
- Cylinder leakage tester

Some Safety Issues to Consider
- You will be working under the hood of a running vehicle. Keep your hands and fingers away from moving belts, fans, and other parts.
- Be sure to only disconnect the proper vacuum hose. Many other hoses look alike but could carry gasoline or hot coolant under high pressure.
- During this test, you may be disabling the ignition or fuel systems. Be sure you do so only for the minimum amount of time to get your readings. Operating the engine with cylinders disabled may lead to damage of the catalytic converter or other parts if done for more than a minimum amount of time. If in doubt, ask your supervisor/instructor.

- If you disable the cylinders by disconnecting the spark plug wires, you may expose yourself to extremely high voltage (up to 100,000 volts). Reduce the possibility of electrical shock by using appropriate insulated spark plug wire pliers.
- When running any vehicles in the shop, make sure you use the shop's exhaust ventilation system to discharge all exhaust gas safely outside.
- Always follow your supervisor's/instructor's directions on how to get the piston to top dead center. Failure to do so could cause injury or damage to the vehicle.
- Use caution when turning the engine to top dead center. If you do this by hand, be sure that your fingers, hands, etc. stay clear of belts and pulleys that could cause severe pinching.
- Make sure the ignition switch is in the "off" position and the key is removed from the ignition switch during this job to prevent someone from inadvertently cranking the engine over while you are working on it.
- Comply with personal and environmental safety practices associated with clothing; eye protection; hand tools; power equipment; proper ventilation; and the handling, storage, and disposal of chemicals/materials in accordance with local, state, and federal safety and environmental regulations.

Performance Standard

0—No exposure: No information or practice provided during the program; complete training required

1—Exposure only: General information provided with no practice time; close supervision needed; additional training required

2—Limited practice: Has practiced job during training program; additional training required to develop skill

3—Moderately skilled: Has performed job independently during training program; limited additional training may be required

4—Skilled: Can perform job independently with no additional training

Time off_____

Time on_____

Total time_____

CDX Tasksheet Number: NN09

1. Disable the ignition or fuel system so that the engine will crank, but not start.

> **NOTE** Some vehicles can be put into "clear flood" mode by depressing the throttle to the floor before turning the ignition key to the "run" position. This prevents the fuel injectors from being activated. If your vehicle is equipped with this mode, hold the throttle down to the floor and try cranking the engine over (make sure you are prepared to turn off the ignition switch if the engine starts). You can also disable the engine by disconnecting the fuel injectors or ignition coils.

2. Crank the engine over for approximately 5 seconds and listen to the cranking sound.

> **NOTE** The engine should crank over at a normal speed. Too fast could mean low compression caused by bent valves or a slipped timing belt or chain. Too slow could mean a seized piston or bearing, or a faulty starting system. An uneven cranking sound may indicate grossly uneven compression pressures in the cylinders.

3. **List your observation(s):**

4. **Determine any necessary action(s):**

5. Have your supervisor/instructor verify satisfactory completion of this procedure, any observations found, and any necessary action(s) recommended.

© 2015 Jones & Bartlett Learning, LLC, an Ascend Learning Company

Performance Rating

CDX Tasksheet Number: NN09

0	1	2	3	4

Supervisor/instructor signature _____ Date _____

Perform engine absolute (vacuum/boost) manifold pressure tests; determine necessary action.

MLR 8A2 | **AST** 8A5 | **MAST** 8A5

Time off_____

Time on_____

Total time_____

CDX Tasksheet Number: C392

1. Find an appropriate vacuum hose to connect into.

> **NOTE** Make sure it is connected to the intake manifold vacuum and that you are not disconnecting anything that will affect the operation of the engine. If possible, use a vacuum tee, which will allow you to take the reading *and* still allow the vacuum to get to its intended device.

2. Running vacuum test

    a. Describe the purpose of this test, the components or functions that this test checks, and what the results might indicate:

    b. Start the engine and allow it to idle. Note the vacuum reading: _____
       i. Is the vacuum gauge needle relatively steady?
       Yes: _____ **No:** _____

    c. Carefully raise the engine RPM to 2000 RPM and note the vacuum reading: _____

    d. Determine any necessary action(s):

3. Have your supervisor/instructor verify satisfactory completion of this procedure, any observations found, and any necessary action(s) recommended.

Performance Rating

CDX Tasksheet Number: C392

0	1	2	3	4
□	□	□	□	□

Supervisor/instructor signature _____ Date _____

▶ TASK Perform cylinder power balance test; determine necessary action.

MLR	AST	MAST
8A3	8A6	8A6

Time off_____

Time on_____

Total time_____

CDX Tasksheet Number: C393

1. Research the best option for disabling the cylinders on this vehicle in the appropriate service information. The following list contains the most common methods. Indicate the method you are going to use.

    a. Disconnect the individual spark plug wires or ignition coils. _____

    b. Disconnect the individual fuel injectors (multi-port fuel injection only). _____

    c. Diagnostic scope to disable cylinders through the ignition primary circuit. _____

    d. Scan tool on vehicles with power balance capabilities. _____

    e. Vacuum hose and test light (option for waste spark ignition systems). _____

2. Determine from the service information whether this vehicle has an idle control system. **If it does, list how to best disable it during this test:**

3. Have your supervisor/instructor check the above answers. **Supervisor/instructor initials:** _____

4. If this vehicle is equipped with an idle control system, disable it and set the idle speed to an appropriate RPM.

    a. **List that RPM here:** _____ **RPM**

5. Disable cylinders one at a time and record the RPM drop (not the RPM) of each cylinder.

    a. **RPM drop:** _____ _____ _____ _____ _____ _____ _____ _____

6. **Determine any necessary action(s):**

7. Have your supervisor/instructor verify satisfactory completion of this procedure, any observations found, and any necessary action(s) recommended.

Performance Rating

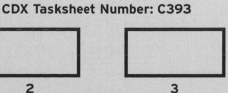

CDX Tasksheet Number: C393

0	1	2	3	4

Supervisor/instructor signature _____ Date _____

© 2015 Jones & Bartlett Learning, LLC, an Ascend Learning Company

► **TASK** Perform cylinder cranking and running compression tests; determine necessary action.

MLR 8A4 **AST** 8A7 **MAST** 8A7

Time off_____

Time on_____

Total time_____

CDX Tasksheet Number: C709

1. Research the procedure and specifications for performing both a cranking compression test and a running compression test on this vehicle in the appropriate service information.

    a. **List the conditions that must be met for the tests to be accurate (you may paraphrase):**

2. Specifications

    a. **Minimum compression pressure: _____ psi/kpa**
    b. **Maximum variation: _____ %**

3. Cranking compression test

    a. **Perform the cranking compression test following the specified procedure. The first column is a standard test. The second column is a wet test using a small amount of clean engine oil. List the readings obtained for each cylinder:**

Cylinder	Standard Test	Wet Test
1	psi / kPa (Circle one)	psi / kPa (Circle one)
2	psi / kPa (Circle one)	psi / kPa (Circle one)
3	psi / kPa (Circle one)	psi / kPa (Circle one)
4	psi / kPa (Circle one)	psi / kPa (Circle one)
5	psi / kPa (Circle one)	psi / kPa (Circle one)
6	psi / kPa (Circle one)	psi / kPa (Circle one)
7	psi / kPa (Circle one)	psi / kPa (Circle one)
8	psi / kPa (Circle one)	psi / kPa (Circle one)

    b. **Calculate the difference between the highest and lowest cylinders (dry test): _____ %**

4. Running compression test. **Caution:** Make sure your assistant is ready to turn off the ignition if the throttle sticks during each snap throttle test.

    a. **Perform the running compression test following the specified procedure. List the readings obtained for each cylinder:**

Cylinder	Idle	Snap Throttle
1	psi / kPa (Circle one)	psi / kPa (Circle one)
2	psi / kPa (Circle one)	psi / kPa (Circle one)
3	psi / kPa (Circle one)	psi / kPa (Circle one)
4	psi / kPa (Circle one)	psi / kPa (Circle one)
5	psi / kPa (Circle one)	psi / kPa (Circle one)
6	psi / kPa (Circle one)	psi / kPa (Circle one)

Cylinder	Idle	Snap Throttle
7	psi / kPa (Circle one)	psi / kPa (Circle one)
8	psi / kPa (Circle one)	psi / kPa (Circle one)

5. Determine necessary action(s):

6. Have your supervisor/instructor verify satisfactory completion of this procedure, any observations found, and any necessary action(s) recommended.

Performance Rating

CDX Tasksheet Number: C709

0	1	2	3	4

Supervisor/instructor signature _____ Date _____

CDX Tasksheet Number: C395

1. **List all of the possible places where compression can leak out of a cylinder:**

2. Remove the appropriate spark plugs to test one cylinder (the cylinder being tested and the adjacent plugs).

3. **Bring that piston up to top dead center on the compression stroke and install the cylinder leakage tester. List the reading you obtain.**

   a. **Cylinder #:** _____
   b. **Cylinder leakage:** _____ %
   c. **Leaking from:** _____

4. Perform this test on one other cylinder. List the reading you obtain. Before removing the cylinder leakage tester, call your instructor over to verify the reading.

   a. **Cylinder #:** _____
   b. **Cylinder leakage:** _____ %
   c. **Leaking from:** _____

5. **Determine necessary action(s):**

6. Have your supervisor/instructor verify satisfactory completion of this procedure, any observations found, and any necessary action(s) recommended.

Performance Rating

CDX Tasksheet Number: C395

0	1	2	3	4

Supervisor/instructor signature _____ Date _____

AST 8A3 | **MAST** 8A3

Time off_____

Time on_____

CDX Tasksheet Number: C390

Total time_____

1. Ask your instructor to assign you a vehicle with an engine noise or vibration concern. **List the customer concern:**

2. Research possible causes of the concern for this vehicle in the appropriate service information.

   a. **List any possible causes:**

   b. **List any specified tests to pinpoint the problem:**

3. With your supervisor's/instructor's permission, operate the vehicle to verify the concern. **List your observations:**

4. Follow the service manual procedure to diagnose the concern. **List your tests and results here:**

5. **Determine necessary action(s):**

6. Have your supervisor/instructor verify satisfactory completion of this procedure, any observations found, and any necessary action(s) recommended.

Performance Rating

CDX Tasksheet Number: C390

0	1	2	3	4

Supervisor/instructor signature _____ Date _____

Engine Performance: Camshaft Timing

Student/intern information:

Name _____ Date _____ Class _____

Vehicle used for this activity:

Year _____ Make _____ Model _____

Odometer _____ VIN _____

Learning Objective/Task	CDX Tasksheet Number	2013 MLR NATEF Reference Number; Priority Level	2013 AST NATEF Reference Number; Priority Level	2013 MAST NATEF Reference Number; Priority Level
• Verify correct camshaft timing.	C400		8A11; P-1	8A11; P-1

Time off _____

Time on _____

Total time _____

Materials Required

- Vehicle or simulator
- Possible need of specialized tools such as a scan tool, etc.

Some Safety Issues to Consider

- Because the vehicle will be running for an extended amount of time, make sure the vehicle cannot move or roll by applying the parking brake and using wheel chocks.
- You will be working under the hood of a running vehicle. Keep your hands and fingers away from moving belts, fans, and other parts.
- Do not rotate the crankshaft or camshaft if the timing belt is removed. Moving the cam or the crank could cause valve or piston damage.
- Comply with personal and environmental safety practices associated with clothing; eye protection; hand tools; power equipment; proper ventilation; and the handling, storage, and disposal of chemicals/materials in accordance with local, state, and federal safety and environmental regulations.

Performance Standard

0–No exposure: No information or practice provided during the program; complete training required

1–Exposure only: General information provided with no practice time; close supervision needed; additional training required

2–Limited practice: Has practiced job during training program; additional training required to develop skill

3–Moderately skilled: Has performed job independently during training program; limited additional training may be required

4–Skilled: Can perform job independently with no additional training

AST
8A11

MAST
8A11

Time off_____

Time on_____

Total time_____

CDX Tasksheet Number: C400

1. Research the timing belt inspection procedure for this vehicle in the appropriate service information. List the following specifications:

   a. **Timing belt replacement interval:** _____ **mi/km**

   b. **Draw a picture or print off a copy of the timing belt alignment diagram:**

2. Following the specified procedure, verify correct camshaft timing. **List your observations here:**

   a. **Is the camshaft timing correct? Yes:** _____ **No:** _____

3. Have your supervisor/instructor verify satisfactory completion of this procedure, any observations found, and any necessary action(s) recommended.

Performance Rating

CDX Tasksheet Number: C400

0	1	2	3	4

Supervisor/instructor signature _____ Date _____

Engine Performance: Engine Operating Temperature

Student/intern information:

Name _____ Date _____ Class _____

Vehicle used for this activity:

Year _____ Make _____ Model_____

Odometer_____VIN_____

Learning Objective/Task	CDX Tasksheet Number	2013 MLR NATEF Reference Number; Priority Level	2013 AST NATEF Reference Number; Priority Level	2013 MAST NATEF Reference Number; Priority Level
• Verify engine operating temperature; determine necessary action.	C398	8A6; P-1	8A10; P-1	8A10; P-1

Time off_____

Time on_____

Total time_____

Materials Required

- Vehicle or simulator
- Infrared temperature gun
- DVOM
- Drain pan

Some Safety Issues to Consider

- Open the radiator cap (or any other part of the cooling system) only with the engine cold. Opening a radiator cap on a warm or hot engine could cause severe burns.
- Electric fans can turn on at any time. Keep hands and fingers away.
- When running any vehicles in the shop, make sure you use the shop's exhaust ventilation system to discharge all exhaust gas safely outside.
- Comply with personal and environmental safety practices associated with clothing; eye protection; hand tools; power equipment; proper ventilation; and the handling, storage, and disposal of chemicals/materials in accordance with local, state, and federal safety and environmental regulations.

Performance Standard

0—No exposure: No information or practice provided during the program; complete training required

1—Exposure only: General information provided with no practice time; close supervision needed; additional training required

2—Limited practice: Has practiced job during training program; additional training required to develop skill

3—Moderately skilled: Has performed job independently during training program; limited additional training may be required

4—Skilled: Can perform job independently with no additional training

Verify engine operating temperature;
determine necessary action.

Time off_____

Time on_____

Total time_____

CDX Tasksheet Number: C398

1. **Research the following specifications in the service information.**

    a. **Thermostat opening temperature:** _____ °F/°C

    b. **Temperature at which the electric fan comes on (if equipped):**
        _____ °F/°C

    c. **Temperature at which the fan clutch engages (on) (if equipped):**
        _____ °F/°C

2. Apply the vehicle's parking brake and secure the vehicle with wheel chocks to prevent the vehicle from rolling.

3. Start the vehicle. Allow the vehicle to warm up while monitoring the engine temperature with the temp gun. Find the spot where the highest temperature reading is found on the engine side of the thermostat housing (on most engines). Monitor the temperature at that spot.

> **NOTE** The temperature should rise to between the thermostat opening temperature and the electric (or clutch) fan "on" temperature (if equipped). If this happens, continue to the next step. If the engine doesn't get that hot, diagnose the problem and go to step 4 below. Do NOT allow the engine to overheat!

    a. **If the engine is equipped with an electric fan, the temperature should vary between the electric fan "on" temperature and the electric fan "off" temperature. Record these temperatures:**

        i. **Electric fan "on" temp:** _____ °F/°C

        ii. **Electric fan "off" temp:** _____ °F/°C

    b. **If the engine is equipped with a clutch fan, the temperature should rise above the thermostat opening temperature but not above the clutch fan engagement temperature. Record these two temperatures:**

        i. **Clutch fan "engaged" temp:** _____ °F/°C
        ii. **Clutch fan "disengaged" temp:** _____ °F/°C

    c. **If the engine is equipped with a mechanical fan without a clutch, the temperature should rise to, or slightly above, the thermostat opening temperature and should remain fairly steady. Record this operating temperature:**

        i. **Engine operating temperature:** _____ °F/°C

4. **If the engine did not reach the specified thermostat opening temperature, list the max temperature reached:** _____ °F/°C

5. **Determine any necessary action(s):**

6. Have your supervisor/instructor verify satisfactory completion of this procedure, any observations found, and any necessary action(s) recommended.

Performance Rating

| 0 | 1 | 2 | 3 | 4 |

Supervisor/instructor signature _____ Date _____

Engine Performance: Ignition System

Student/intern information:

Name _____ Date _____ Class _____

Vehicle used for this activity:

Year _____ Make _____ Model _____

Odometer _____ VIN _____

Learning Objective/Task	CDX Tasksheet Number	2013 MLR NATEF Reference Number; Priority Level	2013 AST NATEF Reference Number; Priority Level	2013 MAST NATEF Reference Number; Priority Level
• Remove and replace spark plugs; inspect secondary ignition components for wear and damage.	C960	8A7; P-1	8C4; P-1	8C4; P-1
• Inspect and test crankshaft and camshaft position sensor(s); perform necessary action.	C663		8C2; P-1	8C2; P-1
• Inspect, test, and/or replace ignition control module, powertrain/engine control module; reprogram as necessary.	C664		8C3; P-3	8C3; P-3
• Diagnose (troubleshoot) ignition system-related problems such as no-starting, hard starting, engine misfire, poor driveability, spark knock, power loss, poor mileage, and emissions concerns; determine necessary action.	C712		8C1; P-2	8C1; P-2
• Access and use service information to perform step-by-step (troubleshooting) diagnosis.	C841		8B2; P-1	8B2; P-1

Time off_____

Time on_____

Total time_____

Materials Required

- Vehicle(s) with ignition-related concern(s)
- DMM/DVOM
- Spark tester
- Problem-specific tools and equipment such as scan tool, lab scope, etc.

Some Safety Issues to Consider

- Diagnosis of this fault may require test-driving the vehicle on the school grounds or on a hoist, both of which carry severe risks. Attempt this task only with full permission from your supervisor/instructor and follow all the guidelines exactly.
- When running any vehicles in the shop, make sure you use the shop's exhaust ventilation system to discharge all exhaust gas safely outside.
- Because the vehicle will be running for an extended amount of time, make sure the vehicle cannot move or roll by applying the parking brake and using wheel chocks.

- You will be working under the hood of a running vehicle. Keep your hands and fingers away from moving belts, fans, and other parts.
- Modern ignition systems are capable of creating extremely high voltage (many over 80,000 volts). While there is a small risk of death directly from the shock, it can cause substantial pain, leading to injury from jerking away from it and into a sharp object or moving belt.
- Comply with personal and environmental safety practices associated with clothing; eye protection; hand tools; power equipment; proper ventilation; and the handling, storage, and disposal of chemicals/materials in accordance with local, state, and federal safety and environmental regulations.

Performance Standard

0–No exposure: No information or practice provided during the program; complete training required

1–Exposure only: General information provided with no practice time; close supervision needed; additional training required

2–Limited practice: Has practiced job during training program; additional training required to develop skill

3–Moderately skilled: Has performed job independently during training program; limited additional training may be required

4–Skilled: Can perform job independently with no additional training

Remove and replace spark plugs; inspect secondary ignition components for wear and damage.

MLR	AST	MAST
8A7	8C4	8C4

CDX Tasksheet Number: C960

1. Research the following specifications in the appropriate service information:

   a. **Spark plug gap:** _____ in/mm

   b. **Ignition coil–primary winding resistance:** _____ ohms

   c. **Ignition coil–secondary winding resistance:** _____ ohms

   d. **Spark plug wire resistance:** _____ ohms

2. Using the recommended equipment and following the correct procedure, inspect and test ignition primary and secondary windings of the ignition coil(s). **List your observations here:**

   a. **Ignition coil–primary winding resistance:** _____ ohms

   b. **Ignition coil–secondary winding resistance:** _____ ohms

3. Following the specified procedure, remove the spark plugs (keeping them in the same order) and inspect them. **List your observations:**

4. Following the specified procedure, inspect the secondary ignition wires. **List your observations here:**

5. Measure the resistance of each spark plug wire. **List your measurements:**

6. Have your supervisor/instructor verify removal of the plugs. **Supervisor's/instructor's initials:** _____

7. Following the specified procedure, gap the spark plugs, apply a small amount of antiseize to the threads if directed, reinstall them by hand, and torque them to the specified torque.

8. Have your supervisor/instructor verify satisfactory completion of this procedure, any observations found, and any necessary action(s) recommended.

Performance Rating

CDX Tasksheet Number: C960

| 0 | 1 | 2 | 3 | 4 |

Supervisor/instructor signature _____ Date _____

Time off_____

Time on_____

Total time_____

CDX Tasksheet Number: C663

Vehicle used for this activity:

Year _____ Make _____ Model_____

Odometer_____ VIN_____

1. **List the crankshaft/camshaft sensor-related customer concern/complaint:**

2. **Research the particular concern in the appropriate service information and list the possible causes:**

3. Using the specified equipment and the correct procedure, inspect and test the crankshaft and camshaft position sensor(s). **List your test(s) and observations here:**

4. **What is causing the customer concern?**

5. **Determine any necessary action(s) to correct the fault(s):**

6. Perform any necessary action(s) and note the results here:

7. Have your supervisor/instructor verify satisfactory completion of this procedure, any observations found, and any necessary action(s) recommended.

Performance Rating

CDX Tasksheet Number: C663

0	1	2	3	4

Supervisor/instructor signature _____ Date _____

Inspect, test, and/or replace ignition control module, powertrain/engine control module; reprogram as necessary.

AST
8C3

MAST
8C3

Time off_____

Time on_____

Total time_____

CDX Tasksheet Number: C664

Vehicle used for this activity:

Year _____ Make _____ Model_____

Odometer_____ VIN_____

1. **List the ignition control module/powertrain control module-related customer concern/complaint:**

2. **Research the particular concern in the appropriate service information and list the possible causes:**

3. Using the specified equipment and the correct procedure, inspect, test, and/or replace the ignition control module or powertrain/engine control module. **List your test(s) and observations here:**

4. **What is causing the customer concern?**

5. **Determine any necessary action(s) to correct the fault(s):**

6. **Perform any necessary action(s) and list the results here:**

7. Reprogram the module in accordance with the manufacturer's procedure if necessary. **List your results:**

8. Have your supervisor/instructor verify satisfactory completion of this procedure, any observations found, and any necessary action(s) recommended.

Performance Rating

CDX Tasksheet Number: C664

0	1	2	3	4

Supervisor/instructor signature _____ Date _____

▶ **TASK** Diagnose (troubleshoot) ignition system-related problems such as no-starting, hard starting, engine misfire, poor driveability, spark knock, power loss, poor mileage, and emissions concerns; determine necessary action.

AST 8C1 | **MAST** 8C1

Time off_____

Time on_____

Total time_____

CDX Tasksheet Number: C712

Vehicle used for this activity:

Year _____ Make _____ Model_____

Odometer_____ VIN_____

1. **List the ignition system-related customer concern/complaint:**

2. **Verify the concern and list your observations here:**

3. **Research the particular concern in the appropriate service information and list the possible causes:**

4. Using the specified equipment and the correct procedure, diagnose the concern. **List your tests and results here:**

5. **What is causing the customer concern?**

6. **Determine any necessary action(s) to correct the fault(s):**

7. Have your supervisor/instructor verify satisfactory completion of this procedure, any observations found, and any necessary action(s) recommended.

Performance Rating

CDX Tasksheet Number: C712

0	1	2	3	4

Supervisor/instructor signature _____ Date _____

▶ **TASK** Access and use service information to perform step-by-step (troubleshooting) diagnosis.

AST
8B2

MAST
8B2

Time off_____

Time on_____

Total time_____

CDX Tasksheet Number: C841

1. The requirements for this task will be met by any number of Engine Performance diagnostic tasks you satisfactorily complete. Ask your instructor if a particular task you have completed, meets the criteria listed in the description of the task above. **If so, list that task number and description:**

2. **List what service information you accessed and how you used it when performing the step-by-step diagnosis:**

3. Have your supervisor/instructor verify your work. **Supervisor's/instructor's initials**_____

Performance Rating

CDX Tasksheet Number: C841

0	1	2	3	4

Supervisor/instructor signature _____ Date _____

Engine Performance: Fuel and Induction System Testing

© 2015 Jones & Bartlett Learning, LLC, an Ascend Learning Company

Student/intern information:

Name _____ Date _____ Class _____

Vehicle used for this activity:

Year _____ Make _____ Model _____

Odometer _____ VIN _____

Learning Objective/Task	CDX Tasksheet Number	2013 MLR NATEF Reference Number; Priority Level	2013 AST NATEF Reference Number; Priority Level	2013 MAST NATEF Reference Number; Priority Level
• Inspect and test fuel pumps and pump control systems for pressure, regulation, and volume; perform necessary action.	C868		8D2; P-1	8D3; P-1
• Check fuel for contaminants; determine necessary action.	C420		8D1; P-2	8D2; P-2
• Inspect and test fuel injectors.	C842		8D6; P-2	8D7; P-2
• Replace fuel filter(s).	C422	8C1; P-1	8D3; P-1	8D4; P-1
• Inspect, service, or replace air filters, filter housings, and intake duct work.	C962	8C2; P-1	8D4; P-1	8D5; P-1
• Inspect throttle body, air induction system, intake manifold, and gaskets for vacuum leaks and/or unmetered air.	C424		8D5; P-2	8D6; P-2
• Verify idle control operation.	C665		8D7; P-1	8D8; P-1
• Diagnose (troubleshoot) hot or cold no starting, hard starting, poor driveability, incorrect idle speed, poor idle, flooding, hesitation, surging, engine misfire, power loss, stalling, poor mileage, dieseling, and emissions problems; determine necessary action.	C713			8D1; P-2

Time off_____

Time on_____

Total time_____

Materials Required

- Vehicle/simulator
- Fuel pressure gauge (higher than specified pressure)
- DMM/DVOM
- 1-quart/-liter fuel container
- Graduated test tube (100 mL is optimal)
- Injector pulsing tool
- DVOM
- Shop vacuum
- Leak detection tool (such as a smoke machine or other appropriate device)
- Problem-specific tools and equipment such as: scan tool, lab scope, etc.

Some Safety Issues to Consider

- When performing this task, you will be exposed to gasoline or diesel fuel. Make sure you use the proper gloves to prevent fuel from coming in contact with your skin.
- This task requires working with liquid fuel. Prevent serious burns or fires by keeping open flame or any other source of ignition far away.
- When running any vehicles in the shop, make sure you use the shop's exhaust ventilation system to discharge all exhaust gas safely outside.
- You will be working under the hood of a running vehicle. Keep your hands and fingers away from moving belts, fans, and other parts.
- Comply with personal and environmental safety practices associated with clothing; eye protection; hand tools; power equipment; proper ventilation; and the handling, storage, and disposal of chemicals/materials in accordance with local, state, and federal safety and environmental regulations.

Performance Standard

0—No exposure: No information or practice provided during the program; complete training required

1—Exposure only: General information provided with no practice time; close supervision needed; additional training required

2—Limited practice: Has practiced job during training program; additional training required to develop skill

3—Moderately skilled: Has performed job independently during training program; limited additional training may be required

4—Skilled: Can perform job independently with no additional training

Inspect and test fuel pumps and pump control systems for pressure, regulation, and volume; perform necessary action.

Time off_____

Time on_____

Total time_____

CDX Tasksheet Number: C868

1. Research the following specifications/procedures for this vehicle in the appropriate service information.

   a. List the type of fuel pump that is used in this vehicle: _____
   b. Fuel pump pressure (key on/engine off): _____ **psi/kPa**
   c. Fuel pump pressure (key on/engine idling): _____ **psi/kPa**
   d. Fuel pump pressure (deadhead): _____ **psi/kPa**
   e. Fuel pump volume: _____ **pt/L/oz/lb per:** _____ **sec/min/hr**
   f. List the steps to relieve the pressure in the fuel system:

2. Have your supervisor/instructor verify your answers.
   Supervisor's/instructor's initials: _____

3. Test the fuel pump according to the specified procedure and list your observations.

   a. Fuel pump pressure (key on/engine off): _____ **psi/kpa**
   b. Fuel pump pressure (key on/engine idling): _____ **psi/kpa**
   c. Fuel pump pressure (deadhead): _____ **psi/kpa**
   d. Fuel pump volume: _____ **pt/L/oz/lb per:** _____ **sec/min/hr**
   e. Does the system hold pressure for at least 5 minutes once the key is turned off? Yes: _____ **No:** _____

> **NOTE** Keep the fuel in the container for the next task, C420/8D1/8D2: Check fuel for contaminants and quality; determine necessary action.

4. **Determine any necessary action(s):**

5. Have your supervisor/instructor verify your conclusions. **Supervisor's/instructor's initials:** _____

6. Perform any necessary actions as approved by your supervisor/instructor and list the results here:

7. Have your supervisor/instructor verify satisfactory completion of this procedure, any observations found, and any necessary action(s) recommended.

Performance Rating

CDX Tasksheet Number: C868

0	1	2	3	4

Supervisor/instructor signature _____ Date _____

Check fuel for contaminants and quality; determine necessary action.

Time off_____

Time on_____

Total time_____

CDX Tasksheet Number: C420

1. Obtain a quantity of fuel from the vehicle into the fuel container.

   NOTE This is best done while performing a fuel pump volume test.

2. Pour 90 mL of gasoline into the graduated test tube.

3. Let this settle for a minute or two. Observe any contaminants in the fuel. **List your observations:**

4. Add 10 mL of water, bringing the total volume to 100 mL.

5. Cap the test tube tightly with a cork or other appropriate device.

   NOTE Be sure you hold the cap firmly in place during this procedure. It will become pressurized, which could force the cap off, spraying fuel a considerable distance.

6. Slowly and carefully agitate the fuel/water mix for 30 seconds to bring the water into contact with the fuel. If there is any alcohol in the fuel, this will allow the water to be absorbed by the alcohol.

7. Allow the mixture to settle for a minute or two. Observe the level of the water in the bottom of the test tube. Anything higher than the initial 10 mL is the amount of alcohol in the fuel. **List your observation(s):**

8. **Determine any necessary action(s):**

9. Have your supervisor/instructor verify your observations. **Supervisor's/instructor's initials:** _____

10. Carefully pour off the fuel in the test tube back to the fuel container. Make sure no water leaves the test tube.

© 2015 Jones & Bartlett Learning, LLC, an Ascend Learning Company

11. Properly dispose of the remaining water/fuel mixture.

12. Have your supervisor/instructor verify satisfactory completion of this procedure, any observations found, and any necessary action(s) recommended.

Performance Rating

CDX Tasksheet Number: C420

□	□	□	□	□
0	1	2	3	4

Supervisor/instructor signature _____ Date _____

AST 8D6   **MAST** 8D7

CDX Tasksheet Number: C842

Vehicle used for this activity:

Year _____ Make _____ Model_____

Odometer_____ VIN_____

1. Research the fuel injector testing procedure for this vehicle in the appropriate service information. **List the following:**

   a. **Specified resistance for the fuel injectors:** _____ ohms
   b. **Fuel pump pressure (key on/engine off):** _____ psi/kPa
   c. **List or print off and attach to this sheet the steps to test the fuel injectors.**

2. Visually inspect the fuel injectors for leaks, damage, etc. **List your observations:**

3. Follow the specified procedure to test the fuel injectors. **List your observations:**

4. If the service information doesn't list a method for testing the injectors, use the following method.

   a. Install the fuel pressure gauge on the fuel rail.
   b. Disconnect the fuel injector electrical connectors.
   c. Connect the injector pulsing tool to one fuel injector, according to the toolmaker's instructions, and set it for the specified amount of time in milliseconds.
   d. Pressurize the fuel rail by turning on the ignition switch for a few seconds. Then turn the ignition switch off.
   e. **List the fuel pressure:** _____ psi/kPa
   f. Activate the injector pulsing tool for the appropriate amount of time. Watch the pressure gauge and record the pressure after the injector has been cycled on and off (one time). List your readings below. Continue this test on each fuel injector, remembering to pressurize the fuel rail each time before activating the injector pulsing tool.
   g. **List your readings for each injector.**

      Injector #1 _____ psi/kPa   **Injector #2** _____ psi/kPa
      Injector #3 _____ psi/kPa   **Injector #4** _____ psi/kPa
      Injector #5 _____ psi/kPa   **Injector #6** _____ psi/kPa
      Injector #7 _____ psi/kPa   **Injector #8** _____ psi/kPa

> **NOTE** Uneven pressure drops indicate uneven fuel flow through each injector.

5. **Determine any necessary action(s):**

6. **Measure the resistance of each fuel injector and list your readings.**

   Injector #1 _____ Ohms   Injector #2 _____ Ohms

   Injector #3 _____ Ohms   Injector #4 _____ Ohms

   Injector #5 _____ Ohms   Injector #6 _____ Ohms

   Injector #7 _____ Ohms   Injector #8 _____ Ohms

7. **Determine any necessary action(s):**

8. Have your supervisor/instructor verify satisfactory completion of this procedure, any observations found, and any necessary action(s) recommended.

Performance Rating

CDX Tasksheet Number: C842

☐	☐	☐	☐	☐
0	1	2	3	4

Supervisor/instructor signature _____ Date _____

▶ TASK Replace fuel filters.

MLR 8C1   **AST** 8D3   **MAST** 8D4

Time off_____

Time on_____

Total time_____

CDX Tasksheet Number: C422

Vehicle used for this activity:

Year _____ Make _____ Model _____

Odometer _____ VIN _____

1. Research the fuel filter replacement procedure for this vehicle in the appropriate information.

   a. List any special procedures and/or tools to perform this task:

   b. Look up the flat rate time for this task: _____ hr

2. Release any fuel pressure in the system by following the manufacturer's recommended procedure.

3. Follow the specified procedure to remove the fuel filter.

4. Have your supervisor/instructor verify removal of the fuel filter. **Supervisor's/instructor's initials: _____**

5. Install a new fuel filter (or reinstall the old one if your instructor directed you to do so).

6. Once the filter is installed correctly, clean up any spilled fuel and dispose of it properly.

7. Apply the vehicle's parking brake and secure the vehicle with wheel chocks to prevent the vehicle from rolling.

8. Turn the ignition switch to run and check for any fuel leaks. Immediately shut off the vehicle if a leak is present. Repair any leaks.

> **NOTE** Ask your supervisor/instructor whether or not to perform the next action before proceeding.

9. Cut the old filter open with a hacksaw to examine the inside. **List what you found inside the filter:**

10. Have your supervisor/instructor verify satisfactory completion of this procedure, any observations found, and any necessary action(s) recommended.

Performance Rating

CDX Tasksheet Number: C422

0	1	2	3	4

Supervisor/instructor signature _____ Date _____

Inspect, service, or replace air filters, filter housings, and intake duct work.

MLR 8C2   **AST** 8D4   **MAST** 8D5

Time off_____

Time on_____

Total time_____

CDX Tasksheet Number: C962

1. Research the procedure and specifications for servicing the air filter, housing, and ductwork in the appropriate service information.

   a. **Specified air filter number:** _____

2. Following the specified procedure, remove the air filter from the filter housing.

3. **Inspect the air filter and list the condition:**

4. **Inspect the filter housing and ductwork. List your observations:**

5. Clean the filter housing following the specified procedure.

6. Have your Supervisor/Instructor verify removal. **Supervisor's/instructor's initials:**
   _____

7. Following the specified procedure, reinstall the air filter, housing and ductwork.

8. Have your supervisor/instructor verify satisfactory completion of this procedure, any observations found, and any necessary action(s) recommended.

Performance Rating

CDX Tasksheet Number: C962

0	1	2	3	4

Supervisor/instructor signature _____ Date _____

Inspect throttle body, air induction system, intake manifold, and gaskets for vacuum leaks and/or unmetered air.

AST 8D5   **MAST** 8D6

Time off_____

Time on_____

Total time_____

CDX Tasksheet Number: C424

Vehicle used for this activity:

Year _____ Make _____ Model_____

Odometer_____ VIN_____

1. Visually inspect the air induction system for any obvious leaks such as cracks, loose fittings, or missing hoses. **List your observations:**

2. Use an appropriate leak detection tool to test for any non-obvious leaks and/or unmetered air. **List your tests and observations:**

3. **Determine any necessary action(s):**

4. Have your supervisor/instructor verify satisfactory completion of this procedure, any observations found, and any necessary action(s) recommended.

Performance Rating

CDX Tasksheet Number: C424

0	1	2	3	4

Supervisor/instructor signature _____ Date _____

AST 8D7   **MAST** 8D8

Time off_____

Time on_____

Total time_____

CDX Tasksheet Number: C665

Vehicle used for this activity:

Year _____ Make _____ Model _____

Odometer _____ VIN _____

1. **List the idle speed control-related customer concern:**

2. **Research and list the desired idle speed:** _____ **rpm**

3. **Research the particular concern in the appropriate service information and list the possible causes:**

4. **Using the specified procedure, verify the vehicle idle speed and list here:** _____ **RPM**

5. Using the specified procedure, test the idle control system operation. **List your test(s) observation(s) here:**

6. **Determine any necessary action(s):**

7. Return the vehicle to its beginning condition and return any tools you used to their proper locations.

8. Have your supervisor/instructor verify satisfactory completion of this procedure, any observations found, and any necessary action(s) recommended.

Performance Rating

CDX Tasksheet Number: C665

0	1	2	3	4

Supervisor/instructor signature _____ Date _____

Diagnose hot or cold no starting, hard starting, poor driveability, incorrect idle speed, poor idle, flooding, hesitation, surging, engine misfire, power loss, stalling, poor mileage, dieseling, and emissions problems; determine necessary action.

MAST
8D1

Time off_____

Time on_____

Total time_____

CDX Tasksheet Number: C713

Vehicle used for this activity:

Year _____ Make _____ Model _____

Odometer _____ VIN _____

1. **List the fuel injection system-related customer concern:**

2. **Verify the concern and list your observations here:**

3. Research the possible causes for this concern in the appropriate service information.

   a. **List or print off and attach to this sheet the possible causes:**

   b. **List or print off and attach to this sheet the procedure for diagnosing the concern:**

4. **Follow the specified procedure to diagnose the concern. List your tests and results here:**

5. List the cause of the concern:

6. Determine any necessary action(s) to correct the fault:

7. Have your supervisor/instructor verify satisfactory completion of this procedure, any observations found, and any necessary action(s) recommended.

Performance Rating

CDX Tasksheet Number: C713

0	1	2	3	4

Supervisor/instructor signature _____ Date _____

Engine Performance: Exhaust Analysis

Student/intern information:

Name _____ Date _____ Class _____

Vehicle used for this activity:

Year _____ Make _____ Model _____

Odometer _____ VIN _____

Learning Objective/Task	CDX Tasksheet Number	2013 MLR NATEF Reference Number; Priority Level	2013 AST NATEF Reference Number; Priority Level	2013 MAST NATEF Reference Number; Priority Level
• Inspect and test catalytic converter efficiency.	C714		8E6; P-2	8E9; P-2
• Diagnose abnormal exhaust color, odor, and sound; determine necessary action.	C391		8A4; P-2	8A4; P-2

Time off_____

Time on_____

Total time_____

Materials Required

- Vehicle or simulator
- Exhaust gas analyzer
- Exhaust hose(s)
- Vehicle with unusual exhaust condition
- Problem-specific tools and equipment, such as stethoscope, compression tester, back pressure gauge, scan tool, etc.

Some Safety Issues to Consider

- When running any vehicles in the shop, make sure you use the shop's exhaust ventilation system to discharge all exhaust gas safely outside.
- Diagnosis of this fault may require test-driving the vehicle on the school grounds or on a hoist, both of which carry severe risks. Attempt this task only with full permission from your supervisor/instructor and follow all the guidelines exactly.
- You will be working under the hood of a running vehicle. Keep your hands and fingers away from moving belts, fans, and other parts.
- This task may require that the engine is loaded while running, which requires the use of wheel chocks to help prevent the vehicle from rolling. Never stand, or allow anyone else to stand, directly in front of or behind the vehicle while performing this procedure.
- Comply with personal and environmental safety practices associated with clothing; eye protection; hand tools; power equipment; proper ventilation; and the handling, storage, and disposal of chemicals/materials in accordance with local, state, and federal safety and environmental regulations.

Performance Standard

0—No exposure: No information or practice provided during the program; complete training required

1—Exposure only: General information provided with no practice time; close supervision needed; additional training required

2—Limited practice: Has practiced job during training program; additional training required to develop skill

3—Moderately skilled: Has performed job independently during training program; limited additional training may be required

4—Skilled: Can perform job independently with no additional training

AST 8E6 **MAST** 8E9

Time off_____

Time on_____

Total time_____

CDX Tasksheet Number: C714

1. Research the catalytic converter testing procedure for this vehicle in the appropriate service information.

   a. **List or print off and attach to this sheet the procedure to test the converter:**

   b. If no procedure is available, there are four generally accepted methods of testing a converter:

      1. The first is a pre-catalyst/post-catalyst emission test (sometimes called an intrusive or intrusion test).
      2. The second is a cylinder ignition–shorting emission test where one cylinder's ignition is disabled and the resulting emissions are measured and compared to the pre-shorted emission readings.
      3. On OBDII-equipped vehicles, using the pre-catalyst and post-catalyst O_2 sensor readings to show a difference in exhaust oxygen content will indicate converter efficiency.
      4. Using mode 6 data from the vehicle's PCM to indicate the number of failure counts for the catalyst

   Ask your supervisor/instructor which method to use, and list it here: _____

   NOTE Some local regulatory authorities mandate a loaded cruise test. This test is hard to duplicate in most shops and is best done on a dynamometer. Unless your shop has this piece of equipment available, it would be best not to perform a loaded cruise test. Also, in some states a no-load cruise test is allowed on certain vehicles. Please note that some vehicles can experience transmission failure if this test is performed. Therefore, we do not recommend performing this test on any vehicle unless it is with your supervisor's/instructor's direct authorization and supervision.

---

2. **Test the catalytic converter following the specified procedure. List your tests and observations:**

3. **Determine any necessary action(s):**

4. Have your supervisor/instructor verify satisfactory completion of this procedure, any observations found, and any necessary action(s) recommended.

Performance Rating

CDX Tasksheet Number: C714

0	1	2	3	4

Supervisor/instructor signature _____ Date _____

Diagnose abnormal exhaust color, odor, and sound; determine necessary action.

AST
8A4

MAST
8A4

Time off_____

Time on_____

Total time_____

CDX Tasksheet Number: C391

Vehicle used for this activity:

Year _____ Make _____ Model_____

Odometer_____ VIN _____

1. **List the exhaust-related customer concern:**

2. **Research possible causes of the concern for this vehicle in the appropriate service information.**

   a. **List any possible causes:**

   b. **List any specified tests to pinpoint the problem:**

3. With your supervisor's/instructor's permission, operate the vehicle to verify the concern. **List your observations:**

4. Follow the specified procedure to diagnose the concern. **List your tests and results:**

5. List the cause of the concern:

6. Determine any necessary action(s) to correct the fault:

7. Have your supervisor/instructor verify satisfactory completion of this procedure, any observations found, and any necessary action(s) recommended.

Performance Rating

CDX Tasksheet Number: C391

☐	☐	☐	☐	☐
0	1	2	3	4

Supervisor/instructor signature _____ Date _____

Engine Performance: Exhaust System Testing

Student/intern information:

Name _____ Date _____ Class _____

Vehicle used for this activity:

Year _____ Make _____ Model _____

Odometer _____ VIN _____

Learning Objective/Task	CDX Tasksheet Number	2013 MLR NATEF Reference Number; Priority Level	2013 AST NATEF Reference Number; Priority Level	2013 MAST NATEF Reference Number; Priority Level
• Inspect condition of exhaust system hangers, brackets, clamps, and heat shields; repair or replace as needed.	C963	8C4; P-1	8D9; P-1	8D10; P-1
• Inspect the integrity of the exhaust manifold, exhaust pipes, muffler(s), catalytic converter(s), resonator(s), tail pipe(s), and heat shields; perform necessary action.	C428	8C3; P-1	8D8; P-1	8D9; P-1
• Check and refill diesel exhaust fluid (DEF).	C965	8C5; P-3	8D11; P-3	8D12; P-3
• Perform exhaust system back pressure test; determine necessary action.	C429		8D10; P-2	8D11; P-2
• Test the operation of turbocharger/supercharger systems; determine necessary action.	C869			8D13; P-3

Time off_____

Time on_____

Total time_____

Materials Required

- Vehicle
- Large Channellock® (arc joint) pliers
- Exhaust back-pressure gauge
- Tachometer (if the vehicle is not equipped with one)
- Diesel Exhaust Fluid refractometer or hydrometer
- Problem-specific tools and equipment such as: scan tool, lab scope, etc.

Some Safety Issues to Consider

- Vehicle hoists are important tools that increase productivity and make the job easier. However, they can also cause severe injury or death if used improperly. Make sure you follow the hoist and vehicle manufacturer's operation procedures. Also make sure you have your supervisor's/instructor's permission to use a vehicle hoist.
- You will be working under the hood of a running vehicle. Keep your hands and fingers away from moving belts, fans, and other parts.
- When running any vehicles in the shop, make sure you use the shop's exhaust ventilation system to discharge all exhaust gas safely outside.

- Diagnosis of this fault may require test-driving the vehicle on the school grounds or on a hoist, both of which carry severe risks. Attempt this task only with full permission from your supervisor/instructor and follow all the guidelines exactly.
- Comply with personal and environmental safety practices associated with clothing; eye protection; hand tools; power equipment; proper ventilation; and the handling, storage, and disposal of chemicals/materials in accordance with local, state, and federal safety and environmental regulations.

Performance Standard

0–No exposure: No information or practice provided during the program; complete training required

1–Exposure only: General information provided with no practice time; close supervision needed; additional training required

2–Limited practice: Has practiced job during training program; additional training required to develop skill

3–Moderately skilled: Has performed job independently during training program; limited additional training may be required

4–Skilled: Can perform job independently with no additional training

▶ TASK Inspect condition of exhaust system hangers, brackets, clamps, and heat shields; repair or replace as needed.

MLR	AST	MAST
8C4	8D9	8D10

Time off_____

Time on_____

Total time_____

CDX Tasksheet Number: C963

1. Safely raise and secure the vehicle on a hoist.

2. Inspect the following parts for damage, wear, or missing components. Also, check the integrity of the pipes by squeezing them with the large arc joint pliers. **List your observations about each.**

    a. Exhaust system hangers, brackets, and clamps:

    b. Heat shields:

3. **Determine any necessary action(s):**

4. Have your supervisor/instructor verify your conclusions.
Supervisor's/instructor's initials: _____

5. Perform any necessary actions as approved by your supervisor/instructor.
List them here:

6. Have your supervisor/instructor verify satisfactory completion of this procedure, any observations found, and any necessary action(s) recommended.

Performance Rating

CDX Tasksheet Number: C963

0	1	2	3	4

Supervisor/instructor signature _____ Date _____

Inspect the integrity of the exhaust manifold, exhaust pipes, muffler(s), catalytic converter(s), resonator(s), tail pipe(s), and heat shields; perform necessary action.

MLR
8C3

AST
8D8

MAST
8D9

CDX Tasksheet Number: C428

1. Safely raise and secure the vehicle on a hoist.

2. Inspect the following parts for damage, wear, or missing components. Also, check the integrity of the pipes by squeezing them with the large arc joint pliers. **List your observations about each.**

   a. **Exhaust manifold(s):**

   b. **Exhaust pipes:**

   c. **Muffler(s):**

   d. **Catalytic converter(s):**

   e. **Resonator(s):**

   f. **Tail pipe(s):**

   g. **Heat shield(s):**

3. Determine any necessary action(s):

4. Have your supervisor/instructor verify your conclusions.
Supervisor's/instructor's initials: _____

5. Perform any necessary actions as approved by your supervisor/instructor.
List them here:

6. Have your supervisor/instructor verify satisfactory completion of this procedure, any observations found, and any necessary action(s) recommended.

Performance Rating

CDX Tasksheet Number: C428

0	1	2	3	4

Supervisor/instructor signature _____ Date _____

► **TASK** Check and refill diesel exhaust fluid (DEF).

Time off_____

Time on_____

Total time_____

CDX Tasksheet Number: C965

Vehicle used for this activity:

Year _____ Make _____ Model _____

Odometer _____ VIN _____

1. On a diesel vehicle equipped with diesel exhaust fluid, research the following specifications in the appropriate service information.

    a. **Specified diesel exhaust fluid:** _____
    b. **Specified replenishment interval:** _____ **mi/km/mo**
    c. **Specified diesel fluid tank capacity:** _____
    d. **Specified urea content:** _____ **% or specific gravity**
    e. **List the purpose of diesel exhaust fluid:** _____

2. Following the specified procedure, obtain and measure the urea content or specific gravity of the DEF fluid. **List your results:**

3. Check the level of diesel exhaust fluid in the reservoir. **List your observations:**

4. If necessary, refill the diesel exhaust fluid to the proper level.

5. Have your supervisor/instructor verify satisfactory completion of this procedure, any observations found, and any necessary action(s) recommended.

Performance Rating

CDX Tasksheet Number: C965

0	1	2	3	4

Supervisor/instructor signature _____ Date _____

Perform exhaust system back-pressure test;
determine necessary action.

AST 8D10   **MAST** 8D11

CDX Tasksheet Number: C429

1. Research the procedure to test exhaust back-pressure on this vehicle in the appropriate service information.

   a. **List the location for installing the back-pressure gauge:** _____

   b. **List the maximum allowable back-pressure:** _____ **in/hg or psi/kPA at** _____ **RPM**

2. Install the back-pressure gauge according to the specified procedure.

3. Measure the exhaust back-pressure, being careful to follow the specified procedure.

   a. **List your readings obtained:** _____ **in/hg or psi/kPA at** _____ **RPM**

4. **Determine any necessary action(s):**

5. Have your supervisor/instructor verify satisfactory completion of this procedure, any observations found, and any necessary action(s) recommended.

Performance Rating

CDX Tasksheet Number: C429

0	1	2	3	4

Supervisor/instructor signature _____ Date _____

Test the operation of turbocharger/supercharger systems; determine necessary action.

MAST
8D13

CDX Tasksheet Number: C869

Vehicle used for this activity:

Year _____ Make _____ Model_____

Odometer_____ VIN_____

NOTE This task is extremely hazardous and should be performed only under close supervisor/instructor supervision. Diagnosis of this fault may require test driving the vehicle on the school grounds or on a hoist, both of which carry severe risks. Attempt this task only with full permission from your supervisor/instructor and follow all the guidelines and laws exactly.

---

1. Research the testing and specifications for this vehicle in the appropriate service information.

    a. **Maximum boost:** _____ **psi/kpa**

    b. **List, or print off and attach to this sheet, the procedure for testing the turbocharger/supercharger:**

    c. Have your supervisor/instructor approve the specifications and testing procedure. **Supervisor/Instructor initials:** _____

2. Following the specified procedure, test the turbocharger/supercharger.
   List your tests and results:

3. **Determine any necessary action(s):**

4. Have your supervisor/instructor verify satisfactory completion of this procedure, any observations found, and any necessary action(s) recommended.

Performance Rating

CDX Tasksheet Number: C869

0	1	2	3	4

Supervisor/instructor signature _____ Date _____

Engine Performance: Powertrain Control System Testing

Student/intern information:

Name _____ Date _____ Class _____

Vehicle used for this activity:

Year _____ Make _____ Model _____

Odometer_____VIN_____

Learning Objective/Task	CDX Tasksheet Number	2013 MLR NATEF Reference Number; Priority Level	2013 AST NATEF Reference Number; Priority Level	2013 MAST NATEF Reference Number; Priority Level
• Describe the importance of running all OBDII monitors for repair verification.	C661	8B2; P-1	8B4; P-1	8B4; P-1
• Retrieve and record diagnostic trouble codes, OBD monitor status, and freeze-frame data; clear codes when applicable.	C659	8B1; P-1	8B1; P-1	8B1; P-1
• Perform active tests of actuators using a scan tool; determine necessary action.	C867		8B3; P-2	8B3; P-2
• Inspect and test computerized engine control system sensors, powertrain/engine control module (PCM/ECM), actuators, and circuits using a graphing multimeter (GMM)/digital storage oscilloscope (DSO); perform necessary action.	C840			8B7; P-2

Time off_____

Time on_____

Total time_____

Materials Required
- Vehicle or simulator (OBDII)
- Scan tool
- DMM/DVOM
- GMM/DSO
- Problem-specific tools and equipment

Some Safety Issues to Consider
- If you need to start the vehicle, you should ensure that the parking brake is firmly applied; if necessary, use wheel chocks to prevent the vehicle from moving when the vehicle is started to verify the completion of this task.
- Only students who have their supervisor's/instructor's direct permission should perform this task due to the safety concerns involved.
- Diagnosis of this fault may require test-driving the vehicle on the school grounds. Attempt this task only with full permission from your instructor and follow all the guidelines exactly.
- When running any vehicles in the shop, make sure you use the shop's exhaust ventilation system to discharge all exhaust gas safely outside.

- Comply with personal and environmental safety practices associated with clothing; eye protection; hand tools; power equipment; proper ventilation; and the handling, storage, and disposal of chemicals/materials in accordance with local, state, and federal safety and environmental regulations.

Performance Standard

0–No exposure: No information or practice provided during the program; complete training required

1–Exposure only: General information provided with no practice time; close supervision needed; additional training required

2–Limited practice: Has practiced job during training program; additional training required to develop skill

3–Moderately skilled: Has performed job independently during training program; limited additional training may be required

4–Skilled: Can perform job independently with no additional training

Describe the importance of running all OBDII monitors for repair verification.

Time off_____

Time on_____

Total time_____

CDX Tasksheet Number: C661

1. Research the following details in the appropriate service information:

   a. **List which OBDII monitors apply to this vehicle:**

   b. **List the parameters the "Catalyst" monitor must meet before showing a "Ready" status:**

   c. **List the parameters the "Evap" monitor must meet before showing a "Ready" status:**

2. **Describe in your own words the importance of running all OBDII monitors for repair verification:**

3. Have your supervisor/instructor verify satisfactory completion of this procedure, any observations found, and any necessary action(s) recommended.

Performance Rating

CDX Tasksheet Number: C661

| 0 | 1 | 2 | 3 | 4 |

Supervisor/instructor signature _____ Date _____

Retrieve and record diagnostic trouble codes, OBD monitor status, and freeze-frame data; clear codes when applicable.

MLR 8B1   **AST** 8B1   **MAST** 8B1

Time off_____

Time on_____

Total time_____

CDX Tasksheet Number: C659

1. **Connect the scan tool to the vehicle in accordance with the manufacturer's instructions; retrieve and record any diagnostic trouble codes:**

2. **List the monitor status for each OBD monitor:**

3. **List (or print off and attach) the freeze-frame data:**

4. Clear codes when applicable. This may not necessarily be now.

> **NOTE** Clearing the codes will also erase the OBD monitor status and freeze-frame data on most vehicles. Clear codes only when the service information directs you to do so.

5. Have your supervisor/instructor verify satisfactory completion of this procedure, any observations found, and any necessary action(s) recommended.

Performance Rating

CDX Tasksheet Number: C659

0	1	2	3	4

Supervisor/instructor signature _____ Date _____

Perform active tests of actuators using a scan tool; determine necessary action.

AST
8B3

MAST
8B3

Time off_____

Time on_____

Total time_____

CDX Tasksheet Number: C867

1. Connect the scan tool to the vehicle in accordance with the manufacturer's instructions and, while using the scan tool directions, perform active tests on at least two actuators. **List the actuators tested and the results of those tests:**

2. **Determine any necessary action(s):**

3. Have your supervisor/instructor verify satisfactory completion of this procedure, any observations found, and any necessary action(s) recommended.

Performance Rating

CDX Tasksheet Number: C867

0	1	2	3	4

Supervisor/instructor signature _____ Date _____

Inspect and test computerized engine control system sensors, powertrain/ engine control module (PCM/ECM), actuators, and circuits using a graphing multimeter (GMM)/digital storage oscilloscope (DSO); perform necessary action.

MAST
8B7

Time off_____

Time on_____

Total time_____

CDX Tasksheet Number: C840

1. Research the following patterns/test procedures for this vehicle in the appropriate service information.

   a. Sketch (or print out) the specified oxygen sensor pattern (front):

   b. Sketch (or print out) the specified fuel injector pattern:

2. Connect the GMM or DSO to the oxygen sensor circuit, start the vehicle, allow the engine to warm up for the specified amount of time, and observe the pattern on the test equipment.

   a. Sketch or print off and attach to this sheet the pattern you obtained here:

   b. List your observation(s):

3. Connect the GMM or DSO to the fuel injector circuit, start the vehicle, allow the engine to warm up for the specified amount of time, and observe the pattern on the test equipment.

   a. Sketch or print off and attach to this sheet the pattern you obtained here:

b. List your observation(s):

4. Determine any necessary action(s):

5. Have your supervisor/instructor verify satisfactory completion of this procedure, any observations found, and any necessary action(s) recommended.

Performance Rating

CDX Tasksheet Number: C840

0	1	2	3	4

Supervisor/instructor signature _____ Date _____

Engine Performance: PCV System Testing

Student/intern information:

Name _____ Date _____ Class _____

Vehicle used for this activity:

Year _____ Make _____ Model _____

Odometer _____ VIN _____

Learning Objective/Task	CDX Tasksheet Number	2013 MLR NATEF Reference Number; Priority Level	2013 AST NATEF Reference Number; Priority Level	2013MAST NATEF Reference Number; Priority Level
• Inspect, test, and service positive crankcase ventilation (PCV) filter/breather cap, valve, tubes, orifices, and hoses; perform necessary action.	C432	8D1; P-2	8E2; P-2	8E2; P-2
• Diagnose oil leaks, emissions, and driveability concerns caused by the positive crankcase ventilation (PCV) system; determine necessary action.	C666		8E1; P-3	8E1; P-3

Time off _____

Time on _____

Total time _____

Materials Required

- Vehicle or simulator with related fault
- Problem-specific tools and equipment

Some Safety Issues to Consider

- You will be working under the hood of a running vehicle. Keep your hands and fingers away from moving belts, fans, and other parts.
- When running any vehicles in the shop, make sure you use the shop's exhaust ventilation system to discharge all exhaust gas safely outside.
- Only students who have their supervisor's/instructor's direct permission should perform this task due to the safety concerns involved.
- Diagnosis of this fault may require test-driving the vehicle on the school grounds. Attempt this task only with full permission from your instructor and follow all the guidelines exactly.
- Comply with personal and environmental safety practices associated with clothing; eye protection; hand tools; power equipment; proper ventilation; and the handling, storage, and disposal of chemicals/materials in accordance with local, state, and federal safety and environmental regulations.

Performance Standard

0—No exposure: No information or practice provided during the program; complete training required

1—Exposure only: General information provided with no practice time; close supervision needed; additional training required

2—Limited practice: Has practiced job during training program; additional training required to develop skill

3—Moderately skilled: Has performed job independently during training program; limited additional training may be required

4—Skilled: Can perform job independently with no additional training

Inspect, test and service positive crankcase ventilation (PCV) filter/breather cap, valve, tubes, orifices, and hoses; perform necessary action.

MLR 8D1 **AST** 8E2 **MAST** 8E2

Time off_____

Time on_____

Total time_____

CDX Tasksheet Number: C432

1. Research the PCV system on this vehicle in the appropriate service information.

    a. **List the service interval for replacing the PCV valve:** _____ mi/km

    b. **List the service interval for replacing the breather filter:** _____ mi/km

2. Follow the specified procedure to inspect and test the PCV system. **List your observations for each component below:**

    a. **Filter/breather cap:**

    b. **PCV valve:**

    c. **Tubes, orifices, and hoses:**

3. **Determine any necessary action(s):**

4. Have your supervisor/instructor verify your conclusions. **Supervisor's/instructor's initials:** _____

5. **Perform any necessary action(s) and list them here:**

6. Have your supervisor/instructor verify satisfactory completion of this procedure, any observations found, and any necessary action(s) recommended.

Performance Rating

CDX Tasksheet Number: C432

0	1	2	3	4

Supervisor/instructor signature _____ Date _____

Diagnose oil leaks, emissions, and driveability concerns caused by the positive crankcase ventilation (PCV) system; determine necessary action.

AST *8E1* **MAST** *8E1*

Time off_____

Time on_____

Total time_____

CDX Tasksheet Number: C666

Vehicle used for this activity:

Year _____ Make _____ Model_____

Odometer_____ VIN_____

1. **List the customer concern:**

2. Research the particular concern in the appropriate service information.

   a. **List the possible causes:**

   b. **List or print off and attach to this sheet the procedure for diagnosing the concern:**

3. Using the recommended procedure, inspect the vehicle and diagnose any oil leaks, emissions, and driveability concerns caused by the PCV system. **List your observations here:**

4. **List the cause of the concern:**

5. Determine any necessary action(s) to correct the fault:

6. Have your supervisor/instructor verify satisfactory completion of this procedure, any observations found, and any necessary action(s) recommended.

Performance Rating

0	1	2	3	4

Supervisor/instructor signature _____ Date _____

Engine Performance: EGR System Testing

Student/intern information:

Name _____ Date _____ Class _____

Vehicle used for this activity:

Year _____ Make _____ Model_____

Odometer_____ VIN_____

Learning Objective/Task	CDX Tasksheet Number	2013 MLR NATEF Reference Number; Priority Level	2013 AST NATEF Reference Number; Priority Level	2013 MAST NATEF Reference Number; Priority Level
• Inspect, test, service, and replace components of the exhaust gas recirculation (EGR) system, including tubing, exhaust passages, vacuum/pressure controls, filters, and hoses; perform necessary action.	C434		8E4; P-2	8E7; P-2
• Inspect and test electrical/electronic sensors, controls, and wiring of exhaust gas recirculation (EGR) systems; perform necessary action.	C435			8E6; P-2
• Diagnose emissions and driveability concerns caused by the exhaust gas recirculation (EGR) system; determine necessary action.	C667		8E3; P-3	8E3; P-2

Time off_____

Time on_____

Total time_____

Materials Required

- Vehicle or simulator with related fault
- Hand vacuum pump (for vacuum-operated EGR components)
- DVOM (for vehicles equipped with electric/electronic EGR components)
- Problem-specific tools and equipment

Some Safety Issues to Consider

- You will be working under the hood of a running vehicle. Keep your hands and fingers away from moving belts, fans, and other parts.
- When running any vehicles in the shop, make sure you use the shop's exhaust ventilation system to discharge all exhaust gas safely outside.
- Only students who have their supervisor's/instructor's direct permission should perform this task due to the safety concerns involved.
- Diagnosis of this fault may require test-driving the vehicle on the school grounds. Attempt this task only with full permission from your instructor and follow all the guidelines exactly.
- Comply with personal and environmental safety practices associated with clothing; eye protection; hand tools; power equipment; proper ventilation; and the handling, storage, and disposal of chemicals/materials in accordance with local, state, and federal safety and environmental regulations.

Performance Standard

0–No exposure: No information or practice provided during the program; complete training required

1–Exposure only: General information provided with no practice time; close supervision needed; additional training required

2–Limited practice: Has practiced job during training program; additional training required to develop skill

3–Moderately skilled: Has performed job independently during training program; limited additional training may be required

4–Skilled: Can perform job independently with no additional training

Inspect, test, service, and replace components of the exhaust gas recirculation (EGR) system, including tubing, exhaust passages, vacuum/pressure controls, filters, and hoses; perform necessary action.

AST 8E4 **MAST** 8E7

CDX Tasksheet Number: C434

1. Research the procedure for inspecting and testing the EGR system on this vehicle in the appropriate service information.

    a. List the type of EGR valve this vehicle is equipped with: _____

    b. List the service interval for replacing any of the EGR system components:

2. Follow the specified procedure to inspect and test the EGR system. **List your observations for each component below:**

    a. EGR valve:

    b. EGR tubing and exhaust passages:

    c. Vacuum/pressure controls:

    d. Filters and hoses:

3. **Determine any necessary action(s):**

4. Have your supervisor/instructor verify your conclusions. Supervisor's/instructor's initials: _____

5. **Perform any necessary action(s) and list them here:**

6. Have your supervisor/instructor verify satisfactory completion of this procedure, any observations found, and any necessary action(s) recommended.

Performance Rating

| 0 | 1 | 2 | 3 | 4 |

Supervisor/instructor signature _____ Date _____

Inspect and test electrical/electronic sensors, controls, and wiring of exhaust gas recirculation (EGR) systems; perform necessary action.

MAST
8E6

Time off_____

Time on_____

Total time_____

CDX Tasksheet Number: C435

Vehicle used for this activity:

Year _____ Make _____ Model_____

Odometer_____ VIN_____

1. Research the procedure for inspecting and testing the electrical/electronic components of the EGR system on this vehicle in the appropriate service information.

   a. List any EGR electrical specifications for this vehicle:

2. Follow the specified procedure to inspect and test the EGR system components. **List your observations for each component below:**

   a. EGR valve, if electrically operated:

   b. EGR vacuum solenoid, if equipped:

   c. EGR flow sensor, if equipped:

   d. Electrical wiring:

3. **Determine any necessary action(s):**

4. Have your supervisor/instructor verify your conclusions. **Supervisor's/instructor's initials:** _____

5. Perform any necessary action(s) and list them here:

6. Have your supervisor/instructor verify satisfactory completion of this procedure, any observations found, and any necessary action(s) recommended.

Performance Rating

CDX Tasksheet Number: C435

0	1	2	3	4
☐	☐	☐	☐	☐

Supervisor/instructor signature _____ Date _____

Diagnose emissions and driveability concerns caused by the exhaust gas recirculation (EGR) system; determine necessary action.

AST 8E3 **MAST** 8E3

CDX Tasksheet Number: C667

Vehicle used for this activity:

Year _____ Make _____ Model _____

Odometer _____ VIN _____

1. **List the EGR-related customer concern:**

2. Research the particular concern in the appropriate service information.

   a. **List the possible causes:**

   b. **List or print off and attach to this sheet the procedure for diagnosing the concern:**

3. Using the recommended procedure, inspect and diagnose any emissions and driveability concerns caused by the EGR system. **List your tests and observations here:**

4. **List the cause of the concern:**

5. Determine any necessary action(s) to correct the fault:

6. Have your supervisor/instructor verify satisfactory completion of this procedure, any observations found, and any necessary action(s) recommended.

Performance Rating

CDX Tasksheet Number: C667

0	1	2	3	4

Supervisor/instructor signature _____ Date _____

Engine Performance: Evaporative Emissions System Testing

© 2015 Jones & Bartlett Learning, LLC, an Ascend Learning Company

Student/intern information:

Name _____ Date _____ Class _____

Vehicle used for this activity:

Year _____ Make _____ Model _____

Odometer _____ VIN _____

Learning Objective/Task	CDX Tasksheet Number	2013 MLR NATEF Reference Number; Priority Level	2013 AST NATEF Reference Number; Priority Level	2013 MAST NATEF Reference Number; Priority Level
• Inspect and test components and hoses of the evaporative emissions control system; perform necessary action.	C870		8E7; P-1	8E10; P-1
• Diagnose emissions and driveability concerns caused by the evaporative emissions control system; determine necessary action.	C844			8E5; P-2

Time off_____

Time on_____

Total time_____

Materials Required

- Vehicle or simulator with related fault
- Hand vacuum pump
- DVOM
- Infrared temp gun
- Smoke machine
- Problem-specific tools and equipment

Some Safety Issues to Consider

- You will be working under the hood of a running vehicle. Keep your hands and fingers away from moving belts, fans, and other parts.
- When running any vehicles in the shop, make sure you use the shop's exhaust ventilation system to discharge all exhaust gas safely outside.
- Only students who have their supervisor's/instructor's direct permission should perform this task due to the safety concerns involved.
- Diagnosis of this fault may require test-driving the vehicle on the school grounds. Attempt this task only with full permission from your instructor and follow all the guidelines exactly.
- Comply with personal and environmental safety practices associated with clothing; eye protection; hand tools; power equipment; proper ventilation; and the handling, storage, and disposal of chemicals/materials in accordance with local, state, and federal safety and environmental regulations.

Performance Standard

0–No exposure: No information or practice provided during the program; complete training required

1–Exposure only: General information provided with no practice time; close supervision needed; additional training required

2–Limited practice: Has practiced job during training program; additional training required to develop skill

3–Moderately skilled: Has performed job independently during training program; limited additional training may be required

4–Skilled: Can perform job independently with no additional training

▶ **TASK** Inspect and test components and hoses of the evaporative emissions control system; perform necessary action.

AST
8E7

MAST
8E10

Time off_____

Time on_____

Total time_____

CDX Tasksheet Number: C870

1. Research the procedure for inspecting and testing the evaporative emissions control system on this vehicle in the appropriate service information.

   a. **List the specified service interval for replacing any of the evaporative emissions system components:**

2. Follow the specified procedure to inspect and test the evaporative emission system components. **List your observations for each component below:**

   a. **Charcoal canister:**

   b. **Purge control valve, if equipped:**

   c. **Thermal vacuum valve, if equipped:**

   d. **Purge control solenoid, if equipped:**

   e. **Hoses:**

3. **Determine any necessary action(s):**

4. Have your supervisor/instructor verify your conclusions. **Supervisor's/instructor's initials:** _____

5. **Perform any necessary action(s) and list them here:**

6. Have your supervisor/instructor verify satisfactory completion of this procedure, any observations found, and any necessary action(s) recommended.

Performance Rating

CDX Tasksheet Number: C870

0	1	2	3	4

Supervisor/instructor signature _____ Date _____

▶ TASK Diagnose emissions and driveability concerns caused by the evaporative emissions control system; determine necessary action.

MAST
8E5

Time off_____

Time on_____

Total time_____

CDX Tasksheet Number: C844

Vehicle used for this activity:

Year _____ Make _____ Model _____

Odometer _____ VIN _____

1. **List the customer concern:**

2. Research the particular concern in the appropriate service information.

   a. List the possible causes:

   b. List or print off and attach to this sheet the procedure for diagnosing the concern:

3. Using the recommended procedure, inspect and diagnose any emissions and drive-ability concerns caused by the evaporative emissions control system. **List your tests and observations here:**

4. **List the cause of the concern:**

5. Determine any necessary action(s) to correct the fault:

6. Have your supervisor/instructor verify satisfactory completion of this procedure, any observations found, and any necessary action(s) recommended.

Performance Rating

0	1	2	3	4

Supervisor/instructor signature _____ Date _____

Student/intern information:

Name _____ Date _____ Class _____

Vehicle used for this activity:

Year _____ Make _____ Model_____

Odometer_____VIN_____

Learning Objective/Task	CDX Tasksheet Number	2013 MLR NATEF Reference Number; Priority Level	2013 AST NATEF Reference Number; Priority Level	2013 MAST NATEF Reference Number; Priority Level
• Inspect and test electrical/electronically operated components and circuits of air injection systems; perform necessary action.	C438		8E5; P-3	8E8; P-3
• Diagnose emissions and driveability concerns caused by the secondary air injection and catalytic converter systems; determine necessary action.	C843			8E4; P-2

Time off_____

Time on_____

Total time_____

Materials Required

- Vehicle or simulator with related fault
- Hand vacuum pump (for vacuum-operated air injection components)
- DVOM (for vehicles equipped with electric/electronic air injection components)
- Problem-specific tools and equipment

Some Safety Issues to Consider

- You will be working under the hood of a running vehicle. Keep your hands and fingers away from moving belts, fans, and other parts.
- When running any vehicles in the shop, make sure you use the shop's exhaust ventilation system to discharge all exhaust gas safely outside.
- Only students who have their supervisor's/instructor's direct permission should perform this task due to the safety concerns involved.
- Diagnosis of this fault may require test-driving the vehicle on the school grounds. Attempt this task only with full permission from your instructor and follow all the guidelines exactly.
- Comply with personal and environmental safety practices associated with clothing; eye protection; hand tools; power equipment; proper ventilation; and the handling, storage, and disposal of chemicals/materials in accordance with local, state, and federal safety and environmental regulations.

Performance Standard

0–No exposure: No information or practice provided during the program; complete training required

1–Exposure only: General information provided with no practice time; close supervision needed; additional training required

2–Limited practice: Has practiced job during training program; additional training required to develop skill

3–Moderately skilled: Has performed job independently during training program; limited additional training may be required

4–Skilled: Can perform job independently with no additional training

Inspect and test electrical/electronically operated components and circuits of air injection systems; perform necessary action.

AST 8E5 | **MAST** 8E8

CDX Tasksheet Number: C438

1. Research the procedure for inspecting and testing the electrical/electronic components of the air injection system on this vehicle in the appropriate service information.

    a. **List any air injection system electrical specifications for this vehicle:**

2. Follow the specified procedure to inspect and test the air injection system components. List your observations for each component below:

    a. **Air injection switching valve, if electrically operated:**

    b. **Air injection bypass or diverter valve, if electrically operated:**

    c. **Air pump, if electrically operated:**

    d. **Electrical wiring:**

3. **Determine any necessary action(s):**

4. Have your supervisor/instructor verify your conclusions. **Supervisor's/instructor's initials:** _____

5. Perform any necessary action(s) and list them here:

6. Have your supervisor/instructor verify satisfactory completion of this procedure, any observations found, and any necessary action(s) recommended.

Performance Rating

CDX Tasksheet Number: C438

0	1	2	3	4

Supervisor/instructor signature _____ Date _____

▶ TASK Diagnose emissions and driveability concerns caused by the secondary air injection and catalytic converter systems; determine necessary action.

MAST
8E4

Time off_____

Time on_____

Total time_____

CDX Tasksheet Number: C843

Vehicle used for this activity:

Year _____ Make _____ Model_____

Odometer_____ VIN_____

1. **List the customer concern:**

2. Research the particular concern in the appropriate service information.

   a. **List the possible causes:**

3. Using the recommended procedure, inspect and diagnose any emissions and driveability concerns caused by the secondary air injection and catalytic converter systems. **List your tests and observations here:**

4. **Determine any necessary action(s) to correct the fault:**

5. Have your supervisor/instructor verify satisfactory completion of this procedure, any observations found, and any necessary action(s) recommended.

Performance Rating

CDX Tasksheet Number: C843

0	1	2	3	4

Supervisor/instructor signature _____ Date _____

Engine Performance: General Driveability and Emission Diagnosis

Student/intern information:

Name _____ Date _____ Class _____

Vehicle used for this activity:

Year _____ Make _____ Model_____

Odometer_____VIN_____

Learning Objective/Task	CDX Tasksheet Number	2013 MLR NATEF Reference Number; Priority Level	2013 AST NATEF Reference Number; Priority Level	2013 MAST NATEF Reference Number; Priority Level
• Diagnose engine mechanical, electrical, electronic, fuel, and ignition concerns; determine necessary action.	C710		8A9; P-2	8A9; P-2
• Diagnose the causes of emissions or driveability concerns with stored or active diagnostic trouble codes; obtain, graph, and interpret scan tool data.	C660			8B5;P-1
• Diagnose emissions or driveability concerns without stored diagnostic trouble codes; determine necessary action.	C711			8B6; P-1
• Interpret diagnostic trouble codes (DTCs) and scan tool data related to the emissions control systems; determine necessary action.	C668		8E8; P-3	8E11; P-3
• Diagnose driveability and emissions problems resulting from malfunctions of interrelated systems (cruise control, security alarms, suspension controls, traction controls, A/C, automatic transmissions, non-OEM-installed accessories, or similar systems); determine necessary action.	C409			8B8; P-3

Time off_____

Time on_____

Total time_____

Materials Required

• Vehicle or simulator with related fault
• DVOM
• Problem-specific tools and equipment such as: scan tool, lab scope, etc.

Some Safety Issues to Consider

• You will be working under the hood of a running vehicle. Keep your hands and fingers away from moving belts, fans, and other parts.
• When running any vehicles in the shop, make sure you use the shop's exhaust ventilation system to discharge all exhaust gas safely outside.
• Only students who have their supervisor/instructor's direct permission should perform this task due to the safety concerns involved.

- Diagnosis of this fault may require test driving the vehicle on the school grounds. Attempt this task only with full permission from your instructor and follow all the guidelines exactly.
- Comply with personal and environmental safety practices associated with clothing; eye protection; hand tools; power equipment; proper ventilation; and the handling, storage, and disposal of chemicals/materials in accordance with local, state, and federal safety and environmental regulations.

Recommended Resource Materials	Materials Required
• CDX Automotive program • Technical service bulletins, shop manuals, and any other information applicable to the specific vehicle or components you are working on • Class notes	• Vehicle or simulator with related fault • DVOM • Problem-specific tools and equipment such as: scan tool, lab scope, etc.

Performance Standard

0–No exposure: No information or practice provided during the program; complete training required

1–Exposure only: General information provided with no practice time; close supervision needed; additional training required

2–Limited practice: Has practiced job during training program; additional training required to develop skill

3–Moderately skilled: Has performed job independently during training program; limited additional training may be required

4–Skilled: Can perform job independently with no additional training

Diagnose engine mechanical, electrical, electronic, fuel, and ignition concerns; determine necessary action.

AST 8A9 **MAST** 8A9

Time off_____

Time on_____

Total time_____

CDX Tasksheet Number: C710

1. **List the driveability-related customer concern:**

2. Research the particular concern in the appropriate service information.

   a. **List the possible causes:**

3. Using the specified procedure, inspect and diagnose any engine mechanical, electrical, electronic, fuel, and ignition concerns. **List your tests and results here:**

4. **List the cause of the concern:**

5. **Determine any necessary action/s to correct the fault:**

6. Have your supervisor/instructor verify satisfactory completion of this procedure, any observations found, and any necessary action/s recommended.

Performance Rating

CDX Tasksheet Number: C710

0	1	2	3	4

Supervisor/instructor signature _____ Date _____

▶ **TASK** Diagnose the causes of emissions or driveability concerns with stored or active diagnostic trouble codes; obtain, graph, and interpret scan tool data.

MAST
8B5

Time off_____

Time on_____

Total time_____

CDX Tasksheet Number: C660

Vehicle used for this activity:

Year _____ Make _____ Model_____

Odometer_____ VIN_____

1. **List the emissions- or driveability-related customer concern:**

2. Research the particular concern in the appropriate service information.

   a. **List the possible causes:**

3. Using the correct equipment, retrieve and record diagnostic trouble codes, OBD monitor status, and freeze-frame data, then interpret the scan tool data:

   a. **List any stored DTCs and their descriptions:**

   b. **List the status of all monitors:**

   c. **List any freeze-frame data:**

4. With the aid of the stored data or active diagnostic trouble codes, diagnose the cause of emissions or driveability concern. List your tests and results here:

5. List the cause of the concern:

6. Determine any necessary action/s to correct the fault:

7. Have your supervisor/instructor verify satisfactory completion of this procedure, any observations found, and any necessary action/s recommended.

Performance Rating

CDX Tasksheet Number: C660

0	1	2	3	4

Supervisor/instructor signature _____ Date _____

Diagnose emissions or driveability concerns without stored diagnostic trouble codes; determine necessary action.

Time off_____

Time on_____

Total time_____

CDX Tasksheet Number: C711

Vehicle used for this activity:

Year _____ Make _____ Model_____

Odometer_____ VIN_____

1. **List the emissions- or driveability-related customer concern:**

2. **Research the particular concern in the appropriate service information.**

   a. **List the possible causes:**

3. Follow the service manual procedure to diagnose the cause of the concern. **List your tests and results here:**

4. **List the cause of the concern:**

5. **Determine any necessary action/s to correct the fault:**

6. Have your supervisor/instructor verify satisfactory completion of this procedure, any observations found, and any necessary action/s recommended.

Performance Rating

CDX Tasksheet Number: C711

| 0 | 1 | 2 | 3 | 4 |

Supervisor/instructor signature _____ Date _____

Interpret diagnostic trouble codes (DTCs) and scan tool data related to the emissions control systems; determine necessary action.

Time off_____

Time on_____

Total time_____

CDX Tasksheet Number: C668

Vehicle used for this activity:

Year _____ Make _____ Model_____

Odometer_____ VIN_____

1. **List the emissions system-related customer concern:**

2. Research the particular concern in the appropriate service information.

   a. **List the possible causes:**

3. Using the correct equipment, retrieve and record diagnostic trouble codes. OBD monitor status, and freeze-frame data:

   a. **List any stored DTCs and their descriptions:**

   b. **List the status of all monitors:**

   c. **List any freeze-frame data:**

4. **Using the data listed above, interpret the DTCs and scan tool data results. List your tests and results here:**

5. **List the cause of the concern:**

6. **Determine any necessary action/s to correct the fault:**

7. Have your supervisor/instructor verify satisfactory completion of this procedure, any observations found, and any necessary action/s recommended.

Performance Rating

CDX Tasksheet Number: C668

0	1	2	3	4

Supervisor/instructor signature _____ Date _____

Diagnose driveability and emissions problems resulting from malfunctions of interrelated systems (cruise control, security alarms, suspension controls, traction controls, A/C, automatic transmissions, non-OEM-installed accessories, or similar systems); determine necessary action.

MAST
8B8

Time off_____

Time on_____

Total time_____

CDX Tasksheet Number: C409

Vehicle used for this activity:

Year _____ Make _____ Model_____

Odometer_____ VIN_____

1. **List the driveability- or emissions system-related customer concern (interrelated system problem):**

2. Research the particular concern in the appropriate service information.

    a. **List the possible causes:**

3. Using the correct equipment, retrieve and record diagnostic trouble codes, OBD monitor status, and freeze-frame data:

    a. **List any stored DTCs and their descriptions:**

    b. **List the status of all monitors:**

c. List any freeze-frame data:

4. Using the data listed above, diagnose the cause of the customer concern. **List your tests and results here:**

5. **List the cause of the concern:**

6. **Determine any necessary action/s to correct the fault:**

7. Have your supervisor/instructor verify satisfactory completion of this procedure, any observations found, and any necessary action/s recommended.

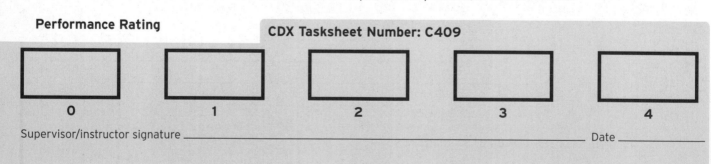

Performance Rating

CDX Tasksheet Number: C409

0	1	2	3	4

Supervisor/instructor signature _____ Date _____

Appendix: CDX/NATEF Correlation Guide

Section AO: General Safety			
CDX Tasksheet Number	NATEF 2013 MLR Reference and Priority	NATEF 2013 AST Reference and Priority	NATEF 2013 MAST Reference and Priority	Corresponding Page(s)
C451	OA1; P-1	OA1; P-1	OA1; P-1	5-6
C452	OA2; P-1	OA2; P-1	OA2; P-1	37
C453	OA3; P-1	OA3; P-1	OA3; P-1	51
C454	OA4; P-1	OA4; P-1	OA4; P-1	53-54
C455	OA5; P-1	OA5; P-1	OA5; P-1	49
C456	OA6; P-1	OA6; P-1	OA6; P-1	7
C458	OA7; P-1	OA7; P-1	OA7; P-1	9-10
C459	OA8; P-1	OA8; P-1	OA8; P-1	11
C460	OA9; P-1	OA9; P-1	OA9; P-1	13
C461	OA10; P-1	OA10; P-1	OA10; P-1	21
C462	OA11; P-1	OA11; P-1	OA11; P-1	23
C463	OA12; P-1	OA12; P-1	OA12; P-1	25
C464	OA13; P-1	OA13; P-1	OA13; P-1	69-70
C895	OA14; P-1	OA14; P-1	OA14; P-1	71
C465	OA15; P-1	OA15; P-1	OA15; P-1	15
C466	OB1; P-1	OB1; P-1	OB1; P-1	29-32
C467	OB2; P-1	OB2; P-1	OB2; P-1	33-35
C468	OB3; P-1	OB3; P-1	OB3; P-1	39
C469	OB4; P-1	OB4; P-1	OB4; P-1	41
C896	OB5; P-1	OB5; P-1	OB5; P-1	43
C472	OC1; P-1	OC1; P-1	OC1; P-1	61
C473	OC2; P-1	OC2; P-1	OC2; P-1	47
C474	OC3; P-1	OC3; P-1	OC3; P-1	63
C475	OC4; P-1	OC4; P-1	OC4; P-1	65
C590	OC5; P-1	OC5; P-1	OC5; P-1	83
C476	OD1; P-1	OD1; P-1	OD1; P-1	55-56

CDX Tasksheet Number	NATEF 2013 MLR Reference and Priority	NATEF 2013 AST Reference and Priority	NATEF 2013 MAST Reference and Priority	NATEF 2008 Reference and Priority	Corresponding Page(s)
C885		1A1; P-1	1A1; P-1	1A1; P-1	89
C002	1A1; P-1	1A2; P-1	1A2; P-1	1A3; P-1	91
C898	1A2; P-1	1A3; P-1	1A3; P-1		105
C004	1A3; P-1	1A4; P-1	1A4; P-1	1A5; P-1	103-104
C005				1A6; P-2	
C541	1A4; P-1	1A5; P-1	1A5; P-1	1A13; P-1	195-195
C899	1A5; P-1	1A6; P-1	1A6; P-1		127-128
C886	1A6; P-1	1A7; P-1	1A7; P-1	1A14; P-1	99-100
C596		1A8; P-2	1A8; P-2	1A15; P-2	197-198
C900	1A7; P-3	1A9; P-3	1A9; P-3		93
C671		1A10; P-3	1A10; P-3	1A12; P-2	119-121
C673		1B1; P-1	1B1; P-1	1B1; P-1	131-132, 134
C674		1B2; P-1	1B2; P-1	1B2; P-1	132-133
C021		1B3; P-2	1B3; P-2	1B8; P-2	137
C723	1B1; P-1	1B4; P-1	1B4; P-1	1B10; P-1	155
C676		1B5; P-1	1B5; P-1	1B11; P-1	129-130
C677		1B6; P-1	1B6; P-1	1B14; P-1	153
C718			1B7; P-3	1B3; P-3	145-146
C675			1B8; P-3	1B4; P-3	199-200
C719			1B9; P-3	1B5; P-3	147
C720			1B10; P-3	1B6; P-3	149-150
C721			1B11; P-3	1B7; P-3	151-152
C722			1B12; P-2	1B9; P-2	139
C724			1B13; P-2	1B12; P-2	141-142
C027			1B14; P-3	1B13; P-2	143-144
C679		1C1; P-2	1C1; P-2	1C14; P-2	125
C029			1C2; P-1	1C1; P-1	159-160
C030			1C3; P-2	1C2; P-2	161-162
C726			1C4; P-2	1C3; P-2	163
C727			1C5; P-2	1C4; P-2	167
C034			1C6; P-3	1C5; P-3	169-170
C728			1C7; P-1	1C6; P-1	175-176
C036			1C8; P-2	1C7; P-2	177
C729			1C9; P-3	1C8; P-3	179
C678			1C10; P-2	1C9; P-2	165-166
C597			1C11; P-2	1C11; P-2	185

CDX Tasksheet Number	NATEF 2013 MLR Reference and Priority	NATEF 2013 AST Reference and Priority	NATEF 2013 MAST Reference and Priority	NATEF 2008 Reference and Priority	Corresponding Page(s)
C040			1C12; P-2	1C12; P-2	187-188
C730			1C13; P-2	1C13; P-2	171-172
C731			1C14; P-1	1C15; P-1	189-190
C578	1C1; P-1	1D1; P-1	1D1; P-1	1D3; P-1	211-212
C598		1D2; P-1	1D2; P-1	1D14; P-1	229
C734	1C2; P-1	1D3; P-1	1D3; P-1	1D4; P-1	213-214
C050	1C4; P-1	1D4; P-1	1D4; P-1	1D7; P-1	219-220
C680		1D5; P-2	1D5; P-2	1D8; P-2	221-222
C052		1D6; P-2	1D6; P-2	1D9; P-2	223-224
C735	1C3; P-1	1D7; P-1	1D7; P-1	1D6; P-1	217-218
C053		1D8; P-1	1D8; P-1	1D10; P-1	225-226
C732		1D9; P-1	1D9; P-1	1D1; P-1	205-206
C737	1C5; P-1	1D10; P-1	1D10; P-1	1D13; P-1	203-204
C871		1D11; P-3	1D11; P-3	1D11; P-3	227
C736		1D12; P-2	1D12; P-2	1D12; P-2	207-208
C733			1D13; P-2	1D2; P-2	181

Section A2: Automatic Transmission and Transaxle

CDX Tasksheet Number	NATEF 2013 MLR Reference and Priority	NATEF 2013 AST Reference and Priority	NATEF 2013 MAST Reference and Priority	NATEF 2008 Reference and Priority	Corresponding Page (s)
C599		2A1; P-1	2A1; P-1	2A2; P-1	237-238
C681	2A1; P-1	2A2; P-1	2A2; P-1	2A3; P-1	235
C682		2A3; P-1	2A3; P-1	2A5; P-1	245
C902	2A2; P-1	2A4; P-1	2A4; P-1		239
C903	2A3; P-1	2A5; P-1	2A5; P-1		241
C740			2A6; P-1	2A6; P-1	257
C743			2A7; P-2	2A9; P-2	273-274
C741		2A6; P-3	2A8; P-3	2A7; P-3	259
C063		2A7; P-3	2A9; P-3	2A8; P-3	261-262
C066		2A8; P-1	2A10; P-1	2A10; P-1	269-270
C600			2A11; P-1	2A13; P-1	265-266
C747		2A9; P-2	2A12; P-2	2A12; P-2	271-272
C904	2A4; P-2				243
C683	2B1; P-2	2B1; P-2	2B1; P-2	2B1; P-2	277-278
C748		2B2; P-2	2B2; P-2	2B2; P-2	281
C601		2B3; P-1	2B3; P-1	2B3; P-1	267-268

CDX Tasksheet Number	NATEF 2013 MLR Reference and Priority	NATEF 2013 AST Reference and Priority	NATEF 2013 MAST Reference and Priority	NATEF 2008 Reference and Priority	Corresponding Page (s)
C905	2B2; P-2				279
C907	2B4; P-1	2B4; P-1	2B4; P-1		245-246
C906	2B3; P-2	2B5; P-2	2B5; P-2		283-284
C604		2C1; P-1	2C1; P-1	2C1; P-1	287-289
C749		2C2; P-1	2C2; P-1	2C6; P-1	291-292
C605		2C3; P-2	2C3; P-2	2C7; P-2	293
C606	2C1; P-3	2C4; P-3	2C4; P-3	2C23; P-3	249-250
C607	2C2; P-3	2C5; P-3	2C5; P-3	2C24; P-3	251
C684			2C6; P-2	2C2; P-1	299-300
C685			2C7; P-2	2C3; P-2	323-324
C686			2C8; P-2	2C4; P-2	315
C083			2C9; P-2	2C5; P-1	331-332
C688			2C10; P-2	2C9; P-1	301-302
C689			2C11; P-1	2C10; P-1	295
C750			2C12; P-2	2C11; P-2	307
C690			2C13; P-2	2C12; P-2	311
C751			2C14; P-2	2C13; P-2	305
C752			2C15; P-2	2C14; P-2	303-304
C753			2C16; P-2	2C15; P-2	313
C754			2C17; P-2	2C16; P-2	325-326
C755			2C18; P-2	2C17; P-2	327-328
C756			2C19; P-2	2C18; P-2	317-318
C757			2C20; P-1	2C19; P-1	319-320
C758			2C21; P-1	2C20; P-1	321-322
C759			2C22; P-2	2C21; P-1	309

Section A3: Manual Drive Train and Axles

CDX Tasksheet Number	NATEF 2013 MLR Reference and Priority	NATEF 2013 AST Reference and Priority	NATEF 2013 MAST Reference and Priority	NATEF 2008 Reference and Priority	Corresponding Page(s)
C101		3A1; P-1	3A1; P-1	3A2; P-1	341
C102	3A1; P-1	3A2; P-1	3A2; P-1	3A3; P-1	339
C901	3A3; P-2				349
C691		3A3; P-1	3A3; P-1	3A5; P-1	351
C105	3A2; P-1	3A4; P-1	3A4; P-1	3A6; P-1	353
C106		3B1; P-1	3B1; P-1	3B1; P-1	369-370
C107		3B2; P-1	3B2; P-1	3B2; P-1	357-358
C608		3B3; P-1	3B3; P-1	3B4; P-1	379-380

CDX Tasksheet Number	NATEF 2013 MLR Reference and Priority	NATEF 2013 AST Reference and Priority	NATEF 2013 MAST Reference and Priority	NATEF 2008 Reference and Priority	Corresponding Page(s)
C111		3B4; P-1	3B4; P-1	3B5; P-1	365–366
C938		3B5; P-1	3B5; P-1		363
C847		3B6; P-1	3B6; P-1	3B6; P-1	375
C848		3B7; P-2	3B7; P-2	3B8; P-2	373
C908	3B1; P-1				359
C909	3B2; P-1				361
C768		3C1; P-2	3C1; P-2	3C6; P-2	391–392
C611	3C1; P-3	3C2; P-3	3C2; P-3	3C17; P-3	343
C609			3C3; P-2	3C4; P-2	383
C693			3C4; P-2	3C5; P-2	385
C887			3C5; P-3	3C13; P-3	387
C132		3D1; P-1	3D1; P-1	3D1; P-1	395–396
C133		3D2; P-2	3D2; P-2	3D2; P-2	401–402
C134	3D1; P-2	3D3; P-1	3D3; P-1	3D3; P-1	399–400
C849	3D2; P-2	3D4; P-1	3D4; P-1	3D4; P-1	397–398
C779		3D5; P-2	3D5; P-2	3D6; P-2	402–403
C100				3E1:1; P-2	
C138			3E1: 4; P-2		415
C889		3E1: 4; P-2	3E1: 5; P-2	3E1:3; P-2	413–414
C780			3E1: 6; P-3	3E1:4; P-2	417
C890			3E1: 7; P-3	3E1:5; P-2	419–420
C781			3E1: 8; P-3	3E1:6; P-2	423
C782			3E1: 9; P-3	3E1:7; P-2	425
C145			3E1:10; P-3	3E1:8; P-2	429
C783			3E1:11; P-3	3E1:9; P-1	431
C147			3E1:12; P-3	3E1:10; P-2	421–422
C148			3E1:13; P-3	3E1:11; P-2	427–428
C784			3E2: 1; P-3	3E2:1; P-3	435
C785	3E1; P-2	3E1:1; P-2	3E1: 1; P-2	3E2:2; P-2	411–412
C911	3E2; P-1	3E1:2; P-1	3E1: 2; P-1		407
C912	3E3; P-1	3E1:3; P-1	3E1: 3; P-1		409
C786			3E2:2; P-3	3E2:4; P-3	437
C153			3E3:5; P-2	3E3:1; P-2	441–442
C154	3E1:1; P-2	3E2:1; P-1	3E3: 1; P-1	3E3:2; P-1	443–444
C155		3E2:2; P-1	3E3:2; P-1	3E3:3; P-1	447
C156		3E2:3; P-2	3E3:3; P-2	3E3:4; P-2	449–450
C850		3E2:4; P-2	3E3:4; P-2	3E3:5; P-2	445
C788		3F1; P-3	3F1; P-3	3F2; P-3	455–456

CDX Taksheet Number	NATEF 2013 MLR Reference and Priority	NATEF 2013 AST Reference and Priority	NATEF 2013 MAST Reference and Priority	NATEF 2008 Reference and Priority	Corresponding Page(s)
C913	3F1; P-3				459
C876		3F2; P-3	3F2; P-3	3F5; P-3	461–462
C914	3F2; P-2	3F3; P-3	3F3; P-3		463
C613		3F4; P-3	3F4; P-3	3F8; P-3	467
C787			3F5; P-3	3F1; P-3	453–454
C878			3F6; P-3	3F7; P-3	465
C875			3F7; P-3	3F4; P-3	457–458

Section A4: Suspension and Steering Systems

CDX Taksheet Number	NATEF 2013 MLR Reference and Priority	NATEF 2013 AST Reference and Priority	NATEF 2013 MAST Reference and Priority	NATEF 2008 Reference and Priority	Corresponding Page(s)
C166	4A1; P-1	4A1; P-1	4A1; P-1	4A3; P-1	473
C851			4A2; P-1	4A2; P-1	475
C168	4A2; P-1	4B1; P-1	4B1; P-1	4B1; P-1	555
C169		4B2; P-1	4B2; P-1	4B2; P-1	557
C170		4B3; P-2	4B3; P-2	4B3; P-2	561–562
C884		4B4; P-2	4B4; P-2	4B4; P-2	549–550
C880		4B5; P-2	4B5; P-2	4B5; P-2	551–552
C173		4B6; P-2	4B6; P-2	4B6; P-2	559–560
C882		4B7; P-2	4B7; P-2	4B8; P-2	533–534
C933	4B1; P-1				529
C883		4B8; P-2	4B8; P-2	4B9; P-2	531
C177	4B2; P-1	4B9; P-1	4B9; P-1	4B10; P-1	511
C178	4B3; P-2	4B10; P-2	4B10; P-2	4B11; P-2	515
C917	4B4; P-1	4B11; P-1	4B11; P-1		519
C180	4B5; P-1	4B12; P-1	4B12; P-1	4B13; P-1	517–518
C181		4B13; P-2	4B13; P-2	4B14; P-2	523
C699		4B14; P-2	4B14; P-2	4B15; P-2	525
C183	4B6; P-2	4B15; P-2	4B15; P-2	4B16; P-2	521
C184		4B16; P-2	4B16; P-2	4B17; P-2	541–543
C185		4B17; P-1	4B17; P-1	4B18; P-1	545–546
C186			4B18; P-3	4B19; P-3	627–628
C700	4B21; P-3	4B19; P-3	4B20; P-3	4B20; P-3	625
C551	4B22; P-2	4B18; P-3	4B19; P-3	4B21; P-3	631
C916	4B8; P-1				539–540
C918	4B7; P-1				537–538
C930					

CDX Tasksheet Number	NATEF 2013 MLR Reference and Priority	NATEF 2013 AST Reference and Priority	NATEF 2013 MAST Reference and Priority	NATEF 2008 Reference and Priority	Corresponding Page(s)
C919	4B10; P-1				569
C920	4B9; P-1				539
C921	4B11; P-1				571
C922	4B12; P-1				595
C923	4B13; P-1				573
C924	4B14; P-1				567
C925	4B15; P-1				597
C926	4B16; P-1				565–566
C927	4B17; P-1				591
C928	4B18; P-1				593
C929	4B19; P-1				615
C202	4B20; P-1				617–618
C852		4C1; P-1	4C1; P-1	4C1; P-1	607–608
C853		4C2; P-1	4C2; P-1	4C2; P-1	609–610
C790		4C3; P-3	4C3; P-3	4C3; P-2	581–582, 587
C791		4C4; P-3	4C4; P-3	4C4; P-2	583, 587
C792		4C5; P-2	4C5; P-2	4C5; P-1	585–586
C192		4C6; P-3	4C6; P-3	4C6; P-2	579, 588
C193		4C7; P-3	4C7; P-3	4C7; P-3	577, 587
C194		4C8; P-3	4C8; P-3	4C8; P-3	603–604
C793		4C9; P-3	4C9; P-3	4C9; P-2	575, 588
C794		4C10; P-3	4C10; P-3	4C10; P-1	599–600
C934		4C11; P-3	4C11; P-3		601–602
C854		4C12; P-1	4C12; P-1	4C11; P-3	619–620
C617	4C1; P-1				637–638
C202		4D1; P-1	4D1; P-1	4D1; P-1	631–632
C203		4D2; P-1	4D2; P-1	4D2; P-1	621–622
C616				4D6; P-2	
C931	4B23; P-3	4D3; P-3	4D3; P-3		629
C206		4E1; P-1	4E1; P-1	4E1; P-1	635, 653
C617		4E2; P-1	4E2; P-1	4E2; P-1	639–640
C618		4E3; P-1	4E3; P-1	4E3; P-1	641, 651
C213		4E4; P-2	4E4; P-2	4E4; P-2	643, 651
C214		4E5; P-2	4E5; P-2	4E5; P-2	645, 652
C216		4E6; P-1	4E6; P-1	4E6; P-1	647, 652
C217		4E7; P-2	4E7; P-2	4E7; P-2	649–650
C795		4E8; P-3	4E8; P-3	4E8; P-3	655

CDX Tasksheet Number	NATEF 2013 MLR Reference and Priority	NATEF 2013 AST Reference and Priority	NATEF 2013 MAST Reference and Priority	NATEF 2008 Reference and Priority	Corresponding Page(s)
C940		4E9; P-2	4E9; P-2		657
C619	4D1; P-1	4F1; P-1	4F1; P-1	4F1; P-1	481-482
C855		4F2; P-2	4F2; P-2	4F2; P-2	505-506
C222	4D2; P-1	4F3; P-1	4F3; P-1	4F3; P-1	483-484
C701		4F4; P-2	4F4; P-2	4F4; P-2	499-500
C796		4F5; P-2	4F5; P-2	4F5; P-2	507-508
C620	4D3; P-1	4F6; P-1	4F6; P-1	4F6; P-1	485-486
C621	4D4; P-2	4F7; P-2	4F7; P-2	4F7; P-2	489-491
C227				4F8; P-1	
C580	4D5; P-1	4F8; P-1	4F8; P-1	4F9; P-1	495-496
C552	4D6; P-1	4F9; P-1	4F9; P-1	4F10; P-1	497
C935	4D7; P-2	4F10; P-2			501-502
C937			4F10; P-2		503-504
C936	4D8; P-2	4F11; P-1	4F11; P-1		487-488

Section A5: Brakes

CDX Tasksheet Number	NATEF 2013 MLR Reference and Priority	NATEF 2013 AST Reference and Priority	NATEF 2013 MAST Reference and Priority	NATEF 2008 Reference and Priority	Corresponding Page(s)
C229		5A1; P-1	5A1; P-1	5A2; P-1	665
C230	5A1; P-1	5A2; P-1	5A2; P-1	5A3; P-1	663
944	5A2; P-1	5A3; P-1	5A3; P-1		667
C251	5A3; P-1	5A4; P-1	5A4; P-1	5C7; P-1	753
C894		5B1; P-1	5B1; P-1	5B1; P-1	775
C622	5B1; P-1	5B2; P-1	5B2; P-1	5B2; P-1	581-582
C704		5B3; P-1	5B3; P-1	5B3; P-1	685-686
C235		5B4; P-1	5B4; P-1	5B4; P-1	687, 691
C236		5B5; P-3	5B5; P-3	5B5; P-2	779-780
C237	5B3; P-1	5B6; P-1	5B6; P-1	5B6; P-1	695-696
C623		5B7; P-2	5B7; P-2	5B7; P-2	697
C624		5B8: P-2	5B8; P-2	5B8; P-2	699-700
C239	5B4; P-1	5B9; P-1	5B9; P-1	5B9; P-1	673
C242		5B10; P-3	5B10; P-3	5B11; P-3	797
947	5B5; P-3	5B11; P-2	5B11; P-2		795
C705	5B6; P-1	5B12; P-1	5B12; P-1	5B12; P-1	677
C625	5B7; P-1	5B13; P-1	5B13; P-1	5B13; P-1	675
946	5B2; P-1				683
C706		5C1; P-1	5C1; P-1	5C1; P-1	739, 755
C800	5C1; P-1	5C2; P-1	5C2; P-1	5C2; P-1	741

CDX Tasksheet Number	NATEF 2013 MLR Reference and Priority	NATEF 2013 AST Reference and Priority	NATEF 2013 MAST Reference and Priority	NATEF 2008 Reference and Priority	Corresponding Page(s)
C626	5C2; P-1	5C3; P-1	5C3; P-1	5C3; P-1	743
C248	5C3; P-1	5C4; P-1	5C4; P-1	5C4; P-1	745, 749
C707	5C4; P-2	5C5; P-2	5C5; P-2	5C5; P-2	747-748
C801	5C5; P-2	5C6; P-2	5C6; P-2	5C6; P-2	751
C251				5C7; P-1	
C708		5D1; P-1	5D1; P-1	5D1; P-1	703, 717
C802	5D1; P-1	5D2; P-1	5D2; P-1	5D2; P-1	705
C803	5D2; P-1	5D3; P-1	5D3; P-1	5D3; P-1	707
C627	5D3; P-1	5D4; P-1	5D4; P-1	5D4; P-1	711
C805	5D4; P-1	5D5; P-1	5D5; P-1	5D6; P-1	713
C628	5D5; P-1	5D6; P-1	5D6; P-1	5D7; P-1	725
C806	5D6; P-1	5D7; P-1	5D7; P-1	5D8; P-1	727, 733
C629	5D7; P-1	5D8; P-1	5D8; P-1	5D9; P-1	731
C630	5D8; P-1	5D9; P-1	5D9; P-1	5D10; P-1	729
C631	5D9; P-3	5D10; P-3	5D10; P-3	5D11; P-3	719
C632	5D10; P-2	5D11; P-2	5D11; P-2	5D13; P-2	709
948	5D11; P-1	5D12; P-1	5D12; P-1		721
C807	5E1; P-2	5E1; P-2	5E1; P-2	5E1; P-2	765-766
C808	5E2; P-1	5E2; P-1	5E2; P-1	5E2; P-1	767
C809		5E3; P-1	5E3; P-1	5E3; P-1	769-770
C581		5E4; P-3	5E4; P-3	5E4; P-3	771-772
C556		5E5; P-3	5E5; P-3	5E5; P-3	689
C267		5F1; P-3	5F1; P-3	5F1; P-1	789-790
C810	5F1; P-1	5F2; P-1	5F2; P-1	5F2; P-1	783-784
C811	5F2; P-2	5F3; P-2	5F3; P-2	5F3; P-2	759
C633	5F3; P-1	5F4; P-1	5F4; P-1	5F4; P-1	761
C272	5F4; P-1	5F5; P-1	5F5; P-1	5F5; P-1	793
C273	5F5; P-2	5F6; P-2	5F6; P-2	5F6; P-2	785-786
C275		5F8; P-2	5F7; P-2	5F8; P-1	787
C274	5F6; P-1	5F7; P-1	5F8; P-1	5F7; P-1	735-736
C634		5G1; P-1	5G1; P-1	5G1; P-1	803
949	5G1; P-3	5G2; P-3	5G2; P-3		801
950	5G2; P-3	5G3; P-3	5G3; P-3		805
C635			5G4; P-2	5G2; P-2	815
C636			5G5; P-2	5G3; P-1	817-818
C812			5G6; P-3	5G4; P-3	809
C637			5G7; P-1	5G5; P-1	811
C639			5G8; P-3	5G7; P-1	819
C813			5G9; P-3	5G8; P-3	821

A. General Electrical System Diagnosis

CDX Tasksheet Number	NATEF 2013 MLR Reference and Priority	NATEF 2013 AST Reference and Priority	NATEF 2013 MAST Reference and Priority	NATEF 2008 Reference and Priority	Corresponding Page(s)
C286	6A1; P-1	6A1; P-1	6A1; P-1	6A3; P-1	827
C951	6A2; P-1	6A2; P-1	6A2; P-1		829–830
C641	6A4; P-1	6A3; P-1	6A3; P-1	6A7; P-1	897
C953	6A5; P-2	6A4; P-1	6A4; P-1		905–906
C291	6A6; P-2	6A5; P-1	6A5; P-1	6A8; P-2	899–900
C295	6A7; P-2	6A6; P-1	6A6; P-1	6A10; P-2	901–902
C289	6A3; P-1	6A7; P-1	6A7; P-1	6A6; P-1	893
C952		6A7; P-1			
C817		6A8; P-1	6A8; P-1	6A12; P-1	851–852
C298	6A9; P-1	6A9; P-1	6A9; P-1	6A13; P-1	903–904
C299		6A10; P-1	6A10; P-1	6A14; P-1	907–908
C643	6A11; P-1	6A11; P-1	6A11; P-1	6A15; P-1	913
C955		6A12; P-3	6A12; P-1		917
C301	6A10; P-1	6A13; P-1	6A13; P-1	6A17; P-1	915
C642			6A14; P-2	6A9; P-2	909–910
C559			6A15; P-1	6A16; P-1	919
C954	6A8; P-1				849
C302	6B1;P-1	6B1; P-1	6B1; P-1	6B1; P-1	835–836
C818	6B2; P-1	6B2; P-1	6B2; P-1	6B2; P-1	837–838
C304	6B3; P-1	6B3; P-1	6B3; P-1	6B3; P-1	841–842
C644	6B4; P-1	6B4; P-1	6B4; P-1	6B4; P-1	843–844
C819	6B5; P-1	6B5; P-1	6B5; P-1	6B5; P-1	845–846
C820	6B6; P-1	6B6; P-1	6B6; P-1	6B6; P-1	847
C561	6B7; P-3	6B7; P-3	6B7; P-3	6B7; P-3	971
C645	6B8; P-1	6B8; P-1	6B8; P-1	6B8; P-1	839
C874	6B9; P-3	6B9; P-3	6B9; P-3	6B9; P-3	973
C309	6C1; P-1	6C1; P-1	6C1; P-1	6C1; P-1	857–858
C310	6C2; P-1	6C2; P-1	6C2; P-1	6C2; P-1	859–860
C311	6C3; P-2	6C3; P-2	6C3; P-2	6C3; P-2	863
C312	6C4; P-1	6C4; P-1	6C4; P-1	6C4; P-1	865
C313	6C5; P-2	6C5; P-2	6C5; P-2	6C5; P-2	861–862
C314		6C6; P-2	6C6; P-2	6C6; P-2	867–868
C315	6D1; P-1	6D1; P-1	6D1; P-1	6D1; P-1	873
C316		6D2; P-1	6D2; P-1	6D2; P-1	879–880
C317	6D2; P-1	6D3; P-1	6D3; P-1	6D3; P-1	871–872
C318	6D3; P-2	6D4; P-1	6D4; P-1	6D4; P-1	877
C319	6D4; P-1	6D5; P-1	6D5; P-1	6D5; P-1	875–876

CDX Tasksheet Number	NATEF 2013 MLR Reference and Priority	NATEF 2013 AST Reference and Priority	NATEF 2013 MAST Reference and Priority	NATEF 2008 Reference and Priority	Corresponding Page(s)
C320		6E1; P-1	6E1; P-1	6E1; P-1	889–890
C956	6E1; P-1	6E2; P-1	6E2; P-1		885–886
C321	6E2; P-2	6E3; P-2	6E3; P-2	6E2; P-2	887
C564	6E3; P-2	6E4; P-2	6E4; P-2	6E4; P-2	883
C646		6F1; P-2	6F1; P-2	6F1; P-1	935–936
C325		6F2; P-2	6F2; P-2	6F3; P-1	955
C327		6G1; P-1	6G1; P-1	6G1; P-1	923
C328		6G2; P-2	6G2; P-2	6G2; P-1	929
C329		6G3; P-2	6G3; P-2	6G3; P-2	927
C330		6H1; P-2	6H1; P-2	6H1; P-1	941–942
C647		6H2; P-2	6H2; P-2	6H3; P-1	945
C333		6H3; P-3	6H3; P-3	6H4; P-3	947
C861		6H4; P-2	6H4; P-2	6H5; P-1	953–954
C335	6F1; P-1	6H5; P-1	6H5; P-1	6H6; P-1	951
C337	6F2; P-1	6H6; P-1	6H6; P-1	6H8; P-1	979
C821		6H7; P-2	6H7; P-2	6H10; P-2	963–964
C648	6F3; P-3	6H8; P-3	6H8; P-3	6H12; P-3	943
C957	6F4; P-1	6H9; P-1	6H9; P-1		933
C958	6F5; P-1	6H10; P-1	6H10; P-1		925
C336			6H11; P-3	6H7; P-3	957–958
C338			6H12; P-3	6H9; P-2	961–962
C340			6H13; P-3	6H11; P-3	965–966
C959			6H14; P-3		967–968

Section A7: HAVC

A. A/C System Diagnosis and Repair

CDX Tasksheet Number	NATEF 2013 MLR Reference and Priority	NATEF 2013 AST Reference and Priority	NATEF 2013 MAST Reference and Priority	NATEF 2008 Reference and Priority	Corresponding Page(s)
C341		7A1; P-1	7A1; P-1	7A2; P-1	981
C342	7A1; P-1	7A2; P-1	7A2; P-1	7A3; P-1	979
C824		7A3; P-1	7A3; P-1	7A5; P-1	989
C825		7A4; P-2	7A4; P-2	7A6; P-2	991–992
C650		7A5; P-1	7A5; P-1	7A7; P-1	1003
C347		7A6; P-1	7A6; P-1	7A8; P-1	1005
C651		7A7; P-2	7A7; P-2	7A9; P-2	1013
C652		7A8; P-1	7A8; P-1	7A10; P-1	1011
C566		7A9; P-3	7A9; P-3	7A11; P-1	1057

CDX Tasksheet Number	NATEF 2013 MLR Reference and Priority	NATEF 2013 AST Reference and Priority	NATEF 2013 MAST Reference and Priority	NATEF 2008 Reference and Priority	Corresponding Page(s)
C653	7B1; P-1	7B1; P-1	7B1; P-1	7B2; P-1	1019–1020
C654		7B2; P-2	7B2; P-2	7B3; P-2	1021
C826		7B3; P-2	7B3; P-2	7B4; P-1	1023
C827	7B2; P-2	7B4; P-2	7B4; P-2	7B5; P-3	983
C863		7B5; P-3	7B5; P-3	7B6; P-3	1015
C355		7B6; P-2	7B6; P-2	7B7; P-2	1025–1026
C959	7B3; P-1				993
C356		7B7; P-1	7B7; P-1	7B8; P-1	995–996
C829		7B8; P-2	7B8; P-2	7B9; P-1	1027–1028
C873		7B9; P-1	7B9; P-1	7B10; P-1	1029–1030
C830		7B10; P-1	7B10; P-1	7B11; P-2	997
C350			7B11; P-2	7B1; P-2	1059
C831		7B11; P-2		7B12; P-3	1037
C832			7B13; P-2	7B13; P-3	1039–1040
C364	7C1; P-1	7C1; P-1	7C1; P-1	7C3; P-1	1045
C370		7C2; P-2	7C2; P-2	7C9; P-2	1047
C362			7C3; P-2	7C1; P-2	1043
C864		7C3; P-2	7C4; P-2	7C10; P-3	1051
C373		7D1; P-1	7D1; P-1	7D2; P-1	1049–1050
C374		7D2; P-2	7D2; P-2	7D3; P-1	1061–1063
C835		7D3; P-2	7D3; P-2	7D4; P-2	1065–1066
C376		7D4; P-3	7D4; P-3	7D5; P-3	1067–1068
C865		7D5; P-3	7D5; P-3	7D6; P-3	1069–1070
C378	7D1; P-1	7D6; P-1	7D6; P-1	7D7; P-2	1071–1072
C655	7D2; P-2	7D7; P-2	7D7; P-2	7D8; P-2	999–1000
C866		7D8; P-2	7D8; P-2	7D9; P-2	1055–1056
C656		7E1; P-1	7E1; P-1	7E1; P-1	1033–1035
C836		7E2; P-1	7E2; P-1	7E2; P-1	1007
C657		7E3; P-1	7E3; P-1	7E3; P-1	1009–1010
C658		7E4; P-1	7E4; P-1	7E4; P-1	1031–1032

Section A8: Engine Performance

CDX Tasksheet Number	NATEF 2013 MLR Reference and Priority	NATEF 2013 AST Reference and Priority	NATEF 2013 MAST Reference and Priority	NATEF 2008 Reference and Priority	Corresponding Page(s)
C386		8A1; P-1	8A1; P-1	8A2; P-1	1081
C387	8A1; P-1	8A2; P-1	8A2; P-1	8A3; P-1	1077
C390		8A3; P-3	8A3; P-3	8A6; P-3	1095-1096
C391		8A4; P-2	8A4; P-2	8A7; P-2	1139-1140
C392	8A2; P-1	8A5; P-1	8A5; P-1	8A8; P-1	1087
C393	8A3; P-2	8A6; P-2	8A6; P-2	8A9; P-2	1089
C709	8A4; P-1	8A7; P-1	8A7; P-1	8A10; P-1	1091-1092
C395	8A5; P-1	8A8; P-1	8A8; P-1	8A11; P-1	1093
C710		8A9; P-2	8A9; P-2	8A12; P-1	1191
C398	8A6; P-1	8A10; P-1	8A10; P-1	8A14; P-1	1103-1104
C400		8A11; P-1	8A11; P-1	8A16; P-1	1099
C659	8B1; P-1	8B1; P-1	8B1; P-1	8B1; P-1	1157
C841		8B2; P-1	8B2; P-1	8B6; P-1	1115
C867		8B3; P-2	8B3; P-2	8B8; P-1	1159
C661	8B2; P-1	8B4; P-1	8B4; P-1	8B9; P-1	1155
C660			8B5; P-1	8B2; P-1	1193-1194
C711			8B6; P-1	8B3; P-1	1195-1196
C840			8B7; P-2	8B5; P-1	1161-1162
C409			8B8; P-3	8B7; P-3	1199-1200
C712		8C1; P-2	8C1; P-2	8C1; P-1	1113-1114
C663		8C2; P-1	8C2; P-1	8C3; P-1	1109-1110
C664		8C3; P-3	8C3; P-3	8C4; P-2	1111-1112
C960	8A7; P-1	8C4; P-1	8C4; P-1		1107-1108
C713			8D1; P-2	8D1; P-1	1133-1134
C420		8D1; P-2	8D2; P-2	8D2; P-2	1121-1122
C868		8D2; P-1	8D3; P-1	8D2; P-1	1119-1120
C422	8C1; P-1	8D3; P-1	8D4; P-1	8D3; P-2	1125
C962	8C2; P-1	8D4; P-1	8D5; P-1		1127
C424		8D5; P-2	8D6; P-2	8D4; P-2	1129
C842		8D6; P-2	8D7; P-2	8D5; P-1	1123-1124
C665		8D7; P-1	8D8; P-1	8D6; P-1	1131
C428	8C3; P-1	8D8; P-1	8D9; P-1	8D7; P-1	1145-1146
C963	8C4; P-1	8D9; P-1	8D10; P-1		1143
C429		8D10; P-2	8D11; P-2	8D8; P-1	1149

CDX Tasksheet Number	NATEF 2013 MLR Reference and Priority	NATEF 2013 AST Reference and Priority	NATEF 2013 MAST Reference and Priority	NATEF 2008 Reference and Priority	Corresponding Page(s)
C869				8D9; P-3	
C964	8C5; P-3	8D11; P-3	8D12; P-3		1147
C869			8D13; P-3		1151
C666		8E1; P-3	8E1; P-3	8E01; P-2	1167–1168
C432	8D1; P-2	8E2; P-2	8E2; P-2	8E02; P-2	1165
C667		8E3; P-3	8E3; P-3	8E03; P-1	1175–1176
C843			8E4; P-2	8E06; P-2	1187
C844			8E5; P-2	8E10; P-1	1181–1182
C435			8E6; P-2	8E05; P-2	1173–1174
C434		8E4; P-2	8E7; P-2	8E04; P-1	1171–1172
C438		8E5; P-3	8E8; P-3	8E08; P-3	1185–1186
C714		8E6; P-2	8E9; P-2	8E09; P-1	1137–1138
C870		8E7; P-1	8E10; P-1	8E11; P-1	1179–1180
C668		8E8; P-3	8E11; P-3	8E12; P-1	1197–1198